AF786967

TRANSITIONAL JUSTICE AND MEMORY IN EUROPE (1945–2013)

SERIES ON TRANSITIONAL JUSTICE

The Series on *Transitional Justice* offers a platform for high-quality research within the rapidly growing field of transitional justice. The research is, of necessity inter-disciplinary in nature, drawing from disciplines such as law, political science, history, sociology, criminology, anthropology and psychology, as well as from various specialised fields of study such as human rights, victimology and peace studies. Furthermore, the research is international in outlook, drawing on the knowledge and experience of academics and other specialists in many different regions of the world.

The series is aimed at a variety of audiences who are either working or interested in fields such as crime and justice; human rights; humanitarian law and human security; conflict resolution and peace building. These audiences include academics, researchers, students, policy makers, practitioners, non-governmental organisations and the media.

All books published within the series are subject to a double-blind peer review by recognised authorities in the field.

The General Editors of the Series are:

- Prof. Stephan Parmentier (Catholic University of Leuven, Belgium)
- Prof. Jeremy Sarkin (University of South Africa)
- Prof. Elmar Weitekamp (University of Tübingen, Germany)

The general editors receive the support from an Editorial Committee and an Advisory Board, consisting of internationally renowned academics and practitioners.

Published titles within this Series:

5. Antoine Buyse (ed.), *Margins of Conflict. The ECHR and Transitions to and from Armed Conflict* (2011), 978-94-000-0157-2
6. Gaby Oré Aguilar and Felipe Gómez Isa (eds.), *Rethinking Transitions. Equality and Social Justice in Societies Emerging from Conflict* (2011), 978-1-78068-003-3
7. Richard Zajac Sannerholm, *Rule of Law after War. Ideologies, Norms and Methods* (2012), 978-1-78068-008-8
8. Nicola Palmer, Phil Clark and Danielle Granville (chief editors), *Critical Perspectives in Transitional Justice* (2011), 978-1-78068-035-4
9. Edda Kristjánsdóttir, André Nollkaemper and Cedric Ryngaert (eds.), *International Law in Domestic Courts: Rule of Law Reform in Post-conflict States* (2012), 978-1-78068-041-5
10. Bas van Stokkom, Neelke Doorn and Paul van Tongeren (eds.), *Public Forgiveness in Post-Conflict Contexts* (2012), 978-1-78068-044-6
11. Ilse Derluyn, Cindy Mels, Stephan Parmentier and Wouter Vandenhole (eds.), *Re-Member. Rehabilitation, Reintegration and Reconciliation of War-Affected Children* (2012), 978-94-000-0027-4
12. Anne-Marie de Brouwer, Charlotte Ku, Renée Römkens and Larissa van den Herik (eds.), *Sexual Violence as an International Crime: Interdisciplinary Approaches* (2012), 978-1-78068-002-6
13. Estelle Zinsstag and Martha Albertson Fineman (eds.), *Feminist Perspectives on Transitional Justice: From International and Criminal to Alternative Forms of Justice* (2013), 978-1-78068-142-9
14. Josep M. Tamarit Sumalla, *Historical Memory and Criminal Justice in Spain. A Case of Late Transitional Justice* (2013), 978-1-78068-143-6
15. Catherine Jenkins (ed.), Max du Plessis (ed.), *Law, Nation building and Transformation The South African experience in perspective* (2014), 978-1-78068-184-9
16. Susanne Buckley-Zistel and Stefanie Schäfer (eds.), *Memorials in Times of Transition* (2014), 978-1-78068-211-2

For previous volume in the series, please visit http://tj.intersentia.com

Series on Transitional Justice, Volume 17

TRANSITIONAL JUSTICE AND MEMORY IN EUROPE (1945–2013)

Edited by

Nico Wouters

intersentia
Cambridge – Antwerp – Portland

Intersentia Publishing Ltd.
Trinity House | Cambridge Business Park | Cowley Road
Cambridge | CB4 0WZ | United Kingdom
Tel.: +44 1223 393 753 | Email: mail@intersentia.co.uk

Distribution for the UK:
NBN International
Airport Business Centre, 10 Thornbury Road
Plymouth, PL6 7 PP
United Kingdom
Tel.: +44 1752 202 301 | Fax: +44 1752 202 331
Email: orders@nbninternational.com

Distribution for the USA and Canada:
International Specialized Book Services
920 NE 58th Ave. Suite 300
Portland, OR 97213
USA
Tel.: +1 800 944 6190 (toll free)
Email: info@isbs.com

Distribution for Austria:
Neuer Wissenschaftlicher Verlag
Argentinierstraße 42/6
1040 Wien
Austria
Tel.: +43 1 535 61 03 24
Email: office@nwv.at

Distribution for other countries:
Intersentia Publishing nv
Groenstraat 31
2640 Mortsel
Belgium
Tel.: +32 3 680 15 50
Email: mail@intersentia.be

Transitional Justice and Memory in Europe (1945–2013)
Nico Wouters (ed.)

© 2014 Intersentia
Cambridge – Antwerp – Portland
www.intersentia.com | www.intersentia.co.uk

Artwork on cover: Author Jan Jordaan, title 'Hurt', medium Linocut, 1999. From the *Universal Declaration of Human Rights – International Print Portfolio*, Article 5, published by Art for Humanity, South Africa, 1999.

ISBN 978-1-78068-214-3
D/2014/7849/31
NUR 828

GPRC
Guaranteed
Peer Reviewed
Content

British Library Cataloguing in Publication Data. A catalogue record for this book is available from the British Library.

No part of this book may be reproduced in any form, by print, photoprint, microfilm or any other means, without written permission from the publisher.

CONTENTS

THE USE OF HISTORY IN THE FIELD OF TRANSITIONAL JUSTICE: A CRITICAL INTRODUCTION

Nico Wouters

In an 2007 article Elizabeth Cole wrote that "history is still to some extent a missing piece in the planning for transitional justice processes".[1] This statement surprises for several reasons. History, both as an academic discipline or in its broader sense, seems to hold an obvious value for the field of Transitional Justice (TJ). To look at past cases and see what policies have (not) achieved the desired effects seems unavoidable for any kind of efficient policy evaluation.[2] Many post-conflict societies today struggle with questions on the intergenerational consequences of certain policies, on the long-lived effects of the sequencing of measures or how and when certain challenges recur. The broad temporal space is precisely what is often lacking in policy evaluation. Many key works in the field are explicitly historical in their approach.[3] The work of sociologist Luc Huyse, this project's initiator, is a prime example.[4] The two volumes edited by Neil J. Kritz offer national historical case studies, not unlike the ones presented in this volume, while the report edited by C.M. Carlos also uses a systematic comparative framework of historical European cases.[5] Jon Elster explicitly writes in his reference work *Closing the Books*: "The main task of this book is to discuss why processes of transitional justice have taken different forms in different transitions and why they have sometimes been absent altogether".[6] Comparative

---

1 E.A. Cole, 'Transitional justice and the reform of history education', (2007), 1 *International Journal of Transitional Justice*, 115–137.

2 O.N.T. Thoms, J. Ron and R. Paris, 'State level effects of transitional justice: What do we know?', (2010), 1/4 *International Journal of Transitional Justice (IJTJ)*, 329–354.

3 For example: A. Barahona de Brito, C. Gonzalez-Enriquez and P. Aguilar, *The Politics of Memory. Transitional Justice in Democratizing Societies*, Oxford, 2001.

4 L. Huyse, *All things pass, except the past*, Amsterdam/Brussels, 2009.

5 N.J. Kritz, *Transitional justice: How emerging democracies reckon with former regimes*, Washington, 1995, 2 vol.; C.M. Carlos, *Study on how the memory of crimes committed by totalitarian regimes in Europe is dealt with in the member states*, unpublished report, Madrid, 2008.

6 J. Elster, *Closing the books. Transitional justice in historical perspective*, Cambridge, 2004, at 79.

pattern seeking – sometimes labelled "transitology" – or longer term outcome evaluation by definition needs a historical dimension.[7] Truth and Reconciliation Commissions (TRCs) and memorial policies (commemorations) are today considered essential parts of the TJ toolkit. Increasingly, historians are engaged as experts in different types of "truth finding" initiatives.[8]

Nevertheless, Cole's statement rings true. Although in her article, she specifically referred to the absence of history *education* as a part of the TJ field, her analysis is transferable to the historic profession (from now on, "history" in this introduction refers to the profession and academic discipline). Arguably the most essential developments of the TJ field in the last decades have been its remarkably successful interdisciplinarity – law, sociology, political sciences, anthropology, psychology – and its integration of many different angles (democratisation, legal approaches, victim reparation etc.). These and other academic disciplines have brought in their specific set of expertise and, in doing so, influenced the course of the TJ field.[9] However, this integration seems more difficult for history as an academic discipline.

This book is the result of a project that ran between 2011 and 2012. The project, titled "*Transitional Justice after war and dictatorship. Learning from European experiences (1945–2000)*" was initiated by Luc Huyse. It was carried out by a joint venture between the *Peace Building Division of the Belgian Federal Public Service of Foreign Affairs* (which provided the financial funding) and the Belgian Brussels-based *Centre for Historical Research and Documentation on War and Contemporary Society* (CEGESOMA).

The first phase of the project, predominantly academic, ran between April 2011 and January 2012. Nine European cases were selected to create a balanced reference group. Belgium, France, the Netherlands and (West-) Germany cover the post-WWII context. Portugal, Spain and Greece are the cases from the beginning of the so-called third wave of transitions to democracy.[10] Germany, Poland and Hungary cover the post-1989 transitions.

Fourteen experts were selected to write nine national case studies.

All authors were asked to analyse the main actors, the key-events that marked certain shifts, the intergenerational aspect, the impact of academic research and the interaction between national and international contexts. All

---

7 Ph. Pham and Vinck, 'Empirical research and the development and assessment of transitional justice mechanisms', (2007), 1 *IJTJ*, 231–248.

8 E. Barkan, 'Engaging history: Managing conflict and reconciliation', (2005), 59 *History Workshop Journal*, 229–236.

9 G. Dancy, 'Impact assessment, not evaluation: Defining a limited role for positivism in the study of Transitional Justice', (2010), 4 *IJTJ*, 355–376.

10 S. Huntington, *The third wave. Democratization in the late twentieth century*, Oklahoma, 1992.

authors used a common checklist of questions to write their respective chapters.[11] For the "central phase" of policy implementation, these questions included the type of preceding regime, the type of transition, the type and duration of this central phase (judicial innovations and continuities, the use of quasi-judicial techniques or non-judicial measures), the numbers involved (of perpetrators and victims), the international contextual factors, the overall evaluation of court justice (swift, fair, severe, etc.) and employed benchmarks. For the longer term developments ("phase three") some common focal points included the reintegration of perpetrators, the measures for victims, reconciliations measures, the development of public debate (initiated by, continuous/discontinuous, open/restricted, issues) and memory irruptions.[12]

This book contains the academic output of the project: the nine national chapters completed with two mutually complementary comparative conclusions.[13] The different outcomes for certain chapters is in part caused by the different research situation in some countries (Portugal and Spain for example). It is also caused by the diversity in academic profiles of the authors. Of the fourteen experts involved, seven were historians while the other seven were social scientists, mostly political scientists. This perfect balance was the result of a coincidence, not of some conscious decision on the part of the organisers. Because of this interdisciplinary mixture, the common checklist was used with different (or overlapping) methodologies, some authors preferring historical description and analysis over social science argumentation. The common checklist ensured the comparability of the cases. This way, the academic diversity worked to our advantage.

During a Brussels workshop (12–13 January 2012) all the authors discussed why the subtitle of the project, *"Learning from European experiences"* was perceived as difficult by the historians involved, while the sociologists or political scientists experienced fewer inhibitions. Apart from enhancing the overall quality of the work, this discussion gave the project a final push towards a reflection on the use of the historical profession in the field of the transitional justice; on the nature and value of historical analysis, on the type of knowledge it can produce as well as the role historians can (not) play as experts in TJ policies.

This book offers a modest contribution toward further cooperation between history and the field of TJ. Before suggesting how this book aims to accomplish

---

11 Organized in three temporal categories: pre-existing legislation or experiences when relevant, the central phase of TJ (the actual core phase of policy development and implementation) and the longer succeeding period.

12 A. Wilde, 'Irruptions of Memory: Expressive Politics in Chile's Transition to Democracy', (1999), 2 *Journal of Latin American Studies*, Cambridge University Press, 473–500.

13 The policy-oriented aspect, what was essentially the lessons learned part of the project, is covered in a separate final report written by Luc Huyse (freely downloadable and available in English, French and Spanish: www.cegesoma.be).

this, I felt it necessary to sketch the larger framework and certain difficulties as part of a critical introduction.

1. IS HISTORY USEFUL?

"Putting history in transitional justice" or "learning lessons from history": quite clearly both are not evident. But why exactly? Is it difficult because of fundamentally opposed principles or systems of value between history and the policy aspects of the field of TJ, because of contradictory aims and goals, because of differing methodologies or simply in an interdisciplinary confusion on basic terminologies? Or all of the above?

The basic questions the field of TJ poses to history are not complex in themselves: what past mistakes should we avoid and what measures in the past have been proven to achieve societal stability? The answers are anything but simple. Even before actually dealing with these questions, one steps on a highly sensitive nerve within history: the question of its practical utility. This is an old debate. Just one important example was new historicism, or the way philosopher Karl Popper renounced deterministic approaches to history and models of thought that set up predictive laws for the course of society based on past events.[14]

The old debate on the utility of history seems to have come back with a vengeance in recent decades.[15] Today, however, debates on the utility of history are often public and popularised.[16] In an opinion piece in the Dutch newspaper *De Volkskrant* (October 2012), for example, journalist (and historian) Rutger Bregman pleaded for a more "relevant" role of historians in society: "there is no academic discipline which is so eager to completely tow down its own relevance. It is high time historians once again do what society needs them to do: draw lessons from the past".[17] Bregman attacks the profession's tendency to hide in niche-themes that only interest "ten people on the planet" [*sic*], without any relevance for current societal issues: "utility, this little taboo word within

---

14 K. Popper, *The open society and its enemies*, Routledge, 1945; idem, *The poverty of historicism*, Routledge, 1957.

15 E. May, *'Lessons' from the past: The use and misuse of history in American foreign policy*, NY/Oxford, 1973; Ch. Meier, *From Athens to Auschwitz. The uses of history*, Cambridge/London, 2005.

16 T. Basiuk, S. Kuzma-Markowska and K. Mazur, *The American uses of history: Essays on public memory*, Frankfurt/Berlin/Brussels, 2011.

17 *'Er is immers geen vakgebied dat zichzelf zo gretig wegrelativeert. Het wordt tijd dat de geschiedkundigen weer gaan doen waarvoor de maatschappij ze nodig heeft: lessen trekken uit het verleden'*. R. Bregman, 'Tijd dat geschiedkundigen weer gaan doen waarvoor ze nodig zijn: lessen trekken uit het verleden', *De Volkskrant*, 3 October 2012.

humanities sciences, should once again be put centre stage".[18] This provoked an immediate response by another historian who objected that, on the contrary, "detachment" was essential to history: "Political scientists and sociologists seek confirmation of their analysis of the present in the past. Their aim is not to know the past but to understand the present. In this way, their aim is the exact opposite of historians".[19] This small example perfectly illustrates the two opposing views on the role of history as well as the sensitivities surrounding the issue.

The past and history are in a peculiar position in current European society: extremely popular and seemingly omnipresent on the one hand, yet under growing pressure and criticism to deliver some kind of "answers" on the other. French thinker François Hartog argues that we currently live in a strongly presentist memorial regime (*régime d'historicité*).[20] Populations and groups feel a growing gap between present/future and 'their' past, which helps explain our current 'turn to history' and all things memorial. Another aspect of these tensions might lie with the enduring impact of post-modern doubts on the value of historical knowledge. Another piece of the puzzle perhaps lies with current neoliberal trends in which "utility" is a universal angle to approach all scientific or scholarly research. This certainly intensified after the Bologna reform of European universities which started after 1999. Another piece might be found in the global rise of the "politics of regret", in which the need to somehow 'repair' past mistakes (for example, offer official apologies) has become a dominant form of political legitimation. Certain authors see in this also a transformation of temporality and historicity, tied to declining nation states' attempts to assimilate their many diverse groups.[21] At a more basic level, one part of the puzzle might be that our inability to develop stimulating visions for the future makes us invest so much energy in re-evaluating the past.[22] Or the digital revolution can be one last element of explanation. Some claim that today, information, images and objects from the past have become so omnipresent and are so simultaneously accessible all the time that historical consciousness has become fundamentally

---

18 Original language quotation: '"*Nut*", *dat verboden woordje binnen de geesteswetenschappen, zou weer op een voetstuk moeten komen te staan*'.

19 '*Politicologen en sociologen zoeken in het verleden bevestiging van hun analyses over het heden. Hun doelstelling is niet om het verleden te kennen maar om het heden te begrijpen. Daarmee is hun doelstelling tegengesteld aan die van historici.*', T. Bogers, 'De historicus moet wars zijn van het heden', in *De Volkskrant*, 11 October 2012.

20 A. Huyssen, *Twilight memories: Marking time in a culture of amnesia*, New York, 1994/London, 1995; F. Hartog, *Régimes d'historicité: présentisme et expérience du temps*, Paris, 2003.

21 J.K. Olick and B. Coughlin, 'The politics of regret: analytical frames', in J. Torpey, *Politics and the Past*, NY, 2003, 37–63.

22 Ch. S. Maier, 'Overcoming the past? Narrative and negotiation, remembering and reparation: issues at the interface of history and the law', in J. Torpey (ed.), *Politics and the past: on repairing historical injustices*. Lanham, 295–304, 303.

decontextualised (or at least has eroded). Presumably, this digital age calls for new kinds of memories.[23]

Therefore, if we try to put history into transitional justice with a project originally titled "learning from the past", we seem to dive headlong into a minefield. This book does not tackle these issues as such. Nevertheless, we do need some clarity. We need to understand what possible tensions or issues move at the background in order to understand how this book positions itself. I would like to distinguish three main points which are continuously present – directly under or right above the surface – when dealing with the relationship between history and TJ. These three issues are:

1° the idea of history as a guide for present and future;
2° the idea of "closure" and its rhetorical connection with "reconciliation";
3° the connection between the concept of justice and history.

2. THE PAST AS A GUIDE FOR PRESENT AND FUTURE

The idea of history as a guide goes back to Thucydides.[24] The modern idea of history has its roots in the 19th century.[25] George Santayana's famous aphorism, "those who forget the past are condemned to repeat it" is clear: if we fail to understand the past correctly, and fail to learn the "proper lessons" from history, we are bound to make the same mistakes (mostly referring to war and mass violence). In this sense, the past becomes some kind of gigantic reservoir of "lost wisdom" that we must try to put to good use.

On a basic level, there is some obvious truth in this. As anyone working in – for example – foreign diplomacy will confirm, a basic knowledge and understanding of the past of the countries you are dealing with is necessary to avoid the many pitfalls history has laid in front of us. In this basic sense, we draw lessons from the past every day.

Nevertheless, the idea of history as a guide goes beyond this. What we mean here is the conscious use of history – rational or emotional – to construct and legitimise current (political) decisions. Probably the most commonly encountered example of this is analogous reasoning. This happens when we draw

---

23 A. Huyssen, *Twilight memories.*

24 M. MacMillan, *Dangerous games. The uses and abuses of history*, New York, 2009 (and especially the chapter: History as a Guide, 139–165).

25 F. Nietzsche, *On the advantage and disadvantage of history for life*, Indianapolis, 1980.

parallels between current situations and past events, and try to come to a decision in the present based on the past outcome of this allegedly similar situation. To a certain extent, this type of analogous reasoning is impossible to avoid. Analogy-based logics are an intrinsic part of human reasoning.

However, we mean the conscious construction of an analogy as authoritative argument. Let us take the perhaps most frequently used historical analogy after 1945: the Munich analogy. This of course refers to the Munich Conference in 1938, when Britain and France agreed on Hitler's annexation of the German-speaking lands of Czechoslovakia. After 1945, the "lesson from Munich" has been used by many politicians, in many different situations and with many different interpretations.[26] Indeed, one can learn different lessons from Munich. Some lessons could be that one should never negotiate with a dictator, that one should negotiate but not yield under pressure, or that one should negotiate early enough (or perhaps go to war early enough). Analogous argumentation connected to World War II and Hitler became highly popular during the "war on terror" after 2001. The American president George Bush, Jr., and the British Prime Minister Tony Blair made frequent use of past analogies, apparently to legitimise an agenda they had already decided upon. Comparing Hussein with Hitler, in particular, proved a powerful legitimising rhetoric: "If President Bush or Prime Minister Blair decides that Saddam Hussein is rather like Hitler, then that suggests ways of dealing with him".[27]

Analogies are tempting: "While it is true that the analogies we draw from the past for present-day analysis often mislead us, it is equally true that policy-makers, journalists and historians cannot resist using them".[28] Indeed, European historians themselves often actively offer analogies (perhaps to enhance the perceived importance of their profession?). This clearly increased after 1989, when the pasts of eastern European countries became "unfrozen". Certainly in Eastern Europe, "[Historians] cast themselves as national preceptors by offering parallels with the past. German scholars, for instance, saw unification in 1990 as, above all, the "chance for the German historians" to offer policy prescriptions [...]".[29] The reason for the popularity of analogies is clear: they are highly useful.[30] Analogies create the illusion that the argument has some kind of (academic) legitimacy. Also, by seeking legitimation in past events, policy makers can to a certain extent abstain from the responsibility to offer present-day based arguments.

---

26 M. MacMillan, *Dangerous Games.*

27 M. MacMillan, *Dangerous Games,* 156.

28 J.-W. Müller, *Memory and Power in Post-War Europe. Studies in the Presence of the Past,* Cambridge, 2002, at 27.

29 J.-W. Müller, *Memory and Power* at7.

30 See also: Y.F. Khong, *Analogies at war: Korea, Munich, Dien Bien Phu and the Vietnam decisions of 1965,* Princeton, 1992.

Clearly, this is one main area of tension. The way history as a profession sees "analogous reasoning" completely differs from the popular use described above. Analogous reasoning by policy makers by definition necessitates extreme simplification. The message needs to be immediately understandable to all. In fact, the whole point is to create some kind of "instant legitimacy".[31] If one were to overcomplicate or add too many layers of context, analogies would lose all rhetorical power and, therefore, use. For historians, comparisons between a past event/situation and a present day one, or systematic diachronic comparisons, are in theory perfectly feasible (although one could discuss the scholarly relevance of such an approach). But as an exercise in comparativism, it would necessitate a complex weighing of contexts and variables between the two cases and/or events (as well as asking the right set of questions; what does one want to achieve with such a comparison?). Therefore: the "past-present analogy" as a commonly used rhetorical instrument is completely opposed to diachronic comparativism as a historic methodology.

There is more to this than analogous reasoning alone. I would like to distinguish two courses of the idea of history as a guide: the first a popular emotional discourse and the second a positivist, scholarly one.

The emotional connections felt with the past are strongly based on constructed identities. The popular heritage craze (or history craze, for that matter) seems in part fuelled by a powerful societal need to find some "lost assurances" in the past. Some theorise that this is tied to the "destabilising" effects of globalisation. Controlling the past becomes compensation for the lack of control over an overly complex present. European heritage policies are sometimes criticised for consciously stimulating this kind of nostalgic use of the past, especially when it joins forces with the economic agenda of the tourist industry.[32] The past becomes something one can "experience" on a Sunday afternoon. Common critical terms for this are the "packaging of the past" or the "staged authenticity".[33] "Dark Tourism" is an accepted subfield of critical heritage and tourist research.[34]

Commemorations of the First World War offer a prime example. In one of the many different tourist walks on the western front in Flanders, visitors can make a tour through trenches while equipped with heavy bags. The aim is to experience what it must have been like for the soldiers on the front. To cite a typical marketing text of a Flemish museum in 2012: "taste and experience the

31 Müller, *Memory and Power*, 27.

32 D. Lowenthal, *The heritage crusade and the spoils of history*, Cambridge, 1998.

33 J.H. Gilmore and B.J. Pine, *Authenticity: What consumers really want*, Harvard, 2007.

34 See the website of the Institute for Dark Tourism Research (University of Central Lancashire); www.dark-tourism.org.uk/.

atmosphere of 'The Great War 1914–18' and WW II. You can feel the terror of the front soldiers and the ordinary population. You can smell the chloral- and mustard gas. You can see and walk in real authentic [*sic*] trenches. You can hear – as well as be surrounded by – bombardments and destroyed cities and this for over 22 museum rooms".[35]

A convergence of education policies, cultural policies, tourist and heritage policies in Europe have stimulated a general societal tendency in which the past is considered to be directly accessible. The intellectual effort necessary to bridge the gap between present and past is downgraded. The most important implication behind this (and certain educational programmes such as remembrance and peace education, for instance) is that the alleged emotional connection with the past is valued much more highly than cognitive knowledge and/or rational understanding. The emotional experience of "what it must have been like" is supposed to create a much deeper and more valuable form of understanding of the past than "mere" rational knowledge ever could. This is the emotional form of the idea of "history as a guide"; seeking comfort and/or confirmation in the past. This is not history, but rather "[...] a postmodern memory steeped in patrimonial reverence for the past, one that promises to tell us who we are rather than to offer insights into where we ought to be going".[36]

The second type of the "history as a guide" idea is rational-positivistic in nature and, as such, might seem the opposite of the above. Here, the underlying idea is that careful and systematic analysis of specific (exemplary) events from the past can enable politicians (or military leaders) to enhance the quality of their policy decisions today. It is a highly popular conviction. The connection with the field of TJ is clear. Colleen Duggan writes: "the transitional justice evidence base that we are accumulating through applied research and evaluation practice should be utilisation focused".[37] The TJ field has a real need for applied research that can provide a solid empirical evidence base to support effective policy decisions and evaluation; or "outcome monitoring and evaluation" on longer term impacts.[38] Indeed, arguably the most essential question from within the TJ field is: "will this policy work?" (to which the only answer is: "that depends on what you want to achieve").

---

35 Original quotation: '*U proeft en beleeft de sfeer van 'Den Grooten Oorlog 1914–1918' en WOII. U voelt de angst van de frontsoldaten en de gewone bevolking. U ruikt chloor- en mosterdgas. U ziet en wandelt in echte authentieke loopgrachten. U hoort en zit middenin bombardementen en vernielde steden en dit over 22* verdiepingen'.

36 N. Wood, *Vectors of memory. Legacies of trauma in post-war Europe*, Oxford, 1999 (quote: 4–5; this quote refers to Pierre Nora's research on *Lieux de mémoire*).

37 C. Duggan, 'Editorial note', (2010), 4/3 *IJTJ*, 315–328.

38 Ph. Pham and Vinck, *Empirical research*, 237–238.

Implemented on history as a profession, this would mean to develop refined scholarly methodologies (diachronic comparativism or systematic correlations between variables and possible outcomes) through which analysis of past events could lead to models with *predictive* qualities.[39] The necessary task is to detect "universal" mechanisms or causalities in the past and at the same time isolate all unique characteristics of past events and their contexts. This idea of "applied counterfactual history" is problematic for historians, in principal as well as methodologically. In principal, the idea of analysing the past in order to look for parallels in present and future negates history's fundamental philosophy as an academic discipline. Simply put, it reverses the order of things. It replaces the discipline's essential main goal of analysing past events in their specific timeframe. More concrete problems arise on the level of methodology. Some argue that counterfactual reasoning is unavoidable for every kind of human analysis to some extent. As an academic methodology to support policy development, however, it is not an accepted part of the historian's toolkit.

The emotional and the rational approaches to this idea of the past as a guide seem opposed. Yet at the heart of both lies the assumption of a continuous linear interconnection between the present and the past; a direct and easy accessibility of the past. This assumption does not take intellectual effort into account, which is needed to bridge the gap between present and past; in fact, it sometimes seems to assume that this gap hardly exists at all.

Few will dispute we can distil useful knowledge from the past. However, this knowledge is bound within strict limits. Perhaps historians working in current contexts should be more explicit in describing these limits, both to themselves and to other disciplines or fields.

3. CLOSURE AND RECONCILIATION: SEARCHING FOR A CONSENSUS ON THE PAST

In her critical editorial from 2009, Christine Bell writes that the "common project" of transitional justice should perhaps not be in "a common pursuit of justice as accountability", but in "the common enterprise of finding a mechanism for "dealing with the past" that will sustain political settlement".[40] Few will disagree with this statement.

---

39 G. Dancy, 'Impact assessment, not Evaluation: Defining a limited role for positivism in the study of transitional justice', (2010), 4 *IJTJ*, 355–376.

40 Ch. Bell, 'Transitional Justice. Interdisciplinarity and the state of the "field" or "non-field"', (2009) *IJTJ*, 3/1, 5–27.

The statement that societies have to "deal with the past" in order to create some kind of stability has become a commonly accepted and frequently used mantra in recent decades. There are variations: "coming to terms" with the past, "overcoming the past" or to translate the German *Wiedergutmachung* ("making things right again") are some examples. They have become highly popularised. Not surprisingly, they are also highly popular in the field of TJ.

The dominance of these terms is the direct result of the violent legacy the 20th century Colonialism and slavery, two world wars and the Holocaust, racism and genocide – in short, mass violence – have made it abundantly clear that today we are far removed from the 19th-century ways of constructing glorious national collective identities based on inspiring past events.[41] The violent legacy of the 20th century has imposed the question of how to "deal with the past" as a seemingly never-ending mission to European societies. This task is especially daunting in Eastern Europe.[42]

"Dealing with the past" or "overcoming the past" are somewhat vague concepts; probably partly the reason for their success and widespread use. The same goes for an even more important series of discourses; the concepts of "closure" and "reconciliation".[43] Reconciliation is also closely interrelated with concepts such as "overcoming the past", "turning the page", "closure", "sealing the past" and "moving on". From a perspective of the relationship between history and the field of TJ, however, it seems essential to have at least a general consensus of what these things could mean.

The wording of "dealing with the past" suggests that the past is a problem which must be "solved", "fixed", or "repaired". By definition the past can never be "repaired", but the underlying message here is that we have to confront the past and not bury it. But should we confront and remember or overcome and forget? Truth can indeed be sometimes in conflict to the notion of reconciliation and societal stability. The idea that "properly" dealing with the past is the necessary precondition for societal reconciliation is strong. On a general level we all understand the same thing when we use the word "reconciliation". On a slightly more concrete level however, it becomes clear that reconciliation means many different things to many different people, nor is there any consensus on how we should actually achieve reconciliation. Would we as a society be able to define exactly when a past could be considered "properly closed"?

---

41 A. Cairns, 'Coming to terms with the past', in J. Torpey, *Politics and the Past*, 63–90.

42 T. Judt, 'The past is another country: Myth and memory in post-war Europe', in Müller, *Memory & Power*, 157–184.

43 E. Daly and J. Sarkin, *Reconciliation in divided societies: Finding common ground*, Philadelphia, 2006; H.M. Weinstein, 'Editorial note: The myth of closure, the illusion of reconciliation: final thoughts on five years as co-editor-in-chief', (2011), 5/1 *IJTJ*, 1–10.

It seems a matter of finding the right balance between forgetting and remembering. In the search for this balance, quite clearly the element of remembering has now become the dominant one. It is an essential characteristic of European society today: "To be against the retrieval of neglected memories or their commemoration is to be out of step with the general public's reverence towards, and willingness to engage in, a wide range of memorial activity".[44]

Historically, trials of (main) perpetrators have in Europe been one of the dominant instruments of reaching some kind closure. Describing the divisive impact of different national/international memories (communism, anti-communism and antifascism) between 1945 and 1989, along with well as divisions of memory in civil societies, Müller states: "In that sense, the period of the Second World War was never quite properly closed, there was no peace treaty as there used to be after conflicts of this magnitude, and despite Nuremberg, there was, overall, no proper justice or reckoning for the guilty".[45] The idea expressed here is that some kind of large scale measure (an internationally endorsed peace treaty, an international trial for major war criminals) is necessary to "properly" close such a period.

Later stage trials in Europe after 1989 – certainly those relating to the Holocaust – are even increasingly explicitly intended (or at least perceived) as instruments of larger societal closure.[46] Clear examples can be found in France, with the trials of Milice member Paul Touvier (1994) and the trial of Maurice Papon (1997) where, amongst others, historian Robert Paxton was called as a "witness-historian".[47] The French justice system and political class attributed to both of these trials (and certainly the Papon trial) – even as the trials were taking place – goals that surpassed the judicial. Both trials were labelled as pedagogical events "for history and memory".[48] French historian Henry Rousso pointed to the ambivalent consequences of this approach: "(…) Once the verdict had been rendered (…) the justice system had to close it – a situation that was not without its contradictions, because this very same justice system had been thought of, over the years, as a guardian of memory".[49]

Modalities and context are essential here. For example, when historians are conscious of the judicial impact their conclusions might have – for instance, that

44 N. Wood, *Vectors of memory*, at 1.
45 J.-W. Müller, *Memory and Power*, at 5–6.
46 D. Bloxham, *Genocide on trial: War crimes trials and the formation of holocaust history and memory*, Oxford, 2001.
47 H. Rousso, 'Justice, history and memory in France. Reflections on the Papon trial', in J. Torpey, *Politics and the Past*, 277–295.
48 H. Rousso, 'Justice, History and Memory in France', 278.
49 H. Rousso, 'Justice, History and Memory in France', 286.

a certain historical analysis might be used by the defence to acquit someone who is probably a war criminal – will this not affect their analysis? Academic autonomy and free access to archives and information seem key conditions. With the French Papon trial, the historians were forced to work in conditions (lack of access to archives and the judicial file, lack of preparation, lack of proper set of questions) that would probably not have been acceptable by "normal" scholarly standards.[50] Rousso is critical of the historians present at the Papon trial: "in the end, this type of expertise served above all to legitimise the supposed historical character of the trial more than to enlighten the court (…)".[51] But what was the alternative? Demand proper conditions under threat of total withdrawal from the proceedings? The risk of isolating the historic profession from important and acute societal developments seems real. At the same time, the risk of delegitimising the historic profession by serving as "lap boy" for other interests is equally real.

Parallel issues arise in the context of historical expert committees who are assigned by political authorities to conduct research on a specific historical subject or a past event. Exact modalities can highly vary, but the political assignment usually entails that the selected historians come up with some kind of "usable" result. The kinds of answers these committees provide largely depend on the political assignment and questions set in the beginning. Despite the specificity of contexts, there is one basic point of tension: is a report ridden with nuances, complexities and ambivalent responsibilities the kind of truth politicians and the general public expect when they mandate (and pay for) a team of historians to provide answers?

There are several recent examples of such commissions for Belgium and France. For the Netherlands, the Srebrenica report is probably the most notorious example. This research on the events prior to, during and after the fall of Srebrenica was carried out by the Dutch Institute for War, Holocaust and Genocide Studies (NIOD). When presented in 2002, the final report directly led to the resignation of the Dutch government. Some Belgian examples include the parliamentary Lumumba-commission (2002, to investigate the circumstance of the murder on Congo's first prime minister, Patrice Lumumba, in 1961) and the research project "Docile Belgium", on the responsibility of the Belgian authorities with regard to the persecution of the Jews.[52] The Holocaust in particular has become an important topic for this kind of research, evidently also through the many national commissions investigating the aryanisation of Jewish property

50 H. Rousso, 'Justice, History and Memory in France', 289.
51 H. Rousso, 'Justice, History and Memory in France', 291.
52 B. Bevernage, 'Geschiedenis in Overheidsopdracht: Wetenschap, Ethiek En Politiek in De Belgische Lumumba-commissie', (2012), 125.1 *Tijdschrift voor Geschiedenis*, 81.

during WWII. Examples of such expert commissions are the Bergier, Wiesel and Tismăneanu commissions.[53]

All these commissions operated in a delicate (national and international) political climate. Their results, in particular the longer term impact, are ambiguous to say the least. Highly parallel issues arise for TRCs that are assigned to establish an "authoritative record": a narrative legitimised by academic authority and officialised by political power.[54] One could be positive and say that the final reports of these (and other) historical expert commissions lead to a result that Michael Ignatieff attributes to Truth Commissions, namely that they "[...] reduce the number of lies that can be circulated unchallenged in public discourse".[55] Indeed, such expert reports offer some kind of (temporary) official truth that could help create broader public awareness on certain past events. However, reality is more complex. The impact of the last three commissions mentioned above, for example, is difficult to assess. The political backlash and polemics after their final reports seem to indicate that this type of "official expert reports" can easily have counterproductive effects on the short or mid-term.[56] The other examples mentioned for Belgium and the Netherlands also provoked heated debate. Therefore, this is about much more than simply creating the proper working conditions (full disclosure of archives, academic freedom and autonomy). Historians should be aware of the public and political expectations and the societal impact their official "truths" can have.[57]

The essential problem is that, frankly, we know little about the effects in society of such authoritative records or expert reports. Indeed: "a report can establish facts and provide information, but it cannot always change people's beliefs, affect how people interpret the information or establish the moral common ground necessary to promote reconciliation".[58] We can assume that "slow science" has a

53 The Swiss Bergier commission (1996), named after the economic historian who lead the team of experts, was an expert commission ordered by the Swiss parliament to investigate the relations between Swiss enterprises and authorities with the Nazi regime during WWII. The Wiesel commission (The International Commission on the Holocaust in Romania, 2003) was installed by then-president Iliescu to investigate Romania's role in the Holocaust. The Tismăneanu commission (Presidential Commission for the Study of the Communist Dictatorship in Romania, 2006) was installed to investigate the communist past and regime in Romania. D. Ursprung, 'The role of historian's commissions between science, politics and public opinion', *Paper presented at IICCMER conference 'Dealing with the Past: The Role of Historians' Commission – The Swiss and the Romanian Experience'*, Bucharest, 14–15. June 2011, www.danielursprung.ch/pdf/commission.pdf [consulted 21 December 2012].

54 E. Daly, 'Truth Skepticism: An Inquiry into the Value of Truth in Times of Transition', (2008), 2/1 IJTJ, 23–41, at 28.

55 M. Ignatieff, *The Warrior's honour: Ethnic war and the modern conscience*, London, 1998 (quote: 188).

56 D. Ursprung, *The role of historian's commission.*

57 E. Daly, *Truth Skepticism.*

58 E. Daly, *Truth Skepticism*, 38.

longer term impact, where a certain scholarly consensus might take decades to seep into the public historical consciousness. But how does such a process work? And can its impact be counterproductive? There is also little systematic knowledge on how to successfully disseminate or translate intellectual academic results to a broader society. These are domains such as history education but also public history projects (museums, artistic projects, etc.) that could be developed after the trials or the work of TRCs.[59]

TRCs share similarities with history as related to the field of TJ.[60] Historians often act as experts at TRCs. Some of the recent criticism on TRCs certainly interests us here; not so much the traditional "impunity-criticism" with regard to the amnesty-for-truth-principle but, rather, the question on the nature of the created "truth" and its societal impact. How do TRCs define truth and more importantly, can this truth deliver the goals set at the beginning?[61] Often, the truth is intended to achieve several – sometimes opposing – things at once.[62]

The issue of the impact of historical analysis is a growing academic debate. Michael Ignatieff wrote: "crimes can never be safely fixed in the historical past: they remain locked in the eternal present crying out for vengeance".[63] However, some authors say that when historians are involved in TRCs or similar initiatives, their work unavoidably leads to burying these "cries for vengeance". Authors such as Verne Harris, Anthony Holiday and Jacques Derrida criticised such commissions and this type of historical analysis for stimulating forgetting in the name of remembering.[64] Belgian theoretical historian Berber Bevernage claims that the turn to history by TRC's is part of a "politics of time", meant to create a clear rupture with the past and, in doing so, lock it away safely. He criticises this process by noting that it benefits the perpetrators more than the victims.[65] Campbell and Connolly state in an article: "It is unnecessary to take the radical constructivist position that all truth is socially constructed to see that truth processes can involve significant degrees of agency, entrepreneurship (including

59 E.A. Cole, *Transitional justice.*

60 'Narrative and negotiation, remembering and reparation: issues at the interface of history and the law', in J. Torpey, *Politics and the Past*, 295–305. For a historical perspective, see also: Conseil International des Archives et Direction des Archives en France, *Mémoire et Histoire: les Etats Européens face aux droits des citoyens du XXIème siècle*, Bucarest, 1998.

61 E. Daly, *Truth Skepticism.*

62 E. Daly, *Truth Skepticism*, 27.

63 M. Ignatieff, 'Articles of Faith', (1996), 25 *Index on Censorship*, 110–122, at 121.

64 A. Holiday, 'Forgiving and forgetting', in S. Nuttall and C. Coutzee (eds.), *Negotiating the past*, Oxford, 2000, 43–56; B. Bevernage, 'Geschiedenis en herinnering aan gewelddadig conflict. Over het onomkeerbare, het onherroepelijke and de productie van "afstand"', (2011), 45/2 *Vlaams Marxistisch Tijdschrift*, 54–65.

65 "Therefore, it indeed can be asked whether the 'historical turn' in the field of transitional justice always serves an ethical cause", B. Bevernage, *History, Memory and State-Sponsored Violence. Time and Justice*, Routledge, 2011, 86–87.

deliberate silences) and resource deployment, both by those attempting to mould truth and by those to whom the truths relate".[66]

Certainly this last point is familiar to historians (and I will revisit the issue in my conclusion). History selects and interprets and inevitably becomes a political arbitrator between remembering and forgetting. But can we reduce the role of history in TRCs, expert commissions, trials and more generally to the field of TJ to that of a political instrument meant to control the past to support current political agendas? That seems highly one-sided. Historical consciousness and collective remembrance develop over a longer term. This process is uncontrollable to a large extent. History plays a much more diverse and complicated role than the one-sided "locking away the past".[67] We are in need of more concrete, empirically driven case studies over a longer-term period, on how these processes evolve; something which this book will try to do.

What society basically asks historians to do in all the contexts described above is to provide a scholarly *consensus* on the past. This is what E. Barkan defends, namely, that after war and conflict, historians should come up with a "negotiated history": a history that all different opposing parties can support and endorse.[68] A consensus on the past is seen as the basis for harmony and reconciliation. What a consensus on the past seems to mean here, is an agreement on basic interpretative elements as well as some kind of fixed, legally decreed decision on this interpretation. The latter is important. Closure as a founding element of societal stability obviously is of little use when the consensus changes every year due to new historical research. Factual details can change, of course, but the fundamental consensus ("the truth") is expected to remain.

This is where I detect one of the basic tensions. This kind of scholarly consensus – or perhaps more precisely the *expectations* created by stakeholders in society around such a consensus – is to a large extent contradictory to history as a profession. Obviously, some kind of basic consensus amongst historians about major historical events will always exist. World War II and the Holocaust are good examples of this. Although still hotly debated and frantically researched, some scholarly consensus on many basic elements exists. Nevertheless, history as an academic discipline is, at its very core, essentially revisionist. Perhaps even more than any other domain within the humanities, history as an academic discipline thrives and advances through the revision of a perceived consensus. Confronting an alleged consensus is basically what historians do. This, then,

---

66 C. Campbell and I. Connolly, 'The sharp end: Armed opposition movements, transitional truth processes and the Rechtsstaat', (2012), *IJTJ*,11–39, at 38.

67 Editorial note, (2012) *The international Journal of Transitional Justice*, 1–10.

68 E. Barkan, *The guilt of nations: Restitution and negotiating historical injustice*, Baltimore/London, 2000, 10.

might help us understand why the idea of closure in the field of TJ is difficult to translate easily to the historic profession. Historians do not want to close the past; they want to continuously search for new ways of opening it. We can find similar echoes, for example, when Maier says historians should write "contrapuntal" and not "harmonic" history: "the historian must create a narrative that allows for contending voices, that reveals the aspirations of all actors […]".[69] This is probably why many historians are so opposed to the idea of controlling the past by law or decree. One might succeed for a certain amount of time to arrange the past by decree, only to find out that elements unearthed by historians will resurface with a vengeance.

From the historian's point of view, an ongoing re-evaluation of the past might be the best type of reconciliation we can get. A state-sponsored report on a historic truth can be perfectly legitimate at one specific moment in time, but only as a step in an ongoing process of revision; a revision that can (and will) lead to heated debates and memory "incidents". A historical take could be that we need to accept these 'memory eruptions', or even conflicts, not as a negative sign that the past still haunts us but as an unavoidable and even positive part of a process. Indeed: "If a new regime is truly democratic and open, it must tolerate continued efforts to challenge the dominant view of history", even if this dominant view has been created by the official 'authoritative record' constructed by the regime itself.[70] Indeed: "A well-documented report can force the debate to move past the question of whether abuses occurred to discussions on how to remedy ongoing suffering and prevent future abuses".[71] Memory incidents should not be considered as failures of the work of a TRC, but should be accepted as unavoidable steps. These memory eruptions betray underlying changing attitudes in society. What is interesting is how and why these "eruptions" occur. Is their impact always positive (or negative) in terms of truth-seeking or reconciliation? Again, it is exactly this question that will be tackled throughout the chapters and the comparative conclusions in this book.

4. JUSTICE AND (HISTORIC) TRUTH

The third and final point of tension is based on the rhetorical connection made between the concept of historic truth and the idea of "justice".

When asked to describe the role of history in the TJ field, many people will probably refer to the element of "truth-seeking". For a historian, "truth" is a

69 Ch. Maier, 'Doing history, doing justice', in R.I. Rotberg and D. Thompson, *Truth v. justice: The morality of truth commissions*, New York/Oxford, 2000, 268.

70 E. Daly, *Truth Skepticism*, 29.

71 E. Daly, *Truth Skepticism*, 33.

difficult concept. Most historians today firmly believe that history is malleable and that 'objective truth' is at best a touchstone in historical criticism. TRCs today also recognise the multiplicity of truth (or better: 'truths'),[72] although they cannot come to clear conclusions on how to deal with this subjectivity and multiplicity.[73] However, within the TJ field, truth (and therefore history) inevitably carries moral implications. Indeed: "Truth, justice and memory (or the prevention of forgetting) have long been closely interwoven concepts".[74]

History is perceived here mainly as an instrument against forgetting (against oblivion). To quote Cubitt again: "historical writing on the Holocaust for example, is frequently intended (…) as an instrument of remembering – a way of holding on to people and events that are in danger of being forgotten or misremembered".[75] Maier writes: "Like reparations, historical narratives are increasingly conceived of as compensatory. (…) They introduce new agents who have hitherto been left in obscurity".[76] The act of writing history itself becomes imbued with a moral element; doing justice by preventing oblivion. Historians become memory-keepers as a moral duty towards the "victims of the past". Martha Minow suggests that this way writing history becomes an essential part of restorative justice.[77] Jeffrey Olick and Brenda Coughlin even suggest a direct correlation between writing history to prevent victim-oblivion and the current trends towards so-called politics of regret (see further).[78]

It holds a particularly powerful appeal to many historians as well, probably because it has deep and broad foundations in the many types of "new history" after 1945 (oral history, social histories, history from below or daily life, gender history, workers history, gay and lesbian history etc.). These fields explicitly originated from the intention to bring to light histories of forgotten groups ("victims of history"). They placed subaltern, hitherto invisible groups at the centre of attention by shifting the focus away from traditional ruling elites. The term "popular memory" was essential here; collective memories that were in need of being preserved. An ideological dimension was often explicit. This was certainly visible in the field of oral history.[79] Rather than

---

72 See also: A. Isaacs, 'At war with the past? The politics of truth seeking in Guatemala', (2010), 4 *IJTJ*, 251–274.

73 E. Daly, 'Truth Skepticism: An Inquiry into the Value of Truth in Times of Transition', (2008) 2/1 *IJTJ*, 23–41.

74 G. Cubitt, *History and Memory*, 55.

75 G. Cubitt, *History and Memory*, 52.

76 Ch.S. Maier, *Overcoming the past?* at 303.

77 M. Minow, *Between vengeance and forgiveness: facing history after Genocide and mass violence*, Boston, Mass., 1998, 81–82. For a take on restorative justice in general: J. Braithwaite, *Restorative Justice and Responsive Regulation*, Oxford, 2002.

78 J.K. Olick and B. Coughlin, 'The politics of regret: analytical frames', in Torpey, *Politics and the Past*, 37–63.

79 P. Thompson, *The Voice of the Past*, London, 1978.

staying a detached observer, the historian was encouraged to become a participator with the aims of creating awareness within populaces of their specific group identities.[80]

New histories obviously interacted with broader societal developments and new takes on commemoration and remembrance. When victim groups gradually became more conscious of the specificity of their wartime experiences, they organised themselves to place certain claims on society. A first part of their post-war agency, however, was always to preserve their memories and this way, get history on their sides. The most explicit political translation of this moralised history regime can probably be found in the growing number of public apologies or statements of regret. An increasing number of public authorities or other formal representatives offer official apologies for past wrongdoings by their predecessors.[81] This also is a type of symbolic reparation. Olick and Coughlin consider regret even as "a form of historical consciousness".[82] The rise of this "culture of regret", according to both authors, is "[...] part of the transformation of temporality and historicity that is tied up with the decline, rather than the triumph, of the nation-state".[83] Essentially, the culture of regret is a political and social product of changing discourses, sensibilities and the rise of the human rights paradigm in Europe. However, history is one big reservoir of things that by today's moral and judicial standards are considered wrongdoings and mass violations of human rights.[84.] The geographical issues (borders) alone are completely insolvable. "When is the past too long ago?", as Peté and Du Plessis ask. These are political decisions within a much broader societal debate that ultimately depend on how one defines reparation and what it is one exactly hopes to repay.

From a historical, academic point of view, however, this is an anachronistic question. Things we consider grave human rights violations right now were considered differently decades ago. Rousso notes the contradiction that on the one hand there is the recognition that certain crimes are irreparable and on the other the increasing demands to offer some kind of reparation. The result is memorial militancy; the idea of an inexhaustible debt to the past which serves to "up the moral ante" but does not necessarily enhance understanding.[85]

---

80 Popular Memory Group, 'Popular memory. Theory, politics, method', in R. Perks and A. Thomson (eds.), *The Oral History Reader*, London/New York, 2006, 32–43.

81 For this see: C. Jenkins, 'Taking apology seriously', in S. Peté and M. DU PLESSIS (eds.), *Repairing the past? International perspectives on reparations for gross human rights abuses*, Antwerp/Oxford, 53–82.

82 J.K. Olick and B. Coughlin, *The politics of regret*, at 52.

83 J.K. Olick and B. Coughlin, *The politics of regret*, at 56.

84 S. Peté and M. Du Plessis, 'Reparations for gross violations of human rights in context', in S. Peté and M. Du Plessis (eds.), *Repairing the past*, 3–28, at 27.

85 H. Rousso, *La Hantise du Passé: entretien avec Philippe Petit*, Paris, 1998.

In this moral approach, history and the field of TJ seem to find evident common ground.[86] In its 2005 set of principles, the UN commission for human rights defined the "right to know the truth" as an inalienable right. Several concrete actions are prescribed: safeguarding archives, making them available, recovering facts and unearthing hidden truths. Dutch historian Antoon De Baets, who uses an ethical approach to history as a profession, equates "the right to history" with "the right to know the truth about past human rights violations".[87] He considers the history of war and dictatorship as essential activities for any democratic society: "A democracy must offer a truthful critique on past dictatorships and conflicts".[88] The notion of history as "a moral duty against oblivion" runs parallel with the current European (and global) trends of claims for reparations (restitution, compensation, rehabilitation, satisfaction and guarantees of non-repetition) by victim groups.[89] TRCs also increasingly see reparation as an inclusive concept, an integrative approach meant to deal with psychic harms and trauma. An active memorialisation policy is an accepted part of this.[90] Next to prosecution of perpetrators, establishing the truth, reparations, institutional reform and reconciliation initiatives, commemorations are one of the basic pillars of TJ policies today.[91] The basic communication texts of the ICTJ in New York say: "architectural memorials, museums and commemorative activities are indispensable educational initiatives to establish the record beyond denial, and prevent repetition".[92]

This moral approach to history implies that forgetting becomes some kind of injustice; some kind of deficiency within democratic capacities in society, a lack to recognise victims, a lack to (literally) do justice to past events.[93] Perhaps the strongest political exponent of this context, is the so-called "duty to remember". This has become an element of cultural and education policies in several European countries, for example in Belgium and France. The duty to remember legally decrees what to remember, how to remember it and what basic message ("lessons") to distil from it. The duty to remember is a political

---

86 Ch. Maier, 'Doing history, doing justice', in R.I. Rotberg and D. Thompson, *Truth v. justice*, 261–278.

87 A. De Baets, *Responsible History*, New York/Oxford, 2009, 68.

88 A. De Baets, *Responsible History*, 70.

89 P. Hayner, *Unspeakable truths: Confronting state terror and atrocity*, Routledge, 2001, 171.

90 B. Hamber, L. Sevcenko and E. Naidu, 'Utopian dreams or practical possibilities? The challenges of evaluating the impact of memorialization in societies in transition', (2010), *IJTJ*, 397–420.

91 L. Bickford, 'Transitional justice', in *The Encyclopedia of Genocide and Crimes Against Humanity*, New York, 2004, vol. 3, 1044–45.

92 ICTJ website (consulted on 20 December 2012). Link: www.ictj.org/our-work/transitional-justice-issues/truth-and-memory.

93 See also: J.W. Booth, 'The unforgotten: Memories of justice', *American Political Science Review* 95:4, 2001, 777–791.

driving force for the field of peace or remembrance education. This field views itself as complementary to historical research. Its main goal is to use knowledge of the past to change values and steer the behaviour of individuals and groups in the present. History has to search for the most clear examples in the past, where underlying societal mechanisms of racism, exclusion, war, violence and even genocide could be projected on today's society. The past becomes a tool for civic education in current democratic value systems.[94] The duty of remembrance and peace education both result from the dominant human rights paradigm. Despite the importance it gives to history, many historians themselves seem to feel uneasy about the political, legal and normative issues this duty to remember raises.[95]

An important distinction to be made here is how one understands the concept of "responsibility". Individual and collective responsibilities carry different meanings for historians, than the decisions on judicial and political guilt by courts and politicians. Responsibilities can be understood by historians as a complex, entangled dynamic process of individual competences and structures, changing contextual factors with a prehistory leading up to the events, individual ideologies and convictions/norms, certain perceptions and (lack of) knowledge of the people who made certain decisions at that time. Putting these (and other) factors together can create a complex picture where individual and collective responsibilities emerge. But this is far removed from the question of who bears the biggest guilt. Historians can provide a broader picture within its historic context, and, as Du Plessis argues, programmes to raise such forms of public awareness can be considered forms of legitimate reparation.[96]

The duty to remember and the politics of regret, however, go beyond raising awareness and stimulating historical consciousness. For many historians, the moral duty to remember needs limits, definitions and a clearer framework. As food for thought, this could also entail reflections on the dynamics of forgetting in society, and the question of how societies can forget in acceptable ways.

---

94 K. Van Nieuwenhuyse and K. Wils, 'Remembrance education between history teaching and citizenship education', in *Citizenship Teaching and Learning*, 2012 (vol. 7, nr. 2), 157–171.

95 Z. Todorov, 'The uses and abuses of memory', in H. Marchitello, *What Happens to History: the Renewal of Ethics in Contemporary Thought*, New York, 2001.

96 M. Du Plessis, 'Reparations and international law: how are reparations to be determined, against whom, and what form should they take?' in S. Peté and M. Du Plessis (eds.), *Repairing the past*, 147–177.

5. TO CONCLUDE: HOW THIS BOOK APPROACHES HISTORY IN TRANSITIONAL JUSTICE

In this introduction I wanted to sketch a broad picture to clarify some of the recurring tensions between the historic profession and the field of TJ. The field of TJ has clearly evolved to be highly interdisciplinary. However, the integration of history seems more difficult than that of certain other social sciences. In this introduction, I wanted to indicate factors that might help to better understand some possible causes.

We believe that history can be beneficial for the current field of TJ. The introduction above can lead to the simple conclusion that history needs to preserve its specificity and in fact use it as a strength. This book wants to be a practical exercise in doing exactly that.

This book uses an empirically driven approach. We use several historic national case studies in a longer term international comparative research. Authors of the chapters were asked to treat three large chronological phases in TJ: first, historical antecedents or precedents of TJ policies (if any); second, the actual main phase of TJ policy development and implementation after war and/or dictatorship; and third, the longer term, intergenerational impact of those TJ policies over several decades. The latter was an important focal point. We worked towards a mutual comparative result. All the authors used a common checklist of topics and questions that offered a guiding analytical framework. This means that despite certain heterogeneity, all of the case studies in this book were written with the same basic set of questions.

The initial premise of the project was that the European perspective had the advantage of the lengthy time span. For many of the European cases involved, decades (and generations) have passed since the examined policies were first designed and executed. By using these comparative case studies based on a mutual framework, we hope to provide insights on the way TJ policies impact the evolutions of collective memories over several decades, or even generations.

The four post-1945 transition chapters, West-Germany (Annete Weinke), France (Marc Olivier Baruch), Belgium (Nico Wouters and Dirk Luyten) and the Netherlands (Peter Romijn and Erik Schumacher), can really use the longer term intergenerational angle to its fullest potential. At first glance, national differences seem to dominate the picture, until one takes the longer term outcomes over several decades as the primary angle and we can gradually see similar mechanisms emerge.

The three following chapters tackle the southern European cases at the beginning of the so-called 'third wave of democracy', Portugal, Spain and Greece. The case of Spain is almost a textbook case for TJ policy evaluation, but the duo of Paloma Aguilar and Clara Ramírez-Barat succeed in offering many new insights based on innovative archival research. They provide a wealth of recent data as well as a critical re-assessment of the alleged "success" of Spain's transition. Much less is internationally known on the transition after dictatorship in Portugal, but the events described by Filipa Raimundo and António Costa Pinto prove we need to pay more attention to this case, certainly in comparison with Spain. In particular, this concerns understanding the mechanisms in which the societal dynamic to deal with the past suddenly lost momentum after 1980 and silence became an accepted part of Portuguese society.

Stefanos Katsikas offers an in-depth analysis of Greece's post-1974 trials of the leaders of the military junta and the so-called EAT-ESA torture trials. One of his focal points is the interaction between Greece's national political context in relation to certain international events.

The last two chapters treat post-1989 transitions in Hungary (written by Renáta Uitz) and Poland (written by Klaus Bachmann). These two cases diverge greatly from the post-1945 transitions. Nevertheless, comparison is interesting exactly because of these divergences, as well as the fact that the TJ process is still much more an ongoing and open process in these two countries.

The book concludes with two complementary chapters. In the first concluding chapter, Luc Huyse offers a general comparative "group photo" of the nine chapters. His comparative search for patterns of recurrent processes visible in the nine national chapters analyses the key factors that influenced TJ policy development, execution and its direct and longer term impacts. My own comparative conclusion uses the issue of the longer term impact as the starting point for a more in-depth look on the process of memory making, including the so-called politics of memory.

WEST GERMANY: A CASE OF TRANSITIONAL JUSTICE *AVANT LA LETTRE*?

Annette WEINKE

1. INTERNATIONAL LAW AND 20TH CENTURY GERMANY

1.1. THE "*LONGUE DURÉE*" OF THE GERMAN "STRUGGLE TO COME TO TERMS"

One of the most extraordinary criminal trials in recent German judicial history ended in Munich in May 2011. There is much reason to believe that this will be the last trial of its kind in the Federal Republic. After fourteen months and more than 90 days of proceedings a court jury delivered a verdict against John (Ivan) Demjanjuk. In July 2009, the former Trawniki guard had been extradited to Germany from the United States, and shortly afterwards the Central office for prosecuting Nazi crimes, located in the state of Baden-Württemberg, had cited him in the course of its investigations into the extermination camp at Sobibór. The Bavarian state attorney's office brought charges against him, not for genocide but for participation in 28,000 simple counts of "murder". On the basis of a legal rationale that is surely unique in the history of German criminal justice for Nazi cases, the court sentenced the 91-year-old defendant to five years imprisonment as an accessory to murder, with the term suspended due to the man's advanced age.[1]

Like in a magnifying glass, the Demjanjuk trial allows us to focus on issues that continue to connect the Second World War with the post-war era down to this day. Covered by the neologism of "transitional justice", these issues now belong to the basic inventory of an enlightened and self-reflective treatment of a dictatorial and violent history. Can a liberal constitutional state take up the

1 A. BENZ, *Der Henkersknecht. Der Prozess gegen John (Iwan) Demjanjuk in München*, Berlin, 2011.

mission of atoning for the state-sanctioned injustices of a defunct predecessor regime by punishing the perpetrators and rehabilitating their victims? By what means can the state assure that the rule of law is not derailed, that the fragile balance is kept between the victims' expectations of justice and the principles of a legitimate legal system? Can the interests of a democracy in consolidation be protected when the institutions of the state itself provide the primary means for pursuing the difficult mission of overcoming the former dictatorship's consequences? Given the fact that both the Nazi regime and the modern communist dictatorships of the 20th century could not have existed without a minimum degree of consent and participation from the society as a whole, should we conclude instead that the overcoming of a totalitarian past, if it is to be successful and lasting, must involve the active participation of large parts of the people? Finally, the question remains of what a concept like "historical justice" can even mean, in the face of millions of murdered victims.[2]

As the boom in the interdisciplinary academic sub-discipline of transitional justice continues, the case of the West German post-war democracy also still holds a relatively prominent place within it. Unlike Japan, the other great field for applying the new humanitarian international law after the Second World War, Germany is thought in many ways to show the best case for a restoration of civilised norms and democratisation. To foreign scholars of German history like the American sociologist John Torpey, the West German case even has set worldwide standards of reckoning with an extreme violent past; according to Torpey, with the beginning of the 21st century '"we are all Germans now" in the sense that all countries (and many other entities as well) that wish to be regarded as legitimate confront pressures to make amends for the more sordid aspects of their past and, often, to compensate victims of earlier wrongdoings".[3] In this view both the overcoming of dictatorship, war and genocide, and the re-education of the Germans into democrats and citizens, are interpreted as the results of an *Aufarbeitung* or "coping" strategy, which was first imposed after 1945 from the outside by the Allies as representatives of the larger international community and later internalised and conducted by the Germans themselves, though in a slow, often contradictory process. A decisive contribution to the successful transformation and self-transformation is attributed to the modernised international law of war.[4] In this reading the Nuremberg criminal justice project was not just a reaction to unique and especially serious historical crimes, but can also be understood as a process of learning from the negative

2 L.H. Meyer, *Historische Gerechtigkeit*, Berlin/New York, 2005.

3 J. TORPEY, *Politics and the Past*, NY, 2003, 3; H. Wefing, *Der Fall Demjanjuk. Der letzte große NS-Prozess*, München, 2011.

4 P. Betts, 'Germany, International Justice and the 20th Century', in (2005) 17/1–2 *History and Memory*, 45–86.

experiences after the First World War as manifest in the subsequent national trials before the *Reich* courts in Leipzig. While historians – usually skeptical of evolutionary patterns of interpretation – stress the ambivalent effects of personnel purges and criminal trials[5], scholars of the law tend to assume close connections between the overcoming of Nazi rule in Europe, the establishment of a universalist human rights regime, and the gradual creation of a civil political culture.[6]

A precise examination of the German experience may be also illuminating because the processes did not end abruptly after the founding of the two republics and the partial restoration of national sovereignty, but were followed by patterns that in certain ways have continued until now, with the case of Demjanjuk as only the latest example. This allows us to analyse the different levels of "politics of the past" (*Vergangenheitspolitik*) and politics of memory, the construction of public and private forms of memorialisation, and historiographic developments within the frame of a *longue durée*.

The indigenous "overcoming of the past" pursued by the German elites after 1948–49 in politics, the justice system and academia was characterised at first primarily by a particular discourse of *Rechtsstaat* (a concept analogous but not identical to the Anglo-Saxon concept of "rule of law,") "reconciliation," and "German honour" that was explicitly understood as a counter-project to the universalist ideas of the Western Allies.[7] As a result of their postulated identity of the Federal Republic as the legal successor to the German *Reich* (a position that in international law contradicted the Allied view of *debellatio*), the late-arriving Nazi trials in the FRG proceeded from restrictive interpretations of national criminal law. This decision *de facto* entailed a marginalisation of the victims and the impunity of high-ranking perpetrators who had held genuine decision-making authority. In reaction to the educational and punitive aims of the Allies, the Federal Republic developed a peculiarly technocratic approach to the past, one justified above all by a "top-down" definition of state and security interests. Both public opinion and demands for justice from those once persecuted by the Nazis were regarded as factors that could be largely treated as negligible quantities.

Some scholars have interpreted this as the attempt by West German legal elites to use the Nazi trials as a primary venue for restoring the concept of the

5 T. Judt, *Die Geschichte Europas seit dem Zweiten Weltkrieg*, Bonn, 2006.

6 R. Teitel, 'Transitional Justice Genealogy', (2003) 16 *Harvard Human Rights Journal*, 69–94.

7 C. Goschler, 'Politische Moral und Moralpolitik. Die lange Dauer der "Wiedergutmachung" und das politische Bild des "Opfers"', in H. Knoch (ed.), *Bürgersinn mit Weltgefühl. Politische Moral und solidarischer Protest in den sechziger und siebziger Jahren*, Göttingen, 2007), 138–156, at 145.

Rechtsstaat.[8] As a matter of fact, it could be argued that the legal-philosophical premises, political functions and moral implications of the trials were closely intertwined. By conducting them on the basis of ordinary statutory law (and not international humanitarian law), one could stick to the fiction of an embattled "legal continuity" and the firm belief that the German state – as the embodiment of a higher "ethical idea" ("as the reality of a moral idea" [*"als Wirklichkeit der sittlichen Idee"*] or "that which is reasonable in and for itself" [*"das an und für sich Vernünftige"*], in the words of Hegel) – had not been infringed in its substance after 1933. In a conservative reading of Ernst Fraenkel's notion of two antagonistic spheres constituting the "Dual State", the "prerogative state" (*Maßnahmestaat*) of Himmler's SS had gained a status of predominance, but had not been able to extinguish completely the sphere of the "normative state" (*Normenstaat*). Instead the latter had survived the Third *Reich* in a form of quasi-hibernation, and the traditional elites had the task to demonstrate that the "rule of law" and brutal violence had coexisted during those twelve years, albeit only in a very awkward and distorted way.

What is remarkable about this interpretation of the past is its defensiveness. It mostly lacked the triumphant tone and the posture of moral high grounds, which had been typical for right-Hegelian state discourses in the tradition of Carl Schmitt. In contrast to the Weimar years, the post-war debate over legal positivism, the status of Nazi law and the role of civil servants and the judiciary in the Third *Reich* never gained the currency of a national *Leitdebatte*. The main reason for this probably was that both the lack of a unified national state and Adenauer's policy of pursuing West Germany's sovereignty by integration prevented the recurrence of mythical state concepts. Disillusioned by their experiences with the "total state" of the Nazi era, the former vanguard of "conservative revolutionaries" like Hans Freyer, Arnold Gehlen, Helmut Schelsky and Ernst Forsthoff had transformed themselves into a bunch of "technocratic conservatives" who replaced their former nationalistic concept of the "ethical" state with the rather profane and pragmatic idea of the "welfare state".[9]

It is also important to see that the trials of Nazi crimes, reparations and restitutions, and delayed personnel purges were never strictly domestic issues. The operative German actors always had an eye on the special "German" situation, which was manifest in the obligations of international alliance and

8 D.O. Pendas, '"Law, not Vengeance": Human Rights, the Rule of the Law and the Claims of Memory in German Holocaust Trials', in M.Ph. Bradley and Patrice (eds.), *Truth claims: representation and human rights*, Rutgers, 2002, 23–42, at 28.

9 J. Hacke, 'Staatsbilder: Einige Konzeptionen des Staates in der Soziologie und Sozialphilosophie der Bundesrepublik', in H. Münkler and J. Hacke (eds.), *Wege in die neue Bundesrepublik. Politische Mythen und kollektive Selbstbilder nach 1989*, Frankfurt a.M., 2009, 65–82.

integration with the West and in the constraints of the German-German system conflict. From a historian's perspective, one of the most surprising phenomena is how a not-very popular judicial and administrative coping process at times became the catalyst for a culture of public debate and a pluralist understanding of history, and how this happened in spite of (or perhaps *because of*) the relatively meager substantive results.[10] Nevertheless, it would take until the late 1980s before the prevailing pattern would again change. Under the influence of the confrontation with the East German communist past and the worldwide wave of institutionalisation in humanitarian international criminal law (e.g., the establishment of the International Criminal Court for Former Yugoslavia [ICTY] and the permanent International Criminal Court [ICC]), Germany underwent a partial rapprochement with globalised or universalist discourses; at the same time, the era following the 1989–91 transition also saw the country clinging to national legal traditions and older patterns of discourse.

1.2. "A PAST THAT WILL NOT GO AWAY..." CONTINUITY AND RUPTURE AFTER 1945

As the Federal Republic is not the only country to have confronted the problem of overcoming dictatorship on its own (and with shifting intensity), a comparative approach using other cases and other nations is possible and in recent years has become more routine.[11] But comparative analysis cannot work without an agreed-upon common frame of analysis and common perspectives for comparison. Developments since the fall of the Soviet bloc have served to render much about the post-Second World War period more obvious: the early post-war purges, the criminal trials against NS regime perpetrators and abettors, the restitutions to the victims, but also the amnesties and exemptions from prosecution can today all be interpreted as integral parts of a secular, transnational transformation process that began immediately after the war and continues today, more than 65 years later.[12] Even if borders cannot always be drawn clearly between judicially camouflaged reprisals and legitimate processes under rule of law, there was an undeniable categorical difference between the countless (European and indeed world-wide) *ad hoc* trials of the early post-war

10 A. Weinke, 'Strafrechtliche Abrechnung als Medium gesellschaftlichen Wandels? Bundesrepublik und DDR', in K. von Lingen (ed.), *Kriegserfahrung und Nationale Identität in Europa nach 1945*, Paderborn, 2009, 131–149.

11 K.-D. Henke, and H. Woller (eds.), *Politische Säuberung in Europa. Die Abrechnung mit Faschismus und Kollaboration nach dem Zweiten Weltkrieg*, München, 1991; Deák, Gross and Judt (eds.), *Politics of Retribution*; N. Frei, (ed.), *Transnationale Vergangenheitspolitik. Der Umgang mit deutschen Kriegsverbrechern in Europa nach dem Zweiten Weltkrieg*, Göttingen, 2006.

12 Lagrou, *The Legacy of Nazi Occupation: Patriotic Memory and National Recovery in Western Europe, 1945–1965*, Cambridge, 2000.

period, which could be viewed largely as expressions of the then prevalent patriotic (or nationalist-chauvinist) moods, and the internationalist approach of the punitive program that the Allies set up for the two perpetrator nations of Germany and Japan. Given this background, it seems to require explanation that many European countries, after a certain lapse of time, adopted similar mechanisms of a primarily legalistic treatment of the past, which tended to run at a similar temporal pace and to pursue similarly socially integrative functions. These parallels are conspicuous and point to a transformation of moral understanding, but also to a change in the relationship between citizen and state. The French historian Henry Rousso recently described these processes as the "legalisation" or "judicialisation" of the past.[13] In this view, the implementation of tribunals and lustration programs signified not so much the closure of a global military conflict as the prelude to a new phase characterised by the emergence of the law and judiciary as "vectors of memory" and authorities of historical narration, with enormous effects on representations of history in the long run.

In the following, before I turn to the specifics of the West German case and describe a few differences and similarities to the parallel experiences in other states, I first wish to briefly define a number of parameters that had decisive effects on its basic structure. While I am reluctant to employ the worn-out trope of a German "special path,"[14] it was significant that the country was subject to different conditions than prevailed in most of the post-war Western European democracies. In a kind of dialectic back-and-forth between occupiers and occupied, the occupation period saw the establishment of a coping strategy in which formal legal procedures dominated, while a defensive attitude against universalist human rights concepts struck deep roots among the German actors.

The particular difficulties with a past "that will not go away" arose primarily from the thoroughgoing upheavals and ravages left in large parts of state and society by the rule of the NS regime from 1933 to 1945. As recent work on the history of West German liberalisation especially has found, the resulting distortions remained long after the transition of 1945, and exercised influence in particular on the politics of the past (amnesties, prosecutions, personnel assessments, reparations and restitutions).[15] The final years of the war brought

---

13 H. Rousso, 'History of Memory, Policies of the Past: What For?', in K. Jarausch and Th. Lindenberger (eds.), *Conflicted Memories. Europeanizing Contemporary Histories*, Oxford/New York, 2007, 23–37; Idem, 'Égo-Histoire. Vichy in Geschichte, Erinnerung und Recht', in H. Rousso, *Frankreich und die "dunklen Jahre". Das Regime von Vichy in Geschichte und Gegenwart*, Göttingen, 2010, 82–178.

14 U. Herbert, 'Europe in High Modernity. Reflections on a Theory of the 20th Century', (2007) 5 *Journal of Modern European History*, 5–21.

15 U. Herbert (ed.), *Wandlungsprozesse in Westdeutschland. Belastung, Integration, Liberalisierung 1945–1980*, Göttingen, 2002.

the complete collapse of political, economic and social structures, and for many Germans, the loss of national sovereignty and great-power status seemed to be the most tangible expression of this. Although a part of the racist *Volksgemeinschaft* at least internally turned away from the political leadership in the latter years of war, their exterior behavior displayed a stubborn mixture of apathy, spite and the will to persevere until the bitter end.[16]

The gradual erosion of the National Socialist promise of order, consumer prosperity and harmony did not lead to effective popular protests or to the formation of a strong opposition movement against the NS regime; and neither did the regime's active inclusion of large strata of the people in the criminal policies of plunder and extermination. In contrast to the various European resistance movements, the German case saw a "resistance without the people", mainly composed of bourgeois and conservative dignitaries.[17] Even with the looming absolute military defeat of the Reich, the NS propaganda machinery was able to present the conspirators of 20 July 1944 as infamous "traitors to the Fatherland". Unlike countries like France or Italy, early post-war West Germany had no national heroic myth of resistance to draw upon in building a new positive identity, or to serve (despite all the legal problems) as the memorial anchor for a successful historical and judicial "self-investigation".[18] And, at first, there were almost no untainted counter-elites who could have shouldered the practical missions of democratic reconstruction or judicial reckoning with the old elites.

Also of great social-psychological consequence was that the radical population policies of the Nazis had created irreversible facts also within Germany itself. In the formerly Nazi-occupied countries of Western Europe, it was possible at least for war veterans and political resistance fighters (if not for the victims of racial persecution) to secure a place in the pantheon of national memory. Aside from a few re-migrants like the famous Fritz Bauer, however, the Federal Republic had almost no people left who could credibly represent the demand for a retroactive "justice" on the basis of their own historical experience.[19] The lack of a counter-narrative to the official discourse of memory was made even greater by the

16 D. Süss and W. Süss, 'Volksgemeinschaft und Vernichtungskrieg. Gesellschaft im NS-Deutschland', in D. Süss and W. Süss, (eds.), *Das "Dritte Reich". Eine Einführung*, München, 2008, 79–100.

17 H. Mommsen, 'Der deutsche Widerstand gegen Hitler: Eine Bilanz', in H. Mommsen, *Zur Geschichte Deutschlands im 20. Jahrhundert. Demokratie, Diktatur, Widerstand*, München, 2010, 235–250, at 235.

18 Ch. Cornelissen, '"Vergangenheitsbewältigung" – ein deutscher Sonderweg?', in Hammerstein, Mählert and Wolfrum (eds.), *Aufarbeitung*, 21–36; N. Frei, 'Die Rückkehr des Rechts. Justiz und Zeitgeschichte nach dem Holocaust', in N. Frei, *1945 und wir. Das Dritte Reich im Bewusstsein der Deutschen*, München, 2005, 63–82.

19 L. Huyse, 'The Criminal Justice System As a Political Actor in Regime Transitions: The Case of Belgium, 1944–50', in Deák, Gross and Judt (eds.), *Politics of Retribution*, 157–172.

competition of systems with the GDR, which served to discredit socialist and communist cultures of resistance *in toto*. Given this background, until the 1960s the discourse of national victimhood, of "German suffering" from the Allied bombing campaign and displacements of German populations in Eastern Europe prevailed, while the problem of active and passive complicity in National Socialist crime was usually ignored.

1.3. THE LEGACY OF "LEIPZIG" AND "NUREMBERG"

All that being said, the factor that most consistently shaped the German relationship to the country's past in the long term was the Allied political presence and their establishment of a new order. They were the ones who initially built an infrastructure for a comprehensive legal and administrative reckoning with National Socialism, and they dictated the frameworks and aims. Above all, the leading position of the Americans meant that the Western zones of occupation followed a specific pattern of *Aufarbeitung* based on an innovative legalism shaped in the United States, a doctrine that intentionally sought distance from the 19th-century Victorian "standard of civilisation".[20] This project was rooted in the New Deal liberalism of the 1930s and 1940s and its zeal for planning and social intervention. The concrete objective was to use the downfall of the German Reich as the opportunity for a fundamentally new interpretation of existing international law, and to create a multilateral security system that would get away from the discredited models of the League of Nations. The Kellogg-Briand Pact of 1928, which called for the international abolition of "wars of aggression," was promptly redefined into a criminal law. New *corpus delicti* such as "crimes against humanity" and new forms of criminal participation such as "conspiracy" were adapted both from the legal traditions of Anglo-Saxon common law and from the sociological analyses developed by German emigrants who had worked at the Office for Strategic Services (OSS) during the war.[21]

Despite their multilateral aims and universalist claims, the American-dominated international law discourse of the 20th century still made recourse to concepts of

20 E. Borgwardt, *A New Deal for the World: America's Vision for Human Rights*, Cambridge/Harvard, 2005; J. Osterhammel, *Die Verwandlung der Welt. Eine Geschichte des 19. Jahrhunderts*, München, 2009.

21 T.B. Müller, 'Die epistemischen Bedingungen der Macht. Wissenschaft, Staatsapparate und Stiftungen im frühen Kalten Krieg: Der institutionelle Kontext Otto Kirchheimers, Herbert Marcuses und Franz Neumanns in Amerika', in R.Ch. van Ooyen and F. Schale (eds.), *Kritische Verfassungspolitologie. Das Staatsverständnis von Otto Kirchheimer*, Baden-Baden, 2011, 35–66; R. Ahrens, 'Kartelle und Verschwörungen. Franz Neumanns „Behemoth" und die Nürnberger Prozesse', in N. Frei and T. Schanetzky (eds.), *Unternehmen im Nationalsozialismus. Zur Historisierung einer Forschungskonjunktur*, Göttingen, 2010, 26–35.

Western superiority and civilization. Just as the British-American human rights declarations during the war assumed the existence of a Western community of values[22], so too did the lodging of charges against the Third *Reich* rest on the assumption that principles like rule of law and due process had survived almost intact through the era of authoritarian and totalitarian regimes. Although the Americans and the British at times espoused entirely contrary ideas with regard to the future of Western-controlled colonial territories, the decline of Europe's colonial regimes and the resulting decolonisation debate provided an important background foil to the Nuremberg project of criminal prosecution.[23] The decision to indict the leading elites of the Nazi regime under international law thus arose from a dual motive. First of all, the Western Allies were concerned with reestablishing the liberal concept of order within their own sphere of influence, after it had suffered great damage from the National Socialist occupation of large parts of Europe. The Germans especially were to be guided firmly back into the fold of "civilised" states. Second, however, the Allies also desired to present a signal against racist ideologies and "superman" fantasies to the colonised peoples who were fighting for their own liberation. Given the perpetual virulence of the "race question," it was thought that a practical adherence to specific norms and rules could in the future help bolster the Western powers' self-categorisation as "civilised" states. Thus the Allied occupation's legalist treatment of the German *Reich* and prosecution of wartime occupation crimes can be read as an attempt to at least partly realise the promise of equality inherent in the modern international law of war through the exemplary punishment of the German elites. That this liberal internationalist legalism did not maintain a solid institutional basis after the end of the acute phase, and that the remarkable experiment's fascination faded quickly as the Cold War escalated, was due to both the continuing importance of the national sovereignty paradigm and the rapid exhaustion of Allied idealism in the bloody colonial wars of the post-1945 period.[24]

Besides the development of new norms for criminal law and the at-least partly successful anchoring of human rights principles in modern international law, the creative potential of the Nuremberg project was embodied especially in its innovative attempt to combine legal rulings, history politics, and a specific form of educational historiography. "Nuremberg" was meant not only to implement a political and legal agenda but also to pursue a historical and cultural mission. The latter was aimed simultaneously at the mass of Germans, the peoples of the Allied countries, and an imagined international public. This too again recalled the period after the First World War, when debates over the criminalisation of

---

22 M. Mazower, 'The Strange Triumph of Human Rights, 1933–1950', (2004) 47/2 *The Historical Journal*, 379–398.

23 F. Klose, *Menschenrechte im Schatten kolonialer Gewalt. Die Dekolonisierungskriege in Kenia und Algerien 1945–1962*, München, 2009.

24 Lagrou, *The Legacy*.

wars of aggression and plans for a tribunal against the government of the German *Reich* had strengthened the idea of "historical engineering" in all of the states involved.[25] The World War I Allies also did not consider it enough to give a legal rationale for the preparation of charges against representatives of the Wilhelmine state. They had also desired to establish an unassailable "context" (in Martti Koskenniemi's sense of the term) to underpin claims that they were delivering a specific "historical truth".[26] From the beginning, the Nuremberg tribunal was planned as a "world trial," aiming in part to compose the very same moral "international community" that until then was largely imaginary, and for this reason it was extremely important to lend a high degree of narrative plausibility and meaningful coherence to the indictment of the Nazi leadership.

That the picture of the Nazi state drawn by the prosecutors and court may seem relatively conventional and one-dimensional from a present-day perspective can be partly explained by the fact that all responsible institutions were concerned with legal politics, trial tactics, and the larger strategies of the occupation. At its core, the interpretation stressed individual intentionality, focusing strongly on the person of Hitler and the political leadership, and stressing the aggressive potential of the National Socialist *Lebensraum* ideology and its linear implementation "from above". Whereas the denazification proceedings – especially in the American zone – began as a personnel purge that would scrutinise millions of people, the instrument of criminal prosecution was clearly led by the sociopolitical goal of achieving an ideal separation between Nazis, elites, and the broad population. The retroactive indictment of functionaries for "conspiracy" to commit aggressive war and to murder "racially inferior" civilians was intended to build a bridge for Germans-at-large to distance themselves from the regime (and their own degrees of participation in it) after the fact. A special irony in the proceedings was that the prosecution was influenced strongly by the analyses of the Marxist, mostly Jewish-German social scientists who worked for the OSS during the war. This group of "enemy aliens" included well-known leftist intellectuals like Franz Neumann, Otto Kirchheimer and Herbert Marcuse.[27] They tended to attribute the rise of fascism mainly to structural deficits in the ostensibly neutral and apolitical liberal state, while also underestimating the consensual character of the German plunder-and-pillage society and the significance of its "redemptive anti-Semitism".[28]

---

[25] K. Wilson, 'Introduction: Governments, Historians and "Historical Engineering"', in K. Wilson (ed.), *Forging the Collective Memory. Government and International Historians through Two World Wars*, Providence, 1996, 1–27.

[26] M. Koskenniemi, 'Between Impunity and Show Trials', in J.A. Frowein, and R. Wolfrum (eds.), *Max Planck Yearbook of United Nation Law* 6, 2002, 1–35.

[27] M. Salter, *Nazi War Crimes, US Intelligence and Selective Prosecution at Nuremberg. Controversies Regarding the Role of the Office of Strategic Services*, Abingdon/New York, 2007.

[28] S. Friedländer, *Das Dritte Reich und die Juden. Verfolgung und Vernichtung*, Bonn, 2006.

Materially, this form of court-based history writing was supported above all by a deliberate and massive use of official documents captured from German archives, expert briefs by historians and academics, and documentary footage taken by Allied film teams took during their military advance (known as "evidence films"). Fearing that conventional judicial forms of representation would fail to convey the monstrosity and non-representability of the Nazi mass murder, the Americans relied all the more on the mechanisms of a "visible justice".[29] Despite the substantive contribution to the prosecution from Jewish refugee organisations, Robert H. Jackson, the American chief prosecutor, rejected their request to submit an *amicus curiae* brief.[30] In place of living victims, whom Jackson considered to be an unpredictable factor, film played the dual function of evidence and witness testimony against the Nazi atrocities. That the visual material outranked the living victims was described as a preference for "hard evidence" (of documents and films) over "soft evidence" (of witness testimonies)[31], and was possible only because in preparing for the International Military Tribunal (IMT) the Western Allies gave themselves the right to relax the traditional procedural rules of the Anglo-Saxon criminal justice system.[32]

Although we look back with almost seven decades of perspective, the ambitious Nuremberg project still cannot be reduced to one simple conclusion or one interpretative framework. Its history of ideas seems to belong within the debate on human rights and humanitarian interventionism that arose after 1918, but its practical implementation often diverged from its ideal goals. In summary we can say that fair-trial principles were followed at least in the Western zones, while in practice human rights receded in importance as a political impetus (if one even wants to attribute it to the Allied trials). Otherwise, how the new punitive principles and guidelines for denazification were applied very much depended on the specifics of the prosecuted criminal frameworks and differed greatly among the occupation zones. Looking back on later developments in the Federal Republic, we can observe that an impressive number of proceedings had already been concluded before the new democratic institutions were even fully established. Much of that work was also done through the West German courts established under Allied supervision in 1946, which handled NS crimes committed against German nationals.[33]

---

29 R. Overy, 'The Nuremberg trials: international law in the making', in Ph. Sands (ed.), *From Nuremberg to The Hague: the future of international criminal justice*, Cambridge, 2004, 1–29.

30 M.A. Lewis, 'The World Jewish Congress and the Institute of Jewish Affairs at Nuremberg: Ideas, Strategies, and Political Goals, 1942–1946', (2008) 36 *Yad Vashem Studies*, 181–210.

31 E. Haberer, 'History and Justice: Paradigms of the Prosecution of Nazi Crimes', (2005) 19/3 *Holocaust & Genocide Studies*, 487–519, at 492.

32 C. Vismann, *Medien der Rechtsprechung*, ed. by Alexandra Kemmerer und Markus Krajewski, Frankfurt a.M., 2011.

33 A. Eichmüller, 'Die Strafverfolgung von NS-Verbrechen durch westdeutsche Justizbehörden seit 1945', (2008) 4 *VfZ*, 621–640.

According to the latest, conservative estimates, up to 100,000 Germans and Austrians were tried before courts in all of Europe after the war on charges of participation in specific crimes or membership in a criminal organisation.[34] That does not include those who were temporarily imprisoned, were forced to forfeit property, or who had their civil rights suspended in the course of internment and denazification measures. In the three Western occupation zones, the US, UK and French military courts and commissions convicted more than 2,000 people for NS regime and war crimes. There were about 2,300 convictions in France itself, and the Netherlands saw 250. Prosecution was relatively less vigorous in Belgium (83), Denmark (77), and Norway (95). In evaluating these figures, it must be considered that the quantitative dimensions alone cannot say how the proceedings were perceived by the German side. As an example, the Belgian trial in 1950–51 of Alexander von Falkenhausen, the former military commander of the German occupation of Belgium, was very much affected by the context of the imminent resumption of diplomatic relations between Germany and Belgium. Von Falkenhausen returned the favor of an early commutation by accusing leading Belgian politicians, like Paul-Henri Spaak, of collaboration. After his return to the Federal Republic, he was celebrated as a resistance hero.[35]

Even today it is often overlooked that West German courts played an important role in judicial *Aufarbeitung* during the five-year occupation. Contrary to the frequent misconception among researchers, the German courts in the American zone delivered more convictions (2,051) than those in the British (1,564), with the (smaller) French zone far behind (740). Most of the convictions involved crimes committed within the original 1937 borders of the German Reich (denunciations, "euthanasia" murders, and other crimes committed in the pre-war period and during the final months of the Nazi regime). By comparison, German courts almost completely ignored the deportations and systematic murder of Jews during the war itself, despite the fact that these also affected about 60,000 German Jews from the original territory of the Reich and the Protectorate, and thus could have been covered under the pre-Nazi German law: Only 13 cases with regard to deportation crimes were brought before West German courts until 1960, most of them ending with acquittals.[36]

---

34 N. Frei (ed.), *Transnationale Vergangenheitspolitik.*

35 Lagrou, 'Eine Frage der moralischen Überlegenheit? Die Ahndung deutscher Kriegsverbrechen in Belgien', in N. Frei (ed.), *Transnationale Vergangenheitspolitik*, 326–350. N. Frei, *Vergangenheitspolitik, Die Anfänge der Bundesrepublik und die NS-Vergangenheit*, München, 1996; N. Frei, 'Amnestiepolitik in den Bonner Anfangsjahren. Die Westdeutschen und die NS-Vergangenheit',*Kritische Justiz* 29 (1996) 4, 484–494.

36 Ch.F. Rüter, 'Ost- und westdeutsche Strafverfahren gegen die Verantwortlichen für die Deportationen der Juden', in A. Klein and J. Wilhelm (eds.), *NS-Unrecht vor Kölner Gerichten nach 1945*, Köln, 2005; S. Friedländer, *Das Dritte Reich und die Juden.*

The legal situation was not the same in all occupation zones, and since German justice was required by Allied edict to use the ex post facto punitive rules of Nuremberg law when applicable (especially by Control Council Law No. 10), German legal scholars and practitioners criticised the practice as a continuation of Nazi justice by other means.[37] Omitting the completely different historical context, these laws were for instance compared with the retroactive emergency decrees of February and March 1933 (Decree of the Reich President for the protection of people and state of 28 February 1933; Law for the implementation and execution of the death penalty of 29 March 1933), both of which were issued in the acute phase of the Nazi seizure of power with the function of suppressing political opposition. Although there were a number of tangible causes for critique of CCL No. 10 (the Allies themselves gave rise to contradiction by also calling on German justice institutions to uphold the principle of *nulla poena sine lege*, or "no penalty without a law") the German scholarly discourse was thoroughly shot through with self-righteousness and self-exoneration. Many of the legal scholars who found the Allied structures and practices to be dubious had themselves participated in the demolition of the rule of law after the NS regime came to power in 1933. And after the founding of the Federal Republic it became all the more obvious that the rejection of "natural law" by most of these conservative judges only applied to the macro-criminality of the NS regime. They saw no contradiction in calling upon a natural "moral law" to justify the criminal prosecution of homosexuals, sexual libertines, teenage crime and "wild rockers".

2. NATIONAL POLICIES OF "*VERGANGENHEITS-BEWÄLTIGUNG*"

2.1. APORIA OF WEST GERMAN "*VERGANGENHEITS-BEWÄLTIGUNG*"

The Federal Republic of the 1950s and 1960s attempted to find its own paths in coping with the National Socialist past. The impulses came partially from its relations with the Western alliance of the United States, Great Britain and France. The Allies' political representatives were prepared to make a few concessions with regard to commuting sentences for a number of the Nuremberg convicts. This consensus for a reconciliation course was always subject to the

---

37 A. Weinke, '"Alliierter Angriff auf die nationale Souveränität"? Die Strafverfolgung von Kriegs- und NS-Verbrechen in der Bundesrepublik, der DDR und Österreich', in N. Frei (ed.), *Transnationale Vergangenheitspolitik*, 37–93; D.O. Pendas, 'Retroactive Law and Proactive Justice: Debating Crimes against Humanity in Germany, 1945–1950', (2010) 43 *Central European History*, 428–463.

limits set by frequent flaring of public outrage in their countries over the elite continuity of the Bonn Republic. Another limiting factor was that the Allied punitive program set in motion a dynamic of "coming to terms" and "shedding light," creating a structure that was soon followed even by critics of the sociopolitical experiment of 'democratisation from above' by way of international law (of war). This constellation explains many of the contradictions and a-synchronicities of the West German politics of the past, to this day. It also explains why the enterprise of *Vergangenheitsbewältigung* (overcoming the past), as the contemporary normative neologism called it, can in many ways be understood as both a conscious counter-project to, as well as an unconscious mirror image of, "Nuremberg".[38]

To the degree that the Western Allies pulled back from the fields of criminal prosecution and judicial historiography starting in the late 1940s, these were gradually taken over by the Federal Republic and integrated into its official politics of the past. The founding of a semi-sovereign West German partial state was seen by most political leaders as a clean break with the concluded era of occupation rule, as made obvious by a series of amnesty and immunity laws whipped through the *Bundestag* by the newly elected coalition government of CDU-CSU and FDP in 1949–50, right after the first West German parliament was constituted.[39] Almost as significant to the Federal Republic's processing of the past, however, was a measure undertaken in relative quiet and under the nose of the parliament. In April 1951 the FRG government requested that the Western allies suspend their requirement that German courts apply CCL No. 10.[40] The initiative came from the FDP-led Federal Justice Ministry, representatives of a few states, and the conservative president of the Federal Supreme Court (*Bundesgerichtshof*), Hermann Weinkauff. In internal consultations it was he especially who pleaded for suspension, arguing that CCL No. 10 was impossible to reconcile with German legal thinking and in any case an inadmissible interference in state sovereignty. Curiously for a former member of the *Reichsgericht*, Weinkauff called it "unbearable" that the West German courts under CCL No. 10 could still deliver the death sentence, given that the Federal Republic had abolished capital punishment two years earlier.[41]

The way the issue of the death penalty was handled after 1949 is another illuminating example of how the coping strategies of the former occupiers and of

---

38 Ch. Cornelissen, '"Vergangenheitsbewältigung" – ein deutscher Sonderweg?', in Hammerstein, Mählert and Wolfrum (eds.), *Aufarbeitung*, 21–36, 2005.

39 N. Frei, 'Amnestiepolitik in den Bonner Anfangsjahren. Die Westdeutschen und die NS-Vergangenheit', (1996) 29/4 *Kritische Justiz*, 484–494.

40 U. Brochhagen, *Nach Nürnberg. Vergangenheitsbewältigung und Westintegration in der Ära Adenauer*, Hamburg, 1994.

41 R. Evans, *Rituals of Retribution. Capital Punishment in Germany 1600–1987*, Oxford, 1996.

the West German state were intertwined. Because all four Allied powers had a long tradition of capital punishment before 1945, they unanimously decided to incorporate it in occupation law and the "new" German penal code, which was basically identical to the old, denazified *Reich* penal code of 1871. Although psychologically understandable, the fact that it was heavily used both in the context of criminal prosecutions of Nazi crimes and offenses against Allied authorities stood in stark contrast to actual suspension of the death penalty in many Northern European countries, as well as to the Allied objective of "recivilising" the German people. However, with the exception of the churches, most West Germans seemed to have accepted this policy as a way to restore law and order in times of chaos and rising (petty) criminality.

To the surprise of Konrad Adenauer (CDU), who at that time held the position of a chairman of the Parliamentary Council (which had the task of drafting a constitution), and who was also a staunch defender of the death penalty, and also to the surprise of the Social Democrats, who had already tried to abolish capital punishment after the First World War, the first legislative steps toward abolition were taken in 1949 by the extreme right. Their argument was not that the abuse of capital punishment under the Nazi regime had discredited it once and for all, which clearly had been the case. Instead, expellee politicians like Hans-Christoph Seebohm and Hans-Joachim von Merkatz from the right-wing German Party (*Deutsche Partei*) claimed that the Allies would use executions as a weapon to install a regime of oppression. In May 1949, half of the Christian Democrats, a majority of Social Democrats and all Communist and German Party representatives voted for abolition in the West German *Grundgesetz* (Article 102 GG). It is unclear if all politicians were fully aware of the nationalistic motives behind the measure. Nevertheless, the end of the death penalty in Germany after 78 years (counting from 1871 onwards) was successful only because it was tied to the concerted effort against "Nuremberg law". Even in the following decades, when the shortcomings of the West German judiciary towards Nazi perpetrators became more obvious, calls for the reintroduction of capital punishment were always justified as a means to combat regular criminality and never as a response to state-sponsored mass crimes during the NS era. While many European countries temporarily reactivated the death penalty in their jurisdiction for war criminals and collaborators, West Germany and Uruguay were the only countries in the post-war era to abolish the death penalty even for political crimes and in martial law.[42]

As government and bureaucracy reintegrated tens of thousands of denazified civil servants, including more than a few former members of the *Reichssicherheits-*

---

42 H.H. Jescheck, *Die Todesstrafe im ausländischen Recht, in: Die Frage der Todesstrafe. Zwölf Antworten*, München 1992, 50–64; R. Evans, *Rituals of Retribution.*

hauptamt (RSHA), Gestapo and *Waffen-SS*[43], and as more and more detainees and prisoners of war held by the Allies were released, West German prosecutors felt little impulse to pursue further investigations against German suspects. The numbers of investigations and convictions in West Germany both sank steadily after 1949, dropping to almost none by the mid-1950s.[44] The winding-down of "Nuremberg" essentially concluded in May 1958, with the early release of the last three SS *Einsatzgruppen* commanders. The same period, however, saw an increasing political and social involvement of the Federal Republic in international affairs. In the early 1950s it had still been impossible to speak of German integration in the Western community, let alone moral rehabilitation, not while the consequences of war and occupation were still very much visible all over Europe. But the commitment to peace and freedom as set forth in the West German (provisional) constitution and Germany's entry to the Western political and military alliances and adherence to the European Convention on Human Rights (ECHR) seemed to assure the FRG's conformity with universal standards of human and civil rights. That the German government was now also seeking to gain a foothold in the international discourse on human rights, however, did not really conform well to the domestic culture of impunity in its treatment of Nazi crime. The continuing defensive posture against "Nuremberg" meant that the Federal Republic joined the ECHR with the curious stipulation that it not actually be required to apply the "Nuremberg principles" insofar as these were included in the ECHR.[45] While pursuing efforts to avoid giving even an implicit recognition to Nuremberg law to the point of embarrassment, West Germany in 1954 became one of the first states to follow Raphael Lemkin's appeal and adopt the UN Genocide Convention as national law (*Bundesgesetzblatt*, part II, 1954). This was primarily a device of symbolic politics: a gesture to the associations of German populations expelled from the territories in Poland and Eastern Europe, who were demanding that their displacement be declared a crime of international criminal law. In comparison, there was never any intent to use the Genocide Convention as the means for retroactive punishment of Holocaust crimes.

One of the many paradoxes of the West German treatment of the Nazi past was that the country's late resumption of criminal prosecutions for NS crime came just as the politicians and groups who most abhorred it were closest to achieving the closure they had sought since the late 1940s. On 9 May 1958, when the gates of the US-run Landsberg War Crimes Prison opened to release three *Einsatzgruppen*

---

[43] C. Garner, 'Public Service Personnel in West Germany in the 1950s: Controversial Policy Decision and Their Effects on Social Composition, Gender Structure, and the Role of Former Nazis', (1995) 29 *Journal of Social History*, 25–80.

[44] A. Eichmüller, *Die Strafverfolgung.*

[45] G. Werle, 'Die Entwicklung des Völkerstrafrechts aus deutscher Perspektive', in G. Hankel (ed.), *Die Macht und das Recht. Beiträge zum Völkerrecht und Völkerstrafrecht am Beginn des 21. Jahrhunderts*, Hamburg, 2008, 97–126.

commanders (Ernst Biberstein, Martin Sandberger and Adolf Ott), it was the end of an era marked by German reaction against American reeducation policies and the Nuremberg trials, and by a tug of war between the Germans and the Allies over the Nuremberg verdicts. The resulting rise of solidarity with the perpetrators had occurred in all German social milieus regardless of status, education, confession, party membership or worldview. It was especially well-anchored in the bourgeois-academic strata, largely because of defensiveness in these circles against the Americans' attempt to hold a few members of their own old and new elites responsible by way of criminal trials.[46] Like in no other realm of politics, this engagement for the highly incriminated "war convicts" showed how elements of national-conservative thinking that were not considered "typically National Socialist" (i.e., unlike anti-Semitism, euthanasia and persecution of churches) survived the transition of 1945 relatively intact.[47]

2.2. RETURN OF THE RULE OF LAW?

To this day one can find the opinion in historical scholarship that "1968" represented a sudden, decisive break with the integrative "politics of the past" that had prevailed in the 1950s and early 1960s. But this kind of schematic periodisation conceals the fact that as early as the late 1950s, signs had multiplied that the era of "silencing" and "harmonising" the past would soon come to an end. In contrast to the self-mystifying narrative advanced by some protagonists of the 1968 movement, this change was *equally* carried out by *both* an increasingly self-conscious citizenry *and* by leaders of the state establishment. Even in the early 1950s, the newly established Federal Constitutional Court *(Bundesverfassungsgericht)* delivered a series of controversial rulings that at least partly questioned the Adenauer era's consensus of memorialisation politics. In a much-criticised 1953 decision, the First Senate of the court underlined its opinion that the majority of civil servants under the Third *Reich* had not been untouched by the Nazi era's political circumstances. On the contrary, it had to be taken as a default assumption that they acted out of ideological duty to Hitler and the NS state. For this reason, "all civil service relations were dissolved as of 8 May 1945," and the Federal Republic did not have an obligation to provide restitutions to denazified civil servants for their resulting loss of compensation.[48]

46 J.K. Olick, *In the House of the Hangman. The Agonies of German Defeat, 1943–1949*, Chicago/London, 2005; K. von Kellenbach, 'Vanishing Acts: Perpetrators in Post-war Germany', (2003) 17 *Holocaust & Genocide Studies*, 305–329; R. Webster, 'Opposing "Victors' Justice": German Protestant Churchmen and Convicted War Criminals in Western Europe after 1945', (2001) 15 *Holocaust & Genocide Studies*, 47–69.

47 U. Herbert, 'Integration der jungen Republik durch Verfassungsrecht?', in M. Stolleis (ed.), *Das Bonner Grundgesetz. Altes Recht und neue Verfassung in den ersten Jahrzehnten der Bundesrepublik Deutschland (1949–1969)*, Berlin, 2006, 85–102.

48 N. Frei, *Vergangenheitspolitik*, 96.

Some historians interpret the developments of the late 1950s, when a more sophisticated and increasingly critical relation to the past arose, as West Germany's delayed adaptation to the transformative processes of cultural modernity.[49] Although comparable homogenisation was also typical for the political cultures of other Western European states, there can be no doubt that support for traditional values colored by Christianity and a strong-handed state was especially strong among West Germans. It took a period of peace and order, combined with stabilisation in economic and international conditions, before that society could turn to the question originally forced by the Allies, of how the criminal history of the Third *Reich* could be integrated into the "success story" of the Federal Republic.

In searching for factors that helped bring about the change in German views of the past, it is obvious that judicial confrontations involving conflicts and issues in the "politics of the past" were often the catalysts for broad societal debates. In this period scholarly history tended to play a diminished role, as an observer, commentator or moderator, although the Western Allies had specifically called to life the Institute for Contemporary History (IfZ) in Munich as a public institution devoted to the research of the Nazi era (and endowed with the expert competence and political curiosity of a younger generation of historians). It almost never happened that a historical monograph or a documentary publication set off any of the many public controversies that broke out over the often-invoked "still not overcome" past – and this although (or perhaps because of) the fact that the German Nazi-era files confiscated by the Western allies were being returned gradually to the Federal Republic, and contained all manner of potentially explosive material.[50] Whether arising from the sphere of civil society or that of criminal justice, the controversies that did break out tended to show a similar moral-political constellation: On the one hand, the West German welfare state had taken intensive pains since the 1950s to achieve professional re-integration and social wages and pensions for millions of refugees, people bombed out of their homes, soldiers, prisoners of war, and also, former civil servants of the Third *Reich*; on the other hand it was increasingly found scandalous that people persecuted by the NS regime, many of whom had suffered psychological and physical wounds, lived in a kind of perpetual marginalisation. One case that became exemplary in this regard was the civil suit brought by Hans Wollheim, a Jewish survivor of the Auschwitz-Monowitz forced labour camp, against I.G. Farben AG in Liquidation.[51] Wollheim, a director of the

49 A. Schildt, *Konservatismus in Deutschland. Von den Anfängen im 18. Jahrhundert bis zur Gegenwart*, München, 1998.

50 A. Eckert, *Der Kampf um die Akten. Die Westalliierten und die Rückgabe von deutschem Archivgut nach dem Zweiten Weltkrieg*, Stuttgart, 2004.

51 W. Benz, 'Der Wollheim-Prozess. Zwangsarbeit für die I.G. Farben in Auschwitz', in L. Herbst and C. Goschler (eds.) *Wiedergutmachung in der Bundesrepublik Deutschland*,

Central Council of Jews in Germany, and Henry Ormond, his re-migrated Jewish lawyer, demanded damages for unpaid wages of just 10,000 marks from the former chemicals combine, which was in liquidation under Allied legal supervision. The suit was a test case, intended to clarify for the first time whether German firms had wrongfully enriched themselves from the manpower of prisoners during the Second World War, and whether the former forced labourers were entitled to assert claims to back pay.

It should be noted that persons subjected to racial, religious, or political persecution by the Nazis were able to demand damages for loss of life, injury to health, deprivation of liberty, loss of property and assets, and damage to professional or economic advancement from the Federal Republic as the legal successor of the Third *Reich* and on the basis of Allied reparations laws and the Federal Supplementary Law (*Bundesergänzungsgesetz*, BErG) of 1953. However, the vast majority of *foreign* civilian workers, POWs, concentration camp prisoners, and Jewish forced labourers in concentration camps had no claim under BErG. This was because, first, the legislature did not view forced labour as National Socialist persecution, but as a war-related and strategically necessary measure.[52] Second, Ernst Féaux de la Croix, the Federal Ministry of Finance official in charge of reparations issues, had put a stop to all civil claims for damages by classifying the compensation for former foreign forced labourers as a legal issue that fell within the scope of general reparations claims. According to the stipulations of the 1952–53 Agreement on German External Debts (known as the London Debt Agreement), however, these claims were regarded as either lapsed or temporarily suspended.

Given this background, it must have come as a shock to the corporate executives sued by Wollheim (some of whom had already been charged during the Nuremberg follow-up trials for their participation in forced labour programs) when the Frankfurt court hearing the case ruled that during the war they should have considered it their duty as corporate fiduciaries to obstruct the orders of the SS camp commanders. The Federal Finance Ministry feared that a wave of damage claims against German industry would follow, and helped mediate an out-of-court settlement of the Wollheim case in 1956–57. With the further mediation of Nahum Goldmann, the president of the Claims Conference, and the German Jewish banker Eric Warburg, a compensation agreement for Auschwitz forced labourers was signed in February 1957. Of the 30 million DM scheduled for compensation payments, 27 million DM was paid to the Claims

München, 1989, 303–326; J.R. Rumpf, *Der Fall Wollheim gegen die I.G. Farbenindustrie AG in Liquidation. Die erste Musterklage eines ehemaligen Zwangsarbeiters in der Bundesrepublik Deutschland – Prozess, Politik und Presse*, Frankfurt a.M., 2010.

52 C. Goschler, *Schuld und Schulden. Die Politik der Wiedergutmachung für NS-Verfolgte seit 1945*, Göttingen, 2005.

Conference, while 3 million DM, administered by I.G. Farben AG i.L. itself, went to non-Jewish forced labourers. Moreover, on the side of industry, consent to this solution was explicitly linked to the provision that it would entail no legal or moral obligations of any kind. This was intended to prevent other plaintiffs from approaching I.G. Farben AG i.L. with legal claims. However, it did not alter the fact that this agreement became the model for a number of similar agreements between large West German corporations and the Claims Conference. However, these settlements were to a large extent motivated by concern at the firms about public opinion abroad, especially in the United States, and about their own business interests, and non-Jewish labourers remained largely excluded from such compensation payments.[53] With the exception of a single case (*Dr. Edmund Bartl v. Ernst Heinkel AG*), the courts also rejected all subsequent individual claims for back pay. In the collective memory of West Germany's economic elites, the repudiation of a legal claim was equated with proof of innocence. Therefore, I.G. Farben AG i.L. was not the only firm to take the point of view that all of the payments rendered were attributable to strictly humanitarian motives. In the international negotiations regarding the establishment of a compensation fund by German business, which were launched in 1999, the negotiators also clung to the defence against liability under criminal or civil law, but not to the rejection of guilt and responsibility that originally accompanied it.[54]

Also the late-1950s resumption of criminal investigations into NS regime crimes originated with a civil law case. Bernhard Fischer-Schweder, a former police chief in Memel and leader of an *SS Sonderkommando* who had ordered mass shootings of Lithuanian Jews in 1941, found a new career after his release from an American internment camp as a government official and director of a refugee camp in Ulm. It was not his membership in the SS as such, but the discovery that he had made false biographical statements when hired that caused his premature release from public service. When Fischer-Schweder sued the state to demand he be re-hired at his old position, the police and the courts begin investigating his role in the events of summer 1941. This was an unusually difficult task for the prosecutors, as there had been almost no investigation until then of Holocaust crimes in Eastern Europe. Practically all of the expertise on historical contexts and evidentiary material that had been accumulated during the Nuremberg war crimes program was lost in the meantime and had to be reconstructed from scratch.

53 C. Goschler, *Schuld und Schulden.*

54 R. Bank, 'The Role of German Industry: From Individual Criminal Responsibility of Some to a Broadly Shared Responsibility for Compensatory Payments', in H. Reginbogin and Ch. Safferling (eds.), *Die Nürnberger Prozesse. Völkerrecht seit 1945. Internationale Konferenz zum 60. Jahrestag*, München/ Saur, 2006, 182–190.

The eventual criminal trial of Fischer-Schweder and nine other members of the Stapo firing squads and SD Tilsit initiated a fundamental shift in the FRG's treatment of NS mass criminality. Prosecutor Erwin Schüle, later the chief of the central office for NS prosecutions in Ludwigsburg, called for an inter-federal agency devoted exclusively to investigating NS crimes. The working assumption was still that under trial procedure rules as of the spring of 1960 the statute of limitations had expired for all NS offenses other than murder. The investigations adopted new structural and contextual assumptions. Until then NS cases had been viewed as regular criminal cases based on suspicion of individual acts. Now, the individual crime was to be treated as part of a greater complex of crimes motivated by National Socialist population, race and extermination policies.

The change in how the historical context was viewed went together with an extension of classical investigation activity. The remit of the Central Office in Ludwigsburg (ZSL) founded in 1958 went beyond intensive study of archive documents to a systematic questioning of witnesses as well as the creation of legal historical briefs and documents.[55] In contrast to the Nuremberg trials, which treated a broad spectrum of crimes and crime scenes inside and outside the German *Reich*, ZSL at first concentrated mainly on SS and police actions under the General-Government in Poland and in the occupied Soviet territories. The focus was almost always on the so-called direct perpetrators who gave orders to shoot or kept the murderous machinery of the extermination camps running. Since German law set very high standards with regard to the "subjective side of the act," the prosecutors were forced to take intense consideration of individual biographies and social-psychological dispositions, while also carefully illuminating the situational environment of the various acts of murder. Until then the perception of the Holocaust in the Federal Republic suppressed realities and details; the Ludwigsburg investigations brought together a completely different picture. The extermination of the Jews now appeared as a collective mass crime with many sources of inspiration and which occurred in many locations that was made possible through the proactive cooperation of many participants, and not simply by a central, top-down "order of the Führer". Its radicalisation came through a constant interaction between center and periphery – an interpretation that seems astonishingly modern in light of the more recent "perpetrator research".[56]

---

55 D. De Mildt, *In the Name of the People: Perpetrators of Genocide in the Reflection of their Post-war Prosecution in West Germany*, The Hague, 1996; A. Weinke, *"Eine Gesellschaft ermittelt gegen sich selbst". Die Geschichte der Zentrale Stelle der Landesjustizverwaltungen (ZSL) in Ludwigsburg, 1958–2008*, Darmstadt, 2008; M. Von Miquel, *Ahnden oder amnestieren? Westdeutsche Justiz und Vergangenheitspolitik in den sechziger Jahren*, Göttingen, 2004.

56 G. Paul, 'Von Psychopathen, Technokraten des Terrors und "ganz gewöhnlichen" Deutschen. Die Täter der Shoah im Spiegel der Forschung', in G. Paul (ed.), *Die Täter der Shoah. Fanatische Nationalsozialisten oder ganz normale Deutsche?*, Göttingen, 2002, 13–90.

Revising a reading of West German *Aufarbeitung* history, which has been predominantly negative, Canadian historian Erich Haberer delivers an extensive tribute to the work of the ZSL. He sees an important sign of progress beyond "Nuremberg," above all in the way that Ludwigsburg consistently intertwined judicial and historical methods of truth-seeking. Their concept of a "criminological history" rejected the historical "myth of coercion" and "putative duress" and allowed a better understanding of both the genesis and the effects of the genocide: "In essence, Ludwigsburg represents the institutional manifestation of the merging of history and criminology in judicial investigation and has provided the cognitive link between the subjective personal and the objective trans-personal as mutually reinforcing elements in the perpetration of genocide".[57]

Following Haberer, can we thus characterise the West German ZSL as an institution that embodied the concept of transitional justice *avant la lettre*? There are reasons to question this interpretation, in my view. First, the resources and authorities of the ZSL were initially so limited that the agency was forced to focus on a few groups of delicts and perpetrators. The fatal effects of this selective investigatory mission became obvious in the late 1960s when nearly the entire leading elite of the RSHA were rendered immune to prosecution via a supposed legislative mistake. The "ideologists of the extermination" profited from the fact that Ludwigsburg at first lacked the jurisdiction to go after the level of central planning and decision-making.[58]

Second, ZSL's ability to inspire a more differentiated view of the past was also limited. The image that the agency propagated of itself and its work was very technocratic. It was removed from reality insofar as the mission was thought to be something that could be wrapped up in a matter of a few years. This corresponded to the idea formulated by the governments in Bonn and at the state level that the investigations were simply the "unfinished business" of the Allies. The strong focus on SS crimes went together with playing down those of the Wehrmacht, and not just implicitly; a factor related to Schüle's own past as a soldier on the Eastern Front. Until the end the ZSL maintained the dichotomy between the "criminal SS" and "respectable *Wehrmacht*," the legitimating *sine qua non* of West German NS investigations in general. Furthermore, in their verdicts, the courts showed a preference for a "context" based on the fiction of legal continuity after 1933 and after 1945. That allowed determination of an individual guilt only in cases when the perpetrators had violated the social

57 E. Haberer, *History and Justice*, at 504.

58 A. Weinke, 'Amnestie für Schreibtischtäter. Das verhinderte Verfahren gegen die Bediensteten des Reichssicherheitshauptamtes', in K.-M. Mallmann and A. Angrick (ed.), *Die Gestapo nach 1945. Karrieren, Konflikte, Konstruktionen*, Darmstadt, 2009, 200–220.

norms of the Nazi era itself. Many NS trials therefore ended with verdicts of not guilty or mild sentences, and contributed to the image of the perpetrators as "pathological," a popular *topos* with a German public still seeking its own moral exoneration.

Third, the cooperation between criminal justice and academic history was limited to just a few major trials. One example was the first Auschwitz trial of 1963–65, when the Frankfurt attorney general Fritz Bauer called in the Munich Institute for Contemporary History for expert testimony. Despite the above-average attention that the trial generated both in Germany and abroad, even then there was a characteristic lack of an intensive exchange toward establishing perpetrator-oriented research. Many historians in the 1960s instead turned once again to largely non-empirical big theories; completely unimpressed by the facts brought to light in the NS trials, "intentionalists" and "functionalists" fought amongst themselves for hegemony of interpretation.[59]

And finally, a big difference from the contemporary image of *Aufarbeitung* was that the trials ended up more intensifying than eliminating the continued disadvantaging of the Nazis' victims. Insofar as they were even perceived as a group, their social status at the time was still defined by their limited structural role as judicial witnesses.[60] Paradoxically, this was taken as a sign that they lacked a readiness to reconcile and still desired revenge. Only very slowly did the Federal Republic develop a climate of empathy that allowed to the until-then ignored and traumatised victims a public acknowledgement as "moral witnesses".[61] Because of the perpetrator-centered approach of German criminal law and even more so because of the country's minimal participation in the international discourse of the time on human rights and humanitarian criminal law, the position of the court witnesses tended to create a marginalisation that they broke through only in a few cases by way of effective public actions (such as the appearance of the Klarsfelds and their French-Israeli support committee at the Lischka trial in Cologne).[62] Although most of the former victims saw the NS trials as an important medium for raising the West German public's awareness of the crimes and their own experiences of suffering, only a few organisations took the opportunity for active intervention in the country's politics of the past.

---

59 U. Herbert, 'Vernichtungspolitik. Neue Antworten und Fragen zur Geschichte des "Holocaust"', in U. Herbert (ed.), *Nationalsozialistische Vernichtungspolitik 1939–1945. Neue Forschungen und Kontroversen*, Frankfurt a.M., 1998.

60 Th. Henne, 'Zeugenschaft vor Gericht', in Fritz Bauer Institut (ed.), *Zeugenschaft des Holocaust. Zwischen Trauma, Tradierung und Ermittlung*, Frankfurt a.M., 2007, 79–91.

61 A. Margalit, *The Ethics of Memory*, Cambridge/Harvard, 2002.

62 B. Brunner, *Der Frankreich-Komplex. Die nationalsozialistischen Verbrechen in Frankreich und die Justiz der Bundesrepublik Deutschland*, Göttingen, 2004.

On the one hand the state authorities recommended against it; on the other, the front lines of the Cold War often blocked energetic, united action.[63]

3. JUSTICE, HISTORY, MEMORY

The semantics and practices of an autochthonous "overcoming of the past" are thus shaped by different tensions, which on the one hand came from the specific dilemmas of the post-National Socialist perpetrator society, but on the other are typical to the model of transitional justice, which – according to some critics – is built on the same assumptions of Western rationality, reason and progress that in some contexts have been used to legitimise oppression and open violence.[64] The "lessons in justice" of the administrative-judicial *Aufarbeitung* were always ambivalent, because the prosecuting agencies proceeded in selective fashion, the courts generally assumed diminished culpability in Nazi crime cases, and many of the perpetrators were shielded by their high social status. Given this background, the question arises of just how far-ranging the effects of various measures were within the society. What should we conclude from the fact that more critical dealings with the past only came late, and that for several decades even these were primarily conducted through the medium of criminal and civil law, while international human rights law only gained a degree of practical importance during the last phase? And in this connection, what was the role of the fundamental transformative processes that took hold in more or less all Western industrial societies by the start of the 1960s at the latest?

In considering West German developments, it is clear that the gradual erosion of a consensual memory culture did not at first lead to more stability and integration in the society as a whole. Events in the 1960s and 1970s were marked by an intensification of domestic confrontations and growing social conflicts that led to open violence.[65] Decisive factors in the increasing polarisation included the specific constellation of generations as well as the remarkable elite continuity after the war. Above all, the civil service, always a premier factor of power thanks to the German tradition of "statism" and "clientele orientation"[66], remained a domain of the compromised old elites into the late 1960s. This was

---

63 K. Stengel and W. Konitzer (eds.), *Opfer als Akteure. Interventionen ehemaliger NS-Verfolgter in der Nachkriegszeit*, Frankfurt a.M., 2008.

64 Ch.J. Colvin, 'Purity and Planning: Shared Logics of Transitional Justice and Development', (2008) 2/3 *The International Journal of Transitional Justice*, 412–425.

65 B.J. Davis, 'Violence and Memory of the Nazi past in 1960s-70s West German Protest', in Ph. Gassert and A. Steinweis (eds.), *Coping with the Nazi Past: West German Debates on Nazism and Generational Conflict, 1955–1975*, New York, 2006, 210–237.

66 M. Ruck, 'Die Tradition der deutschen Verwaltung', in A. Doering-Manteuffel (ed.), *Strukturmerkmale der deutschen Geschichte des 20. Jahrhunderts*, München, 2006, 95–108.

especially visible in the highest courts, where, with the exception of the Federal Constitutional Court, an extremely restorative personnel policy meant that the proportion of former NS regime jurists in the FRG judiciary even reached new records at the beginning of the 1960s.[67]

Continuities of personnel in justice, administration, military, academia and business were no longer accepted silently by the younger generations, however, and were instead taken as indicators of illiberal residues and continuing deficits of democracy. Even if the discussion about the "not-yet overcome past" was to some extent a substitute debate for the blocked chances at promotion among the young, the differing historical experiences of the so-called "skeptical" or "flak-helper" generation (i.e. young men, who were born around 1925 and recruited for military service in the last days of the war) and the "children of war" generation (born around 1945) played a role that should not be underestimated in the growing readiness for social conflict.[68] Among the older generations, the impact of revelations about personnel and the often-scandalised feelings about the weakness of Nazi crime prosecutions gradually dissolved the earlier "post-*Volksgemeinschaft*" feelings of solidarity; even as younger Germans interpreted the unwillingness to even talk about the past among their parents and grandparents as an indirect confession of guilt.[69] This specific complex of accusations relating to the past, and rejections thereof, flowed into a neo-Marxist-inspired critique of capitalism that the GDR constantly lent further impulse to with its own propaganda.

But there was another way in which the epochal change in generations influenced the society's relationship to the past. By the 1970s at the latest, as the former Nazi functionary elites left the stage and a new, less compromised group took charge of business, there was a change not only in the moral and political priorities, but also in the prevailing collective understanding of the era. Gradually there formed a new "historicity regime" (to use a coinage from François Hartog), in which the time-horizon was increasingly focused on the present and the future.[70] With the beginning of the SPD-FDP coalition, the Social Democrats also adopted the credo first invoked in 1963 by CDU Chancellor Erhard, who said that the post-war period had itself reached its ultimate "end". This was combined with the idea that, 20 years after the downfall, the Federal Republic

67 H. Rottleuthner, *Karrieren und Kontinuitäten deutscher Justizjuristen vor und nach 1945*, Berlin, 2010.

68 U. Jureit and M. Wildt, 'Generationen', in U. Jureit and M. Wildt (eds.), *Generationen. Zur Relevanz eines wissenschaftlichen Grundbegriffs*, Hamburg, 2005, 7–26; A.D. Moses, 'The Forty-Fivers: A Generation Between Fascism and Democracy',17 (1999) *German Politics and Society*, 95–127.

69 N. Frei, *1968. Jugendrevolte und globaler Protest*, München, 2008.

70 F. Hartog, *Régimes d'historicité, présentisme et expériences du temps*, Paris, 2003.

had largely managed to earn back its "national honour".[71] The relationship to Israel and the Jewish organisations was also now running on a far more sober basis. Unlike the founder generation, who had understood the restitution process as the reincarnation of a lost "German-Jewish symbiosis," the younger generation looked more to the problems of the Third World and the project of German-Polish reconciliation. This view found the support of a majority of West Germans, for whom the *Aufarbeitung* seemed only to raise discouraging memories of the occupation period.

The politics of history and memory of the 1980s were dominated by a set of contradictory trends. First, starting with the reception to the US television series *Holocaust*, there was a greater preoccupation with National Socialist crimes and various "forgotten" groups of victims who had until then been excluded from the official restitutions processes. Given the massive critique leveled at West German contemporary historians, who were accused of ignoring their mission of public education, they sought cautiously to redefine their own role within the fabric of the public, scholarship, and political education.[72] The many civil society projects in regional and local memorial site-work combined with the interest in a history "from below" and a basic attitude of skepticism toward modernisation, one which saw those persecuted by the Nazis as "victims of an obsolete progress".[73] On the other side, the Kohl government propagated a course of "balanced equilibrium" under the slogan of a "spiritual and moral" change, the vagaries of which however turned into more and more of a risky high-wire act.[74] At first sight it might look as though the left-liberal "dig where you are" movement and the Kohlian musealisation projects had very little in common, but hindsight allows us to see certain similarities despite all the differences. These were manifest above all in the common preference for particularistic identity politics and in the tendency to lose a more detailed confrontation with perpetrators behind broadly-drawn ideas of the victims.

This universalist discourse on victims would take on inflationary proportions in the 1990s, when the fall of the communist regime and the end of the bipolar world order brought an era of confusion to the Federal Republic as elsewhere.

---

71 C. Goschler, 'Politische Moral und Moralpolitik. Die lange Dauer der "Wiedergutmachung" und das politische Bild des "Opfers"', in H. Knoch (ed.), *Bürgersinn mit Weltgefühl. Politische Moral und solidarischer Protest in den sechziger und siebziger Jahren*, Göttingen, 2007, 138–156.

72 F. Bösch, 'Versagen der Zeitgeschichtsforschung? Martin Broszat, die westdeutsche Geschichtswissenschaft und die Fernsehserie "Holocaust"', in *Zeithistorische Forschungen/ Studies in Contemporary History*, Online-Ausgabe 6 (2009) 3, www.zeithistorische-forschungen.de/16126041-Boesch-3–2009 (11.11.11).

73 C. Goschler, *Politische Moral*.

74 A. Wirsching, *Abschied vom Provisorium. Geschichte der Bundesrepublik Deutschland 1982–1990*, München, 2006.

Two developments in particular contributed to a resumption of discussion on how to deal with state macro-criminality. On the one hand the dissolution of the GDR and its subsequent addition to the territory of the Federal Republic raised the question of to what extent it would be possible to compensate the victims or punish the perpetrators of communist rule. On the other hand, the sudden access to Eastern European archives made it possible to resume investigations against certain groups of NS regime perpetrators who had until then gone unpunished because a court case seemed hopeless. This category included the former Trawniki camp guard, the Ukrainian Ivan Demjanjuk, who had illegally immigrated to the United States in the early 1950s.

The Federal Republic was not the only country "coping" at the same time with both the National Socialist and the communist past, as the same was happening in all of the post-communist states that saw themselves in national continuities to the collaboration regimes of the Second World War. Nevertheless, the German constellation of a "dual overcoming of the past" after 1989–90 differed from other transitional societies because on the one hand, it came out of an unusually long and complicated history, and on the other hand it was influenced by the asymmetrical circumstances of the unification process. Both on the intellectual as well as organisational levels, this third wave of *Aufarbeitung* was thus the result of an increasingly self-reflexive "overcoming of the past" that had already begun in the Federal Republic of the late 1980s.[75] This becomes especially obvious when one brings to mind the discursive strategies of leading West German jurists during the post-1989 period. As an example of the historical views and self-image of the "flak-helper" generation of jurists, we might take the public remarks of the Berlin SPD justice minister and later chief of the Federal Constitutional Court, Jutta Limbach. When she was asked in 1991 to explain her support for criminal prosecution of SED misdeeds, she said, "My concern is to make sure we avoid yet another failure of German justice in the overcoming of a 'totalitarian past'".[76]

The fact that the liberal *Aufarbeitung* model prevailing in the West was transferred to the GDR after 1990 without first conducting a broad societal and legal debate provoked fundamental critique. In particular, there were serious doubts that the task of "coping" could be harmonised with the comprehensive social and economic transformation, as it was conducted in all of the new German federal states at that time.[77] Despite a series of calls for amnesty, these objections did not really threaten the hegemonic discourse of *Aufarbeitung*. On

75 V. Knigge, 'Gesellschaftsverbrechen erinnern. Zur Entstehung des Konzepts seit 1945', in V. Knigge and U. Mählert (eds.), *Der Kommunismus im Museum. Formen der Auseinandersetzung in Deutschland und Ostmitteleuropa*, Köln/ Weimar/ Wien, 2005, 19–30.

76 G. Mouralis, *Une épuration allemande. La RDA en procès (1949-2004)*, Paris, 2008, at 284.

77 Ch. Meier, *Das Gebot zu vergessen und die Unabweisbarkeit des Erinnerns*, München, 2010.

the contrary, the public debates over the "unjust state" of the GDR and the belated confrontation over the perpetrators of the Third Reich fed off each other, sometimes even prompting the revival and popularisation of a vulgarised version of the totalitarianism paradigm that the scholarship had for the most part left behind.

In their breadth and intensity, the German measures in the areas of prosecution, lustration, opening of archives and historical education clearly differ from those of other post-communist states. This was not only due to the influence of the East German civil rights movement but also a confession of the Federal Republic's old elites that they had failed with respect to the Nazi past. Transnational factors also had an impact on legal policies, justice and the public.[78] Due to the events in southeastern Europe, the second half of the 1990s saw something of a belated peace-making with "Nuremberg". After the Federal Republic at first endorsed the creation of an *ad hoc* tribunal to prosecute serious crimes in the Yugoslavian civil war, and after the German justice system cooperated closely in this with the UN court located at The Hague, Germany's long-overdue adaptation to the understanding of international human rights law prevalent in the West was only a question of time. In ruling on the shootings at the Berlin Wall, the Federal Supreme Court in 1995 directly cited the Nuremberg principles.[79] This argumentation was then confirmed in 1996 by the Federal Constitutional Court, at the time prompting a minor sensation among German constitutional scholars. When in 2001 the European Court of Human Rights confirmed the German Politburo verdicts by citing the Nuremberg principles, the Federal Republic finally dropped its own objections to those principles after nearly 50 years.[80] We are left to speculate whether this late reconciliation with the idea of international criminal law would have been as frictionless if the ECHR had rejected the FRG's approach to the prosecution of SED injustice.[81]

4. SUMMARY

West Germany is regularly invoked as a "test case" for the pertinence of TJ, as practically all of its instruments were applied there after 1945, although for the most part not simultaneously but consecutively. Starting with the International

---

78 Betts, 'Germany, International Justice and the 20th Century', (2005) 17/1–2 *History and Memory*, 45–86.

79 H. Weber, 'Die Vielzahl von Verbrechen und das "zivilisatorische Minimum"', in G. Hankel and G. Stuby (eds.), *Strafgerichte gegen Menschheitsverbrechen. Zum Völkerstrafrecht 50 Jahre nach den Nürnberger Prozessen*, Hamburg, 1995, 355–383.

80 G. Werle, *Die Entwicklung.*

81 A. Weinke, 'Gesetz Nr. 10 des Alliierten Kontrollrats vom 20. Dezember 1945', in *100(0) Schlüsseldokumente zur deutschen Geschichte im 20. Jahrhundert*; www.1000dokumente.de/index.html?c=dokument_de&dokument=0229_kri&object=context&st=&l=de (12 June 2011).

Military Tribunal in Nuremberg – considered a key precedent for international human rights law – Allied and West German authorities conducted thousands of trials against middle and lower rank representatives of the NS regime. The occupation powers attempted to restructure the German civil service with mass dismissals, rehiring those whom they thought to be least compromised. Before the establishment of the two German successor states, the Western Allies laid the foundation for a legislation of *Wiedergutmachung* (recompensation) and restitution for the Jewish and political victims of the Nazi terror. A consequence of this was the restitution agreement between West Germany and the state of Israel in 1952, which – despite harsh criticism from within – turned out to be a "significant cornerstone" of the newly formed Federal Republic.[82] It is important to note that a broader confrontation with Germany's responsibility for the Holocaust did not start before the 1960s. Even the modest beginnings of West German contemporary history, as manifested in the creation of the Munich-based Institut für Zeitgeschichte, were guided by the political conviction that the historical findings of the Allied war crimes trials should serve as just the starting point for further research and needed to be anchored in the German memory culture.

After the first phase of intense legal, political and historiographical activities, the normative, "top-down" approach of TJ in the Western zones, in combination with its instrumentalisation for brutal power politics in the Soviet zone, led to the solidification of a new German "victim myth". Despite the fact that the provisional constitution of the Federal Republic demonstrated a clear break with the past, the "institutional memory" (Richard Ned Lebow) as propagated by the indigenous political elites underlined continuities between the pre-1933 era and the present, thereby characterising the twelve "dark" years as anomalous. In their attempt to block out their previous involvement in the racist and genocidal policy of the Nazi regime, the judiciary successfully restored their legitimacy by staging a veritable "clash of law cultures," juxtaposing "legitimate" national law versus "illegitimate" international law. This resulted in a culture of impunity with regard to Nazi perpetrators, which went hand in hand with a wave of criminal investigations against members of the prohibited Communist Party. The latter was conducted in part on the basis of retroactive laws, the use of which was taboo in the context of NS criminality. A vivid example of the paradoxes in West Germany's effort to "cope with the past" can be found in how its elites alienated large parts of the electorate by jumping on the abolitionist bandwagon: Not the legacy of approximately 50,000 death sentences during the Third *Reich*, but the record of several hundred capital verdicts under Allied occupation prompted the extreme right to give the decisive impulse against the death penalty.

82 E. Barkan, *The Guilt of Nations. Restitution and Negotiating Historical Injustices*, New York/London, 2000.

At a time when a *cordon sanitaire* had been established around Nazi crimes, both in the public and the private sphere, the integrative politics of the past came to a relatively abrupt end. It is debatable what was more decisive in this respect: incidental events like the *Einsatzgruppen* trial of 1957, the anti-Semitic graffiti of 1959, and the Israeli Eichmann trial of 1961, or structural developments like West Germany's entry in Western political and military alliances and the European Convention on Human Rights (ECHR). The generational change led to an erosion of nationalistic attitudes among representatives of the churches and the media, which had been the main agents of *Vergangenheitspolitik* in the sphere of civil society. But even the partial reintroduction of the rule of law in the 1960s did not trigger a long-term cooperation between "criminological history" as conducted by the Ludwigsburg agency and professional historians of the Third *Reich*. The few trials which attracted broader public attention (like the Auschwitz trial) were mainly the work of a few restless "memory dissidents," to use Wulf Kansteiner's formulation. He wrote: "According to the needs of the courts, these perpetrator-focused histories unraveled the complicated power structures of the Third *Reich* and augmented already existing political histories of the regime".[83]

In contrast to normative approaches of earlier TJ models, the Federal Republic's gradual opening towards human rights and a less nationalistic concept of memory depended on a certain degree of democratic stabilisation and economic prosperity. But even this was no guarantee against possible backlashes and the return to violent confrontations, in which the Nazi past often played a pivotal role. Only when the old compromised elites, who had been the targets of harsh national and international critique, finally left the scene in the late 1970's was their place taken some extent by NS victims who gained attention in the context of a globalised Holocaust memory culture. Although the beginning of the "era of the witness," as claimed by Annette Wieviorka, also had some impact on the West German memory culture – manifest for instance in a growing concern for the so-called "forgotten" victims – it took until the 1990's before references to the victims *and* perpetrators became an integral part of a self-reflexive national memory culture. To some extent this has developed into an element of brand identity for the economically thriving, self-confident Berlin Republic.[84] While the critique of deficits in West Germany's coping strategies after 1949 has become the rough consensus among Germany's new elites, their *rapprochement* with a transnational Holocaust memory and human rights discourse has

83 W. Kansteiner, 'Losing the War, Winning the Memory Battle. The Legacy of Nazism, World War II, and the Holocaust in the Federal Republic of Germany', in R.N. Lebow, W. Kantsteiner and C. Fogu (eds.), *The Politics of Memory*, 102–146, at 114.

84 T. Freimüller, *Exportschlager "Vergangenheitsbewältigung"? Beitrag für das Online-Dossier "Konstruktion der Erinnerung" des Goethe-Instituts*, 2007; www.goethe.de/ges/pok/dos/dos/ern/vgp/de2267663.htm.

created new dilemmas. As the controversial judgment in the Demjanjuk case showed, the need to redress the shortcomings and aberrations of the first TJ phase seems to produce new coping strategies and perpetrator stereotypes. In the end, the Trawniki guard was the only defendant out of the entire Sobibór complex who was found guilty in a court, and his was also the only case in the history of NS prosecutions of a conviction for failing to flee from an extermination camp.

SELECTIVE FURTHER READING

AHRENS, 'Ralf, Kartelle und Verschwörungen. Franz Neumanns „Behemoth" und die Nürnberger Prozesse', in FREI, Norbert and SCHANETZKY, Tim (eds.), *Unternehmen im Nationalsozialismus. Zur Historisierung einer Forschungskonjunktur* (Göttingen: Wallstein, 2010), pp. 26–35.

BANK, Roland, 'The Role of German Industry: From Individual Criminal Responsibility of Some to a Broadly Shared Responsibility for Compensatory Payments', in REGINBOGIN, Herbert and SAFFERLING, Christoph (eds.), *Die Nürnberger Prozesse. Völkerrecht seit 1945. Internationale Konferenz zum 60. Jahrestag* (München: Saur, 2006), pp. 182–190.

BARKAN, Elazar, *The Guilt of Nations. Restitution and Negotiating Historical Injustices* (New York/London: W.W. Norton & Company, 2000).

BENZ, Angelika, *Der Henkersknecht. Der Prozess gegen John (Iwan) Demjanjuk in München* (Berlin: Metropol 2011).

Benz, Wolfgang, 'Der Wollheim-Prozess. Zwangsarbeit für die I.G. Farben in Auschwitz', in HERBST, Ludolf and GOSCHLER, Constantin (eds.), *Wiedergutmachung in der Bundesrepublik Deutschland* (München: Oldenbourg, 1989), pp. 303–326.

BETTS, Paul, 'Germany, International Justice and the 20th Century', 17 (2005) *History and Memory* 1/2, pp. 45–86.

BÖSCH, Frank, 'Versagen der Zeitgeschichtsforschung? Martin Broszat, die westdeutsche Geschichtswissenschaft und die Fernsehserie "Holocaust"', *Zeithistorische Forschungen/Studies in Contemporary History*, Online-Ausgabe 6 (2009) 3, URL: www.zeithistorische-forschungen.de/16126041-Boesch-3-2009 (11.11.11).

BORGWARDT, Elizabeth, *A New Deal for the World: America's Vision for Human Rights* (Cambridge: Harvard University Press, 2005).

BROCHHAGEN, Ulrich, *Nach Nürnberg. Vergangenheitsbewältigung und Westintegration in der Ära Adenauer* (Hamburg: Junius, 1994).

BRUNNER, Bernhard, *Der Frankreich-Komplex. Die nationalsozialistischen Verbrechen in Frankreich und die Justiz der Bundesrepublik Deutschland* (Göttingen: Wallstein, 2004).

BUCKLEY-ZISTEL, Susanne and OETTLER, Annika, 'Was bedeutet: Transitional Justice?', in BUCKLEY-ZISTEL, Susanne and KATER, Thomas (eds.), *Nach Krieg, Gewalt und Repression. Vom schwierigen Umgang mit der Vergangenheit* (Baden-Baden: Nomos, 2011), pp. 21–37.

Colvin, Christopher J., 'Purity and Planning: Shared Logics of Transitional Justice and Development',2 (2008) *The International Journal of Transitional Justice* 3, pp. 412–425.

Cornelissen, Christoph, '"Vergangenheitsbewältigung" – ein deutscher Sonderweg?', in Hammerstein, Mählert and Wolfrum (eds.), *Aufarbeitung*, pp. 21–36.

Davis, Belinda J., 'Violence and Memory of the Nazi past in 1960s-70s West German Protest', in Gassert, Philipp and Steinweis, Alan (eds.), *Coping with the Nazi Past: West German Debates on Nazism and Generational Conflict, 1955–1975* (New York: Berghahn, 2006), pp. 210–237.

Deák, István, Gross, Jan T. and Judt, Tony (eds.), *The Politics of Retribution in Europa. World War II and Its Aftermath* (Princeton: Princeton University Press, 2000).

De Mildt, Dick, *In the Name of the People: Perpetrators of Genocide in the Reflection of their Post-war Prosecution in West Germany* (The Hague: Martinus Nijhoff Publishers, 1996).

Echternkamp, Jörg and Martens, Stefan (eds.), *Der Zweite Weltkrieg in Europa. Erfahrungen und Erinnerungen* (Paderborn: Schöningh, 2007).

Eckert, Astrid, *Der Kampf um die Akten. Die Westalliierten und die Rückgabe von deutschem Archivgut nach dem Zweiten Weltkrieg* (Stuttgart: Steiner, 2004).

Eichmüller, Andreas, 'Die Strafverfolgung von NS-Verbrechen durch westdeutsche Justizbehörden seit 1945',(2008) 4 *VfZ*, pp. 621–640.

Elster Jon, Coming to Terms with the Past: A Framework for the Study of Justice in Transition to Democracy, in: European Journal of Sociology 39 (1998), pp. 7–48.

Evans, Richard, Rituals of Retribution. Capital Punishment in Germany 1600–1987 (Oxford: Oxford University Press, 1996).

Féaux de la Croix, Ernst, Schadensersatzansprüche ausländischer Zwangsarbeiter im Lichte des Londoner Schuldenabkommens, in: Neue Juristische Wochenschrift (1960) 50, pp. 2268–2271.

Frei, Norbert, Vergangenheitspolitik, Die Anfänge der Bundesrepublik und die NS-Vergangenheit (München: Beck, 1996).

Frei, Norbert, Amnestiepolitik in den Bonner Anfangsjahren. Die Westdeutschen und die NS-Vergangenheit, in: Kritische Justiz 29 (1996) 4, pp. 484–494.

Frei, Norbert, Die Rückkehr des Rechts. Justiz und Zeitgeschichte nach dem Holocaust, in: Frei, Norbert, 1945 und wir. Das Dritte Reich im Bewusstsein der Deutschen (München: Beck, 2005), pp. 63–82.

Frei, Norbert (ed.), Transnationale Vergangenheitspolitik. Der Umgang mit deutschen Kriegsverbrechern in Europa nach dem Zweiten Weltkrieg (Göttingen: Wallstein 2006).

Frei, Norbert, 1968. Jugendrevolte und globaler Protest (München: dtv, 2008).

Frei, Norbert, Brunner, José and Goschler, Constantin (eds.), Die Praxis der Wiedergutmachung. Geschichte, Erfahrung und Wirkung in Deutschland und Israel (Göttingen: Wallstein, 2009).

Freimüller, Tobias, Exportschlager "Vergangenheitsbewältigung"? Beitrag für das Online-Dossier "Konstruktion der Erinnerung" des Goethe-Instituts, 2007; URL: www.goethe.de/ges/pok/dos/dos/ern/vgp/de2267663.htm.

Friedländer, Saul, *Das Dritte Reich und die Juden. Verfolgung und Vernichtung* (Bonn: BpB, 2006).

GARNER, Curt, 'Public Service Personnel in West Germany in the 1950s: Controversial Policy Decision and Their Effects on Social Composition, Gender Structure, and the Role of Former Nazis', 29 *Journal of Social History* (1995), pp. 25–80.

GOSCHLER, Constantin, *Schuld und Schulden. Die Politik der Wiedergutmachung für NS-Verfolgte seit 1945* (Göttingen: Wallstein, 2005).

GOSCHLER, Constantin, 'Politische Moral und Moralpolitik. Die lange Dauer der "Wiedergutmachung" und das politische Bild des "Opfers"', in KNOCH, Habbo (ed.), *Bürgersinn mit Weltgefühl. Politische Moral und solidarischer Protest in den sechziger und siebziger Jahren* (Göttingen: Wallstein, 2007), pp. 138–156.

HABERER, Erich, 'History and Justice: Paradigms of the Prosecution of Nazi Crimes', 19 (2005) *Holocaust & Genocide Studies* 3, pp. 487–519.

HAMMERSTEIN, Katrin, MÄHLERT, Ulrich and WOLFRUM, Edgar (eds.), *Aufarbeitung der Diktatur – Diktat der Aufarbeitung? Normierungsprozesse beim Umgang mit diktatorischer Vergangenheit* (Göttingen: Wallstein, 2009).

HASSEMER, Winfried, 'Strafrechtliche Aufarbeitung von Diktaturvergangenheit', 61 (2011) *ApuZG* 35–36, pp. 48–54.

HAUPT, Heinz-Gerhard and KOCKA, Jürgen (eds.), *Geschichte und Vergleich. Ansätze und Ergebnisse vergleichender Geschichtsschreibung* (Frankfurt a.M.: Campus, 1996).

HACKE, Jens, 'Staatsbilder: Einige Konzeptionen des Staates in der Soziologie und Sozialphilosophie der Bundesrepublik', in MÜNKLER, Herfried and HACKE, Jens (eds.), *Wege in die neue Bundesrepublik. Politische Mythen und kollektive Selbstbilder nach 1989* (Frankfurt a.M.: Campus, 2009), pp. 65–82.

HARTOG, François, *Régimes d'historicité, présentisme et expériences du temps* (Paris: Seuil, 2003).

HENKE, Klaus-Dietmar and WOLLER, Hans (eds.), *Politische Säuberung in Europa. Die Abrechnung mit Faschismus und Kollaboration nach dem Zweiten Weltkrieg* (München: dtv, 1991).

HENNE, Thomas, 'Zeugenschaft vor Gericht', in FRITZ BAUER INSTITUT (ed.), *Zeugenschaft des Holocaust. Zwischen Trauma, Tradierung und Ermittlung* (Frankfurt a. M.: Campus, 2007), pp. 79–91.

HESSE, Carla and POST, Robert (eds.), *Human Rights in Political Transitions: Gettysburg to Bosnia* (New York: Zone Books, 1999).

HERBERT, Ulrich, 'Vernichtungspolitik. Neue Antworten und Fragen zur Geschichte des "Holocaust"', in HERBERT, Ulrich (ed.), *Nationalsozialistische Vernichtungspolitik 1939–1945. Neue Forschungen und Kontroversen* (Frankfurt a.M.: Fischer, 1998).

HERBERT, Ulrich (ed.), *Wandlungsprozesse in Westdeutschland. Belastung, Integration, Liberalisierung 1945–1980* (Göttingen: Wallstein, 2002).

HERBERT, Ulrich, 'Drei politische Generationen im 20. Jahrhundert', in REULECKE, Jürgen (ed.), *Generationalität und Lebensgeschichte im 20. Jahrhundert* (München: Oldenbourg, 2003), pp. 95–114.

HERBERT, Ulrich, 'Integration der jungen Republik durch Verfassungsrecht?', in Michael STOLLEIS (ed.), *Das Bonner Grundgesetz. Altes Recht und neue Verfassung in den ersten Jahrzehnten der Bundesrepublik Deutschland (1949–1969)* (Berlin: Berliner Wissenschaftsverlag, 2006), pp. 85–102.

HERBERT, Ulrich, 'Europe in High Modernity. Reflections on a Theory of the 20th Century', (2007)*Journal of Modern European History* 5, pp. 5–21.

Huyse, Luc, 'The Criminal Justice System As a Political Actor in Regime Transitions: The Case of Belgium, 1944–50', in Deák, István, Gross, Jan T. and Judt, Tony (eds.), *Politics of Retribution*, pp. 157–172.

Jescheck, Hans Heinrich, 'Die Todesstrafe im ausländischen Recht', in *Die Frage der Todesstrafe. Zwölf Antworten*, (München: 1992), pp. 50–64.

Judt, Tony, *Die Geschichte Europas seit dem Zweiten Weltkrieg* (Bonn: BpB, 2006).

Jureit, Ulrike and Wildt, Michael, 'Generationen', in Jureit, Ulrike and Wildt, Michael (eds.), *Generationen. Zur Relevanz eines wissenschaftlichen Grundbegriffs* (Hamburg: Hamburger Edition, 2005), pp. 7–26.

Kansteiner, Wulf, 'Losing the War, Winning the Memory Battle. The Legacy of Nazism, World War II, and the Holocaust in the Federal Republic of Germany', in Lebow, Richard Ned, Kantsteiner, Wulf and Fogu, Claudio (eds.), *The Politics of Memory in Post-war Europe* (Duke University Press 2006), pp. 102–146.

Kellenbach, Katharina von, 'Vanishing Acts: Perpetrators in Post-war Germany', (2003) *Holocaust & Genocide Studies* 17, pp. 305–329.

Kenkmann, Alfons and Zimmer, Hasko (eds.), *Nach Kriegen und Diktaturen. Umgang mit Vergangenheit als internationales Problem – Bilanzen und Perspektiven für das 21. Jahrhundert* (Essen: 2005).

Klose, Fabian, *Menschenrechte im Schatten kolonialer Gewalt. Die Dekolonisierungskriege in Kenia und Algerien 1945–1962* (München: Oldenbourg, 2009).

Knigge, Volkhard, 'Gesellschaftsverbrechen erinnern. Zur Entstehung des Konzepts seit 1945', in Knigge, Volkhard and Mählert, Ulrich (eds.), *Der Kommunismus im Museum. Formen der Auseinandersetzung in Deutschland und Ostmitteleuropa* (Köln/Weimar/Wien: Böhlau, 2005), pp. 19–30.

Koskenniemi, Martti, 'Between Impunity and Show Trials', in Frowein, Jochen A. and Wolfrum, Rüdiger (eds.), *Max Planck Yearbook of United Nation* Law (2002) 6, pp. 1–35.

Kritz, Neil J., 'The Dilemmas of Transitional Justice', in Kritz, Neil J., *Transitional Justice: How Emerging Democracies Reckon with Former Regimes*, Vol. I. *General Considerations* (Washington D.C.: USIP Press 1995), pp. XIX-XXX.

Lagrou, Pieter, *The Legacy of Nazi Occupation. Patriotic Memory and National Recovery in Western Europe, 1945–1965* (Cambridge: Cambridge University Press, 2004).

Lagrou, Pieter, 'Eine Frage der moralischen Überlegenheit? Die Ahndung deutscher Kriegsverbrechen in Belgien', in Frei, Norbert (ed.), *Transnationale Vergangenheitspolitik*, pp. 326–350.

Lagrou, Pieter, '1945–1955: The Age of Total War', in Biess, Frank and Moeller, Robert G. (eds.), *Histories of the Aftermath* (New York/Oxford: Berghahn Books, 2010), pp. 287–296.

Law on the Federal Republic becoming a member of the Genocide convention of 9 December 1948 (*Gesetz über den Beitritt der Bundesrepublik Deutschland zu der Konvention vom 9. Dezember 1948 über die Verhütung und Bestrafung des Völkermordes*), *Bundesgesetzblatt*, part II (1954), Nr. 15, p. 729.

Lebow, Richard Ned, 'The Memory of Politics in Post-war Europe', in Lebow, Richard Ned, Kantsteiner, Wulf and Fogu, Claudio (eds.), *The Politics of Memory in Post-war Europe* (Duke University Press, 2006, pp. 1–39.

LEWIS, Mark A., 'The World Jewish Congress and the Institute of Jewish Affairs at Nuremberg: Ideas, Strategies, and Political Goals, 1942–1946', (2008)*Yad Vashem Studies* 36, pp. 181–210.

MAZOWER, Mark, 'The Strange Triumph of Human Rights, 1933–1950', (2004) *The Historical Journal* 47 2, pp. 379–398.

MARGALIT, Avishai, *The Ethics of Memory* (Cambridge: Harvard University Press, 2002).

MEIER, Christian, *Das Gebot zu vergessen und die Unabweisbarkeit des Erinnerns* (München: Siedler Verlag, 2010).

MEYER, Lukas H., *Historische Gerechtigkeit* (Berlin/New York: Walter de Gruyter Verlag, 2005).

MIQUEL, Marc Von, *Ahnden oder amnestieren? Westdeutsche Justiz und Vergangenheitspolitik in den sechziger Jahren* (Göttingen: Wallstein, 2004).

MOMMSEN, Hans, 'Der deutsche Widerstand gegen Hitler: Eine Bilanz', in MOMMSEN, Hans, *Zur Geschichte Deutschlands im 20. Jahrhundert. Demokratie, Diktatur, Widerstand* (München: Beck, 2010), pp. 235–250.

MOSES, A. Dirk, 'The Forty-Fivers: A Generation Between Fascism and Democracy', (1999) *German Politics and Society*, 17, pp. 95–127.

MOURALIS, Guillaume, *Une épuration allemande. La RDA en procès (1949–2004)* (Paris: Editions Fayard, 2008).

MÜLLER, Tim B., 'Die epistemischen Bedingungen der Macht. Wissenschaft, Staatsapparate und Stiftungen im frühen Kalten Krieg: Der institutionelle Kontext Otto Kirchheimers, Herbert Marcuses und Franz Neumanns in Amerika', in VAN OOYEN, Robert Christian and Frank SCHALE (eds.), *Kritische Verfassungspolitologie. Das Staatsverständnis von Otto Kirchheimer* (Baden-Baden: Nomos 2011), pp. 35–66.

OLICK, Jeffrey K., *In the House of the Hangman. The Agonies of German Defeat, 1943–1949* (Chicago/London: The University of Chicago Press, 2005).

OSTERHAMMEL, Jürgen, *Die Verwandlung der Welt. Eine Geschichte des 19. Jahrhunderts* (München: Beck, 2009).

OVERY, Richard, 'The Nuremberg trials: international law in the making', in SANDS, Philippe (ed.), *From Nuremberg to The Hague: the future of international criminal justice* (Cambridge: Cambridge University Press, 2004), pp. 1–29.

PAUL, Gerhard, 'Von Psychopathen, Technokraten des Terrors und "ganz gewöhnlichen" Deutschen. Die Täter der Shoah im Spiegel der Forschung', in PAUL, Gerhard (ed.), *Die Täter der Shoah. Fanatische Nationalsozialisten oder ganz normale Deutsche?* (Göttingen: Wallstein, 2002), pp. 13–90.

PENDAS, Devin O., "Retroactive Law and Proactive Justice: Debating Crimes against Humanity in Germany, 1945–1950," in: Central European History 43 (2010) pp. 428–463.

PENDAS, Devin O., '"Law, not Vengeance": Human Rights, the Rule of the Law and the Claims of Memory in German Holocaust Trials', in BRADLEY, Mark Philip and PETRO, Patrice (eds.), *Truth claims: representation and human rights* (Rutgers University Press, 2002) pp. 23–42.

ROTTLEUTHNER, Hubert, *Karrieren und Kontinuitäten deutscher Justizjuristen vor und nach 1945* (Berlin: Berliner Wissenschaftsverlag, 2010).

Rousso, Henry, 'History of Memory, Policies of the Past: What For?', in Jarausch, Konrad H. and Lindenberger, Thomas (eds.), *Conflicted Memories. Europeanizing Contemporary Histories* (Oxford/New York: Berghahn, 2007), pp. 23–37.

Rousso, Henry, 'Égo-Histoire. Vichy in Geschichte, Erinnerung und Recht', in Rousso, Henry, *Frankreich und die "dunklen Jahre". Das Regime von Vichy in Geschichte und Gegenwart* (Göttingen: Wallstein, 2010), pp. 82–178.

Ruck, Michael, 'Die Tradition der deutschen Verwaltung', in Doering-Manteuffel, Anselm (ed.), *Strukturmerkmale der deutschen Geschichte des 20. Jahrhunderts* (München: Oldenbourg, 2006), pp. 95–108.

Rumpf, Joachim R., *Der Fall Wollheim gegen die I.G. Farbenindustrie AG in Liquidation. Die erste Musterklage eines ehemaligen Zwangsarbeiters in der Bundesrepublik Deutschland – Prozess, Politik und Presse* (Frankfurt a.M.: Peter Lang Verlag, 2010).

Rumpf, Joachim R., 'Norbert Wollheim's Lawsuit against I.G. Farbenindustrie AG i.L.', in Fritz Bauer Institut / Goethe Universität Frankfurt am Main, *Norbert Wollheim Memorial, 2010*; www.wollheim-memorial.de/files/1059/original/pdf_Joachim_Rumpf_Norbert_Wollheims_Lawsuit_against_IG_Farbenindustrie_AG_iL.pdf.

Rüter, Christiaan Frederik, 'Ost- und westdeutsche Strafverfahren gegen die Verantwortlichen für die Deportationen der Juden', in Klein, Anne and Wilhelm, Jürgen (eds.), *NS-Unrecht vor Kölner Gerichten nach 1945* (Köln: Greven Verlag, 2005).

Salter, Michael, *Nazi War Crimes, US Intelligence and Selective Prosecution at Nuremberg. Controversies Regarding the Role of the Office of Strategic Services* (Abingdon/New York: Routledge-Cavendish, 2007).

Schildt, Axel, *Konservatismus in Deutschland. Von den Anfängen im 18. Jahrhundert bis zur Gegenwart* (München: Beck, 1998).

Stengel, Katharina and Konitzer, Werner (eds.), *Opfer als Akteure. Interventionen ehemaliger NS-Verfolgter in der Nachkriegszeit* (Frankfurt a.M.: Campus, 2008).

Süss, Dietmar and Süss, Winfried, 'Volksgemeinschaft und Vernichtungskrieg. Gesellschaft im NS-Deutschland', in Süss, Dietmar and Süss, Winfried (eds.), *Das "Dritte Reich". Eine Einführung* (München: Pantheon, 2008), pp. 79–100.

Teitel, Rudi, 'Transitional Justice Genealogy', (2003)*Harvard Human Rights Journal* 16, pp. 69–94.

Torpey, John (ed.), *Introduction, Politics and the Past. On Repairing Historical Injustices* (Oxford: 2003), pp. 1–34.

Vismann, Cornelia, *Medien der Rechtsprechung*, ed. by Alexandra Kemmerer und Markus Krajewski (Frankfurt a.M.: Fischer, 2011).

Weber, Hermann, 'Die Vielzahl von Verbrechen und das "zivilisatorische Minimum"', in Hankel, Gerd and Stuby, Gerhard (eds.), *Strafgerichte gegen Menschheitsverbrechen. Zum Völkerstrafrecht 50 Jahre nach den Nürnberger Prozessen* (Hamburg: Hamburger Edition, 1995), pp. 355–383.

Webster, Ronald, 'Opposing "Victors' Justice": German Protestant Churchmen and Convicted War Criminals in Western Europe after 1945', in (2001) *Holocaust & Genocide Studies* 15, pp. 47–69.

Wefing, Heinrich, *Der Fall Demjanjuk. Der letzte große NS-Prozess* (München: Beck, 2011).

WEINKE, Annette, '"Alliierter Angriff auf die nationale Souveränität"? Die Strafverfolgung von Kriegs- und NS-Verbrechen in der Bundesrepublik, der DDR und Österreich', in FREI, Norbert (ed.), *Transnationale Vergangenheitspolitik*, pp. 37–93.

WEINKE, Annette, '"Von Nürnberg nach Den Haag"? Das Internationale Militärtribunal in historischer Perspektive', in JUSTIZMINISTERIUM DES LANDES NORDRHEIN-WESTFALEN/VILLA TEN HOMPEL (eds.), *Vom Tribunal zum Weltgericht. Neue Fragestellungen zum Verhältnis von Menschenrechtsverbrechen und Völkerstrafrecht 60 Jahre nach dem Nürnberger Hauptkriegsverbrecherprozess* (Geldern: JVA, 2008), pp. 20–33.

WEINKE, Annette, *"Eine Gesellschaft ermittelt gegen sich selbst". Die Geschichte der Zentrale Stelle der Landesjustizverwaltungen (ZSL) in Ludwigsburg, 1958–2008* (Darmstadt: Wissenschaftliche Buchgesellschaft, 2008).

WEINKE, Annette, 'Amnestie für Schreibtischtäter. Das verhinderte Verfahren gegen die Bediensteten des Reichssicherheitshauptamtes', in MALLMANN, Klaus-Michael and ANGRICK, Andrej (eds.), *Die Gestapo nach 1945. Karrieren, Konflikte, Konstruktionen* (Darmstadt: Wissenschaftliche Buchgesellschaft, 2009), pp. 200–220.

WEINKE, Annette, 'Strafrechtliche Abrechnung als Medium gesellschaftlichen Wandels? Bundesrepublik und DDR', in VON LINGEN, Kerstin (ed.), *Kriegserfahrung und Nationale Identität in Europa nach 1945* (Paderborn: Schöningh 2009), pp. 131–149.

WEINKE, Annette, 'Gesetz Nr. 10 des Alliierten Kontrollrats vom 20. Dezember 1945', in *100(0) Schlüsseldokumente zur deutschen Geschichte im 20. Jahrhundert*; www.1000dokumente.de/index.html?c=dokument_de&dokument=0229_kri&object=context&st=&l=de (12.7.2011).

WERLE, Gerhard, 'Die Entwicklung des Völkerstrafrechts aus deutscher Perspektive', in HANKEL, Gerd (ed.), *Die Macht und das Recht. Beiträge zum Völkerrecht und Völkerstrafrecht am Beginn des 21. Jahrhunderts* (Hamburg: Hamburger Edition, 2008), pp. 97–126.

WILSON, Keith, 'Introduction: Governments, Historians and "Historical Engineering"', in WILSON, Keith (ed.), *Forging the Collective Memory. Government and International Historians through Two World Wars* (Providence: Berghahn, 1996), pp. 1–27.

WIRSCHING, Andreas, *Abschied vom Provisorium. Geschichte der Bundesrepublik Deutschland 1982–1990* (München: Deutsche Verlags-Anstalt, 2006).

CHANGING THINGS SO EVERYTHING STAYS THE SAME: THE IMPOSSIBLE "*ÉPURATION*" OF FRENCH SOCIETY, 1945–2000

Marc Olivier BARUCH

1. THE LEGACY OF EARLIER EXPERIENCES

Since France experienced almost fifteen regimes between 1789 and the effective installment of a parliamentary Republic some 90 years later, she got used to political/military coups, purges, successive and always betrayed oaths and the rest – such as criminal punishment of followers of the fallen regime.[1] So it happened during the French Revolution, when the guillotine was invented and much used, as it did after the revolution of July 1830 (High Court trial of Charles X's ministers in 1832), in 1852 following Louis-Napoleon Bonaparte's 2 December 1851 coup or in the bloody spring of 1871 after the decimation of the Paris' Commune.

In this respect, the period of WWI may seem quieter. Certainly, real or supposed spies were executed, as were soldiers accused of cowardice, desertion or mutiny. In 1917, Clemenceau's government decided to have former Premier Caillaux and former Home Secretary Malvy judged by the Senate meeting as a High Court for having expressed defeatist – i.e. pacifist – opinions. What happened after the end of the war, including trials for "collaboration" in occupied northeastern France or *départements* of Alsace and Moselle that had belonged to the German *Reich* since 1871 is not sufficiently known to the larger public to demonstrate any kind of collective trauma.

If we search for the influence of earlier experiences on post-WWII transitional justice, we should therefore not look at the aftermath of the preceding conflict. It has both older and newer predecessors. As has been magnificently shown by

1 ASSOCIATION FRANÇAISE D'HISTOIRE DE LA JUSTICE, *Les ministres devant la justice*, Arles, 1997.

Anne Simonin in her habilitation thesis[2], the main "innovation" of France's TJ after 1945, National Indignity (*Indignité nationale*, NI) has a long history in French criminal law, stemming from both revolutionary political justice of the 1790s and the Revolution of 1848 – and even further from Roman law civil death (*civiliter mortuus*). It should be remembered – as it was, for instance, by the public prosecution during the High Court trial of Vichy Premier Pierre Laval – that civil death could lead to actual death, since anyone could kill or injure such an ex-felon with impunity.

Since post-WWII TJ succeeded the Vichy regime, which had made blatant exceptions to criminal procedural guarantees (*non bis in idem; nullum crimen, nulla poena sine lege*, etc.), it was of the utmost importance for the new legislators not to suffer the slightest suspicion of putting their feet in Vichy's dirty shoes. Therefore most of the indictments leading to detention were sought in the pre-war penal code, mainly in articles 75 to 86 concerning crimes towards the state, such as treason (*haute trahison, intelligence avec l'ennemi*) and plots against the security of the state (*complot contre la sûreté de l'État*). A special decree taken in the weeks preceding the declaration of war, on 29 July 1939, punished these crimes with death penalty. This could be read as a regression, since France had abolished capital punishment for political crimes in 1848. A provisional law from de Gaulle's government extended the charge to military action against the Allied forces.

The quite vague indictment of high treason as well as intelligence with the enemy, the latter which was easier to define, were of evident use, since there had never been even a draft of a peace treaty between Vichy France and Germany. The very core of Pétain's policies throughout the whole war, collaboration with Hitler's *Reich*, was hence characterised as treason, and therefore legitimated the harshest punishment for the head of the regime and many of his followers. It should be remembered that previously, during the Vichy period, de Gaulle's acts from 17 June 1940 onwards had been read as felony, and the now-head of the French provisional government (*Gouvernement provisoire de la République française*, GPRF) had been sentenced to death by a Vichy military court as soon as in August 1940.

2. TRANSITIONAL JUSTICE IN THE MAKING (1943–1947)

2.1. TYPE OF PRECEDING REGIME

Deciding whether the Vichy regime of marshal Pétain was "domestic or exogenous?", "imposed or not?" is not that obvious, since it depends on whether

[2] A. Simonin, *Le déshonneur dans la République: une histoire de l'indignité 1791–1958*, Paris, 2008.

you look upon the past with today's eyes or, as fair historical methodology suggests, you strive to reconstruct the feelings of the defeated layman of 1940. The difference between these two options has for decades nurtured the French memory debate on TJ.

To be sure, Pétain was no Quisling, as were fascist French leaders such as Doriot, Déat or de Brinon. Imposed by the Nazis he was not; he was instead chosen by President Lebrun under regular procedures to become leader (*Président du Conseil*) of what was to be the last government of the French Third Republic (16 June-10 July 1940). Only after he asked for an armistice, signed on 22 June 1940, did Pétain, with the help of former republican Premier Pierre Laval, manage to have the Republic overthrown by a vote in Parliament, that gave him full powers. Thus did this quite old and famous soldier become, on 10–11 July 1940, the legal dictator of France under the brand-new denomination of Head of the French state (*Chef de l'État français*).

The same logic would have us consider him and his regime as domestic. Yet de Gaulle's incredibly audacious and finally victorious bet was to make France one of the victorious powers that, one day, would necessarily defeat Nazi Germany (*"Il faut que la France, ce jour-là, soit présente à la Victoire. Tel est mon but, mon seul but"*.) For this mostly political gamble to succeed, Pétain could not be a cherished leader; he had to be a Nazi puppet. Hence the Gaullist myth of a mostly resistant France – this construction being often seen today as mere manipulation of the past whereas it was in fact first used as a war weapon, and quite an efficient one.

Moreover, during the exactly five years that elapsed between the launching of the German attack on France through the Ardennes (10 May 1940) and the unconditional surrender signed in Reims, at least seven different authorities dominated, sometimes simultaneously, what was then French soil (including Corsica and Algeria, but not the other overseas territories owned by France, i.e. the *Empire français*). The dense history of the period may be summarised by the metaphor of "communicating vessels" for sovereignty and legitimacy between these powers: German military occupation, Italian military occupation, Vichy and state collaborators, pro-fascist ideological collaborators, the resistance – among which the organised and quite effective sub-group of communist resisters – Allied military forces, de Gaulle and the Free French. One of the main aims of TJ as it was thought, organised and enforced by de Gaulle's government was precisely to merge, as peacefully as possible, this puzzle of powers into a unified, legitimate and centralised state, released from any political (communist) or military (American) influence. France was to be liberated neither by the Allies, in the Italian way, nor by pro-USSR partisans.

2.2. TYPE OF TRANSITION

Hence the famous words of de Gaulle celebrating, on the day when the last German soldiers had left Paris, "An outraged Paris! A broken Paris! A martyred Paris! But… a liberated Paris! Liberated by itself, liberated by its people with the help of the armies of France, with the support and the help of all of France, of the fighting France, of the only France, the real France, the eternal France!" (25 August 1944). This France strong enough to liberate herself – "the help of [her] dear and formidable allies" being mentioned only later in the speech – would in no way negotiate any kind of transition with the Vichy regime. How could it, since it denied juridical, political and even metaphysical existence to a regime whose initial and unredeemable mistake laid in its acceptation of defeat? The "self-professed government of the French state" ("*autorité de fait se disant gouvernement de l'État français*"), as it was called in every official text of the Free French, was to vanish as promptly as it had appeared less than fifty months earlier.

On the same 25 August, when asked by the *Conseil national de la Résistance* to solemnly proclaim the restoration of the Republic, de Gaulle refused by arguing that the Republic had never died. But, simultaneously, it was necessary to deal with what had been done by the authority, whatever its name, which had effectively ruled mainland France under the strict control of the German occupier. This was the aim of an ordinance signed by de Gaulle two weeks earlier (9 August), the first article of which stated, as de Gaulle would repeat in Paris, that "*la forme du Gouvernement de la France est et demeure la République; en droit celle-ci n'a pas cessé d'exister*".

Therefore every text promulgated in mainland France from 16 June 1940 onwards was considered as void; nevertheless, in order not to block the institutions, Vichy's official texts had to be formally repealed to become ineffective ("*Sont nuls et de nul effet tous les actes […] promulgués sur le territoire continental, postérieurement au 16 juin 1940 et jusqu'au rétablissement du Gouvernement provisoire de la République française. Cette nullité doit être expressément constatée*".) Yet many of them, the list of which was annexed to the ordinance, were retroactively validated, because they were either purely technical or considered to be ideologically not dangerous (i.e. public health decisions, or organisation of cultural policies).

The administrative, legal and political transition had been thoroughly prepared by a team of administrators and law professors working for the Free French in London until mid-1943, then in Algiers. The replacement of the upper civil service had also been minutely prepared: in every French department the GPRF, in coordination with the local Resistance, had appointed a prefect who usually met no difficulty succeeding his Vichy appointed predecessor.

Free France and the Resistance had also agreed on the creation of a new level, between prefects and the government: Regional Commissioners of the Republic (*commissaires régionaux de la République*, a title usually simplified in *commissaires de la République*) were appointed in the 18 regions created by the Pétain government. Unlike their Vichy predecessors, who were strictly controlled by the government, they had limitless powers, as long as they could not easily communicate with central authorities. As far as TJ was concerned, they were entitled to pardon, by a special – and very provisional – delegation of de Gaulle, president of the GPRF. Some of these never-met-before appointees wrote that the use of pardon was one of the most difficult things they had to deal with, at a time when revenge often took precedence over justice.

2.3. TYPE AND DURATION OF KEY TRANSITIONAL JUSTICE PERIOD

2.3.1. Before the liberation of mainland France (August 1943–August 1944)

In Algeria from the spring of 1943 on, then in liberated Corsica (September 1943), the first TJ measures decided by the French provisional government were enforced. They were aimed at major collaborators – such as Pierre Pucheu, who was sentenced to death by a Special Military Court (*Tribunal militaire d'armée*) and executed in March 1944 for the part he played as Vichy's Minister of the Interior (a position he held between July 1941 and April 1942), in denouncing communist hostages to the Germans. But minor crimes, misdemeanors and "anti-French attitude" were also prosecuted. An ordinance from August 1943 gave a very large field of interpretation of possible indictments, since it was supposed to concern all elected dignitaries, civil servants and public officials who, since 16 June 1940, have, through their actions, their writings or their personal attitude, supported the enemy, damaged the actions of the United Nations or French resisters, or attacked the constitutional order or fundamental public liberties.[3]

The general, and very severe indeed, aim of the project was "to eliminate from public positions in government and/or civil service all those who took no risk whatever in the Resistance". A difference should be made, added the ordinance, between those who only obeyed orders and those who had an opportunity to decide for themselves.

---

3 Original language quotation: "*Tous les élus, fonctionnaires et agents publics qui, depuis le 16 juin 1940, ont, par leurs actes, leurs écrits ou leur attitude personnelle, soit favorisé les entreprises de l'ennemi, soit nui à l'action des Nations-Unies et des Français résistants, soit porté atteinte aux institutions constitutionnelles ou aux libertés publiques fondamentales*".

The framework was ready, and it would lead the way, with only minor changes for most of the issues, to the process that went along progressively, following the liberation of the territory. Four main texts organised this process: the ordinances of 26 June, 24 August, 14 September and 18 November 1944, each of them being corrected and eventually codified on 28 November.

2.3.2. *Judicial state-initiated and state-executed measures*

On the repressive level, the texts promulgated during the Summer and Fall of 1944 established a three-tier system of judicial courts: a High Court of Justice, which dealt with Vichy ministers and senior officials (ord. 18 November); Courts of Justice (CJ), usually one per department, for other serious cases of collaboration (ord. 26 June); and regular Civic Courts (*chambres civiques*, ord. 24 August) for lesser cases of collaboration, punished neither by jail (or even worse, death penalty) nor financial sanction but by the original National Indignity (NI). A fourth important text concerned the administrative purges of civil service (ord. 27 June).

The decree signed on 26 June 1944 intended to "punish acts of collaboration", as its title said. Yet, by definition, the word was of course not to be found in the pre-war penal code. The exact indictments, as found in article 1 of the decree, concerned "all deeds having occurred between June 16th 1940 and the liberation of France that were breaches of criminal laws effective on June 16th 1940, provided they were intended to help, in any form, the enemy".[4]

The link between violations of pre-war law and collaboration was determined in a short text giving the law's ins and outs: "What collaborators did has always been reproved by conscience, and hence punished by both natural and positive law. The word "collaboration" as such may have not been used, but most of its aspects were criminal offences under French criminal law of the Republic".[5] These explanations meant that collaboration was a crime if and only if it could be assimilated to treason. The influence of the Gaullist vision of Vichy is here very strong, since de Gaulle considered that the major crime of Pétain was his asking an armistice, therefore a refusal to go on fighting, the very opposite of a soldier's duty and honour.

Going back not only to 1939 but to universal and permanent morality could prove politically necessary in order to put the blame on Vichy for having renounced one of the human "natural" prerogatives, the duty to fight to the very last. Yet, on purely juridical grounds, many foresaw that courts could find it

4 *"... les faits commis entre le 16 juin 1940 et la date de la libération qui constituent des infractions aux lois pénales en vigueur au 16 juin 1940 lorsqu'ils révèlent l'intention de leurs auteurs de favoriser les entreprises de toute nature de l'ennemi".*

5 A. Bancaud, 'La construction de l'appareil juridique', in Baruch, Marc Olivier (ed.), *Une poignée de misérables: l'épuration de la société française après la Seconde Guerre mondiale*, Paris, 2003, 61–97, at 74.

difficult to bring all the deeds considered as punishable back to this moral duty. NI was invented to punish those who, without being *stricto sensu* traitors or spies, had proved so un-French as "to have willingly helped Germany and her allies, directly or indirectly; or to have willingly damaged or endangered national unity, liberty or equality of the French people".

These Frenchmen were not considered guilty enough to be sent to jail, but on the other hand not innocent enough to be kept as part of the regenerated Nation, as if nothing had ever happened. They should therefore be considered as second-rate citizens, punished by National Degradation (ND).

This meant they were being deprived, either perpetually or for a period of no shorter than five years, of most of the privileges of citizenship, such as the rights: to vote and to be elected; to belong to the civil service; to be an officer or a non-commissioned officer; to hold a directorial position in business, the banking sector, or the press; to hold any position in teaching, justice or the Bar; and, last but not least, to wear any decoration. Pensions would no longer be paid. Moreover, if the court deemed it necessary, people found guilty of NI could be banned from all or part of France and all their assets seized. ND was therefore harsh enough as a punishment, which could also be pronounced as a secondary sanction by the High Court or Courts of Justice.

It was also an innovation, on two grounds. First, it played with retroactivity, since everyone agreed on the necessity of punishing "obviously anti-national" acts that could not be foreseen by the penal code in order to "purify" the Nation. Second, the mere affiliation to "anti-national" institutions (anti-Jewish administration), organisations (such as those in charge of the anti-Bolshevist, anti-Semitic and pro-Nazi exhibitions) or groups (collaborationist parties) – some of them officially created by the Vichy state – made you automatically guilty of NI, whatever your intention.

For cases judged by the High Court and Courts of Justice, the organisation of repression took some liberty with traditional penal and procedural rules. Quite logically, no suspended sentences could be given.[6] Moreover, the possibility of attenuating circumstances was strictly limited. Had it not been, the exculpatory excuse of obedience to legal orders could have been pleaded systematically by the defence.

The 26 June text thus considered that no civil servant would be responsible provided his deeds could be read as a "mere implementation of orders, exclusive of any personal initiative and void of any willing participation to any anti-national doing", except in the case of very severe actions (such as delivering arms or information to the enemy, denouncing wanted patriots, extreme violence, etc.). Practically, this restriction limited – except in very sensitive parts of the civil service, such as police and justice – repression to the higher levels of

---

6 Original language quotation: "*Aucune peine ne pouvait être prononcée avec sursis*".

governmental and administrative hierarchy. The modification of the text by the corrective ordinances of 14 September and 28 November suppressed this restriction, and even added the possibility of suing public agents who abstained from doing acts that would have helped the Resistance. Leniency was no longer acceptable after the savagery of the Germans and their French collaborators in the retaliation against the Resistance between D-Day and the Liberation of Paris

The procedural rules were strictly defined, since the risk of nullification existed. 61 of the 83 articles of the November text were related to procedure before the Courts of Justice. The exceptionality of the time influenced the selection of the jury: the president was a professional judge, whereas members of the jury were chosen amongst patriots (defined as "*des citoyens qui n'ont cessé de faire preuve de sentiments nationaux*") by a commission chaired by the President of the Court of Appeal and a grouping of representatives of Resistance organisations of the district. Non-professional for sure, the members of the jury were under strict supervision of the president, who was endorsed with all traditional powers of a president of an *assizes* court, the composition of which had served as a model for the CJ.

Since judicial repression is the most solemn, and therefore the most legitimising one (as opposed to administrative sanctions, which can be much more arbitrary and secretive), it was important that the traditional "republican" procedural rules be applied. The defence was to be heard in a public debate. Yet it was impossible to prevent a very heated atmosphere in some cases. One of the former resistance members judging Pierre Laval for instance, shouted to him: "Shut up, bastard, you'll finish with twelve bullets anyway!" Moreover, two procedural dimensions strongly curtailed the right of defence. First, the normally independent investigating magistrate was absent, and his role played by the public prosecutor, who was subordinate to the government. Second, the possibility of "*recours en cassation*" (no appeal was authorised in France, until the beginning of the 21st century, against judgments from assizes courts) was restricted to a very short time.

2.3.3. Quasi-judicial techniques

Serving the state, directly or in one of its many peripheries, is no ordinary job. It was even less so during the dictatorial regime of Vichy, when no political representation was allowed, this role being assigned to public administration.[7] It should therefore not be a surprise that a huge number of civil servants had to justify their deeds before being confirmed by the re-established Republic; around 30,000 of them underwent a disciplinary measure – a figure that high should not surprise, so wide was the list of incriminations:

---

7 M.O. Baruch, *Servir l'État français; l'administration en France de 1940 à 1944*, Paris, 1997, at 213.

1° Having in any way supported the policy of the enemy *(Soit favorisé les entreprises de toute nature de l'ennemi);*
2° Having counteracted the war effort of France and its allies, most notably through informing *(Soit contrarié l'effort de guerre de la France et de ses alliés, notamment par des dénonciations);*
3° Having attacked the constitutional order or fundamental public liberties *(Soit porté atteinte aux institutions constitutionnelles ou aux libertés publiques fondamentales)*;
4° Having consciously drawn or attempted to draw material benefits from the implementation of certain measures that were not in line with legislation in effect on 16 June 1940 *(Soit sciemment tiré ou tenté de tirer un bénéfice matériel direct de l'application de règlements de l'autorité de fait contraires aux lois en vigueur le 16 juin 1940).*

This last sentence could open ways to almost unlimited purges: since Vichy had expelled many civil servants (left-wingers, Jews, Freemasons, women etc.) promotions to those deemed loyal had been numerous. Yet, as has been studied for the judiciary[8], academics[9] or prefects[10] a strong *esprit de corps* protected the majority of those who stayed in the limits of reasonable obedience.

Ministers, who had to take the final decision, generally did so on the report of a commission grouping civil servants belonging to the same administration, and often to the same group as that those they had to punish. In the case of prefects, for instance, the commission proved to be more zealous to oust "intruders" (i.e. prefects chosen by Vichy from outside of the prefectural service, many of them coming for instance from the Navy when Admiral Darlan held both the premiership and the Ministry of the Interior in 1941–42).

Moreover, although de Gaulle and the Resistance agreed on the reinstitution of local liberties suppressed by Vichy, purges in local government were centrally organised, since it had been decided not to organise free elections, either nationally or locally, before all prisoners of war and concentration camp prisoners were repatriated. Central government thus strengthened its hold on all the public sector – and even more since the Minister for Finance and Economic Affairs was also responsible for purges in the public works sector.

---

8 A. Bancaud, 'L'épuration des épurateurs: la magistrature', in M.O. Baruch (ed.), *Une poignée de misérables: l'épuration de la société française après la Seconde Guerre mondiale*, Paris, 2003), 172–203.

9 F. Rouquet, 'L'épuration des universitaires, défense et justification', in M.O. Baruch (ed.), *Une poignée de misérables: l'épuration de la société française après la Seconde Guerre mondiale*, Paris, 2003, 229–242.

10 M.O. Baruch, 'L'épuration du corps préfectoral', in M.O. Baruch (ed.), *Une poignée de misérables: l'épuration de la société française après la Seconde Guerre mondiale*, 139–171.

2.3.4. *Non-judicial*

Yet bureaucracy has no short memory. Numerous measures were taken, in the immediate aftermath of Liberation or many years later, to dismiss or at the least to disadvantage "suspect" civil servants without using the as-yet minimal procedure of the Purge Commission. So it happened, from August 1944 onwards, when all senior officials in central and departmental offices were replaced. A text signed in Algiers in January 1944 gave ministers the rare opportunity to get rid of, without motivation, every civil servant seen as professionally insufficient.

Other types of sanctions occurred over the years. Some, mostly vexatious, created lasting resentments (nullity of civil decorations given by Vichy, cancelled promotions) whereas others (early retirement for instance) proved more efficient to progressively expel people not wanted in the civil service. This happened mainly, after 1946, in the military. Even with colonial wars starting, there were too many people in the armed forces. Some had to leave, voluntarily or not; the paradox was that a piece of legislation initially imagined to get rid of collaborators proved its utility against communists or proto-communists after 1947.

The number of texts regulating TJ in the non-governmental sector is impressive. Only the Churches seem to have escaped direct state intervention in their dirty laundry, as shown in this still very incomplete list of texts:

- Trade unions (27 July 1944)
- Newspapers (30 September 1944)
- Agricultural sector (12 October 1944)
- Private business (16 October 1944), including seizure of illicit profits (18 October 1944)
- Mutual societies and Welfare organisations (12 November 1944)
- Lawyers (6 December 1944);
- GPs' organisations (11 December 1944)
- Students (13 January 1945);
- Health professions (18 January 1945);
- Savings banks (25 January 1945)
- Cooperatives (2 February 1945).
- Family benefits and relief funds (14 February 1945).
- Actors, musicians and opera singers (17 February 1945);
- Accredited experts (10 March 1945);
- MPs, members of local and departmental councils (6 April 1945).
- Accountants (11 April 1945);

- Writers, playwrights, painters, engravers, sculptors, composers (30 May 1945); the resistant writers' organisation (*Comité national des écrivains*, CNE) deciding to draw up a blacklist of forbidden writers, poets and playwrights as well.[11]

Sanctions were very diverse, depending on which sector was concerned. They could be limited to moral criticisms (such as a reprimand) or have more direct effects, up to provisional or permanent professional bans.

Except for the Bar, which had a long-standing tradition of autonomous discipline, ministers had their say in the sanctions, usually through appointees in TJ professional commissions. They sometimes had greater powers: for instance, the minister in charge of public health was the highest authority regarding physicians. The other way round, so was the Minister of Education and the Arts in his domain because he had a right to let a work of art of special interest be published even though its creator was blacklisted.

The government intervened so much because they feared public opinion would not stand the idea of professions being spared from purges – or at least undergoing only very lenient ones – whereas some of their most prominent members had been obvious collaborators.

2.3.5. *Numbers of punished perpetrators*

It is common to say that France did not go through real prosecutions, thanks to the Gaullist myth of a Nation deeply resistant, as if by essence. This commonplace is totally unrealistic, both on the quantitative and qualitative sides. As Henry Rousso wrote as early as 1992, some 350,000 people were, in a way or another, concerned by TJ in France after WWII – even though not all of them were indicted or even heard by a judge or a collective body. This obviously made TJ a huge social event: as Marc Bergère has shown at departmental level, post-WWII France can be described as a "*une société en épuration*".[12]

Precise figures were published in the mid-1950s, which must be read more as an assessment of the work done by organs of TJ than as a real effect of the prosecutions. Many sanctions were alleviated by amnesty or through ministerial decisions whereas, on the other hand, decisions not taken into account kept people furious with their post-Liberation fate.

---

11 G. Sapiro, *La guerre des écrivains: 1940–1953*, Paris, 1999, 571–581.

12 M. Bergère, *Une société en épuration: épuration vécue et perçue en Maine-et-Loire: de la Libération au début des années 50*, Rennes, 2004.

Figure 1. Post-WWII TJ, an official summary in 1950[13]

	High Court	in abs	Courts of Justice	in abs	Civic Chambers	in abs	TOTAL
DISMISSALS							
	42		183,512				183,554
ACQUITTALS							
	3		6,724		19,453		26,180
SENTENCED							
Death penalty	18	*10*	2,853	*3,910*			6,791
Of whom executed	*3*		*767*				*770*
Hard labour (life sentence)	2		454	*2,248*			2,704
Hard labour	6		1,773	*8,864*			10,643
Criminal reclusion			1,956	*88*			2,044
Criminal reclusion (life sentence)	14		22,883				22,897
National Degradation (ND) as main sentence	15		3,559	*19*	40,563	*6,082*	50,238
Of whom exonerated for help to the Résistance	*7*		*not known*		*not known*		*3,184*
Total ND							90,801
			40,969	*15,129*	60,016	*6,082*	
TOTAL	100		55,331		66,282		121,713

2.4. EVALUATION

In my opinion, deciding today whether TJ in France after 1944 was fair or not, severe or not, partisan or not exceeds the professional capacity of a social scientist. We may yet try to find some clues, as was for instance a very detailed point system for blaming or exonerating members of the French prefectural corps.[14]

Any evaluation of the politics of TJ in post-WWII France is double. It may be *our* evaluation, that would insist on issues of justice and morals, but it makes more historical sense to wonder how the people *then* considered it – the result certainly being different whether you take into account de Gaulle or the average man's assessment.

---

13 Figures from: A. Simonin, *Le déshonneur.*

14 J. Elster, *Closing the Books: Transitional Justice in Historical Perspective*, New York, 2004, at 104.

According to the very perceptive analyst Raymond Aron, fourteen months after the Liberation the average Frenchman was bitterly disappointed by TJ: "Such a rare unanimity exists on the idea that the purges are a complete failure that one would not even dare discussing it", a situation Aron tried to explain further on: "The eagerness of the Resistance collided in vain with the government's determined cautiousness. [TJ was] a revolutionary act with legal forms, thus discontenting both revolutionaries and legalists".[15] According to him, governing a country in transition implied making compromises. On the opposite side, at the very beginning of 1945, Albert Camus's editorial in the resistant paper *Combat* had proclaimed that France would miss renovation if it did not go through the purging process.[16]

This was indeed the point – and a structural one in TJ. Was it an opportunity to build a "new France", or had it only to do with comforting the state by putting out of the scene, provisionally perhaps, a few bad shepherds? Revolution or restoration? – as Claude Bourdet, a resistant from the very beginning, would summarise it much later.[17] Because the French state proved unable to answer these questions, France underwent global dissatisfaction that crystallised into myth. Purges were supposed to have hit the weak ("*le lampiste*") and spared the powerful – which happened to be true as far as René Bousquet was concerned, but absolutely false for the whole process.

TJ certainly did not turn out to be swift: as we have seen, some cases were still open by the end of the 1960s, notwithstanding the necessity to judge people sentenced *in absentia* – often very severely, the death penalty being in many cases quasi-automatic when the defendant was on the loose. Yet the idea was to be quickly finished with TJ, so that a "pure" France, or at least a purged society, could go forth. Thus many of the special courts had been created for a short period – often too short a period, so that extensions were needed. The idea was to "go back as quickly as possible to normal political life" (ordinance on National Indignity). For instance, cases were not supposed to be brought to the CJ more than six months after the liberation of the whole French territory, fixed on 10 May 1945. Since too many cases were still to be examined, an extension of twelve more months was granted, but only for the Paris region. On 29 July 1949 the CJ were abolished, but for pending cases and/or for *in absentia* defendants who would return before the end of January 1951. All collaboration cases would then be judged by ordinary courts, until the statute of limitations had run out (after ten years for felonies, three years for misdemeanors).

15 M.O. Baruch, 'Conclusion', in M.O. Baruch, (ed.), *Une poignée de misérables*, 531–547, at 532 and 547.

16 H. Rousso, *Vichy: l'événement, la mémoire, l'histoire*, Paris, 2001, at 551.

17 C. Bourdet, *L'aventure incertaine: de la Résistance à la Restauration*, Paris, 1975.

What also seems difficult to deny is the strong emphasis put on respect of strict procedural rules, and consequently on the important part played by professional judges in the process. As we have seen, de Gaulle's and the government's obsession was to enlarge the grip of the state in post-war society as much as possible. High ranking judges would have a very important role in making sure that normal rules would apply. Thus, for instance, would the President of the Court of *Cassation* preside over the High Court (the republican tradition gave this function to a politician, the President of the Senate).

Moreover, if appeal was not allowed (as it is not for the assizes court, which served as a model for CJ), there remains a possibility for cassation: in many cases, very heavy sentences given by a local court would be repealed and sent to another court, able to judge with much less passion (the French word is *dépaysement*). So it happened, for instance, for prefect Angeli, a very fierce opponent to the Resistance in Lyons until the beginning of 1944. Sentenced to death at the end of 1944 by the CJ of this town, he was re-judged a few months later in Paris, and spent only a few years in prison before being released. The Council of State, especially when new possibilities were open to punished civil servants after 1953, considerably softened immediate post-WWII sanctions, reintegrating expelled people in the civil service and compensating for their financial losses.

3. TRANSITIONAL JUSTICE IN THE LONG RUN, A CHRONOLOGICAL APPROACH

The contradictory ambitions at the core of post-WWII TJ policies – i.e. swiftness, fairness and thoroughness – were naturally not met. On the contrary, France had to deal with transitional justice for quite a long time, even though public opinion quickly lost interest in it: it was not before 1960 that the High Court judged for the last time a former Vichy minister, whereas the Central Commission on Confiscation of Illicit Profits (*Conseil supérieur de confiscation des profits illicites*) met in the Ministry of Finance until the beginning of the 1970s.

Then, while things seemed to settle down by exhaustion of cases, the conjunction of political (resignation of de Gaulle from the Presidency in 1969, followed by his death one year later), historiographical (the film *The Sorrow and the Pity* in 1969, Robert Paxton's *Vichy France* in 1972) and generational factors in the wake of May 1968 riots deeply shifted the relation of Frenchmen to their recent past. As historian Henry Rousso wrote in 1987 in a psychoanalytical reading of the phenomenon (*Le syndrome de Vichy*), the memory of Vichy and collaboration has almost become obsessive in contemporary France, a situation that makes the present very long-term approach to post-1944 TJ particularly relevant for the French case.

3.1. 1947–1954: A TROUBLED TIME OF CHANGES IN TJ POLICY

This is a period during which France seems to have done away with the work of prosecution and purging. Three laws (1947, 1951 and above all 1953) emptied prisons and very generously reintegrated former collaborators and Vichyists, a move made mostly for inner political reasons. This shift is visible in remarkable trials and in reconciliation measures. We further successively discuss the political context; the role of new generations, of academic research and of literary works; the memory eruptions which explain some of these policy shifts.

3.1.1. Trials

In 1949, two opposite trials hit the headlines. The first one was the Kravchenko case ("the trial of the century"), a libel action by Soviet defector Kravchenko against the French Communist weekly *Les Lettres Françaises*. It ended in April with the paper and two journalists sentenced to a not very heavy fine. Margarete Buber-Neumann, the widow of the prominent German Communist leader, who herself had survived both Soviet and Nazi concentration camps, testified that Kravchenko was right when comparing the cruelty of both dictatorships. But the Communists and their followers turned out to be so violent against all the witnesses favorable to the defendant, including some former comrades-in-arms from the Resistance, that it was clear that no unity could ever been found again.

To make things worse, René Bousquet, the head of Vichy police between April 1942 and December 1943 – a man directly responsible for the round-ups, hence the deportation and the assassination of thousands of Jews and for a large part, though not the fiercest that was to happen in 1944, in the repression of the Resistance – was sentenced in June by the High Court to five years National Indignity, from which he was immediately released on the motive he had secretly helped the Resistance. The punishment was incredibly light: many policemen, and some prefects who had obeyed Bousquet's orders had been sentenced to death, and more than one effectively shot. That such a big fish of collaboration (he ranked second to Laval for all police affairs) could escape prison sounded as an absolute defeat of the Resistance.

France was not yet through with painful trials. In the first weeks of 1953, a court in Bordeaux had to judge the SS group who had killed, in June 1944, all the population of the rural village of Oradour-sur-Glane. It happened that twelve of the accused were from Alsace, thus being French before having been conscripted in the German Army when the Nazi Reich annexed Alsace after France's collapse of 1940. After they were sentenced to prison, in order to prevent a geographical-civil war of memory the government of 1953 decided to pass of special law granting amnesty for these Alsatians '*Malgré Nous*' ("Against our will"). This was no big deal, since a general amnesty was already at that time on the parliamentary agenda – the fourth one in six years.

3.1.2. Reconciliation measures

From the beginning of the period of TJ, de Gaulle as head of the provisional government and later his successors made great use of pardon. Amnesty also came quite soon: a French tradition is that a new presidential election leads to an amnesty law. So it happened when socialist Vincent Auriol, a former member of the Popular Front government of 1936, became the first president of the Fourth Republic. The law of 16 August 1947, while formally paying respect to the Resistance, alleviated sanctions for collaboration for minors, French Muslims from Algeria and Alsatians. This law was only a test. On 9 February 1949 minors who had been sentenced for having been members of collaborationist groups – such as the *Milice française*, the cruelest and most efficient opponent of the Resistance – got full amnesty.

The two main parliamentary acts came in 1951 and 1953, one before and one after the general election. The law promulgated on 5 January 1951 excluded from amnesty former Vichy ministers, sentenced in High Court, as well as civil servants. But all people sentenced to NI – there were 48,000 – got total or partial amnesty, except the very few who had also been found guilty of war crimes.

The last act was the law promulgated on 6 August 1953. All collaborators who still had less than five years to spend in jail were released. Only those sentenced for very heavy treason or anti-national acts – i.e. "*qui se sont rendus coupables de meurtre, de viol, de dénonciation ou qui, par leurs agissements ou leurs écrits, ont sciemment exposé ou tenté d'exposer des personnes à la torture, à la déportation ou à la mort ou qui ont sciemment concouru à l'action de l'armée ou des services de police ou d'espionnage ennemis*" – remained in prison or were deprived of their civil rights.

In general terms, the consequences of the National Indignity (NI) were cancelled, and pre-1940 politicians who had rejoined Pétain stopped being ineligible for office. Moreover, for the first time since 1945, civil servants punished because of the part they played in the Vichy regime and state collaboration could ask for a reappraisal of their activities. In the five following years, the Council of State, France's highest administrative jurisdiction, will be very active in redefining what should be seen as an acceptable compromise, the result of which was the reintegration in the public sphere, sometimes at very high level of responsibilities and wages, of former prominent collaborators.[18]

18 A. Bancaud and M.O. Baruch, 'Vers la désépuration? L'épuration devant la juridiction administrative, 1945–1970', in M.O. Baruch, (ed.), *Une poignée de misérables: l'épuration de la société française après la Seconde Guerre mondiale*, Paris, 2003, 480–512.

Thus, in the four years that followed the liberation of France, the number of prisoners who had been found guilty of collaboration decreased dramatically (fig. 2):

Figure 2. The impact of amnesty

	People imprisoned for collaboration
Mid 1946	± 48,000
December 1949	± 8,000
November 1950	± 5,000
Before August 1953 law	± 2,000
After August 1953 law	62

Very few French preferred to forget. Yet on 28 October 1946 a War Damage Law was passed that put forth the principle of full compensation for direct material damage caused by acts of war to personal property, real property and business assets. All victims of events occurring during World War II were eligible for this compensation. These measures therefore benefited both victims of anti-Semitic laws and other war victims. Claims under this act were administered by the Ministry of Reconstruction and Housing. The conditions for compensation of common or family-use personal property depended on supporting documents provided by the claimant.

3.1.3. The domestic and international political context

The broad post-Liberation unanimity, shaken by the sudden resignation of de Gaulle in January 1946, collapsed in May 1947 by the forced resignation of communist ministers. In between, de Gaulle had launched his own party, the Union of the French People (*Rassemblement du Peuple français,* RPF), which met tremendous success in local elections – de Gaulle's own brother being elected as president of Paris's city council.

From then on, unstable coalitions of the heterogeneous parties – Christian Democrats (*Mouvement Républicain Populaire*, MRP), Radicals, Socialists (SFIO), plus minor parties such as former resistants René Pleven and François Mitterrand's UDSR and right-wing Independents, most of them former supporters of Pétain – tried to govern France, with much instability.

The political pendulum swung more and more to the right until, in 1952, right-winger Antoine Pinay, a former member of Pétain's *Conseil national* in 1941–42, became Prime Minister, the first non-resistant head of a French government since 1944. Typically enough, he chose as his main personal adviser a high-ranking civil servant who had belonged to Vichy Finance Minister Bouthillier's staff.

In the context of the Cold War (Berlin blockade, Prague coup, Korean War, violent communist demonstrations), the double opposition from Gaullists and Communists made it very difficult for the centrist government to launch the Franco-German Steel and Coal Community. During the parliamentary debate, Premier Robert Schuman was slandered by PCF as a Vichyist (he was under-secretary for refugees during one month in June 1940) and a "*boche*"' (derogatory word for German, since Schuman was born in then-German Lorraine). Verbal violence went even one step further with the crisis of the European Defence Community (EDC). The project had been agreed in 1952 by the French government as a decent way of re-arming Western Germany, a move very much wanted by the USA in the Cold War context. This was a bold step, but a one that horrified both Gaullist and Communist parties. The very idea of having French and German troops joined under a sole command, less than ten years after the defeat of the *Wehrmacht*, split every party of the governmental majority except Christian-Democratic MRP. Mendès France asked for a vote in Parliament, a decision no government had dared to take before; the EDC project was turned down, to the great anger of MRP.

During the same period, frequent nationalist troubles in French Northern Africa (Tunisia and Morocco) were violently repressed by the police, the army and the colonialist party. French writer François Mauriac (Nobel Prize 1952) publicly compared the repression with Nazi methods, as writer Albert Camus (Nobel Prize 1957) had during the Madagascar riots of March-May 1947.

The situation was even worse in Indochina, where French troops opposed Viet Minh guerillas, helped by both China and the Stalin's USSR. No chance of peace was ever seized because of the intransigent position of hawkish Christian Democrat politicians – most of them former prominent leaders of the Resistance – who held key positions as Premiers, Ministers for Defence or the Overseas. Only the impressive defeat of the French Expeditionary Corps in Dien Bien Phu (May 1954) brought an end to the conflict, when former Popular Front and resistant politician Pierre Mendès France was asked to build a center-left coalition, with François Mitterrand as Minister of the Interior.

3.1.4. The national impact of international developments in the domain of TJ

Following a time when "disregard and contempt for human rights have resulted in barbarous acts which have outraged the conscience of mankind", the international community created under the name of United Nations adopted, on 10 December 1948, the Universal Declaration of Human Rights prepared by Eleanor Roosevelt, widow of the US President, and René Cassin, senior legal adviser of de Gaulle during the war.

In November 1950, the European Convention on Human Rights was signed in Rome, to be enforced in 1953. Yet France did not ratify it until 1974; this fact was vainly used by Maurice Papon's lawyers in 1998.

3.1.5. The role of academic research and of literary works

Academic research was still to come. People interested in the issue only had to remember, or to read part of the huge justification literature (memoirs) produced by participants. Publishers also widely circulated books about the main collaboration cases judged in High Court – whereas Pétain's trial was published *in extenso* by the *Journal officiel*. A first synthesis about the government of occupied France, the *Histoire de Vichy* by Robert Aron (not to be confused with his cousin, sociologist Raymond Aron) was published in 1954. In spite of its bias in favor of Pétain and his followers (opposed to evil-doing Laval and collaborationist proto-fascists), it remained a reference book for almost two decades.

Literary texts such as Albert Camus's *The Plague* (*La Peste*, 1947), an allegory of Nazism, or Jean-Pierre Melville's movie adapted from Vercors's *The Silence of the Sea* strongly struck the public, since they strongly differed from the heroic writings or movies (such as famous *La Bataille du Rail*) offered in the immediate aftermath of the Liberation. A general feeling appeared among the resistants that what most of them had fought for – and many (the best ones, wrote Camus) died for – was being wasted by politicians, who only reflected by doing so the inner wish of the electorate, more or less consciously ashamed of having had such a "wait-and-see" attitude during the Occupation.

3.1.6. Memory eruptions: the public debate

The signs and traumas of recent years – memories of the missing ones, commemorations of terrible events, reconstruction of bombed cities, etc. – were then so present than any event could conjure up a dreadful past. So it happened in July 1951 when the 95-year-old Pétain finally died in his prison at l'Île d'Yeu. Although, as every person sentenced by a criminal court, he had been disbarred from the *Académie française*, he had not been replaced in the (highly hypothetical) case he would be pardoned.[19] To succeed him, the very conservative Academy chose former diplomat André François-Poncet, whose reception speech – traditionally an eulogy of one's predecessor – pronounced in January 1953, was a vibrant call to "national unity"[20], a right-wing euphemism for amnesty, heard as amnesty of all those who "did not know".

---

19 G. Sapiro, *La guerre des écrivains*, 638–639.

20 A. François-Poncet, *Discours de réception à l'Académie française, 22 janvier 1953*, available at www.academie-francaise.fr/immortels/discours_reception/francois-poncet.html, accessed on 10 November 2011.

This was precisely what former resistants could not stand. Jean Cassou, a poet and Companion of the Liberation, who had been seriously wounded in Toulouse a few days before the city's liberation, published a strident pamphlet, *La Mémoire courte*, one of the strongest texts ever on what it meant to be a resistant, during *and after* WWII. Of course, Cassou wrote, it could be possible to act as if nothing had happened, and let Frenchmen go "back to normal" – except for "*ce résidu inévitable: les morts*".

3.2. 1954–1970: A TIME OVERSHADOWED BY GENERAL DE GAULLE

This period may be described as overshadowed by the figure of de Gaulle, especially from 1957 onwards, when the socialist government of Premier Guy Mollet, elected in January 1956, turned out to be unable to peacefully end the Algerian war. Mollet preferred a violent repression, including the use of torture. This gave way to a deep moral crisis, especially among intellectuals and (some) civil servants, who as resistants had suffered torture from the Nazis and their accomplices. Political instability, poor diplomatic skills and ultimately the threat of a military coup brought de Gaulle back to government in June 1958, with special powers to prepare a new constitution, leading to the strong executive he will head until 1969. Gaullism succeeded in ending the Algerian war, stabilising France's institutions and pursuing the economical and technological development of France started by the Fourth Republic. A reconstruction of recent history also took place, culminating in 1964–65 with ceremonies celebrating the twentieth anniversary of the Liberation and the 25th anniversary of de Gaulle's rebellion of 1940.

3.2.1. The domestic and international political context

Arriving to power in the wake of military disaster in Indochina, Premier Mendès France had first to negotiate with the Viet Minh, which lead to the Geneva agreements, signed within four weeks. The government also managed to swiftly give independence to Tunisia, but was less happy with the uprising in Algeria, at the beginning of November 1954 – Interior minister Mitterrand boasting that "Algeria is a part of France, so that the only possible negotiation is war". Lasting seven and a half years, the Algerian War was to be the major event of the years to come, leading to a major political crisis that brought the Fourth Republic to an end and de Gaulle back to power in May-June 1958. But, since the socialist government of Guy Mollet agreed on a violent repression, including the use of torture, it also gave way to a deep moral crisis, especially among intellectuals and (some) civil servants, who as resistants had suffered torture from the Nazis and their accomplices.

After the Évian agreements, which ended the conflict – leaving to their fate dozens of thousands of *harkis*, i.e. Muslims who had fought in the French army against the FLN – de Gaulle swiftly led France on the paths of political and economic modernisation, relying on a very conservative majority in Parliament. Social justice was therefore not much of a priority, until the sudden events of the spring of 1968 proved the deep dissatisfaction of French society, especially in the youngest generations.

Whereas the Fourth Republic had been highly dependent on US economic and military aid, de Gaulle vividly remembered the dreadful relations he had, during WWII, with FDR and the US government. His policy as President of France was consequently built on the absolute necessity of national independence. He therefore developed and adapted to his *Weltanschauung* two important moves made by the preceding regime: building a French nuclear force and entering the Common Market with Italy, the Benelux countries and, above all, Germany. His amity towards German Chancellor Konrad Adenauer also led to a strengthening of the bilateral relations, symbolised by the Élysée Treaty, signed in January 1963. In the transition government he organised in June 1958, he chose as Minister of Foreign Affairs the French ambassador to Western Germany, Maurice Couve de Murville, who was to keep this position for ten years.

Two international developments are relevant here. In 1961, Adolf Eichmann was abducted in Argentina by Israeli agents and brought to Jerusalem where he was tried, sentenced to death and hanged. In December 1964, the French Parliament unanimously voted the suppression of statutes of limitations for crimes against humanity. During the debate, a former resistant, by profession a law professor, explained that if Hitler turned out to be alive (one never knew!), it would be impossible to try him after May 1965 if the law were not changed.

3.2.2. The influence of successive generations, the role of academic research, literary works and movies

Although very present on the political scene, de Gaulle gave free rein to Prime Minister Georges Pompidou in the building of ministerial teams. Thus arrived on the French political scene a generation of young "technocrats", many of them alumni of the *École nationale d'administration* (ENA). The most famous of them is undoubtedly Jacques Chirac, born in 1932 (too young to have played any part in WWII), who started a 40-year political career when entering government in 1967. As both Pompidou's and Chirac's cases show, after de Gaulle's resignation in 1969 the Free French and Inner Resistance generations would be progressively set aside in politics.

During the student revolt in 1968 one of the slogans was CRS=SS (CRS standing for *compagnies républicaines de sécurité* – the anti-demonstration police). This last cry was absurd and shocking enough (no matter how violent the Gaullist police could be, it had nothing to do with what had been experienced some 25 years earlier), yet it showed the strong influence of the legend of the Resistance for a generation lacking heroes and myths. It is also significant that one protest song of the extreme-left was called "We are the new partisans", by reference to the group of communist resistants known as FTP (*Francs-tireurs et partisans*).

Some twenty years after the post-WWII prosecutions and purges, books on this tragic event of the recent past were published on both sides of the Atlantic Ocean. Robert Aron's *Histoire de l'épuration* (four volumes published between 1967 and 1975) was a huge success in France. It was written in the same style and with the same slightly Pétainist ideology of his above-mentioned *Histoire de Vichy.* A fairer account of the events was drawn on a PhD dissertation by a young American historian, Peter Novick, and published as a book three years later. Although Novick could of course not have access to the archives that only started to be opened in the 1990s, his work is a fine one, when explaining the complex organisation, deciphering what was at stake and trying to draw a fair assessment of the processes. Yet – in a striking opposition to the fate of Robert Paxton's book on Vichy seven years later – Novick's work was not translated into French before 1985, and never got a wide audience.

A France shaped by Gaullism was still shy enough about its recent past. Two important works were published at the end of 1960s concerning the ins and outs of collaboration, by professors Eberhard Jäckel, from Stuttgart, and Stanley Hoffmann, who taught at Harvard. When the French academic world decided to organise a conference on the issue, as did René Rémond in the *Fondation nationale des sciences politiques,* not a single word was said of the part played by the French state machinery in the round-ups of Jews, nor even of the homegrown anti-Semitic policy of the regime.

Even if literature still drew much inspiration from the recent tragedy (see for instance André Schwartz-Bart's widely-acclaimed *Le Dernier des Justes*, which won the Goncourt Prize in 1959), it was mostly movies that reflected the magnitude and diversity of the French vision of WWII.

The name of Alain Resnais should be cited first, since he directed three masterpieces during this period: *Nuit et Brouillard* (1955), a documentary film that contained the first images showing concentration camps, round-ups of Jews and the part played in them by the French police; *Hiroshima mon amour* (1959), from a screenplay by Marguerite Duras, an intellectual love story between a Japanese man having survived Hiroshima and a French woman whose head had been shaven as a punishment for having had an affair with a German soldier.

And, the most complex and perhaps most beautiful of the lot, *Muriel ou le temps d'un retour*, (1963), a metaphorical relation between the physical destruction of a town (Boulogne-sur-Mer) though bombings during WWII and the moral destruction of a young man who, as a soldier during the Algerian war, was forced to torture.

Many other films related to occupied France, in very different style – be they dramas *Marie-Octobre*, Julien Duvivier, 1959; *Le jour et l'heure*, René Clément, 1963), historical blockbusters (*Paris brûle-t-il?* René Clément, 1966 – in the aftermath of Darryl Zanuck's superproduction of Cornelius Ryan's *The Longest Day*) and even comedies, the most famous (and the highest financial success) of them being *La grande vadrouille* (Gérard Oury, 1966).

Yet, it was not before 1969, the year de Gaulle left the public scene forever, that the most important film was made on the Resistance, Jean-Pierre Melville's *L'armée des ombres* (*Army of Shadows*). While explaining the very unjust obscurity of the movie ("when *Army of Shadows* was released in 1969, it was denounced by the left-wing Parisian critics as 'Gaullist' because it has a brief scene involving de Gaulle and because it involves a Resistance supporting his cause; by the late 1960s, de Gaulle was considered a reactionary relic".), US film critic Roger Ebert saw it as one of the finest movies ever made on the Resistance: "This is not a war film. It is about a state of mind. [...] Melville, who was himself a member of the Resistance, is not interested in making an action film. Action releases tension and makes it external. His film is about the war within the minds of Resistance members, who must live with constant fear, persist in the face of futility, accept the deaths of their comrades and expect no reward, except the knowledge that they are doing the right thing. Because many die under false names, their sacrifices are never known".

3.2.3. Memory eruptions: the public debate

Throughout the 1960s, France's official memory of WWII and the Resistance was entirely shaped by the Gaullist vision, related both to the legend ("Self-liberated France") and to political instrumentalisation, either domestic (André Malraux used to say, from the 1950s onwards: "There is nothing located on the political ground between Gaullists and Communists") or diplomatic: on 6 June 1964, de Gaulle chose not to go to Normandy, arguing he was not present on the day of the landing (D-Day) and that he was not even informed of the military operations prepared and carried out by the Allies. The climax of the commemoration happened in December of the same year, with the burial of mortal remains of resistant leader Jean Moulin, a former republican prefect, in the Pantheon of Paris, the Nation's Memorial.

Except in 1969, after he had resigned, de Gaulle yet never missed the official 'Gaullist' commemoration of 18 June 1940, the day he first spoke on the BBC.

The ceremony never changed during his presidency: he would go to the Mont Valérien, a memorial built on 18 June 1960 close to the place where almost a thousand of resistants were shot by the Germans. Greeted by the Chancellor of the Order of the Liberation (which he had created in 1941), he would review the troops, bow to the victims of Nazi oppression symbolised by sixteen graves, and go after less than half an hour, without having said a word. Only silence could pay the needed tribute to the martyrs.

3.3. 1970–1994: FRANCE'S TROUBLED MEMORIES

3.3.1. The political context

This period can be read symbolically as the "impossible" de-Gaullisation: of French politics perhaps; of French historical memory for sure.

De Gaulle's successor, Georges Pompidou, had not been a resistant. But he choose 'historical Gaullists' as prime ministers: first, Jacques Chaban-Delmas, one of the youngest Resistance heroes, later Pierre Messmer, who fought at Bir-Hakeim and served from 1961 to 1969 as de Gaulle's Defence minister. Both of them were Companions of the Liberation. As such they were allowed, in accordance to the General's will, to attend his funeral in November 1970 in the rural churchyard of Colombey-les-Deux-Églises – whereas Madame de Gaulle had the coffin of her husband nailed before President Pompidou could see the dead man, a revenge for the pain de Gaulle had suffered when ousted by the French in 1940, a way also to remind Pompidou he did not belong to the heroic phalanx.

Pompidou thought he could break away from the legend. He gave a presidential pardon to former pro-Nazi thug Paul Touvier, an accomplice of the worst Nazi brutes from the region of Lyon, thus enabling him to come to France and regain possession of his personal goods. This move drew attention to Touvier, the first step of a judicial odyssey that would bring him, a quarter of a century later, to the Versailles assizes court, his trial ending with a life sentence for crimes against humanity. Touvier died in jail, the first collaborator for decades to do so.

Touvier's pardon was a huge political mistake on the part of Pompidou. Former resistants, some of them quite influential in Gaullist milieus, protested vehemently. Already ill – he would die in office in April 1974 – Pompidou went so far as to say, during a press conference in September 1972, that it was high time to "throw the veil [...] on this period when Frenchmen did not like one another", a presumably unintentional quotation of pre-war extreme-right leader Charles Maurras. His successor Valéry Giscard d'Estaing, the first non-Gaullist President of the Fifth Republic, also tried to modernise France, including French political culture. His presidency coincided with the 1970s, quite a rich and complex ideological period. Giscard and his prime minister Raymond Barre led a strongly Arab-orientated Middle-East policy, at a time when Holocaust denial rose in France. Their absence of reaction when a terrorist attack hit one of Paris's synagogues in November 1980 was bitterly felt by the Jewish community.

François Mitterrand, France's president from 1981 to 1995, was mostly a man of the past. Even more than his two predecessors, Mitterrand was moved by the idea of settling scores with de Gaulle and Gaullism – ancient scores indeed since they went back to the Resistance period. His two-term presidency ended poorly, first when he refused to acknowledge in July 1992 any responsibility of the French state in the tragic round-ups of Jews held fifty years earlier, saying Vichy had nothing to do with France, so that he himself and the Republic he stood for owed no apology. He was booed for that in July 1992 by Jewish activists at a ceremony marking the fiftieth anniversary of the notorious roundup at the *Velodrome d'Hiver* (Vel d'Hiv). In 1994, when a book by journalist Pierre Péan revealed his official past in the Vichy administration, the shock cover illustration of this book was a picture of Mitterrand, then a young civil servant, shaking hands with Vichy president Pétain.

3.3.2. The role of academic research and culture

The quarter-century starting in 1970 corresponds to vast historiographical projects, either initiated in the USA (Stanley Hoffmann, Robert Paxton, Michael Marrus), in Germany (Martin Broszat and the team of the *Institut für Zeitgeschichte*), UK (Jane Caplan, Ian Kershaw) and France (Jean-Pierre Azéma, Pierre Laborie, Henry Rousso, Denis Peschanski, etc.). The influence of Serge Klarsfeld, both as an historian and as an activist, who managed to have Klaus Barbie extradited from Bolivia to France, and who was at the root of all the trials of the mid-1980s to mid-1990s, should not be minimised.

Two movies have strongly orientated the perception of this past by French society. Released in 1969, Marcel Ophüls's *Le chagrin et la pitié* (The Sorrow and the Pity) was not shown by the French state-owned television that had helped produce it before 1982, after right-wing Gaullist and post-Gaullist parties had lost power in France. Although the film became world famous by word of mouth, the government still considered it too outrageous an image of WWII-era France. What it showed was however well-known, and had been for years – even by de Gaulle and his followers: mainly that the French, although not openly in favor of collaboration, went along rather quietly with the wartime collaborationist governments of Pétain and Laval. Historiography has since then shown that the movie made the pendulum swing too much in favor of accommodation and acceptance of collaboration – as did Robert Paxton's famous book, *Vichy France:*

Old Guard and New Order. Yet was it necessary for Frenchmen of the 1970s to realise the whole range of attitudes that had existed in their country between 1940 and 1944.

On the screens from 1985 onwards, Claude Lanzmann's film *Shoah* also played a great part in France's reappraisal of Vichy's role in the deportation and the killing of Jews from France between 1942 and 1944.

3.3.3. Memory eruptions: the public debate

Several of the events discussed in the section on the political context became sources of memory eruptions. Yet two events, very different in significance and magnitude occurred that may be seen as symbols of the complexity of the time.

In 1978, fanatical anti-Semite Louis Darquier de Pellepoix, Vichy's second High Commissioner for Jewish Affairs (*Commissaire général aux questions juives*) was interviewed in Madrid by a journalist working for the magazine *L'Express*, declaring (the sentence made a scandal in France): "Sure, gas was used in Auschwitz. But only lice were gassed".

There was an even greater unease in 1994 when Pierre Péan's book was published. The publication, *Une jeunesse française*, linked Mitterrand to far-right causes before the war and before he joined the Resistance during the war. It also told of his close friendship with former Vichy Police Chief Bousquet, who provided the Germans with the manpower to carry out the *Vel d'Hiv* roundup. Mitterrand continued to meet with Bousquet until 1986, even though Bousquet's involvement in the roundup had become known in the late 1970s. Bousquet was awaiting trial for crimes against humanity when he was shot dead in June 1993, much to Mitterrand's relief.

3.4. 1995 AND AFTER

Some two months after the right-wing Jacques Chirac defeated socialist leader Lionel Jospin in the presidential election, he made the speech that had been eagerly but vainly awaited from Mitterrand: "These dark hours," he said, when presiding on the *Vel d'Hiv*'s site a remembrance ceremony marking the 53rd anniversary of the first mass arrests of Jews in Paris, "forever sully our history and are an insult to our past and our traditions. […] Yes, the criminal folly of the occupiers was seconded by the French, by the French state. […] France, the land of Enlightment and Human Rights, where people are welcomed and given asylum, on that day, committed the irreparable. It broke its promise and delivered those whom it protected to their executioners. […] We owe them an unremitting debt".

So, France's official discourse was now in accordance with historical findings, at last. This unblocking of a frozen situation had a very important impact, helping other public or private institutions working through their own memory. So it happened for instance with the Catholic Church. Following Pope John Paul II's visit to Rome's synagogue in April 1986, and in accordance with recent trends in theology[21], the French Catholic Church made, on 30 September 1997, a "declaration of repentance" to the Jewish people for its silence in the face of French state collaboration with the Holocaust. The ceremony took place, symbolically, in Drancy, the suburban city were Jews were interned before being deported to death camps.

Both the administrative and the judicial would soon follow. Thanks to Serge Klarsfeld's obstinacy, the question of spoliation of Jewish assets by the French state came then into full light. In order to re-examine the issue of spoliation and consider restitution or compensation by the French government and the institutions that were most responsible for and directly benefited from these events, a commission (*Mission d'étude sur la spoliation des Juifs de France*) was set up by a decree of 25 March 1997 to "research the fate of the confiscated items; determine [their] whereabouts; draw up an inventory of seized assets; make proposals to the government on the future of these assets".

Chaired by Jean Mattéoli, a former industrialist and minister, who had been one of the youngest resistants in occupied France, the commission did an impressive amount of work. In April 2000 it published its 3,000-page report, which stated that $1.3 billion worth of Jewish assets were looted by both the Vichy regime and the German authorities. The report also mentioned that 90 percent of plundered assets were restituted after the war.

The report concluded with several recommendations, including setting up a foundation (created immediately as *Fondation pour la mémoire de la Shoah*, under the presidency of very popular politician Simone Veil) with the objective of keeping alive the memory of those who perished and learning lessons from these events. It also recommended that a commission be set up to handle compensation. The Commission for the Compensation of Victims of Spoliation resulting from the anti-Semitic Legislation enforced during the Occupation (CIVS), was created at the instigation of Prime Minister Lionel Jospin on 10 September 1999, and officially set up on 15 November 1999. Its work is not over ten years later.

Most of these moves had been made possible by the immense influence of the Papon case, the longest trial in French history. Maurice Papon, a centre-left civil servant before WWII, became a sub-prefect in Vichy, survived all the purges and ended his career in the civil service as de Gaulle's prefect of Police

---

21 J. Ratzinger, Press conference, 7 March 2000, available at www.clerus.org/clerus/dati/2001-05/10-6/CTIfaute.html#_Toc514122573, accessed 17 November 2011.

from 1958 to 1966. He then turned into a successful politician, and was Budget minister during Giscard d'Estaing's presidency, between 1978 and 1981.

Evidence of his responsibility in the Holocaust emerged during the 1981 presidential campaign, and charges of crimes against humanity, complicity in assassination and abuse of authority were first brought against him in January 1983. Yet the investigations took an incredible amount of time, as they did for the never-to-be-seen trial of René Bousquet. Lawyer Georges Kiejman, a former junior minister for Justice, revealed later that Mitterrand himself had given instructions to slow down procedural action as much as possible. Papon finally went to trial in October 1997, after 14 years of bitter legal wrangling. His trial was the longest in French history, finishing only in April 1998 when he was convicted and given a 10-year prison term.

Finally, in February 2009, the Council of State, France's highest administrative justice body formally confirmed, as it had discreetly done in April 2002[22] that the French state bore moral and legal responsibility for the deportation of nearly 76,000 Jews during the nation's occupation in WWII. In doing so, the court officially recognised the willful participation of France's collaborationist Vichy government in anti-Semitic persecution that had long been attributed to Nazi occupying powers. It was 65 years after WWII was over. At long last, *la boucle était bouclée*.[23]

4. A FEW WORDS OF CONCLUSION

As head of the GPRF, de Gaulle faced a paradox when he seized power in liberated France. He knew France's thirst for revenge and wanted to channel it through regular state justice. Through his pre-war experience within the French State, he used to trust public institutions and their elites, the importance of which he acknowledged in the French state-building tradition, he was clever enough to realise they had served the Pétain regime without trouble, before adopting a "wait-and-see" attitude when needed.

Overly-severe purges would therefore leave France beheaded, a very dangerous situation since the Communist party might take this opportunity to fill the gaps. Even if this fear, very common among the bourgeois elites at that time, has been much exaggerated as we now know, it would anyway have been dangerous to weaken the state apparatus at a time when France faced huge material and political difficulties. Justice may have been important;

22 A. Bancaud and M.O. Baruch, *Vers la désépuration?*, 512.
23 Meaning: France had come "full circle".

reconstruction of the Nation was vital. And the Nation, for de Gaulle, was the State – even at the price of forgetting all the compromises of principle that had been commonplace in the higher ranks of the civil service from mid-1943 onwards. Who could imagine in 1944–1945 that this "realistic" choice would be dearly paid for half a century later, with France struggling with her past through the Papon trial?

As a matter of fact, the crack was in the metal from the beginning. Post-WWII TJ's failure mainly comes, in our opinion, from the incapacity (or the refusal) to give unequivocal answers to key-questions:

- Which kind of attitudes were to be punished?
- On which foundations should the national community be rebuilt?
- Was punishment meant primarily to permanently expel wrongdoers or should the idea of reintegration be taken into account from the beginning?
- How should one accept the idea of political justice, and how should one enforce it?

A past which has not been worked through is liable to come back. Hence, in the mid-70s, whereas things seemed to settle down by exhaustion of cases, the conjunction of historical (resignation of de Gaulle from the Presidency in 1969, followed by his death one year later), historiographical (the film "The Sorrow and the Pity" in 1969, Robert Paxton's "Vichy France" in 1972) and generational factors in the wake of May 1968 riots deeply shifted the relation of the French to their recent past. As historian Henry Rousso wrote in 1987 in a psychoanalytical reading of the phenomenon (*Le syndrome de Vichy*), the issue has almost become obsessive in contemporary France, a situation that makes the present very long-term approach to post-1944 TJ particularly relevant for the French case.

Starting with the election of Gaullist leader Jacques Chirac as President in 1995, politics, academic history, compensation measures and the law finally converged, very possibly providing a path to a reconciliation of France with her WWII past. This period saw very important moments such as Jacques Chirac's speech on 17 July 1995, the work and proposals of the Commission created by the government in 1997 and chaired by former resistant and Gaullist minister Jean Mattéoli (*Mission d'étude sur la spoliation des Juifs de France*), the long delayed Papon trial (fall 1997-Easter 1998) and its successive civil and administrative issues. Combined with the emergence of international TJ (Rwanda, former Yugoslavia, creation of the International Criminal Court, ICC); this unprecedented series of events made the most recent period one of the most strategic in the sixty-year long history of TJ following WWII in France.

SELECTIVE FURTHER READING

Association française d'histoire de la justice (AFHJ), *Les ministres devant la justice* (Arles: Actes Sud, 1997).

Bancaud, Alain, 'La construction de l'appareil juridique', in Baruch, Marc Olivier (ed.), *Une poignée de misérables: l'épuration de la société française après la Seconde Guerre mondiale* (Paris: Fayard, 2003a), pp. 61–97.

Bancaud, Alain, 'L'épuration des épurateurs: la magistrature', in Baruch, Marc Olivier (ed.), *Une poignée de misérables: l'épuration de la société française après la Seconde Guerre mondiale* (Paris: Fayard, 2003b), pp. 172–203.

Bancaud, Alain and Baruch, Marc Olivier, 'Vers la désépuration? L'épuration devant la juridiction administrative, 1945–1970', in Baruch, Marc Olivier (ed.), *Une poignée de misérables: l'épuration de la société française après la Seconde Guerre mondiale* (Paris: Fayard, 2003), pp. 480–512.

Baruch, Marc Olivier, *Servir l'État français; l'administration en France de 1940 à 1944*, (Paris: Fayard, 1997).

Baruch, Marc Olivier, 'Procès Papon, impressions d'audience', *Le Débat*, 102, Fall 1998, pp. 11–16.

Baruch, Marc Olivier, 'L'épuration du corps préfectoral', in Baruch, Marc Olivier (ed.), *Une poignée de misérables: l'épuration de la société française après la Seconde Guerre mondiale* (Paris: Fayard, 2003a), pp. 139–171.

Baruch, Marc Olivier, 'Conclusion', in Baruch, Marc Olivier (ed.), *Une poignée de misérables: l'épuration de la société française après la Seconde Guerre mondiale* (Paris: Fayard, 2003b), pp. 531–547.

Baruch, Marc Olivier, 'Perpetrator Networks and the Holocaust: The Spoliation of Jewish Property in France, 1940–1944', in Gerald D. Feldman and Wolfgang Seibel (eds.), *Networks of Nazi Persecution. Bureaucracy, Business and the Organisation of the Holocaust*, (Oxford/New York: Berghahn Books, 2005), pp. 189–212.

Bergère, Marc, *Une société en épuration: épuration vécue et perçue en Maine-et-Loire: de la Libération au début des années 50* (Rennes: Presses Universitaires de Rennes, 2004).

Bourdet, Claude, *L'aventure incertaine: de la Résistance à la Restauration* (Paris: Stock, 1975).

Elster, Jon, *Closing the Books: Transitional Justice in Historical Perspective* (New York: Cambridge University Press, 2004).

François-Poncet, André, *Discours de réception à l'Académie française, 22 janvier 1953*, available at www.academie-francaise.fr/immortels/discours_reception/francois-poncet.html, accessed on 10 November 2011.

Gacon, Stéphane, 'L'amnistie de la collaboration', in Baruch, Marc Olivier (ed.), *Une poignée de misérables: l'épuration de la société française après la Seconde Guerre mondiale* (Paris: Fayard, 2003), pp. 465–479.

Mauriac, Jean, *Mort du général de Gaulle* (Paris: Grasset, 1972).

Novick, Peter, *L'épuration française, 1944–1949* (Paris: Balland, 1985), transl. from *The Resistance versus Vichy: the Purge of Collaborators in Liberated France* (London: Chatto and Windus, 1968).

PÉAN, Pierre, *Une Jeunesse française* (Paris: Fayard, 1994).

RATZINGER, Joseph, Press conference, 7 March 2000, available at www.clerus.org/clerus/dati/2001-05/10-6/CTIfaute.html#_Toc514122573, accessed 17 November 2011.

ROUQUET, François, 'L'épuration des universitaires, défense et justification', in BARUCH, Marc Olivier (ed.), *Une poignée de misérables: l'épuration de la société française après la Seconde Guerre mondiale* (Paris: Fayard, 2003), pp. 229–242.

ROUSSO, Henry, *The Vichy Syndrome: History and Memory in France since 1944,* translated by Arthur Goldhammer (Cambridge, Mass.; London: Harvard University Press, cop. 1991), transl. from *Le syndrome de Vichy: 1944–198...* (Paris: Seuil, 1987).

ROUSSO, Henry, *Vichy: l'événement, la mémoire, l'histoire* (Paris: Gallimard, 2001).

SAPIRO, Gisèle, *La guerre des écrivains: 1940–1953* (Paris: Fayard, 1999).

SIMONIN, Anne, *Le déshonneur dans la République: une histoire de l'indignité 1791–1958* (Paris: Grasset, 2008).

SIMONIN, Anne, 'L'indignité nationale, un châtiment républicain', in BARUCH, Marc Olivier (ed.), *Une poignée de misérables: l'épuration de la société française après la Seconde Guerre mondiale* (Paris: Fayard, 2003), pp. 37–60.

Study Mission on the Spoliation of Jews in France: Mattéoli Commission, *Final Report,* April 2000, available at www.ladocumentationfrancaise.r/rapports-publics/004000897/index.shtml, accessed on 18 November 2011.

THOMAS, Yan, 'La vérité, le temps, le juge et l'historien', *Le Débat*, Fall 1998, pp. 17–36.

A CONSENSUS OF DIFFERENCES

Transitional Justice and Belgium's Divided War Memories (1944–2012)

Nico Wouters and Dirk Luyten

1. THE CENTRAL PHASE OF TRANSITIONAL JUSTICE POLICIES (1944–1951)

Belgium experienced transitional justice from September 1944 to 1951, after the country had been occupied by the Germans. Belgium had also experienced the punishment of collaboration after the First World War, when the country lived almost completely under German occupation and was split up politically and administratively on linguistic lines (in the northern part, Flanders, most people spoke Dutch, Wallonia, the southern part, was French-speaking; French was also the high status language throughout the country). Legislation, jurisprudence, judicial doctrines as well as the experience with this first punishment of collaboration have left their mark on transitional justice after 1944. In order to facilitate the comparison with the other countries under review in this book, and to be able to point out what is to be considered as a "judicial innovation", we will start with transitional justice after the Second World War and then indicate where and to what extent the punishment of collaboration after the First World War has had an impact on the post-1944 transitional justice process and to what extent measures taken for the post-1944 period were judicial innovations.

1.1. THE OCCUPATION REGIME

Belgium was invaded by Nazi Germany on 10 May 1940. The entire territory was occupied by German troops, except a small German-speaking part in the East (received as compensation from Germany after 1918), which was annexed to the *Reich*. Belgium was ruled by a military government *(Militärverwaltung)* until July 1944, when a civil government *(Zivilverwaltung)* took over until the

Liberation in September 1944.[1] The King preferred to stay in Belgium, officially as a POW (he was the commander-in-chief of the Belgian army), but tried to play a political role, without much success.[2] The government left the country, established itself in London and was considered by the Allies as the legitimate Belgian government. With the invasion, the Belgian parliament delegated powers of the ministers within the occupied territory itself to the highest-ranking civil servants, the secretaries-general. They formed a committee, governed the country and became the political interlocutors of the German authorities.[3]

Belgium was not entirely Nazified: German rule was exercised by making an appeal to the domestic administrations, organisations and authorities and also to collaborators. The latter could be found in large numbers with the leaders, militants and members of the pre-war fascist and extreme-right parties such as the Flemish National League (*Vlaams Nationaal Verbond*, VNV) (Flanders) and Rex (French-speaking Belgium).[4] Confidants of these parties were appointed in different institutions of the state apparatus at central (secretaries-general) and local levels (mayors).[5] These parties obtained the monopoly of political activity. The Germans recruited Belgian citizens to fight on the Eastern Front. The recruitment campaign was supported by the abovementioned parties.

The second face of German rule was the authoritarian reform of the existing liberal-democratic institutions, basically by removing mechanisms of democratic control, and appointing New Order-members to leading positions.[6]

A third means was the creation of new institutions or mass movements, often a copy of the Nazi model and in any case based on the Führerprinzip (e.g. a single trade union).

A fourth feature of the occupation regime was the increasing bureaucratisation of society: new institutions were created employing many people. This bureaucratisation was ideologically driven, but was also a consequence of the change of economic liberalism into a planned economy and a food rationing system. This planned economy left room for an (extensive) black market, which in its turn legitimated the creation of a specific repressive apparatus of control squads and a special administrative jurisdiction, contributing to the expansion of the bureaucracy.[7]

---

1 E. Verhoeyen, *La Belgique occupée: de l'an 40 à la Libération*, Brussels, 1994.

2 J. Velaers and H. Van Goethem, *Leopold III: de koning, het land, de oorlog*, Tielt, 1994.

3 M. Van den Wijngaert, *Het beleid van het Comité van de sekretarissen-generaal in België tijdens de Duitse bezetting 1940–1944*, Brussels, 1975.

4 M. Conway, *Collaboration in Belgium: Léon Degrelle and the Rexist Movement 1940–1944*, New Haven/London, 1993; B. De Wever, *Greep naar de macht: Vlaams-nationalisme en Nieuwe Orde, het VNV 1933–1945*, Tielt/Antwerp/Ghent, 1994.

5 N. Wouters, *De Führerstaat: overheid en collaboratie in België (1940–1944)*, Tielt, 2006.

6 N. Wouters, *De Führerstaat.*

7 D. Luyten, *Ideologie en praktijk van het corporatisme tijdens de Tweede Wereldoorlog in België*, Brussels, 1997.

The main objectives of the occupation regime were maintaining law and order and the exploitation of the economy of the occupied territory for the German war effort. The occupation regime had a repressive character and much in its functioning was not compatible with the Belgian constitutional order and the principles of liberal democracy. The prosecution of the Jews is one of the most striking examples.[8]

The nature of the occupation regime was such that many people were in one way or another bound to the occupation regime: volunteers for the Eastern Front, leaders and members of the collaborationist parties, leaders and employees of the newly established institutions and Belgian civil servants and businessmen.

1.2. TRANSITIONAL JUSTICE MEASURES

Belgium was liberated by Allied troops in September 1944. The Liberation was a swift operation. The London government returned, but in order to enhance its representative status new ministers were appointed, among others a member of the Communist Party, which had played a leading role in the Resistance. At the Liberation, the Germans had brought the King to Austria. Even in the summer of 1944, the King remained critical of the Allies and the parliamentary system. His position, and as a consequence that of the monarchy, became a heated question (the so-called "Royal Question") in Belgian politics until 1950, opposing the left (Communists, Socialists and a part of the Liberal Party) and the right (the Catholic Party and a part of the Liberal Party). Parliament, composed following the last pre-war election of 1939, was convened again after the Liberation and appointed a Regent to replace the King. Government obtained full powers to legislate in certain fields such as punishment of collaboration.[9] The German-speaking part of Belgium was reintegrated and subject to the same transitional justice measures as the rest of the territory.

1.2.1. Judicial policies: state-initiated and state-executed measures

Transitional justice started with the Liberation. A first measure which should be mentioned and which can be labeled as state-initiated are the internments of people suspected of collaboration, most of them in special internment camps. Internment was possible on the ground of a decree-law of 1918, and a circular letter of the Minister of Justice of August 1944. German citizens or citizens of a state which was an ally of Germany had to be interned. All those who might be supposed to have helped the Germans could be subject to internment. The last

8 R. Van Doorslaer, E. Debruyne, F. Seberechts and N. Wouters, *La Belgique docile: les autorités belges et la persécution des Juifs en Belgique durant la Seconde Guerre mondiale*, Brussels, 2007.

9 M. Conway, *The Sorrows of Belgium. Liberation and Political Reconstruction, 1944–1947*, Oxford, 2012.

category included Belgian collaborators. This internment could be imposed by a judicial authority (e.g. the prosecutor, the military prosecutor), the mayor or agents of the state security service. Internment was an administrative measure and was initially aimed at protecting the liberating troops.[10]

In practice, not only the authorities listed in the law and the circular letter gave orders for internment; many people were arrested and interned at the initiative of the Resistance movements or the population. Internment took place in two phases: the days and weeks following the Liberation and the spring of 1945, when political prisoners returned from Germany. In these periods, (alleged) collaborators were subject to (symbolic) violence by the population: furniture and personal belongings were destroyed and women had their hair shorn.[11] Tens of thousands men and women have been interned, but the exact number is difficult to determine. Figures on the total of people interned are not available; we only possess figures on the number of people in internment at certain dates.

Table 1.1. Number of individuals interned[12]

Dates	Number according to John Gilissen	Number according to Luc Huyse
November 1944		55,000
December 1944	37,697	
1 January 1945	32,490	
February 1945		77,000
Early May 1945		20,000
1 June 1945	40,359	
1 July 1945		40,000
1 August 1945	23,190	
1 September 1945	21,340	21,340
Early October 1945		17,613
1 December 1945	8,607	
1 January 1946	5,686	5,686
Early March 1946		1,114
1 May 1946	405	

10 G. Cassart, *L'internement des suspects et des étrangers: arrêté-loi du 12 octobre 1918 et son application en 1944*, Brussels, 1944.

11 L. Huyse and S. Dhondt, *La répression des collaborations 1942–1952: un passé toujours présent*, Brussels, 1993, at 47–52; C. Van Loon, 'De geschorene en de scheerster: de vrouw in de straatrepressie na de Tweede Wereldoorlog', (2008), 19 *Cahiers d'Histoire du Temps Présent*, 45–78.

12 J. Gilissen, 'Etude statistique de la répression de l'incivisme' in *Revue de droit pénal et de criminologie*, 1951, 621. L. Huyse, 'Cijfers en feiten over de na-oorlogse interneringscentra' in J. Ballinckx and K. Van Deuren (eds.), *P. Longinus De Munter, O.F.M. Franciscaan en fotograaf*, Bruges, 1992, 135–139.

The central mechanism of transitional justice in Belgium was the penal law: Articles 113 to 121*bis* of the penal code punished what were called "crimes and offenses against the external security of the state". This penal code existed since 1867, had been adapted for those crimes and offenses in the First World War, in 1934 and between 1942 and 1944. The four types of collaboration were military collaboration (Article 113), economic collaboration (115), political and intellectual collaboration (118*bis*) and informing (121*bis*).

According to the law, in 1944 the punishment for collaboration was, in principle, the death penalty, except for some types of informing, depending on the consequences the informing had for the victim: from five years of imprisonment if the victim was unharmed to the death penalty if the victim died or was permanently injured. Penalties inflicted by the tribunals however ranged from less than one year of imprisonment to the death penalty. The chief military prosecutor gave instructions to the military prosecutors on the penalty they had to demand and which was not always the death penalty.[13] The final decision on the penalty lay with the tribunals and their assessment of the sentence could also have an impact on the jurisprudence of other tribunals.

Articles 113–121*bis* of the penal code were the judicial instruments with which all the acts of collaboration committed under the occupation had to be punished. These instruments were basically the same as those used to punish collaboration after the First World War. This legislation underwent some changes in the 1930s and the London government also altered the penal law on some points, but the foundations and principles were not put into question.[14] Within this framework, some judicial innovations were introduced, as will be explained further.

Collaboration was defined as helping the enemy and the issue was a patriotic one: Belgian citizens should do nothing that could harm the interest of the Belgian state by helping the enemy. In principle, the nature of the political regime of the enemy state played no role. This was also reflected in the changes of the penal law in 1942. The concept of military collaboration (Article 113) was widened, by an interpretative law, to be able to punish those engaged at the Eastern Front.[15] For political collaboration (Article 118*bis*) and informing (Article 121*bis*) special intent was no longer a condition to be punishable. No new penal offences were added which were directly linked to the Nazi character of the occupation regime. The reasons are not quite clear: there was of course the principle of the non-retroactivity of the penal law. This objection has to be

---

13 L. Huyse and S. Dhondt, *La répression*, 266.

14 J. Gilissen, P. Cassiers and F. Debroux, 'Crimes et délits contre la sûreté de l'Etat' in *Novelles. Droit Pénal, Tome II*, Brussels, 1967, 113–319.

15 Initially Article 113 aimed at military action against Belgium or its allies. The concept of 'allies' was changed as to include the USSR.

nuanced however, since it was possible, under certain circumstances, as shown by Articles 113, 118*bis* and 121*bis* to change the penal law during the conflict. Moreover, the issue of the non-retroactivity of the penal law had been debated before the Courts after the First World War.[16] In 1916 and 1917, the penal law had been changed by the government-in-exile in Le Havre and as a consequence, the question of the non-retroactivity of the penal law was raised in the post-war trials. Even if there was the legal argument that this principle was only defined in civil law, not in penal law, nor in the Constitution and moreover non-retroactivity was not applicable for continuous offences, such as collaboration, the tribunals were prudent and only applied the new legislation if it was established that the punishable act was committed after the date the new law had come into force.[17]

Taking into account this precedent, it was accepted by the London Government (which had full powers) in 1942 that there were no judicial objections against a change of the penal law. As far as Article 113 is concerned, an interpretive law was used, an admissible technique to modify a law without violating the principle of non-retroactivity. For the changes of Articles 118*bis* (political collaboration) and 121*bis* (informing), the new definitions could only be applied one month after their publication, i.e. 29 January 1943. After the war, the legality of the changes in the penal law were contested, arguing that the London government was not entitled to make modifications to the law, that the law lacked the necessary publicity to be valid[18] or that the legislation had a retroactive character. The Court of Cassation, the Supreme Court in the Belgian judicial system, rejected these objections on several occasions.[19]

A convicted collaborator received a punishment, in principle the death penalty, but more often imprisonment or a fine. Moreover, he or she lost a series of civil and political rights for a minimum of ten years, such as the right to vote, to be elected or to be a teacher or a lawyer.[20] If collaboration had been inspired by profiteering, the "spoils" of the crime were confiscated. This Article (123*ter*) was mostly used against economic collaborators, who had to pay back to the state the revenue of the transactions which were proven to be economic collaboration.[21]

---

16 Th. Lemoine and X. Rousseaux, 'La force du droit. Bricolage législatif et réorganisation judiciaire' in X. Rousseaux and L. van Ypersele (eds.), *La Patrie crie vengéance! La répression des 'inciviques' belges au sortir de la guerre 1914–1918*, Brussels, 2008, 67–87.

17 M. Deckers, 'De strafrechtelijke vervolging van het activisme. Deel 1: het wettelijk kader' in *Wetenschappelijke Tijdingen*, (2002) 61, 156–178, at 172–173.

18 A law has to be published in the *Moniteur belge/Belgisch Staatsblad*, the Belgian Official Gazette. The new laws were published in the Official Gazette issued by the London Government.

19 J. Gilissen, P. Cassiers and F. Debroux, *Crimes et délits* 117–118, 175.

20 L. Huyse and S. Dhondt, *La répression*, 25–29.

21 D. Luyten, *Burgers boven elke verdenking? Vervolging van economische collaboratie in België na de Tweede Wereldoorlog*, Brussels, 1996, 33.

Punishment of collaboration was in the hands of the military justice system. The military character was slightly mitigated by appointing two lay judges to sit with three army officers. Since many judges were needed, not only professional army officers but also reserve officers acted as judges. The monopoly of the military justice differed from the post- First World War punishment of collaboration, when collaborators were not only tried by the military courts, but also by the assize courts and the courts judging minor offenses. The judicial procedure in military justice was faster and shorter but offered the accused less guarantees than the non-military penal procedure: the prosecutor and the examining magistrate were the same person, contact with lawyers was often difficult and the long internment left many people for a long period of time in legal insecurity.[22]

Since the legislation was basically the same as that used after 1918, the post-1918 jurisprudence put its mark on the judicial settlement of collaboration after 1944.[23] The impact especially concerned the interpretation of judicial concepts such as "weapons and ammunition" in the field of economic collaboration. Judicial doctrine on the post-1918 jurisprudence concerning punishment of collaboration was also used after 1944.

This does not mean, however, that the post-1918 jurisprudence was simply copied after 1944. This becomes clear in the field of economic collaboration, for example, where using the same criteria as in the post-1918 years would have, taking into account the scale of the production for the German war economy by Belgian industry, led to prosecution and punishment of many entrepreneurs. Therefore, the post-1918 jurisprudence was only one of the elements that shaped the prosecution policy pertaining to economic collaboration.[24] Another qualification can be found in the changes of legislation in 1942: one of the aims was precisely to substitute the limitative interpretation by the post-1918 jurisprudence of certain concepts such as "carrying arms" with a broader interpretation, including all kinds of military activities, responding better to the reality of military collaboration during the Second World War.[25]

An element that must have played a role in the prosecution policy and the assignment penalties was that, under pressure from the Flemish Movement (the movement striving for the emancipation of the Dutch-speaking part of the

22 L. Huyse, 'Transitional justice in Belgium, France, and the Netherlands after World War II: Innovations, transgressions, and lessons to be learned' in A. Czarnota, M. Krygier and S. Wojciech (eds.), *Rethinking the rule of law after communism*, Budapest, 2005, 135–152, 137.

23 J. Dautricourt, *La trahison par collaboration avec l'ennemi occupant le territoire national: étude préparatoire et pratique de la répression, dans le cadre des lois pénales belges, complétées par les arrêtés-lois des 17.12.1942 et 6.5.1944*, Brussels, 1945.

24 D. Luyten, *Burgers boven elke verdenking?*, 31–33.

25 J. Gilissen, P. Cassiers and F. Debroux, *Crimes et délits* 117–118, 175.

country), amnesty had been granted in the interwar period to most collaborators of the First World War. In the post-1944 trials some of the people to whom amnesty had been given were again accused of collaboration and could be labelled recidivists. This amnesty had been a source of political conflicts and an issue for political mobilisation for the Flemish nationalists in the interwar period.[26]

As had been the case after 1918, specific sanctions existed for civil servants[27], the professional purge. A conviction for collaboration could have a direct effect on the professional situation of civil servants. Civil servants convicted for collaboration or subject to the civic purge (see further) lost their job and pension claims. Moreover, even if a civil servant was not convicted for collaboration, a sanction could be imposed following the professional purge. This professional purge was based on the disciplinary rules for civil servants, which were part of the statute of the civil servants which existed since 1937 ("*statut Camu*"). This implies that special commissions with a trade-union representation were in charge. This professional purge cannot be qualified as penal law, but was a disciplinary rule, meaning that not only acts but also professional conduct and attitude were assessed. The state police, the *Gendarmerie*, had a specific system of professional purging.[28]

1.2.2. Judicial innovations

As already pointed out, collaboration had to be dealt with at the Liberation in 1944, using basically the same instruments as after the First World War, when collaboration had been less important from a quantitative point of view.

There was however some difference in the techniques used, which can be considered as judicial innovations. Some of those innovations were introduced after the Liberation. Compared to the First World War, the sanctions for collaborators had much more far-reaching consequences. For the judge in the post-1918 trials, imposing the loss of rights was an option, while according to the decree-law of 6 May 1944 the loss of rights was an *automatic consequence* of the sentence and was not pronounced by a judge. The sanction was the same for all convicted collaborators, making no distinctions as to the nature of the offence. The post-1944 jurisprudence had a more mechanistic character than that of the period following the First World War.

---

26 V. Massin and X. Rousseaux, 'Epilogue ou fausse sortie? L'impossible liquidation de la question incivique (1919–1940)' in X. Rousseaux and L. van Ypersele (eds.), *La Patrie crie vengéance!*, 159–168, at 159–158.

27 L. Huyse and S. Dhondt, *La répression*, 37–40.

28 J. Campion, *Les Gendarmes belges, français, et néerlandais à la sortie de la Seconde Guerre Mondiale*, Brussels, 2011.

Moreover, after 1944 a convicted collaborator lost more rights than had been the case after 1918. In 1918, a person convicted for collaboration only lost permanently the right to hold public offices, to vote or to be elected, to be eligible for a distinction, to carry arms or to serve in the Belgian army. The loss according to the decree-law of 6 May 1944 was more extensive. The aim of this law was to exclude convicted collaborators from public life and to protect the cultural, scientific, spiritual and economic patrimony of the Nation.[29] Therefore, people convicted for collaboration were no longer allowed to be a teacher, a lawyer, a journalist, a leader of a political party or to act as a director or administrator of a company. The duration of the loss of rights depended on the sentence.[30]

The decree-law of 6 May 1944 was in fact an alternative to the loss of nationality, a measure which made it possible to exclude someone from public life. Loss of nationality was considered too radical a measure, creating a large group of stateless persons. Loss of nationality was limited to people accused of collaboration that did not attend their trial and were convicted to five years imprisonment or more.

The decree-law of 6 May 1944 still remained within the framework of the penal procedure: all the people who had lost their rights were brought before a judge.

More innovative, but still derived from the penal law, was the civic purge (*épuration civique*), which was organised following the principles laid down in the decree-law of 19 September 1945. People who had committed minor acts of collaboration, listed in the decree-law, were not brought before a judge but lost a set of civil and political rights, for life or for twenty years, such as the right to vote, to be elected, to become a journalist or a teacher. In contrast to other countries, this "purge" was in the hands of the judiciary: the decision was taken by the military prosecutor. An appeal could be made with the court of first instance. The acts of collaboration listed in the decree-law were in the realm of military, political and intellectual collaboration, propaganda or membership in a collaborationist youth organisation. The loss of rights was not a punishment, but a "security measure of civil nature" aimed at the "exclusion from the right to participate in the public life of the Nation"[31], so it served the same purpose as the loss of rights in the decree-law of 6 May 1944. The decree-law of 19 September 1945 was more or less a copy of this system of loss of rights, in fact, the civic purge "halved" the sanction inflicted on a collaborator who was convicted by a military tribunal in the sense that this person did not receive a penalty.

---

29 Decree-law 1944, 412.

30 J. Gilissen, P. Cassiers and F. Debroux, *Crimes et délits*, 272.

31 Decree-law 1945, 6333.

This civic purge was a judicial innovation compared to the instruments used after the First World War and made it possible to target most of the rank-and-file of the collaborationist political parties and organisations. It had an even more mechanistic character than the decree-law of 6 May 1944: people who met the criteria of the decree-law (e.g. being member of a collaborationist party after a certain date) were listed by the military prosecutor and automatically lost civic and political rights. One could advance the hypothesis that the decree-law was an answer to the nature of Nazi rule and collaboration, implicating many people, too large a number for the classic penal procedure. The civic purge was less time-consuming than a court procedure and made it possible to sanction minor acts of collaboration, which in many cases would have been dropped by the prosecutor, leaving these people the possibility to participate in public life, including the right to vote, while the political elite wanted to exclude those people from political participation.

A parallel can be drawn with the nationality law of 1934. This law made it possible to withdraw Belgian nationality from people who had obtained this nationality by naturalisation and who had seriously failed in their duties towards Belgium. The decision was taken by the Court of appeal[32], while for the civic purge, only the military prosecutor was in charge, with a possibility of appeal that brought the case before a court.

This combination of penal law and civic purge gave the post-1944 transitional justice process a far larger reach than had been the case after 1918: a sanction could be imposed on more people and was more important. In 1918–1921 loss of rights could be for life; in 1944–1948, for 10 or 20 years or for life until 19 September 1945. After this date, loss of rights was for life, but people convicted to an imprisonment of less than five years could obtain restitution of the rights lost (*arrêté-loi* 1945: 6339). The loss of rights as conceived the decree-laws of 6 May 1944 and 19 September 1945 was not considered as a penalty, but as a measure of a civic nature; therefore, the loss of rights could not be undone using the normal instruments of penal law such as grace. Special legislation was needed.

Also new was the influence of the newly-developed international legislation regarding the prosecution of war crimes. The decree-law of 13 December 1944 established the Belgian War Crimes Commission, which was a Belgian homologue of the United Nations War Crime Commission.[33] The commission exchanged information and carried out judicial study in preparation for the

32 Decree-law 1944, 411.

33 N. Wouters, 'The Belgian trials (1944–1951)' in D. Bankier and D. Michman (eds.), *Holocaust and Justice. Representation and historiography of the Holocaust in post-war trials*, New York/Oxford, 2010, 219–245.

Belgian prosecution of German war crimes in occupied Belgium. An important step was the Belgian law of 20 June 1947 concerning the competence of the military tribunals with regard to war criminals. This new law was the foundation for the prosecution of German war criminals in Belgium.

In the post-1944 transitional justice, judicial innovations were used but decision makers had been acquainted with some of the new techniques, such as the change of the penal law, since the First World War. As far as the civic purge is concerned, the control over the instrument remained in the hands of the military prosecutors and an appeal, which brought the case before a court, was possible. Many used this opportunity: 43,093 persons met the conditions of the civic purge and were listed by the military prosecutor. In February 1948, about half of the decisions (50.7%) were maintained after an appeal was made with the Court of First Instance.[34]

"Extreme times lead to extreme measures" is only partly true for the Belgian case: the experience with the punishment of collaboration after the First World War played a role. Some innovations were already introduced during the First World War and assessed by the judiciary after 1918. Another qualification is that the state (the military justice system) had the monopoly of the transitional justice process.

1.2.3. Quasi-judicial techniques

A measure which was on the limit of a judicial technique was the "certificate of civism" (*certificat de civisme*). It was a form issued by the local authority declaring that the person who asked for a certificate had not been implied in collaboration during the war. The certificate can to a certain extent be compared to the certificate of good character, which already existed and was necessary to apply for a job in the civil service. The criteria of civism were not well defined, leaving room for appreciation to the local authority. More and more authorities and institutions asked for the certificate when recruiting employees and it was also needed to register as a student at a public university or to apply for a position of public trust.[35]

Private organisations had their internal mechanisms to impose a sanction on leaders or members who had collaborated or misbehaved during the occupation according to the standards of the organisation. These private sanction mechanisms existed in universities, political parties, trade unions, film makers and among artists.[36]

---

34 J. Gilissen, *Etude statistique*, 84.

35 L. Huyse and S. Dhondt, *La répression*, 40–44.

36 D. Martin, 'L'épuration' in A. Despy-Meyer, A. Dierkens and F. Scheelings (eds.), *25 novembre 1941: l'Université Libre de Bruxelles ferme ses portes*, Brussels, 1991, 197–204; V. Scheltiens, 'Breuk en continuïteit in doen en denken: het geval War Van Overstraeten, 1910–1945' in *Cahiers d'Histoire du Temps Présent*, (2010) 22, 15–54.

Table 1.2. Number of punished perpetrators (including civic purge) (1944–1951)[37]

Persons convicted for collaboration	**53,005**
Persons convicted for collaboration and having lost Belgian nationality	**3,165**
Acquittals	**4,736**
Persons who have lost rights on the basis of the civic purge	**21,889**
(Total Belgian population)	**8,334,276**

Table 1.3. Estimate of punished perpetrators by type of disciplinary measure[38]

Type of punishment, sanction	Number of persons
Pecuniary (financial) sanctions	**6000**
Prison sentences, internment	**50,000–70,000**
Loss of (certain) rights and/or nationality	**97,000**
Exclusion of services, benefits, professions	**> 97,000**

Table 1.4. Number of individual victims[39]

Table of the victims (casualties) of the Second World War in Belgium	Number	%
Racial persecution Jews, who died in prison, were killed in Belgium, deported from Mechelen and Drancy (ca. 28,900) Gypsies (352)	Approx. 29,250	Approx. 39
Civilians *(Military campaign of 1940, military operations of 1944–1945, bombardments, V-bombs, voluntary workers in Germany)*	Approx. 19,000	Approx. 5.3
Repression against the resistance Political prisoners (14,100) Executed hostages (295) Killed by collaborationist militias (150)	Approx. 14,545	Approx. 19.3
Military *Military campaign of 1940 (5,705)* *Prisoners of war (3,000)* *Soldiers in the UK and in Africa (770)*	Approx. 9,700	Approx. 12.9
Deported workers	2,592	3.5
Total	Approx. 75,000	100

37 J. Gilissen, *Etude statistique*, 50.

38 K. Aerts, *Repressie zonder maat of einde*, 599.

39 R. Van Doorslaer, 'Gebruikt verleden. De politieke nalatenschap van de Tweede Wereldoorlog in België, 1945–2000' in G. Deneckere and B. De Wever (eds.), *Geschiedenis maken: liber amicorum Herman Balthazar*, Ghent, 2003, 9.

2. TOWARDS MITIGATION AND REINTEGRATION OF CONVICTED COLLABORATORS

In 1944–1945 there was a consensus among political parties that harsh punishment of collaboration was a political priority. Nevertheless, a political left/right divide emerged immediately. The left (Socialists, Communists and Liberals) favored harsh punishment while the right (Catholic Party), especially in Flanders, was more lenient for the collaborators and their motivations. Moreover, in right-wing milieus in Flanders, transitional justice was criticised as exaggerated and a political operation against Flanders and its elite. The left-right divide dominated Belgian politics in the second half of the 1940s and was linked with the Royal Question.[40]

From 1946 on, the political priorities shifted from punishment to reeducation/resettlement of convicted collaborators. The first initiatives were taken by the Liberal Minister of Justice Albert Lilar. These measures had been elaborated by the administration. They included not only reeducation but also shortening of the detention period through labour (for instance in the coal mines – the days worked were deducted from the detention period). Moreover, the Belgian state could make use of the procedures which existed since the end of the 19th century to release prisoners earlier or conditionally. The so-called "Lejeune law" had already institutionalised the possibility of conditional release. By the end of 1948, 12,801 convicted collaborators had already been released. This had risen to 25,400 by the end of 1949 (the conditions were also extended and liberalised).[41]

Extensive use was also made of the already existing possibility for pardon measures. A pardon was an individual *nominatim* measure that granted the reduction of the punishment and often prison sentence. In 1950 only a small number (about 6%) of the convicted collaborators were still in prison.[42] Pardon measures were also used to commute death penalties to lifelong prison sentences. In 1944–45 only 57% (of 166 death penalties) were pardoned this way. In 1946 and 1947 this percentage grew to 71% (of 399 death penalties), in 1948 to 90% (of 431 death penalties) and in 1949–50 finally to 94% (of 206 penalties).[43]

The main penal consequences (prison sentences) were mitigated and "corrected" between 1948–1950 by the combination of 1) pardons, 2) early and 3) conditional releases of condemned collaborators in Belgian prisons. This illustrated a

40 E. Witte, J. Craeybeckx and A. Meynen, *Political history of Belgium: from 1830 onwards*, Brussels, 2009, 221–248.
41 L. Huyse and S. Dhondt, *La répression*, 140–141, 144.
42 L. Huyse and S. Dhondt, *La répression*, 140–141, 170–172.
43 L. Huyse and S. Dhondt, *La répression*, 142–143.

fundamental shift in political strategy regarding the punishment and reintegration of collaborators. The key figure was the Catholic Minister of Justice Paul Struye, who in 1948 pleaded for the use of mass pardon measures, early releases and even restitution of rights.

This was a fundamental shift in political-judicial strategy in just a few years' time: from harsh punishment and banishment in 1945–46, to mass reintegration/resettlement.[44] Several reasons explain this shift. There were certain practical and financial considerations (the overpopulation in prisons for example), the realisation that a policy of re-education was nonexistent, but more importantly also political and strategic reasons (such as the recuperation of the former VNV electorate by the Flemish Catholic Party). In certain leading circles, there was a strong awareness that the creation of a large and permanent sub-group of ostracised (Flemish) former collaborators would continue to serve as a permanent source of disunity within the Belgian nation state. Indeed, this would prove to be the case.

The international context of the Cold War and anti-communism after 1949 obviously weakened the political influence of the communist network (including the former communist resistance) in Belgium, but this international context had no direct, fundamental influence on the development of transitional justice policy in Belgium. The only clear and direct influence of this international context was felt on the prosecution of German war criminals in Belgium. The law on war crimes was only voted into law in June 1947 and by the time the actual trials against Germans began, the international priorities had changed. The persecution of Nazi war criminals no longer was an absolute priority. On the contrary, the imprisonment and persecution of certain high ranking Germans put strain on international relationships. This was highly relevant for Belgium, because the country had been governed by a "moderate" military occupation regime, lead by several members of the traditional ('non-Nazi') establishment and noble elite. The clearest example was the trial of Alexander von Falkenhausen (the former *Militärbefehlshaber* in occupied Belgium). During his trial, public commotion arose in West Germany and international political pressure was put on the Belgian government. Belgian Prime Minister Van Zeeland actively tried to guide the military public prosecutor towards a release of Von Falkenhausen without condemnation. Van Zeeland used the arguments of the relationship with the Americans, as well as the reintegration of West Germany in Europe.[45] Von Falkenhausen was found guilty and condemned by the Belgian military court in March 1951, but he received an immediate early release.

---

44 L. Huyse and S. Dhondt, *La répression*, 150.

45 R. Van Doorslaer, E. Debruyne, F. Seberechts and N. Wouters, *La Belgique docile*, 956–957.

Generally speaking, this fundamental shift illustrates the lack of a coherent long-term vision on transitional justice in post-war Belgium, as well as the rapidly changing political contexts and priorities among successive governments.

Table 2.1. Pardon measures 1946–1954[46]

Year	Adjustment		Rejections		Internment		Total	
	Total number	Percentage	Total	Perc.	Total	Perc.	Total	Perc.
1946	919	13.53%	2,247	33.08%	3,626	53.39%	6,792	18.50%
1947	6,186	56.67%	3,795	34.77%	935	8.57%	10,916	29.73%
1948	6,394	64.34%	3,544	35.66%	–	–	9,938	27.07%
1949	3,163	66.86%	1,568	33.14%	–	–	4,731	12.89%
1950	1,727	88.02%	235	11.98%	–	–	1,962	5.34%
1951	1,199	93.97%	77	6.03%	–	–	1,276	3.48%
1952	556	98.76%	7	1.24%	–	–	563	1.53%
1953	308	88.76%	39	11.24%	–	–	347	0.95%
1954	181	97.31%	5	2.69%	–	–	186	0.51%
Total	20,633	56.20%	11,517	31.37%	4,561	12.42%	36,711	100.00%

The mitigation of non-penal measures proved more difficult. Several careful attempts were taken in an early stage. As far as article 123*ter* is concerned, from June 1948 on, the state no longer confiscated total revenue but only profits. The law of 14 June 1948 was the first fundamental revision of the law of 19 September 1945, changing the system of the loss of rights. For those sentenced to a penalty of less than five years, the judge could decide on the loss of rights: for those people, the loss of rights was no longer an automatic consequence of the conviction.[47] The conditions to appeal for a restitution of rights were also lowered. Again, this meant a fundamental change of policy in three years' time. These changes provided new arguments for mitigating the sanctions for collaborators on whom a sanction had been imposed according to the more severe pre-1948 legislation. Between 14 June 1948 and 31 December 1949 there were 20,937 requests for modification of the loss of rights before a civil court. This modification was granted in 87% of these cases (5,829 people received full restitution of rights, 12,448 received partial restitution).[48]

46 K. Aerts, *"Repressie zonder maat of einde?" De juridische reïntegratie van incivieken in de Belgische Staat na de Tweede Wereldoorlog'* ["Repression without measure or end?". The judicial reintegration of inciviques in the Belgian state after the Second World War], Unpublished Doctoral Thesis, Ghent University, Ghent, 2011, 149.

47 J. Gilissen, P. Cassiers, F. Debroux, *Crimes et délits*, 163, 273.

48 L. Huyse and S. Dhondt, *La répression*, 149.

Several new measures developed this general tendency further. The second correction law (29 February 1952) would further enlarge the possibility for restitution of rights (more than 10,000 "uncivic" persons would receive full or partial restitution based on this law).[49] The law of 19 May 1949 created the possibility of reappointing previously discharged civil servants (1082 reappointments were carried out in ministerial departments on 3144 discharges).[50] Additional laws (Royal decree of 5 March 1951, law of 23 December 1953) introduced further alterations.

The general problem, however, was that the different measures had created separate but interwoven consequences for those who received sanctions: with regard to (partial) loss of (certain) rights, with regard to pecuniary, financial consequences (fines and damages to be paid to the Belgian state, special taxes, forfeiture of goods, loss of full pension, loss of income), or with regard to the exclusion from certain services, opportunities or benefits provided by the government. The cumulative effect of these measures could become very wide and lead to escalation. To a large extent, the escalating consequences of these measures were also unforeseen by the Belgian legislator. These measures were often imbedded in technical-administrative contexts and fragmented over several ministries. This made a centrally coordinated, general policy of mitigation difficult or nearly impossible.

It proved especially difficult to implement centralised mitigation of the large and continuing impact of the pecuniary, financial disciplinary measures. As opposed to the system in place for internments and prison sentences, there were hardly any existing instruments to mitigate the consequences of these measures. Pardons, for instance, did *not* include financial compensation for damages perpetrators had had to pay to their victims or to the Belgian state. After 1948, the ministry of Finances had already tried to implement a moderate execution of the measures of forfeiture of goods but only the "normalisation law" of 14 July 1960 enabled the ministry of Finances to substantially reduce/annul punishment that ordered the full financial recompensation by convicted collaborators. However, the actual implementation of these financial measures seems to have ground to a halt after 1950, once the Catholic party gained control over the successive governments. The Belgian state therefore, in a form of silent or even hidden decision making, abstained [or refrained] from recuperating the sums which condemned collaborators were supposed to pay. In the end, of the total amount of ca. 20 billion Belgian francs (which was the total sum to be claimed for all pecuniary/financial sanctions/punishments), only approximately 4 billion Belgian francs would be effectively collected by the Belgian state.[51]

---

[49] L. Huyse and S. Dhondt, *La répression,* 167.

[50] K. Aerts, *Repressie zonder maat of einde,* 522–524.

[51] K. Aerts, *Repressie zonder maat of einde,* 608.

Unlike in the Netherlands and France, there never was a collective measure of "pardon" or "amnesty".[52] This was caused both by the extreme political division on the matter of the repression which made a general measure politically impossible, as well as the fragmented and ad hoc nature of many of the different disciplinary sanctions and measures.

The law of 30 June 1961 (the so-called "Vermeylen law", after the Socialist minister of Justice in office at that time) was a crucial milestone for the mitigation policy. There were political reasons for the "pause" between the mitigation measures between 1948 and 1953. The political consensus that had been established in 1948 regarding the mitigation and correction was replaced with a situation of renewed political polarisation after the "royal question" (the referendum regarding the restoration of King Leopold III) and the homogenous Catholic government.[53]

This law – approved under pressure of the European Commission – concerned the restitution of rights (described under 123sexties of the penal code). It combined several measures at once. The lifelong loss of rights was exclusively reserved for death penalties and life sentences (by that time only a marginal minority of cases); the restitution of rights was automatically implemented for the so-called lists of the military public prosecutor (loss of rights) and all of the lighter prison sentences (namely those of three years or less); possibilities for appeal were created for the heavier sentences; the description of the scope of the rights one could actually lose was reduced. In the immediate wake of this law, only about a third of the persons who suffered partial or full loss of rights in December 1946 would not receive full restitution of rights.[54]

To summarise, the most important laws that enabled ever more inclusive categories of former collaborators to appeal for restitution of rights were the laws of 14 June 1948, 29 February 1952 and especially 30 June 1961. Regarding the restitution of nationality, these were the subsequent laws of 1 June 1949, 30 December 1953, 27 June 1960 and 30 March 1962. The chronological periodisation is clear. After 1975, the mitigation grinds to a halt at ca. 5 or 10% of the group sanctioned. This is mostly due to the fact that these were the most radical cases: people still in prison, people who had adopted other nationalities and/or people who were still listed as fugitives.

The difficulty of a mitigation policy was even more glaring regarding the exclusion of state benefits, services or career opportunities for "uncivic" persons.

52 L. Huyse and S. Dhondt, *La répression*, 99.
53 L. Huyse and S. Dhondt, *La répression*, 171.
54 K. Aerts, *Repressie zonder maat of einde.*

These exclusions were often the result of conscious and strategic use of laws and regulations. Concrete examples are: welfare payments such as a disability allowance, financial support to pay for certain war damages, a military pension or other financial compensation of national recognition, certain permits etc. General measures to mitigate these highly different measures proved impossible and more importantly, an automatic mitigation of the concrete consequences of these exclusions did not occur when the initial measure which had caused the disciplinary measure in the first place was reduced or mitigated. Some of these exclusions also proved permanent because the opportunity to ask for mitigation occurred only once. Estimates of the number of people involved or the scope of the different consequences of these exclusive measures are not known.

To summarise: the transitional justice process in Belgium has been criticised on different grounds. On the basis of an analysis of the sentences handed out, Luc Huyse pointed out that punishment was unequal.[55] For those brought before the judge shortly after the liberation, punishment was more severe than for those who were judged later. There also was a geographical inequality: military tribunals in certain districts systematically punished the same offenses with higher sentences than military tribunals in other districts. Punishment of collaboration in Belgium was, according to the same author, politicised and became part of the right-left cleavage of Belgian politics in the second half of the 1940s.

Koen Aerts underscores this point of criticism in his recent doctoral research but gives more contextual factors that help explain these inequalities.[56] There was an overlap of different disciplinary measures that caused a multitude of (often non-judicial) consequences for certain people. The Belgian state lost track of the scope of all these measures and could not exercise central control when it felt mitigation was in order. From 1948 onwards, a policy of gradual mitigation of different types of disciplinary measures was undertaken. This was very manifest and quick for the release policy of condemned collaborators in prisons. The mitigation of certain financial consequences and of loss of rights took more time (one could say approximately 20 years) but a fundamental correction was certainly felt after 1961.

But the effects of certain measures proved impossible to reduce or mitigate. Aerts concludes that the Belgian state – mostly unwillingly and unexpectedly – created a durable administrative category of "uncivic" person. This category was not defined by law but its effects were very concrete for the people who remained excluded from certain state benefits, services and full career opportunities that

55 L. Huyse and S. Dhondt, *La répression*, 261–297.
56 K. Aerts, *Repressie zonder maat of einde*.

"normal" Belgian citizens had. Certain results of this seclusion of a certain group of "uncivic" persons proved to be permanent.

3. POLICY FOR VICTIMS

As was the case for the judicial prosecution of collaborators, the Belgian state could fall back on pre-existing legislation created after WWI, for the compensation and support for the victims of war and occupation. On 20 September 1944, the Belgian government made the legislation on the compensation of non-military victims of WWI applicable to the victims of 1940–1944.[57] The National Work for Veterans, Deportees and Political Prisoners was given the task to coordinate payment to families of people in captivity or who were deceased. Some provisional measures were also taken (the laws of 9 February 1945 and 26 August 1947 regarding compensating pensions and the law of 18 May 1945 regarding a repatriation payment). The system of financial compensation for victims or their families rested on two pillars: pensions and interests. Pensions were meant to compensate for physical damage and were calculated on the percentage of invalidity; interests were considered more as a form of national recognition for (financial) consequences certain patriotic activities had caused. This last aspect was tied to a whole new legislation regarding national recognition after WWII.

The Belgian state was quick to adopt a large amount of different official statutes of national recognition between 1945 and 1948. Some of the most important were: the armed resister (law of 19 September 1945; there were several specific officially recognised groups and organisations); civil resister and objector to forced labour (law of 24 December 1946); the deported forced labourers (law of 24 December 1946); the political prisoner (law of 26 February 1947); the resisters through clandestine press (law of 1 September 1948). This diverse and sophisticated framework of different official statutes concerning resisters would become one of the characteristics of the fragmentation of Belgian collective memory and remembrance (we will discuss this later).

Victims were people who had undergone grave maltreatments such as torture, or who were executed or imprisoned. Generally speaking, the term of 30 days or longer of imprisonment was used as a limit to determine whether someone could be legally considered a victim. The national, patriotic aspect of the persecution suffered and therefore the recognition was primordial. The most "exclusive", morally elevated category was that of the political prisoner. This also meant

---

57 C. Closa Montero, *Study on how the memory of crimes committed by totalitarian regimes in Europe is dealt with in the Member States*, Madrid, 2008, 95.

however, that Jews and Gypsies were excluded from any official category and were not recognised as victims. Compensation for Jewish victims deported from Belgium would only follow in a much later phase when the international balance of power changed overnight after 1989 and the global and European perspective of remembrance shifted. Initially, racial deportees were ignored and excluded from state reparatory measures. The first few years after the liberation, the most essential help to Jewish victims came from the NGO Help to Israelites Victimised by the War (*Aide aux Israélites Victimes de la Guerre*, AIVG). This organisation relied almost exclusively on financial support from the (foreign) Jewish community itself.[58] It played a crucial role in the reconstruction of Jewish life in Belgium after 1945.

Belgium also established an agreement with the Federal Republic of Germany, in the context of its compensation legislation (*Bundesentschädigungsgesetz*) of 1953. On 28 September 1960 Belgium concluded an agreement for 80 million German marks.[59] Belgium based the distribution of this money on the already existing categories (political prisoner etc.). This excluded all racial deportees.

In a later phase, new categories would be added, such as the statute on those forcibly enrolled in the German army (law of 21 November 1974); the fishermen in wartime (Belgian fishermen operating from British ports during the occupation-law of 8 February 1984); the people who had responded to the so-called Recruitment Centre for the Belgian Army (*Centre de recrutement de l'Armée Belge – Recruteringscentrum van het Belgisch Leger*, CRAB-RCBL, law of 12 April 1990); the statute of Jewish Children (law of 19 April 1999) and new measures for war victims (also regarding racial persecution, even for people who did not have Belgian nationality in May 1940, law of 11 April 2003).

The different national statutes were tied to a whole array of different forms and tools of financial compensation (pensions, interests, payments, certain financial advantages, etc.). Political prisoners, for instance, received: a one-time payment of 1,500 Belgian francs per month of imprisonment, an annual payment of 3,000 Belgian francs per six months of imprisonment for four years, an annuity or pension (in case of invalidity), priority treatment with the national society for inexpensive houses (ten years), social contributions were considered paid for the duration of the imprisonment and there were certain other advantages offered such as reduction of fees for public transport and free (higher) education.[60]

---

58 R. Van Doorslaer, E. Debruyne, F. Seberechts and N. Wouters, *La Belgique docile*.

59 C. Closa Montero, *Study on how the memory of crimes*, 125.

60 C. Closa Montero, *Study on how the memory of crimes*, 96.

4. LONG-TERM PROCESSES: ON THE EFFECTS OF TRANSITIONAL JUSTICE ON MEMORY DEVELOPMENT

Belgium is characterised by a strong fragmentation of collective memory regarding the Second World War. The Belgian state failed to impose one dominant unifying national narrative on the legacy of WWII after 1945. This is sometimes presented as some kind of Belgian *Sonderweg* in Europe with regard to the memory on WWII. It is even sometimes presented as one of the factors that would lead to the "failure" of Belgium as a nation state and the creation of a federalised country with autonomous regions (Flanders, Wallonia, and Brussels). The lack of unity in war memory is certainly a reality. We argue that the Belgian case was perhaps not as different from neighboring countries such as the Netherlands and France.[61] On the surface, those countries seemed to have been able to create a strong national consensus after 1945 on the legacy of WWII. However, Henry Rousso, in his seminal work *Le Syndrome de Vichy*, has argued that the national consensus in France after 1945 hid many contradictions and conflicts.[62] To a lesser extent perhaps, it has also become clear that the culture of remembrance in the Netherlands was also much more diverse than the strong national narrative would initially suggest. Recent debates in memory studies as well as European WWII commemoration policies clearly confirm this predominantly pluralistic nature of memory. In this regard, Belgium was not so much an exception rather than the most extreme example of a culture of collective remembrance in Europe that was highly diverse. As such, Belgium can serve as an exemplary case; to investigate, for example, why certain cultures of memory become dominant and others fail.

4.1. DIVIDED MEMORIES AND THE AMNESTY DEBATE

A first essential characteristic of the Belgian memorial regime was that the entire process of transitional justice in Belgium quickly became highly politicised. Initially, this followed the traditional political lines, mainly between the Catholic Party on the one hand and the other political parties (Liberal, Socialist and Communist) on the other, that is to say: between the left and the right. Several political, cultural and social fault lines within Belgian society were at work here. The so-called Royal Question (regarding the return of the contested Belgian King Leopold III to the throne) in 1950–51 would deepen the fault lines between left and right, different social classes, between Flanders and Wallonia, and

61 B. Benvindo and E. Peeters, *Les décombres de la guerre: Mémoires belges en conflit, 1945–2010*, Waterloo, 2012.

62 H. Rousso, *Le syndrome de Vichy, 1944–1987*, Paris, 1987.

between cities and countryside. After the national referendum on the re-installment of the King, these political-ideological differences regarding the legacy of WWII were structurally embedded in Belgian politics. As Conway argues, the *question royale* "(...) was not at heart a dispute about the war. It was a debate about the nature of Belgium itself".[63]

Transitional justice was only one of the many factors that caused the fragmentation and gradual disintegration of the Belgian nation-state. But it played an important part; perhaps less so in its direct influence on societal developments between 1945 and 1950 than in the way it would be mythologised and instrumentalised after 1950.

This is not to say that this direct impact was nonexistent. The renewed Catholic Party in 1945 wanted to capitalise on the electoral potential that the disappearance of the two most important collaborationist movements (Rex and especially the VNV) had caused. This way, Belgium was probably the only European country where the largest and most important national political party – or at least an important wing of this party – would gradually choose to identify itself with the legacy of the collaborationists and not with that of the resistance. The rapid revival of an organised Flemish movement was also an important factor in this regard.

As we made clear, this was the political context in which the legislation for compensation and prosecution was developed. Electoral and political considerations did influence purging legislation in an early stage. In fact, a more severe persecution of collaborators would potentially benefit the Socialist, Communist and Liberal parties. These considerations were in the background, influencing the discussion regarding the implementation and scope of the loss of political and civil rights. The lack of consistency in legislation regarding the prosecution and purges was partly caused by this political struggle as political majorities quickly changed and there was a large governmental instability between 1944 and 1948.

The political fragmentation quickly embedded itself in another, more antagonistic central Belgian cleavage: the Flemish-Walloon fault line. The social nature of collaboration during WWII itself had been different in Flanders than in Wallonia. In Flanders, collaboration was more politically motivated. The main collaborating party in Flanders, the VNV, had not been a marginal, isolated party during the 1930s but had been deeply rooted in the (Catholic) Flemish movement. In fact, with the last pre-war municipal elections the VNV had successfully established local majority coalitions with the Flemish wing of the Catholic Party in over 100 Flemish municipal governments. Contrary to

63 M. Conway, 'The end(s) of Memory. Memories of the Second World War in Belgium', *BTNG/RBHC*, (2012) 3–4, 170–188.

Rex, the main collaborationist party in the French-speaking community in Belgium, the VNV was founded on a structural cleavage within Belgian society (the position of the Flemish sub-nation within Belgium). This cleavage and the political manifestation thereof did not disappear after the liberation. The Flemish wing of the Catholic party was well aware of the danger that a new Flemish nationalist party could emerge and even thrive on the symbolic legacy of the "Belgian anti-Flemish repression" after WWII. As a matter of fact, the perceived lack of adequate response to the question of Flemish 'activism' (the "collaboration" of Flemish nationalists during the occupation of Belgium in WWI) after 1919 had stimulated the rise of Flemish nationalism as a political power in Belgium.

Collaboration in Francophone Belgium was perceived differently, partly because the social origins of collaboration and collaborators had been different. After the war, Catholic and conservative elites in Francophone Belgium wanted to distance themselves as much as possible from Rex, the main collaborationist party there.[64] The idea that the post-war trials were simply the first step to permanently ostracise Rexists and other Francophone collaborationists became firmly embedded in Walloon society. There was and is no societal support of any kind for something like "reconciliation" as we understand it today in the field of transitional justice. This way, Francophone Catholic elites would gradually find themselves in an opposite frame of reference than their Flemish counterparts.

The demand for amnesty did not came to the fore immediately. It arose in the context after 1951. Gradually, the call for general amnesty would become a factor of Flemish-Francophone division in Belgian politics for decades. Amnesty debates echoed the parallel debates after WWI regarding the convicted Flemish "activists". During the 1920s and 1930s, 'amnesty' already was a highly symbolic political issue between Flemish nationalists, Belgian patriots and Walloons. For the Flemish nationalist, amnesty quickly became a highly symbolic point of struggle. A general amnesty would imply that the Belgian state would admit to many of its past mistakes and wrongdoings towards the Flemish movement (and Flanders as a whole). As such, the demand for a general amnesty for convicted collaborators became one of the main mobilising themes for the Flemish movement from the 1950 to the 1980s, to gather political support and mass turnouts. Especially during the 1960s, the Flemish wing of the Catholic Party would gradually embed itself in this culture of remembrance. The main characteristics of this culture were a strong comprehensive attitude and even defensive argumentation with regard to the collaboration in Flanders. Collaboration of the Flemish nationalists during WWII was seen as a wrong yet

64 F. Balace, 'Collaboratie en repressie in Wallonië: anders bekeken?' in J. Gotovitch and Ch. Kesteloot (eds.), *Het gewicht van het oorlogsverleden*, Ghent, 2002, 53–74.

comprehensible choice of Flemish idealists who had to act against a (Belgian) state who had never recognised Flemish rights.

The ideological, national socialist aspects of the Flemish nationalist collaboration were swept under the rug. A remarkably strong culture of remembrance cultivated and supported this image, with pseudo-scholarly books, biographical publications, popular imagery and remembrance through the media, symbolic imagery, the creation of martyrs and the cultivation of victimhood, active organisations of former collaborators and remembrance activities. An entire Flemish elite was raised with the dominating narrative that the collaboration had been a legitimate choice, while the post-war persecution of collaborators had been an excessive repression by the Belgian state with the implicit intent to permanently destroy Flemish nationalism as a political force. Flanders and Wallonia developed radically opposed narratives. To speak in general terms: whereas the French-speaking community identified more with the legacy of the resistance and its myth as keeper of democratic values in Belgium, a significant part of the Flemish (Catholic) elite and public opinion identified with the legacy of collaboration and the myth of the "anti-Flemish repression" after WWII.

In this specific political context, amnesty for convicted collaborators as a measure became a highly symbolic issue that was simply impossible to resolve through a political consensus in Belgium. In the French-speaking community and Wallonia, the political elites and the general populace could not consider amnesty as anything else than negating and washing away the crimes of criminal collaborators and the Nazis. In Flanders however, it was associated with repairing the injustices the Belgian "anti-Flemish repression" had wrought on Flanders. Between 1966 and 1975, 31 propositions were introduced for general amnesty in the Belgian parliament; 24 from the Flemish nationalist party People's Union (*Volksunie*) and 7 from the Catholic party.

Gradually, amnesty lost much of its practical relevance during the 1990s. Most convicted collaborators involved were no longer alive after 1995. The last political attempt at an amnesty measure was the proposal of law by the Belgian Catholic Senator Herman Suykerbuyk in 1996. The proposal wanted to give financial compensation to "victims of the repression" (that is, the prosecution of collaboration after WWII). The proposal also mentioned other categories of "victims of war", but in doing so placed convicted collaborators on the same level as victims of Nazi persecution. The proposal was approved in the Flemish parliament but afterwards annulled by the Belgian Constitutional Court (*Arbitragehof/Cour d'Arbitration*) on technical grounds.

Amnesty would never be implemented as such, although many of the effects (certainly on a penal, criminal level) for the majority of convicted collaborators were quickly corrected or mitigated.

4.2. PATRIOTIC MEMORY COMMUNITIES AND THE BELGIAN STATE

Obviously, Belgium patriotism did exist after the liberation, both as the expression of popular sentiments as well as the conscious politics of certain (political and economic) elites.[65] But the successive Belgian governments between 1944 and 1950 somehow failed to use any existing momentum to create one dominant narrative and to impose this onto a nation. What exactly happened with the patriotic discourse in Belgium after 1945?

Belgium already had strong patterns and paradigms of remembrance created after WWI. Not surprisingly, these patriotic paradigms would strongly determine the lines along which the legacy of WWII would be constructed.

There were some governmental attempts after 1945 to use resistance movements to repair the damaged national consciousness and to strengthen national identity. For their part, the (often sociologically and ideologically very different) resistance movements themselves lobbied for national recognition and financial compensation from the state.[66] This dynamic created the many different official categories of recognition (the most important of which were the armed resister and the political prisoner) during the first post-war years. Through the creation of these different official national categories the (individual) suffering of different memory communities (political prisoners, forced labourers etc.) was institutionalised and "nationalised". This process of patriotic competition and political lobbying further stimulated the political fragmentation with regard to the legacy of WWII in Belgium.

Essentially, many of these groups – both patriotic groups as well as groups of former collaborators in Flanders – fell back on older frameworks that were created after WWI. This was clear for instance in the dichotomy between the patriotic war monuments that were created after WWI. Several patriotic war monuments were integrated in the remembrance of most new post-1945 groups. Local WWI monuments were adapted to the post 1945 situation, which meant that names of fallen resisters were added and placed next to the victims of WWI. The most important patriotic war monuments was the fortress of Breendonk (*SS-Auffanglager* during the war), which was granted the status of "national war monument" by parliamentary decision (1947).

The National Rifle Range *(Tir National / Nationale Schietbaan)* and the Congressional Column *(Colonne du Congrès / Kongreskolom*) were good examples of WWI monuments that became "overwritten" after 1945 with WWII

65 M. Conway, *The Sorrows of Belgium*.
66 P. Lagrou, *The Legacy*.

remembrance. The fortress of Huy and the Memorial of Bastogne also became important WWII monuments. The latter was primarily an American monument in memory of American soldiers who died during the Battle of the Ardennes. Belgium kept 11 November as "liberation day", which means that unlike most other European countries the "liberation" is not celebrated and commemorated on 4 May. The "official" remembrance of WWII by the Belgian state was integrated in the already existing (patriotic) WWI remembrance.

These different post-1945 memory communities and interest groups embedded their remembrance activities in an older symbolic framework and physical landscape. This landscape and symbolism existed already in Belgium and had been founded on the legacy of WWI. As Benvindo and Peeters argue, this was one of the main causes for the fact the fragmentation between different separate memory groups in Belgium happened so quickly after 1945 and remained so strong for many decades.[67] Essentially, collective memory and remembrance would after 1950 become the prerogative of specific well-organised (and often "officialised") groups (political prisoners, deportees, former collaborators, etc.). These different organised memory communities created and maintained the dominant narrative and (social) framework, into which individual memories of the members were forced. The social composition of these different groups was fairly homogeneous and there was hardly any room for internal divergences or discussions.[68] These groups adopted a very competitive attitude against each other, even within the same patriotic field. In part because of their competitive nature, these memory communities were the real driving force of the dynamics of collective memory in Belgium for many decades. This did not bring much success for the patriotic organisations, however. Although several of the dominant patriotic organisations remained highly organised and active, they quickly lost real societal or political influence. To a large extent they (and their narratives) became invisible.

In this regard, it is interesting to analyse how the former resistance lost the battle for memory in Flanders. The former resistance quickly disappeared into the background and failed to enact any significant influence on political or public debate. To explain how this occurred, Aerts and De Wever look at several key factors: 1° the agents (the profile and actions of the resistance fighters themselves), 2° their capacity to produce representative actions in public space, and 3° the role of the government or the authorities.[69] The internal division within the larger group of former resistors clearly was one problem. Resistance

---

67 B. Benvindo and E. Peeters, *Les décombres de la guerre.*

68 B. Benvindo and E. Peeters, *Les décombres de la guerre.*

69 K. Aerts and B. De Wever, 'Het verzet in de publieke herinnering in Vlaanderen', (2012) 2/3 *Belgisch Tijdschrift voor Nieuwste Geschiedenis (BTNG)*, 78–108.

fighters and political prisoners failed to organise a strong, unified "community of memory". This then was detrimental to their ability to create an efficient memory production; symbols, activities, etc. In the 1970s and 1980s they also proved unable to connect their traditional Belgian patriotism with newer societal movements (student movements, movements for homosexual rights, etc.) and therefore to somehow modernise their legacy. This caused a continuous (relative) absence on cultural platforms, such as literature, film and television. The Belgian state, for its part, never took strong measures to institutionalise the resistance memory. Aerts and De Wever even detect a political pattern at key moments, when the Belgian government promised former resistance groups to strategically "sell" a mitigating policy towards condemned collaborators. When the important mitigating law of 1961 (above) was voted, for example, the socialist minister of Justice could pacify patriotic groups by promising several future initiatives and stating that this law came at "(...) a moment where we have to put closure to a certain period in our past [...] paying homage [...] to the resistance".[70] The mitigating law for collaborators was voted, but the promises for the patriotic memory community never became reality.

The Flemish memorial landscape on the other hand went also partly back to WWI. This was most notable in the most important Flemish nationalist monument, the Tower of the IJser *(IJzertoren)* in Diksmuide (West Flanders). This monument commemorated not "Belgian" but "Flemish" soldiers who had fallen during WWI. It had already become a focal point of Flemish nationalism during the 1930s. During WWII, it became a symbolic rallying point for the more radical collaborationist factions. In 1945 and 1946, the tower was destroyed with dynamite, supposedly placed by members from former resistance circles. The tower was rebuilt with funding from Flemish nationalist and Catholic circles. With this legacy after 1945, the tower's function as focal point for radical anti-Belgian Flemish nationalism would grow and strengthen considerably. The annual commemoration ceremony ("pilgrimage") at the tower became the high mass of Flemish nationalism. At these highly politicised annual ceremonies during the 1950s through the 1980s, the demand for general amnesty for convicted collaborators ("victims of the repression") would become the one returning point during the speeches; a tradition in itself. During the 1970s and 1980s, the impact of these annual commemorations should not be underestimated. Important national Flemish Catholic Party leaders were often present at these ceremonies and its political messages resounded on a national level.

Benvindo and Peeters hypothesise that what happened after 1944–45 typifies a Belgian pacification model.[71] The Belgian state seemed to follow the same

---

70 K. Aerts and B. De Wever, *Het verzet.*

71 B. Benvindo and E. Peeters, *Les décombres de la guerre.*

strategy in its politics of memory as it did in its neo-corporatist approach for socio-economic matters; delegating large autonomy and powers to certain intermediary players and groups.

4.3. THE MEMORIES OF WAR ENTER A PERIOD OF TRANSITION (1971–1994)

In other western European countries (such as the Netherlands), the eruption of societal changes during the 1960s and 1970s formed the background of a gradual shift in collective remembrance regarding WWII and transitional justice after 1945. This was also caused by a generational change. In Belgium, the impact of this societal transformation on war memory was not as important, because of the growing impact of the politicised context and the Walloon-Flemish divide. The Flemish nationalist party VU gained moderate electoral successes during the 1960s, at the expense of the Catholic party who came under pressure to strengthen its Flemish profile. The fragmentation in war memory was strengthened during the 1960–1970s.

Another important factor was that there was no scholarly historical research in Belgium that could serve as a foundation for a more historical, critical reading of the legacy of the Second World. In Belgium, scholarly historiography started and developed rather late, after the end of the 1970s. Early governmental attempts to set up some kind of national Belgian war museum or centre after the occupation never succeeded. In December 1967 a Study Centre for the history of WWII was created, but it would take several years for this centre to achieve status and influence.

The dominant tendency during the 1960s and 70s continued to be that different memory communities produced their own self-confirming memory products (publications, narratives, imagery and symbols, monuments, commemorative activities, etc.). These were all self-confirming narratives aimed at maintaining one's own group cohesion and consensus. This was very evident in the networks of former Flemish collaborators, who produced a wide array of apologetic and pseudo-scholarly historiography regarding the collaboration of the Flemish National Union during WWII.

However, academic historiography of the occupation in Belgium gradually began to emerge. We might distinguish a certain key era of essential, innovative scholarly research on the Belgian occupation between 1971 and 1994. The starting point clearly was *l'An 40* by Gérard-Libois and Gotovitch, a watershed work published in 1971 that for the first time instigated public debate in

Belgium based on scholarly research on the occupation.[72] Over the course of slightly more than 20 years, several essential key works were published. The end of this key period could be marked by three books: *Onverwerkt Verleden* by Huyse and Dhondt on the post-war trials in 1991, *Collaboration in Belgium* by Martin Conway from 1993 and *Greep naar de Macht* by Bruno De Wever from 1994 (the last two tackled collaboration in Flanders and Francophone Belgium respectively).[73] Huyse and Dhondt could for the first time offer scientific arguments to counteract the myth of the anti-Flemish repression. While clearly demonstrating some errors in the practical implementation and the policy development regarding the prosecution of collaboration, both authors showed that there was no conscious policy of politically motivated imbalances between the convictions of Flemish and French-speaking collaborators. These last three works coincided and partly stimulated important televised series in Flanders as well as in Francophone Belgium on the occupation during WWII. Certainly in Flanders, the enormous impact of the series of televised documentaries presented by the leftist Flemish journalist Maurice De Wilde during the 1980s and 1990s can hardly be overestimated. It had an enormous impact with the larger public and the political world in Flanders. This TV (and book) series broke the taboo in Flanders with regard to these subjects.

Parallel to this was the rise of scholarly as well as public attention to the Holocaust in Belgium – or, rather, in Francophone Belgium. On a scholarly level, historian Maxime Steinberg played a pioneering role. In 1981, he acted as historical expert during the trial (in Kiel, Germany) of Kurt Asche, one of the main German perpetrators of Jewish deportations from Belgium. The Asche trial did – perhaps for the first time after 1944 – focus broad public attention on the topic of the Jewish persecution.[74] Shortly afterwards, Steinberg would publish several essential scholarly works. His three-volume *l'Étoile et le fusil* (1983–87) was the first comprehensive and critical study on the persecution of Jews in Belgium.[75] It is revealing for the context at that time that his (French) work had a large impact in Francophone Belgium and caused broad public debate, while it was ignored in Flanders. It would take another decade for the persecution of the Jews to gradually become a more important, influential topic in Flanders.

The Auschwitz Foundation (*Auschwitz Stichting/Fondation Auschwitz*) has to be mentioned in this regard. It was founded in 1980 by the Belgian Association of

72 J. Gérard-Libois and J. Gotovitch, *L'An 40: la Belgique occupée*, Brussels, 1971.
73 L. Huyse and S. Dhondt, *La répression*; M. Conway, *Collaboration in Belgium*; B. De Wever, *Greep naar de macht*.
74 L. Saerens, 'Van vergeten naar gegeerd. Dossin en de Joodse herinnering', (2012, 2/3) *Belgisch Tijdschrift voor Nieuwste Geschiedenis (BTNG)*, 10–20.
75 M. Steinberg, *l'Étoile et le fusil*, 3 vol., Brussels, 1983–1986.

Former Political Prisoners from Auschwitz-Birkenau and the Camps and Prisons of Silesia (l'*Amicale Belge des Ex-Prisonniers Politiques d'Auschwitz-Birkenau, Camps et Prisons de Silésie)* as an independent but government-sponsored institution. Before 1980, this particular organisation was rather strict in its exclusion of non-political prisoners. By its transfer of archives and operations to the Auschwitz Foundation in 1980, it shifted its primary focal point to education and increasingly also toward(s) the victims of racial persecution. It was a bi-lingual organisation, but the Francophone influence was clearly strongest. It is important because this Foundation was an early indication of the shift from a patriotic paradigm to a more 'democratic' paradigm (with strong focus on human rights).

The scholarly works mentioned above, as well as their popular translation to wider audiences through television, for example, did not change public perceptions, policies of remembrance or social memory communities overnight. However, they had a sustaining influence. They would gradually become harder to ignore and would inspire new, more critical historical research.

We want to present the period between 1971 and 1994 as a period of transition for Belgian war memory. During this period, we can already see several building blocks of the post 2000 memory regime emerge.

One of these building blocks certainly was a stronger moralised and political use of the legacy of WWII. In a 1996 book analysing the 1995 commemoration programme, historian Alain Colignon was one of the first to recognise this change when he notes a "(…) a memorial rupture" (*une fissure mémorielle)* which had become manifest in the Francophone commemorations.[76] Another building block was the emergence of new critical scholarly research. The deconstructive impact of this historical research would take several decades to become generally accepted. This could happen only at the beginning of the 21st century, when changing national and international contexts created the right synergy.

As a last remark, we hypothesise that Francophone Belgium seemed to follow these developments somewhat earlier than Flanders. Admittedly, there remain large gaps in our knowledge on how new critical insights were transferred to a wider public (for example, with regard to the role of the different educational systems). Nevertheless, traces of what would later become the essential characteristics of the memory regime after 2000 – the sensibility towards the human rights discourse most notably – were visible earlier in Francophone Belgium than in Flanders. It is difficult to pinpoint the exact causes for this.

76 A. Colignon, Ch. Kesteloot and D. Martin (eds.), *Commémoration. Enjeux et débats*, Brussels, 1996, at 64.

Clearly, political as well as deeper societal contexts in Francophone Belgium were more open towards this democratic memorial paradigm – and the interpretation of the entire period through a general human rights discourse – than was the case in Flanders.

4.4. THE GLOBAL HUMAN RIGHTS CULTURE: AN END TO BELGIUM'S DIVIDED MEMORIES?

During the 1990s, a fundamental shift in historical consciousness and collective remembrance regarding the legacy of WWII and collaboration and transitional justice would occur. This was caused by a very effective interaction between several, parallel national and international developments.

On a national level, by 1993 the process of state reform had created both a Flemish and a Walloon sub-region with large autonomy. Both new sub-regions would develop a much stronger central grasp on memory politics than the Belgian nation-state had ever had. This was particularly the case in Flanders. The new Flemish nation, with its own parliament, government, institutions and symbols was no longer the weak and "backwards" region in Belgium. On the contrary, the roles were now reversed. As Wallonia faced structural economic crisis and a decline of political influence within Belgium, Flanders during the 1990s shined with self-confidence and self-consciousness, and one could even argue, with arrogance. The new Flemish political elite had no use for the legacy of collaborationists and their old rhetoric of perpetual victimhood to construct its national identity and legitimation. More importantly, the emergence of the extreme right as a political factor dominated politics during the 1990s in Flanders (and Belgium). The Flemish Bloc (*Vlaams Blok*, later: Flemish Interest or *Vlaams Belang*), a Flemish nationalist party with a strong anti-immigrant program and xenophobe rhetoric, would secure 24% of the Flemish electorate during the (Flemish) parliamentary elections of 2004. Many Flemish politicians, now also within the Flemish movement itself, saw the xenophobic Flemish Bloc as the direct heir of the collaborationist VNV during WWII. In this political climate, the supportive and comprehensive attitude towards former collaborators seemed to evaporate quickly.

This internal Belgian development however, went hand-in-hand with complementary international developments that further stimulated a general shift. On a global and European level, there was the emergence of a dominating framework and narrative of human rights after the 1970s, often tied to the rhetoric and imagery of collective European identity, active citizenship and democracy. The most striking aspect of this development was the emergence of the Holocaust as the dominant subject of global collective memory regarding

WWII. This international context had a somewhat belated influence in Belgium, or rather the Flemish and Francophone sub-regions, after 1993.

The Holocaust gradually gained importance as a central topic in collective remembrance in Belgium. This happened first in Wallonia, through educational schemes and policies. Flanders followed later. Several specific institutions were founded to stimulate Holocaust and/or peace education and remembrance, and Democracy or Barbarism (*Democratie ou Barbarie*, an institution and network for French-speaking teachers regarding lessons in citizenship) in 1995. In 1997, the city of Antwerp erected a monument to the memory of the Jews deported from the city. The broader political backdrop was the so-called "purple" governments, where the Belgian social-democratic and liberal parties could form majority coalitions and rupture the decade-old dominance of the Catholic party. The liberal party led the Federal government (the Verhofstadt I and II governments between 1999 and 2007) and the Flemish government. For several years, a highly confident liberal party – specifically the Flemish liberal party – dominated discourse. Several of the liberal party's leading figures in Flanders displayed a peculiar sensibility to the legacy of WWII, tied to present-day issues such as racism and xenophobia. This was especially relevant for Flanders, where the 'democratic memorial paradigm' with regard to WWII had not been dominant until then. Perhaps the most striking initiative the Flemish government took was the creation of *Kazerne Dossin* (Dossin Barracks) Memorial, Museum and Documentation Centre on Holocaust and Human Rights. This institution, on the site of the central *Sammellager* for arrested Jews in Belgium, was created in 2005 and succeeded the old Jewish Museum for Deportation and Resistance. The Flemish government gave this new institution – which has opened its doors in 2012 – a clear assignment, in which the focus would have to be on 'human rights' (which *Kazerne Dossin* interpreted as the "non-discrimination principle") and on peace education (*Kazerne Dossin* has a coordinating role in the Belgian Forum for Peace Education). The Belgian government decided in December 2004 to declare 27 January (the anniversary of the liberation of Auschwitz) the official Holocaust Remembrance Day.

Things had rapidly changed in Flanders, as the Flemish nationalist politician Johan Sauwens found out to his own dismay. As a minister in the Flemish government, he was forced to resign in May 2001 after he had been present at a meeting of the *St. Maartensfonds*, a group of former members of the *Waffen-SS* and Flemish Legion during WWII. Sauwens seemed genuinely surprised by the outrage of the press and public when this became public. His surprise and lack of political insight was essentially based on the fact that for decades, it had been normal for Flemish nationalist politicians to be present in former collaborationist circles and networks. What Sauwens had failed to recognise was that by 2001 something had changed in Flanders with regard to the public attitude towards the legacy of war and collaboration. It was during the Sauwens incident that the Flemish Minister-President Patrick Dewael (a liberal politician and the grandchild of a Liberal minister who died in 1945 in Bergen-Belsen) openly called Flemish Bloc frontman Filip De Winter and his party "fascist" during the heated debates in the Flemish parliament.

The shift during the 1990s essentially meant that the classic (and post-WWI) patriotic paradigm was replaced with a completely different ideological paradigm. Belgium and Flanders adapted to the European and global paradigm. And in this way, the Walloon and the Flemish memories of the war moved closer together. In this context, there was also a significant rise in critical scholarly historiography. This way, Belgium could make up for the delay of the period between the 1950s to the 1990s. On both sides of the language border, scholarly works that took a critical look at all aspects of the German occupation of Belgium during WWII were produced (although not always read, certainly not on the respective other sides of the language border).

Perhaps the one Belgian politician embodying this new ideological paradigm was the liberal Guy Verhofstadt, Belgian Prime Minister between 1999 and 2008. As prime minister, he publicly apologised for the Belgian responsibility in the Rwandan Genocide (Kigali, 2000), he publicly recognised the Belgian cooperation in the persecution of the Jews in Belgium during WWII (Mechelen, 2002) and again apologised for this same fact in name of the Belgian state in 2005 at Yad Vashem. He did this again in 2007 in Brussels, at the same time the Centre for Study and Documentation on War and Contemporary Society was conducting a scholarly study on the responsibility of Belgian authorities in the persecution of the Jewish people in Belgium (ordered by the Belgian Senate with a resolution of February 2003). The Socialist mayor of Antwerp, Patrick Janssens, apologised in October 2007 for the role played by the Antwerp city police in the roundups of the Jews in the summer of 1942.

This political context and regained political willpower of Belgium also lead to new legislation, sometimes with far reaching consequences. Belgium had signed the Geneva Conventions (the four Geneva Conventions concerning the laws of war and the protection of civilians on 8 December 1949 and on the Prevention and Punishment of the Crime of Genocide on 12 December 1949) and had ratified the Conventions in 1951 and 1952. However, it would take several decades before Belgium would actually explicitly integrate this in national legislation (1993). When this new legislation was finally approved in 1999, this meant a serious enlargement of the existing law on the punishment of war crimes, genocide and crimes against humanity (commonly called the "genocide law" in Belgium). One of the changes implemented by this law was the universal jurisdiction of Belgian courts and the non-recognition of legal immunity. The result was to be expected:

a flood of civil action complaints against foreign heads of state and military/political leaders. This maverick approach caused considerable damage to the international political and diplomatic position of Belgium, to the extent that Belgium was forced to amend the law under enormous international political and judicial pressure. In the end, the law was declared null and void (5 August 2003). Some elements of the law which Belgium wished to see preserved were integrated (in a strongly watered-down form) into Belgian criminal laws. The Belgian approval of the International Court of Justice (28 June 2000) was clearly a better approach. Another law still in existence is the law against Holocaust denial (23 March 1995), largely based on the French law of 13 July 1990.

4.5. ON MEMORY CONSENSUS

What Martin Conway calls "the end of memory" for Belgian war memories is, in large measure, simply a generational shift: the end of an era in which the legacy of war has a direct disruptive influence on Belgian politics.[77]

The issue of amnesty offers the best example. Because the call for amnesty for convicted collaborators after WWII was so deeply rooted in central cleavages in Belgian politics, amnesty automatically implied a debate on "national reconciliation" of some kind. Some early attempts at reconciliation were made during the first decade after the liberation, for instance by the Committee for Action and Vigilance (*Comité voor Actie en Waakzaamheid / Le Comité d'Action et de Vigilance)*, an umbrella organisation of resistance organisations meant to bridge the political gaps (especially between the communists and others). This committee would develop several initiatives to reconcile Flanders and Wallonia between 1947 and 1958. Their attempts ultimately crashed on political realities.

The term "national reconciliation" returned several decades later and was sometimes loosely used during from the 1970s to the 1990s. However, real "truth-seeking" mechanisms were never implemented in Belgium. It was clear that national reconciliation was next to impossible in the polarised Belgian context with fragmentation of different and opposing memory communities, and in fact would be a threat to these strongly organised memory communities themselves.

However, between 1999 and 2002, reconciliation seemed to come back with a vengeance. After the commotion around the Suykerbuyk bill (1998) regarding the "victims of the repression", a group of Flemish intellectuals launched a call for national reconciliation in 1999 under the title "Forward without forgetting; a call for an honest and fair judgment about collaboration and repression in Flanders" (*Voorwaarts maar niet vergeten; oproep voor een eerlijk en rechtvaardig*

77 M. Conway, *The end(s) of Memory.*

oordeel over collaboratie en repressie in Vlaanderen). One of the members of this so-called "Forwards Group", historian Frans-Jos Verdoodt, was also affiliated with the committee of the annual pilgrimage of the IJser Tower Monument. During his speech at the annual Tower "pilgrimage" in August 2000, Verdoodt publicly expressed a "historical excuse" (*historisch pardon*) for the mistakes of the collaboration, a symbolic gesture of a very high importance. The Voorwaarts-group was one of the few (and last) examples of an organised attempt at reconciliation. The Flemish government was quick to act upon this private initiative of the Forwards Group. The Flemish government rewarded the initiative with an official government prize in 2001 and on 9 June 2001, organised a conference in the Flemish parliament that received broad media attention. In 2002, a majority in the Flemish parliament adopted the resolution in which collaboration with the German occupier was clearly condemned. Also, a general amnesty was rejected on principle because it would mean "wiping out the past as if it had never taken place". Certain "excesses" of the punishment of collaborators were recognised but these were explicitly placed on another level than the excesses of collaboration with the Nazi occupier itself. This was an important resolution, because it showed the political acceptance of the mistakes of the collaboration and also the impossibility of a general amnesty in Flanders.

The *Voorwaarts*-initiative lead to an academic book (published in French and Dutch), which gave a well-balanced overview of scholarly consensus on WWII in Belgium.[78] Indeed, scholarly consensus was the guiding principle of this book. Its main message was that Belgian historians, Francophone and Flemish, could reach perfect scholarly consensus based on recent analysis. At the same time, Charta 91 (a civil society organisation founded as a reaction to the landslide electoral victory of the extreme right-wing *Vlaams Blok* in Antwerp in 1991) took a parallel initiative that might be considered a reaction to the *Voorwaarts* group's call for reconciliation. Charta 91 feared that reconciliation might also entail forgetting. They organised a conference (24 November 2001) and published a scholarly book in 2002 in which leading historians published chapters on the legacy of collaboration in Flanders.[79] As a whole, the book was an explicit attempt to use history and historiography to battle the *Vlaams Blok* by making the connection between current anti-democratic ideas and Flemish nationalist collaboration during WWII. The book had strong pedagogic undercurrents. Its basic philosophy was that by informing the general public of recent scholarly insights, one could deconstruct durable myths and "democratise" public debate. Both books, although very different, were strongly indicative of a certain context of 2001–2002, where terms such as "reconciliation" connected to the idea of "closure" were dominant throughout political, scholarly and media discourse. It

---

78 J. Gotovitch and Ch. Kesteloot (eds.), *Het gewicht van het oorlogsverleden.*

79 E. Corijn (ed.), *Collaboratie in Vlaanderen. Vergeven en vergeten?*, Antwerp, 2002.

is relevant to note that especially within the Charta 91 book, the notion of "closure" had different meanings throughout several of the contributions. There was little reflection on the notion of closure or on the alleged role of historians in this process.

A few years after the movement of "historical closure", some leading Flemish historians would clash with the Flemish government over the new Flemish Holocaust Museum and Centre (*Kazerne Dossin*) in Mechelen. The scientific work for the Holocaust museum was rejected by the Flemish government, and all the leading historians involved were banned from the project. At its core, the reason for this incident between politics and the academic world was a fundamental difference in visions on the way in which the Holocaust (and the legacy of war, national socialism and occupation in general) should be treated in a "national museum" with an important pedagogic mission.

There is therefore a certain contradiction between the notion of "general consensus and final closure" of war memory that seemed to prevail in 2001–2002 and the incident over *Kazerne Dossin* several years later. Even with an indisputable human rights paradigm, the notion of "consensus on the past" is an arbitrary construct that can quickly break down on a local, more concrete level.

SELECTIVE FURTHER READING

'Arrêté-loi sur la déchéance de nationalité, la privation et la suspension de certains droits pour infraction commise en temps de guerre contre la sûreté extérieure de l'Etat 6 mai 1944', *Moniteur belge*, 2 September 1944, 410–414.

'Arrêté-loi relatif à l'épuration civique', *Moniteur belge*, 1–2 Octobre 1945, 6333–6341.

Aerts, Koen, '"Repressie zonder maat of einde?" De juridische reïntegratie van incivieken in de Belgische Staat na de Tweede Wereldoorlog', Unpublished Doctoral Thesis, Ghent University, Ghent, 2011.

Aerts, Koen and De Wever, Bruno, 'Het verzet in de publieke herinnering in Vlaanderen', *Belgisch Tijdschrift voor Nieuwste Geschiedenis (BTNG)*, (2012, 2/3), 78–108.

Balace, Francis, 'Collaboratie en repressie in Wallonië: anders bekeken?' in Gotovitch, José and Kesteloot, Chantal (eds.), *Het gewicht van het oorlogsverleden* (Ghent: Academia Press 2002), 53–74.

Benvindo, Bruno and Peeters, Evert, *Scherven van de oorlog. De strijd om de herinnering aan de Tweede Wereldoorlog, 1945–2010*, Antwerp/Brussels, 2011.

Benvindo, Bruno and Peeters, Evert, 'La mémoire de la Seconde Guerre Mondiale comme régulation sociale: une perspective belge', *Belgisch Tijdschrift voor Nieuwste Geschiedenis (BTNG)*, (2012, 2/3), 10–20.

Bourgeois, André and Temmerman, Gilbert, Verslag namens de werkgroep belast met het opmaken van de inventaris van de sociale en menselijke gevolgen voor de slachtoffers van de oorlog, met name ook van de Spaanse burgeroorlog en voor de getroffenen van de repressie- en epuratiewetgeving, 91, *Parl.St.* Vlaamse Raad 1984–1985, stuk 290.

CASSART, Georges, *L'internement des suspects et des étrangers: arrêté-loi du 12 octobre 1918 et son application en 1944* (Brussels: Larcier, 1944).

CLOSA MONTERO, Carlos, *Study on how the memory of crimes committed by totalitarian regimes in Europe is dealt with in the Member States* (Madrid: Institute for Public Goods and Policy Centre of Human and Social Sciences, 2008).

COLIGNON, Alain, KESTELOOT, Chantal and MARTIN, Dirk (eds.), *Commémoration. Enjeux et débats* (Brussels, 1996).

CONWAY, Martin, *Collaboration in Belgium: Léon Degrelle and the Rexist Movement 1940–1944* (New Haven (CT) and London: Yale University Press, 1993).

CONWAY, Martin, 'The end(s) of Memory. Memories of the Second World War in Belgium, *Belgisch Tijdschrift voor Nieuwste Geschiedenis (BTNG)*, (2012, 2/3), 170–188.

CORIJN, Eric (ed.), *Collaboratie in Vlaanderen. Vergeven en vergeten?* (Antwerp: Manteau, 2002).

DAUTRICOURT, Joseph, *La trahison par collaboration avec l'ennemi occupant le territoire national: étude préparatoire et pratique de la répression, dans le cadre des lois pénales belges, complétées par les arrêtés-lois des 17.12.1942 et 6.5.1944* (Brussels: Larcier, 1945).

DEBRUYNE, Emmanuel, SEBERECHTS, Frank, VAN DOORSLAER, Rudi and WOUTERS, Nico, *La Belgique docile: les autorités belges et la persécution des Juifs en Belgique durant la Seconde Guerre mondiale* (Brussels: SOMA-CEGES / Luc Pire 2007, 2 vol.).

DECKERS, Michel, 'De strafrechtelijke vervolging van het activisme. Deel 1: het wettelijk kader', *Wetenschappelijke Tijdingen*, 2002, 61, 156–178.

DE WEVER, Bruno, *Greep naar de macht: Vlaams-nationalisme en Nieuwe Orde, het VNV 1933–1945* (Tielt/Antwerp/Ghent: Lannoo, 1994).

GILISSEN, John, 'Etude statistique de la répression de l'incivisme', *Revue de Droit Pénal et de Criminologie*, 1951.

GILISSEN, John, CASSIERS, Paul and DEBROUX, François, 'Crimes et délits contre la sûreté de l'Etat' in *Novelles. Droit Pénal, Tome II* (Brussels: Larcier, 1967), 113–319.

GOTOVITCH, José and KESTELOOT, Chantal, *Het gewicht van het oorlogsverleden* (Ghent: Academia Press, 2002).

HUYSE, Luc, 'Cijfers en feiten over de na-oorlogse interneringscentra' in BALLINCKX, Jef and VAN DEUREN, Karel (eds.), *P. Longinus De Munter, O.F.M. Franciscaan en fotograaf*, Bruges, 1992, 135–139.

HUYSE, Luc and DHONDT, Steven, *La répression des collaborations 1942–1952: un passé toujours présent* (Brussels: CRISP, 1993).

HUYSE, Luc, 'Transitional justice in Belgium, France, and the Netherlands after World War II: Innovations, transgressions, and lessons to be learned', in CZARNOTA, A., KRYGIER, M. and SADURSKI, W. (eds.), *Rethinking the rule of law after communism* (Budapest: Central European University Press, 2005), 135–152.

LAGROU, Pieter, *The Legacy of Nazi Occupation: Patriotic Memory and National Recovery in Western Europe, 1945–1965* (Cambridge: Cambridge University Press, 2000).

LEMOINE, Thierry and ROUSSEAUX, Xavier, 'La force du droit. Bricolage législatif et réorganisation judiciaire' in ROUSSEAUX, Xavier, VAN YPERSELE, Laurence (eds.),

La Patrie crie vengéance! La répression des 'inciviques' belges au sortir de la guerre 1914–1918 (Brussels: Le Cri, 2008), pp. 67–87.

LUYTEN, Dirk, *Burgers boven elke verdenking? Vervolging van economische collaboratie in België na de Tweede Wereldoorlog* (Brussels: VUB Press, 1996).

LUYTEN, Dirk, *Ideologie en praktijk van het corporatisme tijdens de Tweede Wereldoorlog in België* (Brussels: VUB Press, 1997).

MARTIN, Dirk, 'L'épuration' in DESPY-MEYER, Andrée, DIERKENS, Alain and SCHEELINGS, Frank (eds.), *25 novembre 1941: l'Université Libre de Bruxelles ferme ses portes* (Brussels: Archives de l'ULB, 1991), 197–204.

MASSIN, Veerle and ROUSSEAUX, Xavier, 'Epilogue ou fausse sortie? L'impossible liquidation de la question incivique (1919–1940)', in ROUSSEAUX, Xavier and VAN YPERSELE, Laurence (eds.), *La Patrie crie vengéance! La répression des 'inciviques' belges au sortir de la guerre 1914–1918* (Brussels: Le Cri 2008), 159–168.

SAERENS, Lieven, 'Van vergeten naar gegeerd. Dossin en de Joodse herinnering', *Belgisch Tijdschrift voor Nieuwste Geschiedenis (BTNG)*, (2012, 2/3), 10–20.

SCHELTIENS, Vincent, 'Breuk en continuïteit in doen en denken: het geval War Van Overstraeten, 1910–1945', in *Cahiers d'Histoire du Temps Présent*, 2010, 22, 138–170.

STEINBERG, Maxime, *L'Étoile et le fusil*, 3 vol., Brussels, 1983–1986.

VAN DEN WIJNGAERT, Mark, *Het beleid van het Comité van de sekretarissen-generaal in België tijdens de Duitse bezetting 1940–1944* (Brussels: Koninklijke Academie van België, 1975).

VAN DOORSLAER, Rudi, 'Gebruikt verleden. De politieke nalatenschap van de Tweede Wereldoorlog in België, 1945–2000', in DENECKERE, Gita and DE WEVER, Bruno (eds.), *Geschiedenis maken: liber amicorum Herman Balthazar* (Ghent: Tijdsbeeld / Universiteit Gent, Vakgroep Nieuwste Geschiedenis / AMSAB, 2003), 227–266.

VAN DOORSLAER, Rudi, DEBRUYNE, Emmanuel, SEBERECHTS, Frank, WOUTERS, Nico and SAERENS, Lieven, *La Belgique docile: les autorités belges et la persécution des Juifs en Belgique durant la Seconde Guerre mondiale* (Brussels: SOMA-CEGES / Luc Pire, 2007).

VAN DOORSLAER, Rudi (ed.), *Study on how the crimes committed by totalitarian regimes in Europe are dealt with in the Member States National Report Belgium* (Brussels: SOMA/CEGES, 2009).

VAN LOON, Carolien, 'De geschorene en de scheerster: de vrouw in de straatrepressie na de Tweede Wereldoorlog', in *Cahiers d'Histoire du Temps Présent*, 2008, nr. 19, 45–78.

VELAERS, Jan and VAN GOETHEM, Herman, *Leopold III: de koning, het land, de oorlog* (Tielt: Lannoo, 1994).

VERHOEYEN, Etienne, *La Belgique occupée: de l'an 40 à la Libération* (Brussels: De Boeck Université, 1994).

WITTE, Els, CRAEYBECKX, Jan and MEYNEN, Alain, *Political history of Belgium: from 1830 onwards* (Brussels: ASP, 2009).

WOUTERS, Nico, *De Führerstaat: overheid en collaboratie in België (1940–1944)* (Tielt: Lannoo, 2006).

WOUTERS, Nico, 'The Belgian trials (1944–1951)', in BANKIER, David and MICHMAN, Dan (eds.), *Holocaust and Justice. Representation and historiography of the Holocaust in post-war trials* (New York/Oxford: 2010), 219–245.

TRANSITIONAL JUSTICE IN THE NETHERLANDS AFTER WORLD WAR II

Peter ROMIJN and Erik SCHUMACHER

1. PHASE I (BEFORE 10 MAY 1940): PRE-WAR LEGAL FRAMEWORK

A policy of neutrality, adopted in 1839, helped keep the Netherlands out of the First World War. In 1918, there was a general sense of relief that the fear of warfare on Dutch territory had not come true. In the second half of the thirties, that fear returned as a result of German rearmament and Adolf Hitler's confrontational politics. As before and during the First World War, the Dutch government had to prepare for possible war and occupation. Especially in regard to economic war preparations, it reverted to the experiences and the emergency measures of 1914–1918. Deliberations on the character of a possible German occupation were influenced heavily by memories of the particularly stringent German occupation regime in neighboring Belgium during the First World War. The Dutch government saw no alternative to looking into the settlements of international law regarding the mutual rights and duties in the relation between an occupying power and the interior administration of an occupied country (the Laws and Customs of War on Land, as formulated at the Hague Convention of 1907).

As the general legal framework for the penalisation of civilian collaboration with occupying forces, article 102 of the Dutch penal code forbade "assisting the enemy". The article included as "assistance" services to the enemy like espionage and acting as a guide. There was a similar article regarding collaboration in the military penal code. The position of civil servants under a possible occupation was not legally regulated, but directives regarding this problem were issued. In May 1937, the government formulated a set of "Instructions" (*Aanwijzingen*), which contained rules concerning the correct attitude of governing bodies and civil servants in the case of an enemy attack. The Instructions were similar in meaning to a 1915 memorandum on the same matter. The basic principle was that governmental services should keep on functioning as well as possible in the interest of the general population. The civil servants were instructed to decide for themselves in good conscience if a certain measure served the occupier more than the population. At the municipal level in particular, civil servants were explicitly instructed to refuse cooperation to measures that could directly benefit the enemy's war effort.

2. PHASE II (BETWEEN 10 MAY 1940 AND 1 JANUARY 1952)

2.1. BACKGROUND

On 10 May 1940, Germany invaded the Netherlands. Fighting only lasted five days. The Dutch government, including Queen Wilhelmina, fled to London. Following the refusal of the Dutch government to return under German supervision, the Netherlands was brought under the rule of a German civilian administration, led by the *Reichskommissar* Dr. Arthur Seyß-Inquart. The occupier's most drastic measures were the ban on non-national socialist political activity (1940–1941), the forced mobilisation of Dutch workers to the benefit of the German war effort (1942–1945) and the deportation of circa 100,000 of the 160,000 Dutch Jews, leading to the mass murder of this part of the population (1941–1945).[1] For the execution of these measures, the occupier made use of the machinery of government. Increasingly, the occupier also made use of Dutch political sympathisers, in particular the members of the National Socialist Movement (*Nationaal-Socialistische Beweging*, NSB). The membership of the NSB increased from 30,000 to almost 100,000 during the occupation.[2] Members of the NSB made propaganda for the New Order, served on the Eastern Front and assisted in rounding up and arresting Jews and resistance members. In the civil service and industry, a great deal of cooperation with the occupier occurred, often rationalised by means of the idea that this would produce the "lesser evil". Several tens of thousands of Dutch citizens are estimated to have been active in resistance organisations.[3] At the end of 1944, Allied forces liberated the south of the country. In the first months of 1945, the northeast was also liberated. German forces capitulated on 5 May. In total, an estimated 250,000 Dutch citizens had perished during the Second World War in the Netherlands, Indonesia and elsewhere in the world as a result of warfare and occupation measures.

---

1 G. Hirschfeld, 'Niederlande', in W. Benz (ed.), *Dimension des Völkermords. Die Zahl der jüdischen Opfer des Nationalsozialismus*, München, 1991.

2 L. De Jong, *Het Koninkrijk der Nederlanden in de Tweede Wereldoorlog*, vol. 5, Den Haag, 1974, vol. 10, Den Haag, 1981–1982.

3 L. De Jong, *Het Koninkrijk der Nederlanden.*

After the liberation, the legacy of both collaboration and resistance was perceived by elites as a threat to social order and reconstruction. It was necessary to punish political collaborators in a way that was both legally and emotionally satisfactory. In the longer term, they would have to be reintegrated in a society which would be hostile toward them. Furthermore, a mode of operation had to be found to deal with the widespread and varied forms of collaboration and accommodation in the civil service and the industry. During the occupation, members of the former resistance had developed the ambition of playing a crucial role in prosecuting collaboration and shaping the reconstruction after the liberation. They had powerful opinions on these matters, which could hardly be ignored by politicians. The government-in-exile had foreseen these problems and had already made far-reaching preparations for the transition after liberation. The war cabinets under the leadership of prime minister P.S. Gerbrandy hoped their measures would prevent the resistance from playing an independent political role in peacetime. With the establishment of umbrella organisations for illegal activity like the National Support Fund (*Nationaal Steun Fonds*), the Board of Trusted Representatives (*College van Vertrouwensmannen*) and the Interior Forces in the Netherlands (*Nederlandse Binnenlandse Strijdkrachten*), the government shaped the process of disciplining and subordinating of the resistance under its authority.

In the international context in which the main period of transition took place, three factors were of great importance. Firstly, the Netherlands got involved in armed conflict in the Dutch East Indies. During the war, Imperial Japan had occupied the Dutch East Indies. After the Japanese capitulation of August 1945, nationalist leaders had founded an independent Indonesian Republic. Subsequent Dutch cabinets were unwilling to surrender the colony. A total of around 200,000 Dutch soldiers were sent to Indonesia to restore Dutch authority. After four years of fighting, the Dutch government finally agreed to the transfer of sovereignty in 1949. Together with the economic reconstruction, the war in Indonesia demanded so much attention that the public discussion regarding the punishment of collaborators soon disappeared into the background.[4] Another impact of the war in Indonesia was that guards from the internment camps for political delinquents had to be made available for combat overseas. A second important factor was the Cold War. It produced a cleavage in the former resistance and a change in political priorities. The Communists, who were the most ardent critics of the increasingly moderate government policy, soon found themselves in an isolated political position. A third factor was the gradual change in the Dutch attitude towards Germany. In the beginning of the fifties, the Dutch government agreed that the new Federal Republic of Germany should

4 J.C.H. Blom, 'Jaren van tucht en ascese. Enig beschouwingen over de stemming in Herrijzend Nederland (1945–1950)', in idem, *Herrijzend Nederland. Opstellen over Nederland in de periode 1945–1950*, Den Haag, 1981.

be integrated in the Atlantic alliance. This meant that Germans should no longer be thought of as enemies. This change of perspective brought about a more generous clemency policy towards German war criminals and a more lax attitude towards the German responsibility for war, oppression and genocide.[5]

2.2. NEW LEGISLATION

As early as April 1942, Queen Wilhelmina announced that legislation for the punishment of collaborators was in preparation. The government-in-exile and the resistance were at that time united in the view that these anti-national elements should be removed from society. The preparation of punishment was, in that sense, part of warfare, and was therefore based on maximalist objectives: "absolute standards" regarding "right" and "wrong" were to be applied. This fundamental idea inspired a series of legal measures. The Decree on Extraordinary Criminal Law (*Besluit Buitengewoon Strafrecht*, December 1943) was an expansion of the existing legislation regarding assistance to the enemy. The decree consisted of a series of instructions regarding the interpretation of the existing legislation. For instance, individual membership in national socialist organisations was to be seen as assistance to the enemy. The decree also heightened maximum sentences, reintroducing the death penalty in civil law. In disregard of the Constitution, these measures were passed with retroactive effect. To legitimise these far-reaching measures, the newly created system of Extraordinary Jurisdiction (*Bijzondere Rechtspleging*) was given military features: members of the military were added to the judiciary.

The Purge Decree (*Zuiveringsbesluit*, January 1944) was an expansion of the existing administrative legislation, with the purpose of giving the executive an instrument to fire civil servants guilty of collaboration with the enemy. The Tribunal Decree (*Tribunaalbesluit*, September 1944) was an entirely new legal instrument. It was meant to make it possible for Dutch citizens to judge the behavior and especially the disposition of their fellow citizens during the war outside of the sphere of actual criminal law. The Tribunals had the right to impose internment, the deprivation of civil rights and the confiscation of private property. On top of these decrees, statutory purging measures were introduced for specific occupational groups like journalists, medical practitioners and lawyers.

2.3. ADMINISTRATION OF JUSTICE

For the government-in-exile, one of the main priorities was to prevent chaos and lynch law from occurring during and after the liberation. Thorough preparatory

5 F. Wielenga, *Von Feind zum Partner: die Niederlande und Deutschland seit 1945*, Münster, 2000.

measures helped avert a violent day of reckoning. Relatively little blood was shed in the Netherlands after the liberation. There were some dozens of incidental murders, often inspired by personal grievances or local antagonisms. Women who had had relations with German soldiers were humiliated and abused publically. The homes and stores of members of the NSB were covered with graffiti and looted. Both in the south and in the parts of the country that were liberated later on, "wild" arrests took place and arrested persons were maltreated. Lists had been prepared with the names of people who were to be arrested, but they were ignored in practice. As a result, the internment camps soon became overcrowded. The conditions in the camps were often dire. In retrospect, it is striking that despite all the animosity, Dutch citizens vented their fury upon the enemy's allies mainly through arrests. Those arrests were chaotic in character, but almost always had the purpose of handing the arrested persons over to legal authorities so that they could be put on trial.

During the occupation, the government-in-exile had promised a swift, severe and just reckoning with collaboration. The reality of mass arrests, overcrowded internment camps and administrative chaos did not correspond to that promise. The government's main priority was to combat the chaos. After the government took over responsibility for the internment camps from the Netherlands' Military Authority (*Militair Gezag*, MG), circumstances there soon improved. In the summer of 1945, the Directorate General for the Extraordinary Jurisdiction (*Directoraat-Generaal voor de Bijzondere Rechtspleging*, DGBR) was installed under supervision of the Justice Department, so that the Extraordinary Jurisdiction could also be removed from the responsibility of the MG and taken over by the civil authorities. Around the same time, the five Extraordinary Courts of Justice (*Bijzondere Gerechtshoven*) and the Extraordinary Council of Cassation (*Bijzondere Raad van Cassatie*) were formally installed and most of the nineteen Tribunals began their work. A parallel system of criminal laws, courts and procedures had been formed, based partly on existing legislation (Article 102 of the penal code) and partly on new legislation (the Purge Decree and the Tribunal Decree).

Almost all former members of the NSB were prosecuted. Individual membership was reason for internment. Thousands of other persons suspected of collaboration with the enemy were also arrested. This policy meant that a large group of people were interned. All together, between 120,000 and 150,000 people were interned.[6] The Central Archive for the Extraordinary Jurisdiction (*Centraal Archief Bijzondere Rechtspleging*, CABR) in The Hague keeps more than 500,000 dossiers on individuals who were investigated in this context.

6 G. Hirschfeld and P. Romijn, 'Die Ahndung der Kollaboration in den Niederlanden' in H. Klaus-Dietmar and H. Woller, *Politische Säuberung in Europa. Die Abrechnung mit Faschismus und Kollaboration nach dem Zweiten Weltkrieg*, München, 1991, 281–310.

To convince the general public that the promise of a swift, severe and just reckoning would be kept, a number of prominent members of the NSB were soon put on trial. The National Socialist journalist and radio propagandist M.H.L.W. Blokzijl came first. The fact that he was well-known as well as the intended exemplary function of his trial undoubtedly contributed to the Court's decision to give him the death penalty. On 16 March 1946, Blokzijl was executed by a firing squad. His execution was followed by that of A.A. Mussert, the former leader of the NSB, on 7 May 1946. Another prominent NSB leader, R. van Genechten, was also sentenced to death, but committed suicide while awaiting the verdict of the Extraordinary Council of Cassation.

2.3.1. Minor cases

When the extent of the problem of the persecution of "political delinquents" (to use the newly-minted official term) became apparent shortly after the liberation, the need for pragmatic differentiation was felt in circles of both the government and the former resistance. The swift persecution of a number of NSB heavyweights coincided with government efforts to rouse public opinion in favor of the release of a large group of "minor cases". The government wanted to set the small fry among the interned collaborators free, for the combined purposes of ending the overcrowding of internment camps, making camp guards available for combat in Indonesia, and increasing the pace of the Extraordinary Jurisdiction. Moreover, the government feared an international scandal if it would be discovered that the Netherlands detained people for months solely on the basis of their political convictions. However, the release of the minor cases was not a simple matter, as public opposition had to be overcome. An unqualified release therefore was not an option. There was a strong demand for clear sifting criteria and for supervision of the reintegration of the released political delinquents in society.

In August 1945, the newly elected Social Democrat Prime Minister W. Schermerhorn suggested the release of a large group of detainees for the first time. Due to fierce criticism from the MG and the former resistance, the government decided to let the matter rest temporarily. F.J.F.M. Duynstee, a professor of constitutional law who was a close advisor to Justice Minister H.A.M.T. Kolfschoten, together with a group of other progressive legal professionals persisted in lobbying for a release of the minor cases. In October 1945 the government issued the Decree on Political Delinquents (*Besluit Politieke Delinquenten*, BPD), drafted by Duynstee *et al.*, which consisted of guidelines for the release and the exemption of prosecution of political prisoners. It was emphasised that only detainees who had done nothing or close to nothing to assist the enemy were to be considered for release. It was left to the Public Prosecutor to decide when and under what circumstances exemption from prosecution was appropriate. The BPD made supervision by a probation officer mandatory for released political delinquents. For this purpose, an association for the care and resettlement of former political delinquents was established in October 1945, the state-funded Foundation for the Supervision of Political Delinquents (*Stichting Toezicht Politieke Delinquenten*, STPD). Other forms of alternative punishment that were introduced were temporary disenfranchisement and the duty to report to the police regularly.

Kolfschoten emphasised that these conditions would ensure that the released detainees would not have an easy life. As the most important argument in favor of the BPD, he maintained that it was in keeping with the Dutch legal tradition to give precedence to reason over passion. In Parliament, the BPD enjoyed the support of the majority of representatives. The press was, in general, impartial or positive. The council of churches was also in support of the solution produced by the BPD. The general public agreed with the release, but proved to be above all indifferent to the matter. The circles of the former resistance milieus were more critical, but even here the response was relatively mild. They objected to the extralegal character of the procedure, but after a couple of months expressed support for the idea that a large part of the former political delinquents should be reintegrated in society.

The STPD played an important part in supervising the reintegration of the minor cases in society. Because of the large number of former members of the resistance working with the STPD and the presence of prominent members of society in the STPD's Support Council, the foundation was less susceptible to criticism. The members of the STPD felt compassion with the "small traitors" and wanted to prevent the return of a group of pariahs at the fringes of society, susceptible to political extremism (in this case, communism). The churches also claimed a central role. Because of alarming eye-witness accounts by chaplains in the internment camps, religious leaders complained about the "un-Christian treatment" of political delinquents. They strove to convince their congregations that Christian mercy demanded that the released former political delinquents should be accepted as fellow men and welcomed at worship. They also helped individual detainees bring their cases to the attention of courts and authorities. The Department of Justice denied the churches further-reaching involvement, partly because it did not want to yield responsibility, and partly to prevent detainees from being favored on the basis of their religious convictions.

The introduction of the BDP did not bring about the immediate release of large numbers of "minor cases". In many places, the process stagnated for another six months on account of the chaotic administration and composition of dossiers in the internment camps. Also, the implementation of the decree brought about friction between the parties involved. At the insistence of the STPD and the churches, Kolfschoten pushed the Public Prosecutor to work faster, to delegate more and to shorten the period between release and exemption from prosecution, so that rehabilitation could start as soon as possible. The technocrats at the DGBR proposed that these people should be released collectively and under equal conditions. Soon afterwards, a new cabinet was installed. The new Prime Minister, L.J.M. Beel of the Catholic People's Party (*Katholieke Volkspartij*, KVP), announced the intention to release 40,000 detainees before 1 October 1946, i.e. within just three months.

According to the STPD, this was too much too soon: such measures demanded a level of public support, facilities, employment and supervision that was not yet available. Adding to these practical objections, the STPD maintained that the former political delinquents would view uniform conditions for release as additional punishment, whereas conditions geared towards the individual would come across more as a helping hand in the detainee's return to society. The new Justice Minister, J.H. Van Maarseveen of the KVP, proved susceptible to these arguments. He withdrew the target number of 40,000 and allocated more funds to the STPD. The plan formulated by the DGBR was put aside. As a result of continuing pressure from the STPD, the conditions of release and exemption for prosecution remained geared towards the individual. The target number of 40,000 was reached as late as March 1947, when a total of 25,000 political delinquents remained in internment camps and prisons. The system of individual differentiation served two purposes: surveillance and rehabilitation. On the one hand, case workers had the task of preventing former collaborators from clinging to their national socialist beliefs and regrouping. On the other hand, it was deemed necessary for the former collaborators to recognise their failures in order for them to reintegrate in society. With this strategy, the STPD proved fairly efficient in breaking up the former national socialist milieu.

As evidenced by the development of the policy regarding minor cases, the ideal of systematic strictness on the basis of 'absolute standards' gradually lost ground to a differentiated mildness. In practice, the general public was prepared to accept the reversal as unavoidable and necessary. Thus, an active minority, with the support of societal elites, had succeeded in persuading the passive and largely indifferent majority. This attitude was inspired less by heartfelt mercy than by considerations of general interest. In the discussions concerning the release of the minor cases, social and pedagogical arguments dominated. The interest in the political element of the political offence had faded into the background.

2.3.2. Serious cases

From the summer of 1946 on, the administration of justice to the serious cases got going in earnest, partly because the release of minor cases had lightened the burden for the authorities involved. The fact that the Department of Justice had taken over responsibility from the MG meant that preliminary investigations had been streamlined and had improved qualitatively. Former members of the resistance working for the investigation services had received training or been replaced by professional investigators, and their work had been centralised. Like the minor cases earlier, the serious cases were gradually punished with increasing mildness by the judiciary, politicians and the general public – in that chronological order. Both the Tribunals and the Extraordinary Courts of Justice were eventually concerned more with specific offenses than with the defendant's political persuasion at the time. In doing so, the Tribunals sometimes even explicitly referred to the changing opinions of the general public.

Of the 65,000 suspects remaining after the release of the minor cases, about 8% were acquitted, 16% were released after paying a fine, 60% received a sentence of five years or less in prison, 9% got five to ten years imprisonment and 3% ten to fifteen. In the case of political delinquents, 578 received sentences of more than fifteen years, 148 were sentenced to life imprisonment and 152 were sentenced to death.[7] Because of a clemency policy that was very generous compared to that enjoyed by regular convicts, most sentences were shortened in practice. The generous clemency policy was inspired partly by pragmatic arguments of a social and political nature, but also by a moral argument: there was a feeling that the permanent expulsion of a large group of fellow countrymen would bring about social deterioration.

Because the offenses committed by the serious cases were often shocking, it was necessary to placate public opinion before clemency could be granted. With that purpose in mind, in 1947 a number of leading former members of the NSB issued an "admission of guilt", which was read aloud in churches and published in the newspapers. More than a confession of guilt, the text was in essence a call for reconciliation from both sides. The general public, however, received the document with indifference. Nevertheless, a change did occur in the way political delinquency was viewed by most. Increasingly, people saw the selfless side of treason: perhaps the political delinquents had meant well, and had failed mainly by adhering to the wrong ideals. Was it not a mistake to treat these political opponents like regular criminals? The economic crisis of the years before the war had caused such need, some people argued, that it was understandable that a moment of political digression could occur. To these kinds of arguments, legal professionals added the technical consideration that it was not just that those who had been put on trial first who had been punished more severely. Moreover, eminent experts on criminal law pointed to the magnanimous Dutch tradition of clemency.

---

7 A.D. Belinfante, *In plaats van bijltjesdag. De geschiedenis van de bijzondere rechtspleging na de Tweede Wereldoorlog*, Assen, 1978.

Subsequent Justice Ministers ordered the review of the verdicts in the cases of all political delinquents still in prison. A.A.M. Struycken, who was Justice Minister for the KVP between 1950 and 1951 and defended his clemency policy with an appeal to mercy, was so accommodating in this regard that he threatened the political consensus. War criminals that had received death sentences and now appealed for clemency caused the most controversy. The subsequent Justice Ministers opted for what they called "self restraint". Kolfschoten first voiced the concern that the carrying out of hundreds of death sentences would cause moral damage to the population and would be a stain on national history. At the beginning of the fifties, most death sentences had been commuted to life sentences. The cases that remained were the toughest. Each of them brought about political friction and public commotion. The problematic settling of those individual cases coincided with the completion of the Extraordinary Jurisdiction, and therefore heavily influenced opinions on the general effort to reckon with political delinquents. In the end, out of the 152 death sentences, 40 were carried out, in some cases years after the verdict.[8]

The trials, the implementation of the verdicts and the process of reintegration were hardly perfect. Abusive situations during the arrests and the internment, a lack of balance in the verdicts and the far-reaching politicisation of the clemency policy often gave the impression of a failed reckoning. In general, however, insights dominated that were considered modern and humane by experts on criminal law. Furthermore, the post-war elites put the reconstruction of the constitutional order first, and after initial difficulties, this goal was largely reached. The fact that official and legal procedures had to comply with the standards of constitutional order, brought about a process of nuancing and tempering. On reflection, the recovery of liberal democracy proved incompatible with the exclusion of a large group of fellow countrymen on ideological grounds. In addition, the elites argued that the occupier's immoral politics should inspire a return to – and reinforcement of – trusted and highly moral values like forgiveness and mild punishment after a demonstration of regret. Appealing to such moral principles, elites persuaded the general population, often characterised as indifferent, to reluctantly accept parting with the "absolute standards" of the war.

2.4. REINTEGRATION

Paradoxically, the collective stigmatisation of the former members of the NSB as criminals reflected the depoliticisation of the image of collaboration. The problem of collaboration was soon defined in sociological and criminological

[8] H. Führer, *Nachspiel. Die niederländische Politik und die Verfolgung von Kollaborateuren und NS-Verbrechern, 1945–1989,* Münster, 2005, 80.

instead of political terms. According to criminologists, the war and National Socialism had stimulated the pathological and violent tendencies of the maladjusted and the socially weak. Collaboration was, in their eyes, a pathological deviation from the norm of collective resistance. Therefore, they maintained, under the right circumstances, political and social re-education and reintegration was possible.

In the camps and prisons where collaborators were held, political re-education was part of the program. The idea was that the political delinquents would acknowledge their guilt and would part with their national socialist convictions. But in practice, social reorientation became more important. It proved very difficult to force people to change their political views. Most former political delinquents understood very well that their return to society would be easiest if they chose the line of least resistance and left their options open. As a result, genuine re-education proved unachievable in practice. Nevertheless, the conditions for release were seldom violated, and large-scale political regrouping did not occur. The released political delinquents felt that they were being watched closely and apparently came to the conclusion that it was better not to vent their frustrations in public.

The surveillants working for the STPD established that a widespread feeling of dissatisfaction with the Extraordinary Jurisdiction was taken out on the individual political delinquents returning to society. This aversion expressed itself in insensitivity towards the needs of the former collaborators. Civil servants at the national and the local level were often of the opinion that the released political delinquents were entitled to support only if all "good" citizens were completely satisfied. The former collaborators were sometimes forced to sleep outside or in chicken coops. This was related to the general situation of need in the Netherlands: for a long time after the liberation, there was a shortage of housing facilities, furniture and other bare essentials. In the summer of 1951, the activities of the STDP were brought to an end. The existing associations for the care and resettlement of regular offenders took over the responsibility for the remaining cases.

2.5. PURGING

In many respects, the purge was more complicated than the Extraordinary Jurisdiction, because instead of an investigation of specific offenses, it required an investigation of political convictions. The purge revolved around the general question whether or not professionals should be retained in office on grounds of their behavior during the occupation. Many former resistance workers were of the opinion that the passivity and inadequate patriotism of the masses had been the result of the social and spiritual crisis of the interwar years. They deemed a 'moral regeneration' to be necessary. A first requisite was the complete cleansing of society of all stains of collaboration with the enemy. The government was the first and most extensive sector to be purged. Immediately after the liberation, the attitudes of politicians and civil servants were to be held up against the light, signaling that the return of the government-in-exile constituted genuine regime change.

As a result of the fact that the south was a battlefront for an unexpectedly long time, the purge was a particularly cumbersome process in that part of the country. The MG was in charge as an interim government between September 1944 and June 1945, a much longer period than intended. Adding to the difficulties, a struggle for power arose between the MG and the former resistance, which had already taken purging measures in many places before the arrival of the MG and did not want to surrender the initiative. The MG was forced to allow the involvement of the former resistance in sensitive decisions and to accept measures already taken. Because everyone involved awaited the arrival of civil authorities and also because of the inadequacy of the organisation of the purge, controversies dragged on. Above all, two problems frustrated the purge. Firstly, in practice, the Purge Decree proved insufficiently nuanced as a legal framework. It was only suited to dismiss political collaborators. Secondly, the criteria that were used differed from municipality to municipality. Instead of uniform norms, the question whether an individual still commanded the confidence of the local community prevailed.

In February 1945, Beel was appointed Minister of the Interior. He adjusted the Purge Decree by expanding the possibilities to deal with non-national socialist collaboration and by adding forms of disciplinary punishment apart from dishonourable discharge. In order to strengthen his control of the purge and to force the implementation of uniform norms, he established the Central Council for the Purge of Government Employees (*Centraal Orgaan op de Zuivering van het Overheidspersoneel*, COZO).

The establishment of the COZO worked to the detriment of the influence of the advisory committees of the MG, which included many representatives of the former resistance. The MG and the former resistance did not comply without protest. A tug-of-war came into being, slowing the pace of the purge and undermining the authority of the agencies involved. With the purpose of taking control and pushing ahead the process, Beel entrusted the preparation of purging measures to provincial documentation committees, working under the direct control of the COZO. Again, the former resistance protested: the provincial authorities were expected to be even less strict than the ones in The Hague. Beel, however, persevered and thus brought about a change in the implementation of the purge. It was initially organised bottom-up, allowing room for local contributions, but now became a top-down effort. The purge of the government sector was thus transformed into a purely administrative procedure, eventually revolving around the question whether the minister as an employer still had sufficient faith in a civil servant or administrator. The opinions of citizens were less important. These developments left quite a sour taste with the former resistance. The Great Advisory Committee of the Resistance (*Grote Advies-Commissie der illegaliteit*, GAC) prescribed that the "absolute standards" had been abandoned and persistently objected to government policy, however to no avail.

2.5.1. Purging in practice

As a result of Beel's new policy, pragmatism and the attempt to recover legal certainty came to dominate the purge. Verdicts departed as much as possible from objective criteria and formal rules of conduct. In June 1946, a comprehensive summary of jurisprudence concerning the purge of the government sector was circulated to serve as a detailed guideline for determining which offenses should lead to which punishments. At the same time, the authors of the document emphasised that particular circumstances should be taken account of in every individual case. In general, Beel assigned priority to administrative expediency. The obscurity of such considerations fed suspicion.

For instance, the wartime permanent secretaries of the different ministries (the highest-ranking civil servants in the Netherlands) received very diverse punishments. R.A. Verwey, the Permanent Secretary at the Ministry for Social Affairs, was dismissed on the basis of the Purge Decree. K.J. Frederiks, the Permanent Secretary at the Ministry of the Interior, was punished with honourable discharge on the basis of an additional statutory order outside of the Purge Decree (Decree F 221) designed to apply disciplinary measures in cases of civil servants who had lost confidence of the Minister, even if they could not be accused of collaboration. H.M. Hirschfeld, the Permanent Secretary at the Department of Commerce, was dismissed on the same legal basis. The verdict was, however, reversed in a final appeal, after which Hirschfeld could return to a leading position in government. Only insiders could fathom the considerations behind these verdicts down to the minutest detail. Furthermore, the subtleties involved were a far cry from the "absolute standards" that had until recently dominated the public debate. As a result, many ordinary citizens got the impression that the "big fish" had protected each other by putting all the blame on the "small fry".

The purge of the mayors brought about even more dissatisfaction. This was partly caused by the fact that the public image of a mayor could sometimes run counter to the facts. Especially in circles of the former resistance, verdicts were often vehemently objected to – most of the time because they were deemed too mild, but sometimes also because they were deemed too strict. The GAC had the task of collecting those complaints and deciding whether they should be passed on to central authorities. More often than not, the GAC responded by defending the policy pursued. Most of the time, this did not placate the complainants. In fifty to sixty municipalities, controversy escalated. Those cases drew much attention in the national press, leading to the cumulative impression that the purge of the mayors had failed.

The purge of the police suffered from similar problems. Only the agencies involved knew the acts of which individuals were accused and the criteria laid down. The general public was kept in the dark and suspected the worst. After all, the occupier had used the police as an instrument of persecution. The post-war governments on the other hand were relatively mild to the policemen, referring to the difficult circumstances under which they had been forced to work. An important element in the background was the fact that a consistent purge would necessitate the dismissal of a large part of the officers, and would thus endanger the upholding of public order. The slow pace of decision making further contributed to the bad reputation of the police purge and to the general impression that many "weak" policemen had been spared.

Public misgivings about the purges were inspired by several parallel developments. In the first place, a number of controversial cases dragged on and on, and disseminated a sense of corruption of the process. A huge amount of cases had to be processed and most of them were settled in 1946 or in the beginning of 1947. Looking back, it can be argued that this was relatively soon, but owing to the stagnation in the first period after the war, the general image of the purges was rather negative. The former resistance kept complaining about the pace of the purge and of an overdose of leniency. The cases that dragged on had such a high profile that they heavily influenced the general image of the purge. More and more often, those involved with the purge realised that the general public was getting tired of the purges. Such "purge fatigue" also was related to the fact that the initially strict standards were undeniably mitigated in the course of the purge. The outcome of the purges seemed to imply that it was practically impossible to satisfy all hopes of 'purification of society'. This was a result of both political choices of the time and the logic of the procedures. From case to case, much time and energy was put into the research, resulting in the need for a careful and nuanced assessment of pros and cons. Such technicalities fed feelings of indifference. At the same time those who felt victimised by the purges developed a counter-narrative for the uncompromising attitude of the resistance in face of the enemy. They claimed that a certain amount of collaboration had been unavoidable in order to keep society running. Moreover, for most people the priorities quickly shifted from severely purging collaborators towards more topical issues like the violent decolonisation of Indonesia and the poor standards of living.

The GAC, however, blamed this mitigation on the deliberate undermining of the purge by powers that put personal and group interests above the general interest. In the publications of the former resistance, the purge was often severely criticised. At the same time specific members of the former resistance responded with more consideration, in particular those who had been integrated in the post-war power structures.

2.5.2. Purges in the non-government sphere

The Military Authority, and subsequently the first post-war governments, also took responsibility for purges in those parts of society which did not completely belong to the government sphere. University faculty and staff, for instance, were purged as employees in public service. This could not be true for university students, however, but they were subject to a decree which forbade National Socialist students from continuing their studies. At the same time, the decree installed a purge board to sanction those students who had signed a "declaration of loyalty" during the occupation in which they pledged not to resist the occupying power.

The purging intervention of the state in civil society and private enterprise was generally justified by reasons of state. In this respect the broad legal authority of the military interim administration intervened quite expediently. Thus, the initial purge of the arts, including the performing arts, was founded on maintaining public order. The idea was to avoid riots when artists would perform, or exhibit, who had collaborated or benefitted too much from the occupier and National Socialist cultural policies. Only in April 1946 did the government issue a relevant decree. In its policy towards the periodical press, the Military Authority, and the government subsequently, used the distribution of the scarcely available printing paper as an unofficial instrument of preliminary purging. Political interests blurred the purge of the press, as an important part of the press was connected to political parties and the post-war mood was leaning towards a public regulation of the media. Non-aligned "commercial" media had a better chance at remaining in print under the occupation than did the politicised press. After the war, their commercial character was considered the main reason for collaboration and consequently they were punished. An exception was the orthodox Protestant newspaper *De Standaard*, which was replaced by the resistance newspaper from the same political milieu, *Trouw*.

The purge of the business community was a matter of delayed legislation and much political pressure as well. Economic collaboration had been widespread during the occupation, and in the drive for post-war reconstruction was portrayed as a strategy of national survival. In September 1945 the government issued a decree to punish economic collaboration, while some industrialists were arrested for building warships or fortifications for the German enemy. Initially, the extent of production for the enemy was supposed to be decisive for measuring the degree of collaboration. The business community however started to exert so much pressure on the government that they managed to install a board of appeal that revised many of the earliest sentences and at the same time worked towards new and much more lenient standards to be applied. In the private sphere, like in cases of lawyers or medical doctors, the government transferred the authority of purging towards the professional organisations. Initially, they worked with the military administration and adapted rather harsh standards. After a while, discontent among the purged and parts of the public called for the establishment of councils of appeal. These new bodies revised and mitigated sentences in quite considerable ways.

A most dramatic case was the effort to purge the Dutch Supreme Court (*Hoge Raad*), which had remained in office during the occupation. The Court was one of the highest institutions of the state, but at the same time, the judges did not have the status of public employees under administrative law. The members of the Court who had been appointed by the occupier, most of them sympathisers of National Socialism, were dismissed. The remaining ones, who had been appointed in the pre-war years according to regular procedure, were constitutionally protected against dismissal. Amidst much dissatisfaction about the unprincipled attitude of the Court in face of the occupying power, the exiled government nevertheless prepared to dismiss the judges, calling for a state of emergency. A huge controversy arose, in which the post-war governments refrained from violating the constitutional order. They hoped to convince the remaining judges to step down voluntarily, but this did not happen. In 1946, a final compromise was reached, which allowed the Court to continue under a new President, and fed the general notion of a "spoilt purge".

2.6. COMPENSATION

After the liberation, the Dutch government opted for a neutral and reserved approach to the financial support of the victims of the war. There was no differentiation between various categories of victims. They could all appeal to the same government care, in essence a form of poor relief, which only provided the bare necessities of life. This support was temporary, as the idea was that everyone who made use of it would return to the work force as quickly as possible. P. Lieftinck, the Social Democrat Minister of Finance, pursued a particularly sober financial policy on account of the burdens of the reconstruction and the war in Indonesia. He took the line that the Dutch government could not be held accountable for what the occupier had done. In addition, the welfare state was still in its infancy. The responsibility of the government to provide for its citizens was conceived in economic and social terms, the main social concern was that large groups of paupers could threaten public order. In general, relatively little attention was paid to the needs of individual victims or specific categories. According to the dominant line of reasoning, the Dutch population was collectively victimised during the occupation. In this period, compensation policy was not treated as an important subject in the political debate.

The material damage caused by the war was huge. 14,000 farms and 25,000 other companies were (nearly) destroyed. 90,000 houses were irreparably damaged, another 30,000 were heavily damaged and 390,000 houses were lightly damaged. The Decree on Material War Damages (*Besluit Materieele Oorlogsschaden*) of November 1945 served as the guideline for the compensation of damage suffered during the war. In 1950, it was replaced by a slightly more generous act. The general definition was founded on the principle that people had to be compensated for lost material property, like houses, equipment, furniture, commercial goods and stocks, in order to enable them to rebuild their individual and commercial existence. Not compensated were less tangible, but nevertheless very important assets like loss of employment, losses on the stock market and the like. A total amount of 6.3 billion guilders (1.75 billion dollars) would be paid to claimants. In fact, the taxpayers were to produce the money required for this redistribution of funds. In order to soften that pain, the Minister of Finance conceived extra taxes on capital accumulated during the war.

The Decree on the Recovery of Judicial Matters (*Besluit Herstel Rechtsverkeer*) of September 1944 served as the guideline for the return of stolen properties to the victims. From August 1945 on the Decree was implemented by a newly created legal body, the Council for Rehabilitation (*Raad voor het Rechtsherstel*) under the leadership of wartime Prime Minister Gerbrandy. Representatives of the Jewish community had not been formally involved in the preparation of the decree. It was an uphill struggle for them to stand up for their interests, mainly because the government had decided not to follow the German example by dealing with the Jews as a separate group. The obvious fact that the Jews had been victimised by persecution and spoliation in very special ways was thus grossly overlooked. Anyway, the implementation of the decree with regard to Jewish properties was inconsistent. Controversy ensued from cases concerning people who had acquired stolen Jewish properties during the war and maintained that they did not know it was stolen at the time. The disregard for the interests of the Jewish victims on this matter was telling of the general failing of the care for the Dutch Jews after the war. Only decades later was this "chilliness" denounced, and the attitude of the government changed under the pressure of international interest in the problematic legacy of looting and restitution.

In 1947, the Extraordinary Pension Act 1940–1945 (*Wet Buitengewoon Pensioen* 1940–1945, WBP) was passed: an equivalent to the military pension for members of the former resistance and their surviving relatives. Seeing that the government only wished to take the strictly necessary responsibility for the victims of war, this was an extraordinary measure. Here the Foundation 1940–1945 (*Stichting 1940–1945*) was to play a crucial role. This Foundation was an organised interest group established during wartime by the combined resistance, for the purpose of providing support to the families of the dead and wounded of the resistance. The government mandated the Foundation to play an important part in the implementation of the WBP and put a legal framework in place. In doing so, the government implemented a policy of demobilising and depoliticising the resistance. The general concept that the post-war political class imposed was that the constitutional order had been restored and therefore the resistance should exert no political influence as a movement. From this point of view, only the social element required continued dealing with the former resistance as a collective body. This policy was challenged by the political left wing of the former resistance, but supported by the majority from the political centre and right wing. The government legitimised the WBP with an appeal to the concept of "duty of honour" and by differentiating between "active" and "passive" victims of war. This construction was supposed to prevent other victim groups from lobbying for special pensions of their own.

2.7. EVALUATION

In the 1970s, a committee under the leadership of the historian I. Schöffer researched the failed prosecution of the Dutch businessman and war criminal P.N. Menten. The resulting report distinguished three phases in the purge and the Extraordinary Jurisdiction in the first years after the war: a "wild phase", with mass arrests and dire conditions in the internment camps (until the summer of 1945); an "orderly phase", in which the government took over responsibility from the MG and restored constitutional order (1945–1947); and a "phase of aversion", starting halfway through 1947, in which both former resistance workers and former collaborators vehemently criticised the execution of the purge and the administration of justice.

In part, the phase of aversion followed on logically from the first two phases. The wild phase provided those who had been prosecuted or purged with the ammunition needed to channel their frustrations about their fate into a fundamental criticism of the government approach to the problem of collaboration and accommodation. The transition to the orderly phase meant that a lot of former resistance workers felt sidetracked. The depoliticisation of the former resistance was supported by the pro-government majority of the former resistance and therefore promoted by the coordinating GAC. Former members of the resistance might aspire to leading positions in post-war society, but they learned to do so as individuals. They did not want to endanger their personal influence by committing themselves to autonomously acting organisations of the former resistance.

A sour taste remained, which may also be attributed to the recovery of bureaucratic and legal standards. Inevitably, this recovery gave way to a nuancing of the question of guilt. This nuancing eventually attracted a wide consensus, but it did bring about the fading away of the "absolute standards". Consequently, former resisters could easily claim that principles had been sacrificed to opportunism. The indulgent clemency policy, which had the purpose of closing the book on the past as soon as possible, further strengthened the image of a blemished reckoning with collaboration. Finally, the incidental flaws attracted much more attention than the great majority of cases that were dealt with relatively smoothly and nuanced.

On 1 January 1952, the judicial authority of the Extraordinary Council of Cassation was transferred to the Supreme Court of the Netherlands. This brought a formal end to the Extraordinary Jurisdiction. The members of government looked back at the winding up of the war with moderate satisfaction. Among the former resistance, the former collaborators and the general public however, there was a reservoir of dormant dissatisfaction with the purge and the Extraordinary Jurisdiction. A further potential cause for dissatisfaction, the sparing compensation policy, could easily be interpreted as indifferent to the suffering of the Jewish victims of persecution. In the decades that followed, the slumbering dissatisfaction would flare up.

3. PHASE III (FROM 1 JANUARY 1952)

3.1. PUBLIC MEMORY

The public memory of the Second World War in the Netherlands is inextricably linked to a chain of "memory eruptions". Those eruptions could be caused by affairs concerning individuals, by trail-blazing historical research, by television broadcasts or by developments in foreign countries. Characteristic of this style of remembering is that the public debate is regularly dominated for a short period by a certain affair related to the war, after which the war temporarily disappears again from the center of interest. The eruptions are influenced heavily by the alternation of generations and by the dynamics of public debate. Despite the fact that they are by definition incidental, the memory eruptions provide much insight into the structural developments in the way the Second World War is remembered and conceived. On the basis of the characteristics of the subsequent eruptions, it is possible to discern different phases in the development of the public memory of the Second World War, which each had their effect on war-related subjects like clemency, reintegration, compensation, commemoration and reconciliation.

The reactions to the granting of clemency to the former head of the German political police in occupied Amsterdam, W. Lages, in 1952 showed the extent of the potential of mass indignation related to the memory of the persecution of the Dutch resistance and Jewry. Twenty thousand people participated in a protest march, passing by sites where executions had taken place during the war and ending at the former Amsterdam headquarters of Lages' *Sicherheitsdienst* (SD). Almost sixty thousand people signed a National Petition demanding the guarantee that none of the war criminals with commuted death sentences would ever be released. The affair proved that the punishment of German war criminals was still a breeding ground for political tensions. It deepened the chasm between Catholic and social democrat members of the cabinet of social democrat Prime Minister W. Drees and provided the Dutch Communist Party (*Communistische Partij van Nederland*, CPN) with the opportunity to play a prominent role in a broad protest movement. A new storm of protests blew up when, in the final days of 1952, twelve German war criminals escaped from the Breda prison and managed to flee to Germany. H. Gortzak, a Member of Parliament for the CPN, pronounced the suspicion that the prisoners would have had the assistance of Dutch officials and therefore moved for a vote of no confidence in the responsible Minister, which did not find the support of the majority.

In 1956, the newspaper *Haagsch Dagblad* revealed that F.M.A. Schokking, the mayor of The Hague, had surrendered a Jewish family to the SD on his own initiative in 1942, when he had been the mayor of the small municipality of Hazerswoude. From the very beginning, this affair was of an importance that surpassed local politics. Together with Schokking, the post-war political elite, the purge and the public administration during the war were under discussion. The affair showed that a new generation no longer accepted the compromises made during the occupation and the purge. Communists and members of the former resistance argued that Schokking, like so many others, had enjoyed the protection of friends in the ruling elites during the purge. Big newspapers and prominent figures, among them Beel, once again Minister of the Interior, came to Schokking's defence. Beel appointed a commission of experts, which exonerated Schokking. Subsequently, Schokking filed a complaint against the *Haagsch Dagblad* with the Disciplinary Council of the Federation of Dutch Journalists (*Federatie van Nederlandse Journalisten*, FNJ). The Disciplinary Council ruled against him. This verdict provided the left-wing opposition with ample opportunity to criticise the way Beel had handled the matter. After the debate in Parliament, however, Schokking requested and received honourable discharge. The mechanisms which had served to ward off political crises in the past now proved to be faulty.

As a result of national controversies like the one surrounding Schokking, the general image of what it had meant to be "wrong" changed in the course of the fifties. People were now less concerned with treason and irritating local activities, and more with the question of who had been responsible for the deportation and murder of the majority of the Dutch Jews. Strikingly, the voices of the Jews themselves were not often heard in the public debate. As a result, the Jews were only part of the picture as defenceless victims. They were often depicted as passive and needy, and even as nervous and unreliable. Therefore, attention was paid to the persecuted mostly when others felt they could benefit from acting as their spokespersons.[9]

The mostly dormant dissatisfaction that had persisted through the fifties received new impulses in the sixties. Looking back on the reckoning with collaboration, the question kept reappearing of whether or not the "big fish" had not been systematically spared. The criticism hailed from members of the former resistance, who demanded more attention in the public debate, and from a new generation of politicians that used the matter as a tactical weapon in its battle against the existing order. It was of crucial importance that criticism of the purge was linked up with criticism of the failure of radical social, economic and political reform to materialise during the reconstruction period after the war. The supposed failure of the purge was seen as a symptom of a policy pursued by Dutch elites after the war to limit the post-war reforms to a necessary minimum. This criticism was stimulated by two factors. Firstly, the political atmosphere changed. A generation of politicians stood up that had not been involved with the post-war policy. In general, people based their choices less on their political and religious allegiances. Journalistic publications became less dependent on the political and religious families they belonged to, and therefore became more critical. The second factor was the collective memory of the Second World War. In the forties and fifties, a depoliticised image of the war had been established, according to which the Dutch population had resisted the occupier collectively. In the sixties, the memory of

[9] I. de Haan, *Na de ondergang. De herinnering aan de Jodenvervolging in Nederland, 1945–1995*, Den Haag, 1997.

the war was repoliticised and was brought into connection with the general political and social debate.

The trial of A.O. Eichmann in Israel (1960–1962) and the publication of *The Murderers among Us* (1967) by Nazi hunter S. Wiesenthal renewed interest in the crimes against humanity committed during the war. The rise of neo-Nazism in West Germany fueled concerns that fascism could return. The wars in Algeria and Vietnam brought back bitter memories from the forties. Against this international background the Dutch reflection on the evils of National Socialism and collaboration received new and strong impulses due to specific Dutch causes. The revitalisation of public interest in the Second World War produced internal dynamics in Dutch society which, from the mid 1960s onwards, would continuously remain present and occasionally flare up in emotionally charged affairs. Historiography as a form of public reckoning was very much part of this development. In *Ashes in the Wind* (*Ondergang*, 1965), a history of the destruction of the Dutch Jews during the war, the historian J. Presser asked painful questions from the perspective of the victims about the way that the majority of Dutch citizens had responded to the persecution of their Jewish fellow citizens. The book also posed the question if the right people had been punished in the purge. As usual, that question appeared in the public debate in the shape of an affair. A heated debate developed around the question if F. Weinreb had been made a scapegoat during the Extraordinary Jurisdiction for what others had done and had failed to do. During the war, Weinreb had benefited from false promises he made to fellow Jews about safeguarding them from deportation, but he was defended by Presser in *Ashes in the Wind*.

The pairing of contemporary social dissatisfaction with certain elements of the memory of the war resulted in the image of a failing social-political system that already existed before the war and that had, wrongly, not been parted with after the war. A system in which people were abandoned socially, had supposedly rendered them susceptible to National Socialism before and during the war. A system in which the elite put its own survival above everything, even if that meant that large-scale institutional and economic collaboration with the German occupier was necessary. A system in which the self-preservation of the elite demanded that the so-called "small fry" received most of the blame in the post-war purge and the Extraordinary Jurisdiction, whereas the wrong-doings of the "big fish" were covered with the cloak of charity. What happened in the 1960s was that the public memory of spoiled purges was evoked by a younger generation challenging the political elites who had come to power in the immediate aftermath of the war. From the mid-1940s on, they had legitimised their positions by means of a discourse of "taking responsibility" during the occupation and reconstruction. Now, during the 1960s, their position proved to be more vulnerable than before, when the debate on collaboration shifted from political (i.e. National Socialist) collaboration to collaboration in the administration and civil society. In particular the efficacy of the Nazi persecution of the Jews in the Netherlands was now largely attributed to the failure of Dutch authorities, and society at large, to offer sufficient protection.

This vision was not shared by all, but did take a dominant position in the general debate. It came out strongly in the context of the controversy surrounding two members of the elite in the seventies. In 1976, a series of articles appeared in the press in which the wealthy art dealer Menten – already mentioned before – was accused of having been in the service of the SS during the war, committing war crimes in occupied Poland. These accusations led to Menten's arrest. In 1978, W. Aantjes, the parliamentary leader of the Christian Democratic Appeal (*Christen-Democratisch Appèl*, CDA), was accused in the press of having been a member of the SS during the war. In a press conference that was broadcast live on both television channels, historian L. de Jong, head of the National Institute for War Documentation (*Rijksinstituut voor Oorlogsdocumentatie*, RIOD), stated that Aantjes had been a guard at the prison camp Port Natal near Assen and had served in the *Waffen-SS*. Aantjes subsequently resigned as parliamentary leader. Later, it would become clear that the claims that De Jong had put forth were less tenable than they initially had seemed to be.

Controversial cases like those of Weinreb, Menten and Aantjes were solved in a manner tried-and-true in Dutch political culture: commissions of so-called "wise men" were appointed and prominent historians were called in to get at the truth. Historians also took interest in other matters related to collaboration. The demythologising influence of professional historians brought about an adjustment of the image of the failed reckoning with collaboration. In the report about the Menten case, for instance, it was demonstrated that practical difficulties and historical circumstances had played a much larger part in the purge than possible intrigues. The time was ripe to historicise the memory of the war. In 1983, the historian J.C.H. Blom, who had taken part in the historical investigation of the Menten case, gave an influential lecture in which he challenged historians to be less "hypnotised by right and wrong" and to take a more analytical approach to the Second World War. Blom's lecture contributed to a scholarly paradigm change, but the public response was more diffuse.

Another branch of the academic world also influenced the way in which the war was looked back on from the seventies onwards. More and more often, psychologists and psychiatrists mentioned the concept of persecution trauma as an argument to give more attention to the victims of persecution. The documentary *Begrijp je nu waarom ik huil?* (*Do You Understand My Tears Now?*), which was broadcast on national television in 1972, was a milestone in this regard. In the film, a former inmate of Bergen-Belsen relived his camp experiences under the influence of LSD therapy. In 1973, the Centre '45 (*Centrum '45*) was established, which provided therapy for victims of persecution. The fact that the continued psychological suffering of Jews was now acknowledged gave their opinions on the history of their persecution a power of expression it had lacked before. Jewish voices had been marginalised in the past, but now they held a scarcely contested claim to authority in this matter.

The acknowledgement of the psychological suffering of the Jewish victims of persecution served as an example for other (alleged) victim groups. They established their own organisations, often successfully appealing to government funds. When those subsidies were re-evaluated in the context of the governmental cutbacks of the eighties, a form of competition between the victim groups ensued. The fact that the increased influence of professionals has brought about a less black-and-white image of the Second World War does not mean that the war is now no longer a source of continuous controversy. The social memory of the war is still an explosive matter, as evidenced in the late nineties by the emotional reactions to the discovery of a collection of documents revealing the failings of the post-war restitution policy in minute detail. The revelations were met with great public anger and lead to large-scale historical research on the subject of the 'chilly' reception and treatment of Dutch Jews returning from the concentration camps.

3.2. CLEMENCY

In the first years after the war, a policy of generous clemency was introduced with the intent of swiftly reducing the extent and duration of the punishment of political delinquents. In September 1952, the Social Democrat L.A. Donker was appointed Justice Minister. He took a different stance on clemency than his predecessors had. Donker slowed down the collective pardoning of political delinquents with long prison terms, which was nonetheless continued on an individual basis. The pardoning of those who had been sentenced to death and had since received clemency asserted itself as the biggest problem Donker had to face in this matter. The problem became acute when Donker made the controversial decision to commute the death penalty imposed on Lages as one of the chief organisers of the deportation of Dutch Jewry and persecution of the resistance to life imprisonment. Organisations of the former resistance were for the most part unhappy with the decision, but disunity weakened their lobbying power. The non-communist part of the former resistance feared that the Communist Party would benefit from possible commotion and therefore resigned itself to Donker's decision. The former resistance as a whole did push for a ruling out of further clemency for Lages and other imprisoned war criminals with converted death sentences. The majority of Parliament shared this view. Donker subsequently promised Lages and co. would never be set free.

Donker died in office in 1956. His successors reconsidered his relatively strict policy on clemency once again. As a result, on 1 January 1964 there were only four war criminals with commuted death sentences, all of them German, left in prison. They were the last remaining prisoners in the Netherlands who had been convicted as a part of the Extraordinary Jurisdiction. All four of them – Lages, F. Fischer, F.H. aus der Fünten and J.J. Kotälla – were held at the Breda prison. They became known and notorious as the "Breda Four", later the "Breda Three", later still the "Breda Two" and in collective memory once again the "Breda Three". A number of progressive legal professionals were of the opinion that the Breda Four should also be set free within a short term. They called life imprisonment an inhumane penalty, unfitting the Dutch legal system. They also asserted that it should be taken into account that the Breda Four had committed their crimes under great pressure and in a time of degeneration. Opponents of pardoning stated that it would be inconsiderate of the feelings of their victims if the Breda Four were allowed to walk free.

In 1966, Lages fell seriously ill. Expecting Lages to succumb soon, Social Democrat Justice Minister I. Samkalden decided to have him taken to West Germany for treatment. There it appeared that Lages was not terminally ill after all and his condition was treated successfully. The man would live in freedom in West Germany until his death, five years later. Lages's miraculous recovery did not turn out well for the remaining Breda three. It became almost impossible for the Justice Minister to set them free in the face of death. Furthermore, public opinion had become evermore passionate on the subject of clemency.

Despite the pressure of public opinion, subsequent Justice Ministers persisted in looking for ways to end the imprisonment of the Breda Three, united in the opinion that the Dutch constitutional order could not brook literal life sentences. In 1969, Liberal Justice Minister C.H.F. Polak made preparations for an amendment of the law that would make conditional remission possible. When the press discovered his plans, a heated public debate followed. Although it appeared a majority of Parliament was willing to support his intended policy, Polak decided that the objections of his opponents were too serious to ignore and he withdrew his amendment. In 1972, a new Justice Minister for the KVP A.A.M. van Agt made his attempt at solving the problem. He wrote a letter to Parliament stating his intent to pardon the Breda Three, hoping to find support for this measure. Van Agt claimed that the continued imprisonment of the three no longer served an acknowledged purpose in the Dutch judicial system. By way of exception, he made public the advice of the High Council and of the special chamber of the Amsterdam court, both in favor of pardoning. In a parliamentary hearing representatives of the former resistance and victim organisations took the opportunity to object to the plans, which they saw as a denial of their suffering, making use of emotional references to personal histories. The argument in favor of pardoning met with a wall of incomprehension. Due to public disturbance, the hearing had to be suspended.

Leading up to the decisive debate in Parliament, members of Parliament were put under pressure by demonstrations and thousands of letters urging against pardoning. Days before the debate, the Socialist broadcasting society VARA premiered the documentary *Begrijpt u nu waarom ik huil?* on national television. More and more often and more explicitly the passivity of Dutch civilians during the occupation served as an argument against pardoning: Dutch society should not abandon the victims of prosecution *again*. Some of the victims themselves wrote letters to their representatives in Parliament, stating they would view a vote in favor of pardoning as a form of personal betrayal. During the debate, it appeared that the members of Parliament were sensitive to these arguments. A motion against the pardoning was accepted with 85 votes to 61.

Van Agt, the cabinet minister who carried responsibility for the final decision, promised Parliament that the Breda Three would stay in prison for now, and that further decisions concerning possible pardoning would be made in consultation with a commission made up of representatives of the victims and the former resistance. In practice, this commission soon had a decisive voice in the matter. Its supremacy became especially apparent a year later, when Kotälla suffered an intracranial hemorrhage. The commission refused to grant Kotälla release for medical reasons. Van Agt and his successor, Christian Democrat J. de Ruiter, dared not ignore the commission's veto. In 1979, Kotälla died in prison, severely weakened.

Central to the debate was the contradiction between progressive ideas about perpetrator-oriented criminal law reform on the one hand and the classical principle of retaliation on the other. During the Extraordinary Jurisdiction, the executive branch had kept the initiative firmly in its own hands, so as to render a complex problem manageable as fast as possible. This was achieved with the help of criminal law reformists and their new ideas and methods. From the sixties on, the Dutch government took a step back and the policy concerning war criminals became a matter in which the opinions of victims of persecution and members of the former resistance weighed the heaviest. This reversal worked to the disadvantage of the progressive ideas of legal professionals. With the growing influence of public opinion, a shift took place from a predominantly political and legal debate to an emotional and psychological approach, in which the memory of the war played a central part. It was now widely thought that the release of war criminals amplified past suffering and made victims of the victims once again. The meaning of the concepts of "right" and "wrong" changed. "Right" meant taking the side of the victims and opposing pardoning, whereas advocating clemency was the new "wrong", as it was viewed as a betrayal of the victims. In a way, the Breda Three provided the Dutch with a second opportunity to be on the "right" side in the Second World War.

In the meantime, the matter of the remaining Breda Two kept reappearing in public debate. In 1989, Liberal Justice Minister F. Korthals Altes decided the time had come to finally put the matter to rest. He wrote a letter to Parliament stating that the frequent outbursts of emotional debate were more harmful to the victims than a release of the Breda two would be. He secured the support of a group of prominent resisters and victims of prosecution. According to them, the Breda Two's punishment had lost its purpose and contradicted the same constitutional order that the Allies had fought for during the Second World War. After a closed hearing, the majority of Parliament agreed. Fischer and Aus der Fünten were extradited to West Germany. As a result, severe conflict arose among victims of persecution and former members of the resistance. Before the end of the year, both Fischer and Aus der Fünten had passed away.

3.3. REINTEGRATION

With the abolishment of the STPD, the presence of former political delinquents, no longer primarily a legal and political matter, became first and foremost a problem for society to solve. The "ordinary" Dutch who were now to deal with the reintegration of the delinquents, sometimes had a completely different view on desirability of such than did the political and societal elites. Common interest, societal stability and the possible reappearance of a fifth column often played no part in the considerations of ordinary citizens. They led themselves be guided by their own judgments and not by official policy statements. Such judgments could be strongly determined by private experiences of war and oppression. Quite often, the memory of danger and persecution was dominating, and therefore the gap between "right" and "wrong" could remain almost impossible to overcome. Even if former political delinquents repudiated their past by acknowledging guilt, not all people in their environment would allow them to make a fresh start. Others, however, took their distance from the "socially desirable" stance towards former National Socialists. They remembered their own difficulties in taking the "right side" under the duress of the occupation and treated their former National Socialist neighbors as if hardly anything had ever happened. Recent research shows that the overall image was more diffuse than the often-assumed categorical rejection.

Adding to such differing patterns, the former political delinquents took various approaches to their return to society after their internment. Some remained hostile and rejecting towards the outside world, creating their own little world within the family. Others completely devoted themselves to a new role in society. Some renounced their old national socialist beliefs, others held fast to them. For most of them, the past was something to conceal. Even within most families, a parent's history of political delinquency was a taboo subject. Often, small children in those families only had a vague sense that something had happened which was now to be kept a secret. The silence within families was complemented by silence in schools and in neighborhoods. Everyone knew what had happened, but rarely anyone addressed it directly. Bullies in schoolyards made an exception to this rule. Children of former political delinquents were sometimes singled out because of their parents' history and excluded from activities.

In the mid-fifties, the government decided that former political delinquents who had lost their citizenship due to service in the German army or state, could issue a request to regain their Dutch nationality. This measure, by the way, also applied to left-wing Dutch citizens who had fought on the side of the Republicans in the Spanish Civil War. Around the same time, tens of thousands of former political delinquents regained the right to vote. Thus, formal citizenship of this group was restored. Whether it was actually accepted, is another matter.

For former political delinquents, the frequent occurrence of memory eruptions in the public debate was a painful matter. Those eruptions made it more difficult for them to leave the war behind and carried the risk that they would reflect negatively on them. From the mid-sixties on, the nature of the controversies assured that a strong connection between the "wrong sector" and the Holocaust developed in the public eye. The former political delinquents were not in a position to provide a counterbalance to that development. In some respects, the reintegration of former political delinquents benefited from the Cold War. The major wartime political antagonism between Fascism and democracy was replaced by a new one. But this advantage was limited. The Communists kept appealing to the prestige they had acquired as resisters by keeping the memory of the war alive and by continuously warning of "resurgent fascism" in the face of German rearmament.

Social ostracism as a practice was not accompanied by continued official brandishing. After the abolishment of the social work organisations, like the STPD and the Bureau for Special Youth Care (*Bureau Bijzondere Jeugdzorg*, BBJ), the former political delinquents were no longer subject to specific government policies. Their integration was, as it were, formally put beyond question. As there was no longer a separate policy for this group, the group had officially ceased to exist, leading to the logical conclusion that the problems related to political delinquency had likewise dissolved into thin air. For the former political delinquents, this came as a relief in such a way that it worked against continued official stigmatisation. At the same time, however, they lost the opportunity to highlight specific problems related to their National Socialist past, as for instance the loss of civil rights, or unofficial discrimination on the labour market. They could share such problems with their fellow former political delinquents only. This was one of the reasons for many political delinquents to stay in touch with each other in their post-war lives.

Some of them went so far as to organise themselves in new associations. Advocacy groups tried to draw attention to their complaints, mostly concerning the maltreatment of political delinquents in the post-war internment camps and the difficult socioeconomic position in which they found themselves after their release. The Foundation for Former Political Delinquents (*Stichting Oud-Politieke Delinquenten*, SOPD) was established in 1951 with the explicit goal of looking after the interests of former members of the NSB and the SS. In 1953, the National-European Socialist Movement (*Nationaal-Europese Sociale Beweging*, NESB) was established: an association of former NSB-members with enough political aspirations to justify a ban by the authorities in 1955. Soon afterwards a new variant appeared, with the even more cryptic designation Help for Disabled Former Eastern Front Combatants, Surviving Relatives, Political Prisoners and Others (*Hulp aan Invalide oud-Oostfrontstrijders, Nabestaanden, politieke Gevangenen en Anderen*, HINAG).

The tendency of these organisations to stick with national socialist beliefs and to persist in distinguishing the former political delinquents as a separate group, was diametrically opposed to the implicit government policy to stop addressing former political delinquents as such, so as to ease their integration in society. The police acted against these organisations on the basis of public order laws. The court issued penalties on the basis of the Act for the Abolition of Treasonous Organisations (*Wet op de Ontbinding van Landsverraderlijke Organisaties*) and the ban on the distribution of racist and otherwise insulting propaganda, covered in article 137 of the penal code. Organisations like the SOPD, the NESB and the HINAG received much attention in the press, especially in communist publications, but never reached a sizeable membership.

At the end of the seventies, children of former political delinquents began forming their own bonds. They were also the subject of increasing attention in the press. Since the beginning of the eighties, some of them have been meeting each other in gatherings organised by the organisation of fellow-sufferers, "Workgroup Recognition" (*Werkgroep Herkenning*). Some, who claimed to suffer from mental problems related to their parents' war pasts, asked for the same special government care as victims of persecution and warfare. After initial controversy, they were slowly acknowledged as victims and integrated in the existing arrangements. In autobiographies published by children of former political delinquents, the boundaries between "victim", "perpetrator" and "bystander", between "right" and "wrong" were questioned. Their stories found a sympathetic welcome, because they fit in with general criticism of the tired cliché of nationwide resistance and responded to the interest in authentic personal experiences.

3.4. COMPENSATION

With its reserved compensation policy shortly after the war, the Dutch government had not succeeded in putting the matter to rest. In the following decades, compensation became a recurring subject of emotionally charged debate. The fact that the government refused to make special arrangements for specific groups of war victims only deepened their longing for acknowledgement. Furthermore, the decision to make an exception to the rule of no exceptions for the former resistance members meant that the policy of non-differentiation was doomed from the start. It gave other victim groups the feeling that their suffering was denied. Politicians barely had an answer to this sentiment, even more so because the press was always ready to rally for the cause of the victims. In the course of time, one victim group after the other successfully lobbied for special compensation: the Jewish victims of persecution, the civilian war victims, the former resistance and the victims of persecution in the former Dutch Indies, the victims of forced labour in Germany.

The nineteen sixties were an important turning point in compensation policy. A period of economic boom facilitated the development of the welfare state. With new solidarity laws to the benefit of the elderly (*Algemene Ouderdomswet*, 1956), the unemployed (*Algemene Bijstandswet*, 1965) and the disabled (*Wet op de Arbeidsongeschiktheidsverzekering*, 1967), governmental care became a right, rather than a favor. At the same time, the dominant view of the Second World War changed. Presser made himself a spokesperson on behalf of the 100,000 murdered Jews and charged Dutch society with neglect and worse. For the "protest generation" of war children and baby-boomers, the alleged indifference of older generations to the fate of their Jewish fellow-citizens became a central part of the legacy of the war. New conceptions in psychology of the "late consequences" of internment also contributed to the growing criticism of the existing policy concerning victims of persecution. Following the post-war ethics of stoicism, emotions were emancipated.

Jewish victims of persecution especially highlighted their problems. They felt they had the right to special government care, separate from general welfare.

Where the concept of a "debt of honour" had served the lobby of the former resistance, victims of persecution made an appeal to the concept of "special solidarity". The government was willing to make improvements to the existing arrangements, but strongly opposed a disconnection from general welfare. The egalitarian ideal, an article of faith in the Netherlands, contributed to the aversion to making exceptions. But most importantly, there was the fear that after the victims of persecution, more victim groups would demand special government care. Despite such fear, government eventually budged under public pressure and the lobbying power of the Jewish Social Service organisation (*Joods Maatschappelijk Werk*, JMW). The political refusal to grant special compensation to Jewish victims became untenable. In 1973, the Benefit Act for Victims of Persecution (*Wet Uitkeringen Vervolgingsslachtoffers,* WUV) was passed. The WUV was a considerably more generous arrangement than general welfare. It guaranteed an existence that – within reasonable boundaries – was comparable to personal pre-war circumstances.

The fear that other victim groups would soon follow in demanding special compensation, turned out to be justified. In 1984, the Benefit Act for Civilian War Victims (*Wet Uitkeringen Burger-Oorlogsslachtoffers*, WUBO) was passed, followed by the Benefit Act for the Dutch Indies Resistance (*Wet Indisch Verzet*, WIV) in 1986. The fact that these victim groups were relatively late in securing special compensation was connected to their failure to seize a distinct place in the collective memory of the Second World War, like the former resistance and later the Jewish victims had done. There was never a strong identification with the civilian war victims at a national level. The fact that people in the Dutch Indies had suffered, too, was disregarded for a long time. That disregard was caused partly by racism, but also by the aloofness of the Dutch Indonesian community. Only when the organisation of former inhabitants of the Dutch East Indies Pelita, following the example of the Foundation 1940–1945 and the JMW, started to act as an advocacy group, was a breakthrough reached. The phased and long-winded realisation of compensation arrangements for the different victim groups shows that the Dutch government was persistent in its financial restraint and its dislike of making exceptions. Intense pressure from advocacy groups was necessary for a change of policy to be achieved. The government only budged when there seemed to be no other option left.

Halfway through the nineties, the definitive line encircling the rightful claimants to compensation was finally drawn. For a long time, members of the "second generation" had enjoyed the right to periodical compensation via the WBP and the WUV. In 1994, this form of special solidarity was limited to compensation for the costs of psychotherapy.

The passing of the benefit acts was not the end of the matter. Their implementation gave way to new quarrels. Although the government remained responsible in the end, it delegated the work to special councils, which were created specifically for this purpose. The councils were put under pressure by both the government and victim groups. As a consequence, a process of pushing and pulling from all directions thwarted decision-making. In practice, it proved very difficult to fence off the ideals of the debt of honour and the special solidarity. At the end of the eighties, the implementation of the WUV reached a deadlock due to the unexpectedly large amount of claims, insufficient governing capacity and the increasing emotional involvement with the victims. To force a breakthrough, in 1990 the government decided to centralise the implementation and execution of the WUV and the WIV in an independent governing institution, the Council for Pensions and Relief (*Pensioen- en Uitkeringsraad*, PUR). The existing councils were transformed into council chambers and lost part of their independence. In the years that followed, the PUR also became responsible for the implementation of the WBP and the WUBO. As of 1 January 2011, responsibility for the implementation of the benefit acts was transferred to the Social Insurance Bank (*Sociale Verzekeringsbank*).

In addition to the benefit acts, there were incidental compensation measures, chiefly for the Jewish victims of persecution. In the second half of the fifties, two compensation acts were passed in Western Germany – the *Bundesentschädigungsgesetz* (1956) and the *Bündesrückerstattungsgesetz* (1957) – leading to the payment of an estimated total of 750 million Deutschmark (ca. 675 million guilders) to Dutch Jews. The arrangement was cause for frustration, as the submission of claims was an exhausting process. In 1960 and 1962, West Germany and the Netherlands agreed on two complementary restitution and compensation pacts. West Germany donated a sum of 280 million Deutschmark (ca. 250 million guilders), of which 125 million Deutschmark (ca. 110 million guilders), which was earmarked as a compensation for immaterial damage suffered by victims of persecution and their children. To many Dutch Jews, this was a disappointing amount. At the end of the century, another round of incidental compensation occurred. After the revelation of shocking details concerning the looting of the Dutch Jews, the Dutch government, stock market, banks and insurance companies donated a combined 764 million guilders to the Jewish community. At the same time, the government donated 30 million guilders as compensation to the Roma and Sinti community, and 250 million guilders to the Dutch Indonesian community.

3.5. COMMEMORATIONS

After the liberation, there was a consensus that the experience of war had been of profound significance and as such should be passed on to future generations as a central part of national memory. Efforts were made immediately to facilitate historical research of the war period. On 8 May 1945, the National Bureau for the Documentation of the History of the Netherlands in Wartime (*Rijksbureau voor de Documentatie van de Geschiedenis van Nederland in Oorlogstijd*) was founded by the government. Already, in March 1944, the exiled Minister for Education, Arts and Sciences had summoned the Dutch population to collect materials that could be useful to a future institute for war documentation. The resulting RIOD was the first of its kind internationally.

The fact that war monuments were erected everywhere in the country on the initiative of individuals proved that a profound wish to keep alive the memory of war also existed on a local level. Before the war, a tradition of reservedness had existed in the Netherlands when it came to statues and monuments in honour and remembrance of the national past. Now, there was a proliferation. The government decided to call a halt to this development. A general moratorium on monuments was issued and a special commission was installed to judge proposals for new war monuments. From that moment on, war monuments were characterised by a classical style and chiefly Christian symbols of suffering, martyrdom and eventual victory through perseverance. The fundamental concept was the idea of a suffering that had not been useless. The persecution of the Jews was not absent as a theme, but served only as an illustration of German cruelty and the sorrow that had struck Dutch society as a whole. The most important monument erected in this period was the National Monument on the Dam Square in Amsterdam (1956), which still serves as the main site for war commemoration in the Netherlands.

With commemoration gatherings, a similar development took place. They also originated mainly at a local level, and were subsequently centralised by the government. A tradition soon evolved to commemorate the war for two days in the beginning of May – preferably the 4th and the 5th, but initially, exceptions were made for Christian Sabbath. On the first day, the victims of war and persecution were honoured with a moment of silence. On the second day, the liberation was celebrated. This tradition still exists. The commemoration gatherings in the first period after the war were dominated by the myth of collective resistance. They were usually organised at sites connected to the history of the resistance and mainly honoured military and illegal combatants. Relatively little mention was made of the suffering of "passive" victim groups.

From the sixties on, more and more victim groups demanded a place in the national rites of war commemoration. In 1961, Dutch soldiers who had been killed in action after the Second World War, for instance during the war in Indonesia or the Korean War, were honoured for the first time at the national commemoration on 4 May. This was the result of a lobby by veterans and right-wing politicians. Also in the sixties, more attention was paid during the ceremonies to Jewish victims of persecution during the Second World War. In 1963, the Jewish Sabbat was taken into account for the first time. Despite those changes, some people were still dissatisfied with the official ceremonies. They felt that the ceremonies were too military in character, were exclusive to certain victim groups and paid too little attention to the relevance of the war legacy to contemporary conflicts and developments. As a result, alternative commemoration ceremonies were organised. At those gatherings, contemporary suffering in other parts of the world was given a central role. Homosexuals also organised their own commemoration gatherings, because they were not acknowledged as a victim group at the official ceremony. In the seventies, the government strove to unite the various groups. All victim groups were now explicitly embraced at the national commemoration, during which more attention was also paid to contemporary suffering.

The emancipation of the various categories of victims of persecution also reflected in the monuments that were erected in this period. Most monuments commemorating the fate of the Dutch Jews were erected after 1960. For a long time, such monuments were placed almost exclusively at Jewish cemeteries. In 1962, a commemorative plaque was placed at the *Hollandsche Schouwburg* in Amsterdam, where Jews from Amsterdam and surrounding districts were assembled before being deported. In 1970, the first national monument commemorating the persecution of Jews during the war in the Netherlands was erected at the former transit camp at Westerbork. The first monument for the victims of the persecution of Roma and Sinti during the Second World War was only erected in 1978. It was, nevertheless, the first monument of its kind in the world.

In the eighties, authorities feared that, with the passing away of the war generations, the desire to commemorate would fade away. We know now that this concern was not completely justified. In 1980, there were around fifteen hundred monuments commemorating the Second World War in the Netherlands. Since then, this amount has more than doubled, with the introduction of digital monuments as the most recent development. An active remembrance policy at the government level has contributed to the continued interest in the Second World War. The government had, mainly for budgetary reasons, for a long time been very reserved in granting national holidays and organising national celebrations, but now became somewhat more obliging. From 1980 on, Liberation Day was celebrated on a yearly basis – before, it had been once every five years – although the working population did have to sacrifice a day's leave to take part in the festivities. In 1990, 5 May became a national holiday, and as such a day off for civil servants and many others. The government also took measures to streamline and centralise (national) commemoration ceremonies. For this purpose, the National Committee 4 and 5 May (*Nationaal Comité 4 en 5 mei*) was established in 1987.

The historical legacy of the Second World War is still looked after with much effort. Kilometers of archival material concerning the war period are kept at mostly the Institute for War, Holocaust and Genocide Studies (*Instituut voor oorlogs-, Holocaust- en genocidestudies,* NIOD – the former RIOD) in Amsterdam and the National Archive in The Hague. There are at least 84 museums about the war spread around the country. The museums that were established in the first period after the war were mostly concerned with military matters (for instance the National Museum for War and Resistance at Overloon, founded in 1946, and the Airborne Museum Hartenstein, close to Arnhem, 1949). Later museums focused more on the victims (for instance the Jewish Historical Museum, which reopened in 1955, the Anne Frank House, which opened in 1960, and the National Memorial Camp Westerbork, 1983). The effort to keep the memory of the war alive in the eighties also manifested itself in museum policy, as evidenced by the establishment of large museums in Leeuwarden (Frisian Resistance Museum, 1980), Amsterdam (the Resistance Museum, 1984), Groesbeek (the National Museum for the Liberation 1944–1945, 1984), Gouda (the Zuid-Holland Resistance Museum, 1984), Best (the Museum Park "Wings of Liberation", 1984) and Groningen (the War and Resistance Memorial Centre, 1991).

Much attention is devoted to the history of the Second World War in both primary and secondary education. The specific contents of school textbooks are not coordinated at the government level. The National Committee 4 and 5 May and the Anne Frank Foundation are among several distributors of learning materials. Since 1999, the National Point of Support Guest Speakers WWII (*Landelijk Steunpunt Gastsprekers WOII*) coordinates lectures by eyewitnesses at schools. On a yearly basis, workshops focusing on war education are organised for schoolteachers. In the curriculum, the history of the Second World War is often connected to subjects like intolerance, prejudice, racism and discrimination.

3.6. RECONCILIATION?

Owing to the outcome of the Second World War, the context of practicing reconciliation was subordinated to admitting fundamental guilt on the side of the losers. Ever since the 1947 "admission of guilt", which was not taken seriously by many, there has never been another large-scale attempt to bring about reconciliation between the former members of the NSB and the rest of society. The former political delinquents simply had to admit their guilt, in order to facilitate their return to society. Their return was deemed necessary above all for reasons of utility. The feeling was that it would be harmful to society if a large group were permanently sidetracked. A normalisation of relations was therefore most important: conventions for renewed contact had to be developed. Forgiveness was not a big factor in these considerations. In the case of the children of the former political delinquents however, a ritual form of reconciliation did take place. In 1994, Queen Beatrix mentioned in her Christmas address to the nation that the war had scarred this group, too. The next year, representatives of this group were officially invited to the national commemoration on 4 May for the first time.

In essence, the Dutch political class and institutions have pursued the principle that the former National Socialists could redeem themselves of guilt by explicitly distancing themselves from the past and by continued admittance that they had been "wrong". Thus, they came to depend on the good will of their fellow-Dutch to be accepted as "good citizens", a good will which always would be conditional. No reconciliation but continued admission of guilt was the leading principle in dealing with the former supporters of the enemy.

When, from the sixties on, more attention was paid to the shortcomings of the Dutch government and the majority of the Dutch population when it came to protecting the Jewish community during the occupation and the treatment of Jews returning from the concentration camps after the war, a growing number of people felt that an official admission of guilt was desirable. Material compensations were only partly satisfactory in this regard. However, an official apology was not given. In the nineties, the desire for official reconciliation measures towards the Jewish community increased as a result of growing interest in the treatment of returning victims of persecution. The government responded to this development. In 1995, Queen Beatrix, while speaking to the Knesset, admitted that only a minority of the Dutch population had actively resisted the persecution of Dutch Jews during the occupation. In 2000, Prime Minister W. Kok presented partial apologies for the post-war Dutch governments' treatment of the Jews. During an official visit to Israel in 2005, Prime Minister J.P. Balkenende described the deportation of Dutch Jewry as a "pitch-black" chapter in Dutch history. In 2005, the president of the Dutch Railways (*Nederlandse Spoorwegen*) offered an apology to the Jewish community for his company's contribution to deportations during the war.

After the war, anti-German sentiments persisted for a long time in Dutch society. Consequently, as late as 1995, Wageningen, Arnhem and Millingen aan de Rijn were the first municipalities where German dignitaries were officially invited to the celebrations of 5 May. A year later, German dignitaries were also welcomed at the commemoration ceremony on 4 May in Wageningen. In the years that followed, German dignitaries were invited to 4 May ceremonies in 31 more municipalities, but specifically *not* to the official 4 May commemoration at the National Monument in Amsterdam. In the regular public discussions about this policy, an emotional veto by the victims of persecution and their offspring is still alive, both in respect of the internal and external former enemies.

ABBREVIATIONS

BBJ: Bureau for Special Youth Care (Bureau Bijzondere Jeugdzorg) a branch of the Ministry of Justice.

BBS: Decree on Extraordinary Criminal Law (Besluit Buitengewoon Strafrecht) issued 22 December 1943 (nr. D61) by the Dutch government-in-exile.

BPD: Decree on Political Delinquents (Besluit Politieke Delinquenten) Decree of 26 October 1945 (F 244) establishing the principle of out-of-court settlements in minor cases of collaboration.

CABR: Central Archive for the Extraordinary Jurisdiction (Centraal Archief Bijzondere Rechtspleging, part of the archives of the Justice Ministry, now in the National Archives at The Hague).

CDA: Christian Democratic Appeal (Christen Democratisch Appel) – a political party.

COZO: Central Council for the Purge of Government Employees (Centraal Orgaan op de zuivering van het Overheidspersoneel, COZO), a branch of the Ministery of the Interior.

CPN: Dutch Communist Party (Communistische Partij van Nederland).

DGBR: Directorate General for the Extraordinary Jurisdiction (Directoraat-Generaal voor de Bijzondere Rechtspleging, a branch of the Justice Ministry, responsible for the persecution and punishment of collaborators).

FNJ: Federation of Dutch Journalists (Federatie van Nederlandse Journalisten).

GAC: The Great Advisory Committee of the Resistance (Grote Advies-Commissie der illegaliteit).

GOIWN: Community of Former Resistance Members in the Netherlands (Gemeenschap Oud Illegale Werkers Nederland).

HINAG: Help for Disabled Former Eastern Front Combatants, Surviving Relatives, Political Prisoners and Others (Hulp aan Invalide oud-Oostfrontstrijders, Nabestaanden, politieke Gevangenen en anderen).

JMW:	Jewish Social Service organisation (Joods Maatschappelijk Werk).
KVP:	Catholic People's Party (Katholieke Volkspartij).
MG:	Military Authority (Militair Gezag), the military interim administration, operating under responsibility of the Supreme Headquarters of the Allied Forces in Europe and the Dutch government. (1944–1946)
NEBS:	National-European Socialist Movement (Nationaal-Europese Sociale Beweging), a political movement of former Nazi collaborators in the 1950s.
NBS:	Interior Forces in the Netherlands (Nederlandse Binnenlandse Strijdkrachten), the umbrella organisation for the armed resistance, founded in 1944 under the authority of the Dutch government-in-exile.
NSB:	National Socialist Movement (Nationaal Socialistische Beweging), the main National Socialist political formation in the Netherlands, 1931–1945.
PUR:	Council for Pensions and Relief (Pensioen- en Uitkeringsraad for war- and oppression-related social benefits).
RIOD:	National Institute for War Documentation (Rijksinstituut voor Oorlogsdocumentatie), from 1999 named NIOD (Nederlands Instituut voor Oorlogsdocumentatie), from 2010 named NIOD, Institute for War-, Holocaust- and Genocide Studies.
SOPD:	Foundation for Former Political Delinquents (Stichting Oud-Politieke Delinquenten).
STPD:	Foundation for the Supervision of Political Delinquents (Stichting Toezicht Politieke Delinquenten).
WIV:	Benefit Act for the Dutch Indies Resistance (Wet Indisch Verzet), of 1986.
WPB:	Extraordinary Pension Act 1940–1945 (Wet Buitengewoon Pensioen 1940–1945), of 1947.
WUBO:	Benefit Act for Civilian War Victims (Wet Uitkeringen Burger-Oorlogsslachtoffers) of 1984.
WUV:	Benefit Act for Victims of Persecution (Wet Uitkeringen Vervolgingsslachtoffers), of 1973.

SELECTIVE FURTHER READING

Belinfante, A.D., *In plaats van bijltjesdag. De geschiedenis van de bijzondere rechtspleging na de Tweede Wereldoorlog* (Assen, 1978).

Blom, J.C.H., 'Jaren van tucht en ascese. Enig beschouwingen over de stemming in Herrijzend Nederland (1945–1950)', in idem, *Herrijzend Nederland. Opstellen over Nederland in de periode 1945–1950* (Den Haag, 1981).

BOSSENBROEK, Martin, *De Meelstreep. Terugkeer en opvang na de Tweede Wereldoorlog* (Amsterdam, 2001).

FÜHNER, Harald, *Nachspiel. Die niederländische Politik und die Verfolgung von Kollaborateuren und NS-Verbrechern, 1945–1989* (Münster, 2005).

HAAN, Ido de, *Na de ondergang. De herinnering aan de Jodenvervolging in Nederland, 1945–1995* (Den Haag, 1997).

HIRSCHFELD, Gerhard, *Nazi Rule and Dutch collaboration. The Netherlands under German occupation, 1940–1945* (Oxford, 1988).

HIRSCHFELD, Gerhard, 'Niederlande', in BENZ, Wolfgang (ed.), *Dimension des Völkermords. Die Zahl der jüdischen Opfer des nationalsozialismus* (München, 1991).

HIRSCHFELD, Gerhard and ROMIJN, Peter, 'Die Ahndung der Kollaboration in den Niederlanden' in

HENKE, Klaus-Dietmar und WOLLER, Hans, *Politische Säuberung in Europa. Die Abrechnung mit Faschismus und Kollaboratioin nach dem Zweiten Weltkrieg* (München, 1991), 281–310.

JONG, Loe de, *Het Koninkrijk der Nederlanden in de Tweede Wereldoorlog* 5 (Den Haag 1974), 10b (Den Haag 1981–1982).

MEIHUIZEN, Joggli, *Noodzakelijk kwaad. De bestraffing van economische collaboratie in Nederland na de Tweede Wereldoorlog* (Amsterdam 2003).

MONTERO, Carlos Closa (ed.), *Study on how the memory of crimes committed by totalitarian regimes in Europe is dealt with in the Member States* (Madrid, 2010).

ROMIJN, Peter, *Streng, snel en rechtvaardig. Politiek beleid inzake de bestraffing en reclassering van 'foute' Nederlanders, 1945–1955* (Houten 1989/Amsterdam, 2002, 2nd pr.).

ROMIJN, Peter, 'The image of collaboration in post-war Dutch society' in *1945: Consequences and Sequels of the Second World War, Bulletin of the International Committee for the history of the Second World War* 27/28 (1995) 311–324.

ROMIJN, Peter, '"Restoration of Confidence": the Purge of Local Government in the Netherlands as a Problem of Post-war Reconstruction' in DEAK, Istvan, GROSS, Jan T. and JUDT, Tony (eds.), *The Politics of Retribution in Europe. World War II and its Aftermath* (Princeton, 2000).

VAN DE REIJT, Maud, *Zestig jaar herrie om twee minuten stilte* (Amsterdam, 2010).

WIELENGA, Friso, *Von Feind zum Partner: die Niederlande und Deutschland seit 1945* (Münster, 2000).

WITHUIS, Jolande and MOOIJ, Annet (eds.), *De politics of war trauma. The aftermath of World War II in eleven European countries* (Amsterdam, 2010).

Digital sources

www.niod.knaw.nl/nl/CijfermateriaalDuitsebezetting.htm (statistical data on the German occupation of the Netherlands)

www.joodsmonument.nl (Digital Monument of the Jewish Community in the Netherlands)

FROM RUPTURED TRANSITION TO POLITICS OF SILENCE: THE CASE OF PORTUGAL

Filipa Raimundo and António Costa Pinto

1. THE ANTECEDENTS: THE AUTHORITARIAN REGIME

Portugal experienced a right-wing dictatorship that lasted from 1926, the year in which a military *coup d'état* overthrew the First Republic, until 25 April 1974, when the dictatorship was overthrown by another military coup. There were two different political regimes during this long experience of authoritarianism. Crises and movements calling for the restoration of liberal order blighted the Military Dictatorship established in 1926. Having failed to institutionalise itself, in the beginning of the 1930s, the Military Dictatorship gave way to Salazar's "New State". António de Oliveira Salazar was a conservative Catholic politician and university professor who remained Portugal's dictator until he was incapacitated in 1968. His replacement was one of his disciples, the law professor Marcello Caetano. After a brief period of "liberalisation", the New State was overthrown by the military coup that set Portugal on the path to democracy.

With the restoration of democracy, political scientists found themselves divided between those who classed the New State as "authoritarian", based in the typology developed by Juan J. Linz, or as a type of "fascism without a fascist movement".[1] The Salazarist institutions, created by the 1933 Constitution, formally maintained fundamental freedoms; however, they were successively eliminated by decree. The Constitution retained a directly elected head of state and a parliament (AN – *Assembleia Nacional*) to which deputies were elected from a single list prepared by the single-party, the National Union (UN – *União Nacional*), as well as a corporatist chamber (*Câmara Corporativa*).

1 M. De Lucena, *O Estado da Revolução*, Lisbon, 1978.

According to the 1933 constitution, political crimes were excepted from the prohibition of imprisonment without trial (Article 8); it also permitted "security measures", that is, the extension of prison sentences by administrative decision. With the dictatorship's consolidation, political repression came under the auspices of the regime's political police, the Vigilance and State Defense Police (PVDE – *Polícia de Vigilância e Defesa do Estado*), which was created in 1933 out of the unification of police forces inherited from the Military Dictatorship. Despite two name changes, Salazar's political police maintained a constant presence, and was not abolished until the restoration of democracy in 1974. While formally under the control of the Interior Ministry, its independence increased, dominating throughout the investigation and presentation of cases to the political courts. The PVDE became the spine of the system of repression, arresting, torturing and, occasionally, murdering opponents of the regime. Although this theme will not be developed here, it should nonetheless be noted that the scale of the political police's operations in the colonies grew very quickly between 1961 and 1974, with the development of the colonial wars in Angola, Guinea-Bissau and Mozambique.

In 1927 the dictatorship created the first Special Military Courts (TME – *Tribunais Militares Especiais*), which were established to try pro-democratic rebel officers, and which were soon transformed into what was to be the "authoritarian judiciary" until 1945: the TMEs that tried "political crimes". The use of military courts is a characteristic of many civilian dictatorships; however, in the case of Salazar's "New State" it was also one other facet of the military presence within the authoritarian political system. The press censor, the leadership of the political police and the militia of the "New State", the Portuguese Legion (LP – *Legião Portuguesa*) were all led by members of the armed forces.

The special jails for political prisoners were maintained under the auspices of the political police. There were three such prisons in continental Portugal (Caxias, Peniche and Aljube) and one, in which the conditions were particularly hard, on the Cape Verdian island of Tarrafal, which is where the regime sent mainly anarcho-syndicalists, antifascists, trade unionists and communists in the 1930s. Much academic work has still to be done on the history of political imprisonment in Portugal throughout the authoritarian regime; nonetheless, it is important to stress that the use of extreme violence by the state or the role of the concentration camp as means of controlling the opposition do not particularly characterise the "New State".

Following the victory of the Allies in 1945 and the end of WWII, demonstrations were organised in Portugal calling for the liberalisation of the regime and the closing of Tarrafal. Although no substantial changes occurred in the Portuguese regime following 1945, the truth is that from then, and until 1954, Oliveira Salazar did provide an amnesty to some of the prisoners in Tarrafal, and decided to close down the concentration camp and order the return and imprisonment of the last prisoners in Continental Portugal. On 26 January 1954, Tarrafal was finally closed, only to be opened again in 1962, after the beginning of the colonial wars, to hold the African prisoners of the liberation movements. It is estimated that during the period of 1936 and 1954, the camp received around 340 prisoners, of whom 32 did not survive (AAVV 2006).

Besides imprisonment, the dictatorship also provided itself with legal instruments with which to purge the civil service, allowing it to remove all civil servants who expressed opposition to the government "either in the course of their duties or in their private life". These "purges" were to take place many times, particularly in the wake of legal and clandestine demonstrations. Since 1931 "the active repudiation of communism and of all subversive ideals" came to be a mandatory declaration for those taking a civil service position.

With the end of WWII the New State' underwent some institutional alterations, increasing the 'limited pluralism' within the regime. Opposition to the dictatorship was allowed to operate legally during election campaigns and censorship of the media was less intrusive. The political amnesties that had been granted since the 1930s were now made more extensive. The Tarrafal concentration camp and the prison at Peniche were taken from the political police's control, while the TME were abolished and replaced by civil political courts composed entirely of magistrates: the Plenary Courts (TP – *Tribunais Plenários*) that remained in existence until 1974. It was also in 1945 that the regime established the exceptional application of *habeas corpus*; however, the political police saw their authority strengthened as their monopoly over the trials, and the "security measures", that allowed them to prolong indefinite imprisonment.

There are still no complete figures on the number of political prisoners the regime held during its existence. A commission created in 1977 to collect information on the use of repression by the regime and the number of victims, the Commission on the Black Book on Fascism, estimated that the number was over 30,000 prisoners.

Table 1.1. Political prisoners (1932–74[2])

Period	Prisoners
1932–35	2368
1936–39	9575
1940–45	4952
1949–51	1838
1952–60	3740
1961–74	1132

After the Military Dictatorship, there were some characteristics of the political repression that remained constant during the New State: political repression affected both ideological pro-democratic dissidents and, in particular, the organised clandestine groups. There is a powerful correlation between anti-dictatorship political activism and the subsequent repression. From 1945 political repression was increasingly "judicialised"; opponents were rarely murdered (although a main leader of the opposition, General H. Delgado, was killed by the political police, in Spain), but the political police was able to prolong the imprisonment with almost no restrictions.

Oliveira Salazar was replaced by Marcello Caetano in 1968. Caetano reformulated some of the regime's institutions and allowed the softening of censorship and political repression during the first year of his premiership. Mário Soares, an opposition leader, was authorised to return to Lisbon from exile. But in 1969, after non-free and non-competitive elections, it was clear that Salazar's successor had initiated a process of 'liberalisation' without democratisation.

2. THE PORTUGUESE WAY TO DEMOCRACY: A TRANSITION BY RUPTURE

The Portuguese military *coup* of 25 April 1974 launched the beginning of the "third wave" of democratic transitions in southern Europe. In contrast to what happened in neighbouring Spain, it was a transition without negotiation between the dictatorial elite and opposition forces. The coup was led by middle-rank military, in the midst of a three-front colonial war in Angola, Mozambique and Guinea-Bissau.

The role of the military is not only a unique feature of the Portuguese case; it is also a very important one. The colonels who initially formed the Armed Forces

2 Comissão do Livro Negro sobre o Fascismo (Commission for the Black Book on Fascism).

Movement (MFA – *Movimento das Forças Armadas*) did not hand over power to the civilians immediately after the coup. On the day of the coup, a group of seven Generals formed the National Salvation Junta (JSN – *Junta de Salvação Nacional*), and in March 1975, due to internal conflicts between the Generals and the colonels, the JSN was dissolved and the Council of the Revolution was established (CR – *Conselho da Revolução*). Although the first free elections did take place in April 1975 (to elect the Constituent Assembly) and again in April 1976 (to elect the first constitutional government), the CR was not dissolved until 1982. Consequently, the military became the dominant force behind the provisional governments throughout 1974 and 1975, and maintained constitutional supervision powers until 1982, which is important in understanding some features of the transitional justice process conducted during the first two years of the transition.

Although Portugal experienced a transition by rupture, there was almost no violence. Carnations became the symbol of the revolution. In fact, on the day of the coup, the only site of armed resistance was at a political police headquarters and lasted until the morning of 26 April 1974. The only fatal cases happened outside the Lisbon headquarters of the political police, where four individuals were shot dead (including one political police officer who tried to escape) and 45 were injured.

It was the nature of the transition that created a window of opportunity to adopt punitive measures against the former regime. This was a period marked by the crisis of the state, by powerful social movements and military intervention that shaped social attitudes concerning the punishment of those associated with the old regime, and in which the judiciary played almost no role. Disagreements concerning the nature of decolonisation among the military, the implementation of the agrarian reform, the nationalisation of large economic groups, and the support given to many civil society groups contributed to this crisis of the state. The perception of a power vacuum created a window of opportunity for various types of actors to break with the previous regime and remove from their posts all those associated with it. On 25 November 1975 a communist-inspired coup failed and was countered by the right wing of the army. That event marked the real beginning of democratic consolidation. It was only in 1982, the year in which the Constitutional Court was created, that democracy became consolidated.

As in the majority of European countries, transitional justice in Portugal was a domestic affair. As it will be explained bellow, the main decision-makers were the provisional governments (partly composed of military men) and the military. There is no available information on possible international influences that may have helped shape the process but if such influence existed, it was not decisive.

The next section will present the major phases of the process, the legislation produced to deal with the past, its targets and major outcomes.

3. TRANSITIONAL JUSTICE – TRIALS AND PURGES

3.1. THE FIRST PHASE: TRANSITIONAL JUSTICE BASED ON AN ALLEGED REVOLUTIONARY LEGALITY (APRIL 1974–DECEMBER 1975)

The first and central phase of the transitional justice process occurred between 25 April 1974 and December 1975, after the conservative forces brought the revolutionary period to an end. This period corresponds more or less to the first 20 months of democratic transition following the *coup d'état* and was characterised by an intensive break with the past, facilitated by the state crisis and political radicalisation. Many of the measures adopted during this period were based on an alleged 'revolutionary legality'.

The political elite were the first to be put aside, although it suffered no severe punishment. On 25 April, the president of the republic, the cabinet ministers, the leaders of the single party, and civil governors were immediately dismissed (Law 1/74, Law 170/74 and Decree Law 172/74 of 25 April 1974). Other members of the political elite, such as the MPs, were also dismissed during the following days (Law 2/74 of 14 May 1974). In the majority of cases, these individuals received little more punishment than being prevented from voting or from running in the first free elections, which took place in April 1975. Only a few of the high officials of the regime were sent into exile, including the President of the Republic, Américo Tomás, who was sent into exile to Madeira Island on 26 April by the military. On 20 May, together with his family, Tomás was sent to Rio de Janeiro, Brazil, where he spent four years in exile.

On 26 April 1974 all political prisoners were amnestied, including those accused of violent actions, like the execution of political police informants. On the day of the *coup* there were 85 political prisoners in Caxias and 43 in Peniche.[3] There were also a reduced number of political prisoners in Coimbra and Oporto. They were all liberated between the first and the second day of the transition. Four days later, the armed forces authorised the return of the political exiles (who in fact had already begun arriving). Mário Soares – who would later become Prime

[3] Madeira, J. and Pimentel, I., *Vítimas de Salazar. Estado Novo e Violência Política*, Lisbon, 2007.

Minister – arrived on 28 April, whereas Álvaro Cunhal – Secretary General of the Communist Party – arrived on 30 April.[4]

During this period, transitional justice had two major fronts: first, the legal, and in some cases "wild", purges of the state apparatus (bureaucrats, professors, the armed forces, police forces, etc.); and second, the trials of the functionaries and collaborators of the Information and State Defence Police (*Polícia de Informação e Defesa do Estado* [1945–68], PIDE/DGS) –Directorate General of Security (*Direcção Geral de Segurança* [1968–74]). Whereas the purges were mainly adopted by provisional governments, in the case of the trials against the former political police, the process was mainly conducted by the politico-military institutions created in 1974 and 1975. To a lesser extent, the private sector was also affected by this climate of break with the past, during which the population was particularly active and supportive.

3.1.1. The purge of the military, the civil service, and the judiciary

The first institution to undergo a purge process was actually the military.[5] Immediately after the coup, the MFA handed to the chief representative of the JSN, General Spínola, the names of the 60 generals who had pledged their allegiance to the authoritarian regime, and who were subsequently placed on reserve. Special military commissions administrated the purges. According to decree law 775/74, incompetence became the official criterion for removal, as it became impossible to sustain political criteria such as 'collaboration with the old regime', given that the whole defence establishment had collaborated with the New State during the colonial war. After 11 March 1975 – when an aborted military coup gave strength to the left-wing sectors of the MFA – the purge movement was reinforced and the majority of the officers working with General Spínola, were themselves also removed from their posts. In addition, civilians working in military institutions were as well as the militarised police body, the National Republican Guard (GNR – *Guarda Nacional Republicana*) were also purged. According to the decree law 147C/75, 21 March 1975, those who did not "obey the principles espoused by the MFA" were to be placed in the reserve.

Civil servants were probably the most affected by the radicalisation of popular action and the overwhelming spirit of breaking with the past. It all started

4 There are no figures available on the number of returning exiles. The fact that political exiles coincided in the 1960s with the economic emigration and the colonial wars in Africa makes this task even more difficult.

5 A.C. Pinto, 'Authoritarian Legacies, transitional justice and state crisis in Portugal's democratization', *Democratization*, 13(2006), No. 2, 173–204.

with Decree Law 277/74, 25 June 1974, which declared that civil servants could be purged for three reasons: non-democratic behaviour in the course of duty after the coup, inability to adapt to the new democratic regime and incompetence. The minimum punishment was to be transferred to another post (article 4), while the maximum was immediate and compulsory dismissal (articles 2 and 3). All former officials of the political police were to be dismissed. Maximum penalties were applied according to priorities defined later by the government: membership of the dictatorships' governmental elite; political police collaborators; leading members of either from Portuguese Youth (MP – *Mocidade Portuguesa*), the LP or the single party; and the heads of the dictatorship's censorship's board. The law also determined the creation of an Inter-ministerial Purge and Reclassification Commission (*Comissão Inter-Ministerial de Saneamento e Reclassificação*) to undertake this mission. The commission was linked directly to the Council of Ministers and was charged with the co-ordination of the existing purge commissions in the ministries. At the end of 1974 about 4,300 public servants had been subjected to a purge process.[6]

Again, the purge process was reinforced after 11 March 1975. Consequently, decree Law 123/75 referred to the previous regime as a "fascist regime" and determined that purges could be administrated based on individual political behaviour before the fall of the authoritarian regime. In February 1975, official reports on the purge process stated that approximately 12,000 people had been either removed from their posts or suspended. It is estimated that between March and November 1975 the number of removals and suspensions increased significantly: on 25 November of that year, when purges were interrupted, if one takes into consideration all kinds of institutions and sanctions, the number had risen to 20,000.[7]

Generally speaking, the purge process was not governed by a clear strategy and revealed no coherent pattern, varying greatly from sector to sector. Various institutions were involved in the purge process. Aside from the measures adopted by the JSN and the MFA immediately after the coup, the Portuguese Communist Party (PCP – *Partido Comunista Português*) and other small influential parties of the extreme left were the main actors involved. The purges of the state apparatus were uneven and limited; where strong pressure from trade unions and workers' commissions was exerted, as in the Ministries of Labour and Education, forced removals were more frequent. Indeed, while reports indicate that most of the people purged belonged to the higher levels of

6 Unfortunately, reliable figures are not available in the majority of cases and the existing numbers do not always match.

7 Numbers extracted from different media sources. The exact number is unknown.

the administration, in these cases lower ranking civil servants were also affected, particularly for collaboration with the political police.

It is difficult to determine how the purges affected the state bureaucracy on a quantitative level. The process evolved differently from ministry to ministry, depending on the level of pressure from the trade unions and the limits imposed by the legislation. According to the global analysis made by the commission that co-ordinated the process, the action of the various ministerial commissions was very uneven. Some of the most affected ministries were the Ministry of Labour and the Ministry of Education. The JSN removed all university deans and directors of faculties from their posts, and various high-ranking members of the Ministry were transferred. In the secondary schools, the more radical actions by the student movement forced the military to intervene to protect the accused. It was in the universities, however, that both legal and "wild" purges were most thorough, given the very strong pressures exerted by the student movement. Some members of the commissions quickly resigned in protest against the 'wild' purges, which were sometimes undertaken in the absence of any legal proceedings. Students would simply deny some professors entry to the university following assembly votes, although only a small number of those "condemned" were ever submitted to legal purge proceedings by the purge commission of the Ministry of Education. The most radical 'wild' purges took place in the Faculty of Law of the University of Lisbon, where an assembly dominated by a Maoist party decided to purge some members of the Council of State and leaders of the conservative parties, against the will of PCP students. Legal purge proceedings against professors and education workers were more solidly based on two criteria: holding high-level posts under the dictatorship, or collaboration with repression by the political police by denouncing students and opposition professors. As in the Ministry of Labour, the latter category was the most sought after, and purges affected people in the lower ranks who gave information to the PIDE-DGS. Some professors affected by the purges went into other professional activities and others emigrated to Brazil.

Within the Ministry of Foreign Affairs, the purge process was limited to a few members of the diplomatic corps who had held government posts under the dictatorship. When he was nominated Minister of Foreign Affairs, in May 1974, Mário Soares merely transferred some ambassadors, and the purge commission, although fully constituted, worked only in those consulates where collaboration with the political police had been most notable. This was the case in Brazil and France, for example; countries with large Portuguese immigrant communities, where the consulates had been involved in controlling the activities of political exiles.

One of the least affected ministries was the Ministry of Justice, particularly magistrates and the political courts of the dictatorship, the "plenary courts". A good part of the moderate left elite associated with the Socialist Party (PS – *Partido Socialista*) was made up of lawyers that had participated in the first political trials of the 'New State'. At the same time, the Salazarist elite had a large component of law professors, and the regime had always obsessively attempted to legitimate its acts in juridical terms. In the end, corporate factors and, above all, the moderation of socialist leaders were important elements counteracting this impetus to purge the legal profession and Ministry of Justice.

3.1.2. The political police

The political police (PIDE/DGS) was immediately dismantled, together with the dictatorship's anti-communist militia, the Portuguese Legion (LP) (Decree Law 171/74 of 25 April 1974). Several of its officers were arrested within days and held in preventive detention for a period of more or less twenty months.[8] Others were either helped or simply managed to flee the country, namely to Spain and France. Amongst those who fled the country were many of the members of the upper echelons of PIDE/DGS. In the colonies, the political police was renamed Military Information Police.

The punishment of the former officials and collaborators of the political police was one of the main popular demands, which turned into a "PIDE-hunt". For more than a year, several officers of the political police were arrested by the military, often with the help of the population, who denounced their neighbours and in some cases family members. The arrests were undertaken by the military themselves, through a structure called the Operation Command for Continental Portugal (*Comando Operacional do Continente*, COPCON). The (left-wing leaning) newspapers of that time reported that around 1,000 individuals were arrested but numbers cannot be considered reliable.

In order to proceed with the dismantling of the political police and try its members, the military created the Commission for the Abolition of the Political Police, Portuguese Legion and Portuguese Youth (*Comissão de Extinção da PIDE/DGS e LP*) in June 1974. However, the law that criminalised the repressive institutions was not issued before July 1975. The lack of coordination, the inexistence of specific legislation to punish the wrongdoers and other more

8 F. Raimundo, *The Double Face of Heroes. Transitional justice and the political police (PIDE/DGS) in Portugal's democratization (1974–6)*, Institute of Social Sciences, University of Lisbon, Dissertation, December 2007.

urgent matters led to a lack of decision-making and the postponement of the trials.[9]

Law 8/75 (hereafter "Pide Law") defined the political police as 'an organisation of political and social terrorism' whose goal was to 'prevent the free exercise of civic rights' in Portugal. Given the PIDE's 'arbitrary and inhuman practices' it was necessary to criminalise the institution and punish its members. Their punishment was justified on the basis of a "revolutionary legitimacy". Still according to the preamble of the law, PIDE's 'prolonged existence and the use of physical and psychological torture' attested that "there were publicly known and widespread acts which no officer or collaborator can ever claim not to have been aware of". The goal of the law was to "repair the historical injustice" committed for "dozens of years" and to respond to the "overwhelming demand coming from the collective consciousness of the Portuguese people on the need to punish those responsible for fascist repression".

The law punished individuals not for their actions but for their affiliation or collaboration with the political police. Sentences were applied according to the individual's placement in the hierarchy, from Minister of Interior to collaborator. Sentences could range from two to twelve years of imprisonment. However, the trials did not begin before 1976, as it will be explained later.

3.1.3. The economic elites

During the first two years of the transition, the economic elite were also hit hard by the process of nationalisation and state intervention, as well as by the flight of industrialists and entrepreneurs from the country. The "wild" purges were concentrated in the large enterprises in the industrial area around Lisbon and in the banking and insurance sectors. As early as May 1974, the purge of this elite was the third demand of a group of 149 labour conflicts (the first was minimum wage and the second the right to strike), and it remained on the top of the list of demands made by workers and strikers throughout the following year. The Worker's Commissions (*Comissões de Trabalhadores*) often called for purges, which led to the first self-exiles. These purges were established within businesses independently of the unions, and the PCP shared control of these bodies with the parties of the extreme left. These commissions implemented the great majority of "wild" purges.[10]

---

9 F. Raimundo, *The Double Face of Heroes.*

10 A.C. Pinto, 'Political Purges and State Crisis in Portugal's Transition to Democracy', *Journal of Contemporary History*, 43 (2008) No. 2, 305–332, at 315.

Table 3.1. Transitional justice between April 1974 and December 1975[11]

Measure and source	Period referred to	Number and category
Purges: Removal and suspension including by the initiative of the purge commissions and "wild" (approximate numbers)	May 74–December 74	4,293 civil servants. Education and Culture (1,029), Economy (891), Internal Affairs (737), Social Affairs (329), Labour (317), Environment (303), Inter-territorial Co-ordination (278), Finance (191), Foreign Affairs (87), Justice (59), Presidency of the CM (43), Information (29)
Purges: Removal and on reserve	April 74–December 74	300 officers of all ranks and from the three services, of whom around 103 were navy officers
Removal and suspension, legally and illegally	April 74–February 75	+ 12,000 ministers, armed forces, former corporatist apparatus, public sector, economy
Several measures adopted by Purge commissions	1974–76	2,036 individuals: 289 dismissed 2 dismissed and compulsorily retired 107 compulsory retirement 13 suspended 56 transferred (1,564 unknown situations)
Preventive detention	June 1975	843 former officials and collaborators (only in Alcoentre prison)

The whole process became a milestone of civil society involvement in Portugal, particularly with the active participation of trade unions and workers' commissions, small political groups and parties of different left-wing and extreme-left ideologies. In fact, the actions undertaken by these and other strong grassroots political organisations, plus the growing challenge posed by the extreme left during the crisis, and its influence within the military, were at the origin of the period known as the "Hot Summer" of 1975. This was a period that lasted until November 1975, during which it is often considered that Portugal was close to a civil war.[12] Portuguese society began to polarise, fed by the development of strong grassroots political organisations such as the workers'

11 A.C. Pinto, Authoritarian Legacies; F. Raimundo, The Double Face of Heroes.

12 A.C. Pinto, *Authoritarian Legacies.*

commissions, the growing challenge posed by the extreme Left and its influence within the military. This was followed by the emergence of a strong anti-communist movement in the North of the country, comprising conservative notables, members of the military and the Catholic Church. The end of the "Hot Summer", on 25 November 1975, with the retreat of the communists and the "victory" of the moderate forces (inside and out of the MFA, with the support of the Socialist Party and the Social Democratic Party), corresponds to the end of this phase.

3.2. THE SECOND PHASE: THE ESTABLISHMENT OF DEMOCRATIC LEGALITY (DECEMBER 1975–1982)

The second phase came with the end of the revolutionary period, in December 1975. The new Constitution was approved in April 1976, after which the first constitutional governments were formed. However, political power remained under the tutelage of the Council of Revolution (the military organ that replaced the JSN in March 1975) until 1982. This phase was characterised by two major events: the trials of the former members of the political police – often seen as show trials – and the reintegration of a significant part of those purged during the first months of the transition. This was also the period in which the first rehabilitation measures were passed, although the number of victims was significantly low, and hence the impact of the measures was also limited.

In general, the decisions made during this period entailed a tacit agreement not to condemn some of the excesses of the revolutionary period, while the previous regime's misdeeds were also somehow forgiven. The official discourse of the first two constitutional governments led by the socialist Prime Minister, Mário Soares, and by the first democratically elected president, General Ramalho Eanes, favoured "reconciliation" and "pacification". The goal was now to proceed with the reintegration of a large proportion of those who had been condemned.

3.2.1. The military trials

The establishment of democratic legality meant the release on parole of the former officers of the political police, based on law 18/75.[13] Those who had been arrested in April 1974 had been waiting in preventive detention for 20 months without formal accusation. Under the new legislation, they were not only released on parole but they were also entitled to appeal to the Supreme Court because they had been convicted by the territorial military courts.

---

13 F. Raimundo, *The Double Face of Heroes.*

The trials began in late 1976 and for that reason they have been seen as show trials, meant to silence the voices of those who demanded justice. Special military courts were created in Lisbon; trials took place in Lisbon, Oporto, Coimbra and Tomar. The Military Code of Justice was applied, except for the cases in which crimes had been committed and could be proved, in which the Penal Code was used. The decision was taken based on the files and records of the political police itself, using the following criteria: the period of collaboration, work undertaken in the colonies or not. Letters from relatives, friends and fellow citizens helped to downgrade the sentence. Those who had good military active service reports from the colonial war period received especially benevolent treatment.

The military court sentences were much lighter than the "Pide Law" had initially led many to believe and a significant number of those who were in fact tried did not have to serve any prison terms as a result of the pardons granted by the military in the meantime. A total of 2,667 individuals were prosecuted, including chief inspectors and collaborators. Existing numbers indicate that only five per cent of the 2,667 individuals were absolved and three per cent lost their political rights. The remaining 92 per cent were convicted and given prison terms. Sentences ranged from one month to more than two years. A sample of trial sentences analysed indicates: around 80 per cent of the individuals who were tried belonged to the middle-lower ranks; the large majority were set free, based on the fact that they spent around twenty months in preventive detention; many were given up to 180 days of pardon, which significantly reduced their sentences; and, when this was not enough to prevent them from returning to jail, they appealed to the Supreme Court, where their sentences were frequently reduced.[14]

Although there were public demonstrations and criticism of the sentences meted out, they did serve as notice that judicial legality and the rule of law had been re-established following the "excesses" of the turbulent years 1974–75. In the end, the upper echelons were never punished – even if they were prosecuted *in absentia* – except for very few cases.[15]

Disappointment in the face of light sentences led to the creation of a public body known as the Humberto Delgado Popular Tribunal (*Tribunal Cívico Humberto Delgado*), inspired by the Russell Tribunal. Established in 1977, the tribunal sought to mobilise public opinion for the criminalisation and condemnation of the former regime and in particular its most notorious repressive institution: the

14 F. Raimundo, *The Double Face of Heroes.*

15 The legal aspects of the process of transitional justice against the officials of the political (????) have not been studied so far.

political police The popular tribunal was named after General Delgado, who stood against Salazar in the 1958 presidential elections and was later assassinated by the political police in one of the few cases of political death by Salazar's regime. It declared the regime guilty of violating civil freedoms; political, cultural and economic rights and the right to self-determination. It also condemned the decision to send the former President into exile without being held accountable for the wrongdoings committed by the former regime.

The actual trial of those accused of the death of General Humberto Delgado took place in 1978, at the Santa Clara Court in Lisbon. The final sentence of the court stated that "the PIDE brigade was not there to kill, only to arrest the General", and therefore his death was an accident. Only one of the defendants was considered guilty – Casimiro Monteiro (tried *in absentia*) – while the others were set free.

3.2.2. The reintegration of perpetrators

Between 1976 and the early 1980s, steps were taken to reintegrate those who had been victims of the purges. New legislation was passed and measures were quickly adopted to normalise the situation in the economic arena where "wild" purges had been most severe. Soon after the introduction of these new laws, the Council of the Revolution ordered "all officials of the armed forces who had been assigned to the purge commissions in private enterprises" to return to their barracks. The government followed this up with a series of measures that were designed to allow the return of the exiles who had been forced out by the purges. Decree-law 471/76 declared that the ideologically motivated purges carried out by workers in the private and public sectors between 1974 and 1976, and "which had not observed" the laws that were then in force, were legally null and void.

A Commission for the Assessment of Purge Appeals and Reclassifications (CARSR – *Comissão de Análise de Recursos de Saneamentos e de Reclassificação*) was created in February 1976 (Decree-Law 117-A/76) and continued in operation until the mid-1980s, rehabilitating the vast majority of appellants who came before it. It was composed of legally qualified military officials and civilians with no links with the previous regime. According to a report into its activities, the commission expressed the view that "it is necessary to repair the damage that was done during the 1974–75 period, when many of the purges were 'merely arbitrary'" (*Arquivo Nacional Torre do Tombo/Conselho da Revolução*, CARSR, *Relatório de Actividades*, 1976–1977–1978).

Taking advantage of the new situation, the victims of the purges organised themselves into the Movement for the Reintegration of the Unfairly Dismissed (MPDJC – *Movimento Pró-reintegração dos Despedidos sem Justa Causa*), which could count on the new private newspapers to fight in their corner. The trade union movement protested against the reintegration of those who had been purged by holding strikes and even some sporadic sit-ins. But these actions, which mainly affected the recently nationalised state enterprises and the civil service, were largely unsuccessful.

The purge commissions in the ministries ceased to operate in 1976, and the Council of the Revolution, which took on the role of these commissions as well as the leadership of the CEPML, reinforced legal mechanisms to ensure that a process of rehabilitation took place. A moderate member of the Council of the Revolution, Captain Sousa e Castro, was given responsibility for the entire process. Most of those who had been dismissed during the purges had their punishment altered to compulsory retirement; the remainder often received a payment in lieu of lost earnings and restoration of their seniority for the purpose of calculating pension entitlements. In some cases in which trade union or student resistance to the reintegration was particularly vociferous, those who were to be reintegrated were simply transferred to other institutions or remained at home until emotions calmed down before returning to their posts. In some universities reintegration of those who had been purged did not begin until the early-1980s. One case, that of Veiga Simão, Caetano's Minister of Education, was decided by the Council of the Revolution itself; however, the great majority were left to Sousa e Castro and his CARSR.

Between 1976 and 1978 these commissions reassessed around 3,000 trials within the various government ministries and nationalised industries, most of which concerned officials of the previous regime's political police. In the case of PIDE-DGS agents, the CARSR followed the precedent established by the military tribunals: these tribunals had heard the cases against political police agents, and had decided that "the fact that those being tried were former agents of the PIDE-DGS is irrelevant because it was not illegal in the past to be a member of the political police" (See Table 3.2). This principal restored their rights as public employees to them, but only if they had not 'taken part in illegal activities'.[16]

In 1978, the bank accounts of the last President of the former regime were un-frozen and President Ramalho Eanes authorised his return on the basis of "humanitarian reasons". This gave way to protests from extreme left-wing groups who formed the Unitary Commission against the return of Américo Tomás (*Comissão Unitária contra o regresso de Américo Tomás*). Despite of that, Tomás returned to Portugal on 23 July 1978 were he would die of old age. Similarly, Marcelo Caetano was also put on a plane, first to Madeira, and later to Brazil.

---

16 A.C. Pinto, *Political Purges and State Crisis.*

Caetano was also given the chance to return but he refused to come back to Portugal and would die in Brazil in 1980.

Table 3.2. Trials and reintegration numbers (December 1975–82)[17]

Trials		
Parole	December 75–February 76	640 former political police officers
Military Court Sentences (some were tried *in absentia*; sentences do not consider the period of preventive detention or pardons)	1976–1982	144 - absolved 103 - loss of political rights 995 - less than 1 month of prison 825 - 1 to 6 months of prison 161 - 6 moths to 1 year 396 - 1 to 2 years 43 - more than two years Total= 2,667
Reintegration		
Purge proceedings reassessed by the CARSR	1976–1978	3,351 individuals within the various government ministries and nationalised industries, mostly collaborators of the former political police. From a list of 2,031 trials reassessed: 6 were dismissed 109 were compulsorily retired 175 were suspended 29 were transferred 1,353 were reintegrated 130 had their punishment annulled 196 saw their trials archived (received the same sentence as before)

It can be said that until 1982, Portugal solved most of its transitional justice issues. The measures just described seem to have closed the debate on the past and seem to have generated some sort of catharses. Politically, the fact that the single party was immediately dissolved and the absence of a 'post-Salazarist' party seem to have helped dissipate the issue. In addition, there is one article in the Portuguese Constitution that prohibits fascist ideology and symbols (article 46), which is until today part of the Constitution.[18] Every year, the transition to democracy is celebrated, but there is no major political debate on the past or civil society claim for compensation or acknowledgment of resistance, as it will be explained in the next section.

17 F. Raimundo, *The Double Face of Heroes*; A.C. Pinto, *Political Purges and State Crisis.*

18 In the 1990s, despite criticism regarding its usefulness, it was used by the Constitutional Court to ban a political group (MAN – Movimento de Acção Nacional), formed in 1985 with neo-fascist ideology. The trial had considerable media coverage, as it was the first such case on trial, however the party disbanded itself before the court's decision.

4. THE POST-TRANSITIONAL JUSTICE PERIOD (1982–)

Since democratic consolidation, there have been two main issues on the agenda: the archives of the dictator and of the political police and the acknowledgment of the struggle for democracy and the years of repression. Although some heated debates did take place in the 1990s, overall the past has not resurfaced in Portugal with the same intensity as in other post-authoritarian countries.

4.1. THE ARCHIVES

As is the case with other democratic transitions, the fate of the defeated regime's archives was a topic of heated debate. Given the nature of the regime's fall, the military took possession of the PIDE-DGS archives, which consequently survived almost entirely intact. Perhaps more importantly, Salazar's own personal archive survived. These documents, meticulously maintained by Salazar himself, had been kept in the Presidency of the Council of Ministers' offices following his death in 1970, and contain an account of 40 years of Portuguese political life. Both the PIDE-DGS and the Salazar archives have been deposited in the national archive, where, like all other New State documents, they are open to public inspection.

Parliamentary debates concerning the future of the archive were often heated and passionate, with some parties calling for their destruction. Important public debates about the archives began in the 1990s, when these were opened to the public. One such debate, provoked in 1996 by a former socialist minister who had been a victim of the PIDE-DGS, focused on the return of letters, photographs and other materials confiscated by the political police to their original owners or their heirs. Although some defended this course of action during the parliamentary debates that ensued, the negative reaction of the majority of historians ensured that the collections remained in the national archive. Their incorporation into the national archives, in August 1991, and consequent limited release to the public was a controversial victory for historians and left-wing parties.

The current law determines that if the person identified in the case is still alive, or has been dead for less than 50 years, their file may be consulted only with permission from the individual concerned or from their descendents. The other documents, expunged of names, are open for consultation.

4.2. REPARATION MEASURES FOR VICTIMS

Compensation of victims of the authoritarian regime was regulated for the first time in 1977. Victims had to wait until 1977 for the first constitutional government to acknowledge their "exceptional acts in the defence of freedom and democracy". Ironically, victim compensation was regulated through legislation created during the New State. In 1929, a pension was established to compensate citizens for "exceptional and relevant services to the country" (decree law 17335, 10 September 1929); the law was later changed by decree-law 47084, 9 July 1966. This decree-law was initially used to regulate pensions established by *decree law 171/77*, by the Socialist Prime Minister Mário Soares, for exceptional merits in the defence of freedom and democracy. After the dissolution of the Council of the Revolution, in 1982, new legislation was issued to regulate the attribution of pensions and the most important changed was made in 2003 (see Table 4.1).

Table 4.1. Legislation on pensions for exceptional acts in the defence of freedom and democracy

Decree Law 171/77, 30 April, establishes a pension for exceptional merits in the defence of freedom and democracy
Decree Law 43/78, 11 March, determines that pensions should be attributed according to decree law 47084, 9 July 1966 and adds the requisite of proof
Normative Decree H/80, 9 January, clarifies decree law 171/77 and the subsequent changes
Decree Law 31/81, 28 February, gives the Council of Ministers the possibility of fixing the pensions to be attributed
Decree Law 215/87, 29 May, establishes that pensions are attributed jointly by the Prime Minister and the Minister of Finances
Decree-Law 189/2003, 22 August, clarifies the conditions under which pensions are attributed and revokes all previous decree laws that regulated this specific pension

Source: Own work compiled from www.dre.pt.

The legislation currently in force was issued in 2003, by a Social Democratic government headed by Prime Minister José Manuel Durão Barroso (*decree-law 189/2003*). It added to the previous ones the requirement that the attribution should be preceded by a favourable approval by the Attorney General. It extended the list of potential beneficiaries in case of the death of the proposed recipient. The attribution of the this pension has been often controversial in cases where the pension was given to: a) "deserters", i.e., members of the military who opposed the regime and, instead of fighting in the colonial wars, chose to flee the country; b) individuals responsible for terrorist acts; c) former political police officials. Table 4.2 indicates the number of beneficiaries in the first years after the pension was established (the full list is not accessible).

Table 4.2. Number of beneficiaries of financial compensation (until 2006)

Year	No. of beneficiaries
1981	4
1982	5
1983	3
1984	22
1985	20
1986	1
1987	1
1988–2004	35
2004	18
2005–2006	23
Total	132

Source: Raimundo 2012

In 1997, a Socialist government headed by Prime Minister António Guterres approved a law of compensation for the anti-Salazar opposition in terms of social security and retirement pension entitlements, for the time spent underground or in exile (Law 20/97). In order to qualify, the claimants must be able to provide evidence of "time spent, either within the country or abroad, during which they were victims of political persecution that impeded their ability to engage in normal professional activities and prevented their social insertion into the community because of their membership in a political group, or their participation in political activities destined to promote democracy" between 28 May 1926 and 25 April 1974. The application is analysed by a commission composed of three members from three ministries (Internal Affairs, Justice and Solidarity, and Finances). In case of a favourable decision, the local social security is informed in order to proceed with the payment. Table 4.3 indicates the number of applicants and beneficiaries since 1997.

Table 4.3. Number of applicants and beneficiaries of law 20/97 (1997–2009)

Number of requests	1,329
Number of beneficiaries	908

Source: Numbers provided by the staff of the Portuguese Social Security

4.3. SYMBOLIC REPARATIONS

During these more than 30 years of democracy, successive Presidents of the Republic have publicly acknowledged the anti-Salazar opposition and other individuals with democratic credentials by awarding them the "Order of Freedom". The award was founded in 1976 and it is the 'youngest' of the Portuguese Honourific Orders. It was created to acknowledge "Portuguese or foreign citizens who have distinguished themselves for their love of freedom and devotion to the cause of human rights and social justice, in particular in defence of Republican and democratic ideals". Only the President or a member of government is allowed to suggest individuals to be distinguished. Throughout the years the award has lost some of its meaning, given the multiplicity of people to whom it has been awarded.

Table 4.4. Number of people and institutions that have been awarded the Order of Freedom (as of May 2011)

Nationality	Number
National (individual and collective)	428
International	41

Source: www.ordens.presidencia.pt (retrieved on February 2012)

A number of popular organisations were created after April 1974 to demand support and justice for the victims and political prisoners of the regime, but most of these organisations did not outlive the transition. Two organisations were particularly relevant. One was the Association of Former anti-fascist Political Prisoners (AEPPA – *Associação de Ex-Presos Politicos Anti-Fascistas*), created in 1974 and associated with an extreme-left political party (UDP). Throughout their existence, they published several propaganda brochures on the victims of the regime and they were particularly active in demanding the punishment of the political police. The other was the Portuguese Antifascist Resistant Union (URAP – *União de Resistentes Antifascistas Portugueses*), born from the Commission for the Rescue of Political Prisoners (*Comissão de Socorro aos Presos Políticos*), which opposed the regime. Although this organisation still exists today, its presence has been modest.

Within the Parliament, and throughout the 1980s, the Communist Party was the main force responsible for the acknowledgment and remembering of the victims of repression. In several occasions, as in the anniversary of the creation of the concentration camp of Tarrafal, or the anniversary of the death of Humberto Delgado, a minute of silence was held in Parliament in honour of the victims.[19]

---

19 Several references at http://debates.parlamento.pt.

4.4. REMEMBRANCE AND TRUTH TELLING

Portugal did not experience the establishment of any truth-seeking type mechanisms. The state body that came closest to the classical "truth-commission" was the "Commission for the Black Book on Fascism" (*Comissão do Livro Negro sobre o Fascismo*), which was created in April 1977, thus appearing after the process of purges and criminal proceedings and during the period when Portugal was reconciling with the past and overcoming its legacies. This was a governmental organism built to denounce the abuses of the authoritarian regime; it brought together well-known former opposition members, Socialists, Communists and Freemasons. The commission was responsible to the presidency of the Council of Ministers and was composed of socialist and left-republican intellectuals and politicians. Using all of the dictatorship's archives as a source, the Commission published 22 books containing primary documentation, which, amongst other issues, denounced the regime's repression, the treatment of political prisoners, censorship, and the collaboration between economic groups and the political police.

A project to turn the "Commission on the Black Book on Fascism" into a Museum of the Resistance failed to garner the support of the centre-right government of Cavaco Silva in 1991. Since then, a few groups and organisations were born that partially fill in the gap, such as the Museum of the Republic and Resistance, an initiative of the Lisbon City Council and, to a certain extent, the Mário Soares Foundation, created by the former President of Republic. A new museum called "Museum of Resistance and Freedom" was recently inaugurated in Lisbon in the former prison of Aljube, where several notorious members of the opposition were imprisoned. This was the result of negotiations between the Lisbon City Council, the Ministry of Justice and one civil society organisation: the "Do Not Erase the Memory" (NAM – *Não Apaguem a Memória*).[20]

There is a lack of memorialisation of the dictatorship in Portugal, expressed by the absence of museums and exhibitions. Probably the most important so far dates back to November 1999, with the opening of an official exhibition on the twentieth century in Portugal, with the sponsorship of the Presidency and the government, to celebrate 25 years of Portuguese democracy. It was aimed at large public and at students. The exhibition included examples of the torture chambers of the political police and corridors lined with photographs of political

20 The NAM is a left-wing group that claims to be composed by representatives of the various tendencies, including Socialists, former Communists and the Left-Bloc, has been particularly involved in struggles for the preservation of memory. They claim to react against the attempt to erase the memory of anti-fascist resistance.

prisoners, while opposition figures and the pro-democratic press were celebrated. There was also a threatening corridor dedicated to the colonial war, which ended in a well-lit area celebrating the fall of the dictatorship. In Portugal, the creation of museums about repression and the dictatorship is notably absent. All such projects presented in the first two years of the transition were abandoned because of a lack of interest within civil society, including from political parties such as the PS or the PCP, or a lack of enthusiasm on the part of the state.

Nonetheless, the majority of the acts of memorialisation have been carried out either by specific political groups or municipalities, in particular those in which the PCP governs. Such is the case of the municipalities of Almada and Beja. Such memorials, either in the form of public celebrations or monuments, have been consistently present since the transition. The same applies to street names, (re) named after famous opposition figures – republicans, communists and socialists alike, again mainly in cities or municipalities where the communist party has been in power.

During the last four years, both NAM and URAP have tried to assume the role of petitioning for the preservation of the memory, through means such as: petitions for a common effort for the creation of a national place of preservation and diffusion of the memory of the crimes committed by the New State; collecting signatures against the creation of a museum called 'Oliveira Salazar' in the hometown of the dictator, Santa Comba Dão; protesting against the creation of the former headquarters of the Plenary Courts into a hotel, etc. However, it may not be said that these episodes have generated particular interest from the media and the public opinion. Two of the most visible debates occurred back in 1998 and in 2007.

In 1998, the leader of the PIDE unit responsible for Humberto Delgado's assassination gave an interview to a Portuguese journalist in which he stated that he regularly travelled to Portugal, although he had been sentenced to eight years imprisonment *in absentia*. He was soon found in Spain, where he had been living under a false name; however, the Spanish court refused to allow the Portuguese authorities to extradite him, forcing the court that had originally sentenced him to admit that the statute of limitations applied, and that he was therefore free.

In 2007, a television show broadcast on the Portuguese public channel (RTP) ended with the election of the former dictator, Oliveira Salazar, as the "Greatest Portuguese of All Time". Salazar won over Álvaro Cunhal, former Secretary-General of the Communist Party, and Arestides Sousa Mendes, a Portuguese diplomat that gave several visas to Jewish refugees when the Nazis invaded

France in 1940. The result generated an "eruption of memory" and resulted in a letter written by Portuguese Historians and published in one of the most important newspapers in the country.

It was not before 7 June 2008, that the Parliament unanimously approved Resolution n. 330/X, in favour of the diffusion of knowledge on the resistance against the dictatorship to future generations. The document has no particular effect, besides symbolic meaning, and its unanimous approval supports the idea that there is no major debate on the past in contemporary Portugal.

5. SUMMARY AND CONCLUSIONS

Almost immediately, the Portuguese transition eliminated some of the institutional legacies of the authoritarian regime, and replaced some of the more important members of the elite that the dictatorship could have left for the new democracy. Not only were the regime's most important political institutions dissolved, but the "authoritarian enclaves" that had survived many of the transitional processes of the 1970s and the 1980s were also eliminated, or subjected to complex processes that paralysed them. The dissolution of the more repressive institutions (such as the PIDE and the Portuguese Legion) was accompanied by their purge and the partial criminalisation of their members. All this was possible due, in large part, to the initial interweaving of the MFA in the state's structures and its emergence as an authority for regulating conflicts, which substituted, dispersed and paralysed the classic mechanisms of legitimate State repression.

The strong correlation between the dynamics of the purges, the state crisis and the "opportunity structure" that it afforded is temporally visible: with the 25 November 1975 coup that gave victory to the moderate military, supported by the parties of the right and centre-left, both legal and illegal purges came to an almost immediate end. This, in turn, flowed together into a double legacy for the consolidation of democracy. The narrative of the transition seems to us a much more divisive issue in contemporary Portuguese society then the history of the dictatorship itself.

After the 1980s, the process of dealing with the past lost its momentum and gave way to mere sporadic public debates, parliamentary initiatives, and civil society's eruptions of memory. Since the democratic consolidation, several episodes have brought back the past, but no one of them can be said to have been particularly divisive within Portuguese society.

ABBREVIATIONS

JSN:	Junta de Salvação Nacional: National Salvation Junta
NAM:	Não Apaguem a Memória: Do Not Erase the Memory (Movement)
MDP:	Movimento Democrático Português: Portuguese Democratic Movement
MFA:	Movimento das Forças Armadas: Armed Forces Movement
PIM:	Polícia de Informação Militar: Police of Military Information
PIDE/DGS:	Polícia de Informação e Defesa do Estado/Direcção Geral de Informação: Police of Information and State Defence/Directorate General of Information
PVDE:	Polícia de Vigilância e Defesa do Estado: Vigilance and State Defence Police
TME:	Tribunal Militar Especial: Special Military Court
TP:	Tribunais Plenários: Plenary Courts
UN:	União Nacional: National Union (single-party)
URAP:	União de Resistentes Antifascistas: Portuguese Antifascist Resistant Movement

SELECTIVE FURTHER READING

Almeida, Sónia Vespeira de, 'Vítimas do fascismo. Os camponese e a dinamização cultural do Movimento das Forças Armadas (1974–75)', *Análise Social*, vol. XLIII (4°), 2008, 817–840.

Cerezales, Diego Palacios, *O poder caíu na rua. Crise de Estado e Acções Colectivas na Revolução Portuguesa 1974–75* (Lisbon: Imprensa de Ciências Sociais, 2003).

Cervelló, Josep Sánchez, *A Revolução portuguesa e a sua influência na transição espanhola (1961–76)*, (Lisbon: Assírio & Alvim, 1991).

Comissão do Livro Negro sobre o Regime Fascista, *Presos Políticos no Regime Fascista, 1931–1945*, 3 vols. (Lisbon: Presidência do Conselho de Ministros, 1981–84).

Costa, Artur Rodrigues da, 'O julgamento da PIDE/DGS e o direito transitório à memória', *Revista do Ministério Público*, 78, 199, 37–53.

Cruz, Manuel Braga da, *O Partido e o Estado no Salazarismo* (Lisbon: Editorial Presença, 1980).

Fernandes, Filipe and Santos, Hermínio, *Excomungados de Abril, Os empresários na Revolução* (Lisbon: D. Quixote, 2005).

Lucena, Manuel de, *O Estado da Revolução* (Lisbon: Expresso, 1978).

Madeira, João and Pimentel, Irene, *Vítimas de Salazar. Estado Novo e Violência Política* (Lisboa: Esfera dos Livros, 2007).

Martins, Hermínio, 'Portugal', in Woolf, Stuart (ed.), *European Fascism* (New York: Random House, 1968), 302–335.

Maurício, Artur and Castelo Branco Gonçalves, *Saneamento na função pública* (Lisboa: Diabril, 1975).

Pimentel, Irene (2007), *A História da PIDE* (Lisbon: Círculo de Leitores/Temas & Debates, 2007).

Pinto, António Costa, 'Authoritarian Legacies, transitional justice and state crisis in Portugal's democratization', *Democratization*, 13(2), 2006, 173–204.

Pinto, António Costa, 'Political Purges and State Crisis in Portugal's Transition to Democracy', *Journal of Contemporary History*, 43(2), 2008, 305–32.

Pinto, António Costa (ed.), *Dealing with the Legacy of Authoritarianism. The 'Politics of the Past' in Southern European Democracies* (London: Routledge, 2011).

Raimundo, Filipa, *The Double Face of Heroes. Transitional justice and the political police (PIDE/DGS) in Portugal's democratization (1974–6)*, Institute of Social Sciences, UL, Dissertation, December 2007.

Raimundo, Filipa, *Post-Transitional Justice? Spain, Poland, and Portugal compared*, European University Institute, PhD Dissertation, February 2012.

Rezola, Inácia, *Os Militares na Revolução de Abril. O Conselho da Revolução na transição para a democracia em Portugal* (Lisbon: Campo da Comunicação, 2006).

Ribeiro, Maria da Conceição, *A Polícia Política no Estado Novo, 1926–1945* (Lisbon: Estampa, 1995).

Rosas, Fernando, Pimentel, Irene, Madeira, João, Farinha, Luís and Rezola, Maria Inácia *Tribunais Políticos. Tribunais Militares Especiais e Tribunais Plenários durante a Ditadura e o Estado Novo* (Lisbon: Temas e Debates, 2009).

AMNESTY AND REPARATIONS WITHOUT TRUTH OR JUSTICE IN SPAIN

Paloma AGUILAR and Clara RAMÍREZ-BARAT

Within comparative political sciences, the Spanish transition has been often praised as a model to follow. Spain's democratisation process has been presented as one of the most peaceful and successful democratic transitions in the recent decades. The traumatic memory of the population after a cruel civil war and a long-lasting dictatorship was not easy to overcome. However, for many authors, the democratisation process facilitated 'national reconciliation' among Spaniards. According to the same thesis, the basis for the peaceful and successful stabilisation of democracy in Spain was precisely the decision to leave behind the thorniest aspects of the past.

In the last years, however, different voices have been increasingly claiming that the Spanish transition was not as exemplary as it has been portrayed, mainly because it failed to provide justice and truth to the victims of Francoism. Moreover, and contrary to the most accepted version, it was not a peaceful process either; indeed, political violence was among the features of the democratisation period.[1] Beyond mere description, many of those who defend this new reading of the Spanish transition also claim that it is still necessary today to correct the deficiencies inherited from that period in terms of accountability, truth, and reparations.[2]

1 P. AGUILAR and I. SÁNCHEZ-CUENCA, 'Terrorist Violence and Popular Mobilization: The Case of the Spanish Transition to Democracy', (2009), 37/3 *Politics & Society*, at 428–453.

2 Recent research has demonstrated that, contrary to the most pessimistic expectations sustained by democratization literature, accountability policies against human rights perpetrators have not necessarily contributed to the destabilization of new democracies. In fact, transitional countries with a combination of human rights prosecutions and truth commissions have proved to be less repressive than others. H.J. KIM and K. SIKKINK, 'Explaining the Deterrence Effect of Human Rights Prosecutions for Transitional Countries', (2010), 54 *International Studies Quarterly*, at 939–963, 941.

In this chapter, we examine in detail the origins and later evolution of transitional justice (hereafter, TJ) in Spain, with the aim of contributing to this discussion by looking into how such TJ framework has been progressively evolving in the Spanish case. In the first section we will present the most relevant historical and legal antecedents of TJ policies in Spain before Francoism. In the second section, we will discuss the irruption of TJ policies during the Spanish democratic regime established from Franco's death in 1975 until the creation of the Association for the Recovery of Historical Memory (*Asociación para la Recuperación de la Memoria Histórica*, ARMH) in 2000. In the third section, we will deal with what have been called the post-TJ period, which started in 2000, reaching a peak in 2007 with the approval of the so-called "Historical Memory Law" and remains open until today. In the fourth section, we will offer an overview of the state of Spanish political culture regarding the past. Finally, we will end the chapter with a conclusive summary section.

Within the comparative approach of this edited volume, the main contributions of this chapter to the existing literature on the Spanish case are the following: First, the longer term consideration of the TJ approach in Spain by looking at the historical antecedents of the TJ policies approved before the Spanish transition to democracy; second, this chapter presents a complete account of all the TJ policies that have been implemented in Spain since Franco's death, which includes not only the political measures adopted but also the social developments that have taken place since the beginning of the post-TJ period; third, we also integrate an analysis of the existing political culture within the general socio-political framework where TJ policies were pursued; and, finally, we attempt to provide a coherent narrative that gives sense to this long and erratic process, pointing out the reasons for its successes and failures, framing it in the contemporary TJ literature, and providing some tentative prospects for future developments.

1. HISTORICAL ANTECEDENTS OF THE CURRENT TRANSITIONAL JUSTICE POLICIES IN SPAIN

1.1. TRANSITIONAL JUSTICE IN THE PRE-FRANCO PERIOD (SEPTEMBER 1923–JULY 1936)

The history of amnesties, pardons, reparations, purges, and trials related to past crimes and abuses, or simply resulting from acts of vengeance committed after a regime change, can be traced very far back into history. In this section we will focus on the most relevant antecedents of the Spanish transition in the 20th century.

At the end of the Borbonic Restoration regime (1874–1923) a harsh battle took place in Annual (Morocco) resulting in the death of more than 10,000 Spaniards, about 1,000 northern Moroccans, and the lost of an important part of the Spanish colonial territory. The public outrage was such that, by a Real Order of 4 August 1921, the General Picasso was commanded with the writing of a report that would establish the responsibilities for that tragic episode. In spite of all the pressures exerted by the High Military Command, who was afraid of the consequences of this investigation, General Picasso delivered a report to the Congress on 18 April 1922. The report triggered bitter debates in the Congress and caused a great scandal in the public opinion. The negligence and recklessness of the military command was beyond any reasonable doubt.

In July 1922, 39 officers were indicted as a result of the investigation. One year later, a Responsibilities Commission created in the Cortes "had begun collecting testimony that might have led to an assignment of political responsibilities for the Annual Disaster.[3] However, the political crisis at the time was such that the report could not be debated in the Plenary of the Congress: On 13 September 1923, General Miguel Primo de Rivera organised a coup d'état that inaugurated a seven-year dictatorship.

The dictatorship of Primo de Rivera (1923–1930), consented to by the King Alfonso XIII, ended the debate about responsibilities for the Annual Disaster and passed an Amnesty Law to try to calm down the army. At the same time, the dictator began the prosecution of certain politicians of the previous regime, though in a very unsystematic and arbitrary way. One of the few formal initiatives in this respect was the Decree of 12 October 1923, by which former ministries and ex-presidents of the Chambers were not allowed to join the board of directors of any public enterprise. This measure affected about 30 former politicians. Several initiatives were undertaken to reform and purge the inherited administrative and judicial institutions,[4] but the only relevant judicial process driven by the Dictatorship was the one against Santiago Alba, a former State Ministry. But, in spite of the dictatorship's efforts, the Supreme Court declared Alba innocent of the charges in 1926.[5]

In a climate of great discontent, Primo de Rivera resigned (29 January 1930), and the King appointed another member of the military, Dámaso Berenguer, as head

---

3 C. Boyd, '"Responsibilities" and the Second Republic, 1931–6', in M. Blinkhorn (ed.), *Spain in Conflict 1931–1939. Democracy and Its Enemies*, Sage, London, 1986, at 14–39, 16.

4 M.T. González Calbet, *La Dictadura de Primo de Rivera. El Directorio Militar*, Ediciones el Arquero, Madrid, 1987, at 215–256.

5 M. Martorell, *José Sánchez Guerra. Un hombre de honor (1859–1935)*, Marcial Pons, Madrid, 2011.

of the executive.[6] The brief period between this appointment and the proclamation of the Second Republic (14 April 1931) is known as the "*dictablanda*". Berenguer, trying to distance himself from the former dictatorship, passed a Royal Decree-Law of Amnesty on 5 February 1930. His intention was to benefit those who had opposed the Primo de Rivera dictatorship. At that period, some monarchist politicians also suggested the possibility of passing a "bill of indemnity" for the King, given his complicity with the Primo de Rivera Dictatorship. The difficulties for providing a satisfactory monarchist solution unleashed a regime crisis that facilitated the advent of the Republican regime.[7]

One of the leitmotivs of the opposition movements to the Primo de Rivera regime had been the urgent need to establish its political responsibilities. The people against this initiative were disqualified as "*impunistas*", and, given the great mobilising power of the "responsibilities flag", no Republican party was willing to be suspicious of it. The responsibilities proved to be a crucial issue in the two elections that took place in 1931.[8] As a consequence, the second point of the Constituent Decree of the Provisional Government of the Republic pledged to prosecute all pending issues when Primo de Rivera dissolved the Parliament (in reference to the "Picasso report"), as well as the ulterior military and civilian performance of the Dictatorship.[9]

The parliament of the Second Republic created a special commission for the establishment of political accountability and the subsequent prosecution of the former regime (Law of 27 August 1931). According to Payne, several retired generals or minor civilian bureaucrats were arrested, and even the king – who was in exile at the time – was convicted and his properties were confiscated.[10] In 1932 a special Accountability Tribunal, composed of 21 deputies, was created.

---

6 M. Martorell, 'El rey en su desconcierto. Alfonso XIII, los viejos políticos y el ocaso de la monarquía', in J. Moreno (ed.), *Alfonso XIII. Un político en el trono*, Marcial Pons, Madrid, 2003, at 373–402.

7 Ibid.

8 M. Cabrera, 'Los escándalos de la Dictadura de Primo de Rivera y las responsabilidades en la República: el asunto Juan March', (2000) 4 *Historia y Política*, at 7–30, 7. For the details about the advent of the Second Republic, see S. Payne, *Spain's First Democracy: The Second Republic, 1931–1936*, University of Wisconsin Press, Madison, 1993.

9 "*Para responder a los justos e insatisfechos anhelos de España, el Gobierno provisional adopta como norma depuradora de la estructura del Estado, someter inmediatamente, en defensa del interés público, a juicio de responsabilidad los actos de gestión y autoridad pendientes de examen al ser disuelto el Parlamento en 1923, así como los ulteriores, y abrir expediente de revisión en los organismos oficiales, civiles y militares, a fin de que no resulte consagrada la prevaricación ni acatada la arbitrariedad, habitual en el régimen que termina*". Decreto constitutivo del Gobierno Provisional de la República, 27 April 1931.

10 S. Payne, *Spain's First Democracy: The Second Republic, 1931–1936*, University of Wisconsin Press, Madison, 1993, 69–79.

The action of both the commission and the tribunal were considered acts of "sectarian vengeance", which "established the precedent that at each turn of the political wheel vengeance would be exacted on the preceding holders of power".[11] Regarding the consequences of the commission, other authors have recognised that "[t]he responsibilities campaign divided the governing coalition and created additional enemies for the Republic at a time when building a broad national consensus in support of political and social reforms was of crucial importance".[12]

In spite of all the accountability efforts, the state apparatus was not purged, which means that "the great majority of state employees hired under the monarchy remained in place".[13] As regards grace measures, the first initiative of the Provisional Government of the Republic was to declare an amnesty for political prisoners. The next amnesty was passed after the election of Niceto Alcalá Zamora as the first democratically elected president of the Republic (December 1931). As a result, the people imprisoned by the "responsibilities" issue were released.[14]

On 10 August 1932, General Sanjurjo led a failed coup d'état against the Republican government, for which he was imprisoned. The general elections of November 1933 were won by the right, which explains the approval on 20 April 1934, after a very tense debate, of an Amnesty Law that included "everyone (except the ex-king) who had been prosecuted by the Responsibilities Commission or involved in the Sanjurjo rebellion (…). By early May all those who had been accused, tried, imprisoned, or retired by the Republic between 1931 and 1933 were free and ready to resume political life".[15] Due to the pressures exerted by the left, the amnesty also finally included the "anarchist insurgents of December 1933".[16] As regards the responsibilities issue, "[o]n 10 May the Cortes formally voted to abolish the Responsibilities Commission and to deliver its unfinished business to the Supreme Court".[17]

11 Ibid., 70.

12 C. Boyd, '"Responsibilities" and the Second Republic', 15.

13 S. Payne, *Spain's First Democracy*, 42.

14 C. Boyd, '"Responsibilities" and the Second Republic, 28.

15 Ibid., 33. "Of those previously prosecuted and then amnestied by the legislation of April 1934, all save the ringleaders of the *sanjurjada* were offered the option of retiring, going on the reserve with full pay, or returning to active duty". S. Payne, *Spain's First Democracy: The Second Republic, 1931–1936*, 238. The last option was chosen by some of the would-be leaders of the Francoist coup d'état of 18 July 1936.

16 N. Townson, *La República que no pudo ser. La política de centro en España (1931–1936)*, Taurus, Madrid, 2002, 259.

17 C. Boyd, '"Responsibilities" and the Second Republic', 33.

In the mid-thirties there were high levels of political violence. In October 1934, a revolutionary strike, supported by various leftist political and unionist forces, took place in the north of Spain. In a few days the miners had the control of almost the entire region of Asturias. Very violent confrontations took place between the supporters of the strike and the armed forces. The military repression was particularly brutal. The death toll, according to estimations, was between 1,500 and 2,000, most of the victims being strikers. Also, between 20,000 and 30,000 people were prosecuted after the situation was brought under control by the government.

On 16 February 1936, a broad coalition of leftist parties (the Popular Front) won the general elections. Given that some radical leftists immediately began to personally free, by assaulting the jails, some of the above mentioned revolutionaries imprisoned, a very urgent issue was the official approval of an amnesty law. On 21 February the Parliament passed a general amnesty for all social and political crimes since the 1933 elections; about 15,000 people benefited from this legislation.

Regarding the general legal regulation of amnesties and pardons, Article No. 102 of the Second Republic Constitution (9 December 1931) says: "Amnesties will only be passed by the Parliament. No general pardons will be granted". This article also provided that both the Supreme Court and the President of the Republic could grant individual pardons under certain circumstances. According to some authors, this regulation of the clemency institution constituted a turning point in Spanish history, as it was coherent, for the first time, with the separation of powers principle. As it will be seen, this principle was dramatically violated by the Francoist regime, under which the "unity of power" was installed. In accordance with this, the power to grant clemency was attributed in an exclusive way to the Head of State.[18]

1.2. THE CIVIL WAR (JULY 1936–APRIL 1939)

The failure of the 18 July 1936 coup d'état by general Franco in approximately half of the country triggered a long and bitter Civil War in which both sides committed numerous extrajudicial executions. Several months would have to pass before the political repression began to be applied through legal means.

Two months after the beginning of the Civil War, the Francoist forces passed two very important decrees. Decree No 109 (13 September 1936) granted amnesty to the participants in the coups of both 10 August 1932 (General

[18] E. Linde Paniagua, *Amnistía e indulto en España*, Túcar Ediciones, Madrid, 1976, 40–41.

Sanjurjo and his collaborators), and of 18 July 1936 (General Franco and his supporters). Decree No 108 (13 September 1936) declared illegal all parties and associations related with the Popular Front, as well as all organisations that had opposed the Francoist forces since the coup d'état of 18 July 1936. This allowed the judicial prosecution of all Republicans – or those suspected of being ambivalent regarding the rebels –, for the confiscation of all their private belongings, and also of the properties of all the Republican parties, unions and organisations of various kinds. According to the same decree, public servants and employees of public enterprises could also be dismissed for ideological reasons.

But the most important retributive legislation was the Law of Political Accountability (9 February 1939) and the special Tribunal of Political Accountability that was accordingly created. This was the cornerstone for the extensive purging process that took place and also of the equally extensive confiscation process of the properties of the losing side. About 300,000 people had to face disciplinary proceedings as a result. The retroactive effects of the law went back as far as the revolutionary movement of October 1934. Consequently, it punished both some actions that were not illegal at that moment – in a clear violation of the non-retroactivity principle of the law –, and crimes that had already been prosecuted and later amnestied. This law was completed with the Law for the lustration of Public Servants of 10 February 1939.

1.3. THE FRANCO REGIME (JULY 1939–20 NOVEMBER 1975)

The prosecution and punishment of opponents of the regime were extremely harsh, in spite of the existence of some pardons throughout the period, as we will see.

When the Civil War had ended, the Decree of 30 December 1939 declared null and void all amnesties passed by the Republican authorities during the conflict, particularly, the 22 January 1937 Decree-Law, granting amnesty for social and political crimes, as well as for common and military crimes, committed before 15 July 1936. The groups excluded from this amnesty were all convicted of crimes against the Republic before or after that date, and the people responsible for the repression of October 1934. Also, the amnesty Law of 23 September 1939 nullified all sort of crimes that had been committed by the victors of the Civil War from 1931 till the end of the conflict (April 1939). This law complemented the above mentioned Decree No. 109 and was the only amnesty law of the post-war period with political content; the rest of them had an economic character.[19] Among the other notorious repressive mechanisms of the dictatorship, the Special Tribunal for the Repression of Masonry and Communism (1940–1963) and the Tribunal of Public Order (1963–1977) stand out.

In the mid-40s, the enormous amount of prisoners began to be very difficult to manage. At the same time, the political situation of the Francoist regime at the end of World War II had become very delicate, as it was undoubtedly associated with the defeated side in the international conflict. Both problems led to the pardon Decree of 9 October 1945, though the range of beneficiaries was very limited. More pardons were to follow.

For example, the 10 November 1966 Decree on the Political Accountability Extinguishing Commission (created by an Order of 27 June 1945) proceeded to cancel, in a definitive way, the political culpability of the Republicans. The 31 March 1969 Decree, passed at the 30th anniversary of the end of the Civil War, was one of the most relevant and commented-on pardons in the press. According to the declarations of a Francoist politician at that period (Manuel Fraga Iribarne): "We have definitely buried the remains of past divisions and have put to an end our last Civil War".[20] This was far from the truth for many reasons, as we will discuss later in this chapter. It took a lot of time and a high number of regulations to put the victors and the defeated of the Civil War on an equal foot. Reparations for the victims of the Francoist regime took even longer and are still considered to be incomplete by certain political parties and associations. However, Francoist victims received all sorts of material and symbolic reparations (including the exhumation of common graves, which was not allowed in the case of the Republican victims). Many jobs were reserved to ex-combatants or their families, pensions were provided, plaques were installed and monuments honouring the victors were built in every single village.[21]

Pardons and amnesties during the Franco regime were regulated by Article No. 6 of the Organic Law of the State (10 January 1967) – the closest document to a "constitution" under Francoism. The Head of State exerted the prerogative of clemency.

19 Ibid., 89.

20 Quoted by L. López Rodó, *Memorias. Años decisivos*, Plaza & Janés/Cambio 16, Barcelona, 1991, 474.

21 For more details see P. Aguilar, *Políticas de la memoria y memorias de la política*, Alianza Editorial, Madrid, 2008.

2. TRANSITIONAL JUSTICE POLICIES (1975–2000)

2.1. THE LEGACY OF THE FRANCO REGIME

Franco's dictatorship – an authoritarian and national-Catholic regime, with totalitarian and fascist features in its first years – started being dismantled upon the death of the dictator on 20 November 1975. It is estimated that between 1936 and 1942 nearly 500,000 political prisoners passed through more than 100 concentration camps, and that several tens of thousands of Spaniards were court-martialed.[22] As for fatalities, the latest rough estimates of deaths caused by Francoist repression stand at 130,000 (including some 50,000 after the Civil War), and 50,000 by Republican repression during the conflict.[23] Spain's prison population at the end of the war was approximately 270,000, while around 10,000 were deported to Nazi camps between 1940 and 1945.[24] During the conflict, around 30,000 children in the Republican side (the so-called "children of the war") were sent abroad, many of whom never returned; while after the end of the war hundreds of thousands of people were forced into exile.[25] Although there are no official figures of the subsequent period nor consensus among researchers, some sources indicate that the military jurisdiction enforced 13 court-martial death sentences between 1958 and 1975 (4 by garrote and 9 by firing squad).[26] During the time he stayed in power, Franco forbade thousands of people that were purged during the war from returning to their former jobs. Moreover, he rejected granting compensation or pensions to war mutilated, widows and orphans of the defeated side. In contrast, those that fought or sympathised with his forces were given a preferential treatment in employment, granted compensation measures and pensions, provided with health care benefits, publicly honoured at all levels, and even given the possibility of exhuming the bodies of their family members from common graves to bury them properly.

---

22 J. Rodrigo, *Los campos de concentración franquistas*, Siete Mares, Madrid, 2003.

23 F. Espinosa (ed.), *Violencia roja y azul. España, 1936–1950*, Crítica, Barcelona, 2010, 76–77.

24 B. Bermejo and S. Checa, *Libro memorial. Españoles deportados a los campos nazis (1940–1945)*, Ministerio de Cultura, Madrid, 2006.

25 A. Alted, *La voz de los vencidos. El exilio republicano de 1939*, P. Aguilar, Madrid, 2005.

26 The military played a protagonist role in the repression, particularly in the post-war period. But, on the one hand, ordinary justice also participated in the military jurisdiction. And, on the other hand, ordinary judges played leading role in the second part of the regime through some particular jurisdictions created for the repression of the people who opposed the dictatorship. See P. Aguilar, "Judiciary's Involvement in Authoritarian Repression and Transitional Justice: The Spanish Case in Comparative Perspective", (2013) 7, *International Journal of Transitional Justice*, 245–266.

2.2. THE 'SPANISH MODEL': REPARATIONS AND AMNESTY WITHOUT ACCOUNTABILITY AND TRUTH TELLING

Political change in Spain came through a very long process of negotiation after which a consensus was reached between the reformist sectors of Francoism and the different political forces of the democratic opposition. Almost immediately after Franco's death, calling for the spirit of "national reconciliation", some partial mercy measures were adopted, beginning with the pardon granted on the occasion of the coronation of King Juan Carlos I on 25 November 1975. In July 1976 the first government of the Monarchy passed a Royal Decree-Amnesty Law that included political crimes "only if they had not put in danger the life or the integrity of other persons". However, this measure was so restrictively enforced by the still very conservative judiciary of the time, that it had to be complemented in March 1977 with a general pardon and some additional mercy measures that allowed for some margin of interpretation. Finally, on 20 May 1977 the Council of Ministers approved the release of an important number of the Basque prisoners that still remained in prison, mostly on charges of terrorism.[27]

After the democratic elections of 15 June 1977, the first law approved by the parliament was the Amnesty Law of 15 October 1977. This law covered crimes and felonies of a political nature, as well as civil disobedience. As a result, most of the few political prisoners that still remained in prison were freed, recovering their active and passive rights, and obtaining a cleansing of their criminal records. More interestingly, the law also provided amnesty to those who had been sentenced for committing crimes involving bloodshed until 15 December 1976; and between that date and the democratic elections in the instances in which it was possible to prove that the crimes were committed while furthering the reestablishment of public liberties or to vindicate territorial demands (precisely taking into account the remaining ETA prisoners). The practical majority of the political parties, except the natural heirs of Franco's regime, *Alianza Popular* (AP), supported a very ample amnesty that, in contrast with the above mentioned historical precedents, covered the actions committed by the groups opposing the dictatorship, as well as the violations committed by the public servants and officers of the regime. This way the parliament was seeking to promote "national reconciliation" and probably also to avoid of some of the mistakes that it was believed were committed during the Second Republic – the memory of which was often used in a deterrent manner.[28] Moreover, Spanish

27 P. Aguilar, *Políticas de la memoria y memorias de la política.*

28 Interestingly enough, during the discussion about the Amnesty Law of 1977, Antonio Carro Martínez, the spokesman of the party formed by the reformists of the dictatorship (AP), justified the abstention of his group making reference to the republican precedent: "I should refer to the distinguished socialist Mr. Luis Jiménez de Asúa, the Vice-president of this Chamber and President of the Constitution Commission of the Second Republic at the time,

democracy was moving away from the revengeful and sectarian approach of Franco's dictatorship, the legislation of which, as already explained, not only penalised the combatants and sympathisers of the defeated side, but also exculpated the crimes committed by those who supported the coup of 1936.

The decision not to undertake punitive measures came along with the establishment of several reparations policies for the defeated that, from a purely material dimension, would be the only corrective justice actions undertaken at the time by the democratic government. In general lines, all the reparation measures started by compensating, first, the victims of war that were not repaired by Francoism, recognising the "unequal treatment that was given to the defeated, and offering them the same rights of the victorious",[29] and only later, starting in 1990, those of Francoism.

Albeit never part of a coherent policy aimed at dealing with the repressive past, as Aguilar has argued, since the beginning of democracy several laws were passed aiming to correct or repair some injustices of Francoism.[30] Even before the first democratic elections, and continuing under the government of Franco's former Prime Minister, Arias Navarro, a decree was passed on 5 March 1976 by which the war wounded who served in the republican side were for first time entitled to receive pensions. Under the democratic regime, the first material reparation law was the Royal Decree-Law of 6 March 1978 that granted retirement pensions to the members of the Military and members of the forces of public order of the Republic (or their heirs), who were already serving as such before the coup of 18 July 1936. A second Royal Decree, passed in May 1978, regulated the application of amnesty to public servants of the *Generalitat* (the Catalan government). Thirdly, in December 1978, a Royal Decree-Law was passed to extend the amnesty to those public servants who had been purged from the judiciary. Fourthly, a law granting pensions and medical-social support to war widows as well as other family members of persons who died during the war was approved. To qualify, the victims should have died during the war, by injuries caused during the war, or "as consequence of political and union based actions or opinions", only when the death "was not the result of a death sentence, nor because of a violent action initiated by the deceased". Fifthly, the Law of 8 June 1984 recognised the years spent in prison in relation to the motives included in the Amnesty Law of 1977, as computable in terms of contributing to

and foremost, one of the most important criminalist lawyers of this century. Jiménez de Asúa, who recently died in exile, wrote that the blind and excessive use that was done of mercy at the beginning of the Republic was also the motive of its disorder and fall, Cortes Generales, 24 *Journal of Sessions of the Congress of Deputies* (*Diario de Sesiones del Congreso de los Diputados, DSCD*), Plenary Session No 11, 14 October 1977, 958.

29 P. Aguilar, *Políticas de la memoria y memorias de la política*, 6.

30 See P. Aguilar, *Políticas de la memoria y memorias de la política.*

the social security system; while, sixthly, the Law of 22 October 1984 granted pensions and assistance to those members of the Army and Forces of the Public Order who were already serving before the war, also recognising for first time their "services rendered" to the nation. However, it would only be in 1986, when the members of the military who had received sentences under Francoism recovered their active rights, that one of the most important lacunae of the amnesty law was finally amended, i.e. the reincorporation in the army of those who were members of the Democratic Military Union (*Unión Militar Democrática*, UMD). The fact that it took nine years after the amnesty law to pass this measure reveals the power that the military retained during the first years of democracy. Finally, in 1990 the State General Budget Law (*Ley de Presupuestos Generales del Estado*) granted for first time compensation measures for the years spent in Francoist prisons.

In terms of rehabilitation measures, it should be noted that some of the above-mentioned laws implied both the recuperation of the active rights (reincorporation to their former positions) and the passive rights of the beneficiaries. However, it was necessary to pass several additional measures to cover some gaps, such as the Royal Decree of 1 October 1976 regarding public servants of local administrations, or the Royal Decree of 2 June 2 1977 that reinstated public school teachers to their positions.[31] Finally, there have also been a couple of laws that had the aim of returning the property rights of political parties and unions: In January 1986, a law established the return of the seized properties to unions; and in 1998 a second law, in which an indirect disapproval of the dictatorship was included, established the restitution of goods which had been stolen from the political parties.

According to the data gathered in the General Report (*Informe general de la Comisión Interministerial para el estudio de la situación de las víctimas de la guerra civil y del franquismo)* and prepared by an Interministerial Commission appointed in 2004, until 2005 the government had spent a total of € 16,356 million, either to cover indemnities or pensions for the victims of the Civil War in the Republican side. Together with an additional € 5.1 million that would have been allocated to pay indemnities to prisoners in Francoist prisons, the Spanish state would have spent slightly over € 16,361 million to pay reparations both to the victims of war and Francoism. Although the report recognises that the numbers of pension's beneficiaries has been diminishing over time, during the early 1990s around a 25 percent of the state budget devoted to passive pensions was allocated to victims of the Civil War. Accordingly, the report stresses the

---

31 This was complemented with the Order of the Ministry of Interior of 6 July 1977. Together, both documents, would have aimed to correct the omission of the Royal Decree-Law 10/1976 that didn't refer to this collective.

important effort done by Spanish society to restore the rights of the victims of the war and Francoism.[32]

Despite the economic importance of these efforts, it should be underlined that from 1975 to 2000 no other TJ measures were implemented in Spain. More specifically, none of the following polices were undertaken in the country, either during the democratisation period or (with some exceptions, as will be seen) later:

1. Trials. To date there have been no trials for the crimes committed by Francoism during the war or the dictatorship. Some criminal law experts maintain that the statute of limitations together with the Amnesty Law would not allow these trials to take place. Others maintain that, leaving aside the thorny and unresolved debate about the prescription of these crimes, the obligation of the state to investigate them has not been fulfilled.[33] Some recent developments regarding judicial proceedings will be presented below.
2. Purges: As one author has noted, "one of the most striking features of Spain's (...) transition from dictatorship to democracy has been the absence of a political purge aimed at excluding the beneficiaries of the old regime from participation in the public life of the new. Indeed (...), parties composed of former Franco loyalists played a leading role, producing a somewhat unexpected continuity of personnel between the political class of the dictatorship and that of the new constitutional monarchy".[34] Indeed, only very limited and belated measures, such as the early retirement of some judges and military personnel, and the reallocation and institutional reforms of the police forces, were eventually take.[35]
3. Restitution and confiscation of property. As already said, with the exception of unions and political parties, the democratic regime has not returned the extensive property of individuals that was seized during the war or the

32 Comisión Interministerial, *Informe General sobre la situación de las víctimas de la guerra civil y la dictadura*, 28 July 2006, 57–58. However, as the report itself recognizes there were several categories that were still left unattended and that should be considered in further laws, including the children of the war. Also, it is important to note that because Autonomous Communities also have legislative power, by 2006 there were some inequalities about the benefits that same categories of victims were receiving in different territories.

33 A. Gil *La justicia de transición en España*, Atelier, Barcelona, 2009; S. Carulla Ripol and C. Villán Durán, eds., *Justicia de transición. El caso de España*, Institut Català Internacional per la Pau, Barcelona, 2012; J. Chinchón, "Proceso penal y Derecho internacional. Imposibilidad de castigar vs. Obligación de investigar: Algunas reflexiones y propuestas", *Diario La Ley*, XXXIII, 7845, 2012, at 1–10.

34 C. Boyd, '"Responsibilities" and the Second Republic', 14.

35 See Ana B. Benito, 'Poder judicial, responsabilidad legal y transición a la democracia en España', (2009), XLIX/195 *Foro Internacional*, at 163–179, and D. Palacios Cerezales, 'Repressive Legacies and the Democratisation of Iberian Police Systems', (2010), 15/3 *South European Society & Politics*, at 429–448.

dictatorship. Moreover, this possibility has been ruled out citing juridical security.[36] In contrast, the heirs of Franco not only inherited his fortune, but they still own property that originally belonged to the state.

4. Truth commissions. Although there have been a few civil society-led initiatives and many historical studies on the Civil War and the dictatorship, no official truth or historical commission has been created to date. As a consequence, the Spanish state has yet not made any attempt to establish in an official manner the number of victims that the Civil War and the early days of the Francoist repression left behind.[37] A proposal regarding the need to undertake a report about the events occurred during and after the Civil War in relation to the victims and the disappeared, which was made by *Convergencia i Unió* (CIU) during the debates that took place in the Parliament in June 2004, was never taken into consideration.[38] In 2008 the Basque parliament approved a motion advocating the creation of a truth commission,[39] followed in 2009 by a concrete proposal for the creation of such a body in the Basque Country.[40] In 2012, on the occasion of a commemorative act for the victims of the Civil War celebrated on the 81st anniversary of the proclamation of the Republic, in a public speech, Judge Baltasar Garzón requested the creation of a truth commission at a national level. This proposal has been moved forward by several victim groups that conformed in May of 2013 a Platform for the Creation of a Truth Commission (*Plataforma Comisión de la Verdad*).[41]
5. Symbolic reparations. As regards national monuments erected to the victims of Francoism in this period there was only one, located in the Plaza de la Lealtad in Madrid, which, originally devoted to the heroes of the Peninsular War, was renamed in 1985 to honour all the fallen of the Civil War as well.

---

36 For more information on this respect see Comisión Interministerial, *Informe General*, 2006, 61–69.

37 According to some authors: "The main weakness of the ways in which Spanish democracy has reckoned with the past concerns the truth (...). To know the truth is the first and main pre-condition to accomplishing the needs of justice concerning the atrocities committed by the Franco regime and not yet investigated by the democratic institutions" (See J.M. Tamarit Sumalla, 'Transition, Historical Memory and Criminal Justice in Spain', (2011), 9 *Journal of International Criminal Justice*, at 729–755, 751.

38 S. Juliá, 'Public Policy on Historical Memory', in Fundación Alternativas, *Report on Democracy in Spain*, Fundación Alternativas, Madrid, 2011, at 182–208, 182.

39 "Proposición no de ley sobre la obstaculización de la Fiscalía General del Estado ante la causa contra el franquismo," approved on 28 November 2008. See Parlamento Vasco, 108 *Diario de Sesiones*, VIII Term of Office, 28 November 2008.

40 J. Landa Gorostiza, *Bases para la puesta en marcha de una Comisión de la Verdad en Euskadi*, Dirección de Derechos Humanos Departamento de Justicia, Empleo y Seguridad Social Gobierno Vasco, Vitoria-Gasteiz, 31 marzo 2009.

41 N. Junquera, 'Garzón ataca a la justicia española "agazapada en el rincón de la vergüenza"', *El País*, Madrid, 14 April, 2012 "Asociaciones por la memoria histórica impulsan la Plataforma Comisión de la Verdad", *Público*, 24 May 2013. It should be noted, however, that not all the memory groups support this option as they have no trust in the current government or instead they directly advocate for prosecutions.

> The truth is that it lacks any real symbolic power for most citizens.[42] At the local level, while there are some monuments dedicated to all the victims of the war, there are very few dedicated to the victims of the dictatorship, and even less to those who were killed during the first years of the transition. Exceptions to this rule are the commemorative memorial located in the street of Atocha in Madrid where five lawyers were killed in 1977 by right extremists' groups, and the one in Vitoria dedicated to five people what killed by the police in March 1976. Regarding other symbolic gestures, the president of the Republic, Azaña, whose body is still buried in France, received institutional homage at the Parliament in 1990; also, with the occasion of the law granting the members of the International Brigades Spanish nationality, a commemoration act was organised in 1996 (that was not supported by the PP).

Some authors have pointed out that the Spanish state is not providing the obligations dictated by International Law, such as investigating, judging, sanctioning and, very particularly, repairing. The immediate consequence of all International Law violations is the right to reparation, which implies the acknowledgement that a specific right has been violated and, consequently, the state has the obligation to provide reparation to the victims. If these conditions are not met, the state would not be providing reparation to the victims, but just economic compensations or indemnities as a matter of grace.[43]

As far as the current general regulation on amnesties and pardons, there is no specific indication in the Constitution. The only mention to the subject in the constitutional text says: "the King will be able to apply grace measures according to the law", but "not to authorise general pardons" (article 62). In the Penal Code the pardon is contemplated (Title VII, Chapter I, article 130, 4) as one of the causes for the extinction of criminal responsibility.

3. POST-TRANSITIONAL JUSTICE POLICIES AND MEMORY IRRUPTIONS[44] (2000–2011)

Spain is a paradigmatic case of a successful transition to democracy based on the decision to leave aside the most painful memories of the Civil War and of the Francoist repression. After the reparation measures of the early democratisation

42 See P. Aguilar, *Políticas de la memoria y memorias de la política.*

43 J. Chinchón, "El viaje a ninguna parte: Memoria, leyes, historia y olvido sobre la guerra civil y el pasado autoritario en España", *Revista del Instituto Interamericano de Derechos Humanos (IIDH)*, 47, 2007, at 119–233.

44 To our knowledge, the first author who has used the fortunate expression "irruptions of memory" – applying it to the Chilean case – was Alexander Wilde (1999).

period commented above, the agreement on leaving the thorniest parts of the past behind was respected for many years. However, as is well known, decisions to sidestep history tend to be revised, and memory irruptions are inevitable with the passage of time.[45]

In fact, during the last decade we have witnessed a post-TJ process that has transcended the institutional arrangements established during the Spanish transition to democracy.[46] Two crucial turning points have taken place since then. First, the creation of the ARMH in 2000, as well as various other organisations formed, in most cases, by families of victims of the war.[47] All of these groups have very strongly advocated for the recuperation of the silenced memory of the Republican victims and, specifically, for locating their remains still buried in mass graves all over Spain. With a remarkable dose of perseverance, they have managed to introduce the issue of the past in the political agenda of the country – which has been especially taken up by some parties in the left of the Spanish parliamentary spectrum, like *Izquierda Unida* (IU) or *Esquerra Republicana de Catalunya* (ERC). Second, after the socialist turnover of the government, from 2004 until 2007, the drafting process and later approval of a crucial reparation law aimed at addressing the most important pending issues of the Civil War and the dictatorship has led to the adoption of a series of measures that, as we will see later in more detail, have opened many controversies and brought the issue of memory to the public sphere.

3.1. WHY HAS A POST-TRANSITIONAL PHASE TAKEN PLACE IN SPAIN?[48]

Before providing an account of the specific TJ measures that have been approved in this period, a brief summary of the reasons explaining this post-TJ phase will be presented.

Firstly, the arrival of a new generation to the public sphere has proved to be a crucial variable. This generation counts on a stable democratic regime, is devoid

---

45 A. Wilde, 'Irruptions of Memory. Expressive Politics in Chile's Transition to Democracy', (1999), 2 *Journal of Latin American Studies*, at 473–500.

46 P. Aguilar, 'Transitional or Post-Transitional Justice? Recent Developments in the Spanish Case', (2008), 13/4 *South European Society & Politics*, at 417–433.

47 Although ARMH is the better organized and well-known of these victims' organizations, there are many others, including Forum for the Recovery of Memory (Foro para la Recuperación de la Memoria, created in 2002), Friends of the International Brigades (Asociación de Amigos de las Brigadas Internacionales, founded in 1995), or the Exile Association (Asociación de Descendientes del Exilio, founded in 2002), as well as various former prisoners, ex-combatants, disabled soldiers, and "children of the war" groups, some of these founded in the beginning of the transition.

48 P. Aguilar, 'Transitional or Post-Transitional Justice?'.

of the fears of their predecessors, and happens to be much more identified with the principles of universal justice.[49] An important part of this generation of "grandchildren" of the Civil War do not think that going beyond the institutional arrangements of the transition is going to destabilise the political situation and claim that time has come to fully compensate the victims of the past and to give them public recognition for their suffering.[50]

Secondly, the creation in 2000 of the ARMH for the exhumation of the hundreds of common graves dating from the Civil War and the immediate post-war period has had a decisive impact in giving public transcendence to collective memory issues and in providing visibility to justice claims. This association, founded by people belonging to the above-mentioned generation, has promoted many successful exhumations all over Spain, and a handful of initiatives aiming at the recovery of the memory of the victims of the Civil War and Francoism, that have had a great impact in the media.[51] Their initiatives have been very important for shedding light on the Francoist repressive machinery and for creating a public consciousness on the existing lacunae in terms of victims' reparation.

Thirdly, a strategic political turn towards TJ has taken place in the Spanish Workers' Socialist Party [*Partido Socialista Obrero Español* (PSOE)]. The first movements were observed when the PSOE lost power in 1996, after four legislatures in office (1982–1996) during which time the past was, most of the time, left behind. When the main conservative party, the *Partido Popular* (PP), governed the country for the first time, leftist, Catalan and Basque nationalist parties tried to stigmatise it for its Francoist roots.[52] This process was particularly active during its second legislature in power (2000–2004).[53] The initiatives presented or supported by the PSOE in that period necessarily conditioned its actions when it regained office in 2004. In fact, that legislature (2004–2008) was the most important with respect to historical memory and TJ since the transitional stage. The fact that the PSOE, lacking a parliamentary

49 Not to mention that, "there is no doubt that Rodríguez Zapatero himself, the grandson of a Republican army officer executed during the Civil War, is more acutely sensitive to these issues than other Socialist leaders of an older generation", P. Aguilar, 'Transitional or Post-Transitional Justice?', 27.

50 See P. Aguilar, *Políticas de la memoria y memorias de la política*.

51 For the public impact of the exhumation process, see F. Ferrándiz, 'De las fosas comunes a los derechos humanos: El descubrimiento de las *desapariciones forzadas* en la España contemporánea', (2010), 19 *Revista de Antropología Social*, at161–189.

52 The original name of this party until 1989 was Alianza Popular (AP), which was founded in the transition by relevant political personalities of the dictatorship.

53 The empirical evidence for the turning point that took place in the initiatives regarding the past that were presented at the Parliament can be seen in P. Aguilar, 'Presencia y ausencia de la guerra civil y del franquismo en la democracia española. Reflexiones en torno a la articulación y la ruptura del "pacto de silencio"', in J. Aróstegui and F. Godicheau (eds.), *Guerra civil. Mito y Memoria*, Marcial Pons, Madrid, 2006, at 245–293.

majority, needed to govern with the support of parties that were much more determined than itself to give a strong drive to these issues also helps to explain the important policies that were approved at that time.[54]

Fourthly, the consequences derived from the evolution of international human rights and criminal legislation and the lobbying efforts of certain international organisations have proved to be relevant as well, including NGOs such as Amnesty International,[55] but also institutions such as the United Nations,[56] the Council of Europe,[57] and the European Parliament.[58]

Finally, the importance of fortuitous events, such as anniversaries, should not be underestimated.[59] Another crucial example of a fortuitous event is what has been called the "Pinochet effect". The consequences of the detention in London in October 1998 of the Chilean dictator – on the initiative of the Spanish judge Baltasar Garzón – have been abundantly pointed out in the literature for explaining the recent developments of the Spanish case.[60]

---

54 See P. Aguilar, 'Presencia y ausencia de la guerra civil y del franquismo en la democracia española' and P. Aguilar, 'Transitional or Post-Transitional Justice?'.

55 "Between 2005 and 2006, Amnesty International published three reports urging the Spanish government to fulfil its international obligations", P. Aguilar, *Políticas de la memoria y memorias de la política*.429.

56 The United Nations Human Rights Committee included Spain in 2003 among the countries with cases of forced disappearances. For the time being, this Committee has recognised only two cases, since it only deals with disappearances after 1945, whereas the vast majority of Spanish cases date from the civil war or the immediate post-war period. Nevertheless, these two cases impose a series of unavoidable international obligations on the Spanish State. Moreover, in 2009, the UN Human Rights Committee called on Spain to revoke the 1977 Amnesty Law (Human Rights Committee, CCPR/C/ESP/CO/5, 5 January 2009).

57 On 17 March 2006, the Permanent Commission of the Parliamentary Assembly of the Council of Europe (PACE) unanimously approved the condemnation of the Franco regime and urged the Spanish Government to honour its victims in an appropriate manner. See PACE, 'Need for international condemnation of the Franco regime', Recommendation 1736 (2006)1, 17 March 2006; and the 'Reply from the Committee of Ministers to Recommendation 1736 (2006)', adopted at the 963rd meeting of the Ministers' Deputies 3 May 2006.

58 On 4 July 2006, the majority of the political groups in the European Parliament expressed their condemnation of the Franco regime (P. Aguilar, *Políticas de la memoria y memorias de la política*, 429).

59 2000, 2005 and 2010: 25th, 30th and 35th anniversaries of Franco's death; 2006 and 2011: 70th and 75th anniversaries of the beginning of the Civil War; 2006 and 2011: 75th and 80th anniversaries of the proclamation of the Second Republic; 2009: 70th anniversary of the end of the Civil War.

60 See M. Davis, 'Is Spain Recovering its Memory? Breaking the Pacto del Olvido', (2005), 27 *Human Rights Quarterly*, at 858–880; G. Blakeley, 'Digging up Spain's Past: Consequences of Truth and Reconciliation', (2005) 12/1 *Democratization*, at 44–59; S. Golob, 'Volver: The Return of/to Transitional Justice Politics in Spain', (2008), 9/2 *Journal of Spanish Cultural Studies*, at 127–141 and
O. Encarnación, 'Reconciliation after democratisation: Coping with the past in Spain', (2008), 123/3 *Political Science Quarterly*, at 435–459.

3.2. MEASURES APPROVED FROM 2002 TO 2012

On 20 November 2002, the Constitutional Commission of the Congress of Deputies unanimously approved a declaration stating that "no one could feel legitimated to use violence with the aim of imposing political convictions and establishing totalitarian regimes," and urging the government "to develop an integral policy of recognition for those exiled as consequence of the Civil War" which also included protective economic and social measures.[61] Only one year later, as part of the commemoration of the 25th anniversary of the Spanish Constitution, the Congress organised an act of tribute to the victims of the dictatorship. The homage was not endorsed by the PP, the governing party at the time. On that occasion, the spokesman of the PP argued that by organising such act the opposition was breaking the verbal agreement that was reached in 2002 after the approval of the just-mentioned declaration. According to this agreement, if the PP was for first time in its history "to condemn Francoism", the left parties would have to accept in turn "never to use this topic again for political confrontation".[62] Not surprisingly, only some weeks earlier, the PP had also opposed an initiative submitted by *Eusko Alkartasuna* (EA) – and endorsed by the socialist party, *Convergencia i Unió* (CIU), *Coalición Canaria* (CC) and *Izquierda Unida* (IU) – requesting the government to assist and provide recognition to the victims of the Civil War and the dictatorship, facilitate the access to the archives containing information about the war, support the exhumation of the remains buried in mass graves and reassess the pensions of the so-called "children of the war".[63]

Taking on these demands and several that followed, after the PP lost the general elections in March 2004, and only two months after Rodríguez Zapatero started his first term of office with simple majority, the Congress approved a non-law proposition requesting the government to undertake a study regarding the rights of the victims of the Civil War and the dictatorship's repression that were already recognised by the Spanish legislation, to identify the gaps in such legislation, and to advance specific proposals for ameliorating their economic situation. Moreover, the proposal also urged the government to facilitate the general access to private and public archives that held documentation related to the victims,

---

61 Parliament, 825 *DSCD,* Constitutional Commission, VII Term of Office, 20 November 2002, 20511. This declaration has been often mistakenly considered as the first condemnation of Francoism that was passed in the Spanish Congress. But, even if the texts of some of the first proposals contemplated an explicit condemnation of Francoism, the declaration finally approved only contained the disapproval of all totalitarian regimes. However, it is also true that the repression under Francoism was explicitly named.

62 C.E. Cué, 'El PP, contrario a un homenaje a víctimas del franquismo', *El País*, 24 November 2003. See also, 'Las víctimas del franquismo reciben un homenaje en el Congreso de todos los partidos salvo el PP', *El País*, 1 December 2003.

63 'El PP rechaza una moción sobre ayudas a víctimas del franquismo', *El País,* 15 October 2003.

and to submit a draft bill of solidarity with the victims who suffered personal harm during Franco's regime in trying to exercise the forbidden civil liberties that would be later recognised in the Spanish Constitution.[64] To undertake these requests, the government appointed in September the so-called "Interministerial Commission for the Study of the situation of the victims of the Civil War and Francoism", which was directly chaired by the vice-president of the government at the time, María Teresa Fernández de la Vega.[65] The commission was given the mandate to undertake a study regarding the situation of the victims – especially in terms of reparation – and to submit recommendations to the parliament before the end of the year, as well as to draft a bill on the matter. To undertake this task, the commission was granted an initial budget of € 5 million, part of which was also to be used to fund the exhumation projects that were already being carried out with private funds by civil society associations, such as ARMH and *Foro por la Memoria*.[66] In December 2005 the government passed for first time a public call to fund activities related to the victims of the Civil War and the dictatorship.[67]

During the period that the commission was doing its work, several additional measures were taken, in all cases following the proposals of the leftist and regional parties that, from June 2004, increased the number of initiatives regarding the Civil War and the dictatorship submitted before the parliament. In this vein, in January 2005, after several months of negotiations with associations representing the children of the war, the government agreed to raise their pensions and improved the access to health care of those who were still living in foreign countries, especially in the former Soviet Union.[68] Some months later, responding to the formal request of the Catalan government, a Royal Decree was passed requesting the transfer of the documents that were seized in Catalonia after the Civil War by Franco's regime, and since then kept in the General Archive of the Spanish Civil War (in Salamanca). This decision triggered a very loud public dispute (including several demonstrations in the city of Salamanca).[69] The documents were finally transferred to Barcelona in July 2008.

---

64 See Parliament, 13 *DSCD*, Plenary Session, VIII Term of Office, 1 June 2004.

65 'Royal Decree 1891/2004, por el que se crea la Comisión Interministerial para el estudio de la situación de las víctimas de la guerra civil y del franquismo', 227 *Official State Gazette* (*Boletín Oficial del Estado*, BOE), 20 September 2004, at 31523 a 31524.

66 C.E. Cué, 'El gobierno negocia la ampliación y mejora de las pensiones de los "niños de la guerra"', *El País*, 1 November 2004.

67 Presidencial Order, Bases reguladoras para la concesión de subvenciones destinadas a actividades relacionadas con las víctimas de la guerra civil y del franquismo, 310 *BOE*, 17 December 2005, at 41391–41394.

68 'El Gobierno concede una pensión anual de 6.090 € a 603 'niños de la guerra'', *El País*, 22 January 2005.

69 See 'Royal Decree 2134/2008, de 26 de diciembre, por el que se regula el procedimiento a seguir para la restitución a particulares de los documentos incautados con motivo de la Guerra Civil', 9 *BOE*, 10 January 2009, at 3411–3415.

Other issues that were raised at that moment to no avail included, among others, the revision of the sentences issued by Franco's tribunals, the removal of Francoist symbols from public spaces, the need to implement a public policy to supervise the exhumation and identification of the remains buried in mass graves, and the restitution of Republican stolen property.[70]

Partially reflecting the increase in the number of initiatives, a key event took place in 2006 when the Congress approved a proposition (presented by IU-*Iniciativa per Catalunya Els Verds*) declaring the year 2006 as the *year of historical memory*. The motion, which was once again opposed by the PP, contained a single article stating that "On the occasion of the 75th anniversary of the proclamation of the Spanish Second Republic, 2006 is hereby declared as the *Year of Historical Memory*, as tribute and recognition to all the men and women who were victims of Civil War, or later on, of the repression of Franco's dictatorship, for their defence of democratic principles and values, as well as those who, by their effort in favor of human rights, and the defence of public liberties and reconciliation among the Spanish people, made possible the democratic regime established with the Constitution of 1978".[71]

Finally, on 28 July 2006, the Inter-ministerial Commission submitted to the Parliament two reports (one regarding the situation of the victims of the war and the dictatorship, and a second one on archives), and a draft law.[72] The submission of the bill initiated a long and complex negotiation process between the PSOE and the rest of the political parties. While, on the one hand, the PP manifested a strong opposition to the law during the whole process, accusing the left of "breaking the spirit of reconciliation" of the transition, using the past for political purposes; on the other hand, the left parties, as well as some human rights organisations and victims groups, criticised the draft law for being insufficient.[73]

The bitter debates in the parliament soon reverberated in the public space through the media. While public figures and academics, especially historians, contributed

---

70 S. Juliá, 'Public Policy on Historical Memory'.

71 Law 24/2006 sobre la declaración del año 2006 como año de la memoria histórica, 162 *BOE*, 8 July 2006, 25573.

72 Comisión Interministerial, *Informe General sobre la situación de las víctimas de la guerra civil y la dictadura*, 28 July 2006, available at www1.mpr.es/uploads/media/pdf/6/informegeneral2_1232475655.pdf,, and Comision Interministerial, *Informe sobre archivos*, 28 July 2006 available at www1.mpr.es/uploads/media/pdf/8/informesobrearchivos2_1232475674.pdf. See also Draft Bill, 99–1 *Official Gazette of the Parliament* (*Boletín Oficial de las Cortes Generales*, BOCG), VIII Term of Office, 8 September 2006.

73 Amnistía Internacional, *Víctimas de la Guerra Civil y el Franquismo: No hay Derecho. Preocupaciones sobre el proyecto de ley de "derechos de las víctimas de la Guerra Civil y del Franquismo"*, Madrid, November 2006, S. Juliá, 'Public Policy on Historical Memory' and P. Aguilar, *Políticas de la memoria y memorias de la política*.

with multiple editorials and commentary, issues such as the so-called "war of the death notices" emerged out of private initiative. This "war" started when a series of individuals began commissioning notices in the obituary sections of the main Spanish newspapers honouring the persons who had been extra-judicially executed during the war in both sides. However, despite the existence of this clear two-sided confrontation in the public domain, the truth is that the average Spaniard was hardly involved in the debate. Finally, an amended version of the original text was approved in a Plenary Sitting of the Congress of Deputies on 31 October 2007.[74] Two groups opposed the law: The PP and ERC (which, although it was initially one of the main promoters of the law, finally refused to endorse it because it didn't declare null and void the trials of the Franco era).

Law 52/2007 "which recognises and expands the rights, and establishes measures in favor of those who suffered persecution or violence during the Civil War and the dictatorship" (or the popularly known "law of historic memory") was finally passed by the Senate on 10 December 2007 (127 votes for and 119 against), immediately before the parliament dissolved for that term of office.[75] The text has 22 articles and several provisions that together regulate a handful of issues ranging from material and symbolic reparations, to different aspects relating to the maintenance of the memory of the past that, taking on some of the demands presented by the different parties during the drafting process, exceeded the initial approach taken by the government.[76]

As Aguilar has noted, "in very general terms, this law unravelled the tangled web of prevailing legislation in order to ensure better treatment of the victims of war and the dictatorship, rectified the omissions concerning reparation for certain groups and facilitated access to existing documentation. The aim was to pass a law that would serve to recover the memory of those who had fallen into institutional oblivion in spite of having striven to establish a democratic regime in Spain, including the victims of political violence during the transition.[77] Furthermore, it was the first time that a Spanish law acknowledged human rights violations committed under the dictatorship".[78] It should be noted, however, that although the law constitutes the most comprehensive attempt to date to

74 Parliament, 296 *DSCD*, VIII Term of Office, 31 October 2007.

75 Parliament, 140 *Journal of the Senate* (*Diario de Sesiones del Senado*, DSS), VIII Term of Office, 10 December 2007, at 8871–8904. See also Law 52/2007, de 26 de diciembre, por la que se reconocen y amplían derechos y se establecen medidas en favor de quienes padecieron persecución o violencia durante la guerra civil y la dictadura, 310 *BOE*, 27 December 2007, at 53410–53416.

76 The initial text has suffered some minor modifications: article 10 has been altered twice by the 'Ley de Presupuestos Generales del Estado' of 2009 and 2010 to establish new amounts; while the additional disposition No 8 was amended in March 2010.

77 P. Aguilar and I. Sánchez-Cuenca, 'Terrorist Violence and Popular Mobilization', 428–453.

78 P. Aguilar, *Políticas de la memoria y memorias de la política*, 426.

address the violent and repressive past in Spain, its coming into being and implementation have been marked by the radical opposition of the PP, the deep disappointment of many victims' groups, and the apparent indifference of the great majority of Spanish society.

In general terms it could be said the Law deals with four different issues: First, it provides reparation measures to victims; second, it partially addresses the question of the exhumation of remains of common graves of the civil war; third, it contemplates the removal of Francoist symbols and gives a special consideration to the Valley of the Fallen; and, fourth, it regulates issues regarding the preservation and access to private and public archives containing information of the war. Five different ministries have participated in its implementation – including the Ministry for the Presidency, and those of Culture, Justice, Economy and Defence – and several additional legislative provisions had to be taken to develop further some of its measures. A brief explanation on each of these points will follow, including the principal lines of action taken.

Reparatory Measures. The bulk of the articles of the law (Articles 5 to 10) establish different compensation measures (either determining lump sum payments or reassessing pensions), and recognise some categories of beneficiaries that were not included in previous reparatory laws (also standardising some measures that, because they were being differently applied by the Autonomous Communities, created inequalities over the national territory). Especially interesting is the fact that, for the first time after the transition, the law granted reparations for those who died between 1 January 1968 and 6 October 1977 "defending the Spanish democracy".[79] Likewise, and although it was not initially included in the law, under its general framework, the government has granted indemnities to the so-called "social prisoners" of the regime – i.e., those who were imprisoned because of "their sexual orientation, or social danger" (*sic*).[80]

79 This would be delivered in a onetime payment of € 135,000 that was allocated by an Evaluation Commission created in November 2008 to examine the applications. See 'Royal Decree 1803/2008, de 3 de noviembre, por el que se regulan las condiciones y el procedimiento para el abono de las indemnizaciones reconocidas en la Ley 52/2007, de 26 de diciembre, a favor de personas fallecidas o con lesiones incapacitantes por su actividad en defensa de la Democracia', 276 *BOE*, 15 November 2008, at 45394–45401. From the applications presented 49 were positive, 24 negative and 116 were not admitted. See www.memoriahistorica.gob.es/Prestaciones/mas/IndemnizacionesFallecIncap.htm.

80 The Indemnities Commission for Social Ex Prisoners (Comisión de Indemnizaciones a Ex Presos Sociales) was created within the Ministry of Economy by the General Budget of the State Law of 2009 and the Royal Decree 710/2009 of 17 April 2009. The indemnities are fixed in proportion to the time spent in prison, ranging from 4,000 and up to € 12,010 for three or more years; and € 2,302 additional for each additional period of 3 years. Available at <www.clasespasivas.sgpg.pap.meh.es/sitios/clasespasivas/es-ES/PensionesPrestaciones/Paginas/expresossociales.aspx>, accessed 15 August 2011.

In terms of symbolic reparations, the law includes two fundamental measures: First, article 3 of the bill declares the illegitimacy of all the tribunals that were created during the Civil War and Franco's dictatorship on political, ideological or religious grounds, and specifically declares illegitimate the Tribunal for the Repression of Masonry and Communism, the Tribunal of Public Order, the Tribunal of Political Responsibilities and the Courts-Martial.[81] To complement this measure, Article 4 further recognises the right of the victims to obtain a "declaration of reparation and personal recognition". Such certificates are granted by the Ministry of Justice, which, by May 2011, had already issued 1,011.[82] Its symbolic significance notwithstanding, this measure was highly contested, for victims' groups were expecting that the law would declare the sentences of the Francoist tribunals null and void. Following the report prepared by the Interministerial Commission the government argued, however, that doing so would break the country's constitutional order, and contradict the principle of judicial security.[83] On the other side, the families of those "illegitimately sentenced," some of whom had been trying for years to obtain the nullity of the sentences through judicial procedures, were deeply disappointed.[84] The *Generalitat* of Catalonia and the granddaughter of Lluís Companys (the President of Catalonia who was executed by Francoist forces in 1940) requested that the State Prosecutor (*Fiscal General del Estado*) formally demand the Supreme Court to review the case. On 5 April 2010, after having organised an official Prosecutors' Meeting, the National Prosecutor issued a decree in which it was stated that there was no need to send the case to the Supreme Court, because considering that the Law of 2007 had already declared the illegitimacy of the Franco Courts, it was indeed implied that the sentences were null and void.[85] In June 2011, referring to this decree, ERC-IU-ICV once again requested in

---

81 This is accompanied by a final derogatory clause in the law in which several decrees and laws of the dictatorship are specially derogated.

82 Cortes Generales, 'Speech of the Minister of Presidency at the Constitutional Commission', 767 *DSCD*, IX Term of Office, Sesión No. 27, 4 May 2011, at 3–26, 7.

83 Comisión Interministerial: *Informe General de la Comisión Interministerial para el Estudio de la Situación de las Victimas de la Guerra Civil y el Franquismo*, Madrid, 28 July 2006, 31–36.

84 The only judicial process that has taken place in Spain, the "Ruano case," has contributed neither to revealing the truth nor to accountability. And only on one occasion – in spite of more than 40 review petitions – has the Supreme Court agreed to nullify a sentence of a court martial, in spite of the fact that most political trials of the civil war and the Francoist period were conducted without the minimum guarantees for the defendant. A. GIL *La justicia de transición en España*, at 58.

85 'La Fiscalía se niega a pedir la revisión del juicio a Lluís Companys', *El País*, 23 March 2010. See also, Fiscal General del Estado, *Decreto del Excmo, Sr. Fiscal General del Estado sobre las Resoluciones Dictadas contra D. Lluis Companys i Jover por el Tribunal de Responsabilidades Políticas de Barcelona en fecha 13 de diciembre de 1939 y por el Consejo de guerra de Oficiales Generales en Fecha 14 de octubre de 1940*, Madrid, 5 April 2010. For a more detailed analysis see J. Errandonea, 'Estudio comparado de la anulación de sentencias injustas en España', International Center for Transitional Justice, New York, 2008.

Parliament that the sentences be nullified. The proposal was, however, rejected by the PSOE, PP, CIU, and PNV.[86]

The second fundamental symbolic measure included in the law is the concession of Spanish nationality both to the members of the International Brigades who fought in the Republican side during the war, and to the descendants of those who were forced into exile between 18 July 1936 and 31 December 1955.[87] According to the data provided by the Minister for the Presidency in May 2011, 21 former members of the Brigades have obtained Spanish nationality, while the applications of 187,076 descendants of Spanish exiles have been approved. The great majority of the requests came from Latin America, especially Cuba.[88] The law was modified in July 2011 to include in the provisions the grandchildren of exiled women who had married a foreigner after 5 August 1954, while keeping their Spanish nationality. In the same move, the Senate approved a disposition that had long been requested by memory groups, according to which those who disappeared during the Civil War and the Dictatorship – i.e., those who were executed and buried in mass graves – were to be included in the civil registry as deceased.[89]

The issue of the mass graves. One of the key (if not most important) issues that were regulated in the law was the location of mass graves and the identification of the remains of those who were killed during the Civil War and its aftermath. This was important not only because it constituted one of the major demands of civil society associations, but also because, to this day, there has not been any official attempt to establish a record of the thousands of bodies that are still anonymously buried all over the national territory. Since it was founded in 2000, ARMH, together with other associations, has been particularly active in the location and exhumation of mass graves. However, this activity had been carried in an *ad hoc* and private manner. Consequently, together with the lack of funding, many families have had to surmount administrative and legal challenges to access the places where the burials are located.

Articles 11 to 14 of the law are devoted to different issues regarding the "location and identification of victims of the Civil War who remain disappeared" along

---

86 See 'PSOE y PP vuelven a sumar sus votos para impedir declarar "nulas de pleno derecho" las condenas políticas del franquismo', available at Izquierda Unida's website: www.izquierda-unida.es/node/9031.

87 It should be noted that, although the members of the International Brigades were also granted nationality in 1996, the measure approved then implied that they had to renounce to their previous nationality if they were to acquire the Spanish one. The new regulation, however, solves this problem, and the applicants can retain both nationalities.

88 See 'Speech of the Minister of Presidency at the Constitutional Commission', 4 May 2011, 22; and 'Ciudadanía española para nietos del exilio', *BBCMundo*, 4 September 2009, available at <www.bbc.co.uk/mundo/america_latina/2009/09/090829_ley_nietos_pea.shtml >.

89 'Ley 20/2011, de 21 de julio, del Registro Civil, disposición adicional sexta', 175 *BOE*, 22 July 2011, at 81468–82502.

three lines: The commitment of the government to draft a protocol for the exhumation of the remains, the elaboration and publication of a national map of mass graves, and the establishment of a grant program to economically support such activities. Moreover, the law regulates the relevant procedures to access the sites in which the graves are located (both public and private). However, rather disappointingly, the law left the task of exhuming and identifying the remains in the hands of the civil society, instead of making it responsibility of the state. Victims' associations and human rights groups heavily criticised this provision, while several leftist parties proposed a motion to modify the law, which was, however, rejected in December 2008.[90]

In December 2008, the government passed a law announcing the establishment of an Office for the Victims of the Civil War and the Dictatorship that was to serve as the reference point of information regarding the rights recognised in the law.[91] Among the tasks that were included in its mandate was the elaboration of a "protocol of scientific and interdisciplinary action for the exhumation of mass graves and the elaboration of an integrated map covering the national territory of the inhumation sites".[92] In 2008 a draft version of the protocol was completed and sent to the Autonomous Communities, to the Spanish Federation of Municipalities and Provinces, and to the historical memory associations operating at a national level.[93] In November 2009, the government commissioned the Aranzadi Society of Sciences for a project to elaborate a database of the mass graves of the Civil War that had already been exhumed. An incomplete document listing the exhumations done since 2000 was then produced and published. With the aim of advancing the elaboration of a national map, the Ministry of Justice put forward a proposal to coordinate with some Autonomous Communities, by which the latter would provide data of mass graves located in their territory, and the Ministry would integrate them in a single map. To this end, in January 2010 the Minister signed an agreement with eight Autonomous Communities including Andalucía, Aragón, Asturias, Cantabria, Castilla-La Mancha, Catalonia, Extremadura, and the Basque Country. To date, except in the case of the Balearic Islands that signed an agreement in 2011, those Autonomous Communities governed by the PP, have

90 See Senado, 'Proposición de Ley de Modificación de la Ley 52/2007', *BOCG*, IX Term of Office, Serie III A: Proposiciones de Ley del Senado, Num. 8 (a), 3 December 2008.

91 However, in March 2009, ARHM together with Psychologists without Borders established an Office for Victims of the Civil War and Francoism in Madrid. According to AHRM although the Minister of Justice said they were planning to open the office in 2008, nothing had been done in this respect. 'Las víctimas de la Guerra Civil ya tienen oficina en Madrid,' *El País*, 17 March 2009.

92 'Order PRE/3749/2008, sobre el Acuerdo de Consejo de Ministros para creación Oficina Víctimas de la Guerra Civil y Dictadura', 309 *BOE*, 24 December 2008, at 51900–1.

93 *Cortes Generales*, 'Speech of the Ministry of Presidency at the Constitutional Commission', 668 *DSCD*, IX Term of Office, session No. 22, Madrid, 1 December 2010, 5.

declined to provide such data.[94] Since May 2011 a still-incomplete map of mass graves is available online. The map contains data of around 2000 mass graves including those that were transferred to the Valley of the Fallen during Franco's time.[95] Finally, on 23 September 2011, the government approved a final exhumation protocol.[96] Although this protocol constituted an important development, several victims' associations highly criticised the fact that, after the approval of the law, it had taken the government four years to adopt it.[97]

The idleness of the central government in this respect contrasts, however, with the approach taken by several Autonomous Communities, especially the Basque Country, Catalonia, and Andalucía. In 2002, the Basque Government already established an interdepartmental commission to investigate and locate the mass graves of those who disappeared during the Civil War.[98] As a result the regional government signed an agreement in 2005 with the Aranzadi Society of Sciences to locate and facilitate the exhumation of mass graves.[99] In Catalonia, in March 2003, the parliament requested the government to prepare a register of disappeared persons and a map of mass graves.[100] After the exhumation of the grave of Gurb in 2008, which was to serve as a pilot exhumation to establish a protocol, the regional government approved a rather comprehensive exhumation law on 30 June 2009.[101] Moreover, in 2008 the government established an Office of Attention to Victims that offers historical and juridical advice to individuals, as well as assistance regarding compensation measures, location of the disappeared and exhumation of graves. In Andalucía, after the creation in 2004

94 'Víctimas del Franquismo se preparan para un "recortazo" del PP en políticas de memoria', *El País*, 10 September 2011.

95 The map is available at www.memoriahistorica.gob.es/MapaFosas/index.htm.

96 'Order PRE/2568/2011 por la que se publica el Acuerdo del Consejo de Ministros de 23 de septiembre de 2011, por el que se ordena la publicación en el Boletín Oficial del Estado del Protocolo de actuación en exhumaciones de víctimas de la guerra civil y la dictadura', 232 *BOE*, 27 September 2011, at 101916–101923.

97 'La ARMH lamenta que el Gobierno haya tardado 4 años en redactar el protocolo para las exhumaciones', *Nueva Tribuna*, 8 October *2011*.

98 Consejo de Gobierno, *Creación de la Comisión Interdepartamental para investigar y localizar las fosas de las personas desaparecidas durante la guerra civil*, 10 December 2002.

99 *Convenio de colaboración entre el Gobierno Vasco y la Sociedad de Ciencias Aranzadi para continuar la investigación de personas desaparecidas durante la Guerra Civil en el territorio de la Comunidad Autónoma del País Vasco*, Vitoria-Gasteiz, 26 de septiembre de 2006.

100 Motion 217/VI, Parliament of Catalonia, 'en relación con la recuperación de la memoria histórica especialmente al reconocimiento de las personas desaparecidas durante la Guerra civil y la posguerra', 410 *Parliament of Catalonia Official Gazette*, (*Boletín Oficial del Parlamento de Cataluña, BOPC*), 31 March 2003, 9.

101 Law 10/2009, Localización e identificación de las personas desaparecidas durante la Guerra Civil y la dictadura franquista, y la dignificación de las fosas comunes, 5417 *Generalitat of Catalonia Official Gazzette* (*Diario Oficial de la Generalitat de Cataluña,* DOGC), 9 July 2007, 55065. See also, 'Localizados trece cuerpos en la fosa común de la Guerra Civil exhumada en Gurb,' *El País*, 13 June 2008.

of a Committee of Technical Coordination, the government approved an exhumation protocol on 7 September 2009.[102]

To the extent that the law did not make the state directly responsible for the exhumation of the mass graves of the Civil War – leaving the task in the hands of civil society instead – it did establish, however, that the government would provide economic support to individuals undertaking such activities. To this end, starting in 2005, the government has been passing an annual call for applications. The subsidies have the general aim of "promoting the recovery of the collective memory and the moral recognition of the victims of the Civil War". Addressed to associations, foundations, particular groups, trade unions and, since 2010, also universities, the grants have served to finance different types of projects including the compilation of censuses of the disappeared, exhumations, celebration of tributes, compilation of documents and oral testimonies, production of documentaries, celebration of exhibits and publications. According to the speech that Minister for the Presidency delivered to the Constitutional Commission on December 2010, between 2006 and 2010 the government had granted € 19,475,985 to fund 642 different projects.[103]

Together with the central government, several Autonomous Communities have been especially active in promoting and funding activities related to the recovery of the historical memory in Spain. On 31 October 2007 the Catalan Government passed a law creating the Memorial Democratic, an institution that was to develop public policies in relation to the recovery, commemoration and promotion of the democratic memory regarding the Second Republic, the Victims of the Civil War and the Francoist repression. Together with the policies directly promoted by the Memorial, the government of Catalonia has also been funding civil society led activities every year since 2005.[104] In Andalucía, a Commissioner for the Recovery of Historical Memory was appointed in February 2005, and the government has been funding activities to promote the recovery of historical memory since 2003.[105]

---

102 See Decree 521/2004, por el que se crea la Comisión Interdepartamental para el reconocimiento de las víctimas de la Guerra Civil y del Franquismo en la Comunidad Autónoma de Andalucía, 221 *Official Gazzette of Andalucía* (*Boletín Oficial de la Junta de Andalucía BOJA*), 12 November 2004, at 26254–26255; and Orden de 7 de septiembre de 2009, por la que se aprueba el Protocolo Andaluz de actuación en exhumaciones de víctimas de la Guerra Civil y la Posguerra, *BOJA*, 28 September 2009, at 8–12.

103 Speech of the Minister of Presidency at the Constitutional Commission, 1 December 2010, 5. The provisional resolution of 2011 call for applications was approved on 3 October 2011.

104 Law 13/2007 del Memorial Democràtic, 5006 *DOGC*, 12 November 2007, at 45172–45179. See the government website www20.gencat.cat/portal/site/memorialdemocratic.

105 See Decree 54/2005, por el que se crea la figura de Comisario para la recuperación de la Memoria Histórica, 40 *BOJA*, 25 February 2005, at 7–8, and Coordinación de actuaciones en torno a la recuperación de la memoria histórica y el reconocimiento institucional y social de las personas desaparecidas durante la Guerra Civil y la Posguerra, 236 *BOJA*, 9 December 2003, at 25731–25733.

The Basque Country started funding projects for the recuperation of historical memory on an annual basis in 2006; while Aragón began doing so in 2007.[106] Galicia declared 2006 as the *Year of Historical Memory*, after the Socialists came to power in 2005.[107] On July 2006, the regional government created the Council for Memory (*Consello pola Memoria*) that was to provide recommendations in terms of historical memory and to act as intermediary with civil society organisations; and announced the first call for subsidies for particular associations to organise cultural activities to promote the recovery of historical memory.[108] Finally, in 2005 an agreement was signed between the University of Extremadura and the regional government and is currently funding a historical memory research project.[109]

Removal of Symbols. The removal of symbols commemorating the military rebellion or the Francoist repression – except in those cases in which such symbols have historical meaning, artistic or religious-artistic value, or are architecturally fundamental – was contemplated in Article 15 of the law. In November 2008 an agreement establishing instructions to remove Francoist symbols from official buildings at the state level was adopted by the Council of Ministers.[110] In February 2009, a Technical Commission was established to elaborate a report to fix criteria that were to be used to remove the symbols, as well as to evaluate the process on a case-to-case basis.[111] According to the data provided by the government, the commission has already evaluated 715 symbols from different public institutions, 600 of which have already been removed and

---

106 See 'Subvenciones para la realización de actividades y proyectos de recuperación de la memoria histórica', 92 *Basque Country Official Gazzette*, 17 May 2006, 9793; and 'Adjudicación de una subvención del Fondo Local de Aragón para Proyectos Dirigidos a la Recuperación de la Memoria Histórica de la Lucha por la Democracia en Aragón, o en relación con Aragón, durante el periodo comprendido entre 1931 y 1980', 127 *Aragon Official Gazzette*, 29 October 2007, 14500.

107 Decree Xunta de Galicia, *Declaración institucional a respecto da recuperación da memoria histórica e da rehabilitación moral*, 18 August 2005.

108 Order 'por la que se convocan subvenciones a particulares, asociaciones e instituciones culturales para la realización de actividades culturales relacionadas con la recuperación de la memoria histórica', 116 *Galicia Oficial Gazette* (Diario Oficial de Galicia, DOG),19 June 2006, 9779. Since 2008 there has been no more calls, while the Consello is no longer operative.

109 *Convenio entre la Consejería de Cultura de la Junta de Extremadura, La Excma. Diputación Provincial de Badajoz, la de Cáceres, y la Universidad de Extremadura para la realización del programa "Recuperación de la Memoria Histórica de Extremadura"*, 22 September 2005.

110 Orden CUL/3190/2008, de 6 de noviembre, por la que se publica el Acuerdo del Consejo de Ministros, de 31 de octubre de 2008, por el que se dictan instrucciones para la retirada de símbolos franquistas en los bienes de la Administración General del Estado y sus organismos públicos dependientes, 269 *BOE*, 7 November 2008, 44556.

111 See Orden CUL/459/2009, de 19 de febrero, por la que se crea y regula la Comisión Técnica de Expertos para la valoración de los supuestos determinantes de la excepcionalidad en la retirada de símbolos, 51 *BOE*, 28 February 2009, 20757, and Comisión Técnica: *Informe Preliminar sobre criterios generales aplicados por la comisión técnica de expertos de la ley de la memoria histórica*, Ministerio de Cultura, Madrid, 2011. See www.memoriahistorica.gob.es/Vestigios/enlaces/comisionExpertos.htm.

transferred to storage places and museums.[112] Special attention has been given to the symbols that were located in military buildings. According to the data provided on the Ministry of Defence website, after producing a catalogue, between 2009 and 2010, the Ministry has either modified or removed around 410 symbols and changed the names of 11 military outbuildings.[113] However, despite the provisions of Article 17 of the law, the government has not yet taken any measure to develop a registry of the edifications and constructions done by the *Batallones Disciplinarios de Soldados Trabajadores*, and the *Batallones de Trabajadores y Prisioneros en Colonias Penitenciarias* (Disciplinary Battalions of Working Soldiers, and Battalions of Workers and Prisoners in Penitentiary Colonies). In June 2011, the ERC, IU and ICV presented an initiative requesting that the government compile such a registry within a six-month period.[114] In the same resolution the political groups requested the removal of the Francoist symbols that were still in place, as although the government has removed an important amount of symbols, there are still many left (including those located in municipal or private buildings). Once again, taking a leading role in this respect, the Memorial Democratic of Catalonia has prepared a registry of Francoist symbols in Catalan territory which is available online. The project Bitter Memory (*Amarga Memoria*), established by the government of Aragón, has also compiled a map of Francoist symbols in the autonomous community.[115] However, this situation, despite the clear position of the law in the matter, does not prevail over all Spanish territory; for example, there are still eight municipalities in Spain that maintain in their name a laudatory reference to Franco.[116]

Among the symbols of the Francoist past, the Valley of the Fallen – a religious-funerary monumental complex in which Franco and José Antonio Primo de Rivera (the young leader of the Falange who was executed during the war) are buried – has a quintessential standing. The law provides that the Valley of the Fallen shall not be used to celebrate political rallies (Article 16), while an additional disposition succinctly states that "the Management Foundation of the Valley of the Fallen will include in its mandate to honour and rehabilitate the memory of all those who died during the Civil War or as the result of the posterior political repression". The complex is at the same time a massive grave. According to the estimations provided by the Minister for the Presidency in May

---

112 See www.memoriahistorica.gob.es/Vestigios/enlaces/comisionExpertos.htm, and 'Balance general de retirada de vestigios de la Administración General del Estado'. See also, 'El franquismo se retira al sótano', *El País*, 16 October 2011. According to the article, most of these symbols will be transferred to the Documentary Center for the Historical Memory in Salamanca.

113 A map of these symbols as well as a document with the data of the outbuildings names that have been changed can be found at www.defensa.gob.es/memoriahistorica/actuaciones.html.

114 'ERC, IU, e ICV piden un censo de obras realizadas mediante trabajos forzosos durante la dictadura', *Diario SIGLO XXI*, 29 June 2011.

115 See www.patrimonioculturaldearagon.com/patr/contenido/programa-amarga-memoria.

116 Jerónimo Andreu, 'Las utopías de Franco resisten', *El País*, Ciudad Rodrigo, 11 August 2012.

2011, the remains of 33,847 victims of the Civil War are buried there; from 1959 until 1983 these were transferred from cemeteries and mass graves from all over the territory (the remains of most of the Republican victims were moved without the authorisation of their families). The identity of 12,410 of the remains is still unknown.[117] An initial forensic assessment regarding the situation of the remains and the feasibility of exhuming them was completed in February 2011. Although not free of polemics, according to the report it is impossible to exhume and identify the bodies for technical and economic reasons.[118]

Regarding the issue of converting the Valley in a site of "shared memory and reconciliation", on 27 May 2011, following a proposal of the Ministry for the Presidency, the Council of Ministers approved the creation of an "Expert Commission for the Future of the Valley of Fallen", which was chaired by the Ministry for the Presidency, and composed by 11 other members, including among them 10 Spanish academics and intellectuals (including jurists, historians and philosophers) and a Benedictine monk.[119] Among the guidelines that the Minister gave to the members of the commission are: First, the permanence of the Benedictine community that manages the Abbey, and second, the preservation of the giant cross that sits atop the valley. On 29 November 2011, after 5 months of work, the Commission submitted a final report. Three of the members of the Commission did not subscribe to one of the main recommendations: The relocation of the remains of Francisco Franco in a private cemetery. Moreover, as it was to be expected after the political turn in Spain following the electoral victory of the PP in November 2011, none of the recommendations of the commission has been attended – including the request to change the meaning of the whole monument and the creation of a memorial with a list of all the victims. On the contrary, in May 2013 the government announced a project to restore the portal of the basilica where Franco was buried.

The archives. The final set of issues regulated by the law relates to the preservation and access to private and public archives (Arts. 20–22) that

117 Speech of the Minister of Presidency at the Constitutional Commission, 4 May 2011, 9.

118 Andrés Bedate Gutiérrez, 'Viabilidad de identificación en el enterramiento del Valle de los Caídos', Madrid, 15 February 2011. Available at: <www.memoriahistorica.gob.es/NR/rdonlyres/326E9950-5FDA-482A-BF15-0DE8933D49C9/153421/informeforensevalledeloscaidos.pdf>. The original registry books of the Valley, as well as individual cards with the names of 21.423 victims have been digitalized following an agreement signed by the Ministry of Justice and National Conservation on 6 October 2009.

119 'A propuesta del ministro de la Presidencia, El Consejo de Ministros aprueba la creación de la Comisión de Expertos para el Futuro del Valle de los Caídos', Press Release, Madrid, 27 May 2011; and Orden PRE/1396/2011, por la que se publica el Acuerdo de Consejo de Ministros por el que se crea la Comisión de Expertos para el Futuro del Valle de los Caídos, 127 *BOE*, 28 May 2011, at 53148–53153.

contain information of the war. The law stated the right to access both private and public archives; however, no formal procedure was established. According to the Minister for the Presidency, after receiving requests from historians and associations to access some specific archives, the government has sought collaboration between the ministries for the Presidency, of Justice and of Culture to produce a report, as well as to propose a set of legal modifications to guarantee archive access to historians, families, and individuals, while at the same time preserving the right to privacy.[120] To date – setting aside the archives that already have public access – three steps have been taken in this direction. In 2008, an instruction was approved to regulate the access to death certificates from the civil registry dependent on the General Office of Registries and Notaries (*Dirección General de Registros y Notarías*).[121] In 2009, the government passed a Royal Decree regulating the Military Judicial Archives, and in November 2011, a decree regulating the access to the State Archives was approved.[122] Before the general elections of November 2011, and as a consequence of an initiative of the socialist Defence Minister, Carmen Chacón, around 10,000 documents from the Judicial Military Archives – dating from 1936 to 1968 – were ready to be declassified.[123] However, the Ministry of Defence of the new rightist government announced the cancellation of the process in May 2012, alleging potential diplomatic conflicts.[124] As regards the preservation of archives, articles 20 and 21 of the law establish the setting up of the Documentary Center of the Historical Memory and the General Archive of the Civil War, and declare such collections part of the documentary and bibliographic national heritage. The Center, located in Salamanca, was already announced in 2005, and its mandate is to compile, organise and recover all the documents pertaining to the historical period that goes from the Civil War to the Constitution in 1978; to facilitate individuals' access to the collections of public and private archives; and to promote the research and dissemination of such documentary collections. According to the data provided in its website, the Documentary Center comprises the General Archive of the Civil War and

---

120 Speech of the Minister of Presidency at the Constitutional Commission, May 4, 2011, 9.

121 Instrucción de 4 de noviembre de 2008, de la Dirección General de los Registros y del Notariado, sobre acceso a la consulta de los libros de defunciones de los registros civiles, dictada en desarrollo de la disposición adicional octava de la Ley 52/2007, 285 *BOE*, 26 November 2008, 47218.

122 See Royal Decree 1816/2009 'por el que se aprueba el Reglamento de los Archivos Judiciales Militares', 13 *BOE*,15 January 2010, at 3240–3242, and Royal Decree 1708/2011, por el que se establece el Sistema Español de Archivos y se regula el Sistema de Archivos de la Administración General del Estado y de sus Organismos Públicos y su régimen de acceso, 284 *BOE*, 25 November 2011, at 125573–125592.

123 'Defensa levanta el velo de la historia', *El País*, Madrid, 5 December 2011.

124 Defensa aparca la desclasificación de 10.000 documentos secretos', Cadena Ser, 29 May 2012. Available at, www.cadenaser.com/espana/articulo/defensa-aparca-desclasificacion-10000-documentos-secretos/csrcsrpor/20120529csrcsrnac_1/Tes.

several other collections, both public and private. The General Archive of the Civil War is dated from the Franco times, whereas the Documentary Center's collection is comprised by the "original collections" coming from 1) the Ministry for the Presidency, and 2) the Special Tribunal to Repress Masonry and Communism, and the "incorporated collections", which are those that were included after 1979.[125] Since the approval of the law, the Center has developed several programs to recuperate additional documentary collections from the period of 1936–1978. For example, as the Minister for the Presidency highlighted, it has recently acquired 300,000 digitalised documents from the Spanish Civil War Collection of the International Committee of the Red Cross in Geneva.[126]

Together with the collections of the Documentary Center, there are other archives that are important in relation to the Civil War and the Francoist repression: 1) the General Archive and the Police and Prison Archives, located in the Ministry of Interior; 2) the Central Archive of the Ministry of Economy and Treasury, with documents from the Civil War and the purges of Francoism; and 3) the Military Judicial Archives, with documentation of the summary judgments during the war and dictatorship located in twenty-one different outbuildings under the supervision of the Ministry of Defence.[127]

Finally, the Ministry of Culture has also developed and made available online several databases on Ibero-American migrations, Republican soldiers disappeared during the war, Republican soldiers with military ranks and decorations, and Spaniards deported to Nazi concentration camps.[128] There is also an online site dedicated to the Victims of the Civil War and those who were repressed by Francoism that aims at facilitating the access of the average citizen to the documents relative to the victims of the Civil War, the exile and the dictatorship's repression. As a matter of fact, since 2005 the Ministry of Culture has been undertaking important efforts to recover different types of collections, organising them, and making them accessible to the public.[129]

---

125 See www.mcu.es/archivos/MC/CDMH/Presentacion.html. A charter is available at: www.mcu.es/archivos/docs/MC/CDMH/CDMH_cuadroFondoDocs.pdf.

126 Speech of the Minister of Presidency at the Constitutional Commission, 4 May 2011, 8. On archives see www.memoriahistorica.gob.es/Archivos/.

127 Www.memoriahistorica.gob.es/Archivos/Enlaces/documentacionMilitar.htm. See also www.defensa.gob.es/memoriahistorica/a_militares.html and the press release: 'Defensa impulsa la digitalización de los juicios sumarísimos del franquismo y la guerra civil' of 29 June 2011.

128 See www.memoriahistorica.gob.es/Archivos/Enlaces/mcu.htm. All the information can be requested online.

129 See http://pares.mcu.es/victimasGCFPortal/staticContent.form?viewName=presentacion.

3.3. JUDICIAL INITIATIVES

By the summer of 2006, and after the draft of the bill on historical memory was presented before the Parliament, many victims' associations realised that the law was not going to meet their expectations. In part as a response to this disappointment, on 14 December 2006 five organisations of families of persons disappeared during the Civil War and under Francoism submitted several demands at the National High Court (*Audiencia Nacional*, AN).[130] According to the proceedings issued by the Prosecuting Judge, Baltasar Garzón, on 16 October 2008, these claims denounced "alleged crimes of illegal detention under the framework of a systematic and preconceived plan to eliminate political opponents through multiple deaths, torture, exile and forced disappearances from 1936, during the years of the Civil War and the post-war, that took place in different geographical spots of the Spanish territory".[131] It should be noted here that in the Spanish case, the term disappeared should be understood as those persons who were extrajudicially executed and whose bodies, buried in mass graves, have never been located; although in most cases there is either official record or oral testimony about the execution.[132]

On 29 January 2008, the Prosecutor of the AN issued a document recommending those claims not to be admitted as the crimes considered.[133] However, the Judge of the Chamber, Baltasar Garzón, contradicting the position of the Prosecutor, decided to open an investigation. Some weeks later, on 16 and 17 October, Garzón issued two court orders (autos) declaring himself competent to investigate around 114,266 disappearances occurred during the Civil War and Francoism – making use of the International Criminal Law framework – and

130 Including Nuestra Memoria, Sierra de Gredos y Toledo, Associació per a la recuperació de la Memòria Històrica de Catalunya, Asociación por la Recuperación de la Memoria Histórica en Aragón, Comisión pola Memoria Histórica do 36 en Ponteareas, and Asociación por la Recuperación de la Memoria Histórica de Arúcas. Seventeen additional claims would be presented between 25 December and 6 October 2008. See Juzgado Central de Instrucción No 005, Audiencia Nacional: Diligencias Previas Proceso Abreviado 399/2006 V, Madrid, Auto, 16 October 2008. The Audiencia Nacional (AN) is a National High Court that has jurisdiction all over the territory in relation to serious crimes like corruption and terrorism. It has a system of prosecutor and investigation judges and it admits private application.

131 Audiencia Nacional, Juzgado Central de Instrucción No 5, Auto Diligencias Previas-Procedimiento abreviado 399/2006 V, 16 October 2008.

132 See F. Ferrándiz, 'De las fosas comunes a los derechos humanos: El descubrimiento de las *desapariciones forzadas* en la España contemporánea', (2010), 19 *Revista de Antropología Social*, at 161–189.

133 Audiencia Nacional, Fiscalía, 'Dictamen de la Fiscalía de la AN que concluye en la no admisión a trámite y la solicitud de archivo de las denuncias presentadas por algunas asociaciones de víctimas del franquismo', General Fiscalía No: 00757/2007, Juzgado de Instrucción número 5, DP 399/2006, 19 January 2008. See also, Amnistía Internacional, *La obligación de investigar los crímenes del pasado y garantizar los derechos de las víctimas de desaparición forzada durante la guerra civil y el franquismo*, Madrid, November 2008.

stressing that the facts had never been investigated before by the Spanish justice system.[134] With this move he was admitting the claims presented by twenty-two families of disappeared persons, formally accusing thirty-five members of the leadership of Francoism of the alleged crimes (including Franco), and authorising the exhumation of nineteen mass graves.

The decision of the judge came as a big surprise to many, for the possibility of opening judicial proceedings against Francoism was never before (seriously) considered in Spain. In legal terms, Garzón's position was opposed by the prosecutor of the AN, who presented and appeal against his decision alleging that the judge was not competent to investigate the disappearances that occurred during the Civil War, using several arguments ranging from the inadequate characterisation of the crimes as crimes against humanity and hence the retroactivity of using such framework to deal with them.[135] Moreover, the prosecutor alleged that the crimes, as ordinary crimes, were covered by the Amnesty Law of 1977 and would have been prescribed in any case. In an extraordinary session held on 7 November, the Criminal Chamber accepted the Prosecutor's position, requesting the preventive suspension of the exhumations ordered by Garzón until a final decision was taken. As a response, Garzón issued a third order on 18 November declaring the extinction of the criminal responsibility of the accused, for they had already deceased; recusing himself from the proceedings; and transferring the case to the territorial courts of the places in which the mass graves are located (thus leading to the opening of additional proceedings in sixty-two different local courts).[136] Ten days later, the Criminal Chamber established – with 3 dissenting votes – the incompetence of the judge to investigate the crimes.[137]

Besides the significant reaction that Garzón's action triggered in Spanish public opinion, the issue acquired another dimension when the ultra-right-oriented trade union, Manos Limpias, presented a private complaint against Garzón for intentionally issuing an unjust judgment ("*querella por prevaricación*") before the Second Chamber (criminal) of the Supreme Court.[138] This decision was

134 Audiencia Nacional, Juzgado Central de Instrucción No 5, Auto Diligencias Previas-Procedimiento abreviado 399/2006 V, 16 October 2008 and Auto Diligencias Previas-Procedimiento abreviado 0000399/2006 E, 17 October 2008.

135 Recurso de apelación directo ante la Sala de lo Penal de la AN contra el Auto del Juzgado Central de Instrucción Número 005 en las Diligencias Previas del Proceso Abreviado 399 /2006 de fecha 16 de octubre de 2008 interpuesto por el Fiscal Jefe de la AN, 20 October 2008.

136 Audiencia Nacional, Juzgado Central de Instrucción No 5, Auto, Sumario (Proc. Ordinario) 53/2008 E, 18 November 2008.

137 Audiencia Nacional, Pleno Sala de lo Penal, Rollo de Sala 34/2008, 'voto particular que formulan los magistrados José Ricardo de Prada Solaesa, Clara Bayarri García y Ramón Sáez Valcárcel', 18 November 2008.

138 Tribunal Supremo, Sala de lo Penal, Auto Estimando, Querella, 20048/2009, 26 May 2009. See also, 'El PP ensalza al Supremo por abrir una causa contra Garzón por prevaricación', *El País*,

ratified on 3 February 2010 by the investigating judge of the Supreme Court, Luciano Varela, who argued that Garzón had "consciously decided to ignore" the Amnesty Law of 1977 when declaring his competence to investigate the crimes.[139] Five days later, the General Judicial Power Council (*Consejo General del Poder Judicial*, CGPJ) decided to examine the preventive suspension of the judge.[140] An appeal presented by Garzón was dismissed on 25 March, and thus the possibility of sitting the judge on the dock became real.[141]

While the PP – as well some conservative media – manifested their strong support for the proceedings against Garzón,[142] the situation raised some turmoil within Spanish society and the more liberal sector of the legal community.[143] On 24 April, a large demonstration supporting Garzón was organised in more than twenty Spanish cities. The protests, which became a tribute to the victims and the first demonstration in favor of the recovery of historical memory in Spain, were, however, considered "antidemocratic" by the leader of the PP, Mariano Rajoy (now, President of the Government in Spain).[144] While the leftist parties, IU-ICV and ERC, clearly supported the judge, according to *El País,* Rodríguez Zapatero requested "prudence" in the matter alleging the need to respect judicial independence.[145]

Despite the popular support, on 14 May the CGPJ declared the preventive suspension of Garzón, until the Chamber was to decide whether he was guilty or innocent.[146] This decision caused a widespread reaction both in Spain and

28 May 2009. To the complaint of Manos Limpias, a second one – presented on behalf of the association Libertad e Identidad – was accepted on 24 June 2009. Some months later, on 13 January 2010 a new complaint was presented by Falange Española de las JONS, was accepted by the Court. This last one, however, was later dismissed of the proceeding for formal motives.

139 Tribunal Supremo, Sala de lo Penal, Causa Especial, No 20048/2009, presentado por Luciano Varela Castro, 3 de Febrero de 2010.

140 El Consejo General del Poder Judicial (CGPJ) is the governing body of the judicial power in Spain. Its main function is to guarantee the independence of judges of the other state powers.

141 For more details on this case see J. Chinchón Álvarez, "The challenges posed to the recent investigation of crimes committed during the Spanish Civil War and Francoism", in J. Almqvist y c. Espósito (eds.): *The Role of Courts in Transitional Justice. Voices from Latin America and Spain*, Routledge International, Oxford-New York, 2012, 132–158.

142 'El PP ensalza al Supremo por abrir una causa contra Garzón por prevaricación,' *El País*, 28 May 2009.

143 'La Fiscalía del Supremo pide a Varela que archive la causa contra Garzón', *ABC,* 22 April 2010, and 'Al Supremo le llueven peticiones para que cierre el "caso Garzón', *ABC,* 22 April 2010.

144 N. Junquera, 'El acoso a Garzón desata una multitudinaria movilización', *El País*, 25 April 2010. See also, E.G. Sevillano, 'Las movilizaciones de respaldo al juez azuzan la bronca entre PP y PSOE', *El País*, 26 April 2010.

145 'Zapatero frena a los líderes del PSOE que exigen mayor apoyo a Garzón', *El País,* 24 April 2010.

146 'El Poder Judicial suspende a Baltasar Garzón por investigar los crímenes del franquismo', *El País*, 14 May 2010.

overseas. Wile, international human rights organisations such as HRW or ICTJ issued press releases supporting the judge, a group of internationally renowned legal organisations signed a joint petition requesting the UN to intervene.[147] Likewise, important international media echoed similar concerns, including the *New York Times*, *The Times*, *The Guardian* and *Le Figaro*. In Spain, memory associations strongly aired their preoccupation, together with the Professional Association of the Magistracy and Judges for Democracy (*Asociación Profesional de la Magistratura y Jueces para la Democracia*) and prominent figures of the legal profession. At the political level, several parties (including ERC, IU-ICV, and the mixed group[148]) presented in April a series of motions non-law propositions before the Parliament to modify the Law of Amnesty, so as to exclude from its rulings crimes that constitute genocide or crimes against humanity and, as such, would thus no longer be exempt under the Law of Amnesty.[149] The motions were, however, rejected by the PSOE and the PP. Finally the oral trial against Garzón started in the Supreme Court on 24 January 2012 and concluded on 8 February. In the midst of important demonstrations outside the Supreme Court during the whole process and the mobilisation of human rights groups both within and outside of Spain, as well the explicit concern raised by the UN Special Rapporteur on the Independence of Judges and Lawyers, Gabriela Knaul, as many commentators have emphasised, the proceedings against Garzón had made it possible for the families of the disappeared to provide public testimony and have their cases heard in a courthouse for the very first time in history. Finally on 27 February, the Supreme Court issued a sentence clearing Garzón from abuse of power, considering, however, that he had committed a mistake when interpreting the law, and hence, closing the possibility of investigating the alleged crimes.[150]

Following the sentencing of Garzón, the Supreme Court also established by the end of March that the jurisdiction regarding the mass graves was to be located at the local level courts rather than the *Audiencia Nacional*. Although the Supreme Court did agree that the families of those buried in mass graves could request exhumation through legal procedures for identification purposes, it restated that

---

147 'Re: Judge Garzón. Formal Complaint for Consideration and Action from LRWC, ECCHR, ALRC, LWBC, CCR, FIDH, NLG, IADL and OMCT', 20 May 2010.

148 The mixed group is formed by the MPs of minority parties that cannot have their own distinctive group.

149 'IU propone una reforma de la Ley de Amnistía para no indultar los crímenes franquistas', *El Mundo*, 20 April 2010.

150 J. Yoldi and J.M. Lázaro, 'El Supremo considera que Garzón erró, pero no prevaricó, y lo absuelve', 27 February 2012. While not a consequence of this case, on February 10 Garzón was sentenced by the Supreme Court to 11 years of disqualification accused of being responsible of using illegal wiring to uncover a corruption case of the J.M. Lázaro, 'Garzón dice adiós a la carrera judicial al ser condenado a 11 años de inhabilitación', El País, 10 February 2012.

such crimes could not be considered crimes against humanity, alleging retroactivity and prescription motives.[151] As a consequence, from that moment on, the legal power to exhume mass graves would depend on the position of particular courts, instead of following a national level approach.[152] The situation became even more adverse for the families of the victims on April 3rd, when the European Court for Human Rights (ECHR) declared non-admissible the first claim ever brought in front of such tribunal regarding a Civil War disappearance. Echoing the Spanish judiciary arguments, the Court considered that the claim had been presented too late, according to formal proceedings.[153] While there is another case pending resolution at the ECHR, at this point the hope of victims groups importantly lies in a process that was presented at the Federal Chamber of Buenos Aires on 14 April 2010 and confirmed in September of the same year.[154] As this text is undergoing the final revision before its publication, on September 2013 several Spanish journals announced the decision of the Argentinian judge in charge of the case of requesting the extradition of four members of the Francoist security forces under alleged charges of torture. At the present time, the Spanish authorities are waiting to receive the order from the Interpol.

In the decision that Garzón issued in 18 November 2008 transferring the Francoist case to the territorial courts, the judge also made reference to the question of the "stolen children". In doing so, Garzón was hinting at the possibility of the existence of a "systematic plan" of removal of children of Republican families, whose parents were dead, exiled, in jail or disappeared, and who were not considered "ideologically" adequate to raise their children between

---

151 "El Supremo cierra la vía a la investigación penal de los crímenes del franquismo", *El País*, Madrid, 29 March 2012.

152 Chinchón Álvarez has argued that, as a matter of practice and only with very few exceptions, the great majority of the cases are being archived under the consideration that the crimes have prescribed, despite the fact that no proceedings have been open to scientifically determine the age of the remains. See J. Chinchón Álvarez, "El tratamiento judicial de los crímenes de la Guerra Civil y el franquismo en España. Una visión de conjunto desde el Derecho internacional", Cuadernos Deusto de Derechos Humanos, No. 67, Bilbao Universidad de Deusto 2012. As it happens, for example, in September 2012, the local court of Granada announced its decision to close the case of the grave of Federico García Lorca. A recent report released by Amnesty International denounces that after the Audiencia National decision, local courts are systematically closing the cases transferred to them (Amnesty International, *Casos Cerrados, Heridas Abiertas. El desamparo de las víctimas de la Guerra Civil y el Franquismo,* Madrid, Sección Española de Amnistía Internacional, Mayo 2012).

153 'Estrasburgo rechaza por primera vez un caso sobre las fosas del franquismo', *El País,* Madrid, 3 April 2012. See also: European Court of Human Rights, Third section, Application no. 30141/09: Antonio Gutierrez Dorado and Carmen Dorado Ortiz against Spain, Estrasburg, 27 March 2012.

154 See S. Gallego, 'La querella en Argentina por crímenes franquistas avala a Garzón', *El País,* Buenos Aires, 15 April 2010, and N. Junquera, 'Esperanza por la reapertura en Argentina de la causa del franquismo', *El País,* Madrid, 4 September 2010.

1938 and 1950. Once removed from their families, the children would come under state supervision, and their names were changed.[155] According to Garzón (who estimated around 30,000 cases) these facts would not only constitute crimes against humanity, which are not covered by the Amnesty Law of 1977, but also he alerted about the possibility that most victims of such crimes would still be alive. Accordingly, he requested the State Prosecutor (*Ministerio Fiscal*) and to the competent judges to investigate the crimes, punish those responsible, and compensate the victims.[156]

In January 2009, Garzón referred to several local courts the data he gathered regarding the lost children. On 5 November 2010, after initiating the investigations, three local courts referred the cases back to the AN, considering that the crimes should be dealt under its jurisdiction for they constituted crimes against humanity.[157] Although the prosecutor of the AN considered that the Court did not have the competence to investigate these crimes, the pressure exercised by the *Plataforma Grupos Afectados de Clínicas de toda España de la Causa de Niños Robados* [Platform of Hospital Groups from all over Spain Affected by the Case of the Stolen Children] – which had gathered documentation of more than 300 cases of disappeared children – led him to formally demand the Ministry of Justice to create an office to specifically coordinate the demands of the affected persons through administrative means.[158] The case of the stolen children entered a new phase when a second group, the *Asociación Nacional de Afectados por Adopciones Irregulares* (National Association of those Affected by Irregular Adoptions, ANADIR) presented a different claim before the State Prosecutor. ANADIR reported around 261 alleged cases of children who had been stolen from private and public hospitals all over the national territory from 1920 to 1990, and they accused the professionals of these centres (many of which were administered by the Church) of deceiving the mothers by telling them that the children had been born dead, then giving the children into illegal adoption to other families.[159] The relationship between these two cases, however, is highly contested, for while some consider that the first set of cases were the direct result of the Francoist

---

155 About the stolen lost children of Francoism, see R. Vinyes, *Irredentas. Las presas políticas y sus hijos en las cárceles franquistas*, Ediciones Planeta, Barcelona, 2002; R. Vinyes, M. Armengou, and R. Belis, *Los niños perdidos del franquismo*, Plaza & Janés, Barcelona, 2002 and M.A. Rodríguez Arias, *El caso de los niños perdidos del franquismo: Crimen contra la humanidad*, Tirant lo Blanc, Valencia, 2008.

156 'Garzón reparte la causa del franquismo,' *El País*, 19 November 2008.

157 'Un tercer juez devuelve a la Audiencia Nacional casos de crímenes del franquismo', *Público*, 5 November 2010.

158 'La Fiscalía pide a Justicia que investigue la desaparición de niños del franquismo', *Público*, 7 December 2010.

159 'Piden investigar el robo de 261 bebés desde el franquismo a los años 90', *Público*, 27 January 2011.

repression, the second set was pure criminality (and hence the systematic participation of the state would not be clear); others claim that both issues would be natural concatenated.

The proceedings regarding this second case started in March 2011 in Madrid, where 84 different complaints were submitted and would be, according to the Prosecutor, individually considered. The PP has declared its support for the investigations.[160] By June 2011 there were 849 open investigations all over Spain: 162 cases have been transferred to the competent judges, while another 38 have been dismissed.[161] Meanwhile, the Ombudswoman offered her support to the Plataforma representing the first type of cases for the implementation of a coordinated investigation in the national territory. In April 2012, the government announced the intention to create a census of those affected by this particular situation. Still in a design phase, the census will allow to cross information of parents looking for children and of children looking for their biological parents, as well as data regarding the name of the baby, the date and place of birth, and DNA information.[162] More recently, in October 2012, a judge established for first time, in relation to a case that was dated in the 1970s, that the crime of stealing children does not prescribe.[163]

3.4. SOCIAL INITIATIVES

After almost twenty-five years of "veiled silence"[164], during which democratic Spain centered most of its efforts in the country's economic development and modernisation, the repressive past of the Civil War and the dictatorship has clearly erupted in the public space. Starting with the demands of the families of the victims who began to organise themselves in 2000 – when the March of Memory (Caravana de la Memoria), formed by several victims' groups, traveled over the national territory to tell their stories –, and inserted in the political agenda by some of the leftist and nationalist parties, during the last ten years, Spain has witnessed a gradual irruption of its most recent and tragic history. While a strong – though very fragmented – associative movement has been

160 'Comienzan las declaraciones sobre 'los niños robados' del franquismo', *Público*, 11 March 2011.

161 'Sólo 38 denuncias han sido archivadas por la inexistencia de indicios penales', *Público*, 17 June 2011.

162 'El gobierno creará un censo de afectados por el robo de niños', *El País*, Madrid, 2012.

163 'La justicia establece que los delitos por robo de bebés no prescriben', *El País*, 5 October 2012.

164 As we have explained elsewhere, this silence refers both to the social and political realms, not to the cultural one, where the memory of the Civil War and Francoism has been the object of great attention for a long time. See P. Aguilar, 'Presencia y ausencia de la guerra civil y del franquismo en la democracia española'.

consolidating all over the country (with leading organisations such as la ARMH with regional and local branches, but also with dozens of independent small groups or even numerous internet-base initiatives),[165] during the past years the state – and especially the governments of some autonomous regions such as Andalucía, the Basque Country and Catalonia – have been contributing to bolster a movement that has reverberated in the public space in the form of films, documentaries, novels, research projects and academic programs, monographs or photography or history exhibits about the war and the dictatorship. A good example of these initiatives would be the first Congress of Victims of Francoism, organised in Madrid by Foro por la Memoria on April 2012.[166] More recently, a varied group of associations, including some memory organisations but also left-oriented and cultural groups, has created a new platform, Red Aqua, to support the criminal process regarding two Francoist crimes that was opened in Argentina in 2010.[167] In this respect, it is worth mentioning that beyond the recovery of memory, even if in very small number, some sectors of Spanish society still claim the need to pursue justice. This process or recovery has also provoked stimulating and, occasionally, bitter public debates: for example, in the case of the location of the remains of Federico García Lorca, which pitted the poet's family against the descendants of those whose bodies are buried in the same grave; or, more recently, in Poyales de la Hoya – a small town in Avila – between the mayor (from the PP) and a group of residents of the town regarding the exhumation of 10 bodies located in the municipal cemetery.[168]

The perseverance of the families of those who suffered the repression of Francoism during or after the war, and especially their struggle to locate, exhume, identify and rebury the remains of their loved ones, has played a fundamental role in moving this process forward. According to recent figures, by December 2011 and since 2000, more than 300 mass graves have been exhumed, with an average of around 6 bodies per grave and up to 40 bodies or even 382, as is the case of Uclés in Cuenca. In total, more than 5,700 bodies have been recovered.[169] As part of the same process, especially at a local level, there have also been an increasing number of initiatives to vindicate the memory of the victims through symbolic means in streets, squares and

165 Some of the main associations devoted to the recovery of historical memory are mentioned in Table VI (see Annex).

166 N. Junquera, 'Mi padre figura en la historia como un canalla. Quiero que se anule su juicio', *El País*, Madrid, 20 April 2012. See also, *www*.congresovictimasfranquismo.org.

167 For more information visit the website, http://redaqua.wordpress.com/.

168 'En Poyales del Hoyo no quieren Memoria Histórica', *El País*, 7 August 2011.

169 Universidad del País Vasco, Sociedad Aranzadi and Ministry of Presidency, *Exhumaciones llevadas a cabo en España desde el año 2000* (actualizado diciembre 2012), 31 December 2012.

cemeteries all over the country. This movement has also been supported by some regional administrations. So, for example, in February 2010, the Catalan Government created the Memory Spaces Network (Red d'Espais de la Memoria). The project comprises a series of spaces in the Catalan territory that promote the recovery of democratic memory through artistic and historical means.[170] In February 2011, following the example of Andalucía, the Basque Country and Catalonia, the government of Asturias also began also to officially identify the 353 mass graves that had been located in the province with remembrance signs.[171] In Aragón, a technical commission is currently evaluating the possibility of converting the old concentration camp situated in the city of Miranda del Ebro into a site of memory. The camp, that held around 80,000 prisoners throughout its history, was the last one to be closed, in 1947.[172]

In parallel to the recovery of memory, the most recent developments in Spain have also clearly articulated a message of recognition that was missing in previous policies. However, and in spite of the big steps taken, it should also be outlined that the Law that was approved in December 2007 had important gaps – at least, in regards to the possibility of annulling Francoist sentences, and especially in its failure to put in place a national coordinated policy to exhume the mass graves, leaving instead such responsibility in the hands of the civil society groups – and that the government has not been always as diligent as it would have been desired in implementing some of the measures that were indeed included. Taking this into consideration, it is not surprising that some groups such IU and ERC kept presenting new proposals before the Parliament during Zapatero's second term of office (2008–2011), aiming to amend some points of the law; but also requesting the government to grant the means to fully implement the law it had approved.[173] Likewise, the fact that, despite the huge reaction that the proceeding has caused both internally and internationally, Garzón is the first person that has been judged in relation to Francoism, is also more than telling. In this climate of present economic uncertainty (which, after the change of the regional government, has directly

170 See 'Order IRP/91/2010, de 18 de febrero, por la que se crea la Red de Espacios de Memoria Democrática de Cataluña', 5576 *DOGC*, 26 February 2010, 14651. See also www.espaimemories.cat/.

171 'Asturias comienza a dignificar las más de 300 fosas comunes', *Público*, 23 March 2011.

172 'El franquismo se retira al sótano', *El País*, 16 October 2011.

173 See 'El PSOE acepta garantizar la aplicación de la Ley de La Memoria Histórica', *El País*, 11 May 2010. The points that were to be amended included the creation of the Office of Victims, the approval of a protocol for exhumation, the elaboration of a map of mass graves, the removal of symbols and the reform of the Valley of Fallen.

affected a leading initiative such as the Memorial Democratic),[174] victims' associations are worried that all the steps taken will be interrupted or even reverted, not the least because the PP won the general elections of 20 November 2011 with an absolute majority.[175]

Indeed, as anticipated, one of the first measures adopted by the new government was the closing of the Office of Attention to Victims of Civil War and the Dictatorship.[176] Moreover, in the 2012 general budget the government has reduced by 60% the allocations to support activities related to the recovery of historical memory in Spain, although the monies will be exclusively devoted to the exhumation of mass graves, removing complete support to other activities such as research projects, homages and commemorations.[177] In the general budget of 2013 the law of historical memory was left without funds. Family members and victims associations, however, continue to conduct exhumations with private funds. Finally, it also should be underlined that, while with the passage of time there have been more and more public statements acknowledging the human rights violations committed during the war and the dictatorship and/or the suffering of the victims in Spain, at a national level the PP has not yet condemned Franco's dictatorship in an explicit manner in the Parliament (for the declaration that was approved in 2002 only condemned "totalitarian regimes" in general, but not Franco's dictatorship itself).

4. MEMORY AND TRANSITIONAL JUSTICE IN THE POLITICAL CULTURE OF THE SPANIARDS

When looking at long-term effects we have to pay very special attention to the current state of public opinion regarding memory and TJ policies. According to various surveys, the memories of the Civil War and the Francoist dictatorship are still alive (see Figure 1). In 2000, only 42 percent of the respondents thought the divisions and resentments of the Civil War had been forgotten, and almost 70 percent said that, even if these had been forgotten, the deep mark of Francoism was still present. However, the change of mentality was clearly perceived, as most of the people thought that Spaniards' way of thinking was rather unrelated to the past.

174 'CiU desmantela el Memorial Democrático', *El País*, 21 October 2011. After being for almost a year without a Director the Memorial has suffered cuts from up to 60% of its general Budget. As a consequence, for example, the office for victims that the Memorial opened in 2010 is now closed.

175 'Víctimas del franquismo se preparan para un "recortazo" del PP en políticas de la memoria', *El País*, 19 September 2011.

176 'Suprimida la Oficina de Víctimas de la Guerra Civil y la Dictadura', *Público*, Madrid, 2 March 2012.

177 'El Gobierno dará más dinero para abrir fosas del franquismo que los socialistas', *El País*, Madrid, 8 April 2012.

Figure 1. In Spain nowadays...[178]

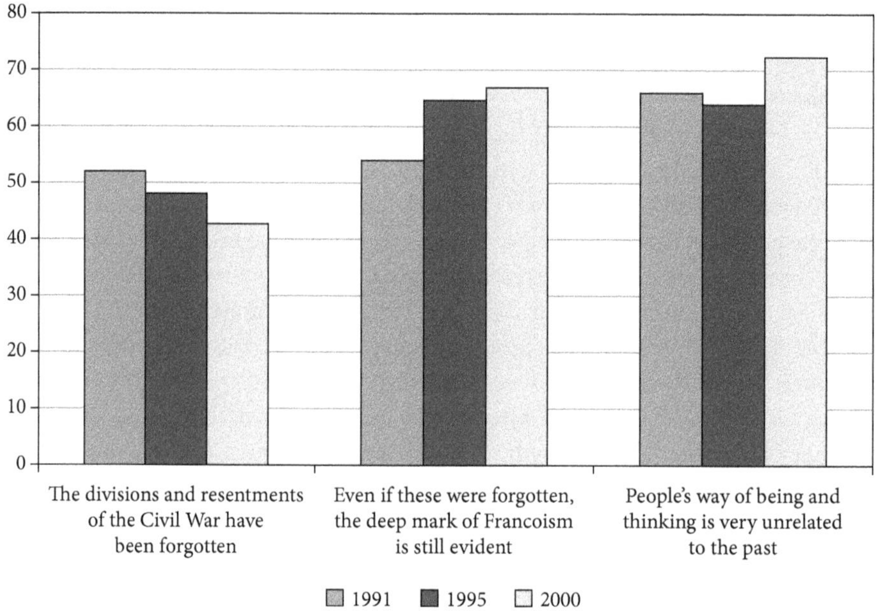

In April 2008, a group of social scientists designed the only monographic survey on collective memory and TJ that has been applied in Spain.[179] In that survey, 53 percent considered the memory of the war was still very vivid in the memory of the Spaniards, whereas 57.5 percent claimed the same about Francoism. It is interesting to point out that more than 30 years after Franco's death, 30.5 percent of Spaniards declare there is still fear of talking about the past. Also, 70 years after the end of the Civil War, 45.6 percent of the population does not think that the divisions and resentment of the conflict have been forgotten. Also, 34 percent agrees with the following sentence: "The best thing is to forget about the past, because if we stir it, a Civil War could happen again". All of this may help to explain why, even today, some social and political initiatives regarding the Civil War and/or the Francoist dictatorship may provoke heated debates, though only a very small proportion of the society gets usually involved in these.

Another interesting result is that every year there are more people who declare that their families fought with the Republicans, and fewer people who claim that their families fought with the Francoists (although the tendency is much

[178] *Centro de Investigaciones Sociológicas*, No. 1984, 2201 and 2401.

[179] P. Aguilar, L. Balcells and H. Cebolla, together with the *Centro de Investigaciones Sociológicas*, No. 2760. All survey data presented in this report for the year 2008 belong to this survey.

more evident in the first case; see Figure 2). It is also worth mentioning that the proportion of people unwilling or unable to answer to this question has decreased from 36 percent to 27 percent since 1980. This may be due to the fact that younger generations feel much less uneasy when dealing with this dramatic episode than their parents and grandparents. It is also true that the more long-established the democratic system is, the less concern about a hypothetical breakdown exists.

Figure 2. As far as you remember, with which of the two sides of the Civil War did your family sympathise more?"[180]

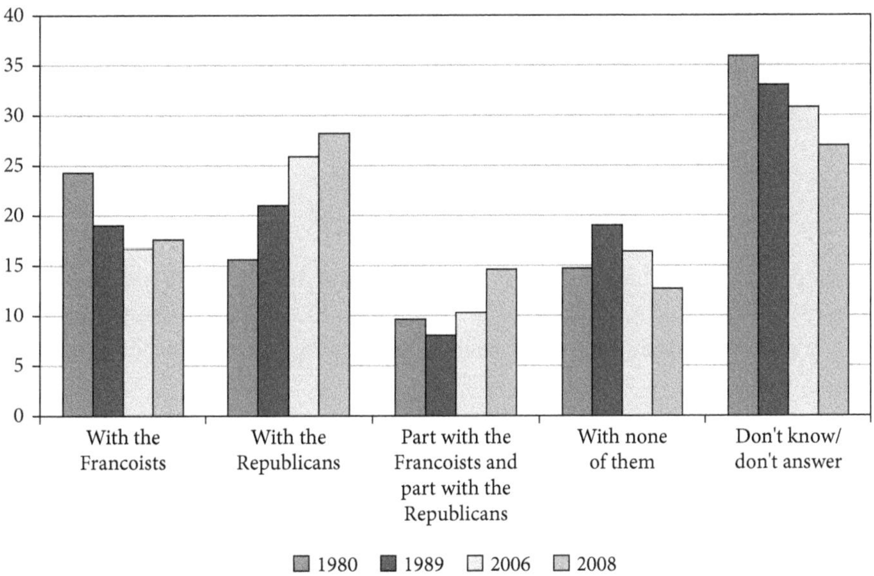

When the interviewed are asked about the most important event of Spanish history, 40 percent of the population chooses the transition, 20 percent points to the Civil War, and less than 10 percent opts for Francoism. There is much more consensus regarding the assessment of the conflict than of the dictatorship. The Civil War is clearly regarded as a tragedy in which both sides committed unjustifiable atrocities (even if, as will be seen, the responsibility is not equally distributed), whereas the verdict of the long-lasting dictatorship is still ambiguous. Even if it is true that the negative assessments have been increasing with the passage of time, and the positive ones have been logically decreasing, most of the Spanish population thinks Francoism had both good and bad aspects (see Figure 3).

180 *Centro de Investigaciones Sociológicas*, No. 1237, 1788, 2632 and 2760.

Figure 3. Historical assessment of Francoism[181]

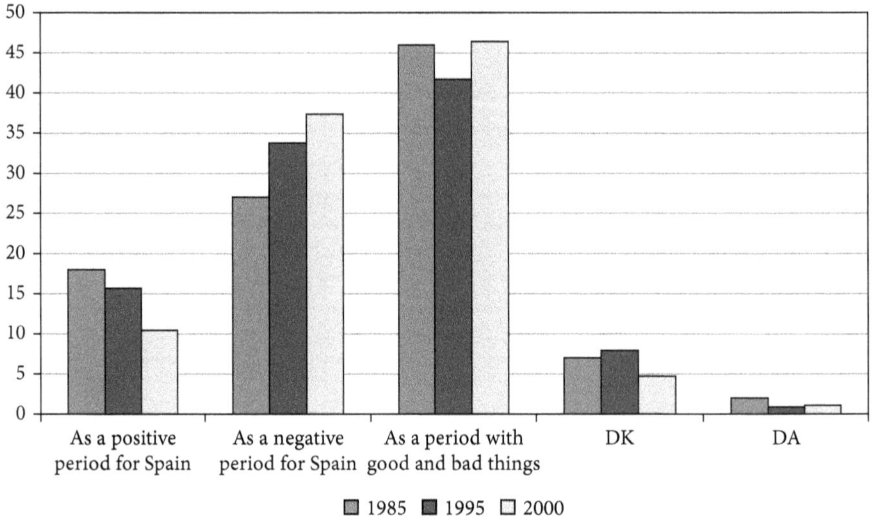

In 2008, in a different formulation of the question, 58.2 percent still chose this ambivalent judgment instead of a straightforward negative response, and 35.1 percent held that during the dictatorship there was more peace and order than nowadays.

Figure 4. How would history judge Franco?[182]

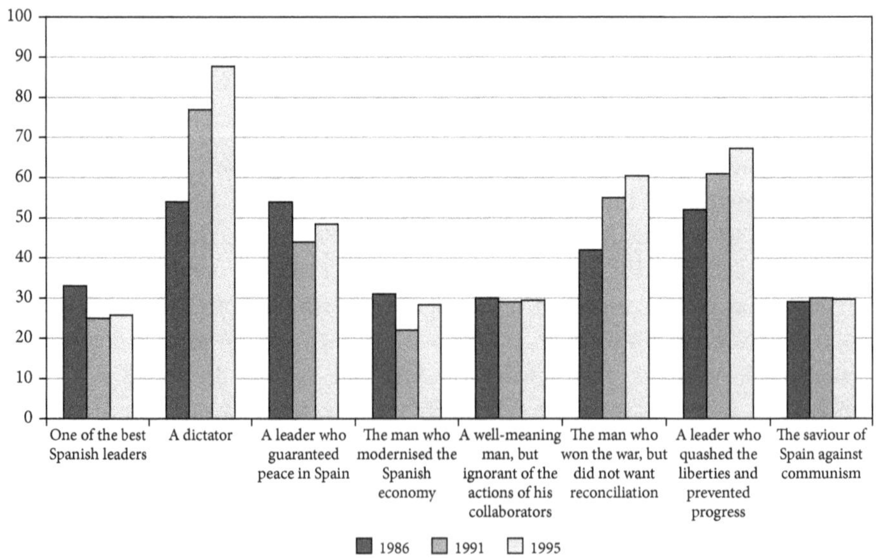

181 *Centro de Investigaciones Sociológicas*, No. 1495, 2201 and 2401.
182 *Centro de Investigaciones Sociológicas*, No. 1558, 1984 and 2201.

Another ambivalent evaluation, though undoubtedly more and more critical as time goes by, is contained in some of the items of Figure 4. When Spaniards are asked about how would history judge Franco, in 1995 50 percent still said as a leader who guaranteed the peace in Spain, 30 percent said as the man who modernised the Spanish economy, another 30 percent as the savior of Spain against communism, and 30 percent as a well-meaning man unaware of the actions of his collaborators. At the same time, the items that received more support were the critical ones: almost 90 percent said as a dictator (it is very interesting that only 54 percent chose this item just nine years before, in 1986), and almost 70 percent said as a leader who smashed quashed liberties and prevented progress.

The most prevalent feelings that the Spaniards link with each of the historical periods under study – Civil War and Francoism – are different, and much clearer in one case than in the other: When asked about the Civil War 55 percent chose "sadness" in the first place, whereas when asked about Francoism 23.5 percent chose "anger" in the first place (the list of available items is identical for both cases).

Also, if 72.2 percent of people affirm that victims of the Civil War received a different recognition according to the side they belonged to (the Republican or the Francoist), only 55 percent hold that victims of the dictatorship have not obtained the recognition they deserve. However, 68.4 percent think the victims of the democratisation period (people who died in demonstrations and strikes) should be recognised. It seems clear that the dictatorial period remains more controversial than other stages of Spanish history. It is interesting to verify that even if people recognise that the dictatorship violated basic human rights (79.6 percent) and that Spaniards did not dare to express their opinion at that period out of fear (88.2 percent), only 55 percent of the respondents are willing to give more recognition to the victims of Francoism – a harsh dictatorship that lasted almost 40 years.

Two factors may account for these somewhat paradoxical results. On the one hand, it is true that many people benefited from the dictatorship: The victors and their heirs enjoyed the numerous benefits that have already been mentioned. Also, many were accomplices of the repression, particularly – though not only – in the post-war period, so many people in Spain have good reasons not to dig very deeply in the past.[183] But, on the other hand, fear, as has been shown, was a crucial feeling during the democratisation period, and some remains of this deeply embedded feeling can be traced until nowadays. Only 49.3 percent of the

---

183 P. Aguilar, 'Judiciary's Involvement in Authoritarian Repression and Transitional Justice: The Spanish Case in Comparative Perspective'.

population declares not to have feared at all, in the 30 years of democracy, the possibility of something similar to a new Civil War.[184] When the interviewed were asked about the reasons why those responsible for human right violations under the dictatorship have not been judged in Spain, 21.4 percent say because these trials could provoke a new conflict among Spaniards.

The verdict for the responsibilities of the atrocities during the Civil War is nowadays clear. It is true that most of the people think there were innocent victims in both sides, and that any homage should include both (82.7 percent). Also, the majority of the respondents (36 percent) declare that the two sides caused the same number of casualties during the Civil War. However, whereas 30 percent declare that Francoists caused more casualties, only 4 percent point to the Republicans. This result is consistent with another question of the same 2008 survey: whereas 40 percent of the respondents consider that both the left and the right were responsible for the outbreak of the Civil War, 30 percent point to the right and only 6.7 percent to the left. Finally, when people are asked in which of the opposing sides of the Civil War they find better represented their current political ideas, even if the plurality says in neither of them (42.6 percent), 31 percent affirms "in the Republican side", and only a 10 percent "in the Francoist one".

Fifty percent of Spaniards think the mortal remains of the losers of the Civil War that still remain in common graves should be identified and transferred to a cemetery; 14 percent consider that these should be identified, but not removed: only a plaque should be installed to identify the place. Finally, only 26 percent of the respondents maintain that nothing should be done; they think it is better to leave things as they are now. Interestingly enough, of the 50 percent in favor of both identification and relocation, 83 percent state that the State should be in charge of this task. However, as we have shown, this has not been the case in Spain: The State is providing public subsidies for the private associations that have decided to assume this task.

The majority of the population (50.4 percent) maintains that the political trials of the dictatorship should be declared null and void; that symbols exalting the Civil War, Franco or Francoism should be retired (55 percent); that a monument devoted to all victims of the Civil War should be built (70.7 percent); and, finally, there should also be a monument to the victims of Francoism (61 percent). However, even if the majority of the respondents consider that people liable for human rights violations under Francoism should be brought to trial, the amount is a bit smaller than in the other cases (48.7 percent). Finally, though the

[184] Only 49.3 per cent of the population declares not to have feared at all, in the 30 years of democracy, something similar of a new civil war.

population is almost split in two, a substantial minority is against the creation of truth commission independent of the government either to investigate the Civil War or the dictatorship (44.8 percent versus 38.9 in the first case, and 42.2 versus 40.8 percent in the second).

A recent article by Aguilar, Balcells and Cebolla has shown that the determinants of the TJ policies, that is, the main variables accounting for its support, are related with victimisation experiences during the dictatorship, family sympathies during the war, age, ideology, and religious feelings (the latter are related with the nature of the Francoist dictatorship, which was very rightist and strongly Catholic). It has also proved that policies that are perceived as being less divisive (i.e. withdrawing symbols) receive more support than others that are thought to entail more controversy (i.e. truth commissions and trials). The study concludes that "individuals do not seem to be forgetful of their history; that is, the mere passage of time does not necessarily contribute to oblivion". In fact, "the lack of appropriate TJ measures may have prevented victims and their relatives from leaving the past behind". Finally, this research shows that "Spaniards are quite supportive of the application of TJ policies", and even that many citizens "would have endorsed a more ambitious legal application of TJ principles than that provided for in the 2007 Law of Historical Memory".[185]

The great amount of books on the Civil War and the post-war repression that have been recently published (some of them have benefited from a better access to archival material), together with the recent advances in terms of reparation and recognition of the victims (numerous exhumations and monuments at the local level, and a more determined political will to give a public recognition to the victims and to explicitly condemn the dictatorship) may have contributed to this somewhat unexpected social verdict. The mobilisation of Spanish society supporting more daring TJ measures has been, until very recently, so scarce, the attitude of politicians regarding both the Civil War and Francoism has tended to be so cautions, and the so called "Spanish model" has been associated so much with forgetfulness, that it was not ease to predict such a clear assessment on Civil War, Francoism, and TJ measures in Spanish society.

5. CONCLUSIONS

TJ has increasingly become recognised as a normative binding framework for countries dealing with legacies of human rights abuses in periods of change

---

185 P. Aguilar, L. Balcells and H. Cebolla, 'Determinants of Attitudes towards Transitional Justice: An Empirical Analysis of the Spanish Case', (2011), 44/10 *Comparative Political Studies*, at 1397–1430, 1420–21.

towards peace and democracy. Yet, it has rarely been considered from a long-term historical perspective. Focusing our attention on the case of Spain, which has recurrently been used in the literature as an example of successful transition without truth or justice, in this chapter we have examined how the Spanish society has in different historical moments during the 20th century dealt with the legacy of previous political violence and unrest, while also considering the most recent developments in what could be called the post-transitional phase, looking over a period of more than 80 years.

As we noted in the first section, historically the Spanish accountability policies have been characterised by analysts as biased and inconsistent. On the one hand, the policies implemented during the Second Republic (1931–1939) have been blamed for contributing to the destabilisation of the fragile regime from its very beginning and for eroding the support of moderate public opinion when it was most needed. Even leftist Republicans who initially supported the creation of the Accountability Commission complained of its inefficiency and the fact that it diverted very important resources and energies from much more urgent questions, particularly given the highly polarised and unstable transitional period. On the other hand, after the Civil War, the Francoist regime promoted accountability in an absolutely sectarian way, with deleterious effects for many thousands of people, while granting immunity for crimes committed by their own supporters. In the past, the institution of clemency was used in most cases in a partisan way; that is, to pardon the crimes and offenses of supporters while allowing adversaries to remain in prison. The most obvious manifestations of this were the exclusive character of the Francoist reparatory policies awarded only to the victims of the victorious side, and the purges of both the Primo de Rivera and Franco regimes, largely inspired by hatred and revenge.

Taking this background into account – and also other well-known constraints that operated during the Spanish transition – it is possible to argue that the political elites of the democratising period after Franco's death in 1975 considered, at least to a certain extent, these historical precedents as the counterexample of what should be done in Spain, particularly the demand of formal accountability. Moreover, the only previous democratic Spanish experience (the Second Republic), given its dramatic failure, was considered, in an almost superstitious way, a precedent to avoid, which eventually implied throwing out the baby with the bathwater.[186] Given that the main priority at the time was to stabilise the new regime in a country that, four decades later, was still traumatised by the memory of the Civil War – which was vividly evoked, given the high level of political violence in the mid-seventies – the politics of "national reconciliation" and "consensus" were considered the best means to

[186] P. Aguilar, *Políticas de la memoria y memorias de la política.*

achieve peace and stability. Not to forget, of course, that the way in which the transition to democracy took place in Spain – with the reformists of the Franco regime playing a leading role in its architecture and the military exerting pressure on the political process – made it unthinkable at the time to punish those responsible for the atrocities committed.

The need to overcome the traumatic memory of the Spanish Civil War, the wish to leave behind the historical spiral of revenge, the desire to leave behind the repressive and discriminatory policies of the Francoist period, the absence of a strong social demand for accountability, the lack of international pressure against impunity, and, finally, the need to appease the ETA terrorist organisation and its supporters help to understand why the Amnesty Law was approved in 1977. The importance of this law lies in the fact that all crimes by the parties in conflict (both during the Civil War and under the dictatorship) were forgiven, a gesture that was presented as the foundations for reconciliation among Spaniards. The symbolic power of such a gesture remains even today so strong that, contrary to the post-TJ developments that have taken place in other countries, in Spain there are no prospects for the annulment of this law. For many, the Amnesty Law is still considered today, together with the Constitution, the cornerstone of the Spanish democracy. The result is that a law which was initially proposed to release the few remaining political prisoners of the dictatorship has ended up being a law which impedes the judicial investigation of the truth (contrary to the interpretation of the amnesty law given by many Chilean judges) and grants impunity to human rights perpetrators.[187]

After two decades in which the young democracy was consolidating, and during which the only TJ policies adopted in Spain proposed an incomplete reparations scheme, this status quo slowly started to be questioned with the creation of a series of victim and families of the victims associations around 2000, which gained notice with support from some of the leftist political formations of the democratic spectrum. Under a new political climate after the general elections of 2004, the party in power, the PSOE, started to negotiate a legislative agreement that finally crystallised in 2007 with the approval of the first comprehensive law on historic memory of the Spanish democracy. Several years after the transition, this law contemplated a series of different measures, including the improvement of some of the previous reparatory measures implemented and, especially, making some symbolic gestures such as the granting of Spanish nationality to descendants

---

187 P. Aguilar, 'The Spanish Amnesty Law of 1977 in Comparative Perspective: From a Law for Democracy to a Law for Impunity', in F. Lessa and L. Payne (eds.), *Amnesty in the Age of Human Rights Accountability*, Cambridge University Press, Cambridge, 2012, at 315–335. A. Gil, 'Spain as an example of total oblivion with partial rehabilitation', in J. Almqvist and C. Espósito (eds.), *The Role of Courts in Transitional Justice. Voices from Latin America and Spain*, Routledge International, Oxford-New York, 2012.

of those who went into exile after the war or declaring the trials conducted by court martials and Francoist tribunals "illegitimate," as well as issuing an "individual declaration of recognition" to those sentenced, upon demand. Using more a memory- than a truth-based approach, the law also contemplated other sets of issues such as the removal of symbols of the authoritarian past (including a special consideration of the Valley of the Fallen), the conservation and access to archives, and, most importantly, the recuperation of the thousands of bodies that remain anonymously buried over the Spanish territory.

Several reasons help to explain why such developments took place in Spain more 30 years after the negotiated transition. First, the new generation had none of the fears of the previous one and identified much more closely with the international human rights law. Second, a victim leads movement was created around 2000, which started the exhumation of the hundreds of common graves dating from the Civil War and the post-war periods. Third, after eight years of conservative government the political system was overturned in 2004 with the victory of the PSOE. Fourth, the international human rights and criminal law framework evolved, and certain international organisations and civil society groups lent support. Finally, there occurred some fortuitous events, such as anniversaries or the detention in London in October 1998 of Pinochet on the initiative of the Spanish judge Baltasar Garzón.

While it should be acknowledged that the 2007 law provided a strong impetus to the recovery of memory in Spain, especially as it was the most comprehensive law ever adopted in the country on this matter, and also very importantly, as it clearly shifted the language of reparations provisions to one of recognition of victims, its coming into being and its implementation have not been unproblematic. While many victims groups and human rights organisations have kept critising the shortcomings of the law in several different issues, the PP has recurrently shown a radical impenetrable opposition to any possibility of looking into the past from a democratic perspective, in part also embedded in a highly politicised discussion with some of the more left-oriented groups, some of which, in turn, have not infrequently used that past to support present political vindications. In this battle, the rather disappointing position of the government of the PSOE, and its failure to take on seriously some of the currently internationally recognised principles regarding legacies of human rights abuse, has been reflected in the apparent inhibition of the great majority of Spanish society not directly connected – mainly for family reasons – to this problematic, which, confronted with a sharp two-sided debate anchored in a distant past, has not been particularly engaged in the debate, despite being mostly in favour, according to the surveys, of the provisions of the law.

As far as political culture is concerned, in spite of all the changes that have taken place in the past years, certain legacies undeniably persist, such as the residual fear of political conflict and a strong support for principles such as "peace and order," two of the most widely publicised political values under Francoism. In 2008, the first political priority that, according to respondents to a nation-wide survey, should be attained by every government still was "keeping order and peace" (chosen by almost 40 percent of the respondents). The rest of the items were: "fighting inequality," "reducing unemployment," "protecting the rights and liberties of the citizens," and "granting economic prosperity". At the same time, support for democracy in Spain is among the highest in Europe, which proves the failure of the most important efforts of the previous Francoist socialisation on the values of the regime. The truth is that legacies of authoritarian regimes and of violent periods are very complex and often generate contradictory memories, among other reasons because of the intrinsic plural nature of social memories. When dealing with these subtle and crucial issues, simplifications should be avoided, and all nuances should be taken into account for a better understanding of TJ processes. Other legacies of the past can be identified in the weakness of Spanish social agency, whereas human rights advocacy has proved to be a crucial determinant of human rights prosecutions.[188] The late and scarce support provided by legal experts to the associations for the recovery of historical memory is essential for understanding its lack of visibility and strength. Furthermore, the lack of sensibility among Spanish judges to recent developments in international human rights legislation and to the principles of universal jurisdiction has been pointed out as an impediment against accountability.[189]

The political and judicial reaction that was triggered against Garzon's attempt to revise the crimes of the Civil War and the first years of Francoism, including the resulting sentence pronounced by the Supreme Court on the case, make further developments in the realm of criminal justice in Spain very unlikely. Of course, the latest developments in Argentina with the indictment of four alleged tortures of Francoism have created an unprecedented situation that is yet to be seen how it will be solved. However, it is extremely unlikely that the amnesty law will be seriously questioned; nor does the establishment of an official, state-sponsored, truth or historic commission seem plausible, at least in the near future (even though civil society and international advocacy on this specific issue have grown importantly). Given some of the demands by memory associations, what might eventually materialise – although probably not in the short term – is the judicial revision of the unfair sentences issued during the

188 H.J. Kim, 'Structural determinants of human rights prosecutions after democratic transition', (2012), 49/2 *Journal of Peace Research*, at 305–320.

189 P. Aguilar, 'Judiciary's Involvement in Authoritarian Repression and Transitional Justice: The Spanish Case in Comparative Perspective'.

Civil War and the Franco regime. For this to happen, however, a radical change of perspective in the judges of the Military Chamber of the Supreme Court will be necessary (although rather unlikely) or the Parliament must pass some reforms of the current law to facilitate the revision of such sentences; it could also decree their annulment, as in Germany.[190] Another area of potential development is granting public access to certain archives pertaining to the military justice. The blocking by the PP in 2012 of the most relevant declassification of secret files in the history of Spain, advanced during Zapatero's second term of office, makes it difficult to imagine that this will happen in the short term. The only Autonomous community that has since the political shift made additional efforts to implement some of the contents of the provision of the law of historical memory is Andalucía.

Despite the important political, social and cultural changes that Spain has experimented with over the past decades, the recent developments analysed here seem to indicate that there is still a strong reticence in the country to undertake justice and truth-seeking measures; the preference seems, rather, to hold onto a framework combining partial reparations – as the only TJ policy possible – and the Amnesty Law – together with the Constitution of 1978 – as the best guarantors of democratic stability and peace in Spain. Recent empirical evidence shows, however, that "transitional countries with human rights prosecutions are less repressive than countries without prosecutions," while at the same time truth commissions have been "associated with improvements in human rights practices".[191] While these studies seem to question, or at least not clearly endorse, the classical thesis among early transitology theory about the high risks TJ measures exercise over stability, what recent developments in Spain seem to show is that, even in consolidated transitions, the past that has been simply set aside has a strong tendency to re-emerge in the public arena. As a statement of fact, the re-emergence of the past in Spain does indeed pose some questions about the shortcomings of the Spanish transition. However, from a normative perspective, another question remains, more intangible and difficult to address, regarding the potential effects that the state's failure to publicly acknowledge the misdeeds of the past and provide redress victims claims for justice might have had in the long run over the quality and dynamics of the Spanish democratic life. While there might be no point nowadays in questioning the political agreements that were undertaken by the political elites back in 1977 in terms of democratic consolidation, there is still ample space to argue that, with a new

---

190 See C. Arangüena, 'La Ley de Memoria Histórica y sus limitaciones: una visión desde la óptica del derecho procesal', in J. Tamarit (ed.), *Justicia de transición, justicia penal internacional y justicia universal*, Atelier, Barcelona, 2010, at 119–142.

191 H.J. Kim and K. Sikkink, 'Explaining the Deterrence Effect of Human Rights Prosecutions for Transitional Countries', (2010), 54 *International Studies Quarterly*, at 939–963, 941.

generation in place and a different national and international landscape, it is a good moment for Spain to reconsider some of its founding ideas. Among the undesirable effects of the impunity of the perpetrators of human rights violations, the lack of redress to victims, and the absence of an official truth commission, the following stand out: a) the unwillingness of judges to contribute to revealing the truth in cases related to the civil war and Francoism, their resistance to review or cancel unfair sentences from those periods, and their lack of sensibility towards international law developments;[192] b) the impunity with which some sectors of the right, even nowadays, refuse to recognise the repressive and dictatorial nature of Francoism (the *Diccionario Biográfico Español*, from the Royal Academy of History, is a good and recent example of this perversion);[193] c) the scarce knowledge among young Spaniards about the Francoist period and about the connivances of important parts of the society, including the judiciary, with its repressive practices;[194] and d) the difficulties and unjustifiable delays in access to certain documents related to repression under the Francoist regime.[195]

ABBREVIATIONS

ANADIR:	Nacional Association of the Affected by Irregular Adoptions (Asociación Nacional de Afectados por Adopciones Irregulares)
AN:	National High Court (Audiencia Nacional)
AP:	Popular Alliance (Alianza Popular)
ARMH:	Association for the Recovery of Historical Memory (Asociación para la Recuperación de la Memoria Histórica)
BOE:	State Oficial Gazette (Boletín Oficial del Estado)

---

192 R. Sáez Valcárcel, 'Los jueces y el aprendizaje de la impunidad, a propósito de los crímenes del franquismo', *Mientras Tanto*, 114, 2010, 41 a 72. Chinchón shows, quoting various sentences, that judges still use to support their decisions the mantra of "reconciliation" and the "need to avoid that any initiative (...) that may promote the opening of old wounds or to rekindle civil confrontation"; J. Chinchón, 'La obligación internacional del Estado de investigar las violaciones a los Derechos Humanos ocurridas en el pasado', in S. Carulla Ripol and C. Villán Durán (eds.), *Justicia de transición. El caso de España*, Institut Català Internacional per la Pau, Barcelona, 2012, at 26–50, 43.

193 T. Constenla, 'Franco no fue dictador, y punto', *El País*, 22 May 2012.

194 The ARMH has repeatedly denounced the scarce attention devoted to the Francoist period in the education system. Also, in a 2008 survey of the *Centro de Investigaciones Sociológicas* (CIS), respondents confirm how rarely they received information about the civil war or Francoism at school; P. Aguilar, L. Balcells and H. Cebolla, *Informe metodológico de la encuesta 2760 del CIS*, Madrid, 2010.

195 M. Jump, 'The Role of Archives in the Movement for the Recovery of Historical Memory in Spain. La Rioja: A Regional Case Study', *Journal of the Society of Archivists*, 33, 2, 2012, at 149–166.

BOJA:	Oficial Gazzette of Andalucía (Boletín Oficial de la Junta de Andalucía)
CIU:	Convergence and Union (Convergencia i Unió)
CC:	Canarian Coalition (Coalición Canaria)
CGPJ:	General Judicial Power Council (Consejo General del Poder Judicial)
DSCD:	Journal of Sessions of the Congress of Deputies (Diario de Sesiones del Congreso de los Diputados)
DOCG:	Official Gazette of the Congress of Deputies (Diario Oficial del Congreso de los Diputados)
DSS:	Journal of the Senate (Diario de Sesiones del Senado)
EA:	Basque Solidarity (Eusko Alkartasuna)
ERC:	Republican Left of Catalonia (Esquerra Republicana de Catalunya)
ETA:	Basque Homeland and Freedom (Euskadi Ta Askatasuna)
HRW:	Human Rights Watch
ICC:	International Criminal Court
ICJ:	International Commission of Jurists
ICTJ:	International Center for Transicional Justice
IU:	United Left (Izquierda Unida)
IU-ICV:	United Left, Intiative for Catalonia and the Greens (Iniciativa per Cataluña- Els Verds)
PACE:	Parliamentary Assembly of the Council of Europe
PNV:	Nationalist Basque Party (Partido Nacionalista Vasco)
PP:	Popular Party (Partido Popular)
PSOE:	Workers Socialist Party of Spain (Partido Socialista Obrero Español)
TJ:	Transitional Justice
UMD:	Democratic Military Union (Unión Militar Democrática)
UN:	United Nations
UPN:	Union of the People of Navarra (Unión del Pueblo Navarro)

SELECTIVE FURTHER READING

Aguilar, Paloma, *Memory and Amnesia. The Role of the Spanish Civil War in the Transition to Democracy* (Oxford: Berghahn Books, 2002).

Aguilar, Paloma, 'Presencia y ausencia de la guerra civil y del franquismo en la democracia española. Reflexiones en torno a la articulación y la ruptura del "pacto de silencio"', in Aróstegui, Julio and Godicheau, François (eds.), *Guerra civil. Mito y Memoria* (Madrid: Marcial Pons, 2006), pp. 245–293.

Aguilar, Paloma, 'Transitional or Post-Transitional Justice? Recent Developments in the Spanish Case', *South European Society & Politics*, 13/4, 2008, pp. 417–433.

AGUILAR, Paloma, *Políticas de la memoria y memorias de la política* (Madrid: Alianza Editorial, 2008).

AGUILAR, Paloma, 'The Spanish Amnesty Law of 1977 in Comparative Perspective: From a Law for Democracy to a Law for Impunity', in LESSA, Francesca and PAYNE, Leigh (eds.), *Amnesty in the Age of Human Rights Accountability* (Cambridge: Cambridge University Press, 2012), pp. 315–335.

AGUILAR, Paloma, 'Judiciary's Involvement in Authoritarian Repression and Transitional Justice: The Spanish Case in Comparative Perspective', *International Journal of Transitional Justice*, 7, 2013, pp. 245–266.

AGUILAR, Paloma, BALCELLS, Laia and CEBOLLA, Héctor, 'Determinants of Attitudes towards Transitional Justice: An Empirical Analysis of the Spanish Case', *Comparative Political Studies*, 44/10, 2011, pp. 1397–1430.

ALMQVIST, Jessica and ESPÓSITO, Carlos (eds.), *The Role of Courts in Transitional Justice. Voices from Latin America and Spain* (Oxford-New York: Routledge International, 2012).

ALONSO, Gregorio and MURO, Diego (eds.), *The Politics and Memory of Democratic Transition. The Spanish Model* (New York/ Cañada Blanch Studies on Contemporary Spain: Routledge, 2011).

AMNESTY INTERNATIONAL, *Casos Cerrados, Heridas Abiertas. El desamparo de las víctimas de la Guerra Civil y el Franquismo* (Madrid: Spanish Section of Amnesty Internacional, 2012).

ARANGÜENA, Coral, 'La Ley de Memoria Histórica y sus limitaciones: una visión desde la óptica del derecho procesal', in TAMARIT, Josep M. (ed.), *Justicia de transición, justicia penal internacional y justicia universal* (Barcelona: Atelier, 2010), pp. 119–142.

ARMENGOU, Montse and BELLIS, Ricard, *Las fosas del silencio. ¿Hay un holocausto español?* (Barcelona: Plaza y Janés, 2004).

ARÓSTEGUI, Julio and GÁLVEZ, Sergio, *Generaciones y memoria de la represión franquista: Un balance de los movimientos por la memoria* (València: Publicacions de la Universitat de València, 2011).

BLAKELEY, Georgina, 'Evaluating Spain's Reparation Law', *Democratization*, 20/2, 2013, pp. 240–259.

BENITO, Ana B., 'Poder judicial, responsabilidad legal y transición a la democracia en España', *Foro Internacional*, XLIX/195, 2009, pp. 63–179.

CAPELLÀ, Margalida and GINARD, David, *Represión política, justicia y reparación. La memoria histórica en perspectiva jurídica (1936–2008)* (Palma de Mallorca: Plural, 2009).

CARULLA, Santiago and VILLÁN, Carlos (eds.), *Justicia de transición. El caso de España* (Barcelona: Institut Català Internacional per la Pau, Barcelona, 2012).

CENARRO, Ánglela, 'Francoist nostalgia and memories of the Spanish Civil War', *International Journal of Iberian Studies*, 21/3, 2008, pp. 203–217.

CHINCHÓN, Javier, 'El viaje a ninguna parte: Memoria, leyes, historia y olvido sobre la guerra civil y el pasado autoritario en España', *Revista del Instituto Interamericano de Derechos Humanos*, 47, 2007, pp. 119–233.

CHINCHÓN, Javier, *El tratamiento judicial de los crímenes de la Guerra Civil y el franquismo en España: Una visión de conjunto desde el Derecho Internacional* (Bilbao: Universidad de Deusto, 2012).

Davis, Madeleine, 'Is Spain Recovering its Memory? Breaking the Pacto del Olvido', *Human Rights Quarterly*, 27, 2005, pp. 858–880.

Encarnación, Omar, 'Reconciliation after democratisation: Coping with the past in Spain', 123/3 *Political Science Quarterly*, 122/3, 2008, pp. 435–459.

Espinosa, Francisco, *Shoot the Messenger?: Spanish Democracy and the Crimes of Francoism. From the Pact of Silence to the Trial of Baltasar Garzón* (Sussex: Sussex Academic Press, 2013).

Ferrándiz, Francisco, 'De las fosas comunes a los derechos humanos: El descubrimiento de las desapariciones forzadas en la España contemporánea', *Revista de Antropología Social*, 19, 2010, pp. 161–189.

Ferrándiz, Francisco, 'Exhuming the defeated: Civil War mass graves in 21st-century Spain', *American Ethnologist*, 40/1, 2012, pp. 38–54.

Gil, Alicia, *La justicia de transición en España* (Barcelona: Atelier, 2009).

Gil, Alicia, 'Spain as an example of total oblivion with partial rehabilitation', in Almqvist, J. and Espósito, C. (eds.), *The Role of Courts in Transitional Justice. Voices from Latin America and Spain* (Oxford-New York: Routledge International, 2012).

Golob, Stephanie R., 'Volver: The Return of/to Transitional Justice Politics in Spain', *Journal of Spanish Cultural Studies*, 9/2, 2008, pp. 127–141.

Jiménez Villarejo, Carlos and Martín, Antonio Doñate, *Jueces, pero parciales. La pervivencia del franquismo en el poder judicial* (Barcelona: Pasado & Presente, 2012).

Juliá, Santos, 'Public Policy on Historical Memory', in Fundación Alternativas, *Report on Democracy in Spain* (Madrid: Fundación Alternativas, 2011), pp. 182–208.

Kovras, Iosif, 'Explaining Prolonged Silences in Transitional Justice: The Disappeared in Cyprus and Spain', *Comparative Political Studies*, 46/6, 2013, pp. 730–756.

Salsench i Linares, Samantha "Francoism facing justice. Enforced disappearances before Spanish courts", *Journal of International Criminal Justice*, 11/2, 2013, pp. 463–483.

Silva, Emilio and Macías, Santiago, *Las fosas de Franco* (Madrid: Temas de Hoy, 2003).

Tamarit, Josep M., *Historical Memory and Criminal Justice in Spain: A Case of Late Transitional Justice* (Cambridge: Intersentia, 2013).

Vinyes, Ricard, Armengol, Montse and Belis, Ricard, *Los niños perdidos del franquismo* (Barcelona: Plaza & Janés, 2002).

OFFICIAL WEBSITES AND OTHER PRIVATE RESOURCES

Name	URL
Official website of the Government	www.memoriahistorica.gob.es/
Oficina para las Víctimas de la Guerra Civil y de la Dictadura	http://leymemoria.mjusticia.gob.es/cs/Satellite/LeyMemoria/es/inicio
Ministry for the Presidency	www1.mpr.es/es/pagina/6/la-ley-de-memoria-historica-y-su-desarrollo.html
Ministry of Economy- Pensions	www.clasespasivas.sgpg.pap.meh.es/sitios/clasespasivas/es-ES/Paginas/inicio.aspx
Ministry of Defence	www.defensa.gob.es/memoriahistorica/index.html
Centro Documental de la Memoria Histórica	www.mcu.es/archivos/MC/CDMH/index.html
Memorial Democratic	www20.gencat.cat/portal/site/memorialdemocratic
ARHM	www.memoriahistorica.org.es
Federación Estatal de Foros por la Memoria	www.foroporlamemoria.info/
Asociación de Amigos de las Brigadas Internacionales	www.brigadasinternacionales.org/
Asociación del Descendientes del Exilio Español	www.exiliados.org/
Asociación de Familiares y Amigos de Represaliados de la II República por el franquismo	www.afar2rep.org/index00.htm
Asociación de Ex-presos y Represaliados Políticos Antifranquistas	www.asocexpresospoliticos.org/
Coordinadora de Colectivos de Víctimas del Franquismo	http://coordinadoravictimas.blogspot.com/
Todos los Nombres	www.todoslosnombres.org/
Desaparecidos de la Guerra Civil y el Exilio Republicano (DESPAGE)	www.nodo50.org/despage/
Amical de Mauthausen	www.amical-mauthausen.org/
Archivo Guerra y Exilio	www.galeon.com/agenoticias/

TRANSITIONAL JUSTICE AFTER THE COLLAPSE OF DICTATORSHIP IN GREECE (1974–2000)

Stefanos KATSIKAS

1. INTRODUCTION

On 23 July 1974 in a meeting between the head of the state at the time, General Phaedon Gizikis, and the country's military leadership (Grigorios Bonanos, Chief of the National Defence General Staff, Andreas Galatsanos, chief of the Army General Staff, Petros Arapakis, chief of the Navy General Staff and Alexandros Papanikolaou, chief of Greek Airforce), it was decided to transfer power to the country's political leadership. The dictator, Dimitrios Ioannidis, was invited to the meeting and was forced to accept the decisions taken by the other members of the meeting. The decision marked the end of the seven year and three month dictatorship in Greece (21 April 1967 – 23/24 July 1974) and the country's transition to the period of democratisation.

An hour later Phaedon Gizikis invited Panagiotis Kanellopoulos, Georgios Mavros, Evangelos Averof, Georgios Mavros, Evangelos Averof, Georgios Novas, Stefanos Stefanopoulos, Spyros Markezinis, Panagiotis Garoufalias and Xenofontas Zolotas, all prominent right-wing and centrist politicians of the pre-dictatorship period, in a meeting to discuss the procedure for the transition. They decided to proceed with the formation of a government of "National Unity" under the leadership of the ex-Prime Minister Konstantinos Karamanlis, who after his disagreement over constitutional reforms with King Paul in 1963, leading to his resignation as Prime Minister, left the country and was living in Paris. The decision was made known to Karamanlis who accepted the offer and returned to Athens in the early hours of 24 July by an airplane which the President of the France, Valéry Giscard d'Estaing, used for state visits. A government of "National Unity" was sworn into office in the early hours of 24 July 1974 under the premiership of Konstantinos Karamanlis with the mandate to prepare the country for a smooth transition to a democratic regime, organise general elections and take the necessary diplomatic steps for managing the crisis in Cyprus after the Turkish invasion of the island on 20 July 1974.

The invasion, which resulted after the junta regime's interference with Cypriot politics, was the main reason for the regime's collapse. The national army regarded itself as the guardian of the country's sovereignty, a view which had often prompted its engagement in Greek politics. After the end of the Greek Civil War in 1949 the national army was seen as the guardian of the state's territorial integrity which was alleged to have been in danger from the country's communists and the Soviet bloc. It was believed that if the country's communists gained power, they would allow the Soviet Union and its East European allies to intervene in Greek affairs at the expense of national interests. The army propaganda had also played heavily on the Greek Communist Party's support for the idea of a regional federation that would have seen the separation of Greek Macedonia and its union with Bulgaria and Yugoslavia within a wider pan-Balkan federal state. Indeed, the launch of the military coup on 21 April 1967 which established a seven-year-long dictatorship in Greece was rationalised by its perpetrators as the only way to "curb the advancement of communists to power" which was alleged to be the result of the policies of the Centre Union government of Georgios Papandreou and the political crisis which had ensued after Papandreou's conflict with King Constantine II, leading to his resignation from the premiership in July 1965. In fact the military plan for launching the coup had the code name "Prometheus" and was provided to be put in motion in case the country was under attack from the Soviet bloc. However, neither the communists nor the Soviet bloc could be blamed for the events in Cyprus. Instead, it was the army who had failed to protect the interests of the nation as, for the first time since 1922 and the Greco-Turkish war in Asia Minor, Greek-inhabited territory had been lost to the Turks.

2. THE COLONELS' REGIME (1967–1974)

The colonels' regime took power on 21 April 1967, less than a month before the scheduled elections and after two years of political turmoil originating, in part, from a confrontation between the young King Constantine II and his Prime Minister, the elder Greek statesman George Papandreou. The confrontation was over the question of royal prerogatives in military affairs. The confrontation led to Papandreaou's resignation in July 1965 and then, because he had commanded the loyalty of the largest single bloc in parliament and had broad public support, a series of caretaker governments supportive of the king was installed. Their bare majorities consisted of 45 breakaway apostate members of Papandreou's Centre Union party and the conservative opposition parties in parliament.[1]

1 R. Clogg and G. Yannopoulos (eds.), *Greece under Military Rule*, New York, 1972; C. Tsoukalas, *The Greek Tragedy*, Harmondsworth, 1969.

At issue were the removal of the monarchy from politics, civilian political control over the military, and the alleged involvement of Papandreou's son, Andreas, in the *Aspida* (Shield) affair, a purported left-wing conspiracy within the army. It was not until December 1966 that Papandreou and Panayotis Kanellopoulos, the leader of the Conservative Radical Union (ERE), agreed to end the crisis and hold elections on 28 May 1967. Although the colonels justified the coup of 21 April on the grounds that it was necessary to save the nation from a government of villains and from an imminent communist takeover, their primary goal was to prevent the May election and the possible return to power of George Papandreou. The charge of a likely communist takeover was completely unfounded.[2]

The coup of middle rank army officers was virtually bloodless and caught the Greek political world and the senior officers of the armed forces completely off balance. The belief that the king and the generals, along with certain political elements, were themselves preparing a coup tended to blunt the significance of the colonels' surprise coup and, indeed, facilitated it. In the remaining months of 1967, many believed that the junta would moderate its position and would soon institute "a new purer democracy". The failure of the king's counter-coup in December 1967 ended that hope, although the junta continued to speak of its role as a parenthesis in Greek history. Colonel George Papadopoulos, the junta strong man, became Prime Minister and gradually concentrated power in his own hands, promising to restore democracy when the Greek people acquired sufficient maturity.[3]

The regime became increasingly repressive. Seeking to justify its brutality, Papadopoulos explained that "if the patient is not strapped to the table, the surgeon cannot perform a successful operation". Parliament was abolished, the constitution was suspended, the press was censored, political opponents were arrested, some were tortured, and abuse was heaped on politicians representing all shades of the political spectrum. The military police assumed the major role in maintaining public order.[4] Wholesale purges were carried out in the armed forces (of mostly royalist officers) and in various ministries and state institutions. Consequently, relations with most West European states reflected increasing strain, and Greece withdrew from the Council of Europe rather than face expulsion for torturing prisoners. The European Community was so repelled by the junta's actions that it suspended Greece's associate membership. However, European Community member states continued to trade with and invest in the colonels' Greece and, along with the USA, refused to expel Greece from NATO.[5]

---

2 G. Katephoris, *I nomothesia ton varvaron (The Legislation of the Barbarians)*, Athens, 1975.

3 Ch. Korizis, *To aftarchiko kathestos, 1967–1974 (The Authoritarian Regime, 1967–1974)*, Athens, 1975; R. Roufos, *Inside Colonels' Greece*, New York, 1972.

4 R. Roufos, *Inside Colonels' Greece.*

5 R. Clogg, *A Short History of Greece*, Cambridge, 2000.

By 1973 Papadopoulos appeared to have consolidated his power at the expense of his fellow conspirators, and civilian technocrats were brought in to replace the military in a number of high government posts.[6] He began to relax the stern rule of high government and promised free elections in 1974, along with the implementation of the regime's 1968 constitution which had replaced that of 1952. Although the regime was clearly unpopular and the bulk of the Greek political world refused to deal with it, relatively little in the way of active organised opposition developed in Greece.[7]

The most serious threat to the regime's stability was an aborted naval mutiny at the end of May 1973 and the defection of the destroyer Velos to Italy. Although the mutineers vehemently denied and indeed resented Papadopoulos's charge that King Constantine had conspired in the plot from his exile in Rome, the regime saw fit to blame Constantine for the mutiny and declared him deposed. In June, Papadopoulos issued a decree abolishing the monarchy and calling for the establishment of a republic.[8] Accordingly, the 1968 constitution was revised. Until then Greece had remained a monarchy under the military regime, although Constantine steadfastly refused to lend legitimacy to Papadopoulos and his cohorts. In July 1973 Papadopoulos, in a controlled referendum, put himself forward as the sole candidate for a seven-year term as President of the Republic, and in the following month he assumed that office.[9]

Papadopoulos' republic was destined to be short-lived. As he began to moderate his policies and attract a civilian following, tensions mounted in the country. In early November, crowds attending a memorial service marking the anniversary of George Papandreou's death were fired on by the police. A few days later, when students occupied the Athens Polytechnic School to protest the rescinding of draft deferments, workers joined in the student general strike, and soon appeals were made to overthrow the dictatorship. Hesitant to use force, Papadopoulos was overruled by his hard-line associates in the military who feared widespread public sympathy for the students unless their action was ended immediately.[10] Troops and tanks were used to evict the students from the Polytechnic in a show of extreme brutality. Scores of students and others were killed, hundreds were wounded, and almost a thousand were arrested. Martial law was re-imposed. Although shaken by these events, Papadopoulos reaffirmed his intention of proceeding with national elections.[11]

---

6 S. Grigoriadis, *Istoria tis Diktatorias (The History of Dictatorship)*, vols. 2 and 3, Athens, 1975.

7 S. Markezinis, *Anamnisis, 1972–74 (Reminiscences, 1972–74)*, Athens, 1979.

8 R. Roufos, *Inside Colonels' Greece.*

9 Ch. Korizis, *To aftarchiko kathestos.*

10 G. Katephoris, *I nomothesia ton varvaron.*

11 Ch. Korizis, *To aftarchiko kathestos.*

At this point, Papadopoulos was removed from power by the more extreme ideologues led by Brigadier General Dimitrios Ioannidis, commander of the hated military police (EAT-ESA) and an original junta member. For some time these men had resented their gradual loss of power under Papadopoulos.[12] They pledged to return the country to the "ideals of the 1967 revolution" and to save it from an "electoral travesty". The constitution was modified, and Lieutenant General Fedon Gizikis was installed as figurehead president along with a civilian government. However, it was clear to all that Ioannidis and his military supporters would remain the real power behind the government. The new regime, unable to govern effectively, employed even harsher measures against dissidents. Also, unable to cope with soaring inflation caused in part by the 1973 oil crisis, it sought to deflect massive discontent at home by instigating a foreign adventure in Cyprus.[13]

3. THE FIRST MEASURES TOWARDS DEMOCRATISATION: "THE GOVERNMENT OF NATIONAL UNITY"

After Konstantinos Karamanlis's arrival and the formation of the government of National Unity events moved fast, and this, in combination with the fact that traditional Greek political and social institutions were weak, was not conducive to a comprehensive strategy towards democratisation. The groups which had resisted the dictatorship were fragmented and the civil society was not prepared to articulate a transition strategy "from below". Therefore the transition to democratisation became a political project which was directed "from above" and whose weight had to fall on the shoulders of Konstantinos Karamanlis.[14] Among the first political measures which Karamanlis took was to legalise the Communist Party of Greece (KKE), which had been outlawed since the time of the Greek Civil War. Its prominent members were forced to flee the country, go underground, or provide a signed declaration that they renounced communism to avoid prosecution under law 508, issued in 1948. In addition, Karamanlis freed all the political prisoners and pardoned all political crimes against the dictatorship. These moves were warmly received by the people, especially those who were long weary of the junta's divisive polemics.

---

12 G. Katephoris, *I nomothesia ton varvaron.*

13 S. Grigoriadis, *Istoria tis Diktatorias.*

14 M. Spourdalakis, *Securing Democracy in Post-Authoritarian Greece: The Role of Political Parties, Stabilizing Fragile Democracies: New Party Systems in Southern and Eastern Europe*, London and New York, 1995, at 168.

On 4 October 1974 Karamanlis formed a new conservative party which was named “New Democracy”. The party won a massive parliamentary majority in the general elections of 17 November 1974 (54.37 per cent of the vote and 220 seats in the 300-seat Greek parliament). The elections were followed by a plebiscite on 8 December 1974 to decide the nature of the country’s political system. The junta had already staged a plebiscite on the 29 July 1973 which resulted in the establishment of the Republic, but after the fall of the military dictatorship, the new government, under Konstantinos Karamanlis, decided to hold another one, as the junta’s legislation was considered illegal. Constantine II, the former King of Greece, who on 13 December 1967 had been forced to flee Greece following an abortive counter-coup against the junta, was banned by the new government from returning to the country to campaign in the plebiscite. An overwhelming majority of 69.18 per cent in the December 1974 plebiscite voted for the abolition of the monarchy and the establishment of the Third Hellenic Republic. 30.82 per cent of the people voted in favour of the monarchy. Following the December plebiscite the newly-elected Greek parliament based on the results of the November 1974 general elections declared a new constitution in 1975 which established Greece as a presidential parliamentary democracy. Konstantinos Tsatsos, an academician, former minister and close friend of Karamanlis and chairman of the parliamentary committee who drafted the Constitution of 1975, served as the first elected President of the Republic from 1975 to 1980.

4. THE JUNTA TRIALS

Within the context of the country’s democratisation Karamanlis also adopted measures to remove collaborators and appointees of the dictatorship from positions they held in public offices. After the fall of the junta and, as the country entered the period of “metapolitefsi” or “transition to democracy” – as Greeks generally term the period of Modern Greek history following the collapse of the seven-year military dictatorship (1967–1974), and before the legislative elections of November 1974 – the government of “National Unity” led by Konstantinos Karamanlis came under growing criticism from the press and the opposition, including Georgios Mavros, the leader of the Centre Union-New Forces, the main opposition party at the time, for being lenient to the members of the recently deposed military junta. For example, the main article of the centre-left Greek newspaper *To Vima* on 24 October 1974 claimed that Dimitrios Ioannidis, who had lead the military coup of November 1973 which overthrew dictator Georgios Papadopoulos and who on 15 July 1974 instigated the military coup against elected President of the Republic of Cyprus, Archbishop Makarios, leading to the Turkish invasion of the island five days later (20 July 1974) '... has disappeared'. At the same time, the article claimed that the five instigators of the 21 April 1967 military coup were 'in exile in the Greek island of Kea'.[15] In addition, on many occasions, Georgios Mavros had demanded the arrest of the junta principals as a necessary condition for cleansing the political life of the country and providing the nation with a 'catharsis' from the political tragedy of the seven-year period of military dictatorship. Mavros often declared that as soon as the new parliament would gather after the November 1974 elections, among its top priorities should be to pass the necessary legislation to annul any automatic immunity laws which the junta might have enacted in order to protect its members.[16] The Greek press further requested an investigation into the role of Dimitrios Ioannidis during the crushing of the student uprising at the Polytechnic School of Athens on 17 November 1973, which many newspapers and political activists described as a 'massacre'.

In response to these demands, on 24 October 1975 the government of 'National Unity' ordered the arrest of the leaders of the military coup of 21 April 1967 Georgios Papadopoulos, Stylianos Pattakos, Nikoalaos Makarezos, Ioannis Ladas and Michalis Roufogalis, who were imprisoned in the Greek island of Kea. They were accused of conspiring against the state again and were to face charges of high treason and mutiny. Immediately after the group of five coup leaders was sent to Kea, the opposition demanded to know the details of the actions of Papadopoulos and his co-conspirators prior to their arrest, while the government denied rumours of pro-junta manoeuvres among the military. In addition, Georgios Papdopoulos, Dimitrios Ioannidis, Michalis Roufogalis, Nikolaos Dertilis, Vassilios Bouklakos and Elias Tsiaouris or Tsapouris (also known as Tsiaparas) were regarded as responsible of the events at the Polytechnic School of Athens and were prohibited from leaving the country, as rumours were circulating that they were planning to escape abroad. During his stay in Kea, Papadopoulos seemed confident that he and the members of his junta would be granted amnesty and would eventually run for office and get elected. However, following a three-month stay on the island, in February 1975, Papadopoulos and the other four junta leaders were transported by a torpedo boat to the port of Piraeus on their way to Korydallos high security prison. By the time Papadopoulos and the other four principals of the 21 April 1967 military dictatorship arrived in Korydallos prison, Dimitrios Ioannidis, who had been arrested on 14 January 1975, was already there.[17]

---

15 *To Vima*, 13 August 1974.

16 *To Vima*, 13 August 2000.

17 V. Nedos, 'O "aoratos dictator" aiteitai tora apofylakisis' (The "Invisible Dictator" Has Now Applied for Prison Release), *Kathimerini*, 22 July 2008.

4.1. THE TRIAL OF THE INSTIGATORS OF THE 21 APRIL 1967 MILITARY COUP

The principals of the 21 April 1967 military coup faced a mass trial which commenced on 28 July 1975 at the Korydallos high security prison. This trial is known as '*I diki ton Protaition tou praxikopimatos tis 21 Apriliou 1967*' (The Trial of the Instigators of the 21 April 1967 coup) – it has often been referred to as 'Greece's Nuremberg', or as 'The Trial of the Instigators', while this trial, together with the 'Trial over the November 1973 Events of the Polytechnic School of Athens' and 'The Trials of the Torturers', which are discussed below, became popularly known as the 'Greek Junta Trials' (*Oi Dikes tis Chountas*). Ioannis Deyannis, who had been appointed as a member of the *Areios Pagos* (Court of Cassation) during the dictatorship years, was the presiding judge of the trial of the instigators of the 21 April 1967 military coup. The mandate of the court was to examine the events surrounding the 21 April 1967 coup, for which Georgios Papadopoulos and over twenty other co-defendants, including the five principal leaders who had been arrested on 24 October 1974, were charged with acts of high treason and mutiny. The security surrounding of the trial was heavy: 1,000 soldiers armed with submachine guns were guarding the jail's perimeter and the roads leading to the jail were patrolled by tanks.

Before and during the trial, Papadopoulos expressed his confidence to reporters that he would not remain incarcerated for long. He assumed full responsibility for the 21 April 1967 coup, but refused to defend himself. Following Papadoloulos example, Stylianos Pattakos, Nikolaos Makarezos and other junta members declared that they would not participate in the trial, while Dimitrios Ioannidis, who was also among those who faced charges in the 'Trial of the Instigators of the 21 April 1967 military coup' stated that, for him, the trial 'was unfortunately not interesting'. The defence justified the decision of their clients not to participate in the trial that this was due to the fact that the Karamanlis government had prejudiced the outcome of the trial by declaring the 1967 coup as a criminal offence. The lawyers of sixteen of the defendants walked out of the courtroom on the first day of the proceedings, declaring that they could not carry out their duties under a climate of terror and violence, to which the presiding judge Ioannis Deyannis replied: "Let all those who wish to leave, leave!".[18]

There was an agreement between the defendants that they would keep silent during the trial and would not issue any statements. The agreement was based on

[18] Ch. Karanikas, 'I anatoli tis dimokratias' (The Dawn of Democracy), *To Vima*, 13 August 2000.

the view on the part of the junta members that they should not politicise the trials because they had nothing to gain out of it politicisation since they lacked support among the Greek public. However, to the surprise of all of them, at some point during the trial procedure, Papadopoulos lost his temper and broke his silence by stating he was the leader of the "Revolution", as the instigators of the 21 April 1967 military coup liked to call their move, and that he was responsible for everything.

The charge of mutiny was contested because even though the colonels had in fact seized power illegally, they did so with the approval of their superior officer, Lieutenant General Grigorios Spandidakis, who even joined the coup and the head of the state, King Constantine II, had finally accepted the coup and sworn into office a junta government. Panagiotis Kanellopoulos, the last legitimate Prime Minister of Greece prior to the coup, acting as witness for the prosecution, testified how he was arrested by machine gun toting soldiers and transported to the palace to meet King Constantine. Kanellopoulos stated that during his meeting with the King he urged the Greek monarch to use his status as commander-in-chief of the Greek military and order loyal officers to crush the coup, but King Constantine refused to do so, fearing bloodshed. Kanellopoulos also stated that, against his advice, the Greek monarch swore in the government of the colonels, a action which had helped to legitimise their rule.

Kanellopoulos's testimony undermined the charge of mutiny. He even accepted responsibility for not pre-empting the coup while in office and claimed that there was no indication at all that the colonels were plotting without awareness of the highest echelons of the army leadership: "I am responsible before history because as Prime Minister of the country I did not succeed in pre-empting what happened. And the reason why I did not succeed in pre-empting it is because there was no indication at all that some colonels were plotting a military coup behind the backs of the highest echelons of the army leadership". But, besides Kanellopoulos's testimony and the support which the military coup received from high-ranking military officers such as Spandidakis, including the very commander-in-chief of the Greek military and head of state King Constantine, the charge of mutiny was also legally contested by the very fact that leader of the first transition-to-democracy government of National Unity, Konstantinos Karamanlis, accepted the invitation of the junta-appointed President of the Republic, Phaedon Gizikis, to return to Greece, which by itself conferred a measure of legitimacy to the junta. In addition, it was Gizikis who swore in Karamanlis as Prime Minister.

During the trial Spandidakis, Zoitakis and Stamatelopoulos differentiated their position from that of the other junta members. This divergence from the common defence line led Georgios Papadopoulos to strongly chastise one of the defence lawyers for trying to question one of Zoitakis's witness. Papadopoulos is reported as claiming: "He is not one of our witnesses. Do not ask him". Papadopoulos himself refused to testify and only declared: "I shall answer only to history and to the Greek people", which led the presiding judge, Ioannis Deyannis, to retort: "Do you think history is absent from his courtroom?", to which Papadopoulos did not respond.

In a period when public anti-US feelings were at its apex over allegations regarding the US government's decision in supporting the coup, there was a demand on part of the press, political activists and prosecutors that the role of a possible involvement of the US Central Intelligence Agency (CIA) in the 21 April 1967 military coup be discussed in the court. This question, which was in line with a widely-held belief in Greece, was not finally answered in the trial. The presiding judge forbade any discussions on the subject with the remark that the mandate of the trial was confined to establish the facts on the day the 1967 military coup was launched. The only testimony about CIA involvement in the coup was given by Andreas Papandreou, son of Georgios Papandreiou, Prime Minister of Greece from 1963 to 1965, and later Greek Prime Minister himself between 1981–89 and 1993–96, who insisted that the colonels worked closely with the CIA.

4.2. THE VERDICT OF THE TRIAL OF THE INSTIGATORS OF THE 21 APRIL 1967 MILITARY COUP

The trial of the instigators of the April 1967 military coup ended on 23 August 1975. Georgios Papadopoulos, Nikolaos Makarezos and Stylianos Pattakos were sentenced to death by firing squad, while Dimitrios Ioannidis received a life sentence. Seven others were sentenced to terms ranging from five to 20 years and two were acquitted. The death sentences were later commuted to life incarceration by the Karamanlis government. This decision was received well by everybody in Greece which on 28 August 1975 led Karamanlis to publicly declare: "When we say life [sentence], we mean life [sentence]", by which he meant that the commutation of the sentences from death to life imprisonment would not be followed by further reductions.

The following table shows the main sentences, according to the verdict of the trial of the instigators of the 21 April 1967 military coup:

Junta Perpetrator	Sentence
Georgios Papadopoulos, Stylianos Pattakos	Dishonourable discharge, Death
Nikolaos Makarezos	Death
Ioannis Ladas, Konstantinos Papadopoulos, Michalis Roufogalis, Dimitrios Stamatelopoulos, Stephanos Karaberis	Life imprisonment
Odysseas Aggelis	Dishonourable discharge, 20 years imprisonment
Petros Kotselis, Nikolaos, Gantonas, Konstantinos Karydas, Evangelos Tsakas	20 years imprisonment
Konstantinos Aslandidis, Alexandros Hadjipetros	Not guilty

5. THE TRIAL OVER THE NOVEMBER 1973 EVENTS AT THE POLYTECHNIC SCHOOL OF ATHENS

On 16 October 1975, in the very same courtroom at Korydallos high security prison in which the trial of the instigators of the 21 April 1967 military coup had taken place, the second trial relating to the seven year period of dictatorship in Greece began. This was the trial investigating the events surrounding the November 1973 uprising at the Athens Polytechnic School. The November Athens Polytechnic uprising was a massive demonstration of popular rejection of the Greek military junta which started on 14 November 1973, escalated to an open anti-junta, anti-US revolt and ended in bloodshed in the early morning of 17 November 1973 after a series of events starting with a tank crashing through the gates of the Polytechnic School.

The trial over the events of the November 1973 Athens Polytechnic uprising lasted fifty-seven days. There were thirty-three indicted in the trial, including Papadopoulos, Ioannidis, Roufogalis, Vassilios Bouklakos, Elias Tsiaouris (or Tsiaparas) and Nikos Dertilis. Papadoloulos, Ioannidis, Roufogalis and Dertilis were already convicted in the trial of the instigators of the 21 April 1967 military coup and serving their sentences from that trial. The only defendant not present at the Polytechnic trial was Elias Tsiaouris, accused of murder, who had escaped custody because he was in hiding.[19] In total, there were 237 witnesses for the prosecution and the defence and about 59 lawyers.[20]

19 G. Papadakou and N. Vasileiadou, *Fovismena anthropakia edeichnan oi sfageis.*

20 G. Kousis, 'Ioannidis-Dertilis: Oi Teleftaioi Egkleistoi Ametanoitoi gia ti Diktatoria' (Ioannidis-Dertilis: The Last Impenitent Imprisoned for Dictatorship), *Eleftherotypia*, 23 July 2008.

The preliminary investigation for the November 1973 Polytechnic events was carried out by prosecutor Dimitrios Tsevas, who submitted the results of his investigation to the office of the prosecutor general on 14 October 1974. In his report, Tsevas stated that Ioannidis and Roufogalis were on the scene during the events and directed their men with the purpose to create, through shooting and violence, conditions which would benefit Ioannidis's planned coup against Papadopoulos.[21]

During the trial a documentary film was shown, produced by Dutch journalists, which showed the three days of events at the Athens Polytechnic School from the time that the students started protesting on 14 November to the very moment of the crushing of the Polytechnic School gates by the tanks in the early hours of 17 November. During the screening, Papadopoulos was not paying attention to the film, mostly looking down, while Ioannidis was reportedly watching the film unperturbed[22], while throughout the trial both men, even though they were sitting close to each other, never exchanged a look. Witnesses such as Antonis Agritelis, the driver of Dertilis's military jeep, testified that he saw Dertilis execute a young man on Patission Avenue. After his action, Dertilis was reported to have entered the jeep boasting to his driver about this. Dertilis disputed Agritelis's testimony but in the end the court partially convicted him on this testimony.[23]

Stylianos Pattakos testified that he called Dimitrios Ioannidis to his office in September 1973 because of rumours that he was planning the overthrow of the Papadopoulos regime. Ioannidis denied the rumours and reassured Pattakos on his "military honour" that he was a supporter of the Constitution and of Papadopoulos regime. Pattakos also mentioned that he was aware of the fact that in the afternoon of 24 November 1973 Ioannidis had been called by Papadopoulos himself and, with Makarezos present, he again vehemently denied any rumours that he was planning a coup. However, despite these reassurances, as Pattakos added, a few hours after Ioannidis meeting with Papadopoulos, around 3:30 am the next day, the tanks appeared in the streets of Athens and Phaedon Gizikis was sworn early that morning as figurehead President of the Republic.[24]

---

21 D. Tsevas, *Porisma Tseva gia to aimatira gegonota tou Polytechneiou ton Noemvrio 1973* (Tseva's Report on the November 1973 Athens Polytechnic Bloody Events), available at www.vrahokipos.net/old/history/gr/polytexneio/Tsevas.htm, accessed 28 September 2011.

22 G. Kousis, *Ioannidis-Dertilis: Oi Teleftaioi.*

23 V. Nedos, *O "aoratos dictator" aiteitai tora apofylakisis.*

24 G. Kousis, *Ioannidis-Dertilis: Oi Teleftaioi.*

On the second day of the trial, Papadopoulos's defence lawyers Karagiannopoulos, Papaspyrou and Steiropoulos raised the objection that the court did not have jurisdictional authority over their client regarding the November 1973 events at the Polytechnic School of Athens, because he enjoyed presidential immunity as President of the Republic during the time of the events, and demanded an immediate ruling from the court.[25] The court went immediately in recess for further deliberations and once the proceedings resumed it announced that Papadopoulos was not immune from prosecution as President of the Republic at the time of the events because the 21 April 1967 coup initiated violence against the Greek state and usurped the power and legal authority of the people. Therefore, all subsequent junta governments were deemed by the court to be products of violence, which meant that Papadopoulos was not a legitimate President of the Republic at the time, and as such not immune from prosecution.

The full unanimous decision of the court, rejecting Papadopoulos's motion for immunity, stated the following[26]:

> The mutinous movement of 21 April 1967, the action of a group of military officers and the resulting situation until 23 July [1974] constituted a *coup d'état*, through which it was intended to usurp the authority and the sovereign rights of the people. The consequent governments were governments of violence. Therefore, it is clearly concluded that anyone who exercised duties of governmental authority under any office including that of the head of state, did not in reality exercise legal authority and consequently they are not protected for their actions during the exercise of such authority under the regulations which define immunity. Accordingly and the standing as accused Georgios Papadopoulos, having exercised duties as President of the Republic during the time the actions were carried out as being attributed to him by the indictment, was not the legitimate President of the Republic and therefore he is not protected under the provisions of immunity.

Following the ruling about immunity, Ioannidis's lawyer Giorgos Alfantakis, made a motion to split and postpone the trial on the grounds that the indictment did not have a complete rationale: although it was mentioned in the order that Ioannidis encouraged and persuaded unit commanders of the state security forces to act in a criminal fashion during the suppression of the uprising, the names of the commanders were not mentioned in the indictment. The court rejected the motion on the grounds that it could not annul the indictment.

---

25 G. Papadakou and N. Vasileiadou, 'Fovismena anthropakia edeichnan oi sfageis…' (The Murderers Appeared Like Scared Little Men), in *Eleftherotypia*, 16 November 2003.

26 G. Papadakou and N. Vasileiadou, *Fovismena anthropakia edeichnan oi sfageis.*

5.1. THE VERDICT OF THE TRIAL OVER THE NOVEMBER 1973 EVENTS AT THE POLYTECHNIC SCHOOL

On 31 December 1975 the five-member court which investigated the events of the November 1973 uprising at the Athens Polytechnic School convicted 20 out of the 32 accused and held Ioannidis as the only person morally responsible for the events. The main sentences are shown in the following table.

Junta Member	Sentence
Dimitrios Ioannidis	Seven life sentences
Georgios Papadopoulos	25 years imprisonment
Stavros Barnabas	Three life sentences
Nikolaos Dertilis	Life sentence
Dimitrios Zagorianakos	25 years in prison
Konstantinos Mavroidis	25 years in prison
Pantelis Karayannis	25 years in prison
Ioannis Lymberis	25 years in prison

6. THE TRIALS OF THE TORTURERS

In addition to the two trials of the instigators and the Polytechnic events, there were another six trials which investigated the use of torture by the dictatorial regime. These trials are widely known as the "The Trials of the Torturers". Two of the trials involved the martial court of the military police (*Ειδικό Ανακριτικό Τμήμα της Ελληνικής Στρατιωτικής Αστυνομίας*, EAT-ESA). The first started on 7 August 1975 at the Athens Permanent Martial Court and the second on 13 October 1975, with the verdict announced on 9 December 1975. Those being prosecuted numbered 18 officers and 14 non-commissioned soldiers who all faced charges of using torture during interrogations with civilians who were suspected of being opponents to the junta regime. The second trial investigated torture allegations with reference to the Bogiati military jail and army units located in the Attica prefecture. These trials were followed by four additional trials which investigated allegations of torture made against members of the Greek security forces and the police. The last of the torture trials started in November 1976. According to a government assessment given to Amnesty International in December 1976, there have been more than 400 torturers' trials held in various towns and cities of Greece since the fall of the military junta. The exact number is difficult to trace due to the lack of centralised records in these trials.[27]

27 Amnesty International, *Torture in Greece: The First Torturers' Trials 1975*, 63.

The charges during the first EAT-ESA torturers' trial were[28]: 'Repeated abuse of authority, violence against a superior officer, unconstitutional detention, ordinary and serious physical injury, repeated insults to a superior, and recurrent moral responsibility for ordinary or serious physical injury'. Each defendant was charged to a varying degree but the only officer to plead guilty to all of the charges was sergeant Michail Petrou, a former guards at the Athens headquarters of EAT-ESA, who returned to Greece from abroad in order to be tried.[29] A problem which the prosecution faced was the theft and destruction of the EAT-ESA files. These files were never recovered and were not used in any of the trials. In fact, documents which were initially exhibited in court by senior EAT-ESA officers later disappeared without ever being found.[30]

During the EAT-ESA trials, the chief of EAT-ESA, Theodoros Theophilogiannakos, pleaded for the non-conviction of any of the accused lower-rank EAT-ESA personnel. His rationale was that such convictions might have encouraged the newly legalised KKE to threaten EAT-ESA men with punishment in case the soldiers executed legally dubious orders. This could demoralise the EAT-ESA personnel who might disobey any order issued by their commanders, when in doubt about the legitimacy of that order. Refusing to obey an order would be illegal from the army's standpoint and would shake the discipline of the military, in Theophilogiannakos' view. "Sentence us, the commanding officers, to death if you wish. All that matters is to save the state", Theophilogiannakos pleaded in the court.[31]

At the close of the trial the prosecutor described the indoctrination process he held responsible for the acts of the defendants. He spoke of those who "used the defendants, fanaticised and toughened them [...]. They are those who inspired in them wrong ideas about our national interests. They are those who for many years, have given thousands of hours' instruction on the fighting of communism without sparing even one hour to the defence of democracy".[32] Speaking of Theofilogiannakos the prosecutor told the court that Theodoros Theofilogiannakos was being guided by a blind anti-communism and he attributed even the slightest opposition to the dictatorial regime to the "communist finger".[33]

28 Amnesty International, *Torture in Greece: The First Torturers' Trials 1975* London, 1977, 13.

29 Amnesty International, *Torture in Greece: The First Torturers' Trials 1975*, 13.

30 M. Haritos-Fatouros, *The Psychological Origins of Institutionalized Torture*, London, New York, 2003, 28–29.

31 M. Hoefnagels (ed.), *Repression and Repressive Violence: Proceedings of the 3rd International Working Conference on Violence and Non-violent Action in Industrialized Societies*, Amsterdam, 1977, 17.

32 M. Hoefnagels (ed.), *Repression and Repressive Violence*, 15.

33 M. Hoefnagels (ed.), *Repression and Repressive Violence*, 15.

Under the colonels' regime nationally minded came to mean "someone who identified himself completely with the dictatorial regime". Ideological devotion was instilled by such measures as forcing the soldiers to kneel to a statue honouring the 21 April 1967 "revolution" which brought the colonels to power. As resistance to the regime spread to wider and wider circles the definition of Greek grew correspondingly narrower. "We are Greece" stated Major Theofylogiannakos in 1970 during the period when he commanded the EAT-ESA. Another commander of this unit stated: "It doesn't interest me what they are saying about us, whether we are torturers [...]. We attend to our job [...]. One thing is real. The Revolution is strong. No-one can shake it".[34]

During the second trial Theophilogiannakos asked the court to disallow testimony from Kostas Kappos, an Member of Parliament of the Greek Communist Party, on the grounds that Kappos was an atheist. Spanos, one of the EAT-ESA officers and torturers, instead of giving a testimony, declared that the "revolution" was betrayed like Cyprus, while another EAT-ESA officer, Hadjizisis, claimed that the EAT-ESA interrogators went through a worse ordeal than the actual interrogation victims. One of the accused, Dimitrios Kofas, was notorious as the "orange juice doctor" because he prescribed orange juice as a panacea for any ailment, including those resulting from torture. In one patient case involving Nikolaos Stapas, an Air Force officer, Kofas prescribed orange juice for haematuria (blood in the urine) caused by severe torture. The "orange juice doctor" was convicted for eleven documented cases for dereliction of his medical duties.[35] In general, the defensive position of all those accused could not perhaps be put in better words than those of one of the prosecutors in one of the EAT-ESA trials who in his closing remarks said: "The torturers wanted to present EAT-ESA not as a place of torture but as a national reformatory. Modestly reserving to themselves infallibility of judgment, they have tried to follow in the footsteps of the Holy Inquisition".[36]

6.1. THE VERDICT OF THE TRIALS OF THE TORTURERS

The following table summarises the verdict and the sentences of the two EAT-ESA trails:

34 M. Hoefnagels (ed.), *Repression and Repressive Violence*, 15.
35 M. Hoefnagels (ed.), *Repression and Repressive Violence*, 15.
36 M. Hoefnagels (ed.), *Repression and Repressive Violence*, 15; Amnesty International, *Torture in Greece: The First Torturers' Trials 1975*, 16; Fr. Wakeman Jr., *Spymaster: Dai Li and the Chinese Secret Service*, Berkeley, University of California Press 2003.

EAT-ESA Member	Sentence (first trial)	Sentence (second trial)
Nikolaos Hadjizisis	23 years imprisonment	7 years imprisonment
Theodoros Theophilogiannakos	20 years imprisonment	7 years imprisonment
Anastasios Spanos	20 years imprisonment	5 years imprisonment
Georgios Tsalas	15 years imprisonment	4 years imprisonment
Dimitrios Kofas (nicknamed "the orange juice doctor")	7 years imprisonment	7 years imprisonment

7. INCARCERATION

In prison the junta principals addressed each other using their former titles such as "Minister", and "President" and showed great deference to Georgios Papadopoulos, who did not readily socialise and preferred to dine alone. The then-warden of Korydallos prison, Yannis Papathanassiou, later published the book *Prison Diary: Korydallos 1975–79*, where he described the amenities that the incarcerated junta members enjoyed, such as air conditioners, television sets and tennis courts. In his book Papathanassiou describes how the Greek Ministry of Justice – under whose jurisdiction the country's prisons, including the Korydallos prison in which the junta members were serving their sentences, fell – being under pressure by junta sympathisers, ordered these special arrangements for the imprisoned members of the Greek junta. Papathanassiou also reveals escape plots organised for these members. For example, the author discusses how, through their lawyers, the imprisoned junta members got involved into the 1977 general election in Greece by supporting a right wing party, National Alignment, founded by hard-right conservative members of Konstantinos Karamanlis's New Democracy, from which these members split in 1977 and under the leadership of Stefanos Stefanopoulos – Prime Minister of the country from 17 September 1965 to 22 December 1966 – managed to win 7% of the vote and five seats in the Greek parliament.[37] Papathanassiou also reveals how the prisoners of Korydallos prison became so incensed about the preferential treatment given to the junta members that they rioted.

Papadopoulos and seven other members of the junta were housed in the maximum-security A block of the Korydallos prison. The leader of the April 1967 military coup resided on the second floor of the compound along with the other members of his regime, while Dimitrios Ioannidis resided on the ground floor. The latter was reported as reading military books and books about the CIA during his incarceration. Because of his involvement in Papadopoulos's

[37] R. Clogg, *Parties and Elections in Greece: The Search for Legitimacy*, Durham, 1987, at 183–84.

overthrow he was accused by the right wing of having betrayed the oath he gave in the summer of 1971 in front of Papadopoulos and another twenty junta members that he would recognise Papadopoulos as the leader of the "Revolution", and thus he was held responsible for the subsequent events, especially the regime's ultimate collapse. For these reasons, Ioannidis did not come in contact with Papadopoulos and the other junta members around him and he spent most of his time alone in an isolated cell. Despite this, he sometimes arranged parties attended by members of the EAT-ESA military policy, who resided on the third floor of the compound.

A plan to grant amnesty for humanitarian reasons to nearly all the jailed former members of the junta members by the Konstantinos Mitsotakis government in December 1990 was cancelled after protests from the public as well as conservatives, socialists and communist political activists. "The universal condemnation both in Greece and Cyprus by the overwhelming majority of the people forced the government to a hasty retreat", said Andreas Papandreou, the leader of the main opposition Socialist Party (PASOK).[38] The government change of heart came at a cabinet meeting and its announcement said that "in order to avoid turning this issue into the object of artificial political tensions, it decided to not advance the procedures for the granting of a pardon".

The former junta rulers themselves never sought pardon or amnesty. But junta supporters have lobbied for an amnesty since the officers were sentenced. Under Mitsotakis's government proposal the only junta member who would not have been pardoned was Dimitrios Ioannidis, who engineered a failed coup in Cyprus by right-wing supporters of the island's union with Greece, which prompted an invasion of Cyprus by Turkey and partition of the island. On Cyprus itself, nearly all political parties condemned the proposal to pardon the leaders. The government spokesman of Cyprus, Akis Fantis, said Cypriots will always hold the Greek military dictators responsible for the island's division.

Although Stylianos Pattakos and Nikolaos Makarezos were let out of jail early due to health reasons, Papadopoulos never asked for clemency and remained in jail until his death.[39] He died in hospital on 27 June 1999, after being transferred there from Korydallos prison. Dimitrios Ioannidis and co-conspirator Nikolaos Dertilis never asked for pardon. By the end of 2005, lawyers representing Ioannidis and Dertilis petitioned the court for their release, but at the same time Ioannidis declared that he did not regret any of his actions. In 2008 Ioannidis was transferred to the General State Hospital of Nikaia from Korydallos prison due to illness. He died on 16 August 2010 from respiratory problems, having

38 *The New York Times*, 31 December 1990.
39 *The Independent*, 28 June 1999.

been taken to hospital the previous evening. He remained incarcerated until his death.

Even in jail, Stylianos Pattakos, exhibited continued devotion to Papadopoulos. It is reported that he enjoyed hearing religious music supplied to him by a monk and in his prison memoirs he describes how he enjoyed tending a small garden and a little pond with 21 goldfish. The two things he mentions in his writings that he did not like was noise pollution at the jail, which he describes a "torture", and that the shape of the pond and faucet combination looked like a hammer and sickle. In another segment of his prison memoirs, Pattakos also mentions an incident involving General Odysseas Aggelis – the Chief of the Armed Forces under much of the junta – and a jail guard. According to Pattakos the jail guard had his radio volume high and Aggelis pleaded with the guard to lower it. The guard not only did not comply but raised the volume higher. Aggelis then asked Pattakos to intervene on his behalf and asked the "noble jail guard again". On 23 March 1987 Aggelis committed suicide in his cell, at the age of 75. Pattakos was released from jail in September 1990 due to "irreparable damage to his health". Nikolaos Dertilis is the last remaining of the principal conspirators of the junta regime currently in jail.

8. RECONCILIATION IN THE AFTERMATH OF THE JUNTA PERIOD (1974–1981)

Transitional justice in post-dictatorship Greece moved beyond trials of the instigators of the 1967 military coup and violation of human rights by the junta regime on its citizens. It also involved the process of reconciliation of the country's political and social division and turbulent past as a result of the devastating civil war of the 1940s. It would be sensible to argue that, while prior to the junta period Greece's political and social life was preoccupied with the process of healing the wounds of the civil war, with any attempts for reconciliation proving to be ineffective, the junta period functioned as a process of "catharses" for the political drama in which Greece lived from the end of the 1940s to the end of the 1960s. In fact, it would be difficult to distinguish between the post-junta transitional justice and the long process of healing the wounds of the 1940s civil conflict which Greece went through during the post-Second World War period.

In the aftermath of the seven-year dictatorship, the Greek political class was not preoccupied with healing the wounds of the country's civil war in the 1940s, but designed a specific political project which aimed to bridge the divides of post-civil war Greek society so as to forge a national consensus. The latter was seen as an important goal to achieve in order to cope with the ethnic crisis with reference to the Cyprus issue and a possible large scale Greco-Turkish war in the future. This project was focused more on the seven-year dictatorship and its aftermath, i.e. the restoration of democracy, than the civil war and as such, it was closely linked to the need to meet the political exigencies of the time and consolidate democratic norms and practices. In line with this, immediately after he was sworn in as Prime Minister, Konstantinos Karamanlis began to speak of the need for a "genuine and progressive democracy" in whose context there would be "room for all Greeks".[40]

The communists, who had been kept outside at the country's political and social life until then, were allowed to participate in the electoral process providing that they registered properly and pledged that they would abide by democratic practices and not use force to come to power. The Greek Communist Party had openly resumed its activities in Greece after the fall of the junta and took part in the 1974 general elections in alliance with the Greek Communist Party of the Interior, which mostly formed by Greek members of the Greek Communist Party who left the Party during the split of February 1968 due to their disagreements with the party's policy to blindly follow the line of the Communist Party of the Soviet Union and reject "Eurocommunism". In the general elections of 1974 the alliance between the Greek Communist Party and the Greek Communist Party of the Interior gained only limited support, taking less than ten per cent of the vote and only eight out of 300 seats in parliament.

In the new period which had just started the foundations for political reconciliation were not to be laid through directly confronting the legacy of the civil war but by rectifying the worst excesses of the Colonels' regime. Immediately upon assuming office, Karamanlis released all political prisoners, abolished the worst prison camps, restored citizenship to all those who had opposed the military regime, removed all orders depriving people of their passports or limiting their right to travel outside Greece and granted a general amnesty for all political offences committed under the dictatorship.[41] Yet, while Karamanlis moved swiftly to reinstate fundamental freedoms, elsewhere his approach was more cautious. The government defended the slow and haphazard search for justice on the grounds that it could not alienate the military at a time when Greece faced the prospect of war with Turkey. In addition, discrimination did not disappeared overnight and the secret services continued to spy on the Greek Communist Party and the parties of the left as it did until then, including the junta period. The certificates of social liability by which Greek citizens had to renounce communism and confirm their loyalty to ideals such as those of family,

[40] *The Times*, 26 July 1974.
[41] *To Vima*, 25 July 1974.

Greek Orthodox religion and defence of the nation and their home country, if needed, in order to have chances of being employed in the public sector, had been officially abolished by law 67/1974. However, old habits seem to have died hard and, if asked, the police were more than willing to continue to issue these documents.[42]

The failures of the past were recognised and effectively a real policy of reconciliation for healing the wounds of the country's civil war in the 1940s instigated so as to facilitate democratisation and deal with a number of pressing foreign policy issues. In this environment, reconciliation was essentially a political project with relatively narrow bounds. The communists were allowed to re-enter the domestic political arena, but splits and the rise of a new leftist political group, the Pan-Hellenic Socialist Movement (PASOK), led by Andreas Papandreou, meant that their electoral impact was limited. Karamanlis's policies also included a search for justice, but this was focused almost entirely on the dictatorship, and by mid-January 1975, 108,000 officials ranging from village councillors to the President of the Supreme Court had been dismissed, transferred or otherwise disciplined as collaborators with the junta regime.[43] It could be that Karamanlis was hoping Greece would follow the Spanish path and close the book on the subject in a pact of oblivion. However, for many Greeks, the search for justice did not stop with the dictatorship. Post-1974, the left was at last able to freely voice its version of the past in both the cultural and political spheres, but rather than healing, this initially laid bare the wounds of the civil war. A new consensus might exist in Greek society, but it was a consensus about the democratic present and, to a more limited extent, the European future, rather than the divisive past.

9. RECONCILIATION IN THE POST-JUNTA PERIOD (1981–1989)

In May 1980, Karamanlis was elected President and resigned as Prime Minister. Georgios Rallis succeeded him as leader of New Democracy but the new Prime Minister was to prove no match for the charismatic Andreas Papandreou in the October 1981 general elections, in which PASOK gained a clear parliamentary majority. The main PASOK slogan was "change", but the term "reconciliation" also featured in the speeches of party leaders. For Papandreou and PASOK, reconciliation meant coming to terms with the past by wiping the slate clean.

42 *Eleftherotypia*, 1 October 1975.

43 H.J. Psomiades, "'Greece from the Colonels' Rule to Democracy'" in J.H. Hertz (ed.), *From Dictatorship to Democracy: Copying with the Legacies of Authoritarianism and Totalitarianism*, Westport, 251–73.

This is to say that the recent history of Greece was to be reappraised. The anticommunist triumphalism of the right, the foundation stone on which the post-1945 Greek state had been built, was to be overturned and the role of the left re-evaluated, so as to bring an end to the discrimination which had excluded large segments of the Greek society from the public life. In other words, reconciliation for PASOK was not a vehicle for building national unity but one for righting the wrongs of the past and, although Papandreou often spoke of "building a government of all Greeks", it was also potentially highly divisive.

References to the period of the junta, reconciliation and the civil war were also useful in reassuring PASOK's more radical supporters that it remained committed to widespread change. Legislation was promised to end the commemoration of civil war victories, discriminations of the past were to be erased, exiles living in Eastern Europe (known in the discourse of the time as "political refugees") would be free to return, and surveillance files would be destroyed within a wider guaranteeing of civic rights. Many of these policies gained broad support, with even the conservative *Kathimerini* newspaper joining calls for the cancellation of ceremonies commemorating the civil war, but there were others on the right who objected. The entire national resistance during the Second World War would be redefined to include all those who took part in military activities against the occupiers during the Second World War. Municipal councils were encouraged to erect monuments to the resistance throughout Greece, and school textbook would henceforth include details of all the different groups. A series of national laws were passed which annulled a series of decrees which had deprived members of the left of political rights and prevented the return of political refugees and their children.[44] Finally, a 1985 law restored pension rights to civil servants who had been dismissed for political reasons.[45]

10. 1989 AND RECONCILIATION BY FIRE

The next major step in the process of reconciliation at the political level was to occur when PASOK lost its majority in June 1989. Once again, reconciliation was linked to a specific political project, this time the cleansing of a corrupt body politic. PASOK lost support following a series of high profile fraud and corruption scandals. The chief theme of the June 1989 elections was the cleansing of PASOK, but there were also calls from the opposition for reconciliation. The Greek Communist Party had voiced such calls before, but following the lead

---

44 D.H. Close, 'The Legacy', in D.H. Close (ed.), *The Greek Civil War, 1943–1950*, London, 1993, 210–21.

45 *Eleftherotypia*, 16 May 1985.

given in 1985, it was now also openly used by New Democracy and the right as well. In the elections, New Democracy gained 145 seats, a tantalising six seat short of a majority. With PASOK holding 125 seats, the balance of power rested with the communists, once again temporarily united in alliance under the name "Coalition of the Left and Progress". Eventually an interim government was formed under the premiership of the New Democracy member of parliament Tzannis Tzannetakis. All of the cabinet were members of New Democracy except for those directly dealing with the financial scandals: the Justice Minister, Fotis Kouvelis, and the Interior Minister, Nikos Konstantopoulos. With veterans from the civil war prominent in both parties, the coalition government symbolised at the highest political level the healing of the divisions of the past. To meet the promise of reconciliation, a new law on the consequences of the Greek civil war was announced that would at last formally remove the term "guerrilla war" from the statute book. Henceforth, the conflict from October 1944 until the end of December 1949 was to be officially termed 'the civil war'. All those convicted for offences relating to their participation in the civil war or political actions between its end and 24 July 1974 were to have their criminal records wiped clean. Pension rights were also extended to all members of the Democratic Army, supported by the Greek Communist Party during the civil war, who had been left disabled or their disabled relatives could establish pension rights. Most spectacularly, on the 40th anniversary of the battle for Grammos, nearly 17 million surveillance files were incinerated.[46] The fate of the files had long been a cause of debate and the decision to burn them was not universally applauded. Some wanted access to their records, possibly to claim compensation and pensions. Partly to forestall such objections, 2,500 files (1,600 selected by the previous PASOK government and the remainder by the government of the day) covering prominent political figures and trails were put aside, not to be opened for many years, but historians continued to criticise what they saw as the destruction of an important archive.

11. EPILOGUE

The successful prosecution of the junta and the heavy sentences imposed on the junta principals sent a message to potential conspirators within the army ranks that the era of immunity from the constitutional transgressions by the military was irreversibly over (*Kathimerini*, 5 January 2008). This was further assisted by the sound project of consolidation of its democratic institutions which the country undertook in the aftermath of the collapse of the junta regime as well of the process of accession to the European Economic Community to which it entered which discouraged any appetites on behalf of the military officers to

46 *The Times*, 30 August 1989.

intervene in politics. In addition, some attempts by the military to launch coups and overthrow the post-1974 elected governments were discovered and the perpetrators punished, which was another factor that kept the Greek army in the barracks. It is debatable how successful those attempts might have been, given that the public prestige of the Greek army had been seriously undermined after the military coup of 21 April 1967 and Turkey's invasion of Cyprus in the summer of 1974.

The EAT-ESA torture trials were acknowledged by Amnesty International as the first trials internationally, after the Nuremberg Trials, to involve prosecution of torture. They were also among the very few trials of torturers in human history and are referred to as the "criminal trials" by Amnesty International. Because it is rare for a country to prosecute torturers, these trials have become the subject of academic research and papers have been published based on their court proceedings. In 1977 Amnesty International published a report about the first torturers' trial in Greece with the dual purpose of documenting the use of torture in a modern oppressive regime and using an example of prosecution of officials who torture, based on a conviction that the Greek experience can benefit the rest of the world.

The dictatorship and its collapse not only fundamentally changed the political landscape of Greece but also, amid continuing urbanisation and other profound social changes, produced the space for a reformulation of the basic norms of society. Something akin to Zalaquett's "foundational time" arose in Greece, when previously unthinkable compromises could occur in the search for a just political system.[47] Following the fall of the colonels' dictatorship and the reassessment of external and internal threats that this brought, a national consensus emerged that henceforth internal political differences should be resolved through non-violent means. Issues connected to the civil war were no longer viewed as existential and instead were accepted as part of everyday politics. Within this environment, although points of dispute remained and actions taken in the name of reconciliation were often exclusive rather than inclusive, all the major political groups of both left and right slowly came to adopt a discourse of reconciliation, even if they continued to have different understandings of its content. Aside from this general acceptance that differences should be settled in a nonviolent manner, a feeling that justice has been done as regards the civil war also seems to have been important. Within the revitalised post-1974 democratic environment, the various political groups were not only able to articulate differing interpretations of the past, but also, using the

---

[47] J. Zalaquett, 'Truth, Justice and Reconciliation: Lessons for the International Community', in C. Arson (ed.), *Comparative Peace Processes in Latin America*, Washington/Stanford, 1999, 341–361.

legitimacy gained in genuinely free democratic elections, they began to right what they perceived as the historic wrongs inflicted on their supporters.

Justice has been found not so much through the courts, although legal actions against members of the colonels' regime after the dictatorship were important in facilitating the process of reconciliation at key moments. Instead, justice has taken a more symbolic and material form, especially with the search for pension rights and equal opportunities within Greek society. Justice has also been about recognition of the role of the various resistance groups who fought during the Greek civil war. It has therefore not been about forgetting the past but forging a new consensus on the bounds of commemoration, as increasingly public ritual has been abandoned in favour of monuments to the national resistance. There have been no truth commissions in Greece or systematic attempts to delineate an agreed narrative. The state no longer claims the right to control memory of the past. Instead, within a revitalised democratic environment, various groups have been free to remember and articulate differing interpretations.[48]

The Greek populace had emerged from the dictatorship more homogenous but also more radical in its views. A remarkably broad national consensus existed in favour of not only the (re)introduction of political freedoms and bringing the defence establishment under civilian control but also of leaving NATO and nationalising key economic sectors.[49] Not only was anti-communism rejected, as the right searched for new legitimacies, but the Greek populace as a whole was also highly receptive to redefinition of political norms and practices. Most importantly, this included an almost universal acceptance that after the excesses of the Colonels' regime, violence, whether by the left or the right, should play no part in politics, and that difference about the past should be expressed peacefully within new normative framework.[50]

In the aftermath of the national crisis with Turkey as a result of the 1974 Turkish invasion of Cyprus, the Karamanlis governments were careful enough not to create new political divisions nor to widen those already existing inside Greece by launching a project of political cleansing of collaborators of the junta regime with the involvement of the country's judicial system. There are individuals who took cases of junta torturers to provincial courts, but the government's role in transitional justice was mainly restricted to the cases discussed above in an attempt to create national unity which would assist it to successfully pursue its

48 *Ta Nea*, 4 September 2006.

49 R. Macridis, 'Elections and Political Modernisation in Greece', in H.R. Penniman (ed.), *Greece at the Polls: The National Elections of 1974 and 1977*, Washington, 1981, 1–20.

50 S. Katsikas and P. Siani-Davies, 'National Reconciliation after Civil War: The Case of Greece', (2009), 46/4 *Journal of Peace Research*, 559–575.

project of democratic consolidation and reorganisation of the country's national defence in the event of a war with Turkey.

There were sections within Greek society which were unhappy in the way that justice towards the junta regime was provided by the post-1974 democratic governments in Greece. On the one hand, conservative members of the Greek police, army, the Greek Orthodox Church and supporters of the extreme right-wing party National Political Union (EPEN) were unhappy with the fact that the protagonists of the colonels' regime were prosecuted and were imprisoned and on many occasions organised protest events, signed petitions and lobbied the government to provide political amnesty to the perpetrators of the junta regime and let them free. On the other hand extreme left-wing groups were unhappy with the scale of political cleansing of the state apparatus by collaborators of the junta regime. Due to this feeling of injustice a number of extreme-left terrorist groups such as 17th November and ELA were formed with the aim of taking the law into their own hand, cleansing the state of collaborators of the junta regime, weakening and finally undermining the country's post-1974 political class which they regarded as continuation rather than a break of Greece's dictatorial past.

The junta regime was to determine the country's post-dictatorship political life in many ways. The democratisation project determined the country's political life. The KKE and sections of the society which were associated with the losing side in the Greek Civil War were legitimised politically and played an active role in the country's political life. Political terms such as "democracy", "democratisation", "national emancipation", by which it meant independent foreign policy which would aim primarily to serve the country's national interests and secondary those of is Western allies, became political banners and came to dominate the country's political rhetoric. The main principles of the narrative of the junta trials, such as consolidation of country's democratic system, freedom of expression, protection of human rights, foreign policy independence continued to dominate the country's political life in the years to come, but their interpretation was influenced by the polarised political climate of the post-junta period. This climate became complicated by the partition of Cyprus in 1974. This, together with the bilateral controversy over the airspace, sea border, and continental shelf, caused Greco-Turkish relations to deteriorate. The fact that the US government officially recognised the junta regime and was regarded by a large part of the Greek political elite as responsible for the territorial division of Cyprus also complicated Greek-US relations and gave rise to anti-US public feelings, which were often inflamed and encouraged by members of the Greek political class. There was a broad consensus on the need for consolidation of a stable democratic regime, non-interference of the army with the country's political life, and the participation of all political parties, including the KKE, in the country's general elections – even the sympathiser of the 1967 military coup EPEN, founded by jailed former junta leader Geogrios Papadopoulos on 30 January 1984, participated (unsuccessfully) in the 1985 general elections, while in the 1984 elections to the European Parliament, the party polled 2.3% of the vote, giving it one of the 24 seats held by Greece in the European Parliament. The junta was seen as the outcome of a long period of political and social division following the Greek Civil War – the Cyprus tragedy and the persecution of both leftist and conservative politicians by the junta regime contributed to such a view, and therefore it was commonly believed that post-junta democratisation could not be completed without a process of reconciliation of the traumas of the Civil War, which would also include the legalisation of the country's communist party.

However, in addition to issues of consensus there were areas of disagreement and, often extreme, polarisation. The demand for foreign policy independence meant that the country should redefine its foreign policy relations with its Western allies. On this subject, while some members of the political class wished to see the country remained allied to the Western bloc, though in a more cautious manner than in the past – for example, it was the founder of the conservative New Democracy, Konstantinos Karamanlis, who withdrew Greece from the military structure of NATO in 1974 – there were periods when other members nurtured more radical views and wished to see Greece break from NATO and the European Economic Community (EEC), which was later renamed to European Union (EU), and become closer with countries of the communist bloc. In addition, while it was a common belief that post-junta democratisation should proceed along with a process of recovering the wounds of the country's Civil War, there was not unanimity at the beginning whether this process should go as far as to officially recognise the anti-Nazi resistance of the Communist Party-controlled National Liberation Front (EAM). For example, in the parliamentary debate for the recognition of National Resistance in 1982, New Democracy walked out of the debate in protest against the Socialist government's intention to recognise the resistance of EAM in the Second World War. Furthermore, within the climate of post-junta democratisation, trade unionism was reinforced, to the extent that the political class has often fallen hostage to trade unions in pursuit of political and economic reforms, political clientelism persisted and extended to include centre-left and leftist members of the society who had been previously at the margins of Greek politics, political populism dominated political life, while resistance during the junta period was among the strongest credentials to establish someone both politically and socially. Finally, the police and security forces were discredited, mainly – but not exclusively – due to their victimisation by the post-junta political class, for being organs of violence and oppression rather than institutions for maintaining public order, as well as for their role in the junta period in violating human rights and restricting any freedom of expression.

The negative image of the junta in the post-1974 period has affected historical research on that period, manifested primarily through silence on the topic. This can be partly explained by the fact that most of the historical archives in Greece and abroad were not declassified for much of the post-1974 period. But even after declassification took place, many scholars, influenced by the negative image of the period – some of them even anxious not to see their democratic and anti-junta credentials being questioned – have systematically avoided researching it. Many publications dealing with that period are personal memoirs or analyses, often politically biased, but there is a lack of research on issues such as the junta's policies towards the Eastern Bloc, the collaboration between members of the country's economic elite and public life and the extent to which those members continue to be influential in the post-dictatorship period, the junta's policies towards ethnic, religious, or social minorities, and other such topics.

ABBREVIATIONS

CIA:	(Central Intelligence Agency)
EAT-ESA:	(Ειδικό Ανακριτικό Τμήμα της Ελληνικής Στρατιωτικής Αστυνομίας, Special Interrogation Department of the Greek Military Police)
KKE:	(Κομμουνιστικό Κόμμα Ελλάδας, Communist Party of Greece)

SELECTIVE FURTHER READING

Amnesty International, *Torture in Greece: The First Torturers' Trials 1975* (London: Amnesty International, 1977).

Clogg, Richard, *Parties and Elections in Greece: The Search for Legitimacy* (Durham: Duke University Press, 1987).

Clogg, Richard and Yannopoulos, George (eds.), *Greece under Military Rule* (New York, 1972).

Close, David H., 'The Legacy', in Close, David H. (ed.), *The Greek Civil War, 1943–1950* (London: Routledge, 1993), pp. 210–21.

Grigoriadis, S., *Istoria tis Diktatorias (The History of Dictatorship)*, vols. 2 and 3 (Athens, 1975).

Clogg, Richard, *A Short History of Greece* (Cambridge: CUP, 2000).

Haritos-Fatouros, Mika, *The Psychological Origins of Institutionalized Torture* (London, New York: Routledge, 2003).

HOEFNAGELS, Marjo (ed.), *Repression and Repressive Violence: Proceedings of the 3rd International Working Conference on Violence and Non-violent Action in Industrialized Societies* (Amsterdam: Swets and Zeitlinger, 1977).

KARANIKAS, Christos, 'I anatoli tis dimokratias' (The Dawn of Democracy), *To Vima*, 13 August 2000.

KATEPHORIS, George, *I nomothesia ton varvaron (The Legislation of the Barbarians)* (Athens, 1975).

KATSIKAS, Stefanos and SIANI-DAVIES, Peter, 'National Reconciliation after Civil War: The Case of Greece', *Journal of Peace Research*, Vol. 46, No. 4 (2009), pp. 559–575.

KORIZIS, Chariton, *To aftarchiko kathestos, 1967–1974 (The Authoritarian Regime, 1967–1974)* (Athens, 1975).

KOULOUMBIS, Theodoros, 'Ellinoamerikanikes Sxeseis 1974–1999' (Greek-US Relations 1974–1999), *Kathimerini*, 5 January 2008.

KOUSIS, Giorgos, 'Ioannidis-Dertilis: Oi Teleftaioi Egkleistoi Ametanoitoi gia ti Diktatoria' (Ioannidis-Dertilis: The Last Impenitent Imprisoned for Dictatorship), *Eleftherotypia*, 23 July 2008.

MACRIDIS, Roy, 'Elections and Political Modernisation in Greece' in PENNIMAN, Howard R. (ed.), *Greece at the Polls: The National Elections of 1974 and 1977* (Washington, DC: American Enterprise Institute for Public Policy Research, 1981), pp 1–20.

MARKEZINIS, Spyros, *Anamnisis, 1972–74 (Reminiscences, 1972–74)* (Athens, 1979).

NEDOS, Vassilis, 'O "aoratos dictator" aiteitai tora apofylakisis' (The "Invisible Dictator" Has Now Applied for Prison Release), *Kathimerini*, 22 July 2008.

PAPADAKOU, Gianna and VASILEIADOU, Nantia, 'Fovismena anthropakia edeichnan oi sfageis…' (The Murderers Appeared Like Scared Little Men), *Eleftherotypia*, 16 November 2003.

PECKHAN, Robert Shannan, 'Orbituary: George Papadopoulos', *The Independent*, 28 June 1999.

PSOMIADES, Harry J., 'Greece from the Colonels' Rule to Democracy', in HERTZ, John H. (ed.), *From Dictatorship to Democracy: Copying with the Legacies of Authoritarianism and Totalitarianism* (Westport, CT: Greenwood), pp. 251–73.

ROUFOS, Rodic, *Inside Colonels' Greece* (New York, 1972).

SPOURDALAKIS, Michael, *Securing Democracy in Post-Authoritarian Greece: The Role of Political Parties, Stabilizing Fragile Democracies: New Party Systems in Southern and Eastern Europe* (London and New York: Routledge, 1995).

TSEVAS, Dimitrios, *Porisma Tseva gia to aimatira gegonota tou Polytechneiou ton Noemvrio 1973* (Tseva's Report on the November 1973 Athens Polytechnic Bloody Events), available at www.vrahokipos.net/old/history/gr/polytexneio/Tsevas.htm, accessed 28 September 2011.

TSOUKALAS, Constantine, *The Greek Tragedy* (Harmondsworth, 1969).

WAKEMAN, Frederic Jr., *Spymaster: Dai Li and the Chinese Secret Service* (Berkeley: University of California Press, 2003).

ZALAQUETT, José, 'Truth, Justice and Reconciliation: Lessons for the International Community', in ARSON, Cynthia (ed.), *Comparative Peace Processes in Latin America* (Washington, DC: Woodrow Wilson Center Press; Stanford, CA: Stanford University Press, 1999), pp. 341–361.

THE INCOMPLETE TRANSITION IN HUNGARY

Renáta Uitz

1. INTRODUCTION: THE "THREE PHASES" IN THE HUNGARIAN CONTEXT

In the case of post-Communist regimes, such as Hungary, the "three phases approach" as envisioned by this book might be somewhat more challenging to conceptualise than for those Western European democracies which did not undergo a regime change after WWII. Therefore, before commencing a detailed analysis, a caveat is necessary.

Hungary began its democratic existence in 1989. At the time, it had two repressive, authoritarian periods to account for (the so-called actual repression phase, phase 1): the older one which was responsible for Hungary's part in the holocaust during WWII, and a more recent one, the communist regime which in addition to being a deeply authoritarian regime was also responsible for at least two major waves of grave injustice: one following the stabilisation of the communist regime after its settling in, and another wave of repression aiming to suppress the 1956 revolution. The period of transitional justice falling between 1989 and 2000 is a dense and intense stretch of two decades wherein the qualities of the central phase (phase 2) and the long-term effects (phase 3) as understood by the project concept often merge. This overlap between the central phase and the long-term effects is far from being over. The incompleteness of the transition project is partly due to the fact that transitional justice measures (including retroactive criminal justice measures, amnesties and rehabilitations) came in waves after 1989, as a result of an intense dialogue between the political branches of the state and the Constitutional Court. Nonetheless, despite the adoption of a wide range of legal instruments, as the politics following the 2010 elections demonstrate, the quest to achieve justice for the past continues.

In order to demonstrate that reconciliation over authoritarian regimes and grave injustices perpetrated by them is far from complete in Hungary, suffice it to mention that the conservative-Christian coalition which won a constitution-making majority in 2010, in the fifth regular democratic election since 1989, declared that the elections amount to a "revolution in the voting booth" which will finally bring so-called "true transition" to Hungary. In this spirit the new constitution passed in the spring of 2011 by this parliament declares in its preamble (entitled "*National Avowal*") that "We do not recognise the communist constitution of 1949, since it was the basis for tyrannical rule; therefore we proclaim it to be invalid. We agree with the members of the first free Parliament, which proclaimed as its first decision that our current liberty was born of our 1956 Revolution" and that "We date the restoration of our country's self-determination, lost on the nineteenth day of March 1944, from the second day of May 1990, when the first freely elected body of popular representation was formed. We shall consider this date to be the beginning of our country's new democracy and constitutional order". These excerpts are clear evidence that the 20-year-old Hungarian democracy is still struggling not only with defining its identity, but also with accounting for the injustices perpetrated by its predecessors.

The complexity and political relevance of Hungary's communist past is further highlighted by the fact that on 30 December 2011 Parliament passed set of Transitional Provisions to the new constitution before its entry into force on 1 January 2012. The first part of the Transitional Provision is entitled "On Transition From Communist Dictatorship to Democracy". In its operative part this document declares the Hungarian Socialist Party (i.e. the political party which governed Hungary for 12 years after 3 democratic elections since 1989) fully responsible for all the acts of the Hungarian Socialist Workers' Party (i.e. the Communist Party). According to this document accountability for the crimes during the communist regime was not asserted after 1989 as the chain of legal continuity was not broken. In addition to calling for the prosecution of crimes, and responsibility for economic injustice, the document also calls for a Committee of National Remembrance (*Nemzeti Emlékezet Bizottsága*).

As an attempt to put the provisions of the freshly enacted document into effect, on 30 December 2011 Parliament also adopted a law lifting the statute of limitations for crimes against humanity, and for certain crimes committed during the communist dictatorship (Act no. 210 of 2011). It was also in the spirit of the Transitional Provisions that, in March 2012, Parliament commemorated with a resolution those who were executed, sentenced for political reasons, interned or suppressed between the autumn of 1944 and May 2, 1990, or were victims of mass deportation in the early 1950s.[1] Nonetheless, despite for the calls for responsibility in rather strong language, when a small opposition party, LMP (Politics Can Be Different) submitted a bill to permit access to the files of

[1] 16/2012. (III. 14.) OGY resolution.

communist secret services in February 2012, this project was not even brought up for discussion due to the resistance of the parliamentary majority (T/5116). The faction leader of the senior coalition party, FIDESZ, said at a press conference on 19 March 2012 that the it was a major flaw of the rejected bill that it was submitted by a person who cannot be regarded as a victim of the previous regime due to the positions of his father and grandfather during the previous regimes. Instead of a bill addressing the issue of the communist secret services, the majority faction leader moved towards establishing the Committee of National Remembrance by the summer of 2012. At the same time, LMP mobilised deputies successfully to schedule a day of debate on the communist secret services in early April 2012.

2. PHASE 1: REPRESSIONS

In the 20th century Hungary experienced two repressive regimes built on (at least traces of) totalitarian ideologies: a conservative nationalist regime which was slipping into a national socialist one while Hungary was an ally of Nazi Germany during WWII, and – subsequently – a communist regime following WWII. Strictly speaking, the national socialist regime lasted a few months right before WWII came to an end, and much of the harm (including the Holocaust resulting in the deaths of half a million Jews and thousands of Roma) is attributable to the preceding conservative nationalist regime which preceded it. The communist regime, while lasting longer, had an early phase of extreme suppression, followed by an intense phase of repression and then by a lighter phase during which Hungary earned the title the "happiest barrack" (*legvidámabb barakk*) in the communist camp. As a result the number of victims of communism is much more difficult to estimate.[2] *The Black Book of Communism* puts lethal casualties of Hungarian Communism at half a million (an estimate which may be accepted as reliable starting point), while other larger groups of victims will be identified in the following analysis.[3]

It is a common characteristic of both repressive regimes that in prevailing popular narratives (which do not necessarily portray historical facts adequately) both are

2 This is so in part due to the fluidity of the term victim. In the case of Communism it is safe to work with a definition where the deprivation of life, liberty or property is the result of a politically motivated act of the government. This definition is closest to some of the statutory definitions which were used in the transitional justice measures in Hungary.

3 Where possible I will try to draw data from multiple sources, available to Hungarian and international audiences. At points where sufficient differences exist, I will make an attempt to reveal potential causes behind the differences. The following factors are important to keep into account: 1) regarding victims of the Holocaust, data differ depending on the territory taken into account, 2) regarding casualties during communist regimes, certain resources became available due to recent declassification of various governmental papers.

often presented as "foreign imposed" or "foreign inspired" in their inception. In such accounts Hungary appears as a helpless victim in the web of world events, and key Hungarian decision-makers are portrayed as doing their best in the circumstances. Such narratives, if used improperly, have the obvious effect of downplaying "Hungarian" responsibility for the events. This is all the more disturbing since Hungarian governmental actors and authorities took an active role in perpetuating atrocities and implementing repressive measures with pain striking efficiency on their own, often without direct pressure from outside. The country report will focus on such wrongs committed in pursuit of totalitarian ideologies by Hungarian governmental actors, and will not cover otherwise appalling injustices which were committed by foreign powers, or were otherwise part of wartime losses.

2.1. FROM ADMIRAL HORTHY'S CONSERVATIVE NATIONALIST TO THE NATIONAL SOCIALIST REGIME

The hard-core national socialist regime of Ferenc Szálasi together with its immediate predecessor, the interwar conservative-nationalist regime during the governorship of Admiral Miklós Horthy remain responsible for preparing and executing the Holocaust in Hungary. Technically, the Hungarian nationalist socialist regime is a relatively short period between the coup d'état which put the national socialist Ferenc Szálasi in place as the "Leader of the Nation" between 15 October 1944 and the end of WWII. In the interwar period the Hungarian conservative-nationalist political regime of Admiral Horthy took several measures which were conducive to the elimination of the Hungarian Jewry and took care of making Hungary "Jew-free" before the national socialist takeover. Therefore, the Horthy and Szálasi regimes have to be covered together in order to get a full picture.

The anti-Semitism of the Horthy era was deep and all-encompassing, consisting of a web of both violent and peaceful anti-Semitic measures in varied fields of economics, culture/education and politics. For instance, the period of the White Terror responding to the 1919 Bolshevik revolution is a clear example of open, government sponsored physical violence against the Jewish Bolsheviks. Karády puts the number of the victims killed by counterrevolutionary commandos without legal authorisation at somewhere between several hundred to a thousand. In addition to the killings, show trials resulting in death sentences were organised. A wave of emigration followed in which important intellectuals (like György Lukács) and artists (like László Moholy-Nagy and Sándor Korda) left Hungary. Romsics counts about a hundred death sentences, followed by 74 executions.[4]

[4] I. Romsics, *Magyarország története a XX. században* (The history of Hungary in the 20th century), Budapest, 2005, 134.

As an important non-violent anti-Semitic measure one has to take note of the fact that it was as early as in 1920 when ethnic *numerus clausus* in higher education was prescribed by law (Act no. 25 of 1920). In the words of Viktor Karády "academic *numerus clausus* was an essential device for the realisation of the much publicised new policy of the "change of the guard" It limited new admissions of Jews in universities and most institutions of higher education to a proportion of 6% of those admitted".[5] This was an important first step followed by many during the period of the so-called "Christian Course" which sought to eliminate the "oppressive influence" of the Jews over Hungarian culture and economy with varying intensity.[6] As a positive development the Hungarian Jewry received representation in the upper house of parliament and *numerus clausus* was revoked in 1928 (Act no. 14 of 1928) – clearly in response to pressure from foreign and international Jewish organisations.[7] In the period from 1938 to 1944 these more moderate years were followed by the years of openly anti-Jewish legislation, the primary aim of which was finding a final solution to the "Jewish question".

Between 1938 and 1944 three "Jewish statutes" were passed.[8] "According to a 1941 census, Hungary, including the recently annexed territories, had a Jewish

---

5 V. Karády, 'The anti-Semitic 'change of the guard' in Hungary. A Case Study in Institutional Violence', as available at http://karadyviktor.uni.hu/keret.cgi?/southampton.htm.

6 V. Karády, 'Different Experiences of Modernisation and the Rise of Anti Semitism. Socio-Political Foundations of the *numerus clausus* and the 'Christian Course' in Post World War I. Hungary', in *Transversal* 4/2 (2003), 3–34.

7 J. Gyurgyák, *A zsidókérdés Magyaroszágon, Politika eszmetörténet* (The Jewish Question in Hungary, A history of political ideas, Budapest, 2001, at 127–130.

8 The so-called "first Jewish statute" (Act no. 15 of 1938 on the more efficient ensuring of the balance of social and economic life [*A társadalmi és gazdasági élet egyensúlyának hatályosabb biztosításáról*]). Under the new law only 20 percent of jobs in the liberal arts (including medical doctors, solicitors, engineers, press workers, actors and artists), commerce or factories could be held by Jews. The bill was viewed as the end of equality before the law. The statute left 5 years for its implementation, and was meant to be enforced by chambers of professionals. Soon the Imrédy government moved for harsher measures in order to solve the Jewish question, and oversaw the preparation of the "second Jewish statute" which was already passed under the Teleki government in 1939 (Act no. 4 of 1939 on the limitation of the societal and economic expansion of the Jews [*A zsidók közéleti és társadalmi térfoglalásának korlátozásáról*]). The second Jewish statute introduced a definition of Jew as a person of Jewish religion, or a person with at least one parent or two grandparents of Jewish origin. The statute makes conversion to Christianity extremely limited: only families with 3 converted generations qualify as non-Jewish. Apart from reintroducing *numerus clausus*, the ceiling for Jewish employment was reduced to 6 per cent, and Jews were completely banned from public administration, the judiciary and teaching positions in secondary education. Jews could not become defining figures in newspapers and theaters. The third Jewish statute was passed in 1941 under the Bárdossy government (Act no. 15 of 1941). The full title of the third Jewish law is 1941 évi XV. törvénycikk *a házassági jogról szóló 1894:XXXI. törvénycikk kiegészítéséről és módosításáról, valamint az ezzel kapcsolatban szükséges fajvédelmi rendelkezésekről* (Act no. 15 of 1940 on expanding and amending Act no. 31 of 1894 on the law of marriage, and race-protection measures necessary in connection with it). It was a clear Nuremberg-type racial

population of 825,000, less than 6 percent of the total population. This figure included 100,000 converts to Christianity who, under Hungarian race laws passed between 1938 and 1941, were classified as Jews".[9] Of them, roughly half a million perished during WWII, in the Holocaust in concentration camps (mostly in Auschwitz) and in forced labour battalions.[10] In addition, approximately 5–50,000 Roma perished in the concentration camps.[11] Until the German occupation, Nuremberg-type laws and forced labour conscription formed the most vicious forms of systematic anti-Semitic measures in Hungary. Note that unlike in other countries in Central Europe, Jews residing in Hungary did not suffer pogroms. While the Kállay government had little problem with anti-Semitic measures, Prime Minister Kállay resisted intensifying domestic radical right wing and German demands to round up and deport the Hungarian Jewry.[12] Evidence that German pressure was intensifying on Hungary in this respect is available in the records of the Wannsee conference of January 1942.

The first two mass killings of Jews in which the Hungarian authorities participated indeed took place well before the German occupation on 19 March 1944, yet these killings were not part of the systematic murder of the Jews. Despite anti-Jewish legislation, in the early years of the war Hungary even temporarily took Jewish refugees from other war-ridden territories. The influx of Jewish refugees led to a most regrettable incident in the summer of 1941, when

law, which qualified as a Jew everyone with at least two Jewish grandparents, and prohibited intercourse between a Jewish man and a Christian woman (but not the other way around). Later, act no. 8 of 1942 altered the status of the Jewish confession (from "adopted" to "recognized") in order to stop government funding thus far paid to the Jewish community, while act no. 15 of 1942 (at times called as the "fourth Jewish statute") prohibited the acquisition of arable land by Jews.

9 Data by US Holocaust Memorial Museum at www.ushmm.org/wlc/article.php?ModuleId=10005457.

10 Estimations differ depending on how the territory of Hungary is calculated for a given period. As Romsics summarizes: the estimate of half a million applies to the 1944 territory of Hungary, while if we take the Trianon boarders, the victims number 300,000. Romsics, *Magyarország története*, at 265 (in Hungarian).
For an important English language study taking the territorial dimension into accounts see Randolph L. Braham, *The Politics of Genocide: The Holocaust in Hungary* (1981), vols. 1–2. For data Braham relies on statistics from *Hungarian Jewry before and after the persecution*, a publication of the statistical department of the World Jewish Congress, Hungarian Section. For a more recent study in Hungarian which is based on archival research see Tamás Stark, "A magyar zsidóság a vészkorszakban és a második világháború után" (Hungarian Jewry during the Holocaust and after WWII), Regio – Kisebbség, politika, társadalom, vol. 4, issue no. 3 (1993): 140–150, also available at http://epa.oszk.hu/00000/00036/00015/pdf/09.pdf (in Hungarian), and his more recent Tamás Stark, *Zsidóság a vészkorszakban és a felszabadulás után (1939–1955)* (Jewry during the Holocaust and after Liberation (1939–1955)), MTA Történettudományi Intézet (1995). Note that while Stark often gives lower ("more cautious") estimates on casualties, his research is highly regarded in the field.

11 I. Romsics, *Magyarország története*, 265.

12 J. Gyurgyák, *A zsidókérdés Magyaroszágon*, 165–166.

about 18,000 Jews – mostly aliens and refugees – were deported from Hungary to German-occupied Galicia and transferred to the Ukraine (to Kamenets-Podolski)[13] who were killed by Nazi *Einsatzgruppen* and local Ukrainian forces on 27–28 August 1941.[14] This event has become known as the first mass killing of Jews in WWII, and Hungarian forces were clearly an auxiliary in the tragic fate of the victims. In another well-known incident in January 1942 which was not directed against Jews the Hungarian military was deployed to Novi Sad region ("Délvidék") to eliminate a partisan cell. Among the 4,000 killed, there were some 700–1,000 local Jews who also fell victim to the military action.[15]

Well before the German occupation, starting in 1939, Jews were conscripted for forced labour via legislation.[16] Then, in 1941, Jews were forbidden from serving in the army, therefore forced labour did not qualify as regular army service, and forced labourers were not entitled to military provisions and rations. Forced labourers typically served in noncombatant units (e.g. digging fortifications, clearing snow, maintaining roads and clearing minefields) in various fronts, including the extremely cold and rough Eastern Front after Hungary declared war on the Soviet Union.[17] Up to 50,000 Jews were deployed in such units until 1943 in the Soviet Union.[18] By 1943 13–15,000 of them died and another 10–11,000 were captured.[19] The copper mines of Bor in Serbia also had about 4,000 Hungarian Jewish forced labourers working there. Before German occupation, at least 27,000 (most likely 34,000) Jewish forced labourers died while on duty.[20] Ironically, with the German occupation of Hungary on 19 March 1944 forced labour became a life-saving alternative to being deported to a concentration camp.

The situation changed dramatically for the worse with German occupation on 19 March 1944 and the disaster became complete when the Hungarian nationalist socialist regime of Ferenc Szálasi and his Arrow Cross movement came into power on 15 October 1944. While historians of this period usually

13 R.L. Braham, *The Politics of Genocide: The Holocaust in Hungary, Condensed edition*, Detroit/Michigan, 2000, at 32.

14 Data by US Holocaust Memorial Museum at www.ushmm.org/wlc/article.php?ModuleId=10005457.

15 T. Stark, *Zsidóság a vészkorszakban és a felszabadulás után (1939–1955)* (Jewry during the Holocaust and after Liberation (1939–1955)), Budapest, 1995, at 17; R.L. Braham, *The Politics of Genocide*, 37.

16 1939 évi II. törvénycikk *a honvédelemről* (Act no. 2 of 1939 on national defence).

17 R.L. Braham, *The Politics of Genocide*.

18 J. Gyurgyák, *A zsidókérdés Magyarországon*, 172.

19 T. Stark, 'A magyar zsidóság a vészkorszakban és a második világháború után' (Hungarian Jewry during the Holocaust and after WWII), in *Regio – Kisebbség, politika, társadalom*, 4/3 (1993), 140–150; J. Gyurgyák, *A zsidókérdés Magyarországon*.

20 Data by US Holocaust Memorial Museum at www.ushmm.org/wlc/article.php?ModuleId=10005457.

argue about the potential impact of the Hungarian political tactic of reluctant cooperation before the German occupation (i.e. whether it saved Jewish lives, and how many), it remains absolutely clear that following the occupation the extermination of the Hungarian Jewry could not have been carried out with such efficiency in such a short time without the measures being meticulously prepared by local forces before the arrival of Adolf Eichmann and his Special Commando (*SS-Sondereinsatzkommando Ungarn*) with the German occupying forces.

Deportations started right after German occupation, in the spring of 1944. The first transport is estimated to have had about 8,000 persons.[21] Between 14 May and 8 July 1944 (thus, before the Arrow Cross takeover) some 430,000 Hungarian Jews were deported from Hungary in 147 trains to Auschwitz by Eichmann, with the assistance of the Hungarian police and the cooperation of the Jewish Council.[22] This meant that with the exception of Budapest, Hungary became "Jew-free" in less than four months following German occupation. In addition, Eichmann also made sure that Jewish property and valuables benefitted the German economy, while the Hungarian government was also claiming its share of the spoils. The creation of Jewish ghettos made this process easier. While deportations from all over Hungary were in full swing, in the summer of 1944 (on 14 June) Eichmann made an offer to Rudolf (Rezső) Kasztner of the Jewish Council to divert a transport of 30,000 Hungarian Jews to Austria to forced labour thus saving them from extermination. Braham estimates that about 75 per cent of these forced labourers who worked in Austria indeed survived.[23]

Although extermination of the Jews (i.e. making Hungary "Jew-free") was a central part of the Arrow Cross ideology, if not an obsession – maybe even more important that winning the war on the German side – the project was completed outside Budapest by the time the Hungarian national socialists came into power in October 1944. Due to earlier developments the anti-Semitic terror of the Arrow Cross militia was taking place in Budapest, where some Jews still survived.[24] The cruelty with which Hungarian Arrow Cross militia treated the Jews (with their 4,000 strong militia), regularly shooting stripped Jews into the Danube from the embankments stunned, even the German occupying forces. As a result, over 100,000 Jews were killed between 15 October 1944 and 13 February 1945.[25]

---

21 R. Hilberg, *The Destruction of the European Jews, Revised and Definitive Edition*, vol. 2, New York, 1985, at 832.

22 R.L. Braham, *The Politics of Genocide*, at 104–152.

23 E. Lappin, 'The Death Marches of Hungarian Jews Through Austria in the Spring of 1945', Jerusalem, 2000, at http://yad-vashem.org.il/download/about_holocaust/studies/lappin_full.pdf; R.L. Braham, *The Politics of Genocide*, 149.

24 R.L. Braham, *The Politics of Genocide*, at 151; K. Ungváry, *The Siége of Budapest, 100 Days in WWII*, New Haven, 2005, at 284–305.

25 K. Ungváry, *The Siége of Budapest*, at 287–288, 291.

Hungary's Soviet liberation seems to have a history of its own, producing further victims and seeds of complicated Communist mythologies. Soviet military presence – while it unquestionably brought an end to German occupation – also had its victims: the Soviet army took its toll on the civilian population, with 100-120,000 captured as prisoners in addition to the 600,000 military men taken in Soviet captivity.[26] Many were taken for the Soviet Union to work and returned after years of hard labour. The terror, often perpetrated by rambling Soviet soldiers who were not disciplined by their commanders, made the position of the emerging Hungarian Communist Party precarious. Rapes committed by Soviet soldiers are estimated to have been ranged between 50- to 200,000 incidents.[27]

While armed resistance to German occupation was minimal, as the Soviet forces were clearing the German army from Hungary, the activity of newly formed and reorganised political parties intensified. The Hungarian Communist party became revitalised as a political force in an emerging yet competitive political sphere. The blessings of Stalin were borne by those who spent time in the Soviet Union before, while those coming from the Hungarian communist underground were not to be trusted – a rift with fatal future consequences.[28] Mátyás Rákosi was the trustworthy Hungarian leader for the time being. On 21 December 1944 (thus, before liberation from German occupation) a temporary national assembly was formed in Debrecen, with the largest faction (39 per cent) belonging to the Communist Party.[29]

2.2. ESTABLISHING THE COMMUNIST REGIME: 1944–1948

In the years following WWII the Hungarian Communist Party slowly consolidated its rule, eliminating its political competitors by 1948.[30] Interpretations largely differ on whether they see this period as a preparation of communism in Hungary, or as period of genuine political competition which resulted in the defeat of democratic forces. Without intending to take sides in this debate it is most important for the present study that measures adopted by dominant political forces in this period – while were varied in form and intensity, and not always primarily punitive in nature – produced large numbers of individuals (victims) who were deprived of their life, liberty or property along the way. It is understood

26 I. Romsics, *Magyarország története*, 270; Kenéz, *Hungary from the Nazis to the Soviets, The Establishment of the Communist Regime in Hungary, 1944-1948*, Cambridge, 2006, at 38 ff.

27 A. Pető, A, 'Átvonuló hadsereg, maradandó trauma. Az 1945-ös budapesti nemi erőszak esetek emlékezete' (Passing army, lasting trauma. The memory of sexual violence cases in Budapest in 1945), in 1–2 (1999) *Történelmi Szemle*, 85–107.

28 Kenéz, *Hungary from the Nazis to the Soviets*, at 20 ff.

29 I. Romsics, *Magyarország története*, 278–279.

30 Kenéz, *Hungary from the Nazis to the Soviets*.

that these deprivations happened in the name of an authoritarian ideology which was gaining increasing prominence between 1944 and 1948, and achieved sole dominance in 1948 in the form of Rákosi's Communist dictatorship.

Allegedly applied as a measure to ensure and strengthen public peace, the new post-WWII governments heavily relied on internment or deportation of elements that were regarded to be dangerous to the new political stability. Internment could be prescribed as a criminal punishment for 6 to 24 months.[31] From 1946, however, it became available as a preliminary measure against persons who were "problematic" from the perspective of preserving the public peace.[32] A secret decree of the minister of interior authorised unlimited internment powers to this effect. A widely accepted estimate puts the number of persons interned at 40,000. In addition to prohibiting fascist political organisations, the new regime slowly closed down all civil society organisations and associations (over 1500 organisations in total). By the autumn of 1946 this was followed by the removal of approximately 60,000 civil servants who were deemed to have reactionary tendencies (the so-called "B lists").[33] A second wave of cleansing followed in 1948 when an additional 80,000 were removed from public service accordingly. Similar cleansings were undertaken in the private sector. Together with wiping out sources of dissent from the civil sector and all ranks of employment, internment had become an important means of ensuring that dissent was silenced and political competition extinguished by 1948.

Serious deprivations of property also occurred in the process of attempts to consolidate the ownership regime. The political forces had to rapidly decide on the consolidation of property, most importantly, the ownership of arable lands. While the incentive came from Soviet orders, all major political forces agreed on property reform being instrumental. In addition to the confiscation of Nazi and Arrow Cross property, large estates and lands owned by banks and commercial entities was effected with minimal compensation. Church property was confiscated without compensation in the process. Property thus confiscated or expropriated was distributed to new owners, whose status was protected against

---

31 On the basis of Article 3 of 81/1945 ME decree on people's courts (81/1945. (II. 5.) ME rendelet *a népbíráskodásról*). Until the enactment of this decree, the legal regime of the interwar period was used as a legal basis for internment (see es8130/1939 ME and 760/1939 BM decrees).

32 This avenue was opened by 1946. évi VII. törvény *a demokratikus államrend és a köztársaság büntetőjogi védelméről* (Act no. 7 of 1946 on the criminal protection of the democratic order and the republic).

33 I. Romsics, *Magyarország története*, 290. For the legal background see 19.5000/1946 ME decree (B-lists for public administration) and 8660/1946 ME decree (B-lists for private sector).This procedure was the outcome of a "screening procedure" prescribed earlier by 15/1945 ME decree, applicable for the public sector. Later 1080/1945 ME decree extended the procedure to the private sector as well.

claims from old owners by act no. 9 of 1946. By 1948, forced collectivisation was used to divest the new owners from private ownership and uniting them in Soviet-type cooperatives. Heavy and light industry was taken into state ownership along with banks. Along with nationalisation Hungary introduced the system of central planning in the economy in 1947.

2.3. 1949–1956: THE YEARS OF COMMUNIST DICTATORSHIP

With the pluralism of the Hungarian political sphere diminished and an all-encompassing political party, the Hungarian Workers' Party (*Magyar Dolgozók Pártja*)[34] overtook both politics and governance, and thus in 1949 Hungary clearly entered a true Stalinist-type Communist dictatorship under the leadership of Mátyás Rákosi (who stayed in power until 1953). With the death of Stalin in 1953 an opportunity for departure presented itself; developments were deemed insufficient and the short-lived 1956 revolution erupted.

The Rákosi regime was true to its Stalinist model down to the requisite personality cult of the leader and systematic elimination of rivals and dissenters, outside and inside the Communist party via show trials, mass prosecutions and mass internment. Show trials were an important means to persecute unwanted prominent allies in groups, among them László Rajk (sentenced to death and executed).[35] In connection with the trial of Rajk another 141 persons were arrested, of whom 14 were executed and 11 were imprisoned for life, while 38 were interned.[36] In the spring of 1950, former social democrats were tried, with 276 interned and 154 jailed in the end. In the spring of 1951, non-Muscovite Communists had their turn, with 21 leaders jailed, among them János Kádár. In 1952 the Communist party was gearing up to 'uncover' a Zionist conspiracy in the party,[37] and the idea was only dropped due to Stalin's death. In addition to the grand show trials, mass prosecutions were organised against the enemies of the regime – mostly to spread fear. Between 1950 and 1953 an estimated one million

---

34 The Hungarian Workers' Party was formed in 1948 by the amalgamation of the Hungarian Communist Party (Magyar Kommunista Párt) and the Hungarian Social-Democratic Party (Magyar Szociáldemokrata Párt).

35 I. Rév, *Retroactive Justice: Prehistory of Post-Communism*, Stanford, 2005.

36 Here I follow Romsics, *Magyarország története*, at 344 et seq. (in Hungarian). Cf. the *Black Book of Communism* giving slightly different numbers (94 arrests which resulted in internment, 14 executions, 11 deaths in prison and 50 long imprisonments are mentioned expressly at 426).

37 On instructions from Stalin, the Communist Party leadership had an unusually high proportion of Jews – who were later purged from the party, which again created an air of anti-Semitism for post-WWII Hungary. For a most insightful analysis in English see I. Rév, *Retroactive Justice*.

indictments were prepared, with charges filed in 650,000 cases and convictions rendered in as many as in 390,000 instances.[38] A new wave of internment started in 1950, affecting the "untrustworthy" on the southern border, resulting in 44,000 class enemies being interned to labour camps (like mines or major building projects). Potential pockets of "Horthyist resistance" were also eliminated in 1951 when the remnants of the aristocracy (some 14–15,000 people) were put in internment camps and their remaining property was confiscated. By 1953, Hungary had approximately 100 internment camps (Recsk and Kistarcsa being the most famous), often referred to as the "Hungarian gulag".[39]

The State Security Agency became an important actor in ensuring the practical operations of terror, with its 40,000 informants. The card system of the Agency carried information on almost a million persons. They were the one to assist with the putting together of charges for the various trials; they were also in charge of running the internment camps and also contained the border control force. Rákosi once referred to it as the instrument over which the Party shall have exclusive control.[40] It is thus not such a surprise that the 1956 revolutionary government decided to shut down the Agency.

2.4. FROM THE SUPPRESSION OF THE 1956 REVOLUTION TO NORMALISATION INTO THE 'HAPPIEST BARRACK'

With the death of Stalin in Hungary Rákosi could not maintain his Communist regime of personal cult. When attempts to consolidate the system failed on 23 October 1956 a revolution erupted. Well-known Muscovite Communist Imre Nagy became the Prime Minister of the attempt to establish democratic governance. This revolution was brought to an end on 10–11 November 1956 by force: Soviet military assistance was provided to János Kádár's side to restore order. By December 1956 the Hungarian Socialist Workers' Party (*Magyar Szocialista Munkáspárt*, or MSZMP) under the direction of János Kádár was in control of the situation. Since the beginning of 1957 this Communist Party was assisted by its own armed force, the Workers' Guard (*Munkásőrség*).

38 Romsics, *Magyarország története*, at 345 (in Hungarian). The estimate of the 1956 Institute also puts the number of indictments at 650,000. See "ÁVÓ" in the Glossary at http://server2001.rev.hu/oha/eng/_6_6.html (in English). In an earlier work Fehérváry gives similar statistics (at least the magnitude is similar) in István Fehérváry, *The Long Road To Revolution: The Hungarian Gulag, 1945–1956* (Pro Libertate, 1989), at 24 (in English). All these data are difficult to corroborate as their sources for statistics are not identified. For an early monograph also covering these trials in Hungarian see also Frigyes Kahler, *Joghalál Magyarországon 1945 1989* (*Justizmord* in Hungary 1945–1989). (Zrínyi, 1993). Cf. the *Black Book of Communism* records 700–800,000 convictions (not prosecutions) for crimes against state property at 400–401.

39 Romsics, *Magyarország története*, at 345 (in Hungarian).

40 On quote in the *Black Book of Communism* at 398.

The 1956 Revolution (which used to be labeled a "counter-revolution" until 1989) was followed by a campaign to restore order – and seek revenge. Revolutionary armed units were disarmed, leaders of the revolution were rounded up (about 200 of them), and courts martial were quickly put in place. In early December the Party's firing squads killed about 100 people. By January 1957 people's courts were handing down sentences against the revolutionaries for conspiracy and for crimes against the state. Between November 1956 and the end of 1959 procedures were commenced against some 35,000 persons, about 10–22,000 of whom were convicted for crimes against the state (of whom some 16,000 received imprisonment) and 200–400 were executed.[41] Among these undoubtedly the most famous trial was that of Prime Minister Imre Nagy and his accomplices, as a result of which the former Prime Minister was sentenced to death. Approximately 13,000 were interned without any court procedure and a few hundred were interned in the Soviet Union. Over 170,000 emigrated from Hungary fearing further persecution. All in all, however, the terror campaign was much more precise than the previous ones.

Mechanisms of social control became much more refined (resulting in lighter casualties) after the wave of revenge over the 1956 revolution ceased by the early 1960s. By and large, show trials and political trials as such ceased. Political dissent was increasingly tolerated and controlled via more gentle interference by the police (often not exceeding asking for "papers" and interrogations which did not result in subsequent procedures), and semi-visible surveillance by the Communist Secret Service, more precisely, by the domestic intelligence division in the Ministry of Interior (known as "Subdivision III/III").[42] The Secret Services interfered with the lives of individuals in two important ways: while the

41 There are considerable differences in statistics in the Hungarian literature, which result at least in part from the time period taken into account and also from the classes of crimes included in the calculation. In a recent study Frigyes Kahler reviews recently used data to find that some contemporary statistics put the number of executed to almost 3,000, while Cseh and Szakolczai write of 229 executed (until April 1958), Zinner counted 367 executions (until 1963), Kahler's own research found 3–400 executions (until 1963) and Gosztonyi's research suggests 453. The total count on convictions depends on the classes of crimes taken into account (only crimes against the state vs. including other political crimes, and also the exact period which was covered). See Frigyes Kahler, '1956 szellemének megtorlása tíz év után, Vaczkó László és Hamusics János ügye', *Aetas* 2006/1: 38–56, at 38–39 (in Hungarian). Romsics's research has numbers within the range provided above in the main text at Romsics, *Magyarország története*, at 406 (in Hungarian). For another recent, comprehensive account in Hungarian see also Gábor Jobbágyi, *Ez itt a vértanúk vére. Az 1956 utáni megtorlási eljárások* (This is the blood of martyrs. Procedures of revenge following 1956) (Kairosz, 1998).

42 As is now known, in its latest composition before the fall of the communist regime in 1989, the State Security Service (*Állambiztonsági Szolgálat*), i.e. Division III of the Ministry of Interior, comprised of Subdivision III/I for external intelligence, Subdivision III/II for counter-intelligence, Subdivision III/III for domestic intelligence (or "internal reaction") and Subdivision III/IV for military intelligence. Previously the various divisions carried different names, such details, however, will not be covered below, unless noted otherwise.

most obvious victims are the ones who were put under surveillance (and as a result were bothered further by the Communist government), many of the 200,000 informers were also pressured into cooperation (e.g. having been blackmailed through their religious convictions or sexual preferences revealed to the Secret Services via preparatory work). Thus, they are to be regarded as perpetrators of injustices as well as victims thereof.

3. PHASE 2: TRANSITIONAL JUSTICE MEASURES

3.1. A PRELUDE TO TRANSITIONAL JUSTICE MEASURES IN 1989: THE FIRST EFFORT IN DOING JUSTICE ABOUT WWII?

Following WWII the newly formed Hungarian government took several steps in order to do justice about the injustices of the war, which resulted in major deprivations for those affected. Although these measures might be understood to belong among the "wrongs of communism," due to their orientation and inspiration it makes better sense to group them together. Among these are the people's courts handing down convictions for genocide and war crimes, and the mass deportations of ethnic groups under and beyond the Treaty of Potsdam.

The emerging Hungarian political elite took to consolidating its rule quickly. On 26 February 1945 radical right-wing organisations were disbanded, the Jewish statutes were abolished and people's courts were established to serve expedited justice on the Hungarian war criminals.[43] These courts were predominantly staffed by laymen, rules of procedure were lax and the procedures definitely do not live up to even the most basic requirements of the rule of law.[44] Between 1945 and 1950 people's courts heard approximately 60,000 cases, in 27,000 of which they found against the defendants, leading to over 10,000 imprisonments and 189 executions.[45] The people's courts were definitely instruments of political revenge-seeking. Following the transition to democracy special legislation was enacted to rehabilitate the illegally convicted. The quality of the records makes these procedures complicated and they often produce stunning results.[46] Due to

43 The people's courts operated between 3 February 1949 and 1 April 1950.

44 L. Karsai, 'The People's Courts and Revolutionary Justice in Hungary, 1945–46,' in I. Deák, J.T. Gross and T. Judt (eds.) *The Politics of Retribution in Europe: World War II and Its Aftermath*, Princeton, 2000, 233–252.

45 I. Romsics, *Magyarország története*, 281.

46 See for instance the rehabilitation of Ferenc Kisbarnaki Farkas in 1998, who prepared the unsuccessful breakout attempt on behalf of Admiral Horthy in 1944, following which he joined the side of Szálasi's Arrow Cross government, as the leader of the National Allocation Government Secretariat (*Országos Elhelyezési Kormánybiztosság*). His role in the extermination of the Hungarian Jewry is unclear. In 1950 he was convicted in absentia for his

the arbitrariness of the procedure and the harsh sentences, it was widely believed at the time that the people's courts were instruments in the hands of revengeful Jews.[47] Starting in 1948, a special unit of the Ministry of Interior, the State Security Agency (*Államvédelmi Hatóság*) assisted the people's courts in their search for war criminals.

On the quality of the procedure and of the surviving records consider what László Karsai, a historian examining the records on behalf of Yad Vashem found: "It was general practice that the People's Courts did not hear the witnesses of the defence. During the past few years, we have found more than fifty persons deserving to be presented with Yad Vashem's award to *Righteous Gentiles* for saving Jews, often in the face of mortal danger. ... [The] reason why the more than fifty *Righteous Gentiles* is a considerable number (and it is continuously growing as a result of our research) is that Yad Vashem has so far honoured less than 400 Hungarians (including 12 foreign diplomats stationed in Hungary, like Raoul Wallenberg) with that award".[48]

Among the victims of the retribution following the war are clearly ethnic Germans who were deported under Article 13 of the Treaty of Potsdam. Under this framework Hungarian authorities expelled an estimated 180–200,000 "ethnic Germans" towards the West.[49] In addition, outside the Potsdam framework, a complicated exchanged of ethnic deportees started between Czechoslovakia and Hungary, after the Czechoslovak government was unsuccessful in seeking approval for a similar unilateral expulsion of ethnic Hungarians from Czechoslovakia. Instead, after tense initial negotiations triggered by deportations of Hungarians in Czechoslovakia, the two

decision as president of a military tribunal convicting one of his underlings, who performed the unsuccessful breakout attempt in 1944. The person convicted was finally not executed. In an interview on 6 December 2006 the eminent military historian Krisztián Ungváry noted: the biggest flow of the rehabilitation process is that it only allows for a formal review of the challenged conviction, but does not have room for an overall assessment of the person's career preceding that conviction. According to Ungváry an entirely new criminal procedure would be appropriate instead of rehabilitation. See www.168ora.hu/cikk.php?id=6741.

47 L. Karsai, *The People's Courts.*

48 L. Karsai, 'Crime and Punishment: People's Courts, Revolutionary Legality, and the Hungarian Holocaust," in 4/1 (2000–2001) *InterMarium*, at http://ece.columbia.edu/research/intermarium/vol4no1/karsai2.pdf.

49 B. Apor, 'The Expulsion of the German Language Population from Hungary,' in S. Prauser and A. Reefs (eds.), *The Expulsion of the 'German' Communities from Eastern Europe at the End of the Second World War*, 1 (2004), EUI Working Paper HEC, at 33, available at http://cadmus.iue.it/dspace/bitstream/1814/2599/1/HEC04-01.pdf; Á. Tóth, *Telepítések Magyarországon 1945–1948 között. A németek kitelepítése, a belső népmozgások és a szlovák-magyar lakosságcsere összefüggései* (Settlements in Hungary, 1945–1948, Connection between the internment of Germans, internal migration and the Slovak-Hungarian population exchange), Kecskemét, 1993.

governments agreed on a bilateral population exchange,[50] as a result of which the Czechoslovak government recruited ethnically appropriate volunteers from Hungary,[51] while Hungary took the ethnic Hungarians expelled from Czechoslovakia. Approximately 76,000 ethnic Hungarians arrived, while approximately 60,000 Slovaks left Hungary, leaving their immovable property behind without compensation.[52]

As is clear from this description of the first phase of doing justice about the past, the measures adopted after WWII clearly resulted in further injustices which potentially needed to be tackled by any democratic regime to come in Hungary, which cared about the impact of the legacies of previous Hungarian governments. These measures which aimed to punish the perpetrators of wrongs – as they were perceived at the time by the incoming communist regime – clearly added new groups of victims to an already long and complicated list.

3.2. THE LEGAL FRAMEWORK FOR TRANSITIONAL JUSTICE AFTER 1989

In 1989 Hungary underwent a negotiated transition to democracy. The communist regime agreed to amend the 1949 Stalinist constitution and to new elections in the spring of 1990, at the Round Table talks. Since the new regime came about without any rupture, as a result of sheer legal and constitutional continuity the new Hungarian democracy shared the past of all the previous Hungarian regimes, the horrors of which were recounted above. To say the least, the Hungarian Constitution is Act no. 20 of 1949 – a profoundly amended version of Rákosi's Stalinist constitution – profoundly amended in its philosophy and contents, but not in its title. This is how the symbolic is intertwined with the pragmatic, the poetic and historic with the legal in the Hungarian context. It is not such a major surprise, therefore, that the Hungarian parliament elected in

50 The population exchange has its own website at www.lakossagcsere.hu/mt200701493.html&d=1(in Hungarian). There is a debate about the numbers (both concerning people and property) which will not be reproduced here. On the population exchange see in Hungarian e.g. Katalin Vadkerty, *A belső telepítések és a lakosságcsere* (Internal settlement and population exchange) (Kalligram, 1998); Katalin Vadkerty, *A kitelepítéstől a reszlovakizációig 1945–1948. Trilógia a csehszlovákiai magyarság 1945–1948 közötti történetéről.* (From Deportation to Re Slovakisation 1945–1948, A trilogy on the history of Hungarians in Czechoslovakia between 1945–1948) (Kalligram, 2007); and László Szarka, "A csehszlovák–magyar lakosságcsere helye a magyar kisebbség tervezett felszámolásában 1945–1948 között" (The role of Czechoslovak Hungarian population exchange in the planned extermination of the Hungarian minority in 1945–1948) Kisebbségkutatás 2007/3, also at www.hhrf.org/kisebbsegkutatas/kk_2007_03/cikk.php?id=1446.

51 Ethnic Hungarians who decided to stay in Czechoslovakia underwent "re-Slovakization".

52 The two governments mutually waived their claims, regarding their long due uncompensated claims to be considered equal.

2010 is still concerned about engineering constitutional continuity, identifying its rightful predecessors and seeking to distance itself from uncomfortable legacies.

The first democratically elected parliament was concerned with (1) punishing perpetrators of past crimes which went unpunished for political reasons (the so-called retroactive justice mission, involving the courts), (1) removing the negative consequences of unjust political convictions of the past regimes (mostly in the form of rehabilitation through the judiciary and compensation measures transferred through the welfare sector) and (3) providing some form of compensation to the victims of various types of past abuses other than unjust or illegal political convictions (e.g. assignment to forced labour battalions). These were issues which more or less genuinely followed from the mission of the first parliament to set the record straight about Hungary's constitutional heritage; this mission was very much in line with the philosophy of the first democratically elected Prime Minister, József Antall, who was a historian himself. Note that doing justice about the Holocaust is not key item on the agenda. This is so because compensation measures were at least in some part in place at the time of transition.

A task which the first parliament was well-aware of, but tried to avoid was (4) addressing the activities of the communist secret services. This task presented at least three potential avenues of access (not all of which are related to transitional justice), i.e. providing access to the files (archives) of the secret services to victims and researches, identifying the agents, employees and collaborators of the secret services, and dismantling the communist secret services in order to build a discontinuous security service for the new democracy. Indeed, due to the surveillance scandal of late 1989 (the so-called Duna-gate) which made it clear that the services kept members of the democratic opposition under surveillance during and even after the Round Table Talks of 1989, this was a problem which bothered many who realised that the unreformed secret services are keeping the new political elite under surveillance irrespective of the changes in the constitutional regime.[53] There was also increasing pressure to clear the new elite from being in the ever longer shadow of former "secret service agents and collaborators" in order to protect the integrity of a still-fragile political system.

The legal framework adopted by the democratic (post-communist) regime in response to the crimes and injustices perpetrated by previous totalitarian regimes was passed incrementally (over an extended period) as a result of a continuing conversation between the political branches and the Constitutional Court. During this extended period which lasted well over a decade, the relevant

---

53 R. Uitz, 'Communist secret services on the screen: The Duna-gate scandal in and beyond Hungarian media', in Apor and O. Sarkisova (eds.), *Past for the Eyes: East European Representations of Communism in Cinema and Museums after 1989*, Budapest, 2008.

legal regime underwent several adjustments until it reached its current form.[54] As a result of judicial as well as non-judicial processes taking several years, transitional justice measures were often shaped by scandals, revelations and realisations which were not apparent (or not even familiar) during the early days of transition. In an interesting twist of events, most recently the European Court of Human Rights handed down two judgments which pin-point the weaknesses of the application of existing legal solutions which need to be addressed by the Hungarian government even if it is determined to close the books on the past.[55]

3.2.1. Retroactive justice measures punishing perpetrators of past crimes

The clearest example of the transformation of a judicial instrument of doing justice about the past into an almost pointless legal and political debacle is the case of the retroactive criminal justice laws. First and foremost, the first democratically-elected parliament intended to punish the perpetrators of "crimes which went unprosecuted for political reasons under the previous regime".[56] The first democratic Hungarian government decided to pass retroactive criminal justice legislation via lifting the statute of limitations.[57] The sponsors of the retroactive criminal justice bill argued that the "rule of law cannot be used to shield injustice".[58] In the early days such measures were seen as necessary largely in order to punish those military and paramilitary officers who ordered the mass killings of usually unarmed civilians during and in the course of the suppression of the 1956 revolution.

---

54 Previous solutions which were either rejected by the Constitutional Court or overcome as a result of policy decisions will be discussed to the extent relevant for the present analysis due to the constraints of the report.

55 *Korbely v Hungary* (Application no. 9174/02, Grand Chamber judgment of 19 September 2008) put an end to the debate between national courts concerning the proper criminal assessment of lethal actions of military and paramilitary units against civilians in the early days of the 1956 revolution. More recently *Kenedi v Hungary* (Application no. 31475/05, judgment of 26 May 2009) reinforced the efficiency of legal measures ensuring access to the documents of Communist secret service in government custody (over the government's insistence that the documents constituted state secrets and as such need to be classified and cannot be accessed or disclosed by a qualified historian).

56 Here I borrow the language of the first attempt at passing a retroactive justice law which was invalidated by the Constitutional Court in 11/1192 (in the famous *Zetenyi-Takacs* decision – which gets its name from the sponsors of the bill.) The full title of the Hungarian retroactive criminal justice bill was "On the Prosecutability of Grave Crimes Committed between 21 December 1944 and 2 May 1990, Which Were Not Prosecuted for Political Reasons". On the making of the bill in English see G Halmai and KL Scheppelle, "Living Well is the Best Revenge: The Hungarian Approach to Judging the Past", in J.A. MacAdams (ed.), *Transitional Justice and the Rule of Law in New Democracies* (Notre Dame, University of Notre Dame Press, 1997) at 158–160.

57 11/1992 (III. 5.) AB decision.

58 J. Kis, 'Az első magyar Alkotmánybíróság értelmezési gyakorlata' (The first Hungarian Constitutional Court's interpretation practice), in G. Halmai (ed.), *The Constitution Found? The First Nine Years of Constitutional Review on Fundamental Rights*, Budapest, 2000.

The Constitutional Court found that retroactive criminal legislation of this kind was unconstitutional. Invoking the principle of the rule of law enshrined in the old Constitution (Article 2.1), the basic premise of the Constitutional Court's reasoning was that of the legality of transition and of constitutional continuity between the previous regime and the emerging democratic system. Although entering a decision which ultimately prevents the prosecution of grave criminal offenses that went unpunished for political reasons during previous oppressive regimes is not a trivial stance to take for a constitutional court in the early phase of democratic transition, the reasoning of the Hungarian Constitutional Court is in the rather abstract language of the requirements of the rule of law and legal continuity. Indeed, the Hungarian Constitutional Court was strongly criticised for its reliance on the conception of the rule of law and its adherence to a continuity rhetoric which falls short of any harsh condemnation of the previous regime. This criticism prompted then-Chief Justice László Sólyom to make an unusual gesture and explain the Constitutional Court's decision, stressing the moral imperatives informing the Court.[59] Importantly, the Constitutional Court indicated that it would find a solution acceptable which permits the prosecution of only such crimes which constituted crimes at the time the acts were committed and for which the statute of limitations has not run out.

Subsequently Parliament succeeded in finding a legal solution which made room for the conviction of previously unprosecuted perpetrators of armed violence during the 1956 revolution, indicting such persons for crimes for which the statute of limitations does not run out under international criminal law.[60] Criminal courts of the ordinary judiciary found it difficult to apply the substantive law to some of the events, as the *Korbély* decision of the ECtHR clearly demonstrates. While there are not too many cases of this kind left, and the ones which are still open do not affect high-ranking Communist Party or governmental officials, Hungarian courts were willing to decide on the merits of the indictments brought before them.[61] One of the cases reached the European Court of Human Rights, wherein the Grand Chamber of that body found that the applicant's conduct did not constitute a crime under the applicable international criminal law rules, and therefore the applicant was convicted in

59 H. Schwartz, *The Struggle for Constitutional Justice in Post-communist Europe*, Chicago, 1999, at 100.

60 The law is Act no. 90 of 1993 (az 1956. októberi forradalom és szabadságharc során elkövetett egyes bűncselekményekkel kapcsolatos eljárásról). While the Constitutional Court rejected parliaments attempts to fiddle with the statute of limitations among the rules of criminal procedure (42/1993. (VI. 30.) AB decision), it allow those bits of the scheme to pass where the limitation issue was resolved with reference to rules of international criminal law (53/1993. (X. 13.) AB decision). See also 36/1996 (IX.4.) AB decision which invalidated the 1993 act but defined rules concerning the applicable substantive criminal law in such cases.

61 M. Morvai, 'Hungarian Criminal Court Cases concerning the (Retribution for the) 1956 Revolution', in A. Sajó (ed.), *Out and Into Authoritarian Law*, The Hague, 2003.

violation of the principle of *nullum crimen sine lege* in violation of Article 7 of the European Convention (*Korbély v. Hungary*). Following the decision of the Grand Chamber, in reopened proceedings the Supreme Court did not find it appropriate to acquit the accused who won in Strasbourg. The Supreme Court in its review decision emphasised that the ECtHR is in a different procedural position and decides on different matters than the national courts. Furthermore, the Hungarian criminal justice system might have several opportunities to test the limits of these lessons in cases concerning Hungarian perpetrators of the Holocaust.

3.2.2. Rehabilitation laws

The rehabilitation laws were far less complicated to pass. This class of measures prominently addressed the victims of political convictions rendered by peoples' courts for genocide and war crimes in the immediate aftermath of WWII, during the early communist show trials and in connection with the 1956 revolution. The first statue was passed already in 1989 by the outgoing communist Parliament. It was followed by Act no. 26 of 1990 on invalidating the illegal convictions between 1945 and 1963 (second rehabilitation statute), and somewhat later by Act no. 9 of 1992 on invalidating of convictions for certain crimes against the state and public order between 1963 and 1989, passed by the first democratically-elected parliament (third rehabilitation statute, also called the "nullification statutes"). Before passing the third nullification law, a committee of experts was convened by the government to review 6,620 criminal convictions and 696 forced medical treatment orders before the concept of law was prepared.[62] The fourth rehabilitation statute – Act no. 130 of 2000 on invalidating convictions in connections with the repression following the 1956 revolution – was passed much later. The last two statutes do not offer a blanket rehabilitation: individual applicants have to approach courts with the documentation of their cases in order seek clearance individually. Therefore, it is clear that the rehabilitation scheme in Hungary also falls among the judicial instruments. The rehabilitation scheme was supplemented by various compensation instruments along the way in connection with the harm the victims of such convictions suffered.[63] Compensation, however, did not mean *in*

[62] F. Kahler (ed.), *A semmisségi törvények, Büntetőjogi tanulmányok* vol. 3 (The nullification statutes, Essays in criminal law), Budapest, 2002, at 190.

[63] The last Communist parliament passed two resolutions (not statutes!) in this respect: 19/1989(XI. 1.) OGY resolution on the compensation for the victims of illegal convictions, internment and displacement (kitelepítés) and 20/1989 (XI. 1.) OGY resolution on remedying the harms cause to the persons who were kept in police custody (interned) or were displaced. This was followed by another resolution of the first democratically elected parliament: 36/1990 (III. 28.) OGY resolution on remedying the harms suffered by the Hungarian citizens who were taken to the Soviet Union of forced labour (jóvátételi munka), and who were convicted by Soviet courts and in the meantime rehabilitate for lack of a criminal offense.

integrum[64] restitution of property which had been confiscated via the nullified criminal conviction.

3.2.3. *The files and activities of the communist Secret Services: Lustration and access to files*

In the Hungarian context lustration (decommunisation) and access to files of the communist Secret Services are deeply intertwined, due to the logic of the first lustration law adopted by the first democratically-elected parliament. It set off an ongoing game of public ping-pong between Parliament and the Constitutional Court, which seemed to have more or less settled only by 2000.[65] The ongoing hullabaloo about lustration is remarkable only because it clearly shows that parliamentary debates on convenient means of persecuting political opponents do not cease. These debates shall also be regarded as litmus tests on the shape of the moral standards of a polity far into the 21st century.

Despite attempts to pass a law from the very beginning, the first bill on lustration was passed in 1994, in the last days of the first parliament. The first democratically-elected government submitted its first bill on lustration on 13 May 1991 (Bill no. 2294), purporting to "promote the clarity of democratic governance" (preamble). In the half-year following the introduction of the bill, over 250 amendments were proposed, prompting the government to withdraw the bill in the summer of 1992. Finally, in the autumn of 1993 the government submitted a different bill on lustration which was then passed into law in the spring of 1994, and entered into force on 5 April 1994.[66] Due to all this procrastination, in which Prime Minister Antall is believed to have had a major role, the first lustration law did not apply to the members of the first democratically-elected parliament.

The lustration law as passed in 1994 calls for the screening of MPs, officials who have to take an oath before parliament and cabinet ministers, among others. The aim of lustration is to reveal if the person concerned was a career officer working for the internal division of the state security services specified in the law, supplied the state security services with reports as informants via network assignments (collaboration), or was in a position to receive reports from the services. In addition, the screening extends to state security units of the armed

64 From the Latin 'restitution in integrum', meaning full restoration to the original situation.

65 Act no. 93 of 2000.

66 The full title of the law is "Act on Background Checks to be Conducted on Individuals Holding Certain Important Positions", Act No. 23 of 1994. Available in English in Neil Kritz (ed.), *Transitional Justice, How Emerging Democracies Reckon with Former Regimes*, Vol. 3, Washington, D.C., United States Institute of Peace Press, 1995, 418 et seq.

forces during the 1956 revolution, and members of the Hungarian Nazi Party.[67] The lustration procedure itself was performed by a panel of lustration judges. The panel examined the files of former domestic security services, while persons subjected to screening were not required to make depositions. Collaboration with the domestic intelligence services was established if a "statement of intent" on cooperation is found, together with proof that the person received remuneration for cooperation. When ascertained, collaboration with former internal state security services is disclosed, unless the public official concerned decides to resign from office.

Central provisions of the 1994 lustration act did not pass constitutional scrutiny.[68] In its decision the Constitutional Court made clear that by 1994 the point has passed where lustration could possibly serve as a means to protect peaceful transition from the interference by the security services of the former regime.[69] Rather, the lustration law is meant to ensure the transparency of public affairs and public offices, and as such it should be subject to constitutional scrutiny under the ordinary terms of constitutionality (i.e. there is no room for transitional justice-like considerations).[70] The Constitutional Court presumed that someone's collaboration with the communist secret services falls within the realm of private information. Following this premise the justices rejected the argument that learning about a public office-holder's previous cooperation with the communist state security services would per se amount to such a public interest where the act on data protection[71] allows the disclosure of private data.[72]

Note that on the clearly relevant matter of access to the files of the Communist secret services the Constitutional Court found that Parliament violated the right to informational self-determination when it failed to regulate access to the archives of former secret services. Thus, the Court held that parliament committed an unconstitutional omission and set 30 September 1995 as a deadline for legislation to be adopted. Note that at the time the files of the communist secret services were not deposited in a public archive but were in the custody of the national security establishment of the day. At the time the national security services still operated under a Cabinet decree from 1990 which set up the interim infrastructure of the national security services.[73]

---

67 Such information was available from other, open sources. Thus, there was no need to consult the archives of the state security services.

68 60/1994 (XII. 24.) AB decision.

69 60/1994 (XII. 24.) AB decision; ABH 1994, 350.

70 60/1994 (XII. 24.) AB decision; ABH 1994, 350–1.

71 Act no 63 of 1992 on the protection of personal data and public access to data of public interest.

72 60/1994 (XII. 24.) AB decision; ABH 1994, 354.

73 Cabinet decree 26/1990. (II. 14.) MT on the interim regulation of the performance on national security tasks.

In 1996, well past the deadline set by the Constitutional Court, the Socialist-dominated parliament amended the lustration law. The 1996 amendment significantly narrowed the scope of mandatory lustration. The lustration law thus amended defines agents as persons who were (open or "top secre"") career officers of subdivision III / III of the communist Secret Services (i.e domestic intelligence) or its predecessors;[74] and persons who signed a declaration of intent to cooperate with the communist state security services and supplied reports there under; persons who received some remuneration (payment or benefit) from the state security services, and signed a declaration of intent to cooperate or supplied reports; whose name appears in the network records of subdivision III / III, and received some remuneration (payment or benefit) from the state security services or signed a declaration of intent to cooperate.[75] A sunset clause introduced at the time aimed to end lustration in 2000.

In 2000, Parliament, dominated by the conservative Alliance of Young Democrats – Hungarian Civic Party, extended the scope of lustration well beyond the coverage adopted in 1994.[76] As a result, editors working in the electronic and printed media became subject to mandatory lustration along with leaders of political parties receiving funds from the central budget. In addition, the amendment opened the possibility of voluntary lustration for attorneys, notaries, religious leaders and media workers not subjected to mandatory lustration. In 2001, the sunset provision on mandatory lustration was extended until 2004.

Legislation allowing access to files of the communist secret services to victims and researchers, creating the Agency for History (*Történeti Hivatal*), was adopted as an afterthought to the lustration scandals, forced upon Parliament by the Constitutional Court. With major amendments to rules on access to the files of the former secret services victims of the communist intelligence services also gained meaningful access to files containing information on their lives with legislative amendments in 2001.[77] The Medgyessy scandal of 2002 (when it turned out that the Prime Minister who previously was cleared by lustration has indeed worked for the communist Secret Services) confirmed the weaknesses of the existing legal regulation on lustration, and forced the reconsideration of lustration and informational reparations. The Medgyessy cabinet was so intent

---

74 Act no 23 of 1994Article 1(1)(a).

75 Act no 23 of 1994Article 1(1)(b).

76 Act no 93 of 2000.

77 Act no. 67 of 2001. This act did not affect the scope of lustration. Instead, it introduced a number of clarifications in the act which made it somewhat easier for victims to access their files deposited with the Agency for History. Furthermore, it was the first in the line of lustration bills to define such terms as "person under surveillance", "career employee", "network person", and also third party and relative.

on setting the record about secret service agents and files straight, that it even convened an independent committee of experts, headed by László Sólyom, the former president of the Constitutional Court who later became President of the Republic. In the spring of 2003 a new law entered into force on access to the archives of former secret services, transforming the Agency for History into the current Historical Archives of the Hungarian State Security (*Állambiztonsági Szolgálatok Történeti Levéltára*).[78]

3.3. THE CONTEXT OF TRANSITIONAL JUSTICE MEASURES FOLLOWING 1989

The process of transition to democracy in Hungary owed a lot to a number of international factors such as the Polish Round Tables (which were closely followed in Hungary and were perceived as a model) and the opening of the Iron Curtain (which in practice assisted a wave of East German citizens who spent their vacation in Hungary, at Lake Balaton, to flee to the West through Austria), as well as the willingness of the World Bank / IMF to provide a loan to the enormously indebted Hungarian economy upon the request of Communist Party Secretary Károly Grósz.

The impact of the Polish negotiated transition and the Round Table Talks would be difficult to underestimate. It served as a model for handling the crisis in a negotiation. Since Hungary did not have a well-organised opposition with a long tradition of cooperation (such as Poland) the events in Poland also were highly informative for the leaders of the emerging opposition on how to operate and what to demand. One of the most prominent participants of the round table talks, János Kis, argued recently that the Hungarian opposition was assisted by the success of the Polish opposition greatly, as the achievements of Solidarność served as the bare minimum to be presented to the Hungarian Communist Party.

4. PHASE 3: LASTING IMPACT

4.1. REINTEGRATION OF PERPETRATORS

In the Hungarian case it would be an exaggeration to speak about the reintegration of perpetrators for various reasons. Firstly, because many of the

[78] Act no. 3 of 2003 on the disclosure of the secret services activities of the Communist regimes and on the establishment of the Historical Archives of the Hungarian State Security available in English at the website of the Historical Archives at www.abtl.hu/html/en/acts/ABTL_4_2003_evi_III_tv_e.pdf.

key perpetrators of the Holocaust, and even of the violence which was part of the repression following the 1956 revolution were not alive anymore in 1989 and later. Due to the delays with passing the framework of the retroactive justice laws it is essentially pointless to talk about the reintegration of even those who were convicted by the democratic regimes.

Secondly, provided that the category of perpetrators includes those who collaborated with the communist secret services it is crucial to note that there are several prominent examples of politicians who refused to resign after the nature and extent of their involvement with the repressive apparatus of the previous regime was exposed (notably Prime Ministers Gyula Horn and Péter Medgyessy).

Thirdly, in case one were to open up the definition of perpetrators to also include Communist politicians who took part in key decisions of the previous regimes, one has to note that the Communist Party has not been banned in Hungary in or after 1989. Therefore, those politicians who intended to remain in the public sphere could test themselves in the new parties in democratic elections. In their case it seems pointless to talk about reintegration.

4.2. MEASURES FOR VICTIMS

4.2.1. Compensation

Compared to the rehabilitation laws, compensation of victims who lost their lives or liberty to the illegal governmental actions motivated by political reasons was a much longer process. Most importantly: the Constitutional Court ruled in the early days of transition to democracy that the Hungarian government was under no obligation to pay compensation and that under the Constitution such a right did not exist.[79] In addition to stressing the *ex gratia* nature of compensation, the Constitutional Court noted that compensation can take place in several steps, in installments and does not have to provide full restitution.[80] In constitutional terms the result was that the Constitutional Court accepted a very

---

79 The first decision of the Constitutional Court on the matter intended to clarify the differences in principle between re-privatization, property restitution and compensation for lost property – concepts which were used interchangeably in early policy concepts. On this see 21/1990 (X. 4.) AB decision.

80 The Constitutional Court was consistent about one limit on the legislature's discretion: the returning of arable lands to their previous owners (re-privatization) while offering partial restitution for loss of property to all other owners violates equal treatment; reaffirmed in 28/1991 (VI. 3.) AB decision. Nonetheless, in practice the Hungarian solution on the restitution of church property closely resembles re-privatization. The respective rules were reaffirmed in 4/1993 (II. 12.) AB and 35/1994 (VI. 24.) AB decisions.

deferential standard of review over compensation measures to come, essentially not preventing more than outright arbitrariness of compensation measures. Over the years numerous compensation measures were passed to remedy harm caused to private property and also non-material damages (i.e. deprivation of life and liberty) in the form of compensation statutes to which several amendments were passed even as late as in 2006 (some in response to Constitutional Court decisions).

The scheme addressed deprivations of private property, and various forms of moral (non-material) harm. Property claims were separated into compensation for lost arable lands and compensation for other types of lost property.[81] Compensation for moral harms included victims who lost their lives or deprived for their liberty during previous unjust repressive regimes in the period of March 1939 and 23 October 1989.[82] Over 900,000 decisions were taken on compensation for deprivation of life or liberty until November 2006. In addition to one-time compensation payments some of the victims qualified for long-term payments. Separate legal measures ensured the adjustment of pensions for persons whose limited access to pension-worthy employment for politically motivated reasons deprived them from agreeable payments from the state pension system.[83]

The first general deadline for compensation claims under the 1991–1992 schemes ran out quickly. Due to the relatively high number of late applications the deadline for applications was reopened between mid-February and mid-March 1994. Another round of applications for those deported and/or perished in the hands of foreign powers was opened by Act no. 29 of 1997, until 7 October 1997. The deadline for compensation of deprivation of life or liberty was subsequently reopened for an additional 4 months in 2006.[84] During the reopened application

---

81 Act no. 25 of 1991 on compensation for lost property, also Act no. 24 of 1992 (on property compensation) and under Act no. 2 of 1994 (on the extension of the deadline). Altogether over 1.3 million decisions were rendered on property compensation cases alone until November 2006. Statistics on compensation are provided by the Central Justice Affairs Office at www.kih.gov.hu/alapterv/karpotlas/statisztikak/statisztika2009.html.

82 The main statute is Act no. 32 of 1992 on the compensation of persons who were illegally deprived for their life or liberty for political reasons between March 1939 and 23 October 1989. Note that the compensation claims of Jews drafted for forced labour battalions were added to this scheme only as late as by Act no. 29 of 1997. A separate statute, Act no. 52 of 1993 was enacted on national care (*nemzeti gondozás*), compensating those who lost 67 per cent of their capacity to work in the national resistance of 1944–45 or during the 1956 revolution.

83 The legal basis for pension review was created by a series of government decrees: 93/1990, 52/1992 and 174/1992 (all passed during the first democratically elected parliament). Of the 467.209 applications 118.459 were rejected (as of 29 October 2007).

84 By Act no. 47 of 2006. In the first quarter of 2009 over 13,000 decisions were taken, roughly one third of which accepted the claims. See www.kih.gov.hu/alapterv/karpotlas/statisztikak/statisztika2009.html.

procedure it was possible to resubmit applications which were previously rejected for lack of evidence. With access to Soviet military archives it became significantly easier to provide adequate evidence of internment and forced labour in the Soviet Union which resulted in loss of life or liberty. In practice it became extremely difficult to prove the duration of deportations: the Supreme Court, in a decision to preserve the consistency of jurisprudence (*jogegységi határozat*), started to insist on requiring proof to be submitted in notarised documents (*közokirat*), a rather strict formal requirement for acceptable documents.[85]

Instead of providing full compensation or restitution, the solution was to provide partial compensation in the form of vouchers which lost their market value rapidly. In addition, over the years several lower level, discretionary executive measures were adopted to allocate and distribute one-time allowances to a select group of victims which the Constitutional Court refused to classify as compensation in the above sense.[86]

In order to administer the compensation process the first democratically-elected government established a specialised agency, the so-called Compensation Office (in its full name *Központi Kárpótlási és Kárrendezési Hivatal*, or Central Compensation and Claims Office) which was closed down on 1 April 1998 when the mass of the applications was handled. The remaining tasks of the Compensation Office were taken over first by the Central Claims Office (*Központi Kárrendezési Iroda*) of the Office of Justice (*Igazságügyi Hivatal*). Initially the operation of the Compensation Office was supervised by a ministerial council which included the supervising minister appointed by the Cabinet, the Minister of Agriculture, the Minister of Justice, the Minister of the Interior, the Minister of Finance, the president of the Compensation Office and the president of the Societal College on Compensation. In 1994 supervision of compensation was entrusted to the Minister of Agriculture. In 1998 it was transferred to the Ministry of the Regions, and in 2000, to the Ministry of Justice. Since the early days compensation cases were handled with the assistance of the Societal College of Compensation (*Társadalmi Kárpótlási Kollégium*) which assisted a range of governmental actors in matters of compensation with expertise on the historical context of particular claims.

---

85 1/2002. KJE decision of June 27, 2002, available in Hungarian at www.lb.hu/joghat/jk0102.html.

86 See e.g. 267/2000 (XII. 26.) Korm. (Cabinet) decree on financial assistance to certain victims who suffered long-term deprivations of liberty. In 10/2003 (IV. 3.) AB and 11/2003 (IV. 9.) AB decision the Constitutional Court emphasized that the cabinet decree introduced a welfare scheme and the benefits paid as a result did not qualify as compensation.

4.2.2. *Victims' organisations*

With the emergence of the potential for democratic transition, several civil society initiatives appeared to bring recognition and justice to the victims of past oppression. It would be impossible to give a complete list of these organisations and associations; therefore the analysis will cover the most prominent and active ones which contributed visibly to exploring and exposing the injustices of oppressive regimes in Hungary. Among these organisations the most vocal and lasting ones are devoted to exploring, documenting and exposing the memory of the 1956 revolution. The reburial of executed Prime Minister Imre Nagy of the 1956 revolutionary government was a crucial symbolic event of transition to democracy, and the organisations of victims had a key role in setting the record straight about the revolution and raising awareness about its achievements.

The most prominent among the groups are the Committee for Historical Justice (*Történelmi Igazságtételi Bizottság*) founded in the spring of 1988 in the apartment of András B Hegedűs, and whose founders included Árpád Göncz (the first president of the new democracy, who had been sentenced to life imprisonment for his involvement in 1956, and was released in 1963) and Erzsébet Nagy (the daughter of executed Prime Minister Imre Nagy). Miklós Vásárhelyi (who was also sentenced to 5 years imprisonment for 1956) gave the group its name.

Another prominent 1956 imprisonment victim, Jenő Fónay, founded the Organisation for the Former Political Prisoners and Forced Labourers (who spent their time) in the Soviet Union (*Szovjetunióban Volt Magyar Politikai Rabok és Kényszermunkások Szervezet*, or POFOSZ) in 1989. According to their mission statement "POFOSZ unites not only 1956 revolutionaries, but others who were imprisoned for political reasons – such as the ones taken on forced labour (*malenkij robot*), deported, doing front service, political prisoners from before '56, sentenced to gulag by Soviet courts".[87]

By and large, victims' organisations became less visible in the public sphere with the completion of the compensation process. Note that several victims' organisation which were devoted to exploring the record of 1956 and recast its memory remained active; due to the unsettled record of 1956 some of these groups became active alongside radical-nationalist fringe groups after 2006.

4.3.3. *A largely unfulfilled promise: access to files*

Victims of surveillance by the Communist secret services were left behind by the delays in providing meaningful access to the files. Since this was a widespread

87 See their website at www.pofosz.hu/.

violation of human rights in the private sphere, very often through the (coerced) activities of the friends and family members of the victims, addressing this need and building a wide-scale societal dialogue over the matter would have been instrumental to coming to terms with the communist past. Instead of a wide-scale effort, Hungarians were left with a gradually developing legislative framework on access to files, followed by a lengthy transfer of files, and then cataloging of files. In the meantime, often scandalous accounts on the surveillance of public figures were in the center of reflection. Accounts on the less than completely prominent subjects of surveillance (such as musicians) which might make the subject accessible to the general public started to appear only recently, due to the delays with access to files.

As was already mentioned, upon the urging of the Constitutional Court, the 1996 amendment to the lustration law finally established an archives (called the Agency for History), thus allowing access to the archives of former secret services.[88] Under the original version of the law access to files was rather limited. As a rule, one could only request secret surveillance data about oneself, and, even then, the names of informers and cell-mates were deleted. Persons who cooperated with the secret services could not get access to the reports they supplied the services with.

The 1996 law made it the duty of current secret services to transfer all files generated by the domestic intelligence division of former secret services before 1980, which do not pertain to the carrying out of duties pertaining to the current secret services. The law did not contain review procedures for challenging declassification decisions, or the lack thereof. Although files were supposed to be handed over in 60 days following the entry into force of the law, the transfer of documents was completed by 2000. Pre-1980 files were declassified and handed over without much hesitation. Still, the military and counter-intelligence services declassified and handed over roughly 5% of those post-1980 files which these intelligence agencies received in 1990.

A set of amendments to the law on the Agency for History was instituted upon the request of the Agency itself in 2001. Until the passage of these amendments the legal status of the Agency was unclear, as it did not qualify as an archive under Hungarian law.[89] Particularly important from the perspective of victims' rights, it was only at this time that the law on access to files distinguished between victims and perpetrators (agents), allowing them different levels of access to the information contained in their own files. This amendment was

88 Act no. 67 of 1996.
89 Among other respects, this status affects rules of receiving researchers and releasing information to them, for scientific purposes.

requested by the Agency for History and was also found acceptable by the parliamentary commissioner (ombudsman) for data protection. The rationale behind the amendment was that victims should be able to learn all information about their own cases contained in the records of the state security services, which would have been available to them at the time they were under surveillance. In addition, the amended rules allowing access to researchers allowed more information to be left on the materials supplied by the agency.

In the wake of the Medgyessy scandal the political elites refashioned the Agency for History, turning it into the Historical Archives of the Hungarian State Security in 2003.[90] The law, which entered into force on 1 April 2003, calls for the establishment of the Historical Archives of the Secret Services, an institution which is to become the integrated archives of the files produced by all Hungarian intelligence agencies between 21 December 1944 and 14 February 1990.[91] As a general rule, such documents and their copies shall be presented to the Historical Archives within 30 days – unless they contain state secrets. The transfer of documents is supervised by a committee of three, the members of which are nominated by the government, the Hungarian Academy of Sciences and the Hungarian Historical Society, respectively. At the end of 2011 the Archives had almost 4,000 meters of documents.[92]

Although documents containing state secrets are withheld, a list of such documents has to be submitted to the Historical Archives. The law specifies 12 grounds on the basis of which documents may be withheld due to containing state secrets. The classification may be challenged in the Metropolitan Court, and the burden of proving that the document contains state secrets is on the government. Judicial review of classification is an important step towards providing access to the files of former secret services. Still, the list of exceptions is lengthy, and the grounds are phrased in rather general, over-inclusive terms. The new law allows broader access to the files held by the Historical Archives. Finally, the person under surveillance finally may learn the identity of the person or agent reporting on her, as well as the identity of their official contact.

Due to such delayed and fragmented access to the file of secret services, the Hungarian public debate on collaboration with the communist secret services was far from comprehensive. Essentially, during the first twelve years of the new democracy, the debate was dominated by a quest to identify agents and lists of agents of the communist secret services. Agents were vilified by the lustration

90 Act no. 3 of 2003.

91 Act no. 3 of 2003.

92 As reported on the website of the Archives at www.abtl.hu/kutatoterem/alt_tajekoztato (in Hungarian).

debates, and debates on the significance of working for the services in whatever capacity were tainted by the fact that prominent political figures whose involvement was uncovered through lustration or otherwise refused to resign from office, essentially, because they did not feel that they had done anything 'wrong'. As a result, the debates surrounding lustration became increasingly value-laden, and all politicians for the democratically elected Socialist Party were invariably turned into "communist agents" (whatever that means). This rhetoric neatly fit in the deeply polarised Hungarian political sphere, where conservative forces are ready to pull the communist card on their opponents any time, for no particular reason.

Due to perpetual scandals and agent lists flooding the public square, it became apparent that the holdings of the Historical Archives are incomplete. In July 2007 the Prime Minister of the Socialist government at the time requested a committee of experts under the leadership of eminent historian János Kenedi to assess the amount and whereabouts of documents not deposited with the Historical Archives. Their report was published in 2008.[93] The aim of the review was to declassify and make the widest array of former secret services documents available with the fewest restrictions. More recently a second Kenedi committee was commissioned (by the outgoing Socialist government) to assess the conditions and accessibility of a collection of magnetic tapes which were believed to contain operative information from the later days of the communist secret services, including a list of agents. The contents of these tapes were printed on some 3,800 pages. This second Kenedi committee was disbanded in December 2010 by the current government, before it could publish its final report or make the information on the tapes available to the broader public.

To date, very little was said of what made ordinary people collaborate with the communist secret services. Some important, yet marginal reflection was offered on account of a few cases involving prominent intellectuals as either victims or as perpetrators.[94] These cases and the ensuing exchanges were crucial milestones in triggering a more informed debate; nonetheless, they did not manage to move the public discourse to overcome those rhetorical patterns which by then were deeply engraved by all the noise about the need to assemble agent-lists.

---

93 The full text of the report is available in Hungarian at http://mek.oszk.hu/08400/08450/08450.pdf.

94 See prominently Peter Esterházy's *Javított kiadás* (2002), a novel-diary on the author's finding out that his father collaborated with the Communist Secret Services. Also the Kenedi case in ÉS (an exchange between historian János Kenedi and his protege, the writer Sándor Tar who turned out to be reporting on him) and the case of film director István Szabó who was found to have collaborated with the services during his youth, after the 1956 events.

The documentary film of Zsigmond Gabor Papp on the communist secret services (*The Life of an Agent*, 2004, 84 minutes) is an important effort in providing an opportunity to understand the regime and the secret services better. The work is based on archival footage of educational films, originally prepared for training purposes, and obtained from the film library of the communist secret services. Instead of focusing on particular prominent victims, the documentary focuses on the operational logic of the services themselves, exposing the almost comical sense of self-importance which characterised their ethos. Clearly accessible to generation born after the transition, this documentary is excellent example of the possibility of thematising the characteristics of the communist regime in a manner which permits ample reflection on the role and responsibility of collaborators of the former secret services.

4.3. REMEMBERING: THE POLITICS OF MEMORY

The politics of memory has been central to the Hungarian transition to democracy, and to positioning particular political agendas in the Hungarian scene from the earliest days. It has been repeated many times in the literature that the Hungarian transition commenced when a prominent figure of the Communist Party, Imre Pozsgay, openly suggested that the 1956 counterrevolution might have been a revolt or an uprising indeed. This statement is often viewed as the gesture from the reform wing of the Communist Party which clearly signaled that the road was open for a negotiated transition to democracy.

The significance of this gesture was elevated to a new dimension with the exhumation and subsequent public reburial of illegally executed Prime Minister Imre Nagy on 16 June 1989.[95] It is not an exaggeration to claim that from the perspective of transitional justice measures the carefully manufactured reburial of Imre Nagy attained deeper significance in the Hungarian context than the collapse of the Berlin Wall and the opening of the Iron Curtain on the Hungarian-Austrian border, although the latter events undoubtedly had a broader international significance and also tell more about the international context and interrelatedness of the collapse of communist regimes in Central and Eastern Europe in 1989. Pozsgay's statement and the reburial may sound like largely symbolic gestures; nonetheless, one has to keep in mind that the rehabilitated historical event left behind thousands of victims suffering as a result of governmental oppression, who were eager to see their stories told and dignity restored. Victims' organisations were formed which became very active in exploring and establishing the historical record, as well as in seeking the

---

95 I. Rév, *Retroactive Justice.*

rehabilitation of victims of politically motivated judicial persecution in the aftermath of the revolution.

The reburial of Prime Minister Imre Nagy was the first major peaceful public demonstration in support of political changes at a central location, Heroes' Square (*Hősök Tere*) in Budapest (which is home to historic leaders and rulers of Hungary, and which also saw numerous 1 May parades taking place at the adjacent space formerly known as Parade Square [*Felvonulási tér*]). Such a display of support had the utmost significance as the emerging democratic opposition which was most successful in getting the Hungarian Communist Party to negotiate the terms of transition with them did not have any democratic legitimation – the newly emerging parties of 1989 are best understood as Budapest-based intelligentsia circles. The events of the reburial were transmitted in Hungarian state television and numerous recordings survive in the documentary canon of the transition[96] which suggests that the reburial was an emotional and deeply moving event which had the potential of inducing reconciliation instead of shaming and blaming. Indeed, it is emerging from the records of the communist Secret Services that agents on the scene were instructed by their handlers to move the mood towards reconciliation themselves.

Thus, the first democratically-elected parliament set course on a complex mission, in which symbolic and practical (mostly judicial) measures were also present. The first parliament passed on act to preserve the significance of the 1956 revolution.[97] The day of 23 October, when the revolution erupted (and the same day on which the new democratic republic was announced) was made into a day of national commemoration. Somewhat ironically, the name of Imre Nagy did not make it to the statute. He had to wait until 1996.

It was in 2000 when Parliament finally passed legislation on Holocaust memorial day and the memorial day of the victims of communism.[98] These measures are somewhat ad hoc and are often inspired by visible or assumed political gains, instead of the need to foster sincere commemoration. Take the memorial day of the victims of communism.[99] It was proposed in response to the decision of the

96 Most famous are the recordings of the independent studio Black Box(*Fekete Doboz*) which are staples in any visual material on transition. Recently a documentary compilation from the Archives of Black Box was reissued on dvd.

97 Act no. 26 of 1990 on acknowledging the significance of the 1956 revolution and freedom-fight.

98 58/2000. (VI. 16.) OGY határozat a kommunista diktatúrák áldozatainak emléknapjáról (58/2000. (VI. 16.) OGY decision on the memorial day of the victims of Communist dictatorships).

99 In the following year, Parliament made 1 March into the Day of Civil Security Services (Polgári Nemzetbiztonsági Szolgálatok Napja).

Minister of Education (Zoltán Pokorni of FIDESZ), also supported by Parliament, to turn 12 April into a Holocaust memorial day. The initial proposal for the memorial day of the victims of communism was also competing for a spot in early April, on the day when Bishop Vilmos Apor was killed by Soviet soldiers. During the parliamentary debate this date was exchanged for 25 February, the day in 1947 when – in an unprecedented move – Soviet military forces removed Béla Kovács (the leader of the Smallholders' Party) from the Hungarian political scene to the Soviet Union, in order to allow more room for maneuver for Rákosi's Communist Party.

On the one hand it is clear that two memorial days of the kind in April make the calendar of horrible memories somewhat crowded. And while picking a good date to commemorate is not easy, Béla Kovács is an unlikely subject of veneration in the light of his subsequent political career following his return to Hungary from Soviet internment in 1955: he was a member of the Imre Nagy (revolutionary) cabinet and while he refused a cabinet position in the incoming Kádár administration, he remained an MP until his death in 1959.[100] Note that these days are not national holidays, but memorial days which are observed in the form of commemorative events in secondary schools.[101]

A similar instance of political mud-slinging surrounded the institution of the Day of Hungarian Freedom, which was introduced during the conservative FIDESZ government to commemorate June 19 – the day when the last Soviet soldier left Hungary – as the Day of Hungarian Freedom.[102] The lengthy preamble of the bill recalls highlights of Hungarian history with adding "The former German occupation was exchanged for Soviet occupation, and in the shadow of Soviet bayonets enabled the installation and 4-decade long persistence of a communist dictatorship causing un-assessable suffering and harm. Our Nation suffered the nearly half-century-long lack of her sovereignty with lagging behind Europe, entering an economic and social dead-end street and the shattering of moral values". The bill was adopted with the support of MPs from all sides.

When the Socialist-liberal coalition came into power in the year after in 2002, as early as the autumn the Ministry of Justice took the time to introduce a bill which would turn 19 June into a public holiday to commemorate the Day of Independence, thus, effectively renaming the freshly anointed Day of Hungarian

100 I. Rév, *Retroactive Justice.*

101 I. Pető, 'Hol lakik a kommunizmus?' (Where does Communism live?), in *Mozgó Világ*, 22/2 (2002), 91–95.

102 See Act no. 17 of 2001 on the significance of regaining the freedom of the country and on the Day of Hungarian Freedom.

Freedom. In the general debate the lead speaker for the opposition did not hesitate to point out: the sole aim of the Socialists now in government was to remove the preamble of the statue which reminds them of the past deeds of their party.[103] This government's bill was withdrawn in the end[104]; nonetheless, the incident truly demonstrates the tone and nature of the exchange. The banality of this debate is not toned down by the fact that on the same day, right after this bill, the same Socialist government successfully proposed commemorating the day of the execution of Prime Minister Imre Nagy and the martyrs of the 1956 revolution (16 June), in addition to commemorating 23 October, the day on which the 1956 revolution erupted.[105] Indeed, the speakers on the opposition side did not miss an opportunity to remind the Socialist government that they work for a party which is the legal successor of the Communist Party which is guilty for calling Soviet tanks to suppress the 1956 revolution.[106]

5. CONCLUSIONS

Hungary is a good case for analysing an incomplete transition. Despite most elaborate statutory frameworks being in place, accompanied by a nuanced constitutional jurisprudence grounding these measures in a democratic constitutional framework, a democratically-elected government in 2010 found it necessary to manufacture a revolutionary rhetoric to position itself as the embodiment of the "true transition" yet to come. The current government's memory project involves not only a new constitution which selectively declares discontinuity with past regimes (regarding which transitional justice measures were undertaken in numerous respects), but also a reheated retroactive justice debate for those wrongs which had not yet been undone, and the need to rebuild the square in front of the Parliament building (complete with several historic monuments) to reflect Hungarian history better. In the meantime, "communist" remains a routine denigration in politics, while the conservative side is making attempts to restore the legacy of problematic interwar politicians and intellectuals. Therefore, it seems clear that the implementation of legal measures seeking to foster transitional justice alone do not bring reconciliation, much less generate coming to terms with the past, no matter how compatible these measures may be with principles of the rule of law and with constitutional rights.

103 Speech no. 252 of László Salamon, Fidesz on Day 17, 10 September 2002, at www.parlament.hu/internet/plsql/ogy_naplo.naplo_fadat?p_ckl=37&p_uln=17&p_felsz=252&p_szoveg=p_felszig=252 (in Hungarian).

104 See the parliamentary record on bill T/464 in the term 2002–2006.

105 59/2002. (IX. 20.) OGY decision.

106 Speech no. 298 of Dénes Kosztolányi, Fidesz on Day 17, 10 September 2002, at www.parlament.hu/internet/plsql/ogy_naplo.naplo_fadat?p_ckl=37&p_uln=17&p_felsz=298&p_szoveg=&p_felszig=298 (in Hungarian).

SELECTIVE FURTHER READING

APOR, B. (2004), 'The Expulsion of the German Language Population from Hungary', in PRAUSER, S. and REEFS, A. (eds.), *The Expulsion of the 'German' Communities from Eastern Europe at the End of the Second World War*, EUI Working Paper HEC no. 2004/1 (2004), available at http://cadmus.iue.it/dspace/bitstream/1814/2599/1/HEC04-01.pdf.

BÉLA, R. (2006), A 'Duna-gate' ügy jelentősége a rendszerváltás történelmében (Politológiai értelmezési lehetőségek) (The significance of the Duna-gate case in the history of transition, Attempts at interpretation in political science) Szegedi Tudományegyetem Állam- és Jogtudományi Karának Tudományos Bizottsága, Acta Juridica et Politica, Tomus LXVIII. Fasc. 19, Szeged.

BRAHAM, R.L. (2000), *The Politics of Genocide: The Holocaust in Hungary, Condensed edition,* Wayne State University Press in association with the United States Holocaust Memorial Museum, Detroit, Michigan.

GYURGYÁK, J. (2001), *A zsidókérdés Magyarországon, Politika eszmetörténet* (The Jewish Question in Hungary, A history of political ideas), Osiris, Budapest.

HALMAI, G. and SCHEPPELLE, K.L. (1997), 'Living Well is the Best Revenge: The Hungarian Approach to Judging the Past', in MACADAMS, J.A. (ed.) *Transitional Justice and the Rule of Law in New Democracies*, University of Notre Dame Press, Notre Dame.

HILBERG, R. (1985), *The Destruction of the European Jews, Revised and Definitive Edition*, vol. 2, Holmes & Meier Publishers, Ltd., New York.

KAHLER, F. (ed.) (2002), *A semmisségi törvények, Büntetőjogi tanulmányok* vol. 3 (The nullification statutes, Essays in criminal law), Kairosz, Budapest.

KARÁDY, V. (s.d.), 'The anti-Semitic "change of the guard" in Hungary. A Case Study in Institutional Violence', as available at http://karadyviktor.uni.hu/keret.cgi?/southampton.htm.

KARÁDY, V. (2003), 'Different Experiences of Modernisation and the Rise of Anti Semitism. Socio-Political Foundations of the *numerus clausus* and the 'Christian Course' in Post World War I. Hungary', *Transversal* (Graz), vol. 4, no. 2, pp. 3–34.

KARSAI, L. (2000) 'The People's Courts and Revolutionary Justice in Hungary, 1945–46,' in DEÁK, I., GROSS, J.T. and JUDT, T. (eds.), *The Politics of Retribution in Europe: World War II and Its Aftermath*, Princeton University Press, Princeton.

KARSAI, L. (2000–2001), 'Crime and Punishment: People's Courts, Revolutionary Legality, and the Hungarian Holocaust', *InterMarium*, vol. 4, no. 1, at http://ece.columbia.edu/research/intermarium/vol4no1/karsai2.pdf.

P. KENÉZ, *Hungary from the Nazis to the Soviets, The Establishment of the Communist Regime in Hungary*, 1944–1948, Cambridge University Press, Cambridge, 2006.

KIS, J. (2000), 'Az első magyar Alkotmánybíróság értelmezési gyakorlata' (The first Hungarian Constitutional Court's interpretation practice)', in HALMAI, G. (ed.), *The Constitution Found? The First Nine Years of Constitutional Review on Fundamental Rights*, indok, Budapest.

LAPPIN, E. (2000), 'The Death Marches of Hungarian Jews Through Austria in the Spring of 1945', YAD VASHEM, Jerusalem, at http://yad-vashem.org.il/download/about_holocaust/studies/lappin_full.pdf.

Morvai, M. (2003), 'Hungarian Criminal Court Cases concerning the (Retribution for the) 1956 Revolution,' in Sajó, A. (ed.), *Out and Into Authoritarian Law*, Kluwer International, The Hague.

Pető, A. (1999), 'Átvonuló hadsereg, maradandó trauma. Az 1945-ös budapesti nemi erőszak esetek emlékezete' (Passing army, lasting trauma. The memory of sexual violence cases in Budapest in 1945), *Történelmi Szemle* 1999, nos. 1–2, pp. 85–107.

Pető, I. (2001), 'Hol lakik a kommunizmus?' (Where does Communism live?), *Mozgó Világ*, vol. 22., no. 2, pp. 91–95.

Rév, I. (2005), Retroactive Justice: Prehistory of Post-Communism, Stanford University Press, Stanford.

Romsics, I. (2005), Magyarország története a XX. században (The history of Hungary in the 20th century), Osiris, Budapest.

Schwartz, H. (1999), The Struggle for Constitutional Justice in Post-communist Europe, The University of Chicago Press, Chicago.

Stark, T. (1993), 'A magyar zsidóság a vészkorszakban és a második világháború után' (Hungarian Jewry during the Holocaust and after WWII), *Regio – Kisebbség, politika, társadalom*, vol. 4, no. 3, pp. 140–150.

Stark, T. (1995), *Zsidóság a vészkorszakban és a felszabadulás után (1939–1955)* (Jewry during the Holocaust and after Liberation (1939–1955)), MTA Történettudományi Intézet, Budapest.

Szarka, L. (2007), 'A csehszlovák–magyar lakosságcsere helye a magyar kisebbség tervezett felszámolásában 1945–1948 között' (The role of Czechoslovak Hungarian population exchange in the planned extermination of the Hungarian minority in 1945–1948), *Kisebbségkutatás*, vol. 16, no. 3, pp. 415–430.

Tóth, Á. (1993), *Telepítések Magyarországon 1945–1948 között. A németek kitelepítése, a belső népmozgások és a szlovák-magyar lakosságcsere összefüggései* (Settlements in Hungary, 1945–1948, Connection between the internment of Germans, internal migration and the Slovak-Hungarian population exchange), BKMÖL, Kecskemét.

Uitz, R. (2008), 'Communist secret services on the screen: The Duna-gate scandal in and beyond Hungarian media,' in Apor, P. and Sarkisova, O. (eds.). *Past for the Eyes: East European Representations of Communism in Cinema and Museums after 1989*, CEU Press, Budapest.

Ungváry, K. (2005), *The Siége of Budapest, 100 Days in WWII*, Yale University Press, New Haven.

Vadkerty, K. (1998), *A belső telepítések és a lakosságcsere* (Internal settlement and population exchange), Kalligram, Bratislava.

Vadkerty, K. (2007), *A kitelepítéstõl a reszlovakizációig 1945–1948. Trilógia a csehszlovákiai magyarság 1945–1948 közötti történetérõl* (From Deportation to Re-Slovakisation 1945–1948, A trilogy on the history of Hungarians in Czechoslovakia between 1945–1948), Kalligram, Bratislava.

THE POLISH PARADOX: TRANSITION FROM AND TO DEMOCRACY

Klaus Bachmann

1. TRANSITIONAL JUSTICE IN POLAND DURING AND AFTER WORLD WAR II

1.1. INTRODUCTION

For various reasons it is difficult to compare Polish experiences with Transitional Justice to those of other countries. First of all, Transitional Justice is usually used as a notion for mechanisms and processes which societies experience on their way from a dictatorship to a democracy. If the notion of Transitional Justice is to be used in a non-normative way, it should also be applied to forms of extraordinary justice which occur when a country goes through a transition from a democracy to a dictatorship. This is the case of Poland between 1944 and 1948. Poland emerged from the war as a very fragile multiparty democracy, occupied by the Soviet Army.

Due to pressure of the USSR and Poland's Western allies, the multiparty interim government which was ultimately formed comprised members of the (anti-Soviet) Socialists and of the Polish Peasants' Party, whose members were subsequently coerced out of the public administration, the security sector, the local administration and finally also out of government. The most prominent representative of the non-communist anti-German resistance, Prime Minister Stanisław Mikołajczyk, decided to flee to Britain and form (once again) a government in exile, while his supporters in the country were being murdered, abducted or jailed by Polish and Soviet security organs. During the second part of the forties, the country was embroiled in a kind of internationalised civil war, during which the Soviet Union strongly supported the weaker communist movement, whereas Poland's Western allies only reluctantly gave assistance and support to the stronger part, the pro-Western non-communist parties.

Unlike the situation in most Western European countries, which had been liberated by US and British forces, power in Poland was strongly contested and the question of the country's geopolitical orientation and its future political system remained unsolved until 1948, when the pro-Soviet communist movement took power and launched the Stalinisation of all spheres of public and (to a large extent) private life.[1]

The second reason why post-war transitional justice in Poland is difficult to compare to other countries is linked to Poland's geopolitical shift to the west, which was accompanied by massive forced migration and exchanges of population between Poland and its Eastern Soviet neighbors, the Lithuanian, Byelorussian and Ukrainian Soviet Republics. As a result of the military balance of power, of the absence of Western troops in Poland and the acquiescence of Britain and the US during the final phase of World War II, the USSR was able to keep Poland's eastern territories, which it had taken over as a result of the Ribbentrop-Molotov Pact in 1939 and – after extensive ethnic cleansing and systematic terror against representatives of the local upper classes – had annexed as Soviet republics. In order to make the country a bulwark against Germany and keep it within the Soviet sphere of influence after the war, Poland was given a large part of Germany's eastern territories, which were subsequently depopulated and then resettled with Poles from Poland's pre-war eastern territories. Between 1943 and 1947, Poland's new western and central parts were also repopulated with people of different ethnic origin, who had left their home territories either as a result of ethnic cleansing or due to specific bilateral agreements between the Polish government and the governments of the neighboring Soviet republics (except for the Kaliningrad region, where population exchange and expulsion did not affect Poles). That way, the governments involved in these exchanges secured the transfer of ethnic Poles from Ukraine, Byelorussia and Lithuania to Poland, and at the same time, the "return" of ethnic Lithuanians, Ukrainians and Byelorussians to their homelands. It should be kept in mind that the majority of these people had never before lived in those territories. These measures were far from being entirely successful, since many people managed to evade resettlement, but they reduced the percentage of ethnic and religious minorities on both sides of the border considerably and accelerated assimilation.

Both developments – Poland's "shift to the west" and its repopulation – had far-reaching implications for the analysis of Transitional Justice measures carried out during the last phase of the war and during the immediate post-war period.[2]

First, as far as collaborators with the German occupier were concerned, the Polish authorities could only prosecute, judge and punish perpetrators of whom

1 S. Courtois (ed.), *Une si longue nuit. L'apogée des regimes totalitaires en Europe 1935–1953*, Paris, 2003.

2 T. Snyder, *The Reconstruction of Nation Poland, Ukraine, Lithuania, Belarus 1569–1999*, New Haven/London, 2003, 154–178.

they could get hold in the territory of post-war Poland. In other words: The crimes which were to be punished had been committed on another territory than the one where these crimes actually could be punished. Both territories (occupied Poland and post-war Poland) overlapped partly, but perpetrators who stayed in the former eastern territories of (pre-war) Poland, were not punished by the Polish authorities and according to Polish laws, but instead fell under the jurisdiction of Soviet authorities and Soviet laws. This considerably changes the overall statistical outlook of prosecutions, trials, extralegal measures and administrative punishment for collaborators as compared to countries which did not undergo such radical territorial and demographic changes.

These changes have yet another implication for the assessment of the relative scope and consequences of transitional justice. Due to the political instability, the penal punishment of collaboration became inextricable from the battle for power between the anti-Soviet and pro-Soviet forces in the country. Collaboration with the Soviet occupier never was an issue for the judiciary. During the Stalinist period, mere participation in anti-communist or anti-Soviet organisations during the war became a reason for prosecution (and often enough even for extralegal executions), despite the fact that all anti-Soviet clandestine movements had actually also conspired or fought against the German occupier. The charge of collaboration was abused for the fight against anti-communists or people whom the new regime regarded with suspicion.

1.2. ANTECEDENTS

The post-war definition of collaboration was further obfuscated by two other factors. The first has only a societal and discursive relevance and has to do with the fact that the anti-Soviet opposition also misused the notion of collaboration for its political battle and used it to denounce not only wartime cooperation of Polish communists with the Soviet authorities but also attempts of the post-war Polish authorities to protect ethnic and religious minorities and the Polish Jewry from pogroms. Since the far-right underground was strongly anti-Semitic and ethnically exclusionist, it usually took sides with the perpetrators of pogroms against minorities and regarded state protection for them as a form of collaboration with enemies of Poland.

The second factor which contributed to the collaboration imbroglio was linked to the war time situation of occupied Poland. Between 1939 and 1941, the country had been occupied by Germany (west of the rivers San and Bug), and the Soviet Union (east of both rivers) and then, in summer 1941 completely by Germany. After 1943 its eastern parts had been gradually liberated (or, in the eyes of the London-based government-in-exile and the anti-Soviet resistance) reoccupied by the Red Army. This meant a dual occupation by two powers which were regarded as traditional enemies by the overwhelming majority of the political establishment and the population. Getting support from Poland's traditional Western allies like Great Britain or the US was extremely difficult, since arms could only come through either German or Soviet occupied territory or by air. Any clandestine movement which strove for military efficiency was – to a certain extent – forced to cooperate with one occupier in order to be able to fight the other one. Armed resistance in Poland was doomed to fail if it did not take into account the overall balance of power in the country and adapt to it in time. That is why, at different points in time, Polish partisans coordinated their actions with the Red Army, or at other times, with German troops, why they joined arms with Ukrainian partisans (against whom they later fought) and why they accepted arms from German authorities in order to fight Ukrainians and Soviet partisans, and later became members of Soviet special units, whose aim it was to extinguish Ukrainian nationalist partisans and German troops which were withdrawing from the eastern territories. From this perspective, any successful resistance against one occupier required collaboration with the other one. This distinguishes the meaning of "collaboration" from its homologue in Western Europe, where resistance could be efficient without cooperation with a totalitarian occupier. Most non-communist resistance movements in Western European states obtained support from Great Britain, the US or sometimes from their unoccupied colonies. For them, collaboration was the antonym of resistance. In Poland, refusing collaboration while resisting an occupier would have condemned a partisan movement to marginalisation and total inefficiency. Such movements did exist; they were mostly created by members of Poland's pre-war nationalist far right and were anti-German as well as anti-Soviet and anti-Western and tried to get support from Fascist Italy or to rely solely on themselves. None of them had any measurable impact on the course of war.

There is yet another conceptual problem linked to the use of the notion of 'collaboration' and transitional justice. Usually, transitional justice is meted out to perpetrators, who are regarded as members of the same group, community, society or nation, which prosecutes them. Unlike in France, Belgium or the Netherlands, collaborators in Poland were not accused of "uncivic" (*incivique*) behavior or high treason *vis-à-vis* the state or the government-in-exile. They were accused and judged because they had betrayed the Polish nation. This national rather than civic or political concept of treason enabled the post-war authorities to garner additional legitimacy for (often politically motivated) verdicts of treason; it also enabled them to extend the accusation to people who could not reasonably be blamed for betraying a state to which they had never belonged (for example *Wehrmacht* officers, citizens of the Third *Reich* or Germans from Germany's former eastern territories, who had never belonged to the Polish nation). Last but not least, the notion of "national treason" reflected the dominant trend of Polish society, to interpret the battle against the occupier as a fight for national sovereignty and independence rather than for democracy and pluralism.

1.3. THE PREPARATION OF TRANSITIONAL JUSTICE MEASURES

Measures to be carried out after the liberation of Poland were planned and formulated by two competing political camps. First, there was the government-in-exile in London, which consisted of a coalition of different pre-war parties, among them anti-communist left wing parties (Socialists and Peasants' Parties) and the national democratic right. Second, there was an ad hoc liberation commitee, which had been created in Moscow and comprised Polish pre-war communists from the radical, clandestine party and took over power in the territories which had been conquered by the Red Army and over which the Soviet Union did not claim supremacy. The émigré government was the highest authority for the non-communist resistance, which until 1943 limited its actions to small sabotage, incidental assassinations and espionage for the Western Allies. After the defeat of the *Wehrmacht* at Stalingrad 1943 and the gradual withdrawal of German troops from the East, the government-in-exile and the military leadership of the Polish "Home Army" (*Armia Krajowa*, AK) elaborated plans for an insurrection in case the front would move back to Polish territory. The government-in-exile also compiled and issued a code of conduct for Polish citizens under occupation, which was based on the pre-war criminal code and intended to criminalise collaboration with the enemy. The code of conduct never played any role in post-war Poland, since the government-in-exile was deprived of sufficient influence in the security sector and could not enforce it in practice. However, it did play a role before the country was conquered by the Red Army, because it was used as a legal basis for clandestine courts, whose verdicts were carried out against alleged traitors and informants. The exact number of these verdicts is unknown, since the legally required procedures were not actually carried out in all cases, but archival research indicates that 3,000 death penalties were issued during the occupation, of which 2,500 were carried out.[3]

Competing jurisdiction over Poland was claimed by the "Polish Committee for National Liberation" (*Polski Komitet Wyzwolenia Narodowego*, PKWN), which declared itself the official interim government of Poland once it had conquered the first big Polish city on the Red Army's way westwards, Lublin. Due to its

---

3 W. Borodziej, 'Hitleristische Verbrechen. Die Ahndung deutscher Kriegs- und Besatzungsverbrechen in Polen', in N. Frei (ed.), *Transnationale Vergangenheitspolitik. Der Umgang mit den deutschen Kriegsverbrechern in Europa nach dem Zweiten Weltkrieg*. Göttingen, 2006, 408–437, at 408.

close relationship with the USSR and to the cooperation of many of its members with the Soviet occupier in eastern Poland between 1939 and 1941, the so called "August decree", issued in summer of 1944, contained only provisions about the punishment of collaboration with the German enemy and remained mute about collaboration with the Soviets. It was that decree which ultimately was used by the courts when they decided guilt and innocence during the post-war collaboration trials.[4]

An exceptional, numerically marginal, but politically highly salient case of transitional justice was the trial against 15 Polish high-ranking politicians of the Polish non-communist underground and General Leopold Okulicki, the commander of the Home Army. The so called "trial of the sixteen" took place after the men had been lured into secret consultations with Soviet emissaries, abducted and then transported to Moscow. There, they were put on trial for sabotage. Some of the accused were acquitted; others were sentenced to prison terms between four months and ten years (the latter applied to Okulicki). The Red Army and the Soviet special services had already conducted large scale arrests of Home Army officers, who had sought contact with Red Army units during the latter's advance into Polish territory. By leaving their hiding places, the Polish partisans had intended to test the intentions of the Soviets, to offer their duties in the fight against the withdrawing Wehrmacht and to emphasise the government-in-exile's claim to the disputed eastern territories.

If one includes these rather unorthodox and dubious cases, the main actors carrying out transitional justice in an organised and institutionalised manner were the Polish non-communist underground (the AK), the transitional government and the Soviet authorities. Their temporal and territorial jurisdiction partly overlapped until the country came under the complete control of the Soviet authorities. By then, the non-communist members of the transitional government had lost control over the security sector and the judiciary. The only measures of transitional justice which were being applied were the ones meted out first by the interim government and then by the authorities of the Polish People's Republic.

These actors wielded jurisdiction over a number of different categories of suspects. The Soviet authorities were mainly interested in political and military leaders and their measures were mostly concentrated on actors who potentially could constitute a security threat to the Red Army and who endangered the stability of the new order. The Polish underground concentrated its efforts on traitors, informants and spies who worked for the German police, Gestapo or SS and on German middle- and high-ranking officials whose actions were

4 W. Borodziej, *Hitleristische Verbrechen*, 408–409.

detrimental for the Home Army's military and political interests, or who were loathed by the local population because of their ruthless behavior. However, the degree of brutality or of their military and political significance was not the only criterion for making a German official (or a traitor) a target of the underground courts. Another was the likelihood of retaliation by the German authorities and the damage such retaliation could inflict on the interests of the Home Army or local population. The German authorities tended to strike back by taking hostages, carrying out summary executions or – in the case of partisan attacks – by destroying the closest village and killing or deporting the inhabitants. Retaliation was more likely the more prominent and the more influential a target was. This mechanism limited the reach of the Home Army's heavy hand to middle- and low-ranking informants of the occupier, whose activities harmed the underground's interests disproportionally, but who were not very important for the Germans.

1.4. THE SCOPE OF JUSTICE

Transitional justice in a narrow sense was carried out on the basis of the "August decree" against Germans, Poles and members of the pre-war national and ethnic minorities. Since the applicable statistics from the archives do not distinguish between occupiers and traitors, the actual scope of justice meted out against Polish citizens is difficult to assess. It also must be kept in mind that most Polish publications about the issue only deal with ethnic Poles' (and, in Upper Silesia, members of the higher categories of the so-called "*Volksliste*")[5] collaboration with the German authorities and do not include information about Ukrainians, Byelorussians and Lithuanians, who were mostly prosecuted by the Soviet authorities, who obtained jurisdiction over Poland's eastern territories once they were conquered again by the Red Army.[6]

Until 1948 about 110,000 people were interned, half of which were German soldiers who had been left behind by the withdrawing Wehrmacht and had been captured either by the Soviets or the Polish Army and security services. The special courts, which had been created for the punishment of traitors of the nation, had to rule on 12,529 indictments, half of which led to convictions. The

5 With the Volksliste, the German authorities in territories annexed to the Reich gave privileges to people who declared their loyalty to the German Nation by accepting a category of the Volksliste. At the same time, they risked recruitment into the German Army. The policies of the different Gauleiters in the annexed territories varied strongly and so did the behavior of the population affected by these policies.

6 According to Dean 2003, about half of all members of the Schutzpolizei in Byelorussia and Ukraine were punished after the war by Soviet authorities. M. Dean, *Collaboration in the Holocaust: Crimes of the Local Police in Belorussia and Ukraine, 1941–1944*, London, 2003.

reluctance of the judges evoked discussions in the government on whether the judiciary was still infected by bourgeois tendencies. The special courts were dissolved and their cases transmitted to the regular courts. At the end 631 suspects were sentenced to death. This number rose until 1956 to 1,212, but the existing fragmentary sources do not reveal how many of these verdicts actually ended with the execution of a suspect and whether all these verdicts were based on charges of treason and collaboration. About 18,000 persons were convicted of collaboration and war crimes according to the "August decree". But this number includes cases of collaboration (pertaining to Polish citizens) and of war crimes (of which mainly Germans were accused).[7] The majority of people convicted for collaboration had been members of the "Blue Police" (*Granatowa Policja*), an internal Polish police force, whose members had been drawn from both pre-war policemen and from new recruits, who were often used to secure deportations, to guard the ghettos and carry out raids against black marketeers and to organise street raids against the resistance movements. After the war, Gestapo informers and so-called *szmalcowniki* were also punished. The latter category comprised people who had blackmailed Jews in hiding outside the ghettos or who had sold information about such hiding places to the Gestapo. The same happened to Poles who had been found to be working for German-inspired propaganda publications. In general, the scope of transitional justice applied against collaborationists was, compared to the measures in West European countries, rather narrow, especially if confronted to the number of potential suspects and the size of the pre-war and post-war population.[8]

Judges were less hesitant to convict and punish German officials who had either been apprehended during the final phase of the war by Polish or Soviet authorities, or had been extradited from Allied-occupied Germany, Austria and Czechoslovakia to Poland. These extraditions usually went smoothly; they became more time consuming and bureaucratic once the Allied Powers had granted sovereignty to West Germany and Austria. A famous case of transitional justice against a major German perpetrator was the trial and subsequent public execution of Arthur Greiser, the loathed *Gauleiter* of the Wartegau in summer 1946.

Executions of high ranking German officials were among the most spectacular ones, but they were statistically marginal. By 1945, 51,000 German soldiers had been imprisoned, 35,000 members of the Volksliste had been interned and were waiting for their deportation to occupied Germany.[9] Many of them died, due to bad treatment, torture or just malnutrition and diseases which spread among

---

7 W. Borodziej, *Hitleristische Verbrechen*, 412–437.

8 K. Bachmann, *Vergeltung, Strafe, Amnestie. Eine vergleichende Studie zu Kollaboration und ihrer Aufarbeitung in Belgien, Polen und den Niederlanden*. Peter Lang International, 2011, 317–336.

9 W. Borodziej, *Hitleristische Verbrechen*, 412–430.

the crowded camp populations. Germans who had failed to escape with the German authorities when the Wehrmacht withdrew from Poland and Germany's eastern territories were often submitted to humiliating treatment and forced to wear special signs. Many of them were used as forced labour. Their number decreased rapidly, after the Potsdam agreement was signed by the Allied Powers, which foresaw the expulsion of most of Poland's German population. Immediately after the eastern territories of Germany had been conquered by Soviet troops and a provisional Polish administration been installed, local mayors, militias and Polish army units had proceeded to the "wild" and unorganised expulsion of the German population, which was forced across the Oder and Neisse border.

These measures affected between 400,000 and 1.2 million people. However, it is difficult to categorise them as transitional justice, since these people were not accused of any wrongdoings, they could not be charged with treason or collaboration (since they had never been citizens of Poland and Germany had never "occupied" their territory) and no judicial procedures were put in place to punish them. Officially, they were removed for geopolitical reasons and because the new government of Poland was convinced that their continuing presence would destabilise post-war Poland and lead to a renewal of ethnic conflicts. Later on, the Polish authorities also claimed to need the soil and the buildings left behind for the resettlement of Poles from Poland's pre-war eastern territories. The expulsion was regarded as a punishment by those affected by it, but from the perspective of the Polish authorities, it was certainly not linked to individual guilt.

1.5. NON-JUDICIAL MEASURES AND POPULAR PURGES

While in France and Belgium, a rather clear line can be drawn between immediate post-war purges on the one hand, and the beginning of judicial procedures against collaborationists on the other, it is quite difficult to distinguish between both developments in Poland. There are only very scarce sources which provide information about immediate popular and spontaneous purges in Poland and there is no evidence for the kind of symbolic cleansing described, for example, by Virgili in her book about the forced shaving of women and girls in liberated France.[10] Much of the energy which went into such spontaneous actions in Western Europe was apparently channeled into the imprisonment and expulsion of Poland's pre-war German population.

Purges in the administration and the media started some time after the war had ended, but they were due to political rather than judicial considerations. They were mostly undertaken in the order to facilitate the Polish Workers' Party's

10 F. Virgili, *La France "virile". Des femmes tondues à la Libération*, Paris, 2000.

takeover of power in the country. The charge of collaboration was used in this fight for power in a way that makes it very difficult to distinguish between judicial and political measures, between punishment for actual wrongdoings and politically motivated purges directed against those who were suspected of resisting the imposition of a communist dictatorship. Subsequently, members of the leftist parties who refused to merge with the Polish Workers' Party (*Polska Partia Robotnicza* (PPR)) were fired from the security sector and the local administration; the central administration was taken over step by step by PPR loyalists and the non-communist members of the government were marginalised. Individual members and the entire hierarchies of non-communist parties were arrested or killed by "unknown perpetrators". By 1948 the communist leadership had weakened the opposition in the country to such an extent that it could proceed to the cleansing of the party's own ranks. By then, the leaders of the main opposition parties had already fled abroad and founded exile parties. What followed is best described as a Stalinist takeover and the introduction of a terror regime, rather than as an attempt to reckon with collaboration.

Nevertheless, the topic was frequently used in the political struggle and for propaganda purposes in order to discredit potential opponents of the country's Stalinisation. Therefore facts, persons and events linked to non-communist resistance against the German occupier were literally erased from public life, the media and even from scholarly research. Poland's new rulers introduced an extremely exclusive interpretation of the recent past, which left space only for communists and Soviet partisans and attempted to extinguish the AK and the nationalist underground organisations from collective memory. The same happened with respect to the Polish Western Army, whose members had fought in the ranks of the British Army during the battle over the Channel, the Normandy landing and, most prominently, at Monte Cassino. The Warsaw Uprising, which had been condemned by Stalin, became a political taboo. Instead the (mostly leftist, but hardly communist) insurgents of the Ghetto Uprising, which had taken place in 1943, were declared national heroes and the anniversary of the uprising was commemorated with great expenditure. Neither the insurgents, nor their supporters, nor their families nor their successors were capable of challenging the new government's power, since their number was too small, they had died during the uprising or had fled abroad after the war. This was different with respect to the Armia Krajowa's members, whose ranks were ten times larger than those of the communist partisan movements. They were hunted down, imprisoned or killed during raids and, after an amnesty in August 1945, kept away from key parts of the state administration and monitored and intimidated by the state security. The public condemnation of the AK was based on an interpretation of the past which presented the Home Army as reluctant and hesitant in the fight against the Germans and which regarded its leaders as responsible for the launch of the Warsaw Uprising, which had been crushed by the German Army. The actual reason for the prosecution of Home Army members was the potential threat that their mere number constituted to the rule of the Polish United Workers' Party (*Polska Zjednoczona Partia Robotnicza*, PUWP).

1.6. REINTEGRATION AND THE IMPACT OF DEMOGRAPHY AND RECONSTRUCTION

The exclusionist phase slowly waned, beginning from the early sixties. During the Stalinist terror regime, the country underwent a huge forced industrialisation, accompanied by urbanisation and strong economic pressure on the agricultural sector. This coercive model of modernisation was partly successful, but reached its limits during the first half of the fifties. After Stalin's death and Khrushchev's self-criticism in 1956 the PUWP sidelined its Stalinist leadership and opened its ranks for "national communists", who previously had been ousted and imprisoned because of alleged nationalist deviation. The new leadership withdrew from the coercive policy vis-à-vis private farmers, who started to leave the cooperatives into which they had been forced during the late forties. The Party began a prudent and slow rehabilitation of former members of the non-communist resistance groups. More and more of them were released from prison and allowed to meet each other. Many were even admitted to the lower segments of the state administration and the offices of state-run enterprises. Their rehabilitation was furthered by a power struggle in the PUWP, which reached its peak in the second half of the 60s. In this power struggle, a nationalist fraction challenged the power of the incumbent party leadership by attacking them for their supposedly Jewish origin. This fraction, led by the Minister of the Interior and the head of the communist combatants' Union[11], Mieczysław Moczar, took advantage of the frustration of a large part of the party administration, whose possibility to advance further in the hierarchy had been blocked after 1948 by Polish communists who had come to Poland with the Red Army and taken over key positions, due to the fact that Stalin had trusted them more than the communist partisans who had fought in the Polish

11 In Polish, *Związek Bojowników o Wolność i Demokracji* (ZBOWiD, Union of Fighters for Freedom and Democracy). The name reveals a policy. Since the number of communist "fighters for freedom" was about ten times lower than the number of the non-communist resistance movements, ZBOWiD inflated its ranks by including retired members of the post-war security sector, which, according to the communist interpretation of the recent past, had also fought for freedom and democracy, by protecting the country from a return to power of the allegedly discredited forces of "Polish fascism" and from a "nationalist revenge" and by securing the achievements of the "revolution", which, according to this version of history, had taken place when the Red Army had re-conquered the country in 1944.

underground. Moczar and his supporters managed to channel their frustration, the dissatisfaction of large parts of the youth with the government and the striving of former anti-communist partisans for their rehabilitation into one political movement. He opened the ranks of his combatants' Union to former AK members and promoted a new, nationalist interpretation of the Poles' fight against the German occupier. Where the Stalinist version had stressed the "righteous and uncompromised fight of the progressive forces of the Polish left" against the Germans and "fascist Polish elements" at one hand and the Home Army's reluctance to fight on the other hand, the new version reconciled the whole underground under the common roof of an alleged "resistance movement", to which communists and non-communists had allegedly belonged. This was much more inclusive than the old one, and it enabled the nationalist aisle of the PUWP and ZBOWiD to strengthen their ranks with the support of the AK members and their families.

1.7. THE LOGIC OF INCLUSION

This inclusive strategy was a huge political success for ZBOWiD, the PUWP and for those who had spent the preceding decades as second class citizens, who could talk about their war experiences only among their families and closest friends. It brought both the ZBOWiD and the PUWP an unprecedented surge in new members. The biggest increase occurred after March 1967, when the police suppressed students' and pupils' protests in Warsaw and the nationalist wing of the Party launched a campaign against the alleged "Zionist" instigators of the riots. The anti-Semitic campaign against students and intellectuals and the nationalist propaganda of the Moczar faction within the PUWP leadership considerably strengthened the legitimacy of the Party. Part of this policy was a more and more inclusive approach to former non-communist and anti-communist members of the Polish anti-German and pro-Western resistance movement. By 1965, the proportion of former AK members having entered ZBOWiD was estimated at about 60,000 out of 200,000 ZBOWiD members in total.[12]

Still, the leadership of the AK (which was either dead or had emigrated and had no influence on the ongoing power struggle in Poland) was officially regarded with hostility and ritually condemned in speeches and handbooks, but rank-

12 The data about PUWP and ZBOWiD membership were retrieved from the annual statistics of the Warsaw based Main Statistical Agency (*Główny Urząd Statystyczny*). I am grateful to the staff of the GUS archives in Warsaw for assistance.More information about the data can be found in: K. Bachmann, *Repression, Protest, Toleranz. Wertewandel und Vergangenheitsbewältigung in Polen nach 1956*, Dresden/Wrocław, 2010.

and-file members of the pro-Western partisans were now admitted as full members and sometimes even courted by the ZBOWiD leadership. Many of their memoirs were published, from which paragraphs about the Warsaw Uprising and other anti-Soviet stains usually were erased.

There is a pattern in the way official history was interpreted. The more severe economic problems became and the more the regime came under political and social pressure, the more it tried to extend its legitimacy by shifting from internationalism and social demagogy to a patriotic or even nationalist discourse. During the last phase of its path from almost total symbolic exclusion to almost entire symbolic inclusion, General Wojciech Jaruzelski created a "Military Council for National Salvation" (*Wojskowa Rada Ocalenia Narodowego*, WRON), which formally imposed martial law on Poland in December 1981 and declared "the fatherland" to be "in danger". In the second half of the nineties, the number of publications about the Warsaw Uprising peaked. A wave of patriotic memoirs of former AK members who had fought during the Uprising flooded the bookshops, making the Uprising a great national narrative. By then, only the members of the radical right-wing and anti-Semitic "National Armed Forces" (*Narodowe Siły Zbrojne*, NSZ) were exempt from the officially recognised heroic tradition. Compared to the other clandestine units operating during World War II, they were a small minority.[13]

1.8. HISTORICAL POLICY, HISTORIOGRAPHY AND THE MEANING OF COLLABORATION

In 1946, the communist writer and intellectual Jan Kott already defined the mainstream approach of Polish society to the issue of collaboration during the war, by coining a quote which has remained famous until today. In an article in the 46th edition of the weekly *Przekroj* in 1946, he claimed that "collaborationism is a foreign word. During occupation, no single word emerged which would describe cooperation with the Germans. It did not show up, because there was no need for such a word. We are rightly proud of not having created our own Hácha or Quisling, that there was no single Polish party which collaborated with the occupier and that even among our pre-war fascists, only a few believed in the civilizing mission of the German people. There is no such expression in Polish as 'collaborationism', because there was no collaboration. There were only traitors and special courts, which dealt with them".

---

13 K. Bachmann, *Repression, Protest, Toleranz. Wertewandel und Vergangenheitsbewältigung in Polen nach 1956*, Dresden/Wrocław, 2010.

For decades, Kott's allegation was taken as the starting point of nearly every author who wrote about the conditions in German-occupied Poland. Even during the Stalinist period, when the PUWP's propaganda accused the Home Army of hesitance and cowardice, the "C-word" was not mentioned. It was sometimes used in order to discredit the members of the nationalist right-wing organisations which had fought against the German and the Soviet occupier and remained in the underground throughout the forties, rejecting amnesty. Official propaganda simply associated them with fascism, and fascism with National Socialism. But in general, nationalists, anti-communists within the Polish emigration, PUWP members and many mainstream historians would agree that "collaboration" had not played a significant role in occupied Poland, as opposed to Vichy France and many other countries of Western Europe. Some of the nationalists would have probably pointed to the cooperation of Polish leftist intellectuals with the Soviet occupiers in eastern Poland between 1939 and 1941, but this was only a topic for the intellectual communities of the Polish Diaspora in the West and the flourishing cultural underground of the eighties. For people like Jan Kott (who actually had collaborated with the Soviets in Lwów[14] before 1941), this was a total non-issue.

For all post-war societies, defining the meaning of collaboration was the basis for establishing the scope of post-war retribution. In Poland, this definition remained extremely narrow. If we regard the notion of "collaboration" or "collaborationism" (as it sometimes was called) as the result of a social process of constructing a picture of the past, we will be able to observe the specific measures which were taken in order to keep this notion as narrow as possible. First, in public discourse, the use of the notion of collaboration was limited to individual or collective behavior during the German occupation. Second, it was restricted to ethnic Poles. The latter approach excluded all ethnic minorities whose members actually had cooperated with the German authorities in many ways, from "the Polish nation", which, thanks to this approach, remained untainted. This approach was also applied with respect to those people (mainly, but not exclusively, in Upper Silesia) who had ascribed themselves to one of the four categories of the "Deutsche Volksliste" and had taken advantage of the material benefits which had been the result of adherence to the German nation. In a next step, public discourse (and historiography) declared the few remaining people who undisputedly had been ethnic Poles and had collaborated with the occupier as a few rotten apples in a healthy barrel. What emerged from all these approaches was the picture of a heroic nation, which had suffered and resisted evil, and, by doing so, had become a unique example in a Europe of dirty

14 Lwów is the Polish name for the town in today's western Ukraine, which now is called L'viv, and once was soviet Lvov and, before WWI, belonged to the Habsburg Empire under the name of Lemberg.

compromises, collaboration and acquiescence. This picture was seldom challenged. There were some attempts to question the heroism and sense of the Warsaw Uprising during the sixties and seventies, but they remained quite restricted and hampered by censorship and the impossibility to discuss openly the implications of Soviet politics for the Uprising.

1.9. MEMORY ERUPTIONS – THE QUESTION OF ANTI-SEMITISM AFTER THE WAR

In the relatively liberal atmosphere of the late eighties, liberal catholic weekly *Tygodnik Powszechny* launched a debate about the wait and see attitude and moral indifference of ethnic Poles vis-à-vis the Holocaust of the Polish Jewry during the war. But while this debate put in doubt whether Poles had been heroes or bystanders, it did not raise the issue of active collaboration. In Poland, the question of continuity between pre-war anti-Semitism, collaboration in the Holocaust and post-war anti-Jewish pogroms had never been publicly debated in terms of "collaboration", as it often had been in US, French and other foreign publications. This changed when Jan Tomasz Gross published his polemical reckoning with Polish anti-Semitism in 2000 under the quite innocent title of *Neighbors*.[15] In the book, he described one of the biggest pogroms on Polish territory, which occurred during the German advance against the Red Army in 1941, when parts of the Polish, Lithuanian and Ukrainian populations took revenge on alleged "Soviet collaborators" among the local Jews (who had not fled eastwards with the Red Army). As a result of Gross' book, a mass grave was excavated in Jedwabne, a long and fierce debate among historians and the media started about the scope and meaning of "Jedwabne" and finally Polish president Aleksander Kwaśniewski issued an apology during a commemoration ceremony in Jedwabne. Nevertheless, the debate focused on anti-Semitism rather than collaboration, which might have been due to the fact that many well-known pre-war Polish anti-Semites had been victims of and fighters against the German occupation and some of them had even saved the lives of Jews hiding outside the ghettos. Actually, Gross's subsequent books, and the debates they initiated in Poland, remain one of the rare indicators for a retrospective societal value shift from the very inclusive, patriotic memory, whose roots can be traced back to the sixties, to a more exclusive, critical post- materialist memory, which began to develop in Western Europe during the seventies. But still, this is not the mainstream. The shift is taking place among the members of small, relatively well-educated and increasingly cosmopolitan cohorts, which transcend age groups. Another indicator of this shift is the rising number of respondents who

15 T. Gross, *Neighbors. The Destruction of the Jewish Community in Jedwabne, Poland*, Princeton, 2001.

answer in the affirmative to the question in opinion polls of whether there is "something" in Polish history of which "Poles should be ashamed".[16]

2. TRANSITIONAL JUSTICE AND DEMOCRATISATION DURING THE NINETIES

2.1. INTRODUCTION

Poland was a rather exceptional example of transitional justice after World War II, but it is in the mainstream with respect to its transition in 1989 from a one-party communist dictatorship to a liberal and market-oriented democratic system. There is some controversy in the literature (and the political discussion) about when exactly transition started, and according to some authors, one should go all the way back to 1980 (the emergence of Solidarity (*Solidarność*), the first independent trade union), to the second half of the eighties (when Mikhail Gorbachev was elected head of the Central Committee of the CPSU (Communist Party of the Soviet Union) and the Polish leadership released all political prisoners, opening the way to a negotiated transition) or to the actual start of transition negotiations in 1988, which led to the Round Table talks and the June election in 1989. The overwhelming majority of historians and political scientists dealing with the 1989 transition in Poland regard the regime of General Wojciech Jaruzelski as a communist one-party dictatorship. However, there are also voices which place Jaruzelski's regime into the neighborhood of Latin American military dictatorships, due to the important role the military played in politics after the imposition of martial law in 1981. These are only minority voices in the discussion, though. The character of this transition and of Poland's further development are also contested: Was it actually a transition to democracy and a liberal market economy, or did it lead to a postcommunist sham-democracy, where all important decisions are taken behind the curtain between important stakeholders of the *ancien régime* and members of the new political establishment and are then formally approved by democratic bodies, which are manipulated by these clandestine networks?

2.2. THE PREPARATION OF TRANSITIONAL JUSTICE MEASURES

One of the biggest differences between Poland's rather violent post-war transition and the country's negotiated power sharing deal in 1989 consists of the total lack

16 These questions are asked in the framework of the so called "Polish Social Diagnosis" (Polska Diagnoza Społeczna). The data can be retrieved from the Polish Social Data Archive (*Archiwum Danych Spolecznych*): www.ads.org.pl.

of any plans for retribution. Whereas both governments-in-exile had detailed plans for the punishment of collaborators and German war criminals, it is difficult to find any considerations in the democratic opposition and the communities of Polish emigrants about punishment for the leadership and supporters of the oppressive regime during the eighties. Retribution for perpetrators was no issue for the underground and it was, of course, no topic for the negotiations which led to the Round Table talks. At the Round Table, debates about how to punish the "other side" of the table would have certainly led to the breakdown of the talks, which were held in an atmosphere of limited mutual trust and common aims. The Round Table was actually similar to many Truth Commissions throughout the third wave of democratisation, much more concerned with the future and the solution of problems than with dealing with the past. Since both sides agreed to carry out "non-confrontational elections" in order to legitimise the power sharing agreement concluded at the Round Table, it would have been detrimental to their deal if they had engaged in blaming the other side for past wrongdoings. During the transitional phase between the elections in June 1989 and summer 1990, when the communist generals resigned from their government posts, any attempt to prosecute leaders and followers of their former regime would have had to overcome some insurmountable obstacles:

- The public administration, including the security services and the army, were still dominated by officials who had been socialised and educated under the *ancien régime*;
- The new government needed the support of the former PUWP's members in the *Sejm* and Senate in order to pass the package for economic reform, since the former opposition had no majority there and the situation of the country required very speedy, swift and efficient decisions. For months, the Sejm and its committees acted like a "voting machine" for the government, with endless night sessions, extraordinary procedures and bills passed without (or with only a minimum of) debate.
- The new government dissolved the Secret Police (*Służba Bezpieczeństwa*, SB), whose officers could apply for jobs at the police or the newly created "State Protection Agency" (*Urząd Ochrony Państwa*, UOP). About 4,000 former SB officers lost their jobs as a consequence of this procedure, which came close to a purge of the SB staff. In order to protect their informers and themselves from penal consequences, officers in the Ministry of the Interior began to destroy secret files, burning them on distant waste dump sites outside Warsaw.[17]
- The new government refrained from similar screening procedures for public prosecutors and judges. Hence, existing networks remained in power in the judiciary. As it would turn out, judges and prosecutors would apply strictly

17 L. Stan, *Transitional Justice in Eastern Europe and the Former Soviet Union. Reckoning with the communist past*, London/New York, 2009.

> positivist and legalist approaches to prosecuting and sentencing, which, under conditions of limited access to evidence, was extremely convenient for suspects, since it excluded the possibility of retroactive punishment.

A gulf between elite and popular opinion about transitional justice became visible. A strong strand of the media, supportive of the new government, opposed retribution in the name of national reconciliation and reconstruction. Since the economic and technological backwardness of Poland and the inability to reform the economy had been the main reasons why the *ancien régime* had lost legitimacy and popular support, this was no banal argument. In his first address to the Sejm, Tadeusz Mazowiecki, a hesitant, prudent and politically moderate Catholic intellectual, drew "a thick line between today and the past", suggesting he would refrain from holding the former leadership legally accountable for crimes and failed decisions in order to secure support for his reforms and for a swift economic recovery of the country. Subsequent governments followed this line, and retribution actually remained restricted to a very few cases of middle-range officers of the Ministry of the Interior who were sentenced to jail for torturing political prisoners during Stalinism. All attempts of prosecutors and later of the newly created Institute for National Remembrance (*Instytut Pamięci Narodowej*, IPN) to judge the authors of martial law and the subsequent human rights violations were unsuccessful. Either the trials were delayed by clever defence lawyers, or they had to be postponed due to the illness of the main suspects or, in some cases, verdicts were reversed by higher courts or referred back to the lower courts for procedural reasons. Both generals, Jaruzelski and Kiszczak, due to their high positions, could only be charged by a special "state tribunal" created right after the introduction of martial law in 1982 and designed to judge violations of the constitution. According to the amended version of the so-called "small constitution" of 1947, the assent of a qualified majority of the National Assembly would have been necessary to try Kiszczak and Jaruzelski, a threshold that was never met due to the resistance of the postcommunist Alliance of the Democratic Left (*Sojusz Lewicy Demokratycznej*, SLD), whose members of parliament had already blocked such motions on the level of the parliamentary committee for constitutional responsibility.

2.3. NON-JUDICIAL MEASURES AND POPULAR PURGES

Due to the negotiated character of Poland's transition, there were no popular purges comparable to the "*épuration*" in France and Belgium, to the executions and persecutions in Italy or to the civil war-like mass executions which followed the regime changes in Yugoslavia. Despite the emergence of new forms of (organised) crime, which was the consequence of economic transition rather than a reaction to political change, the police and the army remained firmly in control of the process.

There were administrative measures against perpetrators linked to the former regime as well as attempts at truth-telling, which are quite unknown until today. Several schemes can be distinguished:

- a Polish Truth Commission with the status of an extraordinary investigative Sejm-committee, led by a former member of the democratic opposition, which conducted enquiries into almost a hundred cases of abductions, disappearances and killings of opposition members, which had taken place during martial law. The committee did not play any major part in the transition process. The majority of cases which the committee referred to the prosecutors were discontinued by the latter.
- a scheme which compelled prosecutors to confess former political misbehavior to their superiors if they wanted to keep their job. The scheme had some similarities with the truth-telling mechanism of the South African TRC ("tell all you know and go free"), but was deprived of the latter's impact. Confessions were neither public nor were they accompanied by any truth-telling procedure for victims.[18]
- a lustration attempt, which totally failed, and several bills whose content was watered down in parliament, and which introduced legal procedures for the screening of candidates for political positions, high government posts and "professions which require public confidence". Parts of the relevant laws were rejected by the Constitutional Court, whose judges also followed the general line of legalism and the prevention of retroactive punishment.

Despite the Mazowicki government's attempts to avoid retribution in the name of national unity and reconstruction, the issue resurfaced quickly, together with the huge social cost the population had to bear as a result of economic reform and the breakdown of intra-Comecon trade in 1991. Unemployment rose to 10 percent of the workforce, mass bankruptcies of huge state enterprises followed and farmers faced an explosion of their debts when the government reformed the banking sector and withdrew subventions to the farmers' loans. Populist parties emerged and the postcommunist SLD gained new support – from supporters of the *ancien régime* as well as from those who saw themselves as the losers of transition and watched the careers of new businessmen and former members of the communist establishment with rising suspicion and scorn. In this atmosphere, demands for retribution (often presented as a compensation for the hardships of the transition for "ordinary people") came uniquely from right-wing parties. They basically concerned two different notions: lustration and decommunisation.

---

18 L. Stan, *Transitional Justice in Eastern Europe.*

Lustration was understood as the totality of legal means which would aim at the exclusion of former secret police informers from public life. According to this demand, the files of the secret police should be made available to the public, or to a special agency, whose task it would be to assess the gravity of the misbehavior of "informers" and then to pass sentence. Decommunisation was understood as a program which would aim at the elimination of former (leading) communists from public and political life, comparable to the West German "*Berufsverbot*" during the early years of the Federal Republic of Germany. In some cases, there were also requests for the confiscation of property illicitly acquired under communism, often called economic decommunisation. People who had occupied key posts under the *ancien régime* should be prevented from taking advantage of their connections in order to continue their careers, enrich themselves and their families and exercise power after transition. Economic decommunisation never left the status of bills. Attempts to vote on such bills were mostly curtailed by the successive governments, which regarded them as detrimental for economic development. Political decommunisation also was prevented by the strength of postcommunist parties which held blocking positions in the party system, by human rights commitments, which Poland had to respect due to external pressure and by the legalist Constitutional Court. Therefore, lustration was the only measure which was ever actually applied, but only to a very limited extent.

The first attempt to expose the new political establishment to its alleged political misbehavior in the past took place in 1992, when a rather politically isolated right-wing populist managed to get a resolution passed in the *Sejm* which ordered the Minister of the Interior to deliver a list of those members of government and parliament who, according to the Ministry's archives, had collaborated with the communist secret police and secret services. The motion was vague, and the result was a political earthquake. A few days later, the Minister (who was also a supporter of lustration) delivered a confidential list of 64 members of parliament, government and the presidency (by that time held by Lech Wałęsa), which immediately leaked out to the press. It left unanswered the question of what the people on the list actually were accused of, since – as it later turned out – some of them had signed a contract with the secret police, but never complied with it, others had only been registered by the police as informers, but no records about their actual behavior were available, while still others had worked with the external secret services (and hence had spied on foreign countries rather than on Poles). Some might have been totally innocent (even according to the minister's criteria), others might have betrayed their friends and colleagues or might have harmed the democratic opposition – but the material delivered by the Minister did not provide enough substantiation for conclusive judgment. One of the persons he had depicted as "secret police informer" was Wałęsa himself. He reacted by inspiring a vote of no confidence against the government (which had already lost its parliamentary majority), and, after the government had been voted out of office, he immediately appointed a new prime minister, who failed to form a new government, but managed to fire the previous members of the cabinet, including the Minister of the Interior. A committee of enquiry was set up to elucidate the circumstances under which the Minister had delivered his list to the chairmen of the political clubs in the *Sejm*. The committee never dealt with the veracity of the accusations, only with the political and legal circumstances of what was described as an act of wild lustration, and with the questions of whether lustration had been used in order to blackmail members of the opposition and whether it had been part of a plan for a coup d'état. Later on, the committee concluded that lustration had been illegal and part of a plan to stabilise the ailing multiparty government of Jan Olszewski, but no evidence of an attempted putsch could be found.

After the fall of the Olszewski government and the rise to power of the postcommunist "Alliance of the Democratic Left", which, in 1995, was followed by a stunning victory of left-wing candidate Aleksander Kwaśniewski in the presidential elections, lustration remained an issue for public debates and media discourse, but no legislation was passed. The only legal measure which foresaw the screening of citizens about their behavior under communism was a provision in the election law which required MEP and presidential candidates to sign declarations about their contacts with numerous state agencies, such as the Secret Police, the (communist) Border Guards and the Military Intelligence. However, secret informers were not punished as such. It was not collaboration which was criminalised, but giving false information about collaboration. Despite the overwhelmingly repressive attitudes of Polish society at that time, which favored retribution over prevention and supported lustration, a tainted past did not automatically discredit a candidate in the eyes of the voters. In 2000, Andrzej Olechowski, a liberal non-partisan candidate for the presidency who had openly admitted his cooperation with the communist secret service abroad, managed to get enough votes to surpass the leading candidate of the right and obtained second place after Kwaśniewski, who was elected with an absolute majority.

It was only in 2006 when a populist right-wing multi-party coalition passed a law which required all professionals whose jobs involved public confidence (such as lawyers, notaries and even university professors) to submit declarations about their contacts with communist agencies. The attempt to launch a campaign which could have led to the elimination of a large part of Poland's political and business elite from certain professions and from public life failed due to the resistance of the Constitutional Court, who declared the relevant provision unconstitutional. Since then, lustration has been limited to candidates for important public positions and politicians.

2.4. REINTEGRATION AND THE IMPACT OF DEMOGRAPHY AND RECONSTRUCTION

With respect to the communist system, Poland refrained from any large scale attempts at retribution. Former perpetrators, no matter how important, were not excluded from society, punished or even officially blamed and therefore no measures had to be undertaken to reintegrate them. This restorative, rather than retributive approach to Transitional Justice has been very controversial in society, politics, culture and the media. Supporters of this approach usually point to the need for reconciliation and unity and argue that the lack of retribution has contributed to the social and political integration of members of the *ancien régime,* who reconciled with democracy, human rights and a liberal market economy and refrained from any attempts to reinstate the old system or menace democracy. Even from the opposition benches, the postcommunist left has often saved government bills which lacked sufficient support from the ruling coalition, supported privatisation schemes and the foreign policy of Poland's different multiparty coalitions.

Opponents of Mazowiecki's "thick line" point to the lack of a clear symbolic separation between a bad past and a good future and blame the lack of retribution for rising populism and punitive tendencies in Polish society. Populist politicians claim the lack of retribution and "moral cleansing" to be the main cause for a relativist society and the multiple problems of transition which the country had to deal with in the aftermath of 1989. In their eyes, the silent and smooth integration of former communists into the new order compromised the latter and surrendered Poland's democracy to the poison of post communism, allowing members of the *ancien régime* to keep their social and financial capital and enabling them to corrupt the elites of the new order. Crime, corruption, moral ambiguity, economic scandals and lack of patriotism are rooted in the negligence of the transitional governments to assess the past in clear moral terms and to condemn communism as a crime and the order of the People's Republic as a criminal system.

2.5. MEMORY ERUPTIONS AND THE PREVALENCE OF INCLUSION AND THE NATIONAL PARADIGM

Between 1990 and the end of the century, there was a dichotomy in Poland between an elitist majority, blocking attempts for far-reaching lustration and a popular majority, which favored punishment for former perpetrators. Memory eruptions took place, when prominent cases were judged by the ombudsman of public interest, a de facto prosecutorial position, held in the second half of the nineties by a prominent supporter of lustration, whose task was to check lustration declarations of politicians, whom the lustration law required to produce such a declaration. In 2005 a journalist published a huge record of alleged secret informers, which he had downloaded in the archives of the Institute of Public Remembrance. His file actually contained random information, which had not yet been analysed by the Institute. But the mere fact of publishing tens of thousands of names of alleged informers already led to a fierce debate between supporters and opponents of lustration. The journalist, Bronisław Wildstein, was at first fired by his editor, but two years later was elected head of the State Television Administration by the (pro-lustration) cabinet of Kazimierz Marcińkiewicz.

2.6. THE ROLE OF HISTORICAL AND SOCIOLOGICAL RESEARCH

Unlike the historiography about World War II and the question of collaboration, scholarship does not play a large role in Poland's reckoning with the legacy of its secret police. Although the issue has inspired a huge amount of journalistic, non-academic and mostly normative accounts, lustration has become an issue for foreign researchers rather than Polish academics and most academic analysis of Poland's transitional justice measures actually come from abroad.[19] The internal Polish debate about lustration, its justification and consequences and the implications of the "thick line" was dominated mostly by historians and lawyers, and a small but quite active number of sociologists. However, this is a political rather than a scholarly debate, and some of the participants even actively engaged in partisan politics. As opposed to the debate on collaboration with the German occupier, the debate on lustration has been shaped much more by politicians and political commentators and public intellectuals than by academics.

ABBREVIATIONS

AK:	Home(land) Army (*Armia Krajowa*)
IPN:	Institute of National Remembrance (*Instytut Pamięci Narodowej*)
NSZ:	National Armed Forces (*Narodowe Siły Zbrojne*)
PKWN:	Polish Committee of National Liberation (*Polski Komitet Wyzwolenia Narodowego*)
PPR:	Polish Workers' Party (*Polska Partia Robotnicza*)
PUWP:	Polish United Workers Party (*Polska Zjednoczona Partia Robotnicza*, PZPR)
SB:	Security Service (*Służba Bezpieczeństwa*)

19 M. Nalepa, *Skeletons in the Closet. Transitional Justice in Post Communist Countries*, New York, 2010.
L. Stan (ed.), *Transitional Justice in Eastern Europe*.

UB: Security Agency (*Urząd Bezpieczeństwa*)
UOP: State Protection Agency (*Urząd Ochrony Państwa*)
US: United States
USSR: Union of Socialist Soviet Republics (Союз Советских Социалистических Республик, SSSR)
WRON: Military Council for National Salvation (*Wojskowa Rada Ocalenia Narodowego*)
WW I: World War I
WW II: World War II
ZBOWiD: Union of combatants for Freedom and Democracy (*Związek Bojowników o Wolność i Demokrację*)

SELECTIVE FURTHER READING

Bachmann, Klaus (2010a), *Repression, Protest, Toleranz. Wertewandel und Vergangenheitsbewältigung in Polen nach 1956*, Dresden, Wrocław.

Bachmann, Klaus (2011), *Vergeltung, Strafe, Amnestie. Eine vergleichende Studie zu Kollaboration und ihrer Aufarbeitung in Belgien, Polen und den Niederlanden*, Peter Lang International.

Bernard, Chiari, *Die polnische Heimatarmee. Geschichte und Mythos der Armia Krajowa seit dem Zweiten Weltkrieg* (with collaboration of Jerzy Kochanowski), München, pp. 111–150.

Borodziej, Włodzimierz (2006), 'Hitleristische Verbrechen. Die Ahndung deutscher Kriegs- und Besatzungsverbrechen in Polen', in Frei, Norbert (ed.), *Transnationale Vergangenheitspolitik. Der Umgang mit den deutschen Kriegsverbrechern in Europa nach dem Zweiten Weltkrieg*, Göttingen, 408–437.

Borodziej, Włodzimierz (2010), *Geschichte Polens im 20. Jahrhundert*, München, 2010.

Courtois, Stéphane (ed.) (2003), *Une si longue nuit. L'apogée des regimes totalitaires en Europe 1935–1953*. Paris, 2003.

Dean, Martin (2003), *Collaboration in the Holocaust: Crimes of the Local Police in Belorussia and Ukraine, 1941–44*, London.

Gross, Tomasz (2001), *Neighbors. The Destruction of the Jewish Community in Jedwabne, Poland*, Princeton University Press.

Nalepa, Monika (2010), *Skeletons in the Closet. Transitional Justice in Post Communist Countries*, New York.

Snyder, Timothy (2003), *The Reconstruction of Nation Poland, Ukraine, Lithuania, Belarus 1569–1999*, New Haven, London, 154–178.

Stan, Lavinia (ed.), *Transitional Justice in Eastern Europe and the Former Soviet Union. Reckoning with the communist past*, London, New York, 2009.

Virgili, Fabrice (2000), *La France "virile". Des femmes tondues à la Libération*, Paris.

COMPARING TRANSITIONAL JUSTICE EXPERIENCES IN EUROPE

Luc Huyse

This comparative analysis of policies of dealing with the past is based on ten cases of transition to democracy: Belgium, France, (West-)Germany, and the Netherlands after WWII; Greece, Portugal, and Spain in the 1970s; and Germany, Hungary, and Poland in the post-1989 era (Hungary and Poland after WWII experienced the rise of a dictatorial regime which puts these cases outside the current transitional justice paradigm. They are for the greater part left out of the comparison).[1]

This chapter first compares policies through the description of a number of recurring turning-points in transitional justice decision-making. All countries that are part of the book have gone through episodes where crucial decisions had to be taken in extremely intricate matters. The challenges were common, but did the answers vary? Five such crossroad issues and the multiplicity of responses they generated are discussed. The second section then presents four contextual factors that have shaped both homogeneity and heterogeneity in policy making and implementation. The third section argues that similarities in content and form of policies are more prominent than has often been thought.

1. SAME CHALLENGES, BUT DIFFERENT ANSWERS?

Since the 1990s, practice and scholarship have led to the conclusion that almost all cases of justice after transition are unique. This section tests the alleged diversity through the discussion of a number of recurring turning-points in European transitional justice decision-making. The primary choice bears upon the question of accountability: to punish or close the books. If a policy of

1 The authors of the country case chapters have made possible the writing of this comparison. They delivered essential information and thorough analysis. I also thank them for their critical and insightful comments on a first draft. The usual disclaimer applies.

prosecutions is developed, new options arrive. Dealing with the perpetrators of state crimes, of collaboration with an occupying army, or with the repressive order requires a choice between two logics: the first leads to their exclusion, the other to inclusion and/or reintegration. That is the second issue. Criminal justice after transition differs from ordinary justice because it addresses simultaneously a political and a legal agenda. Blending the two is a third challenge. Then, there is the question of who should receive privileged attention in tackling the pain of the past: those who are responsible for the sorrow, or the victims. Finally, finding an acceptable balance between forgetting and remembering is a fifth critical challenge.[2]

1.1. A DEVIL'S CHOICE: TO PUNISH OR TO LET BYGONES BE BYGONES

Those who emphasise the beneficial effects of accountability measures tend to bring forward two crucial reasons. Firstly, punishing the perpetrators of heinous crimes advances the cause of building or reconstructing a morally just order. The second reason has to do with the consolidation of the regime that succeeds the authoritarian order or of a just-won peace.[3]

Putting back in place the moral order that has broken down requires, it is argued, that "justice be done". It is seen as a moral obligation to the victims of the repressive and brutal past. It serves to heal the wounds and to repair the private and public damage which the antecedent regime or a cruel conflict has caused. It also paves the way for a moral and political renaissance. It is a sort of ritual cleansing process through which national self-respect is restored. It allows the society to debate publicly and firmly establish standards in the area of the rule of law and of human rights. It can be a vast exercise in decoding codes of just political and judicial conduct. A country, it is said, in which such cleansing remains unfinished will be plagued by continuous brooding and pondering. Judicial and administrative action also serves very immediate goals. Between September 1944 and May 1945, when parts of Belgium and Holland were still occupied by the Germans, wholesale internment of suspected collaborators was seen as a necessary protection against sabotage "from within". In addition, the arrest of tens of thousands of suspects was considered to be an adequate measure for preventing summary executions and other unlawful and disorderly behavior.

---

2 The list of the five recurring challenges is principally an analytic instrument. In the presentation, each issue has been isolated from the others. But in a real-world situation they are intimately interlocked. In addition, a certain amount of diversity among countries remains in the intensity with which these dilemmas emerged.

3 L. Huyse, 'Justice after Transition: On the Choices Elites Make in Dealing with the Past', (1995) 1 *Law & Social Inquiry*, 51–78.

A further important goal of accountability actions is the consolidation of the new regime and/or a fragile peace. Screening and, eventually, punishing the collaborators of the defeated order is then greatly needed.

In contrast, opponents of systematic retribution argue that there will no solid peace and democratisation without a national reconciliation (and thus impunity or, at least, tolerance in the handling of past abuses). Purging the society of its bad elements can, they say, jeopardise the transition. In addition, punitive justice can considerably disturb other issues on the transition agenda, such as economic reconstruction.

At first sight the choices that have been made in the national cases greatly differ. At one end of the range is Spain, which, after the demise of the Franco regime, chose to definitely turn the pages. At the other end are the four post-WWII countries. Immediately after the war ended they gave priority to prosecutions. In the case of Germany, that decision was taken by the allied occupying forces. But in West-Germany it was soon reversed by domestic political leaders. Two, three years after their liberation, Belgium, France, and the Netherlands also changed track. Selective clemency replaced absolute severity. In the 1970s Greece decided to limit punishment to the main leaders of the Junta. The successor elite in Portugal first initiated systematic prosecutions but made a U-turn after some eighteen months. Poland, according to Klaus Bachmann, kept to the "thick line between today and the past", the policy which was initiated by Tadeusz Mazowiecki, the first democratically elected president. That choice meant refraining from prosecutions. "Subsequent governments", Bachmann writes, "followed this line, and retribution actually remained restricted to a very few cases of middle-range officers of the Ministry of the Interior". In her report on Hungary, Renata Uitz notes that no definite decision has yet been taken. As for post-communist Germany, Annette Weinke concludes that in their breadth and intensity, the measures "(...) in the areas of prosecution (...) clearly differ from those of other post-1989 states. She sees this deviating position as "(...) a confession of the Federal Republic's old elites that they had failed with respect to the Nazi past".

1.2. EXCLUSION VERSUS INCLUSION OF PERPETRATORS

With regard to the position of suspects and convicts, these societies have had to find a balance between two different scenarios. The first is the systematic expulsion of the perpetrators, based on the logic of exclusion. The other is directed towards their effective reintegration.

A striking similarity in the strategies of Belgium and The Netherlands was the outspoken desire, especially evident in the months before and shortly after the Liberation, to expel the perpetrators – including the rank and file – from their societies. A much-heard expression in political speeches was that "there was no place left for those who had betrayed their country". Portugal, at least in the first months after the April 1974 coup, went the same severe way. Another resemblance lies in the initial tendency to judge the population under absolute standards of good and bad. Sensitivity to the many shades of grey between "black" and "white" was very low. The purges often implied one or another form of "national indignity": a series of civic disqualifications, a prohibition on various kinds of professional activity, prohibition of residence. Belgium, France, and Holland also confiscated the personal goods of unpatriotic citizens. In France, in contrast, General "(...) de Gaulle faced a paradox when he seized power in liberated France. He knew France's thirst for revenge and wanted to channel it through regular state justice". But he realised that "(...) overly-severe purges would (...) leave France beheaded, a very dangerous situation since the communist party might take this opportunity to fill the gaps".

Post-Franco Spain is a case of total absence of purges. The velvet revolutions in post-communist Europe too have, with the exception of Germany, not been followed by a notable physical and/or social removal of the exponents of the old order. In Poland and Hungary, for example, lustration attempts have failed or were blocked by the Constitutional Court.

No post-WWII initial policy of exclusion was a success.[4] The management of the operation was inadequate, uniform screening criteria were absent, politicisation ran very high. The risks of keeping tens of thousands of citizens outside the realms of society soon became apparent. A first danger lurked in the creation of subcultures and networks which in the long run could turn out to be hostile to the newly reinstated democracy. In addition, an *en masse* expulsion of civil service and managerial manpower was felt to be counterproductive because it endangered the badly needed administrative and economic reconstruction. Less than three years after the purge process started, a battery of reintegration-oriented measures was introduced: provisional release, parole, conditional or selective amnesty, rehabilitation. This major policy shift was based on a variety of considerations. Some were of a politico-moral order. Governments viewed clemency as a way to correct and efface shortcomings of the judicial process. One such shortcoming was the considerable inequality that had arisen because punishment had been much harsher in the first months after the war than two or three years later. But pragmatism and politico-strategic motives were dominant.

4 L. Huyse and K. Hoflack, 'Life after prison: the purge and the reintegration of wartime collaborators in Belgium, Holland and France (1944–1994)', (1995) *Bulletin du Comité international d'histoire de la Deuxième Guerre mondiale*, 257–282.

The prisons had to cope with an over-population. The many thousands of convicts exerted an untenable pressure on public resources. And, the thirst for revenge in the population had waned. Other worries, such as the poor standards of housing, came to the forefront. The Cold War too modified the domestic political and public agenda. Communist parties, the most zealous supporters of systematic prosecutions, were expelled from government. Closing ranks in the face of a foreign enemy, the Soviet bloc, was now more important. In the meantime, some WWII countries became involved in colonial wars. In such a situation, internal divisions are a major concern. That too opened the door for a more clemency-oriented policy towards the perpetrators of wartime crimes.

The inclusion-oriented measures, however, were no guarantee for a swift and easy reintegration. Return into society was thwarted by the cumulative character of a cascade of administrative sanctions. Those were extremely difficult to neutralise. The long-term impact of this type of punishment turned out to be a much higher threshold for reintegration than prison time.

1.3. BLENDING *REALPOLITIK* AND RESPECT FOR THE RULE OF LAW

Once a post-conflict society has decided to pursue systematic prosecutions and purges, an additional challenge arrives. Annette Weinke presents it as follows: "By what means can the state assure that the rule of law is not derailed, that the fragile balance is kept between the victims" expectations of justice and the principles of a legitimate legal system?" The problem a new or reinstated democracy faces is to give prosecutions as much political impetus as possible while still conforming to the rule of law – especially when the successor elites have publicly and firmly condemned the legal derailments of the former regime. Tipping the balance in favor of politics very probably leads to legal transgressions. The outcome can even be victor's justice. Undiluted respect for the rule of law may, however, considerably weaken the political effects of the fight against spoilers. It may, in addition, frustrate the victims. The country reports show how difficult it is to walk the thin line between biased and fair justice.

A first intricate problem arises when parts of the behavior which the courts or administrative agencies have to judge is of a purely political nature, e.g., publicly advertised approval of totalitarian ideas.[5] The question can be illustrated by looking at the Belgian, Dutch, and French cases. Pre-war treason legislation did

5 See O. Kirchheimer, *Political Justice. The Use of Legal Procedure for Political Ends*, Princeton New Jersey, 1961.

not cover the many forms of political action which only in the context of the total warfare of WWII took on a collaborationist dimension. Simple extension of the scope of penal law was not self-evident, since part of the political behavior in question could be seen as falling under the constitutional right of freedom of opinion, speech, or association. A second conflict arises between the legal legacy of the past and the newly enacted laws and/or reinterpreted existing regulations. It involves the *nullum crimen sine lege* principle. A third dilemma-like problem touches the principles of the separation of powers and of judicial impartiality. Who will man the courts and administrative tribunals? Two preoccupations have to be reconciled: respect for the traditional guarantees of fair justice, and the desire of the victims to play a role in the operation. A crucial question here is the eventual victim participation in the activities of tribunals. Such special courts can become instruments of partisan vengeance. They are also vulnerable to governmental control. A final problem arises out of a crucial characteristic of the criminal justice system: it tends to work in a dichotomous mode. Judges have to decide whether a penal law is valid or is not valid in a particular case. But in extreme times, behavior is seldom of the black-and-white type. There are a thousand shades of grey. Borderline cases abound. In its early phases transitional criminal justice is often emergency justice, and that makes it blind to the many nuances. The climate is then seldom well suited for a scrupulous sorting out of all the gradations.

Most national cases have been well aware of the dual agenda in criminal justice after transition. Their official discourse often stipulates that trials and lustration must and will be "swift, severe and fair". The reality is that political concerns of swiftness and severity initially received total primacy. France has, according to Marc-Olivier Baruch, been a post-war exception. The author says that it is difficult to deny "(...) the strong emphasis put on respect of strict procedural rules, and consequently on the important part played by professional judges in the process". The reason, he writes, is clear: "Since post-WWII transitional justice succeeded the Vichy regime, which had made blatant exceptions to criminal procedural guarantees (*non bis in idem*, *nullum crimen*, *nulla poena sine lege*, etc.), it was of the utmost importance for the new legislators not to suffer the slightest suspicion of putting their feet in Vichy's dirty shoes". They did, however, not always respect that intention – as will be discussed in the following paragraph. In the 1970s, priority for politics motivated the initial actions of the successor regime in Portugal and in Spain's choice for closing the books. In post-communist Hungary and Poland, the Constitutional Court was a crucial actor in dealing with the dual agenda. Renata Uitz writes: "The legal framework adopted by the democratic (post-communist) regime in response to the crimes and injustices perpetrated by previous totalitarian regimes was passed incrementally (over an extended period) as a result of a continuing conversation between the political branches and the Constitutional Court". But here, just as was the case in Poland, transitional justice decision-making continuously risked infection by partisan interventions, even out of electoral tactics.

Politically motivated choices were driven mostly by the firm conviction that the chaos, caused by the transition, had to be replaced by order as soon as possible. Speedy restoration of the hegemony and legitimacy of state institutions was another strong motive. Thus, *force majeure* and intense time pressures were invoked to justify exceptional legal and administrative techniques that were, in the words of Weinke, judicially camouflaged reprisals.[6] In most post-WWII countries, retroactive criminal legislation was introduced through interpretive modifications of existing laws and through newly created legislation. The death penalty was reinstituted. The introduction in France of "national indignity" as a sanction played with retro-activity. The principle of collective guilt was brought in. People were disqualified, not as individuals but for their membership in any organisation that supported the former regime. The right of defence was curtailed through restrictions on access to appeal courts, on contacts between lawyers and their clients, and in the form of prolonged internments. The possibility of attenuating circumstances was strictly limited. Finally, lay judges sometimes participated in the activities of the tribunals that tried the collaborators.

The exceptional times argument has, however, a limited plausibility. The question of when these times ended could not be avoided. After two or three years, rule of law concerns gradually seemed to rise on the transitional justice agenda. This shift clearly lies in the line of what was noticed in the discussion of the two previous challenges: flexibility led to a reversal of the initial choices.

1.4. PERPETRATOR- OR VICTIM-CENTERED ATTENTION?

Perpetrator-oriented policies were dominant. This is easy to understand for countries where trials were at the heart of justice after transition: that approach was embedded in criminal-law procedures.

True, all national cases developed a policy of financial and symbolic forms of reparation for victims. But, for a number of years the "(...) compensation policy was not treated as an important subject in the political debate", as the report on

---

6 L. Huyse, 'Transitional justice in Belgium, France, and the Netherlands after World War II: Innovations, transgressions, and lessons to be learned', in A. Czarnota, M. Krygier and W. Sadurski (eds.), *Rethinking the Rule of Law After Communism*, Central European University Press, Budapest, 2005, 135–152.

the Dutch situation concludes. It was not different in most other cases. (Note that up to the late 1980s, specific victim-oriented instruments, such as truth commissions and public hearings, were not available.) And when measures were taken, they were often selective for many years. Scarce resources were one reason. Victim competition was another.[7] There was, indeed, much rivalry in the market for sympathy and understanding. A great deal was at stake: compensation, positive discrimination in education and housing, appreciation in the form of monuments, medals, museums and commemorations, and a place in the collective memory. The most tragic outcome of such competition was the exclusion of Jewish, Roma, and homosexual victims – long after WWII had ended. Total absence of the gender dimension in victim policies also created discrimination.

In a number of countries, self-victimisation of perpetrators became apparent soon after retribution operations started. In the Netherlands "(...) those who felt victimised by the purges developed a counter-narrative (...). They claimed that a certain amount of collaboration had been unavoidable in order to keep society running". In Belgium, even the notion of victimhood was hijacked. Convicted collaborators called themselves "victims of the post-WWII repression". The phrase developed into an accepted expression in the Flemish region of the country. The same happened in Portugal. Those who were involved in the 1974–1975 purges also named themselves victims. And in Hungary, as Renata Uitz notes: "It is a common characteristic of both repressive regimes that in prevailing popular narratives (which do not necessarily portray historical facts adequately) both are often presented as "foreign imposed" or "foreign inspired" in their inception. In such accounts Hungary appears as a helpless victim in the web of world events, and key Hungarian decision-makers are portrayed as doing their best in the circumstances". Annette Weinke writes: "Until the 1960s the discourse of national victimhood, of "German suffering" from the Allied bombing campaign and displacements of German populations in Eastern Europe prevailed, while the problem of active and passive complicity in National Socialist crime was usually ignored".

It would take almost twenty years before the public and political acknowledgment of comprehensive victimhood in its many forms became a reality.

1.5. TO FORGET OR TO REMEMBER?

The past is an extremely complex and chaotic universum of facts and events. Historical myths structure, bring order and give sense to that intrusive legacy.

7 J.M. Chaumont, *La concurrence des victimes: génocide, identité, reconnaissance*, Editions la Découverte, Paris, 2010.

Some myths are officially fabricated. The report on France shows how such tales originate: "(...) France's official memory of WWII and the Resistance was entirely shaped by the Gaullist vision, related both to the legend ("Self-liberated France") and to political instrumentalisation". They also are often accepted by the population, because they are in tune with its own interpretation of what has happened. Sometimes, however, myths miss the ingredients essential to serving their expected function. That was the case in Germany. Annette Weinke says: "Unlike countries like France or Italy, early post-war West Germany had no national heroic myth of resistance to draw upon in building a new positive identity, or to serve (despite all the legal problems) as the memorial anchor for a successful historical and judicial "self-investigation"". In some of the national cases, narratives have been utterly divisive. The authors of the Belgian report write that the country "(...) is characterised by a strong fragmentation of collective memory and remembrance regarding WWII and by the lack of a unifying national narrative. Flanders and Wallonia developed radically opposed narratives". The report on Portugal concludes that the memory of the hectic transition years (1974–1982) is a "(...) much more divisive issue in contemporary Portuguese society than the history of the dictatorship itself".

Selective remembering is a crucial component of any historical myth. The hagiographic legend of a "self-liberated" France is one example. For the Netherlands, Peter Romijn refers to the "(...) well known image of a nation united in resistance, at least in the spirit of resistance, which had managed to purge itself from the anti-national elements". But selective forgetting is even more important. It eliminates unpleasant memories: the derisive defeat of the French army during the German invasion, the collaboration of Dutch civil servants and entrepreneurs, the widespread passivity of the Belgian population towards the German occupier, the part the military played in the rise of the authoritarian regimes in Spain and Portugal. According to Tony Judt "(...) Europe's astonishing post-war recovery would not have been possible (...) without a considerable amount of forgetting in the way war and after-war were remembered".[8]

A narrative, thus, is a negotiated mix of selective remembering and selective forgetting. That compromise is continously changing because of the never-ending confrontation with later societal experiences and with the output of historical research. That is what Marc-Olivier Baruch hints at when he writes: "And the Nation, for de Gaulle, was the State – even at the price of forgetting all the compromises of principle that had been commonplace in the higher ranks of the civil service from mid-1943 onwards. Who could imagine in 1944–1945 that this "realistic" choice would be dearly paid for half a century later, with France struggling with her past through the Papon trial?"

---

8 T. Judt, *Post-war. A History of Europe since 1945*, Penguin Books, New York, 2005, 60–61.

2. CONTEXTUAL FACTORS THAT SHAPED POLICIES

This section discusses four contextual factors that have shaped both homogeneity and heterogeneity in policy making and implementation.

2.1. THE PRECEDING REGIME

The pre-transition regime in the national cases varies indeed considerably. In some it was imposed by way of a military occupation (Belgium, The Netherlands, and Poland during WWII). In others, such as Nazi-Germany, Greece, Portugal, and Spain, it was indigenous. The third type is a mixed one: imported by domestic elites in collaboration with a foreign regime (France, Hungary both during and after WWII, communist Poland). Judging a political system of the second and third brand is an intricate and complex operation. It usually permeates large segments of the political and civil society, both in terms of the institutions and of the population. A full purge becomes almost impossible. An additional problem is that the judiciary, a major actor in transitional justice, too has been wholly or in part closely associated with the outgoing regime.

A second distinction is based on the duration of the previous order. An important consequence relates to the survival of pre-totalitarian, viz., democratic structures. This is clearly visible in the case of Belgium, France, Greece, and The Netherlands. Pre-war institutions and their personnel were shattered, but not eliminated. Once the war was over, they were revived very quickly. Moreover, the occupation was too brief to install an authoritarian political and legal culture. In contrast, in Portugal, Spain, and the former Soviet-dominated countries, almost none of the institutions of the pre-totalitarian past had survived after what was a very long-lived regime. Collaboration or, at least, accommodation pervaded most of the population and did so for at least generations, making it extremely difficult to draw the line between good and bad citizens.

A final factor is the kind and the gravity of the committed crimes and how far in the past they occurred. One relevant example is the fact that the repression in the communist countries was, from the 1970s on, more psychological than physical in nature. The passage of time may have blurred the memories and may have led to a more moderate attitude towards those held responsible for what happened during the last two decades of the system.

2.2. EARLIER EXPERIENCES

Preceding experiences with accountability for state crimes, reintegration, and patterns of remembrance form a legacy that may be expected to interfere in transition justice decision-making. The way such a legacy was present in the national cases varies. Belgium, France, and Holland mobilised pre-war legal codes and frameworks. According to Annette Weinke, the Western successor regime revived pre-Nazi legal principles. In Spain, Hungary, and Poland, earlier experiences with sectarian accountability measures caused extreme cautiousness with regard to trials.

2.3. THE TYPE OF TRANSITION

The regime transitions in the national cases were affected in a variety of ways. A rupture through a military coup or victory is a first type. That was the case in post-WWII Belgium, France, Germany, Holland, and Poland and, later, in Greece and in Portugal. A second type is a negotiated compromise between governing and opposition groups as in Spain, after a few months in Portugal, and in the post-communist countries. Each type created a different balance of power between the former and the new political forces. Rupture guarantees the largest choice of strategies, as it opens the widest windows of opportunity. The consequence of a reform or compromise type of transition is that the agreement between the old and the new forces implicitly or, more rarely, explicitly promises the outgoing authorities a safe passage in return for their total or partial abdication. One significant rationale for such policy of clemency is the need to avoid confrontation with the still present leaders of the former regime. Constraints on decision-making are then very extensive.

2.4. THE INTERNATIONAL CONTEXT

The international context at the time of the transition is another influencing factor. The post-WWII policies were developed in an age when supranational codes and institutions with respect to human rights and the rule of law were either weak or absent. The range of tested transitional justice mechanisms was limited; it was still so at the time of the Greek, Portuguese, and Spanish transitions. This has changed considerably since then.[9]

Yet, the Nuremberg tribunal had set a huge precedent. One major step, compared with the approach in the past, was that guilt and punishment no longer affected

---

9 L. Huyse, *All Things Pass, Except the Past*, AWEPA, Brussels, 2009, 56–70.

an entire society but was aimed at individuals. After 1918, the responsibility for atrocities had fallen on Germany as a nation. In addition, an obstacle in the battle against impunity was partially removed. Until 1945, criminal law answered to an exclusively territorial logic. Every country was master of the decision as to who was guilty or innocent within its borders. That situation now changed. It was to be expected that national tribunals in Belgium, France, Germany, and Holland would operate under the influence of that double development.

On 9 December 1948 the General Assembly of the United Nations adopted a convention providing for the punishment of genocidal acts. A new step was taken on 12 August 1949. On that day, under the auspices of the International Red Cross, the four Geneva Conventions saw the light of day. Simultaneously another set of normative standards was created through the Universal Declaration of Human Rights (December 1948). The European Convention on Human Rights followed in November 1950. All these developments came too late, however, to exert decisive influence on the initial design of transitional justice policies in post-WWII Western Europe. However, Spain and Portugal will demonstrate in the 1970s, by preferring reconciliation to punitive measures, that the effect of transnational laws and conventions overall remained limited.

Since the late 1980s a full-fledged transitional justice paradigm, including a set of international hard and soft laws and, more importantly, implementation-oriented institutions and techniques, has been put in place. In addition, the Latin American experiments with truth and reconciliation commissions had broadened the choice of instruments.[10] This created an international context for the post-communist countries that was utterly different from the one in the preceding decades. The pressure of the outside environment was both direct and indirect. Governments, parties, judges, and legal scholars have regularly invoked international conventions on human rights when preparing or reviewing criminal or lustration laws. In Poland, for example, a local Helsinki Committee has been set up, and its proposals for procedural guidelines have received great attention in the first debates on screening. In Hungary the Constitutional Court has been asked to review two articles of the February 1993 law (on the lifting of the statute of limitations) for their conformity with article 7.1 of the European Convention of Human Rights and with article 15.1 of the International Convention on Civil and Political Rights. A strong motive for not neglecting the signals coming from abroad was the possibility that violations of rule of law codes might compromise the countries" membership in the Council of Europe.

---

10 See D. Bloomfield, T. Barnes and L. Huyse, L. (eds.), *Reconciliation After Violent Conflict. A Handbook*, International IDEA, Stockholm, 2003.

3. SIMILARITIES

What follows is a tentative list of matching choices, strategies, and processes in European experiences. The first five cover the time of the transition and the years that come immediately after it. The remaining three touch upon the whole life cycle of transitional justice policies in Europe.

3.1. A CHAOTIC START

The way policies were discussed in section II may lead to a misunderstanding. The impression has perhaps been created that decision-making regarding the five challenges was reasoned, rational, and led to a planned execution. The reality is different. Most country reports speak about improvisation, indecision, ad hoc measures, failing legislation, extrajudicial executions, uncontrolled purges, and problematic military and political "domestication" of former resistance movements – at least in the early years of the post-transition period. A recurring problem, particularly in the purging operations, was the absence of a clear framework for coordinating programs and actions undertaken on the ground. It critically undermined the impact of later reintegration measures.

These shortcomings are easy to understand. War and repressive regimes leave a society, its (state) institutions, and its population vastly damaged. Furthermore, the end of a violent conflict creates a complex and evolving agenda – achieving a stable peace, recovering the political space by re-installing internal legitimacy and the monopoly of force, restoring the political machinery and the civil service, holding free elections, drafting a new constitution, guaranteeing a minimum of physical security, stabilising the currency, rebuilding the economic infrastructure, demobilising the former armed resistance, helping the victims, keeping the international community on-side, and finally tackling the transitional justice questions of accountability, reconciliation, and reparation. All of this had to be done. It was impossible to take on everything at once. Time and scarce resources imposed painful choices. Adding complexity was the unavoidable conclusion that decisions in one area would impact on others. A confused decision-making was unavoidable.

3.2. PRAGMATIC AND ADAPTIVE DECISION-MAKING

There was, however, no shortage of pragmatism. In less than three years after the transition, seven of the national cases had, confronted with organisational failures and the fast changing national and geopolitical context, partially or wholly adapted their policies. Several of these societies had travelled full circle in their reaction to critical challenges.

3.3. PERPETRATOR-CENTERED POLICIES

Procedural criminal law at the time of the transition entailed, given its focus, a *de facto* marginalisation of victims. Another common feature is the badly organised return into society of those who were punished.

3.4. SELECTIVITY IN ACCOUNTABILITY AND REINTEGRATION MEASURES, AND IN REPARATION POLICIES

Official discourses promised fairness and equity in the implementation of punishment of perpetrators. However, retribution impacts on macro-processes that are crucial in any transition from war or repression, such as the reconstruction of the state apparatus and the economy. Considerable leniency in the dealing with suspected administrative and economic elites permeated the actual policy, leading to grave inequality in punishment. Selectivity in designing victim policies was the product of the inevitability of scarce resources, the outcome of victim competition, and self-victimisation.

3.5. POLITICO-STRATEGIC CONCERNS DOMINATED

Authorities claimed that their decisions were built both on strictly political and moral grounds. In reality, particularly in the early years of the process, choices were predominantly based on politico-strategic deliberation.

3.6. A LONG-TERM PROCESS[11]

"Like in a magnifying glass", the report on Germany notes, the trial (in 2011) of former concentration camp guard Ivan Demjanjuk "(...) allows us to focus on issues that continue to connect the Second World War with the post-war era down to this day". In Spain, the authors of the country report write: "(...) from 2004 until 2007, the drafting process and later approval of a crucial reparation law aimed at addressing the most important pending issues of the Civil War and

11 Of course, it may seem a bit too early to predict an analogous life cycle for the post-communist countries. But a number of signs are already there.

the dictatorship has led to the adoption of a series of measures that (...) have opened many controversies and brought the issue of memory to the public sphere". The two citations are exemplary for what appears as the main similarity in the experiences in Europe: dealing with a painful past is a process that stretches over several generations. The continent still struggles to leave WWII behind. Spain is nowadays literally and figuratively exhuming its past of civil war and repression. Accountability questions, the core business of transitional justice, are being asked in almost all countries. Reconciliation, truth seeking, and reparation – the other faces of the process – also remain unfinished. Annette Weinke speaks of "(...) a secular, transnational transformation process that began immediately after the war and continues today, more than 65 years later".

The process never came to a standstill. But the pace of its course accelerated brusquely from the mid-1960s on for the post-WWII countries, and in the late 1990s for Spain. History started to take revenge. In both cases the leap came some twenty-five years after the transition period. At first sight, Portugal and Greece look like the exception to the rule. According to the report on Portugal, occasional memory eruptions do arise. They are provoked by unresolved cases or by new revelations. But the authors write that these are "(...) however ephemeral and do not involve the general public". Nonetheless, the future of the Salazar period archives has led to bitter debates. And the memory of the chaotic transition years is still a divisive topic in Portuguese society. In Greece, sections within the society are unhappy with the way accountability was dealt with after the Junta regime.

Two questions arise. What were the core manifestations of what looks like a never ending looking back? And why did they happen?

3.6.1. What?

Substantial issues are at the heart of the return of the past. Marc-Olivier Baruch writes that in France "(...) the crack was in the metal from the beginning. Post-WWII transitional justice's failure mainly comes (...) from the incapacity (or the refusal) to give answers to key-questions". Indeed, quite a few of the challenges that immediately after the transition had been on the political and public agenda were revisited.

Then the initial preference for a perpetrator-centered approach, a first example, came under heavy fire. The German Federal Republic only very slowly developed "(...) a climate of empathy that allowed to the until-then ignored and traumatised victims a public acknowledgement as 'moral witnesses'" (Annette Weinke). It was the birth of what this author calls a "universalist discourse on victims". In other post-WWII countries, part of the publicly voiced criticism in the 1960s and 1970s was directed at the selectivity of the erstwhile victim policies. Compensation and the acknowledgment of the suffering of Jews, Roma, and homosexuals would at last follow. What started a quarter of a century after WWII is in certain ways still present. Marc-Olivier Baruch notes that in February 2009 the French Council of State "(…) officially recognised the willful participation of France's collaborationist Vichy government in anti-Semitic persecution that had long been attributed to Nazi occupying powers. It was 65 years after WWII was over". It took the political elites in The Netherlands almost sixty years to present apologies for the post-war Dutch governments" treatment of the Jews. In Spain the identification and exhumation of mass graves today provide visibility to victim's claims.

Another issue dealt with the question of accountability. Several aspects of the initial policies were now criticised: the lack of respect for rule of law principles, the clemency for certain categories of perpetrators (e.g., captains of industry), or, in the case of Spain, the total absence of punishment. In Belgium an eventual amnesty for those who collaborated with the Nazis still regularly appears at the political agenda. Also, the search for a proper balance between forgetting and remembering the past was reopened.

Such continuous resurgence of challenges even seems already to mark memory politics in post-communist societies.

3.6.2. Why?

A number of factors have played a role. Epochal change in generations, the report on Germany says, "(…) influenced the society's relationship to the past. By the 1970s at the latest, as the former Nazi functionary elites left the stage and a new, less compromised group took charge of business (…)". A similar development occurred in Spain. Many witnesses who experienced the greatest excesses of the dictatorship at first hand are now in their seventies and eighties. They have always remained silent, saying nothing, for example, about where the mass graves were located. Now that their end is in sight, they are willing to share this information. Then, there is the generation of young forty-somethings. Their attitude to the legacy of the old regime is more distant, freer. Now that their cohorts are occupying the political arena, the bars built by the authorities around the past are gradually disappearing. Was it still necessary to keep the collective memory locked down? Was Spain not mature enough to confront its past without fear? Had the time not come to hunt down some of the myths that had grown up? "Intergenerational justice", a recently coined expression, justly characterises these developments.

Other causes transcend age groups. They are linked with global changes in the area of justice after transition, such as the effect of evolving international human rights norms and visions on fair trial; the availability of a critical mass of profound historical research and media reporting; the coming of a new transitional episode in the post-communist countries; new trials of WWII perpetrators (Eichmann in Israel, Barbie and others in France) as catalysts; and the echo-effect of similar developments in neighboring countries.

Some of the wide-ranging societal changes since the 1960s and 1970s are another source of the shifts in the vision of transitional justice. The time's tendency to call for far-reaching political, social, and economic reforms led to critical questions about the complete failure of the post-war successor elites to realise such radical transformation. In addition, elite-inspired and -induced silence on the way the initial challenges had been tackled had kept the immediate post-WWII episode out of the public debate for many years. The rising demands for transparency in political life were retroactively projected on the past. Holland is a remarkable example. The authors of the Dutch report show that the early policy choices were taken mostly in silence, hidden from the public. An open debate was avoided by restricting the flow of information and by emphasising the urgent need to close ranks. Those who had sympathised with the enemy were "treated" by professionals: judges, civil servants, professors of criminal law or criminology, probation officers, and psychiatrists. From the 1970s on, though, the forced silence could not be kept intact. The foundations, on which the post-war verdicts were based, had not become part of the collective memory, which again and again led to questions of "how" and "why".

3.7. COMMON CHALLENGES

The issue of justice after transition confronts a society with a set of unavoidable and recurring challenges, which in some cases are almost dilemmas. No national cases has escaped these crossroad choices: prosecute or forgive, exclude or include perpetrators, prioritise political rationale or respect for the rule of law, develop a perpetrator-centered or a victim-oriented approach, forget or remember.

3.8. THE CONSIDERABLE IMPACT OF THE OUTSIDE WORLD

The role of international interference has been continuously apparent during the whole period that the book covers (1945–2000). This may be surprising for what are called the first (post-WWII) and second waves (the 1970s) in the history of justice after transition. But, as Annette Weinke concludes, in the case of (West) Germany of the late 1940s national "... trials of Nazi crimes, reparations and restitutions, and delayed personnel purges were never strictly domestic issues. The operative German actors always had an eye on the special "German" situation, which was manifest in the obligations of international alliance and integration with the West and in the constraints of the German-German system conflict". The obligations of alliance that resulted from the Cold War situation were a factor of influence in other national cases too. Involvement in colonial wars, as in France and The Netherlands, was another source of external influence. In Portugal and Greece the regime transition and its immediate aftermath were affected by the military engagement in Southern Africa (Portugal) and in Cyprus (Greece).

TRANSITIONAL JUSTICE AND MEMORY DEVELOPMENT IN EUROPE

Nico Wouters

1. HOW TO APPROACH TRANSITIONAL JUSTICE AND MEMORY?

Henry Rousso marks the post-Nuremberg period as the era of the "judicialisation" of the past, in which the legal domain became one of the dominant "vectors of memory".[1] I agree, but the essential question remains how the judicial vector of memory interacted with the other vectors. This conclusive chapter considers the impact of transitional justice (TJ) policies on longer term memory development. These are often perceived to be separate. It is assumed that states in transition first entered a TJ phase to "turn the page" and afterwards developed a politics of memory to consolidate the status-quo their TJ policies had created.[2] I would like to connect TJ policies and longer term memory development by assuming that TJ policies have had a profound impact on the way societies dealt with the legacy of the dictatorial/war past on the longer intergenerational term.[3] The nature of TJ measures – their broadness/inclusiveness, their timing, the specific nature of the measures, their long-lived effects, their political use (instrumentalisation, etc.) – had a lasting impact on subsequent memorial regimes. The historic European TJ policies are in this sense part of a larger societal settlement that continues to shape collective memories today.

---

1 H. Rousso, 'History of Memory, Policies of the Past: What For?', in K. Jarausch and T. Lindenberger (eds.), *Conflicted Memories. Europeanizing Contemporary Histories*, 2007, Oxford/New York at 23–37; H. Rousso, *The Haunting Past: History, Memory, and Justice in Contemporary France*, Philadelphia, 2002, 286.

2 J.K. Olick and D. Levy, 'Collective Memory and Cultural Constraint: Holocaust Myth and Rationality in German Politics', *American Sociological Review* (1997) 62, 921–936.

3 We derive the term 'memory making' from Heidi Grunebaum. She investigates how the narrative on the past constructed by the TRC impacts the everyday lives of ordinary South Africans (and how this narrative is reinforced or contested). H. Grunebaum, *Memorializing the past: everyday life in South Africa after the Truth and Reconciliation Commission*, Somerset/NY, 2011.
See also: E. Naidu, 'Review Essay. Memory beyond transitions: the role of memory in long-term social reconstruction', 2012), 6 *IJTJ*, 161–171.

I will use the national chapters in order to detect, analyse and explain certain longer term patterns. This is not an easy feat for several reasons. First, because of the heterogeneity and specificity of our historic cases. There are three groups of case studies (post 1945, the 1970s and post-1989), each with different temporal contexts and lengths. Several authors stress the "uniqueness" of their case. Indeed and by definition, national specificities predominate in these national case studies. A second problem simply lies in the fact that international pattern-analysis spanning several decades involves a staggering amount of potentially relevant variables and tropes, such as the politics of memory, public history, private and public memorialisation, the role of the media and the influence of scholarly research, the role of civil society and self-organising mnemonic communities, developments in judicial contexts and changing public norms. These (and other) aspects all operate within autonomous (and therefore sometimes contradicting) dynamics. Yet they are all relevant to some degree.

It is clear that we first need concepts and methodology, even with regard to terms such as "longer term" or even "transitional justice" itself. There is a real danger of anachronistically projecting the latter on our historic cases. We have to bear in mind that for the post-1945 cases, the term (let alone the field) "transitional justice" was non-existent.

How do we define and limit the "longer term"? Several authors have attempted to establish a sequenced TJ life cycle model, for example John Torpey. His four concentric circles represent large successive chronological phases of TJ policies: first a period of transitional justice policy implementation, followed by reparations, followed by apologies (a phase characterised by the gradual interaction between victims and perpetrators) and then to conclude with what he labels a phase of "communicative history". He defines the latter as "a history oriented toward mutual agreement by the various parties that participate in re-writing historical narratives on the basis of a claim that they are (most) directly affected by the history in question". According to Torpey, this contains memory development, memorials and historical consciousness.[4] Torpey seems to suggest a TJ life cycle with certain universal chronological sequencing.

The term "memory" has already been mentioned ("communicative memory", "memory making", "the politics of memory"), and indeed, we need to define it. What we now call memory studies is a body of literature as impressively large as it is heterogeneous. It treats memory in all its forms and its often difficult relationship with the historic profession.[5] Many "types" of memory have been distinguished over the years; social memory, collective memory, cultural

4 J. Torpey, *Politics and the Past*, NY, 2003, 6.

5 G. Cubitt, *History and Memory*; U. Raulff, 'Marktwert der Erinnerung: Ein Historiker bekämpft den aktuellen Gedächtniskult', in *Frankfurter Allgemeine Zeitung*, 5 May 1998.

memory and public memory, to name but a few.[6] The terms "remembrance", "recollection" or "commemoration" have come to gradually replace "memory". Jay Winter and Emmanuel Sivan, for example, prefer the term "collective remembrance" over "collective memory", to stress the importance of "agency, activity, creativity".[7] It is exactly to focus on the latter that I will treat memory not as a "thing" or a content embedded in certain *lieux de mémoires* or as a collective product of a mnemonic community but, rather, as a dynamic social-cultural process.[8] This is an open and integrated concept. It includes "(...) the operations of power that leave their mark not just on the representations of the past that are produced within society, but on the social relationships that govern transmission".[9] I will not put the memorial products or the social activities themselves centre stage but will emphasise the process: the continuously evolving societal negotiation on the past and its changing dynamics between several actors and variables, in this case related to war/dictatorship and TJ policies.[10]

Struggle and power are essential parts of this process: "if particular representations of the past have permeated the public domain, it is because they embody an intentionality – social, political, institutional and so on – that promotes or authorises their entry".[11] Obviously, political power is an essential focal point in this.[12] However, what is commonly known as the "politics of memory" cannot be equated with this social process; rather it is part of it. To look at collective memory/remembrance as a dynamic social-cultural process of struggle for memory creation may seem evident, but in reality not many studies use this as basis for empirical study.[13] We obviously have the advantage of nine case studies, which gives us the possibility for an empirical approach. From the

---

6 R.N. Lebow, W. Kansteiner and C. Fogu, *The Politics of Memory in Post-war Europe*, London, 2006, at 28.

7 The first phrase of Winter's and Sivan's introductory chapter is: "collective remembrance is public recollection"; J. Winter and E. Sivan, *Setting the Framework*, 7.

8 G. Cubitt, *History and Memory*, Manchester/New York, 2007 (quotation 16). "social memory is a process (or set of processes), and processes are composed of social and cultural practices, which combine over time to produce effects in human consciousness and human social relationships" (quotation Geoffrey Cubitt, *History and Memory*, 18).

9 G. Cubitt, *History and Memory*, 178.

10 J. Winter and E. Sivan, *Setting the Framework*, 9.

11 N. Wood, *Vectors of memory*, 2.

12 J. Habermas, 'The public uses of History', in (1988) 44 *New German Critique*, 40–50. "To a large extent, the conflict between remembering and forgetting involves the undecidable political question of how to relate the temporal dimensions of the past and present". B. Bevernage, *History, Memory and State-Sponsored Violence. Time and Justice*, Routledge, 174.

13 'For all the present obsession with 'memory thinking', there have been almost no studies of the nexus between memory and political power (...)'. J.-W. Müller, *Memory and Power in Post-War Europe. Studies in the Presence of the Past*, Cambridge, 2002, at 1–2. The author himself gives two good examples of such studies on the power-memory nexus: N. Frei, *Vergangenheitspolitik: Die Anfänge der Bundesrepublik und die NS-Vergangenheit*, Munich, 1996; J. Herf, *Divided Memory: The Nazi Past in the Two Germanies*, Cambridge, 1997.

nine national chapters I distilled five cluster-themes or -questions which I will use for the analysis below:

1. Is there a universal sequenced phasing in European TJ life cycles?
2. What was the impact of the national politics of memory?
3. What kind of TJ-related issues invoked memory incidents/irruptions?
4. What was the role of local memories and civil society memory agency?
5. How do we explain the large shifts in memory regimes?

These questions are highly interrelated and even overlapping. They mainly serve as an analytical framework, to be placed on our nine case studies. Our case studies will hardly answer all of these questions satisfactorily. Nevertheless, where they lack sufficient depth or detailed research data, they can at least suggest relevant questions for further research.

This approach can be considered to "historise" memory.[14] Memory (or remembrance) becomes a historical political, cultural and social process like any other.[15] Therefore, and to pick up some issues of the introduction, this historisation of memory could be the asset the historic profession brings to the field of TJ.

2. CAN WE SEE A SEQUENCED TJ LIFE CYCLE?

Do our cases reveal some kind of universal fixed chronology; a succession in the way Torpey suggests (from top-down TJ policies, to memory incidents and irruptions, to growing dialogue and finally a historic consensus)? And if so, how can we define these phases and separate the specific-national from the universal-transnational?

National specificities are clearly dominant in our case studies. This matches current views on international memory development. R.N. Lebow, W. Kansteiner and C. Fogu conclude from their comparative research that there was never a "European collective memory" on WWII, "(...) nor is there any generalisable similarity in the phases identified by our authors as characteristics of each nation's politics of memory".[16] Indeed, our cases also show that realities are much more complex than sequenced models. If perhaps we might still

14 See: B. Benvindo and E. Peeters, 'La mémoire de la seconde guerre mondiale comme régulation sociale', in (2012) 3–4 *BTNG/RBHC*, 10–19.

15 Perhaps countering the often formulated criticism on the 'turn to memory' that the latter constitutes a retreat (or flight) from 'real' historical research towards more 'presentist' issues. G. Cubitt, *History and Memory*, 21.

16 R.N. Lebow, W. Kansteiner and C. Fogu, *The Politics of Memory*, 294.

distinguish some kind of first "core phase" of TJ policies, in which TJ policies were developed and implemented, we immediately encounter problems when trying to outline a second phase. When the focal point of policies shifted towards the direct consequences of trials and purges (early releases, pardons, re-integration of perpetrators etc.), this could be considered a new (second) phase, but how should we distinguish it from a third or fourth one (a "post-TJ phase", to use the term Paloma Aguilar and Clara Ramírez-Barat use for Spain)? Annette Weinke talks about "(...) the contradictions and asynchronicities of the West German politics of the past", while Renata Uitz explicitly writes about the "merger" of different TJ phases for Hungary. Phases overlap and merge, developments regress and memory incidents seemingly disappear, only to resurface again. So indeed, all of our cases (more or less explicitly) show that the reality of memory development is too complex to be locked up in neat transnational phases.[17]

When we keep in mind that we do not want to create a transnational fit-all model, comparing the cases in order to analyse phases is useful and even necessary. Let us begin with post-1945 cases. First, there is a short phase in which trials and purges (1945–1947) co-develop with the larger transition (the priorities of political and socio-economic restoration first and foremost). Already during this phase, there seemed to be a general feeling of disappointment (Baruch says for France: "global dissatisfaction"). The purges were considered too lenient by some and too harsh by others. Even as they were being developed, TJ policies (mainly trials and purges) seemed to be immediately recognised as failing to fill the hopes for some grand scheme of "national renewal", built up by 1944–45.

During the following years (1947–51), the political-judicial machine took over. In general, persecution was mitigated with counter-measures such as early releases, pardons and to a certain extent re-integration. Peter Romijn and Erik Schumacher talk about a "differentiated mildness" that replaced the initial overall severity in the Netherlands. This shift happened in all four cases after 1947 with a series of measures between 1947–53. Generally speaking, it was implemented by the judiciary first, endorsed by the political elite second and finally, (grudgingly) accepted by the general public.[18]

This gave way to the third phase after 1951. Political-judicial, material and cultural traces of the war/occupation are so omnipresent that memory incidents occur on an almost daily basis, but without stirring much public interest anymore. The

---

17 G. Cubitt, *History and Memory*, 176–178.

18 This didn't mean a small number of trials were still underway and could go on for years (in France until 1960 for example), but mostly only the heaviest cases remained.

acute transitional phase was over, and the politics of memory took centre stage (which was clear in France, the Netherlands and West Germany). This coincided internationally with the Cold War, whose framework would end the initial "liberal internationalist legalist" ideals implemented in Nuremberg. National elites began to direct the legacy of occupation. For France and the Netherlands, this meant creating political consensus around one unifying narrative. For France, this was the myth of the Resistance and the self-liberating France. Baruch describes this entire era as "overshadowed by General de Gaulle". This does not mean that memory incidents – such as trials or early releases of perpetrators – did not occur during this phase. In France for example, public protest arose in 1949 when René Bousquet received a light sentence and again in 1953 when the Alsatian perpetrators of the SS massacres in Oradour-sur-Glane received special amnesty. There were also other headlines, such as the death of the imprisoned Pétain in 1951. There are also many Belgian and Dutch examples. In this phase, the past was still dominantly present but could not rupture national policies.

In this era, these West European states created national counter-movements against the internationally imposed legal frameworks (Nuremberg, the Universal Declaration of Human Rights, etc.). National states took the politics of memory into their own hands and created solid national myths in which victim recognition was pushed aside. This could be considered as one large phase encompassing TJ policies to consolidating politics of memory. As such, the "technocratic" approach Weinke distinguishes in West Germany after 1949 could be considered the specific West-German version of this development. West Germany could not fall back on any resistance-related narratives, but it had other means. German elites ("technocratic conservatives") strategically connected the idea of the *Rechtsstaat* to the old German *Normenstaat* who allegedly had survived the perceived "anomaly" of the Nazi era. The judiciary and political elites contrasted "legitimate" German national laws with the imposed illegitimate international ones, leading to a de facto culture of impunity against Nazi perpetrators. This policy was "(…) justified above all by a 'top-down' definition of the state and security interests. Both public opinion and demands for justice (…) were regarded as factors that could be largely treated as negligible quantities" (Weinke). Amnesty and immunity laws (as well as the suspension of the mandatory application of CCL nr. 10 by German courts) were quickly implemented. The abolition of the death penalty was politically legitimised as a "counter-Nuremberg". The release of the three last *SS-Einsatzgruppen* commanders in 1958, along with the general support and solidarity they received, marks the success of the consensus reached.

We entered a decidedly new phase during the 1960s. Several factors converged to create the first true large paradigm shift (see below). Again, this was evident in

France, West Germany and the Netherlands (but less so in Belgium). It was perhaps most clear in France, where things were so strongly connected to De Gaulle and the political system he represented. When different trends converged, the legacy of WWII was used to attack a system and the "national-conservative" post-war elites that represented it. Memory incidents suddenly grew stronger. Books, films and documentaries contesting the constructed consensus and revealing 'hidden pasts' surfaced regularly. Elites found it increasingly difficult to suppress these incidents. In France, President Georges Pompidou's pardoning of Paul Touvier – and the protests it engendered – was indicative of the new period. It would later culminate under Mitterand's presidency when the president himself became involved in several larger incidents (Jewish protest in 1992 and especially in 1994, when Mitterand's own Vichy past, and his continued contacts with Bousquet until 1986, were put centre stage). This clash of generations was also clear in West Germany. Also in this phase, the Holocaust began its gradual rise as the "iconic memory vector" it would later become (also in West Germany, where attention to the Holocaust was minimal prior to the 1960s). This large phase would continue for over two decades (until about 1989). Memory incidents over war and TJ-related issues continued to occur. Although separated by many years, we can consider the French documentary *Le Chagrin et la Pitié* (1969, yet not shown on French public television until 1982) and Lanzmann's film *Shoah* (1985) as belonging to the same larger period. As individual memory incidents, these public debates can be isolated, but taken together with all other incidents, they characterise a larger era. Indeed, Lebow, Kansteiner and Fogu write that "(...) the revision of World War II collective memory in Eastern Europe started in the mid-1980s, well before the fall of the Berlin Wall (...)".[19] This runs parallel with what we see in Western Europe, where the 1980s in our four post-1945 cases were a decade of increasingly stronger memory incidents building up to a new paradigm shift after 1989.

After 1989–94, another phase emerged. Eastern European memories became "unfrozen" and a global human rights culture became the foundation for a new memorial regime on war and TJ. This phase was characterised by strong memory irruptions (see below), which gave way to new policies of memory and reparation (a policy of apologies, for example). While socialist president Mitterrand still encountered trouble in 1994 and refused to apologise for the Jewish roundups by the Vichy police, merely one year later right-wing president Jacques Chirac could resurrect unresolved TJ issues by apologising for the same event in the name of France, "(...) the land of Enlightenment and Human Rights, where people are welcomed and given asylum (...)". As Baruch writes: "France's official discourse was now in accordance with historical findings at last". Although this particular shift from Mitterrand to Chirac was obviously specifically French, it marked a

[19] R.N. Lebow, W. Kansteiner and C. Fogu, *The Politics of Memory*, 295.

European shift observable in all other cases. Flanders, in particular, was very similar to France in this regard. Decades-long consensus-constructions – albeit French-national or Flemish nationalist – were quickly replaced by another memory regime. Notably, the perceived shortcomings of the first TJ phase became one of the bases for the new memorial paradigm. Weinke sees the emergence of a "self-reflexive memory culture" and "brand identity" for the newly united Germany.

In the three 1970s cases, TJ policies were broader and from the outset explicitly part of a larger political settlement aimed at stabilisation, normalisation and democratisation. Certainly in the case of Spain, they were the outcome of a relatively well-prepared negotiation process. For all three countries, national reconciliation was a common political goal. This meant, in general, relatively few purges and trials in Greece and, to a lesser extent, also in Portugal. In Portugal there was a short initial phase of "wild purges" and radicalisation, which affected the military, the judiciary and especially the civil service; a period also of improvisation and lack of coherent policy vision. It was quickly controlled, but the final consolidation of democratic institutions would come only in 1982 (with the creation of the Constitutional Court, Raimundo and Pinto). For Greece, the core phase ran from 1974 to 1980. National consensus and reconciliation was constructed with "normalisation" as a priority, meaning democratisation. This determined TJ policies, with a stress on victim-reparations, a strategic selection of high-profile trials of junta figureheads and a de-criminalisation and re-integration of the communists as a legitimate political party in Greece. Trials were indeed strategically focussed, and the purges were consciously downsized.

Spain went even further. The country did not include trials or purges (or anything akin to a truth commission) in its TJ policies. The amnesty law of October 1977 was meant to close this past for good. As in Greece and Portugal, reconciliation (and amnesty) had to make a clean break with the dictatorial past. It was essential to show and prove that parliamentary democracy had the capacity to unite and stabilise, rather than divide and create violence. All three countries developed a parallel reparation policy for gradually increasing categories of victims. This was not a "coherent policy" from the beginning, but it clearly followed a general upwards curve. In Spain, several reparation laws between 1976 and 1984 would further recognise victim categories (victims from Francoism first, but gradually from either side during the Civil War) and offer different forms of reparations and rehabilitation.

Essentially, TJ policies and the politics of memory emerged from this general political programme of reconciliation. This was not fundamentally different from the mechanics of the politics of memory that France, the Netherlands and West Germany developed after 1951. Impunity, lack of specific victim-recognition and constructed silences were part of those settlements as well.

In the three 1970s cases, this consensual policy seemed to have worked for several decades. For Spain, Aguilar and Ramírez-Barat mark a shift around 2000. They write that Spain enters a "post-TJ phase" at this time. It was marked by the traditional things we also saw in the post-1945 cases after the 1960s: a succession of larger memory irruptions and a crumbling of the consensual memory policies. Some Spanish autonomous communities adopted new reparation and memory policies earlier than the central state. They took several reparation and memorialisation measures from 2003 onwards, initiatives that seem closely linked with the global human rights culture (the "Memorial Democratic" in Catalan in 2007, appointment of a commissioner for the recovery of historical memory in Andalucía, the creation of the council for memory in 2006 in Galicia and other measures). For some autonomous community governments, the "recovery of memory" related to civil society initiatives seems crucial. The central Spanish parliament itself in 2007 approved the "law of historic memory" (as it is popularly known). This was a landslide law which marks the replacement of the previous memory consensus. This law contained several basic elements: reparation, subsidies for exhumations and civil society led projects, removal of Francoist symbols and preservation and access to archives. If we project parallels with the post-1945 cases, we might assume that in Spain the dam has been punctured and the country has now entered a prolonged period of continued memory incidents. In this sense, the 2007 law was not the end but the beginning. Indeed, Aguilar and Ramírez-Barat write that civil society groups have already critised the law and proposed new additional legal initiatives.

The two post-1989 cases (Hungary and Poland) have their own specificities, most obviously the fact we have two distinct successive authoritarian periods as well as a very recent transition.[20] Both post-1989 cases had what Renáta Uitz called a "prelude" to post-1989 TJ measures between (mainly trials between 1945 and 1950).[21] This meant that earlier TJ measures had to be re-assessed after 1989. The ambivalent legacy of such a "prelude to transitional justice" casts a shadow over current TJ measures. As in Spain, Hungary and Poland had a negotiated transition with the aim of achieving a consensual national "reconciliation" and

---

20 One could point to the ambivalent democratic nature of the political systems in Hungary and Poland during the first years after 1989: see the chapters of Bachmann and Uitz in this volume.

21 The communist regime took several measures themselves to deal with the former regime, primarily with trials and purges of perpetrators (for Hungary for example, 27.000 people were convicted by people's courts between 1945 and 1950) and ethnic cleansing (of Germans, most notably). Similar specificities exist for Poland, where the first phase TJ policies were complicated by the dual Soviet-German occupation(s) during WWII, internal political power struggles between 1945–1948, the massive forced migrations and relocations of populations after 1945 and the way the new Soviet powers after 1948 used TJ policies to combat anti-communism.

"national unity" (cf. the Polish Round Table talks). Here also, concerns about the future by far surpassed the will to address the past. Polish prime minister Tadeusz Mazoiecke metaphorically underscored this by drawing a "(...) thick line between today and the past". As in the 1970s cases, this led to a TJ policy primarily concerned with creating a sound and stable basis for a future society rather than retributive policies (or full truth-seeking policies). There were hardly any trials or purges (only rare cases of certain middle-range officers suspected of torture) leading to large elite-continuity after 1989. In Poland and Hungary, the popular media supported this strong reconciliatory mindset. Both cases would also be caught up in the global human rights culture and the influence it extracted on TJ policies and memory development (see below).

These phases – descriptive as they may be – nevertheless show several things. They confirm the problems of neatly phased ruptures and universal sequencing. If we take the "iconic" year of 1968 as the moment of rupture, one would ignore the memory incidents and signs of change present during the 1950s. The paradigm and memorial changes of the 1960s and the 1990s did not fall from the sky. Basic elements that constituted their rupture were already active at work during the 1950s and the 1970s–1980s. For West Germany, Weinke characterises the 1980s as a decade with "contradictory trends", with a large impact of the TV series *Holocaust*, the rise of regional-local memorial activities and with historians who tried to redefine their societal role. The 1980s laid the foundation for the "inflationary proportions" of the human rights paradigm during the 1990s (Weinke). This is explicit in Belgium, the Netherlands and Spain. This descriptive chronology points to something we will tackle further below: the importance of generational shifts and the importance of the emerging global human rights culture (or the re-emergence of it, if one considers the International Military Tribunal in Nuremberg as the beginning of this era). The descriptive chronology also shows one large parallel in the ways these different states tried to construct national consensus by means of a politics of memory. It also indicates how, when and why such a consensus could gradually crumble. To conclude: although this chronological overview does not offer universal-transnational sequences it does offer universal mechanisms of memory development.

3. WHAT WAS THE IMPACT OF THE POLITICS OF MEMORY?

The "politics of memory" refers to institutional memory: the "(...) elite constructions of memory" that "shape the memories of groups and individuals", the "(...) efforts by political elites, their supporters, and their opponents to construct meanings of the past and propagate them more widely or impose them on other members of society".[22] Politics of memory are essential because "(...) the state remains relevant both as the carrier of the brunt of warfare (...) and as a major producer and choreographer of commemoration".[23] In a broad sense, the politics of memory can include many different types of policies aimed at the creation or reinforcement of a national memory. Its impact is difficult to determine, because "(...) it is notoriously difficult to determine the actual effects of attempts to influence public opinion even in micro cases".[24] Politics of memory is therefore juxtaposed to bottom-up civil society agency, and to local and popular memories. The struggle between the top-down consensual politics of memory and alternative memories is an essential dynamic. Powerful as this national institutional memory might be, it is it is clearly far from all-controlling. Politics of memory cannot always produce "effective mental shackles". Popular and local memories are hard to control.[25]

An interconnected aspect is the politicisation of TJ-related memory development. With politicisation I mean the injection of current political agendas on memory- and TJ-related policies; or the way these policies were used to support or settle current political scores (most typically between the political left and the right).

For the post-1945 cases, France and the Netherlands seem textbook cases for a strong politics of memory. Central politics of memory emerged quickly. Indicative in the Netherlands was the founding of the National Bureau for the Documentation of the History of the Netherlands in Wartime on 8 May 1945 (!), resulting in the *Rijksinstituut voor Oorlogsdocumentatie* (RIOD). Internationally, this institution of "national historiography" was the earliest of its kind. In France, the national resistance myth was later institutionalised by Gaullism. West Germany obviously lacked this "heroic myth of resistance". This was further enhanced because of the de-legitimation of socialist and communist resistance. Unlike in the Netherlands and France, there was no "memorial anchor" for positive national identity. Also, the de-nazification proceedings were quickly used to detach a relative small group of "Nazi elites" from the bulk of the German population. The result was a different unifying narrative, that of 'German victimhood' (focusing on topics such as the Allied bombings and the displacement of German populations in Eastern Europe). This was to West Germany what the 'heroic resistance myth' was for France: a dominant underlying narrative used to build a consensual politics of memory.

---

22 R.N. Lebow, W. Kansteiner and C. Fogu, *The Politics of Memory*, at 10 and 13 respectively.
23 J. Winter and E. Sivan, *Setting the Framework*, 38.
24 R.N. Lebow, W. Kansteiner and C. Fogu, *The Politics of Memory*, 10.
25 R.N. Lebow, W. Kansteiner and C. Fogu, *The Politics of Memory*, 15.

The three 1970s cases deal with an entirely different context, with a much longer era of dictatorship and with strong elements of civil war (Spain, Greece). The priorities of these countries after 1974 were to "normalise" the country, integrate it politically and diplomatically and consolidate democratic norms. Reconciliation was not a utopian dream but a hard political necessity. This context created a larger willingness from different political sides to create an early consensual political settlement around national reconciliation as part of TJ policies.

Spain constructed an initial unifying narrative on the peaceful nature of transition itself. In Greece, "national reconciliation" was the general aim of a politics of memory from the start (as Stefanos Katsikas writes: "reconciliation was essentially a political project with relatively narrow bounds"). Indeed, the politics of memory designed in 1974 in Greece explicitly saw the seven years of dictatorship as some sort of 'cathartic finale' of a longer era of internal division and civil war, from the 1940s to the 1960s. The first governments failed to implement a cohesive politics of memory. Local civil war commemorations for instance, simply kept taking place. Only after 1981 – when Papandreaou's party gained a full majority in 1981 – would a stronger politics of memory gain ground. New reparation measures for certain victim categories (including also dismissed civil servants in 1985) were taken, while responsibilities during the junta-past were avoided. The Greek central foundational *lieux de mémoire* of this politics of memory became the narrative of "national" resistance during the Civil War, repeated in legal texts, local monuments, schoolbooks and *musea*. Similar to France and the Netherlands, the Greek 'national resistance during WWII' received a broad an inclusive "national" definition. No more divisive local commemoration services: "municipal councils were encouraged to erect monuments to the resistance throughout Greece, and school textbooks would henceforth include details of all the different groups" (Katsikas). Greece reinforced this after 1989 (broader pension rights, erasing criminal records) with a stronger memory politics on the civil war and the Resistance, for instance with a law that formally removed the negative term "guerilla war". In general terms, the pillars of Greece's organised consensus were: 1) a strategic selection of trials and purges (swift trials of the main figureheads, the "instigators" and the "torturers" for example, combined with relatively narrow purges); 2) a strategic policy of reparations for main victims; and 3) a strong politics of memory based on an older, pre-dictatorial national foundational myth (resistance during WWII) meant to avoid possible divisions in society over the more recent dictatorial experience.

As in Spain, this seems to have worked relatively well for several decades in maintaining some kind of consensual silence. There were some heated debates in parliament (for instance, an incident during debates in 1982 on the recognition of the anti-Nazi resistance of the Communist National Liberation Front), but no real memory irruptions. However, there are signs that the national consensus could be gradually crumbling. Katsikas considers the Greek politics of memory as not very strong, going as far as to write that "the state no longer claims the right to control memory of the past. Instead, within a revitalised democratic environment, various groups have been able to remember and articulate differing interpretations" (Katsikas). Apparently, civil society memorial activity is very much alive in Greece, and the essential question is how durable the current consensus or balance is.

The first two Portuguese constitutional governments also put "reconciliation" and "pacification" centre stage (Raimundo and Pinto). In terms of TJ policies, this meant re-integrating "a large proportion" of people condemned after 1974; a mitigation and re-integration policy that continued in the first half of the 1980s. Like Greece, Portugal tried to use trials/courts to satisfy public sentiments. In Portugal's case, this was the Humberto Delgado Popular Tribunal (established in 1977, with trials in 1978). Also as in Greece, strategic reparation policies (compensation such as pension rights, symbolic recognition) were more important than accountability. After the initial purges/trials, to some extent uncontrolled, a strong policy of re-integration of condemned people was carried out between 1977 and 1982.

Portugal seems to be characterised by a lack of a central politics of memory. There are some local and bottom-up initiatives, which try to fill the gap. During the 1990s, a Museum of the Republic and Resistance (a local Lisbon initiative) was opened. Lobbying from a civil society organisation "Do Not Erase the Memory" led to the opening of Museum of Resistance and Freedom, again in Lisbon (in a former prison). A November 1999 exhibition that celebrated 25 years of Portuguese democracy paid some attention to the dictatorship. But in general, António Costa Pinto and Filipa Raimundo write: "(...) the creation of a museum about repression and the dictatorship is notably absent. All such projects presented in the first two years of the transition were abandoned because of lack of interest within civil society, including from political parties (...) or a lack of enthusiasm on the part of the state". In June 2008, the Portuguese parliament unanimously approved a resolution that confirmed the importance of passing on knowledge and memory of the "resistance against the dictatorship", but this was purely symbolic.

Raimundo and Pinto write that the re-integration of convicted perpetrators "solved" all the TJ issues, and these measures "(...) seem to have closed the debate on the past". As they write: "(...) there is no major political debate on the past or civil society claim for compensation or acknowledgement of resistance".

The absoluteness of this statement is rather remarkable, as is the suggestion that this is a permanent situation.

Hungary started its politics of memory only very gradually and prudently. Only in 2000 was memorialisation put centre stage, when parliament voted both the Holocaust Memorial day and the Victims of Communism memorial day (both of these days were put in April, but were not granted the status of fully fledged national holidays). Subsequent commemoration days were approved as well, including a Day of Hungarian Freedom (commemorating the day the last Soviet soldier left Hungary).

Belgium seems a peculiar case. Despite the fact that during the 1920s and 1930s Belgium was able to develop a fairly strong centralised politics of memory around a unifying patriotic war-memory (for example, surrounding the "King-Soldier" Albert I), and despite the fact that after WWII this pre-existing patriotic landscape of memory strongly influenced memory making of the new war, Belgium was unable to develop a central politics of memory after 1945. Belgian war memory, especially over TJ issues, became strongly divided among political and linguistic lines.

The Netherlands and Belgium are often represented as completely opposite cases with regard to their memory politics.[26] Although these differences are real, we should avoid an all-too-strict schismatic model. Under the surface of differing state policies are many local similarities. To paraphrase Baruch, the "cracks in the metal" that divided Belgium after 1945 were also present in France (and in the Netherlands, for that matter). Even a strong consensual politics of memory did not exclude local and individual diversity. Romijn and Schumacher explicitly note this, when they write that even during the first years of TJ policies Dutch citizens "(...) let themselves be guided by their own judgments", often "strongly determined by private experiences". A strong central memory paradigm was accepted but not always interiorised. Romijn and Schumacher write about the Netherlands: "Recent research shows that the overall image was more diffuse than the often-assumed categorical rejection". Indeed, in the Netherlands, early memory incidents revealed ongoing tensions. The lack of victim recognition would remain dormant for several decades, only to come back with a vengeance during the 1970s. Also, Romijn and Schumacher mention that local memorial initiatives were present from the very beginning in terms of memorial activities/ gatherings as well as the erection of monuments: "Before the war, a tradition of

26 Lagrou, *The Legacy of Nazi Occupation: Patriotic Memory and National Recovery in Western Europe, 1945–1965*, Cambridge, 2000; B. De Wever, 'Goede Belgen, foute Vlamingen, grijze Nederlanders', in E. Corijn, *Collaboratie in Vlaanderen: vergeten en vergeven?*, 2002, Antwerp, 51–62.

reservedness had existed in the Netherlands when it came to statues and monuments in honour and remembrance of the national past. Now, there was a proliferation". The Dutch state simply succeeded in controlling and centralising this bottom-up memorial activity, inscribing it in the national myths. The centralised Dutch and French politics of memory were successful for several decades because they could incorporate local memorial initiatives. The "national" monument on the Dam in Amsterdam started as a local initiative but was quickly co-opted and inscribed in a national policy.[27]

During the gradual memorial shift of the 1960s, specific local dynamics became intertwined with the agency of newly emancipating social groups and organised victim groups. Because there was no place for them in the unifying, egalitarian state politics of memory, various groups began to organise alternative commemoration ceremonies. One good example is homosexuals. Exactly the same happened in Belgium, albeit perhaps several years later. The central Dutch politics of memory initially tried to respond by incorporating these groups, the Jewish victims first and foremost and gradually other groups as well (the first monument for the victims of the persecution of Roma and Sinti was erected in 1978).

An interesting question therefore is what conditions allow for a politics of memory to be successful for a certain amount of time. Most of our cases show that a strong politics of memory can come under pressure on several fronts. Most important are: bottom-up civil society agency (see below) and political instrumentalisation and division. Here we will limit ourselves to political division.

Belgium is interesting as an "anti-case". If any successful politics of memory needs a political consensus around some national narrative or unifying myth, Belgium is a case where this was not there to begin with. A political right-left divide on TJ policies emerged quickly after the liberation, during the early phase of TJ policy development itself (Luyten and Wouters). Once the opportunity was missed in 1945, a re-launch proved impossible. Political divides between the left and right and between Wallonia and Flanders only deepened after 1951. Each linguistic and political group became a separate memory community within the Belgian state. Each political initiative relating to the memory of war and TJ (amnesty, reparations, recognitions and memorial activities) was immediately politicised along political-linguistic lines. This was reinforced during the 1960s, 1970s and 1980s, when the federalisation of the Belgian nation-state gradually began.

---

27 B. Benvindo and E. Peeters, 'La mémoire de la Seconde Guerre mondiale comme régulation sociale: une perspective belge', in XLII/2–3 (2012) *BTNG/RBHC*, 10–20; R. Van Ginkel, *Rondom de stilte; Herdenkingscultuur in Nederland*, Amsterdam, 2010.

Several other cases show what happens when national political consensus gives way to party interests. It happened in all post-1945 cases, such as in France when successive presidents tried to deconstruct Gaullism after the 1960s. But it is especially clear in other cases, whose politics of memory started out with a national reconciliatory and consensual politics of memory. As Aguilar and Ramírez-Barat note, the post-2000 memorial legislation (as well as other measures) and the memory irruptions leading to it happened in Spain under strong political polarisation between left and right. Indeed, both authors clearly conclude that political and legal resistance to more broad legal initiatives (trials of perpetrators, declassification of archives but also truth-seeking mechanisms) after 2010–11 remains very strong, certainly after the conservative party gained an absolute parliamentary majority in November 2011. Both authors conclude that there still remains a strong and broad reticence among many circles to recognise the repressive aspects of Francoism. The Garzón incident (a true memory irruption, see below) had a strongly polemical effect, polarising the left and the right over how to deal with the authoritarian legacy (and especially whether or not to annul amnesty and prosecute perpetrators).

In Hungary, things became highly politicised when the conservative-Christian coalition government in 2010 used the notion of "true transition" to support and legitimise a fundamental political project, supported by a grand "memory project". This involved a new constitution (in 2011, replacing the communist 1949 constitution and confirming the political rupture), reinforced politicisation of the memory debate between left and right and to a lesser extent increased memorialisation policies (new memorial holidays, rebuilding the square with new monuments in front of the Parliament building). True transition meant re-opening the debate on accountability and at the same time de-legitimising the socialist party as heirs of the communist regime. Attempts to adapt the recently installed Day of Hungarian Freedom lead to heated parliamentary debates between the left and the right, perhaps indicating that the area of memorialisation policies will also become a field for further political tension between left and right.

In Poland, demands for retribution and accountability quickly resurfaced; as in Hungary in a highly politicised context. Many groups saw former communist networks maintaining themselves (also economically) after 1989 and felt they had somehow "lost" the transition. Demands for a renewed TJ policy based on accountability (meaning a large-scale as opposed to very individually limited lustration policy as well as de-communisation) primarily came from right-wing parties. After the first 1992 lustration incident (when a resolution was passed to list members of government and parliament who had "collaborated" with the communist secret police and secret services), lustration (and to a lesser extent de-comunisation) became a recurring political topic of debate in Polish parliament (without any significant legal "solution"). In 2006, a populist right-wing multi-party coalition made an attempt to implement large-scale lustration measures, yet this was halted through the Constitutional Court, which declared the measure unconstitutional. Certain right-wing parties continued to use the lack of retributive policies to explain certain current societal problems, politicising the memorial debate.

So also a reconciliatory negotiated transition can easily lead to politicisation and division, often over (the lack of) accountability. But quickly the entire legacy of authoritarianism is at stake (persecutions and accountability, truth seeking, preservation of memories and reparations). Few cases (only Portugal and Greece, in fact) lack this fervent politicisation, at least so far.

The consensual politics of memory always includes organised (partial) silence: silence on the role of groups of perpetrators, silence on specific suffering of victims but also silence on certain large events. Nancy Wood uses the concept *Lieux d'Oubli* to indicate the prolonged and structural existence of these organised silences.[28] The most outspoken example is the Holocaust. Despite the enormity of the event, post-1945 TJ policies paid no specific attention to it in terms of accountability or victim-reparation. Group-specific recognition of Jewish victims did not fit into the patriotic memorial paradigms. Between roughly the 1950 and 1970, the Holocaust was a *Lieux d'Oubli* in France and Belgium, and to a lesser extent the Netherlands and West Germany.

The case of Spain shows that silence can work in several ways; it could also be broad tolerance for the continuation of symbols from the Francoist past (the Valley of the Fallen being only the best known example). One of the key elements of the 2007 law was this systematic removal of symbols on the local level and a conversion of the Valley of the Fallen, transforming it into a new *lieux de mémoire* with new meaning.

Greece offers a remarkable example in this regard. In August 1989, on the symbolic anniversary of the battle for Grammos, an enormous archive (personal security and surveillance files) was destroyed in order to neutralise the divisive effect it might have on society in the future. This could be labelled a "politics of oblivion". The post-1945 cases seem to indicate that this type of measure will not have its desired effect in the long run. It is not so much the actual knowledge on the facts itself that is at stake – people will have way of unearthing this when they want to, even when parts of the archives are destroyed – but the underlying context; the readiness of society to address and acknowledge these facts. In this

28 N. Wood, *Vectors of memory*, 11.

sense, history seems to show that destroying archives to avoid divisive debates makes little sense (and it will be interesting to see how Greek society itself will look back on this destruction within one generation).

Organised silence is part of (and partially explained by) a strong national politics of memory. For a certain period, a certain dominant national paradigm seems to be able to sustain a resilience against alternative or contesting interpretations and memory incidents, including bottom-up civil society and local memory initiatives. In such a context, local- or group-memories are doomed to remain locked up in their rather limited social range (within a framework following separate "social scripts" of memory).[29]

4. WHAT KIND OF TJ-RELATED ISSUES INVOKED MEMORY INCIDENTS/IRRUPTIONS?

Luc Huyse uses malaria as a metaphor to describe the longer-term process of memory development: years of calm are replaced with sudden, often unforeseen, periods of strong tension ("high fever"). However, it seems that under the surface of a national consensual politics of memory, controversies over war- and TJ-related issues were always present, without necessarily evolving into larger scale events.

Let us simply assume that a period of relative calm is a period in which a general consensus with a strong founding myth is accepted within a national context. This consensus outlines the limits of a certain interpretative framework that has a resilience towards alternative dissident narratives and visions. This dooms dissident voices to remain "locked up" in their specific mnemonic community. A period of calm therefore presupposes a certain balance between the elite politics of memory and local and/or group-specific initiatives.

A "memory incident" occurs when this consensus is fundamentally contested on a national societal or political scale. The dissident narrative escapes the boundaries of its closed memory subgroup. Memory incidents trigger some kind of (brief) national political or public debate. I will define a "memory irruption" simply as the step beyond this; a memory incident that becomes so strong and uncontrollable that it fundamentally damages or ruptures the existing consensus, in the longer run marking the shift towards a new memorial regime. It is therefore a matter of both scale and nature: the incident has to be large enough, and it has to be indicative of certain underlying societal changes or shifts.

---

29 J. Winter and E. Sivan, *Setting the Framework*.

What type or kind of TJ-related issues instigated memory incidents or even irruptions and why (not)? What type of TJ-related issues created the most discussion? Is there a pattern in this type of "triggers"? And how were they transmitted? On this, Lebow, Kansteiner and Fogu write: "the catalysts for such debates were diverse, as were the fora where they took place".[30] Indeed, this diversity is clearly confirmed by our case studies.

During the immediate post-1945 phase, memory incidents were still a direct result of TJ-policy decisions (protests against early releases of notorious war criminals is the most important example). But after 1951, memory incidents become highly diverse.

In Belgium, the post-war trials and purges were the real cause for memory incidents and irruptions rather than the war/occupation past itself. Here there quickly developed one magnet for memory incidents/irruptions: the demand for amnesty for convicted collaborators (in Flanders).

Weinke observes the importance of "judicial confrontations" as catalysts for societal debates in West Germany; these confrontations were the result of the increasing tension between the extensive reparation policies for (amongst others) Third *Reich* soldiers and civil servants on the one hand, and the lack of reparation policies (material, symbolical) for many groups of Third Reich victims on the other. This became more relevant during the second half of the 1950s. Weinke places a moment of change in 1956 with the Fischer-Schweder trial and another in 1958 with the foundation of the Central Office in Ludwigsburg. These events started a new kind of investigation into the Nazi era (Weinke). This was not yet a true irruption of memory and a shift (it did not quite yet rupture the neglect and marginalisation of different victim groups for example).

Romijn and Schumacher distinguish several types of memory incidents in what they call Dutch "public memory": first, scandals surrounding key figures relating to their individual wartime past (when their collaborationist past was unearthed, resulting in the so-called Dutch "affairs"); second, "trail-blazing" historical research; and third, influential television broadcasts.

In the Netherlands, the role of Dutch national elites was tied relatively early on (during the 1960s) with the Nazis' persecution of the Jews. Another recurring issue for public debate throughout the 1960s was the fate of the last remaining war criminals in Dutch prisons (the four – later three and two – of Breda). This issue continued to provoke heated public debates whenever pardoning was on the political agenda. Such was the case in 1972, when societal forces were mobilised against pardoning. Days before the debate, an influential victim-

30 R.N. Lebow, W. Kansteiner and C. Fogu, *The Politics of Memory*, 21.

oriented documentary was broadcast. The underlying rhetoric was revealing: "Dutch society should not abandon the victims of persecution *again*". The matter, by the way, would never be successfully resolved until the convicted war criminals perished in prison. Two "unresolved" TJ-related issues were consciously linked during the 1960: the failure of the purge itself and the failure of radical social, economic and political reform. The main recurring question basically was whether the wrong persons had been purged (and whether the real perpetrators had escaped punishment). Romijn and Schumacher write: "The supposed failure of the purge was seen as a symptom of a policy pursued by Dutch elites after the war to limit the post-war reforms to a necessary minimum". With this shift, the issue of specific recognition and compensation/reparation came to the fore as central issue. In the Netherlands, this also gradually became a "recurring subject of emotionally charged debate".

Memory incidents/irruptions continue to today. In the 1990s, documents revealing the inhumane nature of the post-war restitution policy caused much public anger (and, in typical Dutch fashion, new historical research). The issue of differentiated victim-recognition was also strong in the Netherlands and France, two countries whose TJ and subsequent memorial policies had initially been based on non-recognition of different victim-groups. The evolution in these countries mapped a gradual change from perpetrator-oriented incidents (scandals around pardoning of war criminals, scandals around the hidden war-past of public officials) to victim-oriented memory incidents/irruptions (cold treatment of victims by society, lack of recognition).

Aguilar and Ramírez-Barat note a distinct rise of memory-related debates and initiatives in Spain after 2000: political declarations and homages in 2002 about more recognition of victims of the civil war and the dictatorship, the appointment of an Inter-Ministerial Study Commission (on the victims of civil war and Francoism) in 2004–06 and political debates on additional measures (new reparation measures for certain victims in 2005; transfer of seized archives in 2008). The year 2006 was proclaimed as the "Year of Historical Memory". These political memory-initiatives were developed in a context of rising political tensions between Spain's two main political parties. The reports of the Inter-Ministerial Study Commission in 2006 caused strong divisive political debates on how to proceed and "(…) the bitter debates in parliament soon reverberated in the public space through the media". At the same time, Aguilar and Ramírez-Barat report, "despite the existence of this clear two-sided confrontation in the public domain, the truth is that the average Spaniard was hardly involved in the debate". There is one incident, however, which both authors seem to label as a true broader societal debate, and it is important to note that this issue at its core was related to the (lack of) prosecution of perpetrators. This was the incident that arose over the decision by Spanish Judge Baltasar Garzón to support the judicial claims made by several families of "disappeared persons" and therefore open the case against 35 former leading members of the Francoist regime. In doing so, Judge Garzón basically tried to circumvent the 1977 amnesty law. He explicitly used international human rights legislation to legitimise his decision. The National High Court resisted this decision, and Garzón himself was indicted by a an extreme right-wing organisation for abuse of power. This incident did what apparently many memory incidents before had failed to do: it sparked a broader debate (primarily between the political left and the right) which was a true societal memory irruption. On 24 April 2010, widespread demonstrations took place in more than twenty Spanish cities in support of Garzón, which both authors label as "(...) the first demonstration in favour of the recovery of historical memory in Spain". Garzón's indictment also led to wide international protest and involvement in the discussion, internationalising this Spanish incident and showing how truly global the human rights culture had become. For a detailed analysis of this debate (and its outcome), see the Spanish chapter in this book; suffice it to say here that this 2008–11 debate was a true memory irruption that began to shake the 1977 "amnesty paradigm" for the first time in Spain.

For the Portuguese case, Raimundo and Pinto note as the most important recent Portuguese memory incidents a debate on the use of the archives of the dictatorial regime (and the political police) in 1996–97, a scandal in 1998 when a well-known perpetrator publicly admitted he could freely travel between Spain and Portugal and the election in 2007 during a TV-show of dictator Salazar as "greatest Portuguese of all time". These things, especially the last, caused heated public debate. Yet, these memory incidents clearly did not rupture current memorial regimes. The incidents quickly faded out, without lasting effect (so far). As such, they were isolated incidents. But at the very least they show that the dictatorial past does have the potential to instigate (brief) heated debate.

In Hungary, memory incidents initially focused on secret service member-lists and archives. The symbolic reburial of former Prime Minister Imre Nagy (executed during the 1956 revolution) can perhaps be labelled as a first important memory irruption. Uitz even writes: "It is not an exaggeration to claim that from the perspective of transitional justice measures the carefully manufactured reburial of Imre Nagy attained deeper significance in the Hungarian context than the collapse of the Berlin Wall and the opening of the Iron Curtain on the Hungarian-Austrian border". The event also had lasting effects. It reinforced the visibility and agency of victim organisations in Hungary and enhanced broader popular support for democratic consolidation. As such, Uitz suggests this was a memory irruption that triggered a paradigm shift (also, for example, pushing the communist movement towards transition and "reconciliation"). This event seems to have had political and public impact. As Uitz writes: "TJ measures were often shaped by scandals, revelations and realisations which were not apparent (or not even familiar) during the early days of transition". Uitz characterises these issues as "crucial milestones" in triggering public debate. However, the debate did not tackle deeper mechanisms (about the broader, everyday societal involvement with the communist regime). Uitz characterises this as a "fragmented" debate, aimed at identifying agents and pushed forward by individual scandals and memory incidents. It is probably much too early for this. Nevertheless, we might hypothesise that we can detect a "dormant" memory irruption waiting to happen here. Therefore, perhaps this is the outline of some future memory irruption.

In Hungary, rehabilitation and compensation did not seem to cause fundamental discussions. On persecution however, Uitz writes that after 2000 "(...) parliamentary debates on convenient means of persecuting political opponents do not cease". The debate (1994–2010) seems to have been only between political powers (parliament) and the Hungarian Constitutional Court. The latter resisted lustration policies as well as accountability measures, for example, causing ongoing legal debates about the legality, the depth and width of lustration.[31]

There were also some more public debates, which transcended the purely legal discussions. These more public debates (and the most likely candidate for real memory irruptions) primarily concerned the activities of the communist secret services (dismantling or continuity, access to archives and identifying and purging agents). Uitz confirms this: "Scandalous accounts on the surveillance of public figures were in the centre of reflection". Lustration and access to communist files did cause some public scandals/debates, for example when it was revealed that prime minister Medgyessy, who had previously been cleared by lustration, had worked for the communist Secret Services. In fact, several prominent politicians refused to resign after their involvement with the repressive apparatus of the communist regime was exposed (notably Prime Ministers Gyula Horn and the aforementioned Péter Medgyessy). This type of scandal – the past catching up with public (political) figures – is very similar to what we saw in the post-1945 cases (France and the Netherlands most notably), which show that this type of scandal/memory incident could continue for many decades (for example, the case of Mitterand after 1994).[32] Uitz writes: "Accounts

---

31 Hungary bypassed the remarks made by the Constitutional Court on the retroactivity of the TJ measures argued by the Constitutional Court by using international criminal law (indicting people for crimes for which the statute of limitations does not run out under international criminal law; sometimes with some difficulties; see the chapter of Uitz in this volume.

32 'Perpetrators' in this context for Hungary relates to the communist past, since perpetrators of the Second World War era (and the Holocaust) and of the 1956 revolution were not alive or active anymore after 1989.

of the less than completely prominent subjects of surveillance (such as musicians) which might make the subject accessible to the general public started to appear only recently, due to the delays with access to files". The issue of full disclosure of these archives remained present in the public forum (Uitz talks about "perpetual scandals and agent lists flooding the public square"); leading to the instalment of two successive expert-committees in 2007 and 2010 charged with investigating the whereabouts and conditions of parts of the archives. Remarkably, the last committee was disbanded (December 2010) before it could publish its final report. The files of the Hungarian Communist secret services could have played an instrumental role in creating some kind of wider-scale societal dialogue. So far, this debate has not occurred, but the potential is clearly there.

In Poland, memory incidents/irruptions were few and far between. In fact, Klaus Bachmann mentions only two that seem to meet the criteria. Perhaps the most well known irruption abroad was the controversy incited by J.T. Gross's book *Neighbours* (2001). Exhumations were undertaken on the Jedwabne site (where the pogrom had taken place in 1941), and Bachmann writes: "a long and fierce debate among historians and the media started about the scope and meaning of "Jedwabne" and finally Polish president Aleksander Kwaśniewski issued an apology during a commemoration ceremony in Jedwabne". The essential topic of this debate was Polish anti-Semitism. Gross's subsequent books continued to incite public and political debates. Another memory incident was somewhat of a Polish wiki-leaks incident, when in 2005 a journalist published records of (alleged) secret informers. The journalist had downloaded the information from the Institute of Public Remembrance. This again caused public/political "lustration" debates.

Bachmann writes the lack of retribution was "controversial in society, politics, culture and the media". He also writes that a 'popular majority' became gradually more in favour of retributive policies. There also seem to have been some movement towards re-assessing the TJ policies.[33] However, Bachmann doubts whether the memory incidents and irruptions so far have caused a true paradigm shift in Poland (such as Polish collective remembrance "catching up" with the global human rights culture). His conclusion seems to be that "the shift is taking place among the members of small, relatively well-educated and increasingly cosmopolitan cohorts, which transcend age groups" (Bachmann). Is this the first stage of a more broader and popular shift in Poland?

---

33 The Polish 'Ombudsman of Public Interest' (described by Bachmann as a 'de facto prosecutorial position'), responsible for public-figures' declarations following lustration legislation, fueled public attention on lustration. The Institute for National Remembrance would try to open up cases against main perpetrators (failing to instigate an efficient stream of trials). Bachmann also mentions several interesting Truth Commission-like initiatives after 1989.

Most memory incidents/irruptions we detected in our cases could be traced back to unsuccessful TJ policies, unsuccessful in that they were retroactively perceived by certain parts of the population as having been unsatisfactory. If we consider memory irruptions as unresolved TJ issues in this sense, we can distinguish two important topics in the four post-1945 cases and in both post-1989 cases: the persecution of the Jews (ignored as a separate issue during the national TJ measures in 1945–51) and the collaboration of national elites with the occupational/dictatorial regime. The patriotic TJ and memory policies in all post-1945 cases protected the interests of the nation-state, therefore avoiding all critical assessment of the roles played by traditional state elites (civil service, police forces, politicians etc.). Many of the scandals/memory irruptions that occurred later were a direct result of elite continuity which TJ policies had consolidated after 1945 and 1989.

These unresolved issues, however, were injected with new meaning, retroactively becoming an implementation of new political, legal and moral values and norms. The best examples are probably the second wave trials during the 1980s and 1990s, for example in France and Germany. On the most basic level, these trials could be considered as revisiting "unfinished business", but in reality they were about much more. They took place in different contexts and gained additional meanings. The much-delayed Papon-trial in France in 1997 was even at that time recognised as a watershed "memory-making event".

When dealing with the nature of memory incidents/irruptions, we have to consider the modes of transmission as well. What fora and media transmitted memories and turned issues into memory incidents and irruptions? Were popular books, films and documentaries important as triggers of memory incidents/irruptions? And what role did historiography play?

We can assume that some memory incidents/eruptions occur when hitherto unknown facts are made publicly known. This is the case, for instance, when archives remain closed for scholars and the public. Reality is complex. In fact, many historic European cases show that silence was not necessarily the same as not knowing the facts. In many cases, a consensual silence existed while the facts themselves were either known or at least available to anyone who wanted to access them. Why would it take until 1994 before Mitterand's war past was "made public"? The most obvious example of such a silence, again, is the Jewish persecution. That the Antwerp police actively rounded up thousands of Jews during the summer of 1942 was hardly a secret. Nevertheless, it would take several voluminous scholarly works during the 1980s, 1990s and after 2000 before the Jewish roundups in Antwerp would become a recurring topic of public debate in Flanders and Belgium (and would get central attention in the high profile Holocaust Museum in

Mechelen which opened in 2012). So, more than having access to the facts, the real issue is the broader societal acknowledgement of the events.

A classic view on the role on historiography in TJ-related issues is given by Charles S. Maier, who describes a cyclical pattern in historiography from consensus to revision to a post-revisionist phase. He writes: "Historical controversies finally end, in fact, not when there is agreement on one narrative; this is usually never achieved. They end where clarification is reached on two or perhaps three basic stories, whose representatives understand the issues that separate them (…). Such an agreement forms the basis of the contrapuntal narrative (…)".[34] In other words, history creates a consensus where there is agreement on which things parties should disagree about. In literature, the impact of historiography as a trigger for memory incidents/irruptions is often downplayed. J. Winter and E. Sivan simply write: "Professional history matters, to be sure, but only to a small population".[35] It is clear that public history (the popular and broader transmission of knowledge to a wider audience such as movies or *musea*) has a much wider appeal. There is rightly so a lot of attention to broader cultural vectors of memory: novels, films, television, *musea* and social and digital media.[36] Lebow, Kansteiner and Fogu also give great importance to the popularised forms of history representation, claiming that "(…) almost across the board, films, plays and television series were catalysts for revisiting the past (…)".[37] But is the size of the audience always a reliable criteria to measure societal impact? Perhaps academic research has a slower and more gradual impact. We have very little impact-measurement, and, in fact, we know very little about the way historical knowledge and discourse are reinforced, distributed, multiplied, transformed and received to and by a larger audience.

Our cases show (again) large diversity in this regard. In the first phase, the dictatorial/war past was still so omnipresent that it was represented almost daily, through different media: "the memory trace was so powerful that no rehearsal was needed initially to recall it".[38] Once the temporal distance became greater, however, the frequency and manner of representation of the events became more essential for its commemorialisation.

---

34 Ch.S. Maier, 'Overcoming the past? Narrative and negotiation, remembering and reparation: issues at the interface of history and the law', in J. Torpey (ed.), *Politics and the past: on repairing historical injustices*, Lanham, 295–304.

35 J. Winter and E. Sivan, *Setting the Framework*, 8.

36 N. Wood, *Vectors of memory*, 6; A. Huyssen, *Twilight Memories: Marking Time in a Culture of Amnesia*, London, 1995.

37 R.N. Lebow, W. Kansteiner and C. Fogu, *The Politics of Memory*, 34–35.

38 J. Winter and E. Sivan, *Setting the Framework*, 14.

In the Netherlands, early scholarly historiography (1950–70) mattered a lot, but primarily because it could be considered as an integral part of the central politics of memory. Historian Lou de Jong and "his" RIOD-centre had an explicit political mandate to write a national war-history in which good and bad were clearly set apart, consolidating the post-TJ memorial regime. In the Netherlands, historiography had a strong influence (both authors call it "a form of public reckoning"); either through individual research and influential publications, or through their involvement in the resolution of certain individual scandals or affairs. From the 1960s to the 1980s, the Dutch often relied on commissions of "wise men" to resolve matters (which could be labelled as some kind of truth-seeking mechanism, albeit rather *ad hoc*). "National" historian De Jong played an essential part in this. No such thing existed in Belgium, where historiography on WWII would only slowly begin to rise as late as the 1970s. When historian Hans Blom gave a lecture in 1983 in which he appealed to transcend the right-wrong approach to WWII, this also created a paradigm shift in historiography (although only partially in public memory). In the Netherlands, historiography also played an important role in bringing (early) wider attention to the persecution of the Jews. So here we have a case where historiography did matter to a certain extent. Portugal also attempted something like an official historiography. A "Commission for the Black Book on Fascism" gathered data and published 22 volumes on repression during the regime. This commission was primarily composed of former opponents of the regime, mostly with a leftist political affiliation.

In our four post-1945 cases, truth-seeking mechanisms were never implemented as such. Mitigation and amnesty policies aside, true reconciliation was never achieved. In the Netherlands, a remarkably early "admission of guilt" (1947) was proclaimed by former leading members of the *Nationaal Socialistische Beweging Nederland* (NSB). This early attempt at reconciliation was rejected by the Dutch population. It would take until 1995 for children of Dutch collaborationists to be invited to the national 4 May commemorations. In Flanders, reconciliation was put on the political agenda between 2000 and 2002. In the wake of the large human rights memorial shift, several large memory incidents occurred, and the legacy of the war and TJ policies were suddenly at the centre of political debates again. Perhaps for the first time in Flanders, "reconciliation" became an explicit term used to launch several societal and political initiatives. Reconciliation was achieved in this sense, that a certain human rights memorial consensus was indeed established in a new Flemish politics of memory.

Belgium offers a nuanced look on the impact of historiography. It played a key role in certain developments but never caused or instigated major incidents/irruptions in itself. The absence of any scholarly-standard Belgian historiography on the legacy of WWII and TJ policies probably was one factor in the fragmentation of war memories and the failure to create a stronger Belgian politics of memory. The fact that the dominant myths surrounding the "anti-Flemish trials" were not debunked by scholarly research until the 1990s is the best example. There were several watershed works that clearly played a crucial role in a (partial and gradual) certain paradigm shift; the works of José Gotovitch and J. Gerard-Libois in the early 1970s caused the first public debates on the cooperation of the Belgian elite (one of the basic "unresolved TJ issues" mentioned above). The works of Maxime Steinberg (on the Jewish persecution) during the 1980s first brought public attention to and debate on the Jewish persecution in Belgium, another major unresolved TJ issue at that time. The works of Luc Huyse and Steven Dhondt (on post-war trials and purges in Belgium) and Bruno De Wever (on Flemish-nationalist collaboration) in 1991 and 1994 respectively were also essential. Yet in Flanders, it was not a scholarly work but a televised documentary series (*The New Order*, by journalist Maurice De Wilde) that caused a true memory irruption in Flanders during the 1980s. This televised series fell back on new scholarly insights but reached audiences of which these scholarly works could only dream. A general assessment on Belgian scholarly historiography is that its impact (and its absence/presence in public debate) were highly dependent upon its interconnectedness with the political and societal context. Some historians followed and made use of ongoing developments rather than determining them themselves.

Likewise, Weinke considers that historiography had little importance for West Germany, defining its role as "(...) a diminished role, as an observer, commentator or moderator; (...) It almost never happened that a historical monograph or a documentary publication set off any of the many public controversies that broke out (...)" (Weinke). Also, regarding the shift that occurred during the 1960s, for example, Weinke quotes Kansteiner who says these 'memory dissidents' gained momentary attention but failed to endanger the existing political history of the regime.[39]

In his analysis of France, Baruch gives a lot of attention to films/documentaries, but historiography (certainly in the first decades after 1945) seems not to have triggered larger debates. The critical work of Peter Novick[40] from 1968 on the post-war trials and purges in France was not translated into French until 1985 (!), while equally critical works of Eberhard Jäckel and Stanley Hoffmann failed to rupture the national consensus as well. Robert Paxton's book came some years later. The many films, however successful, did not turn into memory triggers during the 1960s. Revealingly, Baruch writes: "it was not before 1969, the year de

39 W. Kansteiner, 'Losing the War, Winning the Memory Battle. The Legacy of Nazism, World War II, and the Holocaust in the Federal Republic of Germany', in R.N. Lebow, W. Kansteiner, and C. Fogu, (eds.), *The Politics of Memory*, 102–146, at 114.

40 Novick, *L'épuration française, 1944–1949*, Paris, 1985; transl. from *The Resistance versus Vichy: the Purge of Collaborators in Liberated France*, London, 1968.

Gaulle left the public scene forever, that the most important film was made on the Resistance" (Baruch). We can assume that the large impact of this film depended not solely on its intrinsic qualities but also on its timing; the end of the era "overshadowed by de Gaulle".

For Hungary, Uitz mentions an important documentary film (*The Life of an Agent*, 2004) that used archival footage of the communist regime, although its exact impact on the societal debate remains unclear. In Greece, Katsikas points primarily to silence on the topic. There is reluctance among Greek historians to tackle the history of this period, apparently out of fear of getting mixed up in political debates. In Spain, in contrast, historians played a key role during the large public debates that gradually erupted after 2002. However, as in other cases, historians did not seem to have played a significant part in triggering the "post-TJ phase". For Poland, Bachmann is clear: "scholarship does not play a large role in Poland's reckoning with the legacy of its secret police". Polish academics are present on the so-called "thick line debat" (and lustration debate), but "(...) this is a political rather than a scholarly debate, and some of the participants are even actively engaged in partisan politics". In Poland, it is still primarily foreign researchers who tackle TJ measures and the Polish communist past, apparently with little direct impact on Polish society.

5. WHAT WAS THE ROLE OF LOCAL MEMORIES; CIVIL SOCIETY AGENCY AND MEMORY ACTIVISM?

Civil society related to remembrance is defined by Winter and Sivan as the domain between the family and the state where voluntary social groups, led by secondary (or third order) elites, help shape the process of remembrance.[41] In the context of this conclusion, the essential aspect is the juxtaposition between these civil society memory groups and the national politics of memory.[42]

The importance of civil society agency has already been noted above. Modern civil society memorial traditions emerged after WWI, when social groups and victim groups felt the need to develop new ways of collective mourning and demanded compensation from states.[43] Local civil society agency was

41 J. Winter and E. Sivan, *Setting the Framework*, 28–29.

42 "We may suggest that the dialogue between agents working within civil society and state institutions is an ongoing process of contestation and is likely to remain on of the permanent features of remembrance", M. Van Creveld, *The Transformation of War*, NY, 1991, at 39.

43 R. Bastide, 'Mémoire collective et sociologie de bricolage', *Année sociologique* 21 (1970), 65–108; J. Winter and E. Sivan, *Setting the Framework*, 32.

flourishing after 1918, although national states more or less succeeded in integrating local memory activism into central politics of memory (this was the case even in Belgium). These memory-groups were important because of the agency they could develop. Indeed, these groups became true mnemonic communities; creating specific narratives that through reproduction and rehearsal became memorial frameworks. Individual members within the group had to adhere and conform their individual memory.[44] Memory and remembrance became strongly anchored in social networks.

Therefore, a civil society tradition of remembrance and memory development can be said to have been firmly in place in several European states before 1945.[45] For the post-1945 cases, Belgium is the only country where organised victim groups received specific recognition and financial compensation very early on (in fact, group-specific recognition was an essential part of Belgium's TJ policies; with the Jews being a notable exception). However, this success in terms of recognition and reparation did not necessarily mean these groups (different resistance groups, political prisoners, deportees) could also direct a national politics of memory in their favour. The organised resistance, for example, failed to impose a patriotic paradigm. This early recognition policy institutionalised the victim competition and internal divisions France and the Netherlands would only encounter on a large scale much later. Because of this, Belgium developed a memorial landscape which is often characterised as primarily local.[46] Larger cities (Brussels specifically) have their own local memory culture, although several other cases also note specific urban memory cultures (Aguilar and Ramírez-Barat note the same urban-specific memory for Spain for example).[47]

But this was also more or less the case in France and the Netherlands. In these countries, initial disunity among the former resistance weakened the political impact of these groups. In France, the Netherlands and West Germany, the integration of TJ policies in a national politics of memory led to a lack of victim recognition. The Cold War enhanced this, as victimhood of communists remained difficult. In West Germany, victim groups were marginalised for decades.

Local and civil society memory activism played an important role in the gradual shifts during the 1960s and afterwards, an evolution we could describe in memory and TJ terms as the shift from a perpetrator-oriented to a victim-

---

44 B. Benvindo and E. Peeters, *Les décombres de la guerre: Mémoires belges en conflit, 1945–2010*, Waterloo, 2012, at 220.

45 J.-W. Müller, *Memory and Power in Post-War Europe*, 4.

46 M. Conway, *The end(s) of Memory*.

47 Ch. Kesteloot, 'Toponymie et mémoire de la Seconde Guerre mondiale: Les noms de rues à Bruxelles', in (2012) 2–3 *BTNG/RBHC*, 108–137.

oriented memorial paradigm. This was visible in all countries. Romijn and Schumacher write for the Netherlands: "From the sixties on, the Dutch government took a step back and the policy concerning war criminals became a matter in which the opinions of victims of persecution and members of the former resistance weighed the heaviest". In France, new trials were "the result of militant activity" (with individuals such as Serge Klarsfeld for example).[48] The gradual "second wave of trials" was instigated by individual activists and civil society organisations, not by the state or the judiciary. This impacted the meaning of these trials. During the 1970s and 1980s, the "political and legal debate" was replaced by an "emotional and psychological approach. (...) The meaning of the concepts of "right" and "wrong" changed. "Right" meant taking the side of the victims and opposing pardoning, whereas advocating clemency was the new "wrong" (...)". From the end of the 1970s and during the 1980s, self-organised children of former Dutch political delinquents also asked for recognition as victims: "their stories found a sympathetic welcome, because they fit in with general criticism of the tired cliché of nationwide resistance and responded to the interest in authentic personal experiences". The victim-oriented agency throughout the 1990s led to several new Dutch benefit acts and a new financial-legal framework.

Jewish victims played an important role. Despite early attention to the Jewish persecution in the Netherlands, Jewish victims themselves only came to the fore gradually in the 1970s. Specific recognition and compensation measures by the Dutch state in 1973 happened only after intense pressure and lobbying.[49] In general, Jewish agency paved the way for other organised victim-groups: "In the course of time, one victim group after the other successfully lobbied for special compensation: the Jewish victims of persecution, the civilian war victims, the former resistance and the victims of persecution in the former Dutch Indies, the victims of forced labour in Germany" (Romijn and Schumacher). This coincided with further development of the welfare state in general. States were initially very reluctant to follow this course. The continued effort and memory activism by victim (lobby) groups, therefore, were determinants in reinforcing this shift.[50]

---

48 H. Rousso, *Justice, History and Memory in France*, 284.

49 See the chapter by Romijn and Schumacher in this volume: "Where the concept of a 'debt of honour' had served the lobby of the former resistance, victims of persecution made an appeal to the concept of 'special solidarity".

50 See the chapter by Romijn and Schumacher in this volume: 'The phased and long-winded realization of compensation arrangements for the different victim groups shows that the Dutch government was persistent in its financial restraint and its dislike of making exceptions. Intense pressure from advocacy groups was necessary for a change of policy to be achieved'.

Perhaps the most clear example of the impact of civil society memory activism is Spain. Here, organised victim groups played a crucial role Families of victims began to organise themselves after 2000, and "with a remarkable dose of perseverance, they have managed to introduce the issue of the past in the political agenda of the country (...)". In Spain, "a strong associative movement has been consolidating all over the country". This has strong local roots. This civil society network of regional-local organisations created a "production of memories" through films, documentaries, novels, research projects, exhibitions etc. Civil society organisations were given an essential role in the actual implementation of the 2007 law (especially with regard to the exhumation process), but they did not stop there. These civil society organisations – who are mainly based on the family of victims – created memory incidents and could push towards a true memory irruption through kick-starting the Garzón-incident.[51] Although Aguilar and Ramírez-Barat note that "the great majority of Spanish society" was initially not "particularly engaged" in the many political memory debates in parliament (for example relating to the 2007 "law on historic memory"), the role of civil society organisations in rupturing the consensus and moving towards a new phase can be described as "fundamental".

In Portugal, the victims of purges organised themselves in a reintegration movement, while the trade union movement organised (largely unsuccessful) protests between 1976 and 1980. There was substantial civil society involvement in the purges as early as 1975, which was later controlled centrally by the state. Nevertheless, despite the fact that Raimundo and Pinto write that these issues are "solved", they also indicate a continued bottom-up, local civil society still trying to instigate an active process of memory-making. We already mentioned two recent musea openings in Lisbon (see above). Raimundo and Pinto write: "(...) the majority of the acts of memorialisation have been carried out either by specific political groups or municipalities, in particular those in which the PCP governs". They also note that these memorial activities (celebrations, monuments, street names) "(...) have been consistently present since the transition". Both authors indicate that in recent years, this civil society lobbying for stronger memorialisation increases. This might indicate Portugal could still encounter a "post-TJ phase" memorial shift similar to the Spanish case.

Civil society organisations (victim organisations) also played an important role in Hungary. Several such civil society organisations were essential in "exposing"

51 Although the ARMH (2000) is the most important one, there are obviously many other ones. Aguilar and Ramírez-Barat list some organizations in footnote 47 of their chapter in this volume.

individuals and events, primarily with regard to the memory of the 1956 revolution. They also stimulated some visible, symbolic actions, such as the reburial of former Prime Minister Imre Nagy (executed during the 1956 revolution). Uitz also points out that several of these victim organisations became intertwined to a certain extent with more radical-nationalist groups, suggesting they have become involved with intense political polarisation, making their attitude towards transitional justice as a whole somewhat ambivalent. In any case, access to files and archives was a priority for many civil society (victim) organisations, and one of them, the Agency for History, in fact received official status when parliament transformed it into the Historical Archives of the Hungarian State Security in 2003. This happened, by the way, in the slipstream of the above-mentioned Medgyessy scandal.

So in most cases, civil society memorial activity played an essential role in pushing towards new memorial regimes. A last interesting question might be why in some cases it fails to resonate? Why do certain organised groups win the struggle for memory: simply because of their organisational and mobilising capacity?

When we consider the case of the "failure" of the resistance memory in Flanders, we see a combination of reasons. For decades, the resistance memory was opposed to the dominant memorial regime in Flanders. Martin Conway says that a "(...) protective political subculture" for the resistance in Flanders was missing, suggesting civil society groups need such a protective political culture (with perhaps certain political powerbrokers willing to support their claims) in order to obtain a certain societal impact.[52] Secondly, there were clearly internal divisions that continuously hindered the resistance's ability to produce effective narratives and weigh on public opinion. Also, there were no real individual key figures to represent their group. Flemish resistance memory had a second "missed appointment with history" during the 1970s and 1980s, when it failed to connect with newly emerging victim groups. There was a telling incident during the September 1978 national commemorations at the former concentration camp in Breendonk, when former resisters and political prisoners were less than happy with a group of young homosexuals asking for recognition of their victimhood. Belgian patriotic groups in Belgium failed to connect their narratives and memories to broader societal developments. The case of the resistance in Flanders suggests that group-specific factors – organisational capacity, unity, strong individual leaders with access to political power, effective public memory production – are essential for the impact civil society groups can have on memory irruptions and shifts.

52 M. Conway, 'The end(s) of Memory. Memories of the Second World War in Belgium', in (2012) 3–4 *BTNG/RBHC*, 170–188.

6. HOW DO WE EXPLAIN SHIFTS IN MEMORIAL REGIMES?

This is arguably the most fascinating and ambivalent issue. If we can attribute basic characteristics to a certain consensual interpretive framework that appears dominant during a certain time, when, how and why does this situation evolve into something else? How do we explain the lack of shift in certain cases?

The most important lesson we take from the issues tackled above is certainly that even a so-called consensual memorial regime hides a large memory-diversity right under its surface. From the beginning, there were many (in the words of Cubitt) "(...) hidden contestations, sullen resistances and silent oppressions of memory that can lurk beneath the surface of an apparent acceptance of common structures".[53]

These alternative memories, however, lacked the "fertile ground" to come to full fruition.[54] In France, Belgium and West Germany, local memory activism was present from the beginning. Memory incidents were semi-continuously happening during the 1950s. Two concrete Dutch memory incidents in 1952 were the protest march and petition against the pardon for the former German head of the German political police in occupied Amsterdam and the escape of 23 German war criminals from the Breda prison. In 1956 a newspaper revealed that the then-current mayor of The Hague had surrendered a Jewish family in 1942. Even as early as 1956 this scandal became a broader political and public debate on the war and the purges. Characteristic for the Netherlands is that the persecution of the Jews even arose early on as a major topic for memory incidents (without, by the way, the Jewish voice itself playing any part). Weinke gives similar examples for Germany, such as the Federal Constitutional Court's decision in 1953 to rule out the obligation to restitute de-nazified civil servants, based on the reasoning that Third Reich civil servants had to be considered as complicit to the regime by default. This was a high-profile contestation of national TJ and memory politics.

Yet these and many other incidents that occurred failed to become irruptions or triggers for memory changes. Clearly, one needs the proper political, social or cultural context in order for memory incidents to be able to resonate more

53 G. Cubitt, *History and Memory*, 125.

54 When nations and peoples can feel a strong identification with a certain vision on the past, alternative or dissident visions are felt to be a threat; perhaps these dissident visions will first have to justified in terms of the larger interests of the nation. See: T. Snyder, 'Memory of sovereignty and sovereignty over memory: Poland, Lithuania and Ukraine, 1939–1999', in J.-W. Müller, *Memory and Power in Post-War Europe*, 39–59.

broadly and permanently.[55] Memory irruptions and memory shifts over several decades take place in the context of larger societal evolutions. Weinke labels the entire period between 1945 and 1989 as a one big "(...) secular, transnational transformation process that began immediately after the war and continues today, more than 65 years later", one large "transformative process of cultural modernity".[56] The main question, therefore, concerns the relationship between the memory incident and the underlying societal changes they reflect. Does a certain memory incident trigger certain societal changes, or is it the other way around? Can several memory irruptions enforce a memorial shift through their dominant force, or are they allowed to become important because they express underlying societal shifts?

This is a classic but difficult question. When tackling the shift around 1960 in West Germany, Weinke writes: "it is debatable what was more decisive in this respect: incidental effects like the *Einsatzgruppen* trials of 1957, the anti-Semitic graffiti of 1959, and the Israeli Eichmann trial of 1961, or structural developments like West Germany's entry in Western political and military alliances and the European Convention on Human Rights (ECHR)". For the same period in France, Baruch labels the following important "triggering events": the Eichmann trial of 1961, the French suppression of statutes of limitations for crimes against humanity in December 1964, somewhat later (and especially) the resignation and death of Charles De Gaulle (1969 and 1970 respectively), the Sorrow and the Pity in 1969 but also a scholarly work such as Robert Paxton's *Vichy France* of 1972.

When looking at the ongoing "post-TJ phase" in Spain, Aguilar and Ramírez-Barat first point to the generation change and then to the creation of the Association for the Recovery of Historical Memory (*Asociación para la Recuperación de la Memoria Histórica,* ARMH) for the exhumation processes. Exhumations were one of the major issues of civil society victim organisations in Spain. Perhaps the nature of this issue determined its resonance in society and politics. As both authors write, the ARMH had a "decisive impact in giving public transcendence to collective memory issues and in providing visibility to justice claims". "Visibility" and "transcendence"; both terms suggest that perhaps memory incidents were already present in the earlier phase, but that the specific agency of the ARHM forced a "final push"; it launched enough critical societal mass to act as a leverage to enter a new phase.

---

55 "Past events can only be recalled if they fit within a framework of contemporary interests", R.N. Lebow, W. Kansteiner and C. Fogu, *The Politics of Memory*, 290.

56 A. Schildt, *Konservatismus in Deutschland. Von den Anfängen im 18. Jahrhundert bis zur Gegenwart*, München, 1998.

There are clearly several important factors at work during a memorial regime shift. Can we distinguish a hierarchy of causes?

Like we already said, civil society memory agency was clearly essential to explain a memorial shift. This was the case in all post-1945 cases, and certainly also in Spain. We already discussed this above. There are notable cases where civil society has not succeeded in causing memory incidents/irruptions (Greece, Portugal), despite their local presence. We lack sufficient information to see what is going on there, but the reasons probably lie in a combination of national reasons: lack of a "protective political culture" and internal division (lack of organisational capacity, lack of political lobbying power, lack of effective public memory production).

A second key factor is the relationship between the national-domestic and the international. Lebow, Kansteiner and Fogu focus on the national level. They write: "(...) each country's language and culture is more than a setting in which contestations of the past take place; they are key to understanding the often idiosyncratic ways in which the past has been constructed and contested in their respective countries".[57] Further on they write: "the first result of our comparative analysis is that politics of memory take place primarily within a national framework of reference that does not wither even before historic events of supranational magnitude".[58] They conclude: "Although outside pressure sometimes served as a catalyst, its influence should not be overvalued".[59]

Our national cases confirm this. In Hungary, the internal political context seemed more important than international changing norms. There was a new set of TJ measures in 2011–12, dealing with accountability, a Committee of National Remembrance (summer 2012), the lifting of the statute of limitations for crimes against humanity (and certain crimes committed during the communist dictatorship) and commemoration activities for victims (of the entire period between the autumn of 1944 and 2 May 1990). All of this happened, however, in a specific Hungarian context of high political tension between left and right. The debate focused on "exposing" politicians from the left as "communist agents". Uitz writes: "This rhetoric neatly fit in the deeply polarised Hungarian political sphere (...)". When certain prominent politicians refused to resign, this further deepened the left-right divide and further polemised the TJ debate. So the "catching up" of certain European countries with regard to mobilising collective

57 R.N. Lebow, W. Kansteiner and C. Fogu, *The Politics of Memory*, 27.
58 R.N. Lebow, W. Kansteiner and C. Fogu, *The Politics of Memory*, 293.
59 R.N. Lebow, W. Kansteiner and C. Fogu, *The Politics of Memory*.

memories in the construction of new nationhoods can be "hijacked" by national party politics.[60]

Does this mean national dynamics can "overrule" international developments? Without minimising the importance of national-domestic contexts, I believe this is too absolute a schism. Larger international shifts were essential as well (the Cold War and 1989, the global human rights culture and the Holocaust-attention being the obvious examples).[61] However, their impact translates differently in national cases; in timing and in concrete policy-impact.

The gradual rise of the global human rights culture can not be underestimated. This modern global human rights culture started at the IMT of Nuremberg in 1945. Although slowed and derailed, it slowly returned to the fore during the 1980s. In all post-1945 cases, this global human rights culture offered a new foundation for a new politics of memory, with new TJ-related measures such as reparation and apologies. This is clear in all post-1945 cases, certainly with reparation policies and apologies relating to the Holocaust.

In the Netherlands it seems to be this global human rights paradigm that ended the "old" politics of memory and gave a boost to a newly invigorated politics after the 1990s: an enormous increase in monuments, new digital initiatives, musea and heritage projects and educational initiatives. In West Germany, the Cold War is cited by Weinke as one of the causes that strengthened the continued marginalisation of victim groups while the rise of the international human rights paradigm gained importance only relatively late; probably due to the continued legacy of the counter-Nuremberg, where national law gained dominance over the imposed Allied legislation. The two things that gave the final push were, obviously, the dissolution of the German Democratic Republic (GDR) (the opening of archives, the issue of how to deal with victims of communist rule) and also the Yugoslav civil war and the recognition of the UN court in The Hague. Weinke writes that these (international) factors gave the final push towards integration of the "long-overdue adaptation" to international human rights law in domestic national legislations.

A third key factor is the role of generational change. The generational shift has been recognised and underscored by others.[62] This also runs completely parallel with the findings of Lebow, Kansteiner and Fogu. Based on their comparative

---

60 J.-W. Müller, *Memory and Power in Post-War Europe*, 9.

61 T.G. Ash, 'Trials, Purges and History lessons: treating a difficult past in post-communist Europe', in J.-W. Müller, *Memory and Power in Post-War Europe. Studies in the Presence of the Past*, Cambridge, 2002, 265–283.

62 J. Pilcher, 'Mannheim's Sociology of Generations: An Undervalued Legacy', in *The British Journal of Sociology*, 45/3 (1994), 481–495.

research they conclude that "(...) change is related to demography. The wartime generation appears to have had a very different set of political and psychological needs than the generations that followed. Those needs more or less precluded any honest public discussion of national wartime roles and activities by a majority of the population".[63] They pinpoint focal points of change at the late 1960s and the mid 1980s, stressing "(...) the importance of generational relay during this fifteen-year period".[64]

Indeed, our four post-1945 cases show that the largest memory shifts (1968, 1994) coincide with the coming of new elites in power. This was the case in West Germany, where the civil service (and highest courts) in particular was marked by a strong elite continuity after 1945. This was increasingly contested by a younger generations (the Flak-Helper generation, or "war children" generation): "continuities of personnel in justice, administration, military, academia and business were no longer accepted silently by the younger generations (...)" (Weinke). The analysis of the Spanish case underscores this. Spain is interesting because here, the "paradigm shift" has been triggered and the "second phase" (or as Aguilar and Ramírez-Barat call it: "the post-TJ process") is fully underway. And indeed, when explaining this shift ("why has a post-transitional justice phase taken place in Spain") both authors write; "firstly, the arrival of a new generation to the public sphere has proved to be a crucial variable" (Aguilar and Ramírez-Barat).

For Greece, Katsikas points out that when new coalitions were formed in 1989, civil war veterans were still present in both major political parties. This meant that on both sides of the political spectrum, the political elite still consisted of the "post-dictatorial elite". The rejection of the dictatorship was still a strong mutual "project" on both sides of the political spectrum. This strongly facilitated the ability to compromise and reach a consensual political settlement during the 1990s and beyond.

Belgium, however, shows that generational effects do not have a uniform effect. The 1960s generational shift primarily reinforced the political divisions that had grown during the 1950s. In this sense, the new generations (political elites, children of perpetrators and victims) adopted the memories created by their predecessors and parents and further reinforced them. In this sense only, international trends had less influence on Belgian developments. A true memorial shift in Belgium and especially Flanders would only come during the 1990s. In contrast, what was happening in France and the Netherlands during and after the 1960s was the gradual deconstruction of a centralised politics of memory that had never existed in Belgium in the first place.

63 R.N. Lebow, W. Kansteiner and C. Fogu, *The Politics of Memory*, 32.
64 R.N. Lebow, W. Kansteiner and C. Fogu, *The Politics of Memory*, 297.

International factors can have unforeseen national consequences. The annulment of the statute of limitations for crimes against humanity in France (1964) – according to Rousso "(...) a major turning point in the conception of the past in France's collective memory"[65] – was implemented under European pressure. But as Rousso writes: "originally it was not in any sense intended to reopen trials against French collaborators, who had benefited from amnesty laws in 1951 and 1953 (...)".[66] Nevertheless, this legal innovation would end up leading to the unforeseen wave of high profile trials during the 1980s and 1990s.

Romijn and Schumacher also combine national and international causal factors: international developments, the alternation of generations and what they call the "dynamics of public debate" (which is the national-domestic factor). They see two main reasons for the gradual 1960 shift: the coming of age of new political elite and more open societal debate on the legacy of the war. The latter also occurred under the influence of international events: the Eichmann trial in Israel (1962), the publication of *The Murderers among Us* (1967) by Nazi hunter S. Wiesenthal but also the wars in Algeria and Vietnam. So national memory incidents were inscribed in a larger international context. According to them, the generational effect was essential during the 1960s, when "(...) a new generation no longer accepted the compromises made during the occupation and the purge. [...] For the "protest generation" of war children and baby-boomers, the alleged indifference of older generations to the fate of their Jewish fellow-citizens became a central part of the legacy of the war" (Romijn and Schumacher). Romijn and Schumacher even note that renewed memorial activity during the 1980s was partly caused by concerns that memories would fade away, especially in the younger generation. This too, could be labelled a generational factor.

Therefore, when explaining larger memorial shifts, the key concept is probably "convergence": convergence of the national and the international and of the generational shift with other aspects. No one factor – not even a generational change – explains a paradigm shift. A consensus can hop to the next generation, and a memorial shift can skip a generation. A large and fundamental shift seems to happen only when several strong underlying mechanisms are able to reinforce each other.

For the post-1945 cases, this is clear in the two large paradigm shifts, around 1968–72 and 1989–94. In both these shifts, both international and national (internal-domestic) played an essential role. This is clear in France. De Gaulle's departure marked this shift, which converged with international changes and the position of France within Europe, a generational change but also internal

---

65 H. Rousso, *Justice, History and Memory in France*, 282.
66 H. Rousso, *Justice, History and Memory in France*, 281.

domestic policies. De Gaulle's successors were, as Baruch writes, moved by the idea of "settling scores" with Gaullism. President Mitterand. especially, found out through several memory incidents that he had a hard time reconciling his presidency with the legacy of Vichy (see above).

For Spain, Aguilar and Ramírez-Barat isolate five main causes for the shift to the "post-TJ phase": the generational shift, the actions of the ARHM, new political stances within the Spanish Worker's Socialist Party, the global human rights culture and lastly what they call 'fortuitous events' such as anniversaries (which could also be considered as memory irruptions and triggers). In their analysis, the convergence shines through; the development of a strong victim civil society network, a useful political context after 2004 with the Workers Socialist Party of Spain (*Partido Socialista Obrero Español*, PSOE) who strongly supported a new political settlement and also the international global culture of human rights (which clearly at least in part determined the Garzón-incident).

Baruch writes that with Chirac's excuses, France's politics of memory were finally in accordance with historiography (and the global rights culture), and we see a parallel and similar development in Flanders. Flanders had cultivated a particularly strong sub-memory around WWII and especially the "anti-Flemish repression" by the Belgian state after 1944. This dominant view was remarkably consistent between 1951 and 1989, in this sense "skipping" the larger shift that occurred in neighbouring countries. A rather sudden memorial shift would happen between roughly 1994 and 2001, in which Flemish war and TJ memories would come in accordance with the global human rights memorial culture. No one main cause can explain this sudden shift, however. Several factors converged: the international context, national political developments, a generational shift and new critical historiography. To explain the shift in Flanders between 1994 and 2001, the national and international were hard to separate in terms of causality. The memorial shift happened earlier in Francophone Belgium than in Flanders. Here, the human rights culture, the democratic paradigm and the dominance of the Holocaust came to the fore already during the 1980s. The context was more receptive, probably because the dominant resistance narratives of the 1960s–70s already foreshadowed the more moral human rights approach and democratic paradigm of the 1980s and 1990s.

The case of Flanders shows that a convergence of these factors can create a relatively sudden and quick shift in memorial regimes, despite the existence of a decades-long consensual context. As we saw, Raimundo and Pinto write that the Portuguese politics of memory "solved" all the TJ issues, and these measures "(...) seem to have closed the debate on the past". However, looking at our post-1945 cases, one could ask how durable this calm actually is. Spanish transition initially seemed to have set the example for how to successfully stabilise society and permanently close the past. There seemed to be no "crack in the metal" (to paraphrase Baruch); the transition seemed firmly consolidated. But from their in-depth Spanish analysis, Aguilar and Ramírez-Barat simply conclude: "(...) memory irruptions are inevitable with the passage of time". Therefore, it will be interesting to see what will happen in Greece or Portugal if and when national civil society agency, the generational factor, domestic political contexts and the homogenising global human rights culture converge in a process of mutual reinforcement.

7. TO CONCLUDE AND SUMMARISE

Most of our historic cases confirmed that core phase TJ policies became interconnected with national politics of memory early on. It was hard to disentangle both, even in our post-1945 cases.

We could not distinguish a clear transnational sequenced phasing related to the impact of TJ policies on European memory development. Yet certain phased mechanisms of memory development are clearly distinguishable, even between the different groups of national cases.

In most countries, states were able to develop a strong central politics of memory (1945, 1970s, 1989). Its essential building blocks were: a political consensus between the left and right on a national project (often reconciliation) and a unifying national narrative or myth related to the dictatorial past. In very general terms this meant 1° TJ policies aimed at avoiding broader elite-accountability, 2° strategic victim reparation and 3° a politics of memory based on this inclusive national myth.

A strong politics of memory should not be understood as strong mental/cultural shackles that exacted perfect control over local memories. A strong politics of memory should be viewed as a context of continued resilience against dissident narratives/memories. It is a context in which dissident (local, group-specific) memories simply drop dead after a certain amount of time; they are unable to gain enough momentum to transcend the confounds of their own specific memory group. A strong politics of memory by definition needed to incorporate and neutralise the many local memorial initiatives. However, even in cases that succeeded in building a strong national consensual memory regime, memory incidents stayed present right under the surface. In the words of Mark Mazower: "History has never left Europe nor returned to it".[67] Alternative memories were never buried or forgotten but simply dormant or invisible (meaning: not easily perceivable). Even during periods of prolonged calm,

[67] M. Mazower, *Dark Continent: Europe's Twentieth Century*, London, 1998, 402.

smaller memory incidents occurred regularly. The generational shift of the 1960s in our post-1945 cases were foreshadowed by memory incidents during the 1950s, just as the shift after 1989–94 was foreshadowed by developments during the 1980s. The memory incidents (the "headlines") are not essential as such; what is essential is to understand how and why they suddenly become memory irruptions and coincide with larger paradigm shifts.

An essential condition of a successful politics of memory was the prolonged political consensus that could be constructed around this national unifying myth/narrative. When this national narrative and political consensus came under pressure from bottom-up civil society agency or through political instrumentalisation and division, the central politics of memory quickly crumbled and gave way to either fragmentation or another dominant memorial paradigm that replaced the previous one.

No one factor explained such a memorial shift. Larger shifts in memorial regimes and paradigms happened when several factors converged. Our cases clearly show that the main factors are: 1° civil society agency of particular memory communities, 2° elite-generational shifts and 3° national political division/instrumentalisation.

In all countries where significant memory shifts took place, local civil society agency played an important role in triggering the preceding memory irruptions. In a general sense there was a European memory civil society in place after 1944 that could fall back on the modern tropes of memory build after 1918. Political division is also essential. When one major party (from the left or the right) starts to use the political capital of the legacy of the past, the entire consensual house of cards quickly crumbles.

Historiography should not be underestimated, but is a secondary factor at best. It played a significant yet never essential or determining role. The main problem is that we have little reliable impact measurement data on this topic. Also, we know little about the relationship between academic historic research and the popular platforms of public history (cultural vectors of memory; films, television, musea, literature, digital media).

National, domestic events are certainly the most visible causes of change. As such, they seem to overrule international trends and developments. However, one should not underestimate the impact of international events (the Cold War, the iconic years 1968 and 1989, and the global human rights culture). Large international changes and the large transformative process towards cultural modernity in post-Nuremberg Europe provide essential contextual background. The gradual emergence of a unifying global human rights culture and the emergence of the judicial-legal vector of memory are also absolutely essential.

This had legal, political-moral and cultural effects. The gradual, slow and sometimes contradictory re-assessment of TJ policies in Europe cannot be detached from this. However, we see that the exact nature of these meta-changes, as well as their exact timing, differed greatly among nations. National factors clearly determined the exact nature as well as timing of memory irruptions. As such, national cases did not neutralise international trends but could show great resilience against them.

Most memory incidents/irruptions could be traced back to TJ policies that were perceived as being unsuccessful (unsatisfactory). In fact, the majority of memory incidents/irruptions over the legacy of war and dictatorship in Europe could be traced back to "unresolved TJ issues". The nature of issues that are perceived as unresolved depend on the gradually changing contexts, wherein in post-1945 cases, perpetrator-oriented issues (scandals around the pardoning of war criminals or around the hidden war-past of public officials) gradually gave way to more victim-oriented issues ("cold treatment" of victims, lack of recognition). On a basic level, this was about points that were swept under the rug in the original TJ policies (acceptable victim recognition for the initially neglected Jewish victims, for example).

One of the major issues was traditional elite-complicity with the dictatorial regime (the collaboration of elites with the dictatorship). Indeed, the issue of elite-continuity after the different transitions (1945, 1970s and 1989) turned out to be one of the most important general recurring hot topics for memory incidents/irruptions. This re-assessment of "unresolved issues" was much more than simply re-considering unfinished (legal) business. TJ policies became part of memory development itself. Perceived unresolved TJ issues were retroactively used to defend and implement new cultural and moral values perceived as important at that time. As such, re-assessed TJ policies became part of new memorial regimes.

The absence of European TRC's and related (state sponsored) truth-seeking mechanisms is the most obvious difference with the Latin-American and African continents. No European country installed a fully fledged TRC. This was clearly the legacy of the "Nuremberg model" where the criminal judicial system was meant to create truth out of legal justice. This was considered compatible with a democratic culture of open debate wherein "truth seeking" did not become a state-sponsored project but was rather left to follow its own societal course: as long as it did not fundamentally question the previously established "legal truth".

However, longer term developments show many parallels. In European cases (specifically also the post 1945 cases) the one sided legal agenda of large-scale prosecutions was quickly replaced by policies of re-integration. Societal demands quickly broke through the boundaries of the "legal truth" created by the prosecution and purges. Central politics of memory were set in motion that ultimately tried to steer the public debate towards national unity (and reconciliation). After 1989, several European societies initiated reconciliatory projects, also referring to aspects of truth seeking. The new wave of trials in the post-1945 cases were more about memory and retroactively establishing some kind of moral truth than any strict legal agenda. This also seems to be applicable for national and international procedures for the purpose of providing reparations to the victims of (racial) persecution. Here also, moral redress was a more important discursive component than the principle of material compensation. The later phenomenon of official historical expert-commissions in Europe (although mostly much more limited in mandate) are basically in exactly the same vein as TRC's.

Many parallels occurred on the level of non-state sponsored, civil society or local initiatives (certainly after the 1980s) as well. In Africa and Latin-America, the truth seeking of TRC's was always a combination of official authorative records with broader societal debates and local/civil society agency. This is not unlike the European contexts. Open public debate, and involvement of broader actors (education, cultural actors, civil society actors), of local authorities and of victim organisations clearly took centre stage after 1989. As such, it created processes that ran parallel with patterns of truth seeking mechanisms in other continents.

So I would like to argue that the absence of TRC's in Europe is perhaps more about institutional context, form and shape than about actual underlying societal processes. Europe remained defined by the historical judicial Nuremberg model – of course – but gradually sidestepped to broader truth seeking processes (without TRC's). The German concept *Vergangenheitsbewältigung* started narrowly but gradually came to include many different aspects. Both in east- and western-Europe, the concept of reconciliation was strongly present after 1989 and was explicitly connected to truth seeking (public access to archives, for example). An in-depth comparison between European truth seeking mechanisms and other continents would in – my view – probably gain more by considering the parallels rather than complying to a strict "contrast-model".

If we accept that any type of durable reconciliation needs to be preceded with a painful self-investigation of an in-depth dealing with the past (*Aufarbeitung*) – including painful memory debates/irruptions – we might conclude that Greece and Portugal have been able to momentarily obtain some first-phase consensus but not yet a durable reconciliation. In this sense, the Portuguese silence is bound to shift in the future. Subjects that have been left untouched by research in Greece, according to Katsikas, are: the junta's policy towards communist Eastern Europe, the complicity of the economic and political elite with the junta regime and the junta's policies towards minorities. Indeed, these are exactly the classic issues that caused memory irruptions in the other historic cases. Our other cases seems to show, therefore, that it is only a matter of time before the aforementioned factors will converge to create memory irruptions that can cause the period of calm or consensus in these countries to shift quickly and fundamentally.

ABOUT THE AUTHORS

Paloma Aguilar (Spain) is an Associate Professor of Political Science at the *Universidad Nacional de Educación a Distancia* (UNED) in Madrid. She has published *Políticas de la memoria y memorias de la política* (2008) and *Memory and Amnesia. The Role of the Spanish Civil War in the Transition to Democracy* (2001). She has co-edited the volume *The Politics of Memory. Transitional Justice in Democratizing Societies* (2002). Her main research fields are transitions to democracy, memories of violence and repression, legacies of authoritarian regimes, transitional justice mechanisms, political violence and nationalism.

Klaus Bachmann (Poland) is a Professor of political science at the Warsaw School of Social Sciences and Humanities. He has published on European Integration, International Criminal Tribunals, value changes and reckoning with the past in Germany, Poland and the Balkans and is the author of *Vengeance, punishment, amnesty. Collaboration and dealing with it in Belgium, the Netherlands and Poland* (2011). He has been teaching and doing research at Stellenbosch University, South Africa, Johns Hopkins University, Washington D.C., the Universities of Bordeaux, Renmin (Bejing), Vienna and Wroclaw (Poland).

Marc Olivier Baruch (France) started his professional career in the higher French civil service before becoming an academic in the mid-1990s. In 1997, he was heard as a witness by the Bordeaux criminal court in charge of the Maurice Papon case. Elected in 2003 as *directeur d'études* in the School for Advanced Studies in the Social Sciences (Paris), he specialises in the history of the State in 20th century Europe. He edited a book on French society and post-WWII purges (2003) and is currently working on another one on history, law and politics in contemporary France.

António Costa Pinto (Portugal) is a Research Professor at the Institute of Social Sciences at the University of Lisbon. His research interests include authoritarianism, political elites, democratisation and transitional justice in new democracies, and the comparative study of political change in Europe. His most recent publications include 'Authoritarian Legacies, Transitional Justice and State Crisis in Portugal's Democratization', *Democratization*, Vol. 13 (2), 2006, pp. 173–204 and *Dealing with the Legacy of Authoritarianism: The "Politics of the*

Past" in Southern European Democracies (2011, co-edited with Leonardo Morlino).

Luc Huyse (Belgium) was a Professor of sociology and sociology of law at the Leuven University Law School. He has written and taught extensively on the various dimensions of justice after transition. He has been a consultant to governments and NGO's in Burundi, Ethiopia, South Africa and Zimbabwe. He is co-editor of *Reconciliation after Violent Conflict. A Handbook* (2003) and of *Traditional Justice and Reconciliation after Violent Conflict. Learning from African Experiences* (2008), and author of a book on dealing with the past.

Stefanos Katsikas is Director of Modern Greek Studies programme at the University of Illinois in Urbana-Champaign. He holds a BA in History from the Ionian University (Corfu, Greece), a MA in Southeast European Studies and a PhD in Social Sciences from the University College London (UCL). Prior to his appointment in the University of Illinois, he taught as visiting and full-time lecturer in various universities in the UK – UCL, University of Nottingham, Goldsmiths College, University of London. From 2008 to 2010 he was a John S. Latsis research fellow at the Department of History and Archaeology, University of Athens (National and Kapodistrian University of Athens). His research interests focus on the study of democratisation, reconciliation and regional security in Southeastern Europe in both contemporary and historical settings. Recent publications include: *Negotiating Diplomacy in the New Europe: Foreign Policy in Post-Communist Bulgaria* (2011), which received a Scouloudi publication award from the Institute of Historical Research in London. He is the editor of *Bulgaria and Europe: Shifting Identities* (2010), co-editor of *State-Nationalisms in the Ottoman Empire, Greece and Turkey: Orthodox and Muslims* (1830–1945); and guest editor of *European Modernity and Islamic Reformism among Muslims of the Balkans in the Late Ottoman and Post-Ottoman Period (1830s-1945)*, special issue of the *Journal of Muslim Minority Affairs* 29 (4) (December 2009).

Dirk Luyten (Belgium) is a Researcher at CEGES/SOMA. He published extensively on social-economic policy, the history and ideology of corporatism and the trials in Belgium regarding economic collaboration after WWII. Within CEGES/SOMA, he leads the interuniversity cooperation project '*Socio-political history of the Belgian judicial system*'.

Filipa Raimundo (Portugal) holds a PhD from the European University Institute Department of Social and Political Sciences. Her dissertation is titled "Post-Transitional Justice. Portugal, Spain and Poland in comparative perspective". She wrote a chapter on dealing with the past in Central and Southern European Democracies in Laure Neumayer and Georges Mink's *History, memory and* *politics in Central, East and South East Europe* (2012). Her interests include democratisation, transitional justice, post-conflict reconciliation, authoritarianism and European politics.

Clara Ramírez-Barat (Spain) is a Senior Research Associate at the International Center for Transitional Justice. She obtained a PhD in Philosophy at the University Carlos III of Madrid in 2007, with a thesis on transitional justice. She holds a BA in Humanities from the same university, and an MA in Philosophy from Columbia University. For the past ten years, her research has focused on different aspects of transitional justice, human rights, and democratic theory, and she has authored several publications in these topics. Her most recent research has focused on outreach programmes for transitional justice measures and the relationship between transitional justice and the socio-cultural sphere.

Peter Romijn (the Netherlands) is Director of Research of the NIOD Institute for Holocaust and Genocide Studies in Amsterdam. His work includes studies on the persecution of the Jews in Nazi-occupied Holland, Dutch local government under German occupation, and the politics and legitimacy of occupational regimes in Europe. In 2002, he was co-responsible for the publication of a historical study commissioned by the Dutch government on the 1995 Srebrenica genocide and the involvement of Dutch peace-keepers. Peter Romijn also is a part-time Professor of History at the University of Amsterdam.

Erik Schumacher (the Netherlands) studied history at the University of Amsterdam. Together with Josje Damsma, he is the author of *Hier woont een NSB'er* (2010), a study on ordinary members of the Dutch national socialist party in wartime Amsterdam. He is currently working as a freelance historian and journalist. His participation in this project is on behalf of the NIOD Institute for War, Holocaust and Genocide Studies in Amsterdam.

Renáta Uitz (Hungary) is a Professor of law and chair of the Comparative Constitutional Law programme at the Central European University in Budapest. Her teaching covers subjects in comparative constitutional law in Europe and North America, transitional justice and human rights protection with special emphasis on the enforcement of fundamental (human) rights. Theories and practices of good governance in and after democratic transition, and the role of courts in constructing the constitutional subject are at the centre of her research interests.

Annette Weinke (Germany) is an Academic Assistant at the Historical Institute of the Friedrich Schiller University in Jena. From 2006 to 2010 she worked for the Independent Historians' Commission appointed by the German Foreign Minister in 2006 to investigate the history of the German diplomatic service during the Nazi regime and in its aftermath. Her focuses of research are amongst others the effects of the Nazi past on societies of GDR and FRG as well as the history of international humanitarian law during the 20th Century.

Nico Wouters (Belgium) is head of the Academic Activities section at the Centre for Historical Research and Documentation on War and Contemporary Society (www.cegesoma.be) and a Guest Lecturer at the Department of History at the University of Antwerp (Research Unit on Political History). He is co-editor-in-chief of the *Journal of Belgian History* and editorial board member of the *Low Countries Historical Review*. Between 2004 and 2006 he was a member of the team of researchers asked by the Belgian Senate to determine the responsibilities of Belgian authorities in the persecution of the Jews in Belgium during WWII.

www.ingramcontent.com/pod-product-compliance
Ingram Content Group UK Ltd.
Pitfield, Milton Keynes, MK11 3LW, UK
UKHW051913100926
8556IPUK00006B/867

9 781780 682143